# The Last
# Two Years of
# Salvador Allende

# The Last
# Two Years of
# Salvador Allende

NATHANIEL DAVIS

CORNELL UNIVERSITY PRESS

*Ithaca and London*

*Library of Congress Cataloging in Publication Data*

Davis, Nathaniel.
    The last two years of Salvador Allende.

    Bibliography: p.
    Includes index.
    1. Chile—Politics and government—1970–
2. Allende Gossens, Salvador, 1908–1973.  I. Title.
F3100.D36  1985    983'.0646    84-23774
ISBN 0-8014-1791-0  (alk. paper)

First published 1985 by Cornell University Press.

Printed in the United States of America

*The paper in this book is acid-free and meets the guidelines for
permanence and durability of the Committee on Production Guidelines
for Book Longevity of the Council on Library Resources.*

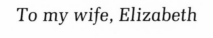

*To my wife, Elizabeth*

# Contents

# Maps

# Preface

IN his 1970 election campaign Salvador Allende offered to lead his countrymen to socialism along a peaceful "Chilean Way." He would seek office through democratic elections; he would carry out the country's political, social, and economic transformation legally, through established Chilean institutions; and he would achieve the transition without violence, without the dictatorship of the proletariat, and without the millions of deaths experienced elsewhere when the road to socialism was traversed by force. In his advocacy of the "peaceful road to socialism" Allende liked to quote Friedrich Engels on a possible "peaceful evolution from the old society to the new in countries where the representatives of the people have all the power and can do what they desire in accordance with the constitution, from the moment when they attain the majority in the nation."[1]

With Allende's election to the Chilean presidency, he was hailed as the first Marxist anywhere on the globe to be so selected through democratic balloting.[2] Allende himself believed that he would go down in history alongside Marx, Engels, Lenin, and Mao. Chile's contribution to world socialism would be unique and lasting.

Because of the aspiration represented in the Chilean Way, the Allende government in the 1970s took on an international role that resembled the one played by the Spanish Loyalist government in the 1930s. Just as many of the world's progressives believed that the Spanish civil war had defined "antifascism" and had posed the issues that later became those of World War II, so many people around the world reacted to the Chilean Way as a test of the U.S. orientation toward reformist, left-leaning regimes and of U.S. willingness to accept and cooperate with them. This is not to associate Allende's government with Loyalist positions or the United States with fascist ones, but it is to point out the great symbolic role that the two experiences in different times assumed in world politics and ideological thought. Moreover, there was a widely sensed poignancy in Salvador Allende's dream, and his personality exerted a great additional pull.

The fall of the Allende government became a judgment on the viability of the democratic road to socialism. The military coup that overthrew President Allende in 1973 seemed to constitute a melancholy verdict on the chances of Eurocommunism and other Marxist political movements that advocate parliamentary struggle rather than violent revolution. Hundreds of millions of the world's men and women had been caught up in the Chilean adventure; much venom permeated subsequent recriminations. The coup was not simply one more in history's long series of military interventions. It was traumatic. The sudden end of the Allende government lighted up the night sky like sheet lightning, exposing a stark landscape we might rather not have seen.

For the people who were supporting Allende's successes and hopes, Allende *had* to succeed. Many were not ready to accept his failure, and they were particularly reluctant to accept the idea that Allende's tragedy had indigenous Chilean roots, even in part. External force must, they thought, have caused Allende's fall. And the foreign agent must have been the United States.

The sense of American responsibility was felt particularly strongly within the United States itself. We Americans tend to be societally ethnocentric—almost narcissistic—exaggerating the influence of both our positive and our negative actions in the world. This American self-importance was superimposed on the progressive world's conviction that Allende's Chilean experiment, left alone, would have triumphed because it was good.

American reactions reflected another quirk of national character. Americans tend to think that political problems have solutions if only one is smart enough to find the right answers. Favored by geography, nature, and history, Americans have tended, historically, to think that almost any difficulty can be worked out. Modern world history tells us otherwise, but our American inclination to underestimate the world's intractability led us to particularly resentful self-examination when the Chilean experiment ended in disappointment.

The political morality play staged in America, with Chile as its subject, exposed basic dilemmas of American foreign policy and its domestic premises. The role and limits of covert action remain a central issue in our public debate—an issue on which there is still no broad consensus. In addition, we have not made a clear choice between activism in the world and a systematic reduction of our foreign commitments. New, searing fires of controversy may sweep across America in the years ahead as these issues are fought out in an atmosphere of increasing discord.

One of the laments of the Vietnam era was that "people lost friends over it." The issue became so important, morally as well as politically, that bonds of friendship and civil discourse sometimes did not survive the strain. People have also lost friends over Chile; and they will lose more, because the ghost of Salvador Allende will not rest.

There are those who believe that America is moving toward ideological polarization, including a McCarthyism of both the right and the left. A flavor of betrayal, or at least disloyalty to America's basic values, too often accompanies "wrong" beliefs. Everybody must wear a white hat or a black one, and heroes and villains must not change roles. Until recent years American foreign policy had been seen as morally steadied, a little the way ocean liners used to be stabilized by the great gyroscopes built into them to reduce their pitching and rolling. This sense characterized our thinking in the golden age of American power and certitude after World War II. Then came a series of jolts, starting with Iran in 1953, Guatemala in 1954, and Vietnam—always Vietnam. In the 1950s, however, Eisenhower's benign persona and the relative moral simplicity of the time protected America from any great sense of having sinned. In the 1960s came the Bay of Pigs, the Dominican Republic, the Congo, and still Vietnam; and Lyndon Johnson was not Eisenhower. In the 1970s we had the Kurds, Cambodia, more Vietnam, and Watergate, with a seemingly endless flow of shameful revelations about our society and its ways of doing business at home and abroad. The Chilean story produced still another bump in our fall from grace, more guilt-laden than some of the earlier ones because Salvador Allende had more going for him than Arbenz, Bosch, Lumumba, or Mossadegh. Allende's vision was more compelling in ways that engage the intellect and evoke commitment.

Americans emerged more cynical, resentful, pessimistic, and withdrawn. The Chilean experience became part of what is a national, almost Freudian, burden, and we should now heed the Viennese teacher's advice. In order to liberate oneself from the suppressed tyranny of the past, one must first understand it and measure its reality. In the end, it would not be healthy for our society to succumb yet again to the "historical amnesia" that George F. Kennan characterizes as a fatal American disease.

When reviewing a diplomatic memoir recently, Charles R. Foster expressed the opinion that "diplomats ought not to write memoirs unless they are entertaining and can serve as suitable reading material for the beach or plane, or unless they provide important new material for diplomatic historians."[3] I cannot achieve Lawrence Durrell's or Charles W. Thayer's heights of diplomatic banter, so I must strive for "important new material." I do hope, however, that this account will find an audience more general than the diplomatic historian. The issues exposed and Allende's Chilean experiment deserve a wider readership.

The dilemma remains: is this a memoir or a monograph? It is both. It would be foolish to pretend that I can remove myself from this volume. I was the U.S. ambassador in Chile during Salvador Allende's last two years, and that is a large part of the reason for this account. Yet my personal experiences in Chile do not justify a book. This volume can be worthwhile only if the observations made here throw light on the larger reality of Allende's Chile.

This book addresses two central questions: First, what political and economic developments in Chile produced the 1973 coup? Second, what was the U.S. role in this sequence of events and in their culmination? I try to show the causes of change and the logic of Chilean events.

The treatment is roughly chronological but not uniformly so. The copper compensation question, for example, could be treated in virtually every chapter, but that would result in a great deal of sausage-slicing; it seems better to discuss copper more analytically and at no more than two or three points in the narrative. On the other hand, a strictly topic-oriented organization would probably sacrifice the dynamic change that characterized the onrush of events in Chile during those turbulent times.

Why does this book, except for the essential background given in chapter 1, cover only the last two years of Allende's three-year presidency? The initial answer is that it covers the time when I was in Chile and experienced events firsthand. The last months of 1971 provided a reasonable break between the earlier period and the time covered in these pages. The Allende government reached a turning point after about a year, both in the political and in the economic sense.

I left Chile about seven weeks after the coup. While this volume covers those weeks, its subject is Allende's government, not the government of his successors. One academic observer, Mark Falcoff, has remarked that "there is no reason to assume that the virtues of a vanished regime increase in direct proportion to the iniquities of its successor."[4] He is more than half right, and Allende's Chilean experiment should be judged on its own terms.

Objectivity is a goal I strive for in these pages. I do have a point of view, of course, and I hope I acknowledge biases openly. Dame Rebecca West recently asserted cheerily that "historians are notorious liars."[5] We live in an age of advocacy journalism and advocacy scholarship. Perhaps it has never been otherwise; nevertheless, too much recent scholarship on Allende's Chile has been written by leftists shouting their case, by liberals who can see no bad in Allende and no good in his enemies, by conservatives who think the distinction between authoritarianism and totalitarianism justifies Pinochet, and by rightists who see only the Red Menace. With luck, this volume might confound a few stereotypes.

The strictures imposed by having held a public trust mean that I am not always able to "reveal all." A few sections related to U.S. intelligence activities, most notably parts of chapters 12 and 13, have been crafted with these inhibitions in mind. I have clearly identified the places where discretion about "intelligence sources and methods" has been necessary, however, and this book contains only truthful statements and interpretations, so far as I have been able to discover the whole truth. No false impressions have been knowingly created by artful omission.

Some commentators have suggested that a professional diplomat should let considerable time pass before writing, and a dozen years

have now passed for me. There are a few who think a Foreign
Service officer should never publish, but rather—as in the old
days—serve out his career to a ripe old age and then retire to his dry
martinis and reminiscences with friends. But we have to recognize
that the idea of mute professionalism in American diplomacy is in
a state of flux. The change in values is impelled by the current
politicization of appointments, by the phenomenon of crack journalists and polemical scholars pursuing alternating careers in government and public advocacy, by the growing popularity of the in-
and-out-of-government route to a successful diplomatic career, by
the 1980 Foreign Service Act's removal of tenure at the top, and by
the lost expectation of a chance to serve until retirement age. So the
premises of old-fashioned, silent diplomatic professionalism are
eroding; but that is another subject.

Maybe the time has come when the story told in these pages may
be heard more willingly than it might have been a few years ago.
John Le Carré, the great spy novelist, has observed that "markets, as
economists know, tend to produce counter-markets. In fashion, the
search for reaction is endless. Nothing is surer than that those who
dressed as dandies yesterday will appear as tramps tomorrow."[6]
Perhaps the moment for this volume is approaching, in fashion's
great tomorrow.

My wife, Elizabeth, and my daughter, Margaret Mainardi, have
read and reread this manuscript. Where the argument was incom-
prehensible, they told me to make it clear; where it was wrong, they
told me to make it right. Margaret also typed the text. The following
friends and former colleagues read the typescript and made many
valuable suggestions: Geraldine P. Biller, Joel W. Biller, Arnold M.
Isaacs, Judd L. Kessler, Alice M. Lowenthal, William Lowenthal,
David A. Phillips, and my sister, Louise F. Davis. The following
colleagues commented on substantial portions of the text: Hal S.
Barron, Alvin H. Bernstein, Ray E. Davis, John W. Fisher, James
Halsema, John E. Karkashian, Jack B. Kubisch, George W. Landau,
David H. Popper, Robert W. Scherrer, and Harry W. Shlaudeman.
Other friends and colleagues, both Chileans and North Americans,
have read and checked portions of the text for accuracy.

I also wish to express my gratitude to Lawrence J. Malley,
Marilyn M. Sale, Roger Haydon, and other members of the Cornell

University Press community for their help and warm encouragement. Mr. Haydon has greatly improved the manuscript in the
course of editing and cutting it, a surgery performed without anes-
thetic, where he had to place sole reliance on diplomacy to relieve
the pain.

NATHANIEL DAVIS

*Claremont, California*

# The Last
# Two Years of
# Salvador Allende

**Map 1.** Chile, schematic

# Chapter 1

# The 1970 Elections and Allende's First Year

IN 1970 Chile boasted one of the world's oldest parliaments. The government of Eduardo Frei Montalva had for six years been the showpiece of the Alliance for Progress, and in the Alliance years more American aid money per capita had been spent in Chile than anywhere else in the hemisphere.[1]

The half-century-old Chilean Communist party was one of the most powerful in the West. The Socialist party boasted a thirty-seven year history and an impressive record in and out of Chilean government. The presidential elections of 1970 would be the fourth time Salvador Allende Gossens had run for the presidency. In 1952, supported by only a faction of his own Socialist party, he had been essentially the candidate of the then-outlawed Communists. He received less than 6 percent of the vote.[2] In 1958 Allende ran again, as standard bearer for the country's combined leftist forces. In a very close race he lost to Jorge Alessandri Rodríguez. Alessandri received about a third of the vote, 35,000 ballots more than those won by Allende's Frente de Acción Popular (FRAP). If a defrocked Marxist priest, Antonio Raúl Zamorano, had not entered the race and taken 40,000 votes, Allende might have won. The Christian

Democrats amassed one-fifth of the vote, and the Radicals (anticlerical and pro-Masonic) about one-sixth.[3]

In 1964 two coalitions were formed: Allende's FRAP once again, and Julio Durán's coalition of his own Radical party, the United Conservatives (traditionalist Catholics), and the Liberals (also conservative but somewhat more reformist). Frei's Christian Democrats had grown in popularity, and they stood alone with only splinter-group support.

Before the 1964 presidential campaign got under way, a by-election in Curicó intervened. Durán's coalition was ignominiously defeated by the FRAP and broke up, although Durán was prevailed upon by party colleagues to remain on the ballot, largely to prevent Radical voters from giving their support to Allende. In essence the presidential election became a two-man race between Frei and Allende. Both sides spent lavishly, in part because the Christian Democrats, Duran's Radicals, and private citizens' groups were receiving funds from the U.S. Central Intelligence Agency (CIA) and from Christian Democratic parties and groups in Western Europe, and in part because Allende's FRAP was receiving money from Communist Bloc and other foreign leftist sources. Frei received 56 percent of the vote as against Allende's 39 percent and Durán's 5 percent.[4]

Chilean postwar history shows, therefore, that since 1958 Allende's coalition had had a good chance of winning a plurality in any three-cornered race. Only a concentration of anti-Marxist votes behind a single, strong centrist candidate defeated Allende in 1964.

## The 1970 Elections

In 1969, with Frei barred constitutionally from succeeding himself, the Christian Democrats nominated Radomiro Tomic Romero, of the left wing of their party, for president. The United Conservatives, Liberals, and smaller conservative groups had banded together in 1966 to form the National party, and Jorge Alessandri was emerging in 1969 as the candidate the Nationalists supported. The aging bachelor had proved an incorruptible and relatively popular president between 1958 and 1964, and the prospect of a left-wing Christian Democratic candidate had guaranteed that conservatives would not support the Christian Democrats' man.

In 1970 the main body of the Radicals joined Unidad Popular

(UP, or Popular Unity), a reconstituted leftist coalition that had taken the place of the FRAP. The anti-Marxist Radicals, led by Durán, had lost a furious battle over party leadership at the Radicals' 1969 party convention and had been expelled from the party. They subsequently formed the Party of Radical Democracy and supported Alessandri in 1970.[5]

The U.S. government did not sink money into anybody's campaign, although $425,000 in covert expenditures by the CIA were approved in March and June 1970 for anti-Allende and anti-UP propaganda. This spoiling operation focused on the dangers of a leftist victory. As later revealed, Richard Helms of the CIA had expressed serious reservations about the U.S. strategy, deploring the bad sense of thinking one could "beat somebody with nobody."[6]

Alessandri's chances of defeating Allende were clearly better than Tomic's. Part way through the campaign, however, Alessandri unwisely subjected himself, in a state of fatigue, to a disastrous television appearance, where poor makeup and lighting magnified a visual impression of decrepitude. The voters, already concerned that the 74-year-old candidate was too aged to conduct a vigorous presidency, were further put off.

On 4 September 1970 the Chilean people gave Salvador Allende a plurality of 36.3 percent, followed by Alessandri's 35 percent and Tomic's 27.8 percent. Allende's margin over Alessandri was 39,000 votes out of three million.[7]

The Chilean constitution passed power to elect the president to the Chilean Chamber of Deputies and Senate, acting in joint session, if no candidate achieved 50 percent of the valid ballots. This arrangement could have resulted in the selection of a candidate other than Allende, as the UP parties were a minority in both chambers. There was a strong tradition in Chile, however, that the man with the plurality was always confirmed when the joint session met, seven weeks after the nationwide election.

### The Seven-Week Hiatus and the U.S. Reaction

Chilean election results were greeted with sinking spirits in quite a number of capitals around the Western Hemisphere. In Washington, it appears, Richard M. Nixon and Henry A. Kissinger were furious. Kissinger, in describing the president's reaction to the 4

September voting in Chile, says that "Nixon was beside himself," adding that the president blamed the State Department and Ambassador Edward M. Korry for the outcome. According to Kissinger, Nixon also resolved to "circumvent the bureaucracy" thereafter.[8]

Thomas Powers, in his book on CIA director Helms, recounts a meeting in mid-October, five weeks after the Chilean election, between President Nixon and Ambassador Korry:

> Kissinger . . . asked Korry if he'd like to talk to the President. . . . Nixon met them at the door and startled Korry, as the door closed behind them, by pounding his fist into the palm of his hand and saying, "That sonofabitch, that sonofabitch!" The expression on Korry's face halted Nixon in mid-expletive. "Not you, Mr. Ambassador. . . . It's that bastard Allende."
>
> Nixon then commenced a monologue on how he was going to smash Allende, but afterward Korry repeated the warnings he had given to Kissinger [that U.S. support for a military coup in Chile might backfire], and despite Nixon's determination to block Allende, he appeared somewhat taken aback.[9]

As recently as 1977 David Frost, preparing to interview the former president, was warned by his colleagues that Nixon had a "short fuse" on the subject of Chile.[10] Writing himself, Nixon recalls that "an Italian businessman who called on me before the Chilean election had cautioned, 'If Allende should win, and with Castro in Cuba, you will have in Latin America a red sandwich. And eventually, it will all be red.' "[11] The businessman's "red sandwich" would have been quite a Dagwood Special: four thousand miles of heterogeneous societies and regimes would lie between those two slabs of Marxist pumpernickel. I do not mean that I think Salvador Allende's election had no effect on U.S. interests. It obviously did. But I do not believe that it put South America in a Cuban-Chilean sandwich. In any case, Nixon clearly detested Allende and his works.

Henry Kissinger has been much quoted as having said at a secret White House meeting, on 27 June 1970, that "I don't see why we need to stand by and watch a country go Communist due to the irresponsibility of its own people."[12] Seymour M. Hersh, the investigative reporter, quotes Roger Morris, a colleague of Kissinger's on the National Security Council staff until a few months before the Chilean elections, as commenting:

I don't think anybody in the government understood how ideological Kissinger was about Chile. I don't think anybody ever fully grasped that Henry saw Allende as being far more serious a threat than Castro. If Latin America ever became unraveled, it would never happen with a Castro. Allende was a living example of democratic social reform in Latin America. All kinds of cataclysmic events rolled around, but Chile scared him [Kissinger]. He talked about Eurocommunism [in later years] the same way he talked about Chile early on. Chile scared him.[13]

On 16 September 1970 Kissinger gave a briefing to newspaper editors during which he said:

I have yet to meet somebody who firmly believes that if Allende wins, there is likely to be another free election in Chile. . . . There is a good chance that he will establish over a period of years some sort of Communist Government . . . in a major Latin-American country . . . [ad]joining . . . Argentina . . . Peru . . . and Bolivia. . . . So I don't think we should delude ourselves that an Allende take-over . . . would not present massive problems for us, and for the democratic forces and pro-U.S. forces in . . . the whole Western Hemisphere.[14]

Henry Kissinger's background press briefing of 16 September was given the day after a secret White House meeting at which Richard Nixon had instructed his CIA director to "save Chile" from Allende. The president's order to Helms had probably been triggered in its turn by a meeting on the fourteenth between Nixon and the Pepsi Cola Company's chairman, Donald M. Kendall, and a breakfast meeting the next day where Kendall, Kissinger, Attorney General John Mitchell, and Agustín Edwards discussed Chile. Edwards, the owner of *El Mercurio*, Santiago's great conservative newspaper, had left Chile after the 1970 elections. He had also owned a Pepsi Cola bottling plant, which associated him with Kendall, and Kendall was close to President Nixon. At the breakfast Edwards prophesied general disaster.

In the early afternoon the president summoned Helms and, with Kissinger and Mitchell present, instructed him to "leave no stone unturned . . . to block Allende's confirmation." Helms was later to testify to Senator Frank Church's Select Committee on Intelligence: "If I ever carried a marshal's baton in my knapsack out of the Oval

Office, it was that day." Helms also carried a single page of hand-written notes that captured the tone of his instructions:

> One in 10 chance perhaps, but save Chile!
> worth spending
> not concerned risks involved
> no involvement of embassy
> $10,000,000 available, more if necessary
> full-time job—best men we have
> game plan
> make the economy scream
> 48 hours for plan of action[15]

The CIA program that Helms launched in order to carry out Nixon's instructions came to be called "Track II." Helms was enjoined from giving any information about it to Ambassador Korry, to the secretaries of state and defense, or even to the Forty Committee, the interagency group chaired by Kissinger that was supposed to consider all covert action programs. It was for this reason that the program was said to be moving on a second, ultrasecret track.

The idea that the CIA hit upon to carry out its charge was to instigate a coup d'état before Allende could be confirmed by the Chilean Congress on 24 October. The CIA was not well organized to carry forward this plan, however, because Ambassador Korry had forbidden the station in Santiago to keep in touch with dissident military officers. The agency thus had to rely heavily on Col. Paul M. Wimert, Jr., the well-connected U.S. Army attaché in Santiago. The result was that both the CIA station and the attaché's office operated behind the ambassador's back.

Through Wimert the CIA developed contacts with two Chilean generals: retired brigadier general Roberto Viaux and Brig. Gen. Camilo Valenzuela. Viaux was former commander of the Tacna Regiment, and he and his troops had almost launched a coup against President Frei in 1969—at which time the president had been defended by loyal garbage-truck drivers who massed their vehicles outside the Moneda Palace. Valenzuela was a better prospect than Viaux in almost all respects, and he was still on active duty and commanded the key Santiago military district.

Both Viaux's and Valenzuela's groups planned to kidnap the commander-in-chief of the Chilean Army, Gen. René Schneider Chereau, who was a firm constitutionalist. Their hope was that the

Chilean military leadership would step in and seize power if the general were abducted. Between 5 and 20 October the CIA had twenty-one contacts or meetings with military and police officers, many of them with members of the two groups of plotters. It is alleged that the CIA and Wimert were offering $100,000 for a successful kidnapping of the Chilean Army commander-in-chief.

As early as 6 October, the CIA was having second thoughts about Viaux and was instructing its Santiago station to advise him to postpone action. On the 17th, seven days before the Chilean Congress was to vote on the presidency, a CIA officer apparently tried to convince Viaux to cancel his plans to abduct Schneider, advice that Viaux did not heed. On that same day other plotters associated with Valenzuela asked Wimert for three submachine guns, ammunition, and a few teargas grenades. Their idea at the time was to kidnap Schneider on the night of 19 October, after a military dinner. On 18 October, Wimert delivered six teargas grenades to the "dinner plotters." Apparently the CIA in Washington had not been able to send guns in time, but the next day Washington despatched three submachine guns, "sanitized" to disguise their origin. They arrived in Santiago via the U.S. diplomatic pouch on 20 or 21 October.

Why was the CIA "cooling off" Viaux while ordering weapons and delivering teargas grenades to other plotters? Powers believes that Washington, while concluding at about this time that Viaux was unreliable, was still anxious to work with plotters thought to be associated with Valenzuela. Church Committee investigators reached the same conclusion.[16]

Kissinger, according to his own testimony, instructed the CIA on 15 October to turn off Track II altogether, and he said that all subsequent CIA Track II operations were unauthorized. While Kissinger's deputy at the time, Alexander Haig, testified in support of Kissinger's assertion, the CIA officers involved in Chilean operations did not. Church Committee investigators note this discrepancy in their report on *Alleged Assassination Plots*, while Hersh directly charges that Kissinger and Haig testified falsely.[17]

In any case, General Schneider left the dinner of 19 October in a well-guarded private car rather than in his limousine, thus eluding the dinner plotters. The same conspirators then told Wimert that another attempt would be made on the twentieth, but that also failed. At two o'clock in the morning of 22 October Wimert delivered the submachine guns, which had by then arrived, to an army officer associated with General Valenzuela.

At 7 A.M. on the same day a group of military conspirators associated with Viaux assembled in secret to make final plans for General Schneider's abduction. An hour or so later they waylaid the general's car, and Schneider was shot and fatally wounded.

U.S. Senate investigators note that the Viaux and Valenzuela groups were in contact with each other and not discrete entities. Therefore, the fact that the CIA was working with Valenzuela's group and trying to discourage Viaux does not altogether relieve the agency of a connection with the actions of Viaux's group on 22 October. Nevertheless, General Schneider was killed by a handgun—not by one of the CIA-provided submachine guns—and the CIA had abduction rather than assassination in mind. In light of these considerations the Church Committee more or less absolved the CIA of responsibility for Schneider's death. Other commentators, including Powers and Hersh, are less generous.[18]

Hersh suggests that Track II plotting in the U.S. government had another dimension, the assassination of Salvador Allende himself. According to Hersh, papers and contingency plans that included this possibility were prepared, and intelligence officers suspected such purposes. Hersh's source for the options papers is Yeoman Charles E. Radford, Rear Adm. Rembrandt C. Robinson's National Security Council staff aide. Hersh writes that he confirmed the existence of "contingency plans" with a senior member of the Washington intelligence community. He also says that Colonel Wimert told him in 1980 that he "figured" that CIA operatives who came to Chile with false, non-U.S. passports in September and October 1970 were there to arrange for Allende's death. Hersh quotes Wimert as asking: "Why else would they be there?" Lastly, Hersh quotes a close associate of CIA director Helms as saying that Helms knew that Richard Nixon wanted him to have Allende killed, even though the president did not actually instruct him to take this action in their 15 September 1970 meeting. Hersh's description is reminiscent of Henry II asking who would rid him of "this troublesome priest."[19]

A close reading of Hersh's account is somewhat less conclusive, however, than the atmospherics might cause one to believe. Hersh presents no evidence that Allende's physical elimination was authorized by anybody in the White House. The presence in Chile of

CIA agents with false passports is explained by Church Committee investigators in terms of liaison with Viaux, not in terms of any assassination plan. Helms testified to the Church Committee in 1975—as Hersh acknowledges—that he had already made up his mind when he became CIA director that the agency would have no part in assassinations and had made that position clear to his colleagues, "and I think they will tell you this."[20] Hersh refers to options papers, contingency plans, surmise, and speculation, but he nowhere shows that anybody ordered Allende killed or took action to further that end.

If the foregoing was Track II, what was Track I? Track I encompassed a number of anti-Allende covert initiatives. The essential distinction was that Track I action proposals were considered in the Forty Committee and pursued with the knowledge of the State Department and the U.S. ambassador to Chile, while Track II proposals were not.

The most noteworthy of these Track I ideas was dubbed the "Rube Goldberg" stratagem. It was designed to frustrate Allende's confirmation by vote of the Chilean Congress and to engineer the reelection of Frei by overcoming the Chilean constitutional bar to consecutive terms. On 14 September, the day before Track II was launched, the Forty Committee discussed several versions of the same basic idea. The first variant would be to convince Christian Democratic congressmen to vote for Alessandri, the runner-up to Allende and therefore the other candidate presented to the joint session of the Chilean Congress on 24 October. Alessandri would serve as president for a day or so and resign, opening the door to a new election in which Frei would be, it was thought, constitutionally eligible to run. The second variant would be to persuade Frei to resign before the end of his term. His minister of interior would then become acting president, pending new elections. The third variant, the "Frei gambit," would be to convince key ministers in Frei's government to resign and induce their colleagues to follow suit. Frei could then appoint a military cabinet and step down himself, so the military would hold power in a kind of sanctioned coup until new elections could be held.[21]

The Forty Committee instructed Ambassador Korry to meet with President Frei and discuss the Rube Goldberg stratagem. It also authorized the expenditure of $250,000 for "projects which Frei or his trusted team" deemed important, which could include bribes to Chilean congressmen. Ambassador Korry states that he rejected the money and declined to discuss the Rube Goldberg stratagem with Frei, although some indirect consultation appears to have taken place. Korry has also said that Frei would not have had his party's support anyway had he run for the presidency in these circumstances. Lastly, an agreement already existed between Tomic and Allende to ask their followers to support whichever of them survived to confront Alessandri in the congressional vote. The Rube Goldberg plans had virtually no chance of success.[22]

In another Track I initiative the Forty Committee approved a propaganda campaign to influence the Chilean Congress through scare tactics, which apparently included predictions of financial and economic disaster should Allende be confirmed. The committee also authorized financial support for visits to Chile by anticommunist foreign correspondents.[23]

There was what might be called a third track, although it was never called Track III: the initiative of International Telephone and Telegraph (ITT). The corporation had a particular interest in Chile because it owned 70 percent of the Chilean Telephone Company (Chiltelco), with an interest valued by ITT at more than $150 million. In June 1970 the ITT Board of Directors had considered Chiltelco's vulnerability to nationalization should Allende win and had asked one of its members, John A. McCone, former CIA director and then still a consultant to the agency, to inquire about the U.S. government's assessment of Chilean electoral prospects. McCone talked several times with CIA director Helms in the ensuing weeks and arranged for the CIA's Western Hemisphere Division chief, William C. Broe, to talk with ITT's chief executive officer, Harold S. Geneen, on 16 July 1970. Geneen reportedly offered a seven-figure sum to help stop Allende's election. Broe responded that the CIA could not disburse ITT funds, but he promised to advise ITT on ways to channel them. ITT later passed $350,000 to the Alessandri campaign and $100,000 to support the newspaper El Mercurio.[24]

The ITT board discussed Chile again on 9 September after Allende had gained his plurality. Geneen told McCone privately that he was prepared to put up a million dollars to assist any U.S. government plan to block Allende's election in the Chilean Congress. McCone passed this offer on to Kissinger and Helms but got no known response from either man.[25]

On 29 September Broe, at Helms's instruction, met with Edward J. Gerrity, ITT's senior vice president, and proposed a plan to stimulate greater economic disorder in Chile. U.S. companies and banks would be encouraged to delay credit and slow down deliveries of goods and spare parts to Chile; technical assistance from the United States would also be withdrawn. By this time, however, Gerrity had received mixed signals from his own representatives in Chile, including appeals for caution and advice that it would be dangerous to be "identified openly with any anti-Allende move." In a confidential comment on the meeting with Broe, Gerrity pointed out to Geneen that Broe's plan would require ITT to press the U.S. corporations to help carry out the plan, a matter somewhat different from asking the U.S. government to take action. Besides, ITT was concluding that the plan was impractical. ITT apparently made a few soundings with other corporations but declined to become heavily involved in carrying out Broe's proposal.[26]

The situation in late September and October was complicated by continuing consultations between the U.S. government and ITT at various levels, both in Washington and in Santiago, and by a considerable seepage of information and attitudes back and forth, including hints about Track II.[27] News of the consultations, including the hints, would be leaked to columnist Jack Anderson, and he publicized them in the spring of 1972.[28]

ITT and the U.S. government never successfully coordinated their efforts. The courtship between the two giants during those crucial seven weeks seemed always to find that the responding flame was flickering out when the suitor's ardor burned most brightly. So the three tracks pursued in the U.S. government had one thing in common: none of them led to any desirable result.

### The Seven-Week Hiatus in Chile

President Nixon wanted the Chilean economy to "scream," and scream it did in the days after 4 September 1970. Chileans almost immediately started a run on the banks and savings associations. Prices slid on the stock exchange, the black market grew, and sales of some durable goods dropped by 50 to 80 percent. Finance Minister Andrés Zaldívar estimated publicly on the twenty-third that nearly a billion escudos in bank deposits, the equivalent of $80 million, had been withdrawn in the two weeks following the 4 September election. In order to keep the money supply flowing, he reported, the Frei administration had printed 304 million escudos.

In mid-October the central bank restricted sales of dollars to Chileans traveling abroad, explaining that $43 million had already been sold in the seven weeks since the election—for a country of ten million people, a lot of money for foreign travel.[29] Many of the rich were fleeing.

Hersh attributes the bank run to the CIA, noting that within two weeks of the election, "twenty-three journalists from at least ten countries" were brought into Chile, and "more than 700 articles and broadcasts" carrying scare stories were produced, inside and outside Chile, before 24 October.[30] I am skeptical, however, that the transition would have been smooth, with or without CIA machinations.

The Christian Democrats glimpsed the outlines of their strategy within two or three days of the 4 September elections and confirmed their position at a party convention in the first days of October. They felt little disposition to overturn the expressed preference of the Chilean electorate, but they were anxious to commit Allende to democratic guarantees that would protect Chile from a drift toward leftist dictatorship. They called publicly for such an agreement, and they made their support of Allende in the congressional runoff conditional on reaching one. By 9 October an agreement had been concluded.[31]

The agreement provided for the formal passage of constitutional amendments that would extend basic guarantees. The right of free association in political parties would be protected, and all parties would be assured equal access to state-controlled media (Article 9 of the Constitution, as amended). The media could be expropriated only by a law approved by an absolute majority of the full membership in each house of Congress. There would be no arbitrary discrimination in the "sale or supply" to press, radio, and television of "paper, ink, machinery, or other elements for their operation" (Art. 10-3). Private, nonprofit education was guaranteed, supported by state funds if necessary and free from political interference in admissions, texts, curriculum, and appointments of teachers. (Art. 10-

7. This provision protected Catholic education, which was supported by public funds.)

With respect to the armed forces, the key provision held that "the forces of public coercion consist solely and exclusively of the armed forces and the corps of carabineros [national police]— institutions that are essentially professional, heirarchically organized, disciplined, obedient, and nondeliberative" (Art. 22). These sentences were designed to protect the "monopoly of force" of the military and police and to protect the chain of command, the integrity of the services, and their nonpolitical ("nondeliberative") role.

The Christian Democrats had initially suggested a provision that all promotions would be made by the respective commanders. Allende with good reason regarded this proposal as an infringement of presidential prerogatives. The final agreement restricted military and police appointments at the officer level to graduates of the cadet schools (Art. 22). Only Congress would be authorized to change the strength of the armed forces or the national police (Art. 22). These last two provisions were designed to prevent leftist infiltration and the grafting of a people's militia onto the regular army.[32] The amendments embodied in the Statute of Guarantees were added to the Constitution on 9 January 1971.

The new constitutional guarantees were important political factors throughout Allende's presidency. They became a standard of conduct against which governmental actions were measured, and opposition disenchantment began quite early. Within several months of Allende's agreement to the guarantees, Régis Debray, Allende's confidant, quoted the president as having said that he had signed them as a tactical necessity to gain power.[33] The president's reported attitude outraged the opposition. His reported statement came, in fact, on top of his public assertion that he was "president of Unidad Popular," not of all Chileans. Allende later clarified this remark, saying that he would defend the rights of "all Chileans" and be the president of all the people, even though he was not the president of speculators, mercenaries, plotters, and the murderers of General Schneider. The explanation helped some, but there were still quite a few who feared that he had expressed himself accurately the first time.[34]

Observance of the constitutional guarantees eroded over time, and this development ultimately became a central element in the alienation of the Christian Democrats, along with other initially friendly political and military leaders. One must appreciate the solemnity of the commitment Allende made in amending the Constitution and the importance of the guarantees in the eyes of the opposition to understand the disillusionment that spread like a cancerous growth through the Chilean body politic between 1970 and 1973.

On 22 October, later in the same day when General Viaux's group of militants fatally wounded General Schneider, the commanders of the Chilean armed forces, after an emergency meeting, declared that the militants' "despicable action" would not change "the permanent determination of the armed forces to fulfill their mission." Gen. Carlos Prats González became acting commander-in-chief of the army, and military and civilian constitutionalists closed ranks. On the twenty-fourth the Chilean Congress voted to elect Allende president, in a secret ballot that gave Allende 153 votes to Alessandri's 35. The next day Schneider died, and on the day after that President Frei and President-elect Allende stood side-by-side at Schneider's funeral. On 3 November 1970 Salvador Allende took the oath of office as president.[35]

### Allende's First Year

Allende had proclaimed during his election campaign that he wanted to alter the political institutions of the country. He proposed the substitution of a single "people's assembly" for the Chamber of Deputies and the Senate, a change that would free him from dependence on an opposition-controlled parliament. There was only one way Allende could accomplish this institutional transformation legally, however, and that was through a national plebiscite, which the president had the authority to call under Article 109 of the Constitution.[36] In order to set the stage for a successful plebiscite, Allende had to convert his plurality of a bit over a third of the Chilean electorate into 50.1 percent.

Allende had a lot going for him. Chile traditionally gave the incoming president a "honeymoon" during which he was accorded the benefit of the doubt. Chileans soon realized, moreover, that Salvador Allende did not have visible horns and a forked tail, and life went on without confirming the direst predictions of the "mummies," as the opponents of progress were called.

In the best Keynesian tradition the new Unidad Popular government turned to "pump priming," stimulating the economy through expenditure to increase purchasing power and employment. The government mandated higher wages and salaries in both nationalized and private enterprises, with the result that most people had extra money to spend.

With approximately half of Chilean industry already in state hands when Allende took power, and additional formal or de facto nationalizations expanding the public sector day by day, the government could give jobs to tens of thousands of pro-UP workers. The SUMAR textile plant, for example, took on one thousand workers in 1971, increasing its employment rolls to 3,500; Cervecerías Unidas, the Santiago brewery, more than doubled its work force after it was nationalized in 1971; and the copper mine El Teniente added some 4,000 workers in 1971 to the 8,000 already employed.[37] It was also open season on political appointments throughout the official state bureaucracy, down to the janitorial level. To give one example, the staff of a single government agency, the Municipal Works Corporation (CORMU), was reported to have increased from 200 to 12,000 during Allende's time. These newly hired employees also had money to spend.[38]

Land reform and what was effectively a government-financed rural dole also allowed poor farm workers to buy goods they previously could not afford. It was summer in the southern hemisphere, and the living was easy.

The supply of goods seemed to expand to accommodate demand. Chilean industrial plants had apparently been operating at less than 70 percent of capacity when Allende took office, and new hires enabled many enterprises to increase output. The government reported a 12 percent increase in industrial production in 1971, the largest jump in many years.[39]

High international copper prices had made it possible for the Frei government to accumulate about $350 to $400 million in foreign reserves. The UP government drew down these reserves in a consumer-goods buying spree that filled the shelves of Chilean stores with imports.[40]

With increased employment, higher use of plant capacity, and more commodities being imported, supply more or less kept up with the increased purchasing power of the population. As a result, the inflationary effect was moderate. Price controls also helped. In

April 1971 the consumer price index was only 20 percent above the prices of a year earlier, while the index for the Frei administration had been running about 35 percent above comparable year-earlier prices.[41]

Nationwide municipal elections were held on 4 April 1971, and Unidad Popular did well. Parties supporting the government won 49.7 percent of the total vote, compared to 48 percent for the opposition, with the remainder for minor candidates and blank and null ballots. The UP had gained more than 13 points since the presidential elections the previous September.[42]

Three months later, on 18 July 1971, a by-election was held in Valparaíso to replace a deputy who had died. The UP candidate and his Christian Democratic challenger each received almost exactly the same percentage of the vote as their parties had won in the April municipal elections. Between April and July it looked as if Unidad Popular was holding almost exactly 50 percent support in the electorate.[43]

As events unfolded, it became clear that these four or five months in 1971 had been the high point in UP popularity. It was probably Allende's best moment to call a plebiscite and have a chance at victory. Allende himself said so in a speech on 20 January 1973, when he counted his failure to call a plebiscite soon after his election as one of his crucial mistakes.[44] In 1971, however, the president was not prepared to throw the dice in the high-risk political gamble the plebiscite would have represented.

I think Allende was right in 1971 and mistaken when he looked back on an apparent opportunity. It is one thing to have 50 percent for one's candidates; it is another to ask the Chilean electorate to dismantle its parliamentary institutions. Socialist party secretary Carlos Altamirano Orrego more realistically called the April 1971 elections a "stalemate." Allende never gave up the idea of the plebiscite, however, and he kept returning to it in subsequent months.

Lord Keynes warned that deficit spending and the stimulation of demand will "prime the pump" of recovery only to the point where idle plant capacity is put to use and full employment is reached. Then stimulation becomes inflation. His warning held for Chile. While the hiring of new workers in state enterprises initially put idle machines to work, the later effect was featherbedding, underemployment, and payrolled workers who produced little or nothing. Labor discipline sagged, for workers felt that "their government" was in power and would protect them. The government for its part needed the workers' votes in its drive for a nationwide majority and was reluctant to crack down.[45] Frequent and interminable political meetings in the factories and factional disputes within UP ranks aggravated the problem.

Even though it had a workers' government, Chilean labor did not hesitate to strike. The coal miners went out in July 1971 for higher pay, and railroad workers struck for almost two months in mid-1971 for the same reason. Miners at the country's third-largest copper mine, El Salvador, walked out in August 1971, in still another wage dispute.[46]

In 1971 world demand for copper slid downward, and copper prices at the end of that year were only about two-thirds of what they had been in 1970. Since most of Chile's export earnings came from copper, Chilean foreign-exchange earnings declined sharply. Moreover, the government resisted devaluation through most of the year, and an overvalued currency depressed the volume of exports and further stimulated the importation of what became very cheap foreign goods.

By November 1971 the Chilean government had spent the bulk of its foreign-exchange reserves, and it declared a moratorium on the payment of interest and principal on most of the country's foreign debt. It also moved to restrict imports, requiring a large deposit before capital and consumer goods could be purchased abroad.[47] These were palliative measures, however, and economic policies remained unchanged.

As for inflation, the rate of increase in the consumer price index declined steadily until September 1971, when it stood at only 15.6 percent above the index the previous year. September, however, was the turning point, and thereafter consumer price increases began to accelerate.[48] By the final months of 1971 impressive short-term success was becoming increasingly severe economic embarrassment, and these economic troubles began to contaminate the political atmosphere.

The shift in attitude of the Christian Democratic party was crucially important to the turbulent political events of Allende's first year in office. On 10 May 1971 the party announced a policy of permanent dialogue with the UP and a stance of "constructive" opposition, which meant that the UP government would be supported "in everything that contributes to the national interest." With Radomiro Tomic's poor showing in the 1970 elections, Renán Fuentealba emerged as leader of the party's loyalist left wing, and later he became president of the party. Fuentealba championed cooperation with Unidad Popular on measures of socialist transformation, in liberty and in accordance with Christian values.[49]

June saw the start of an irregular but deteriorating trend in the CD-UP relationship. Frei's vice president, Edmundo Pérez Zújovic, was murdered on 8 June by extremists of the Vanguardia Organizada del Pueblo (VOP), an ultra-leftist terrorist group. Most of the group's leaders were soon killed in a shoot-out with government detectives, and the circumstances were such as to cause rumors that the VOP leaders had been eliminated deliberately in order to prevent them from revealing their ties to government personalities. The subsequent, heated Valparaíso by-election campaign in June and July further dramatized the differences between the government and the Christian Democrats.[50]

By September the Christian Democrats were becoming increasingly resentful of what they regarded as slanderous attacks from the UP news media. Propaganda assaults directed personally against Frei provoked the former president to speak out on 22 September, charging that the Communists were using the same tactics that had reduced other countries to communist slavery. Christian Democratic youths and UP supporters clashed, and a particularly sharp encounter, where the two sides assaulted each other with rocks and sticks, occurred outside the Christian Democratic party's headquarters on the twenty-fourth. On the same day Senator Osvaldo Olguín, acting CD party president, declared that the party would have to revise its policy of "making the government's job easy."[51]

The closing months of 1971 thus brought a political turning point as well as an economic one. Such honeymoon as there might have been between the UP and the Christian Democrats was ending, and the successes of the first year of Unidad Popular government were turning sour.

## U.S.-Chilean Relations during the First Year

U.S. covert intervention in Chilean politics neither started nor stopped with the seven-week crisis of September and October 1970. Three million dollars in financial support had been allocated to the Christian Democrats in the 1964 elections, and smaller sums had been approved for the congressional elections of 1965 and 1969 and for other political purposes. The CIA had been authorized to spend approximately $425,000 for antileftist propaganda during the 1970 election campaign itself. In January 1971 the Forty Committee approved $1.24 million for the purchase of radio stations and newspapers and to support anti-UP candidates in the April municipal elections. Between January and July 1971 the Forty Committee authorized half-a-million dollars more, mostly to help the Christian Democratic party. For the July by-election in Valparaíso, the Forty Committee voted an additional $150,000. In September the committee approved $700,000 to support *El Mercurio*. During the first year of Allende's presidency these subventions came to slightly more than $2.5 million.[52]

So far as Track II is concerned, it is difficult to be sure when it stopped. The assertion of most U.S. government spokesmen of the time is that it petered out in the months that followed Allende's congressional confirmation and assumption of office. However, Thomas Karamessines, head of clandestine operations of the CIA between 1970 and early 1973, testified that so far as he was concerned, "Track II was really never ended. . . . What we were told to do was to continue our efforts. Stay alert, and to do what we could to contribute to the eventual achievement of the objectives and purposes of Track II. That being the case, I don't think it is proper to say that Track II was ended."[53] Ambassador Korry later said that some operations continued to be carried on behind his back in early 1971, and Hersh reports that CIA documents and intelligence officers' recollections support Korry.[54] I discuss U.S. covert action in Chile systematically in chapters 12 and 13, and here it suffices to note that during Allende's presidency an ongoing U.S. program gave covert financial support to opposition parties, media, and several other opposition organizations. This activity was carried on in the political subculture of the U.S.-Chilean connection.

National Security Decision Memorandum (NSDM) 93, issued by Henry Kissinger on behalf of the president on 9 November 1970, established a policy of applying unacknowledged pressure on Allende's government to prevent its consolidation and to limit its ability to implement policies contrary to U.S. interests and those of our friends. The memorandum ordered that no financing, assistance, or government guarantees of private investment be initiated and that existing assistance be reduced or terminated if possible. The United States was to use its influence in international financial institutions to limit credit and other financial assistance to Chile and was to advise private U.S. businesses with investments or operations in Chile of U.S. policies and concerns. Except for humanitarian programs, no new bilateral economic aid was to be committed. The memorandum also called for an examination of the possibilities of reducing, delaying, or terminating existing bilateral economic aid commitments.[55]

Lastly, the memorandum reportedly ordered a review of possible steps to drive down the world price for copper. So far as I know, nothing came of this last study directive, perhaps because the idea was likely to provoke strong opposition from U.S. mining interests if discovered. Well-informed businessmen in the world copper industry, whom I have consulted, confirm that it would have been extremely difficult for the U.S. executive branch to have manipulated the price of copper through stockpile disposal or other measures because of U.S. congressional restrictions, and U.S. domestic producers and those in friendly countries would have been vigilant and soon noisy had such efforts been initiated. Largely because of the winddown of the Vietnam War, world copper prices did decline in the early months of the Allende administration, and the Chilean government and foreign leftists predictably voiced the suspicion that the United States had pushed down the market.

On 30 December 1970 the Senior Review Group (SRG) of the U.S. National Security Council approved several specific unpublicized economic measures against Chile, including reductions of aid and credit. The Export-Import Bank, for example, while not terminating its loan guarantee program, did drop Chile to its lowest credit-rating category.[56]

NSDM 93 had another aspect, its public face. To avoid giving Allende an easy foreign target that would help him rally support, both domestic and international, U.S. policy called for the maintenance of a "correct" outward posture. The Senior Review Group decided on 19 November to take the following overt position: "We have no wish to prejudge the future of our relations with Chile, but naturally they will depend on the actions which the Chilean government takes toward the United States and the Inter-American system."[57] In February 1971 President Nixon articulated U.S. public policy with respect to Chile in his annual foreign-policy report to the Congress: "Our bilateral policy is to keep open the lines of communication between the U.S. and Chile. . . . In short, we are prepared to have the kind of relationship with the Chilean government that it is prepared to have with us."[58]

The somewhat contradictory elements of secret and declared policy were never clearly explained even within the U.S. government. The chief of naval operations, Adm. Elmo Zumwalt, complained in his memoirs that "no one in Defense, not even Mel Laird or Tom Moorer I conjecture—I cannot be absolutely sure—knew precisely what administration policy toward Chile was [in late 1970 and early 1971] because Henry [Kissinger] had made an elaborate point of not telling them." Zumwalt also discerns a lack of coordination between the State Department, with its "moderate position," and the White House, with a harder line.[59]

Another question deeply influenced U.S. policy. The Chileans moved to expropriate U.S. investments, particularly in the copper mines. Copper was and is Chile's bread and butter. In the early years of the present century the Braden Copper Company, the Guggenheims, and the Kennecott Copper Corporation developed El Teniente, the world's greatest tunneled copper mine, and Chuquicamata, which became the world's largest open-pit copper mine. In later years the Anaconda Copper Mining Company bought Chuquicamata and developed El Salvador and other mines. A few smaller U.S. copper companies also established Chilean operations.

Minerals are a nonrenewable resource, of course, and politically sensitive Chileans reacted against the great multinational corporations, which they perceived as carting off their patrimony year after year, at great profit. Frei's government successfully negotiated Chilean acquisition of a 51 percent interest in the greatest mines, to be accompanied by an ambitious program of mine expansion. That achievement was not enough, however, for the newly victorious Allende government. Within seven weeks of taking office the president introduced a constitutional amendment to nationalize all of Chile's large mines.

On 11 July 1971 a joint session of the Chilean Congress unanimously approved the UP government's copper amendment. The measure provided for compensation to copper companies within thirty years at not less than 3 percent interest. It also gave the president authority to determine whether copper company profits since 1955 had been "excessive" and whether equipment had been allowed to deteriorate, and to deduct such excessive profits and damage from the compensation figure. On 28 September President Allende determined that past profits had indeed been excessive. Excess-profit deductions exceeded the total value of the three largest mines, leaving Anaconda and Kennecott without any compensation for these properties.[60]

Had profits been excessive? Frank R. Milliken, the president of Kennecott, candidly said that his company's Chilean subsidiary had been "a very profitable company." Between 1965 and 1970 Kennecott appears to have received slightly over $20 million a year remitted in profits from its Chilean subsidiary, Braden. Book value of Kennecott's ownership interest in El Teniente *after* half the operation was sold to the Chileans had been declared at approximately $120 million.[61] Milliken made the points that his company had been operating legally under the then-current laws of Chile and that an ex post facto determination of excess profits changed the rules after the game.

John B. M. Place, president of Anaconda, expressed similar sentiments. Anaconda had the additional point that profits and losses at El Salvador had gone up and down like a roller coaster ride; it was unfair to deduct high profits in good years without taking the bad years into account. Anaconda's Chilean investments were even greater than Kennecott's, and Anaconda declared in 1971 that its interest in the Chuquicamata and El Salvador mines had a book value of $303 million. Anaconda also had fewer North American operations than Kennecott and was more dependent on its Chilean mines. Anaconda stock on the New York Stock Exchange plummeted from a high of more than $32 a share in 1970 to $12 a share in 1971.[62]

Personally, I believe that the problem created by foreign development of nonrenewable resources has only one long-term solution: to build gradual payoff of equity into the initial arrangements between multinational corporations and Third World countries.

Such advice would have been of little help to Ambassador Korry, however, as he turned his resourceful intellect and formidable talents to the problem at hand. He tried ingenious formulas, negotiated with Allende, negotiated with the copper companies,

discreetly lobbied the Chilean congressional opposition, offered a
U.S. Treasury guarantee of long-term Chilean bonds, explained,
argued, and cajoled everybody who would listen. But nothing
changed the result.[63]

The U.S. government had a more immediate stake in Chilean
nationalization politics: the heavy exposure of the Overseas Private
Investment Corporation (OPIC), the semiautonomous insurer of
U.S. investments in the Third World. Set up by the U.S. government to encourage development through private U.S. investment,
the organization had begun life in 1948 as part of the U.S. government's regular foreign-assistance bureaucracy, but it was partially
detached from the Agency for International Development in 1971
in order to give the program a more business-oriented leadership.
The activity had suffered difficulties ever since its inception, and it
had never been, strictly speaking, an insurance company that covered calculated risks from premium income. Some of OPIC's premiums had even been diverted to other U.S. government accounts
and were not available to meet claims. The managers of the program had tended to look to the diplomatic clout of the U.S. government to cover their bets. They had also insisted on negotiating
state-to-state umbrella agreements with countries hosting U.S. investment. In these agreements the host countries had to make binding commitments *not* to nationalize U.S. investments without
appropriate compensation.

In the particular case of Chile, OPIC had two additional problems, problems that had grown out of American enthusiasm for
Frei's experiment in democratic progress. First, the U.S. government had granted investment guarantees in Chile without getting
an airtight state-to-state agreement on compensation for
nationalized enterprises. Second, the United States had put too
many eggs in the Chilean basket. If Anaconda, Kennecott, and ITT
had been able to collect all the investment insurance they claimed,
amounting to over half a billion dollars, they would have bank-
rupted OPIC several times over. OPIC's accumulated reserves from
premiums and the original congressional grubstake—with payouts
and diversions deducted—fluctuated in the neighborhood of $100
million. So OPIC's interest in Chilean developments was
incandescent, and its activism in U.S. policy toward Chile was
considerable.[64]

It should be added that OPIC had had a few lucky breaks as well as woes. For one thing, in 1969 Anaconda's chairman, C. Jay Parkinson, had tried to save some premium money by putting a part of his OPIC coverage on "standby." He had also worked out the stock sale to the Frei government without full consultation and approval from OPIC.[65] The legal questions involved in trying to determine whether Parkinson's actions let OPIC off the hook as Anaconda's insurer were complex, but OPIC's full exposure was at least arguable. With lawyers skilled in broken-field running, OPIC was in a situation that was unenviable but not hopeless.

One last aspect of the U.S.-Chilean relationship during Allende's first year needs a word of explanation: military cooperation between the two countries. The Allende government was prepared to continue the cooperative military relationship, and the trouble came from clumsy U.S. efforts to put the Chileans at arm's length. Allende knew that the Chilean military wanted to maintain arrangements with the United States and did not wish to turn to the communist bloc for weapons and support. As Allende was most anxious to strengthen military loyalty, he was willing to accommodate the generals and admirals on the question of ties with the United States, but for a brief moment in 1970 the U.S. government had considered breaking these links. According to the Church Committee report, Ambassador Korry was authorized in September 1970 "to make his contacts in the Chilean military aware that if Allende were seated, the military could expect no further military assistance (MAP) from the United States. Later, Korry was authorized to inform the Chilean military that all MAP and military sales were being held in abeyance pending the outcome of the congressional election on October 24."[66]

Then there was the Easter Island incident. A U.S. facility there and two others on Chilean territory were closed down, and U.S. personnel were hastily withdrawn, in the days before Allende assumed office in November 1970. The U.S. government version of the episode was that these three meteorological and ionospheric observation centers, on Easter Island, at Punta Arenas, and at Quintero, near Valparaíso, were closed for budgetary reasons. The decision had been made in early 1970, some months before the Chilean elections. Hersh has published a somewhat different version, to the effect that the bases' atmospheric testing was merely a cover for their main activity, which according to Hersh was the monitoring of Soviet and French nuclear tests and ballistic missile firings in the Pacific, watching for submarine-launched missiles, and the interception of low-frequency Soviet submarine communications. Hersh wrote that evacuation was ordered "overnight" when the Chilean Congress elected Allende.[67]

Matters became more complicated when Ambassador Korry absented himself from the diplomatic corps' farewell party for the retiring Christian Democratic foreign minister, Gabriel Valdés, and showed up on Easter Island, either to supervise the dismantling of the facility or to distribute food parcels to the islanders (depending on the version one accepts). Outgoing Frei administration officials took offense. They accused the Americans of having failed to give Chile appropriate notice of the closings and of removing equipment without giving the Chilean Air Force the customary opportunity to purchase at least some of it. The incoming Allende people were virtually bystanders during this contretemps, but the episode left a bad taste with them as well.[68]

By this time the United States was perceived as having a dog-in-the-manger attitude, while the new Allende government was apparently forthcoming. U.S. policy makers soon came to understand, however, that U.S. recalcitrance might drive the Chilean armed forces into the waiting arms of the Soviets and Eastern Europeans. The Chilean military was growing concerned at the Peruvian "threat" as the hundredth anniversary of the War of the Pacific drew closer, and there was no question but that the Chilean military leadership would seek technical military assistance and training from somewhere. It should be noted, however, that the United States was not the Chileans' only possible Western arms supplier. The Frei government had actually turned to Britain more than to the United States for purchases of naval vessels and military aircraft, because credit terms had been better. In 1971 Chile owed the British about $150 million for frigates, submarines, Hawker Hunter aircraft, and other items.[69] Nevertheless, the Soviets did stand ready to exploit any deterioration in the relationship between Chile and the United States.

By early 1971 the White House had shifted position. The State Department was instructed to terminate previous "hold" instructions and release some M-41 tanks Chile had purchased.[70] Then the *Enterprise* incident occurred, once again setting back cooperation. In February, shortly after the White House's easing of policy on the

tank sale, Adm. Elmo Zumwalt visited Chile as a part of a Latin
American tour. When he was in Valparaíso, President Allende,
who happened to be there too, invited Zumwalt to call on him. As
later became clear, Chilean naval commander-in-chief Raúl Montero Cornejo had put the president up to suggesting the call and had
primed Allende to tell Zumwalt that Chile would welcome a port-
call by the nuclear aircraft carrier *Enterprise*, which was then cruis-
ing around South America. Zumwalt subsequently briefed
Ambassador Korry, and they both telegraphed Washington urging
that the *Enterprise* visit Valparaíso. Supported by the State Department and the CIA, Kissinger judged that acceptance would constitute a heartier embrace of Chile than the president had in mind.
Before a response could be made to the Chileans, however, Allende
made the invitation public. On 28 February 1971 the United States
publicly rebuffed the overture, reportedly on the direct order of
President Nixon.[71] Allende turned the other cheek. While expressing regret that Chilean hospitality had been spurned, he refrained
from throwing out the U.S. Military Group (MILGROUP), and he
continued to support military collaboration between the two countries. On 29 June 1971 the United States extended an arms credit of
$5 million to Chile for the purchase of C-130 transport aircraft and
paratrooper equipment.[72] The Chilean military, with Allende's
concurrence, welcomed the new loan. Over Allende's first year, in
brief, the Chilean president maintained a benign posture on military relationships. While the U.S. attitude sometimes looked chur-
lish, Washington supported the Chilean military and continued
assistance to it.

### A Change of U.S. Ambassadors

On 20 November 1970 I received a telegram in Guatemala from
Secretary of State William P. Rogers and the assistant secretary for
Inter-American affairs, Charles A. Meyer. They advised me that
they were recommending to the president that I be sent to Chile.
Had I been wiser, I might have declined the honor. At the time,
however, I had no knowledge of U.S. covert action in Chile and
little knowledge of the depth of hostility to Allende in the White
House, although I realized that the U.S. government regarded Allende's election as a sharp setback to U.S. interests.

My specializations in the U.S. Foreign Service were communist

Eastern Europe and Latin America. I had served in the Soviet Union, Czechoslovakia, and Bulgaria and had worked on relations with the Soviet Union and Eastern Europe when assigned to the State Department and the National Security Council staff at the White House. I had also served in Latin America, with postings in Venezuela and Guatemala, and had worked with Latin American programs during three years' service with the Peace Corps. I had filled in as Peace Corps director in Chile during the 1962 winter there and knew the country. Santiago would be my third post as chief of mission.

My family and I returned from Guatemala on home leave in December 1970, and I went straight to Washington for consultations. There I was told that the Chilean assignment was off, canceled for reasons that no one was prepared to discuss. I left Washington for my Christmas leave somewhat bemused. I returned to Washington after Christmas for last-minute consultations before returning to Guatemala City—uncertain, in fact, whether I would be authorized to continue serving anywhere. Just as mysteriously as before, I was advised that the Chile appointment was back on track.

I later learned, informally, what had happened. It appears that I had been mixed up with another Davis, Richard Hallock Davis. I had worked for this Davis—an extraordinarily fine man. With his wife Harriet, Davis had been assigned by the Johnson administration as chief of mission in Romania. During his time there Richard Nixon—then a private citizen—had come through Bucharest. Invited to the embassy residence, the former vice president had gazed around at the daring, contemporary paintings that decorated the walls. Nixon reacted negatively. Reportedly, he put his arm around Harriet and said: "Honey, where did you get the crap on your walls?"

The elections of 1968 resulted in Richard Nixon's victory. Three weeks later Drew Pearson and Jack Anderson publicized the president-elect's critical artistic judgment,[73] which Pearson had learned of while visiting Bucharest shortly after Nixon had been there. It is not clear whether the president-elect felt he had been embarrassed by the story and held the leak against Ambassador Davis, whether Nixon and Davis had disagreed on some policy issue when Nixon was visiting Bucharest, or whether Nixon had sensed the Davises' discomfiture at being told that they had covered their walls with "crap." In any case, Ambassador Davis was sent to the Naval War

College in Newport, Rhode Island, in due course and never received another ambassadorial appointment.

When the secretary of state's formal proposal of my assignment to Chile reached the White House, President Nixon had apparently looked at it and asked an aide, "Didn't Davis serve in Eastern Europe?" The aide answered, "Yes, Mr. President." The President had marked the nomination "Disapproved." Secretary Rogers had not really known me, and I assume he had been relying on Charles Meyer's recommendation and that of my professional colleagues. The secretary, to his credit, apparently took the trouble to go back to the president and ask what the problem was. I assume that the president then explained—for which I am also grateful, as presidents in such circumstances do not always do so. The confusion was cleared up.

The appointment then went forward, though slowly. It was decided in Washington that the April 1971 elections in Chile were of great importance—as indeed they were—and that a change of ambassadors should not be made until the elections were history. The Chileans carried out their municipal elections on 4 April. Immediately, the planned shift in ambassadors leaked in Washington and appeared in the American press. The publicity did not make things easier for anybody, least of all for Ambassador Korry in Santiago. He had opened some delicate negotiations about copper nationalization, and Washington decided that the planned shifts should be deferred a bit longer.

On 5 July 1971 Jeremiah O'Leary of the *Washington Star* publicly described me as being in a holding pattern to go to Chile.[74] The senior management of Kennecott and Anaconda were by this time waiting anxiously on Ambassador Korry's negotiations, hoping that he might ease their great problems.[75] It is said that copper company executives telephoned Secretary of State Rogers all the way to Cairo on one of the secretary's foreign trips, urging that Ambassador Korry not be withdrawn "quite yet." Finally, in late July, my appointment was forwarded to the U.S. Senate for confirmation, and I was ordered up from Guatemala for consultations.[76]

Consultations before going to a new post involve an endless series of calls. Among the more useful ones in my case were visits to the New York City offices of Anaconda, Kennecott, ITT, and several other companies. At ITT I called upon John W. Guilfoyle, Latin American chief of operations. I never met Harold Geneen; he sent me the largest, most expensive Christmas card I have ever received, but that was the extent of our contact.

Chilean foreign minister Clodomiro Almeyda, who was in New York for the opening of the UN General Assembly, called on Secretary Rogers during this time, and he also talked with Henry Kissinger at a dinner at the Chilean Embassy in Washington on 6 October. I wrote up the memoranda for the record, which I remember because I was enjoined from passing a copy of the Kissinger write-up to the State Department. This latter conversation entered mythology as having produced a "face-saving agreement on compensation [for expropriated copper]," later torpedoed.[77] None of this was true. Almeyda and Kissinger probed each other's positions, but that was all that transpired.

I went out to Langley and talked briefly with Richard Helms. He seemed pessimistic about American interests in Chile and their prospects; at one point he said, "It's your problem now."[78]

Senate confirmation hearings are a hazardous passage between a rock and a whirlpool. The Foreign Relations Committee heard me on 21 September 1971, and Senator Fulbright was in good form. He questioned me about an Ex-Im Bank refusal, then widely publicized, of a $21-million loan and guarantee to the Chilean national airline, LAN-Chile. I had met with Ex-Im Bank chairman Henry Kearns the previous day, and I told the committee that the chairman had advised me he had not rejected the loan request but had asked the Chilean government for answers to several questions— including a clarification of Chilean expropriation policy. Of course, the Chileans had correctly interpreted these inquiries as a turndown.[79]

I was sworn in on 4 October, but I was still far from sure that I would be going to Chile. The copper ntionalization question was coming to a head. President Allende had announced his "excess profits" finding on 28 September. The constitutional amendment on copper nationalization gave the Chilean comptroller general two weeks to issue a formal ruling on compensation, and I had visions of American outrage expressed in the suspension of relations at the ambassadorial level.

In the first days of October the chiefs of the State Department's Inter-American Bureau told me that they thought it would be a good idea for Ambassador Korry and me to confer. I suggested that my family and I fly to Rio de Janeiro and talk to the Korrys there, as

they planned to pass through Rio on their way home. My colleagues in Washington assented, and my family and I flew south on
9 October. Ambassador Korry's departure date, however, continued
to slip.

On 11 October the Chilean comptroller general announced that
Anaconda and Kennecott should receive no compensation for their
three great mines. American business and governmental leaders
were, as expected, outraged, and Ambassador Korry telegraphed
Washington and Rio, urging that I put off my arrival in Chile. Washington maintained a beatific silence.

My family and I were booked to fly to Santiago very early on the
morning of 13 October, and the Korrys' latest plans would bring
them to Rio in the mid-afternoon of the twelfth. The plane came in,
we met it, and no Korrys emerged onto the tarmac. Word then came
that the Korrys had taken a later plane and would land at about 9
P.M. We found the Korrys and went straight to the embassy residence for a 10:30 P.M. dinner, served by a patient butler (at the
invitation of Ambassador Rountree, who was not in the city). Edward Korry was morose, and he made it clear that he did not think I
should go to Santiago at all.

At about 2 A.M. Elizabeth and I returned to our rooms and our
four sleeping children. Approximately an hour remained before we
would have to get up; I slept a few minutes, but Elizabeth stayed
up.

We flew south, stopping in Montevideo and then in Buenos
Aires. At each stop I waited for an embassy officer with instructions
to return to Washington. No such messenger came, however, and
my heart soared as the jetliner passed over the great Argentinian
pampas and rose over the Andes on a sparklingly clear day. The
gestation period for my assignment to Santiago was almost eleven
months—not as long as for an elephant, but quite long enough for a
human being.

# Chapter 2

# Castro and the Empty Pots

THE last two-and-a-half months of 1971 witnessed two resonating political events in Chile: a three-week visit by Fidel Castro in November and early December, and a march by about five thousand mostly middle-class Santiago housewives, protesting shortages that they claimed kept their pots empty. Other important events were taking place, of course, but many of the developments in the economic field were deceptively easy to procrastinate about. The country's internal political life had something of the same quality. This breathing spell in October and November was a blessing for a newly arrived U.S. ambassador.

## Arrival and Settling in

A slightly disheveled Davis family landed at Santiago under the azure Chilean sky on 13 October 1971. Four Davis children, ages ranging from thirteen to two, three of them carrying humpty-dumpty pillows, provided footage for the Chilean TV cameras. The Chilean deputy chief of protocol was warmly cordial.

A week later I presented my credentials to President Allende, in the Red Room of the Moneda Palace. The ceremony lasted twenty-two minutes—fifteen alone with the president and Foreign Minister Almeyda, and seven more after the president admitted a large crowd of press photographers. One news photographer caught Allende, Almeyda, and me as we rose from our ornate chairs, leaning forward with bent knees, rumps lifted, heads almost bumping, and eyes looking down. The resulting comical photo was later used on front pages with the caption: "Where has my ration card dropped to?"[1] The leftist newspaper *Clarín* fantasized in print that my chiefs in Washington had instructed me as follows: "Smile whenever you can; be as ingratiating as possible; talk with the journalists. . . . The gringo followed instructions to the letter." Gonzalo Cruz of the conservative paper *La Tribuna*, noting that I had studied at the Universidad Central in Caracas, observed: "He knows, then, that the Latin Americans are less inflexible than they seem, however stubbornly anti-Yankee they show themselves. He knows that all of them—not excluding Castro—long for and are fond of the United States. . . ."[2]

The U.S. ambassador is inevitably a symbol, as I was throughout my time in Chile. So had my predecessor been. Graham Greene, visiting Santiago, had observed Ambassador Korry in the cathedral on 18 September 1971, and he wrote: "I was standing just behind the retiring American Ambassador, remarkable for the size and fatness of his earlobes, who symbolized perhaps the outside aggression." Greene also characterized my appointment as a "hardly-veiled menace."[3]

The symbolic role of an ambassador works both ways. To those who loved the United States and hated Allende, the American ambassador appeared "good," probably for reasons no better than Greene had for deprecating ambassadorial earlobes. The fact that I walked alone to appointments at the Moneda Palace attracted favorable press attention from opposition journalists. A visiting American newsman talked with some anti-UP Chileans and reported to the world that I had come to be known in Santiago as the "good uncle."[4]

I was occasionally lucky with the progovernment press, but still for symbolic reasons. When in January 1972 the diplomatic corps visited the site where a new building was to house the UN Conference on Trade and Development, a leftist journalist asked if I thought the palace would be completed in time for the April UNCTAD meeting, as there was malicious speculation that it would not be. I responded that I was "absolutely sure" that the edifice would be ready. Though I would have been soft-headed to say anything less, I was a hero for a day in the press. As it transpired, the Chileans did get the building done in time.[5]

The symbolic element in an ambassador's actions also makes it perilous to display a sense of humor. On Chilean Air Force Day in 1972 I sat next to Chief Justice Ramiro Méndez Brañas, charmingly described in the leftist press as one of Chile's "most antique mummies." I laughed at something Méndez said, and sure enough *Clarín* published my picture with the stern complaint that its lens had "caught" me in the act of laughing at a solemn official occasion.[6] When I addressed the 1972 Fourth of July luncheon of the American Society in Santiago, I started my remarks with a series of one-liners, in one suggesting that the American businessmen present might feel like travelers on the great plains, their Conestoga wagons in a circle, watching friends dropping to left and to right. "It is a diminishing experience," I remarked, as it indeed was for the American colony in Santiago in those days. Juan de Onís, a fine reporter, converted my joke into the peg for a news story, although I had not meant it as a political statement. On another occasion, in a speech on U.S. aid and development, I had started, "There is an old saying that money isn't everything. . . . Love is the other two percent." The audience laughed, but the international progressive press did not. Periodicals and books quoted me as in deadly serious exposition of America's values. Diplomacy is a hazardous trade.[7]

The life of an ambassador and his wife is laced with a great many social engagements. Some are a waste of time, but diplomacy is a profession of communication and understanding, and its rituals have their uses. For example, at one of the early diplomatic dinners in Santiago, hosted by the Argentinian ambassador, Javier Teodoro Gallac, I got to know the commander-in-chief of the Chilean Army and many of his fellow generals. I was grateful to our host, an old friend, because while it was obviously a good idea to be acquainted with General Prats and his military colleagues, it would hardly have been politic for the U.S. ambassador to have invited Chile's most senior army officers to his house at that time.

The core of diplomatic social activity is the business of meeting, knowing, and listening to the people of one's host country—one-to-one whenever possible. (One cannot be effective without good language skills, and it continues to mystify me why U.S. political leaders determinedly resist this simple truth as they make diplomatic appointments.) Receptions and dinners do not put a diplomat in touch with the poor and ill-used of a foreign land, of course, but such contacts are also possible. Visits to Peace Corps volunteers, missionaries, and development workers at distant sites furnish such opportunites, and I have found these Americans ever generous in furnishing their country's ambassador with the chance to talk with local people.

Senior Chilean government people were good-spirited in their welcome. Foreign Minister Almeyda and his wife, in particular, invited us to dinner three days after I presented my credentials. The Almeydas lived in an unimposing suburban house, and Irma Almeyda served the dinner without help. She also reached out in friendship to my wife.

Clodomiro Almeyda Medina was a remarkable man. He was a relatively short, stumpy figure with a round face, small brush mustache, and thick glasses, which gave him an owlish look. He was known as a Maoist, a theoretical mentor of the revolutionary vanguard. Even so, Almeyda stood close to Allende, and his practical outlook served the government well. His good sense in day-to-day matters seemed to count for more than his theoretical urges. In a regime where there were all too many ideologues and posturers, Almeyda was a force for balance and broad judgment.

I found Almeyda straightforward, as did my diplomatic colleagues. Chile's foreign policy in Allende's time was notaby successful, at least in part because of Almeyda. It was not that he compromised his principles. There were soon missions in Santiago from North Vietnam, North Korea, and other countries unrepresented elsewhere on the South American continent. At the same time the government found support throughout the Americas and the world community, and even maintained good relations with—and received generous loans from—ideologically incompatible countries such as Argentina.

## The U.S. Embassy in Santiago

The main U.S. Embassy offices occupied the top three stories of a nine-story office building in downtown Santiago, across the street from the Hotel Carrera and diagonally across Constitution Square from the Moneda Palace. Our building had a grayish look, although our landlords dazzlingly polished the brass plaque announcing the presence below us of the offices of former president Jorge Alessandri's great paper and pulp company, La Compañía Manufacturera de Papeles y Cartones, known as the Papelera. One entered the embassy spaces from an elevator lobby through great, ancient metal doors. The doors might have withstood a howling mob, a prospect I occasionally contemplated as I went through them. The ambassador's office I remembered from my earlier time in Chile. It had struck me as more cavernous than grand, and the impression was augmented by the ubiquitous brown wood paneling and the heavy, dark curtains on the windows. (The latter would prove convenient during the sniper firing in the days after the 1973 coup.)

The consulate was housed in the faded elegance of a Victorian mansion overlooking the Forestal Park and the Mapocho River, eleven blocks from the embassy's main offices. In earlier days the mansion had housed both the ambassador's apartment and the embassy and consular offices. It even had a little chapel with stained glass windows, which served as the agricultural attaché's office in my time. Being more accessible than the embassy's downtown offices, the consulate had become a favored target of leftist students and radical agitators. Demonstrators had taken delight in hurling paint bombs at the venerable structure, decorating its yellowish, sandy exterior with garishly satisfying splotches. My predecessor, not renowned as a meek and forbearing man, had decreed that the building would not be cleaned off, to remain as a visible reproach to barbarians.

When I arrived, the splotches were still conveying their message to the world. I was warned that cleaning them off would present a new and pristine canvas to the Jackson Pollocks of the MIR and the Socialist Youth. I asked that the building be cleaned, however, and it was. There it remained until my departure, unbesplotched. This may have been pure luck—or an illustration of the old truth that human events almost never simply repeat themselves.

The consular section of the embassy was the only consular office the United States maintained in Chile. The U.S. government once had consulates in the great ports of Chile's three-thousand-mile coastline, but one by one they were closed down, suffering the fate of consulates all over the world. Indeed, the U.S. State Department appears to be drawing in its antennae throughout the globe. We think that we can understand a country from its capital city. We even seem to think we can understand a foreign society while sitting unaided in Washington. Of course, there were U.S. activities in quite a few locations in Chile outside Santiago. The Military Group had offices in Valparaíso, and U.S. Information Service (USIS) binational centers represented us in several cities. These establishments constituted windows of rapport and communication in important communities.

As for work in the embassy itself, reporting was the core responsibility of both the political and economic sections—true generally of countries where stakes are high but relations are not good. In more friendly environments U.S. diplomatic energies tend to be absorbed in operational problem solving and in conducting assistance programs. I soon discovered, moreover, that there were substantial differences in outlook within the embassy. Several officers believed that the political and economic deterioration in the country was a problem the Allende regime would surmount. Some others, including me, perceived a more basic downward slope, which would probably end in crisis. These differing views produced some reporting that went to Washington as the expression of the individual officer's own perspective, rather than an embassy position.

So far as the service attachés' activities were concerned, Col. Paul Wimert's spectacular role in connection with Track II has already been described. He had left Santiago before my arrival, however, and I had occasion to meet him only briefly, in the Office of Chilean Affairs at the State Department. He was amiable but discreet, revealing nothing of his past exploits. Capt. John E. Tefft, the defense and naval attaché, and Col. William M. Hon, the army and later defense attaché, were less flamboyant personalities, which probably was just as well. Lt. Col. Lawrence A. Corcoran, the air attaché, had served earlier in Santiago and had requested and been given a return tour. He knew the language fluently and had many friends in the Chilean Air Force.

The U.S. Military Group—about a dozen officers and enlisted men from all U.S. services—was headed first by Capt. Albert F. Betzel, U.S.N., and later by Capt. Ray E. Davis, U.S.N. (no relation of mine). Captain Betzel resided in Valparaíso, the main home port of the Chilean fleet, but Captain Davis, with my encouragement, established himself in Santiago, where his American colleagues and principal Chilean contacts were located. Several MILGROUP officers had desks in the Ministry of Defense, and some U.S. naval officers had office space in the Chilean naval headquarters in Valparaíso. Critics have alleged that this circumstance must have meant that American officers were involved in plotting the 1973 coup, but that conclusion does not necessarily follow. After all, Allende's minister of defense, other UP officials, and the generals and admirals who became involved in the 1973 plotting always worked in closer propinquity than U.S. and Chilean officers did.

USIS informational and cultural activities continued undiminished throughout the Allende years. The exchange visitor program, library operations, the teaching of English, the circulation of films, contacts with Chilean media, and all the other activities carried out in any Western country were pursued in Chile. The Chilean government made no significant effort to restrict visits in either direction by witholding visas or exit documentation, and binational boards for the selection of grant recipients operated without hindrance. The government lowered no iron curtain.

The Agency for International Development conducted a shrinking activity. In October 1972 there were seven U.S. citizens and eighteen Chilean nationals still working in the AID program. When the able and broad-gauged AID director, Joel W. Biller, moved up to act as my deputy in June 1973, he was replaced by Judd L. Kessler, a resourceful young lawyer who had been serving as regional legal advisor. AID's most important continuing program, sustained throughout Allende's time, was the supply of nonfat dried milk to school children. The "half-liter" milk program was a major UP campaign plank in 1970, and the United States maintained this program without interruption in spite of its obvious political utility to the UP government. AID in fact provided all the milk and milk-substitute beverages served in Chilean elementary schools throughout Allende's three years as president.

The Peace Corps also continued operations throughout the Allende period, which may be to the credit of both U.S. policy makers and the Allende government. Ending the Peace Corps program would have been a cheap and easy demagogic gesture for either side. As luck would have it, I was greeted on my arrival in Santiago by Peace Corps director Donald M. Boucher, whom I had myself welcomed to Santiago in 1962 when he was a newly enrolled volunteer. In 1971 and 1972 Peace Corps volunteers were working throughout the country in forestry science, animal husbandry, the study of Chilean animal species for both scientific and industrial purposes, oceanography, and other technical fields.

The embassy's labor-oriented activities were under the leadership of attaché Arthur B. Nixon, III (no kin to the president) and Robert J. O'Neill of the American Institute for Free Labor Development. AIFLD activities in Chile were controversial, as was true throughout Latin America. Free trade unionism is usually a politically sensitive matter, and Allende's Chile provided no exception. In its main Chilean program AIFLD granted scholarships to Chilean labor leaders to come up to the institute's facility at Front Royal, Virginia, for training in organizing and other union skills. AIFLD was able to carry on its Chilean program at a moderate level with no destructive political blowups. Later, however, politically progressive commentators would seize on AIFLD's training of Chilean trade unionists as evidence of supposed U.S. complicity in the antigovernment strikes of 1972 and 1973.[8]

The NASA tracking station fifteen miles north of Santiago was important because it was one of very few such facilities available to the United States in the Southern Hemisphere. It was a superb installation, used for tracking nonmilitary satellites and other vehicles in space. Worth a hundred million dollars or so, it would have cost a great deal more to build a station with equivalent capabilities elsewhere. There were recurring alarms to the effect that the government was considering closing down the NASA station, but it never did.

These various ongoing activities show considerable forbearance on the part of Allende and his government. What was significant was the U.S.-Chilean programs the Chileans did not shut down, did not throw out, did not dismantle or harass. It is clear that Allende did not want to cut all his ties with the United States. He understood that a relationship that was cooperative in some degree was more desirable than total reliance on assistance from the Russians, Cubans, Chinese, and East Europeans. Besides, he was not sure how generous his communist friends were going to be or how comfortable a total bear hug would feel. There was also a mixture between deliberate restraint and procrastination, inattention and distraction. The mixture probably varied within the Chilean government and with respect to one kind of U.S. activity and the next. For example, Chilean policy toward military cooperation with the United States was, as already indicated, deliberate, closely monitored, and highly influenced by the relationship between Allende and his own military establishment. In other sectors, however, the UP government's motivations were less well defined. The Chileans closest to and best informed about specific American activities—NASA tracking or Peace Corps technical work, for example—were usually also those sympathetic to the activities' continuance. The left extremists in the Socialist party, while undoubtedly aware that NASA and the Peace Corps were still in Chile, were not intimately involved with them and were much occupied with other issues. Allende himself harbored no ill will toward NASA and the Peace Corps. So things went on in a way that would have been inconceivable in an East European "people's democracy."

## Fidel Castro's Visit

Fidel Castro arrived in Santiago on 10 November 1971, for what the Chilean government described as a "ten-day visit."[9] He stayed over three weeks, in an extraordinary display of high-level tourism, thinly disguised meddling, and shrewd commentary on the Chilean scene. It was a circus.

The Chileans' reception of Castro was not uniformly flattering. The opposition press subjected Castro to a campaign of invective that must have jolted the Cuban, accustomed as he was to a captive press in Havana. A chance episode touched off some of the grossest of the opposition onslaughts. Shortly after his arrival Castro was the guest of honor at a workers' club and dance hall in a town north of Santiago. In high spirits, Castro apparently grabbed the arm of his official host and led him through a twirl or hop around the dance floor. That was all the opposition press needed to launch the insinuation that Castro was a homosexual. The word for a gay in Chile is maricón and Castro soon visited a town that has the misfortune to bear a name almost indistinguishable from this word. The anti-UP press simply headlined Castro's name, linked by a dash to the name of the town. There were other headlines with more explicit allusions—unsuitable for dissemination by a university press.

Castro and his Chilean hosts revealed some interesting contrasts. Castro brought the Caribbean with him, including a mixture of bravado, flair, candor, and ebullience. At the same time Castro clearly had a private inner self, and the Chileans sensed a curtain between their visitor and themselves. As for the Chileans, while manifesting their traditional high-spirited vulgarity, they also displayed their usual sophistication and style. They seemed to regard Castro as a yokel from the tropics.

What were the purposes of the visit? For Castro, the visit showed the world that Cuba was no longer alone. Without question, Castro stayed so long because he wanted to form his own opinion of the Chilean experiment and judge its chances of success. He said so, and he certainly formed such judgments. Moreover, the visit gave him the opportunity to talk with many of the revolutionary activists of South America who had congregated in the Chilean sanctuary following Allende's accession to power. There was even speculation at the time of Castro's visit that he was hoping for some revolutionary development in Uruguay or a nearby country and wanted to be among the revolutionary activists in Chile if and when such a break occurred. Perhaps Castro's visit really was a kind of vacation, a change of pace and circumstance, and a chance to tour Latin America's second socialist country—a land justly famous for its beauty. All of these explanations may contain some element of truth.

For Allende, the visit would serve, he hoped, as a visible demonstration of political support. President Allende wanted to dispel the impression of his own isolation, just as Castro did. More important, Allende clearly hoped to use Castro's influence with the Movement of the Revolutionary Left and other extremist groups on the left fringes of Unidad Popular to drive home counsels of discipline and restraint. Castro did meet with MIR leaders at the University of Concepción and a few other places. His statements in support of Allende were probably of some assistance, but their effect was ephemeral, blown away when Castro later proved critical of Allende's political strategy.[10]

By the time Castro departed, the Chileans clearly believed he had overstayed his welcome and had complicated Unidad Popular's problems. Castro was aware of this belief and was reported to have complained on the day he left that he thought Unidad Popular was not happy with the results of his visit, despite the fact that he did everything his hosts wanted. He also acknowledged that many UP leaders thought he had stayed too long and had talked too much.[11]

Two speeches provide a dramatic juxtaposition of Allende's and Castro's views of the Chilean experiment. The first, given by Allende on 21 May 1971 (about six months before Castro's visit), is the highest and most optimistic expression of Allende's aspiration for the "Chilean Way." The second, Castro's farewell speech of 2 December 1971, gives the Cuban's candid and prescient judgment that the Chilean experiment was already failing. Allende said in his 21 May speech:

> Our revolutionary course, the pluralist way, was anticipated by the classical Marxists, but never before realized. . . . Today Chile is the first nation on earth called to fashion a new model of transition to a socialist society . . . built according to a democratic, pluralist, and libertarian plan.
>
> In the revolutionary process we are experiencing, there are five essential principles on which our political and social struggle is based: legality, institutionality, political liberties, the prevention of violence, and the socialization of the means of production. . . .
>
> The obligation to organize and regulate society according to the rule of law is an integral part of our institutional system. . . .
>
> At an opportune time we shall submit a proposal to the sovereign will of the people to transform the present liberal bourgeois constitution into a socialist-oriented one and to change the bicameral congress into a single chamber.
>
> Political liberties . . . must be upheld, including respect for freedom of conscience . . . economic freedom . . . and protection for small and medium-sized businesses.
>
> The Popular Government . . . respects the political liberties of the opposition and carries out its own program within institutional confines. . . .
>
> However, . . . should violence, internal or external, in whatever form, physical, economic, social, or political . . . threaten . . . the conquests of the workers, then . . . the rule of law, political freedoms, and pluralism will be placed in the greatest of danger. . . .
>
> If violence is not unleashed against the people, we shall be able to change the country's basic capitalist structures in democracy, pluralism, and liberty . . . without unnecessary physical force, without institutional disorder. . . .
>
> No country has achieved an acceptable measure of economic development without huge sacrifices. . . . We are offering . . . to build that society at the least possible social cost. . . . [12]

Six months later Castro had come to Chile. He was neither convinced nor reassured by what he saw. Disorders and demonstrations had marred his stay. His Chilean hosts had not succeeded
even in amassing a respectable turnout in the Santiago national
stadium for farewell speeches and ceremonies on 2 December. Castro reportedly regarded the rally as a disaster and complained that
some of his listeners left the gathering before he had finished speaking.[13] With Allende beside him in the bleachers, Castro said:

> We have already learned more than enough about . . .
> bourgeois, capitalist liberties. . . .
> All decadent social systems . . . have defended themselves
> with tremendous violence throughout history.
> No social system has ever resigned itself to disappearing of its
> own free will. No social system has resigned itself to revolu-
> tion. . . .
> In Cuba . . . we were not representative democrats! . . .
> May the anarchronisms be swept out as soon as possible! . . .
> The revolutionaries are not the inventors of violence. . . . The
> inventors of violence have been the reactionaries. . . .
> Who will learn more and sooner? The exploiters or the ex-
> ploited? . . . Are you completely sure that you have learned
> more than your exploiters have? [Shouts of "yes" from the
> crowd.] Permit me, then, to disagree in this case with your mass
> view. . . .
> The confidence of your enemies is based on weaknesses in the
> revolutionary process here, on weaknesses in the ideological
> battle, on weaknesses in the mass struggle, on weaknesses in the
> face of the enemy! . . .
> In fact, we could say that it is the result of weaknesses in your
> effort to consolidate your forces, to unite them and to increase
> them. . . .
> The fascists are trying to . . . beat you to the streets. . . .
> I will return to Cuba more of a revolutionary than when I
> came here! I will return to Cuba more of a radical than when I
> came here! I will return to Cuba more of an extremist than when
> I came here![14]

In the Santiago stadium on that summer evening Allende's cheeks
must have burned.

Castro was not alone in feeling that Allende was not radical
enough. Marx and Lenin were on Castro's side, even though a few
of Marx's later pronouncements could be construed as admitting

the possibility of a peaceful road. As the *Communist Manifesto* stated, "the Communists disdain to conceal their views and aims. They openly declare that their ends can be attained only by the forcible overthrow of all existing social conditions."[15] Castro had Allende's friend Régis Debray with him as well. Debray's position—following Mao—was that "political power grows out of the barrel of a gun."[16]

Castro also had the secretary general of Allende's own Socialist party with him. Carlos Altamirano Orrego, a high-strung, young, patrician Socialist politician who was on the radical left wing of the already leftist Socialist party, had been elected secretary general, with Allende's support, in January 1971. Altamirano served in that position throughout Allende's presidency, leading the ultra-left of the UP coalition in frequently expressed opposition to Allende's policy line. At its January 1971 congress the Socialist party had also been frank in saying that the special conditions under which Unidad Popular came to power obliged it to observe the limits of the bourgeois state "for now," but the party called on its followers to prepare for "the decisive confrontation with the bourgeoisie and imperialism."[17]

A number of influential North American Marxists also agreed with Castro, Debray, and Altamirano. Allende's strategy had been sound through the 1970 election campaign and the first few months in office, they held, but he should have broken with the bourgeois institutional system at the peak of his strength, which they identified as the time of the municipal elections of April 1971. Then he should have "unconditionally" broken Chile's military ties with the United States, trained his own ideologically committed militia, sharpened the class struggle, and radicalized the revolution.[18]

Of course, this was also the position of the ultra leftists in Chile who were politicking against Allende's policies from outside the UP coalition. After the 1973 coup Miguel Enríquez Espinoza, the secretary general of the Movement of the Revolutionary Left (MIR) put his criticism this way:

> The reformist strategy attempted by the Popular Unity government was imprisoned within the rules of the game of the bourgeoisie. . . . It did not seek support in the revolutionary workers' organizations. . . . It rejected an alliance with soldiers

> and noncommissioned officers and instead sought to fortify it-
> self within the capitalist state. The Popular Unity government
> looked for an alliance with the officers of the armed forces and
> with a fraction of the bourgeoisie. The reformist illusion per-
> mitted the dominating classes to fortify themselves. . . .[19]

In hindsight Castro, Debray, Altamirano, and Enríquez were right—in the sense that Allende failed. But it is another question whether the extremists' course would have succeeded, and it is still a third question whether the ultra leftists did not themselves pre-cipitate Allende's failure. As so often, people tended to analyze the situation in accordance with their previously established convic-tions. If history then proves them right, their reasons become en-shrined as truth.

Castro's visit had a considerable influence, and it was a significant impelling force in the polarization of Chilean political life. Castro encouraged the left extremists and strengthened their voices within the councils of government, intensifying the class struggle in Chile and raising the level of ideologically motivated strife. As events worked out, this change did more to solidify the opposition than to broaden or deepen the government's support. Previously sympathetic non-UP politicians became more critical. For example, Senator Fuentealba, who was by then president of the Christian Democratic party, told a rally two weeks after Castro's departure that the Christian Democrats were prepared to collabo-rate in the construction of a Chilean-style socialist society but not of a "Cuban-style socialism that Chileans cannot accept."[20]

Castro's visit enraged many in the armed services. The corps of cadets at the Military School in Santiago developed a sudden mass "illness" when Castro was scheduled to visit the school, and their commandant, Col. Alberto Labbé Troncoso, was summarily re-moved and later retired as a result.[21] Other senior officers were more circumspect but hardly more pleased with Castro's antics and policy line.

To sum up, Castro failed to convert Allende to his own radi-calism but helped to undermine the Chilean Way. He pushed Al-lende further into a fatal compromise between the moderate institutionalists and the left-extremist revolutionaries. This was Al-lende's dilemma.

## The March of the Empty Pots

It was a smallish demonstration to have had so great an impact. On Wednesday afternoon, 1 December 1971, about five thousand women marched through the streets of Santiago beating pots and pans with spoons and sticks, protesting food shortages. The women were escorted by about eighty club-carrying youths from the Christian Democratic and National parties—and, allegedly, also some young militants from the ultra-rightist group known as Patria y Libertad. The demonstration occurred on the day before Castro's farewell at the Santiago national stadium, and it was also a protest against his visit.

As *New York Times* correspondent Juan de Onís described it, "the march apparently turned out to be bigger than the Government had expected"—the biggest since Allende had taken office. "There were grandmothers and young girls in slacks and blouses, teachers and housewives. There appeared to be a significant number of women from working class neighborhoods."[22]

Although the march began peacefully, if noisily, young Communist, Socialist, and MIR youths apparently began throwing rocks at the women and their escorts. Riot police fired off many rounds of tear gas and hosed down the demonstrators and the battling youths. The marchers scattered, but some of them re-formed and marched on. Street skirmishes, later mostly between Marxist and anti-Marxist young men, continued through the night. Shortly after daybreak on the second the president declared a state of emergency in Santiago province, and the commander of the Santiago garrison, Gen. Augusto Pinochet Ugarte, declared a curfew from 1 to 6 A.M. on 3 December.

My wife and I ended up at the edge of the melee, amidst the teargas volleys. On that Wednesday evening the Chilean Foreign Ministry was celebrating an anniversary of its establishment, so the cars of the diplomatic corps of Santiago, after speeches at a downtown theater, became part of one vast traffic jam. We saw the women march by; my impression was that the number of women from "working class neighborhoods" was not all that great. Several Chilean women in the U.S. Embassy and residence staff had gone off to march (without any encouragement from us), and I suspect that loyal or gentrified maids from the better suburbs made up more of the "working class" contingent than women of the shantytowns and poorer districts.

The march was well organized. The women of the more prosperous suburbs had spent hour after hour on the telephone spreading the call. It should be added that the march was less a hunger protest than a political act. In December 1971 food shortages were real and queues were maddening, but the women who marched were not then suffering great hardship.

The march had a symbolic effect considerably greater than the reality of approximately five thousand people walking in the streets—although one should not ignore the fact that so many women, largely from privileged households, marched through tear gas and pelting rocks. Together with Castro's visit, the march of the empty pots brought a change in Chilean politics, from the relative normality and social accommodation that had prevailed in preceding weeks to a greater spirit of confrontation.

### Salvador Allende Gossens

What kind of man was Salvador Allende? I saw a good deal of the president during my two years in Chile, meeting him every two or three weeks in one context or another. Our contacts ranged from an inauguration when he gleefully crammed me and the Chinese ambassador on either side of him in the back seat of a small Chilean car to the funeral of his beloved sister Inés when he suffered wretchedly. I introduced American astronauts, generals, admirals, and politicians to him; I sat with him at a small, round table while our dinner host, the Mexican ambassador, performed a quite creditable hat dance.[23] We conversed at receptions without number, pisco sours in hand, and there were serious times when I had to make unwelcome representations to him on copper and ITT. And there were many other occasions, although an American ambassador cannot really aspire to become an intimate of a Marxist Latin American president. Personal contact was not my only source of information about President Allende, however, as he dominated the Santiago scene, and much of the political talk among Chileans and diplomats in the capital was about him.

Allende had extraordinary and appealing human qualities. He had plied the trade of politics for almost forty years and had collected hardly an enemy in the process. He had the social and socializing instincts of a long-time, top-drawer political personality. His resilience and energy were phenomenal, and he maintained an exhausting schedule in spite of a chronic heart condition and the inescapable inroads of more than sixty years of living. Pedro Ibáñez, a right-wing National party senator, commented after Allende's death that "Allende was an old-style politician . . . loyal to all those who gave him their political support. . . . In private he was unaffected and nice. . . . In the forty years that I knew him, and in spite of the intensity of our political battles, I never saw him act with deliberate ill will or become the slave of hatred or incurable resentments. . . ."[24]

Like all of us a mixture of strengths and human weaknesses, Salvador Allende was not a weak personality, and those around him knew it. After his death, Germán Picó, an old friend of his and an owner of the Santiago newspaper *La Tercera*, commented: "Allende was always very sound and strong, almost arrogant." Ibáñez put it in other words: he was "ambitious and tenacious." Gabriel García Márquez, the Nobel laureate in literature, put the same qualities still another way, saying that Allende "was a perfect Leo: . . . firm in his decisions, and unpredictable."[25]

Allende was vain, as are most national leaders. Ibáñez went on to say that Allende looked in public "like a patent leather dandy." Not a tall man, the president tended to strut when he felt himself on display.[26]

Allende liked fine wines and collected objets d'art—I remember his relish as he showed me the paintings and sculptures at his Tomás Moro residence. The military authorities counted forty suits in his wardrobe closets after his death and took some pleasure in describing his liquor cellar. Reportedly Fidel Castro, an observer of a different inclination, complained at the end of his 1971 visit that "UP leaders live too well and are not under sufficient tension to take the offensive." He called Allende "physically spent."[27]

Throughout Allende's four decades in politics he made no secret of the fact that he liked women. As García Márquez rather delicately put it, "he loved life, he loved flowers, he loved dogs, and he was a gallant with a touch of the old school about him, perfumed notes and furtive rendezvous." Ibáñez was less kind, referring simply to "his licentious manner of living." Allende had married Hortensia Bussi, a teacher in Valparaíso, in 1939, but it was said that she did not regularly spend her nights at Tomás Moro Avenue with the president. Señora Tencha Bussi de Allende displayed an intense personal and political loyalty to her husband, it should be added, and even many cynics were prepared to acknowledge that she loved him deeply to the end. It was also widely known that the president's eye had wandered to the person of his personal secretary, Miriam Contreras Bell, "La Payita." Apparently it was for La Payita, and in her name, that Allende purchased El Cañaveral, a property in El Arrayán suburb outside Santiago. This estate also served as a training site for the president's bodyguards, a political meeting place, and, allegedly, an intimate hideaway where sex films were shown and the president, UP bigwigs, and their girlfriends cavorted—and had themselves photographed as they did so. These stories did not greatly influence Chilean politics, other than providing gossip, during Allende's presidency.[28]

Ingratiating and winning as Allende was in his personal relationships, few of his friends have ever claimed that he was altogether truthful in his political dealings. In praising his endearing qualities, Ibáñez noted in an aside that he was "not absolutely scrupulous."[29] For myself, I liked the president wholeheartedly, but I did not always believe him.

Former ambassador Korry has testified to the U.S. Congress that Allende "for many, many years" was "personally" financed by foreign communist bankrollers. According to Korry, Allende also accepted bribes from multinational corporations, including a mining company that gave the president "as much as $500,000."[30] No one should conclude, however, that Allende was "bought" in terms of his policies or his convictions. If he was "rented," the rent was high, and the leases were short if observed at all.

In political style Allende was famous for his *muñeca,* the Chilean word for a flexible wrist—the clever ability to manipulate things and slither through. He had a flair for maneuver and compromise and an impressive ability to be all things to all men. As Ibáñez put it in his bitter-sweet obituary, Allende, "knowing human weaknesses only too well, knew how to manipulate them." Like all politicians in greater or lesser degree, Allende was an opportunist.[31] It was in Allende's nature to make political bargains rather easily, always with the possibility of being able to wiggle out of them later. This touch of frivolousness with respect to undertakings may have been Allende's greatest political weakness over the long term, even as it was an immense asset in immediate situations.

Turning from Allende's personal characteristics and style to his political philosophy, there is an inescapable question: was Salvador Allende a democrat? Did he genuinely want to bring Chile to socialism through legal and institutional means? Was he sincere when he presented his vision of the Chilean Way in his May 1971 address to the Congress? I believe that the answer is "yes"; Allende wanted these things. More than two decades previously, in 1948, Allende had criticized the Soviets' restriction of individual liberty and their negation of "rights which we deem inalienable to the human personality."[32] During the intervening years most of his positions were consistent with this assertion. It was only the road *to* socialism, however, that Allende wanted to make democratic and institutional. He did not envisage the Chilean people voting exploitative and capitalist institutions back into power. Once "the people" took over in the complete sense, Allende believed that they would continue to rule.

Salvador Allende had another important political conviction, which had grown directly out of his and his fellow leftists' experience during the Radical party presidency of Gabriel González Videla. González Videla had been elected in 1946 with communist support in a Popular Front candidacy and had included three Communists in his cabinet. He had discharged these communist ministers in 1947, however, and had outlawed the party in the following year, relying on centrist and antileftist forces to continue governing. None of the leftist party leaders ever forgot what they regarded as González Videla's betrayal of Chile's progressive forces. Allende had kept this experience vividly in mind when he had entered into the negotiations that resulted in his own selection as UP standard-bearer in 1970. In fact, he promised to "consult" the UP parties in important decisions if he were elected, giving them what was almost a policy veto. Allende was utterly determined not to go down in Chilean history as another González Videla.[33]

Another element in Allende's political philosophy was his tie to Chilean Freemasonry—that powerful lodestone of fidelity in Latin anticlerical circles. His grandfather, Ramón Allende Palilla, had been a serene grand master of the Chilean Masonic Order, and Allende joined the Valparaíso lodge about five years after he had helped found the Chilean Socialist party in 1933. His political opponents used the alleged inconsistency between Marxist and Masonic principles to torment Allende, but he remained loyal to both commitments throughout his lifetime and stoutly defended their compatibility.[34] Allende's Masonic tie cut in more than one direction, of course, and influenced his political fortunes in various ways. It was a channel of brotherhood to many Radical party leaders and voters, but it added to the suspicions of the Christian Democrats and other committed Catholics.

In his diary General Prats records that the most strained discussion he ever experienced in his relations with the president was when he tried to convince Allende to dismiss a fellow Mason, Brig. Gen. Hermán Brady, as politically unreliable and perhaps disloyal to the UP government. Prats failed, and Allende saved Brady—a man who would later become a key commander of the 1973 coup.[35] Prats seems to have been right, and Allende apparently let his Masonic loyalties cloud his judgment.

Allende had been something of a Trotskyite in his youth. Even when he was president, he maintained family ties to the left wing of the Socialist party and even to the left-extremist MIRistas who opposed the UP government. His sister Laura Allende was a Socialist deputy and close political ally of Carlos Altamirano; his nephew Andrés Pascal Allende was a leader of the MIR, with which some of Allende's bodyguards were also associated.

Allende's rightist opponents in Santiago alleged that fear for his own life was a factor in Allende's "soft" attitude toward the MIR, but this charge is doubtful. It is considerably more likely that Allende's unwillingness to repudiate even the most extreme leftists sprang from conviction. His own bourgeois life-style only reinforced his compulsion to be true to his leftist attachments. On more than one occasion the president went personally to shantytowns to parlay with rebellious squatters, "on foot" and without official protection, as Régis Debray points out.[36] When one police raid in a slum area degenerated into bloody fighting between MIR activists and police, with one worker killed by the carabineros, the outraged president suspended the Socialist investigative police chief and his Communist deputy. For its part, the MIR noticeably failed to reciprocate the president's consideration; but even that disappointment did not change Allende's resolve.[37]

Allende was a romantic. Debray says "he saw himself as a knight of hope, a Robin Hood. . . ."[38] Professor Paul Sigmund is probably right when he suggests that Allende was a frustrated revolutionary gladiator, one who privately wished to come out of the mountains and seize power at the point of a gun like Castro or Che Guevara. This romantic illusion is captured in the photograph of Allende on the morning of the 1973 coup. He is dressed in a cardigan sweater and tweed jacket while wearing a helmet, with Castro's gift submachine gun in his hand. Allende's yearning for revolutionary heroism lived side by side in his breast with his genuine attachment to the Chilean Way.[39]

Allende's enemies could truthfully point to many flaws. He fully participated in government by legerdemain and condoned the violation of Chile's liberties, laws, and Constitution. His "flexible wrist" and propensity to renege on commitments, his willingness to let dirty work be done, his dissembling—all were part of Salvador Allende. But Allende was also called by some "the First Dreamer of the Republic"; and he dreamed marvelous, soaring dreams.[40] His aspiration was for a better Chile and for happiness and fulfillment for his compatriots. Not just personally, but in the selfless political sense, he loved the women and children of Chile and had labored over a lifetime for their welfare and opportunity. He unfailingly displayed great, generous, and compelling personal attributes. Few people are altogether consistent in outlook, and Salvador Allende revealed more contradictions and anomalies than most. Nonetheless, he was an extraordinary leader and a profoundly impressive human being.

# Chapter 3

# Chilean Politics and Troubles to the North

FOLLOWING opposition gains in by-elections held in January 1972, Allende attempted to extend his base of support toward the moderate center, but extremist left-wingers in the Socialist party ultimately defeated his initiatives. Nationalization policy became a central issue as the Christian Democrats tried to amend the constitution to set limits on the government's power to seize private enterprises.

In the United States, meanwhile, Jack Anderson published an exposé of ITT machinations in Chile. Allende then introduced an amendment to the Chilean constitution that would permit the nationalization of ITT's main Chilean assets. At the same time the Chilean president had some success in steering an agreement on the renegotiation of his country's foreign debt past suspicious creditors assembled in Paris.

### By-elections, Political Maneuvers, and Expropriation Policy

The outcome of two by-elections held on 16 January 1972 changed the political landscape. In the provinces of O'Higgins and Colchagua, Rafael Moreno, a Christian Democrat who had headed

Frei's Agricultural Reform Corporation (CORA), defeated Héctor Olivares, a Socialist, for the seat of a deceased senator. The split in the main blocs' vote was 53 percent for Moreno, 47 percent for Olivares—Unidad Popular had slipped to a trailing position from its slight lead in voting nine months earlier. The results are even more striking when one considers that the miners of the great copper mine El Teniente were among the voters and the UP candidate had been a union officer in the mine. In Linares a National party candidate, Sergio Diez, who had become famous on a TV political talk show, defeated the Left Christian candidate, María Eliana Mery. Diez received 59 percent of the main blocs' vote to Mery's 41 percent; compared to results in April 1971 the government had dropped five points from 46 percent.[1]

As in the past, the government pulled more votes among men than among women, but the decline in UP strength showed up everywhere. Although salaried employees and wage earners throughout Chile had received pay increases of more than 50 percent in 1971, only partly offset by 20 percent inflation, both groups appear to have been more influenced by increasing shortages of goods, stronger signs of inflation, and sharpening political crisis. Also, the Christian Democrats had pushed land reform seriously when in power. Voters noted their past successes, in which Moreno had been directly involved, and compared them favorably with the disorder, violence, and demagoguery that were starting to characterize the Chilean rural scene. In both city and countryside, socialist restructuring and the UP's menacing rhetoric, plus ultraleftist agitation, were frightening swing voters who had previously supported Allende.[2]

The links of iron that would later unite the opposition parties were not yet forged. There was no formal agreement between Christian Democrats, National party members, and Radical Democrats in the O'Higgins-Colchagua race, though the latter two groups did refrain from putting up a candidate and mostly campaigned and voted for Moreno. The Christian Democrats "returned the compliment" in Linares, advising their supporters to use "freedom of action" in deciding how to vote. In the person of Sergio Diez, the National party had sensibly presented a nondoctrinaire candidate, which made it easier to attract Christian Democratic support.

The Christian Democrats' reluctance to tie themselves to the National party notwithstanding, Unidad Popular soon pushed them into it. In a 7 February 1972 speech Allende proposed that all UP candidates run in a single party list in the March 1973 congressional elections, which would favor them over a fragmented opposition. The Christian Democrats countered with a constitutional amendment requiring that all candidates have a full year's inscription in their party before presenting themselves for election in its list. The Christian Democrats knew that the UP parties could never work out their ticket-splitting arrangements by 4 March 1972—one year before the congressional elections—so the amendment would have spiked Allende's new "single-list" party. In ensuing negotiations between government and opposition a two-tiered system of alliances was worked out. The arrangement forced the Christian Democrats to join formally, if somewhat ambiguously, with more conservative parties about eight months before the congressional elections.[3] It thereby solidified the opposition.

Unidad Popular's postmortem on the January election results was marked by acrimony, intensified by the underlying philosophical differences between the two parties—with the Socialist leaders being left extremists, or close to it, and the Communists being relatively moderate institutional gradualists. The Communists, led by Orlando Millas, expressed concern over accelerating inflation and lack of factory discipline. As for the election results, they blamed the losses in Linares on the violence the MIR had whipped up in the province. In a secret report that leaked, the Communists advocated curbs on the MIR and further work to "neutralize and win over the social base of Christian Democracy" through "dialogue with that party."[4] The Socialist party's Central Committee, on the other hand, took the position that the economic base of the anti-Marxist forces, which was in private enterprise, "must be destroyed." This destruction could be accomplished only by encouraging workers to seize factories remaining in private hands, a leaked Socialist report said. The report was explicit in advocating that Chilean workers use their "political domination" to "seize total power" and establish the "dictatorship of the proletariat."[5]

The UP parties convened at El Arrayán in late January for "self-critical" brainstorming. The secret conclave apparently turned into a cat-and-dog fight. Allende wanted to broaden his government by giving cabinet appointments to Felipe Herrera, former president of the Inter-American Development Bank (IDB), one or two other prestigious figures, and at least one military man. The Communists and the Socialists both opposed the idea. Allende retorted grumpily that the new cabinet "wouldn't last long" but gave in to the pressure. He countered, however, by successfully imposing Herrera as the UP candidate in upcoming elections for rector of the University of Chile.[6]

A cabinet reshuffle had become necessary in any case, because of a quirk in Chilean constitutional law. A simple majority in the Chilean Chamber of Deputies had the power to impeach a cabinet officer, and a majority of the Senate had the power to convict and remove him. Impeachment of the minister of interior, José Tohá González, had been initiated in December 1971, at which time Tohá had been charged with failure to crack down on ultra-leftist groups such as the MIR. He was suspended by the Chamber of Deputies on 6 January 1972, and the president almost immediately decided, in defiance of the spirit but not the letter of the Constitution, to appoint Tohá minister of defense. The incumbent defense minister, Alejandro Ríos Valdivia of the Radical party, thus had to be moved to another cabinet post, which turned out to be the Ministry of Education. That bumped the incumbent minister of education, another Radical—and there was still the need to appoint a new minister of interior. Allende chose Hernán del Canto, until then secretary general of the Central Trade Union Confederation and the losing candidate in the recently contested Valparaíso by-election.[7]

The cabinet reorganization was consummated on 28 January 1972. Allende's most significant move was to bring the Radical Left party (Partido Izquierda Radical, or PIR) into the government. The PIR had been established in mid-1971 when the Radicals had held a national convention and declared the party "Marxist" rather than centrist. Alberto Baltra and Luis Bossay, both senators and former presidential candidates, had bolted over this Marxist adherence and had formed the more centrist PIR. In the January cabinet reshuffle Allende appointed two PIR representatives: Manuel Sanhueza as minister of justice, and Mauricio Yungk Stahl as minister of mining.[8]

As a further response to the by-election defeat, Allende authorized Sanhueza, his new minister of justice, to open negotiations with the Christian Democrats. The issue was the government's continuing campaign to nationalize private enterprises. Sanhueza reached agreement on a list of firms that would be nationalized, offering other firms security in private hands. He signed the understanding, thinking he had the president's authorization to do so, but Altamirano objected violently, citing Allende's 1970 promise to the Socialist party leaders to consult them on policy. Allende gave in again, as he had at El Arrayán. He repudiated Sanhueza's accord, and on 6 April he announced that he would veto crucial provisions of a constitutional amendment on nationalization policy that opposition leaders had pushed through the Congress. The two PIR ministers presented their resignations, and the PIR left the government. Calling this action a "dirty stabbing," Allende appointed Jorge Tapia Valdés of the historic Radical party as minister of justice and an army engineer, Brig. Gen. Pedro Palacios Camerón, as minister of mining.[9]

Nationalization policy had been developing as a central political issue since the latter months of 1971. The National party was then urging the impeachment of Pedro Vuskovic Bravo, the minister of economy. The Christian Democrats agreed to withhold support for Vuskovic's impeachment if Allende would submit a bill to the Congress that would establish rules and limits on nationalizations. On 19 October 1971 Allende duly did so, specifically listing 150 enterprises to enter the "social" sector. Firms with less than 14 million escudos (about $1 million) in assets as of the end of 1969 would be exempt from expropriation. There would be "three areas" of industrial ownership: state or "social" enterprises, mixed ones with some stock in state hands, and private companies.

None of the opposition parties found the government-proposed bill satisfactory. Christian Democratic senators Juan Hamilton and Renán Fuentealba responded with a constitutional amendment of their own. This draft granted state ownership to mining, most transportation, communications, gas, petroleum, cement, steel, nitrates, iodine, and arms production—all either important to defense or nonrenewable natural resources. It required all nationalizations and allocations to a partly private and partly government-owned "mixed" sector to be carried out by legislation, and it made this provision retroactive to 31 October 1971.[10] The CD amendment also addressed another issue that was greatly agitating the opposition: the use of "loopholes" in old laws to achieve the government's political ends. Eduardo Novoa Monreal, Allende's legal adviser, was a master at this game. For example, a decree of

1932 gave the executive authorities power to requisition a plant if production was not maintained. Designed as a temporary expedient during the Great Depression to prevent layoffs and plant closings, the decree was resuscitated in 1971. A leftist-inspired strike would interrupt production, the government would "requisition" the enterprise, and a government-appointed manager would then administer the factory until further notice—thereby producing an effectively nationalized industry.[11]

Requistions had to be registered by the comptroller general. If he thought them unconstitutional or illegal, and declined to register them, he could be obliged to do so by a "decree of insistence" signed by the president and cosigned by all cabinet ministers. Besides requisitions under the 1932 decree, Novoa also found dusty legal provisions enabling the government to "intervene" in the administration of an enterprise, appointing an "intervenor" to run the place in much the same way as the government manager ran a requisitioned plant.

The Hamilton-Fuentealba draft limited and regulated requisitions and interventions, and it also nullified retroactively government acquisitions of shares bought after 14 October 1971 for the purpose of taking control of an enterprise. This restriction was the direct outgrowth of a government campaign to buy a controlling interest in the Papelera, the great pulp paper and newsprint company. The Papelera issue became a great popular cause in Santiago's wealthy suburbs, and Chileans with money either held on to their Papelera stock or bid against the government for shares on the stock market. This noisy and impassioned struggle for a controlling interest in the company had been going on since early October 1971, when the Chilean state Development Corporation (CORFO) had started buying Papelera shares.[12]

The draft passed its first reading in the Chamber of Deputies and the Senate at the end of 1971, and the Congress, meeting in joint session, passed the proposed amendment on 19 February 1972. This Hamilton-Fuentealba constitutional bill on the "Three Areas" of Chilean enterprise superseded the president's original draft, but it still lacked the president's signature.

With this background, we can return to the main story. Sanhueza's abortive talks with the Christian Democrats had taken place in March 1972.[13] In April the president repudiated

Sanhueza's agreement and vetoed the Hamilton-Fuentealba amendment. A complicated but transcendingly important constitutional crisis ensued. It revolved around the plebiscite clause in the Constitution, which Allende had been hoping to use to install a unicameral People's Assembly. The plebiscite clause had been enacted in January 1970, during Frei's last year in power, and at that time the Congress had also established a special Constitutional Tribunal and eliminated an earlier constitutional provision requiring a two-thirds majority to override a presidential veto of a constitutional amendment. The 1970 amendment (Art. 108) said a constitutional amendment would go through the same procedure as an ordinary bill except as thereafter provided. An ordinary bill still took a two-thirds majority for an override (Art. 54), but Article 108 went on to say that a constitutional amendment could be approved by a simple majority, first by each chamber and then in joint session. Article 109 then established the plebiscite as a means to resolve conflict between president and Congress over a constitutional amendment "whenever" it might arise. The stage was set for an immense argument.[14]

The president asserted that it made no sense for a constitutional amendment to need a lesser majority than an ordinary bill. The opposition retorted that the president's remedy was a plebiscite, as articles 108 and 109 of the Constitution made clear. The president argued further that the new Constitutional Tribunal was the appropriate authority to decide the matter, but the opposition countered that the tribunal's job was to judge the constitutionality of laws and plebiscites, not to overturn amendments to the Constitution itself. Each side was favoring the mechanism that would produce the result it wanted, of course; the opposition knew how risky a plebiscite would be for the president, and the president knew that three of the five members of the Constitutional Tribunal were his own appointees.[15]

Maneuvering continued until June 1972, when Minister of Justice Tapia entered into negotiations with Fuentealba in a renewed effort to find a compromise solution. The legislative time limit for a Senate override of Allende's veto expired, however, forcing the Christian Democrats to break off the effort. Agreement had seemed fairly close, and the negotiators had apparently worked out a tentative list of industries to be nationalized. But the Papelera remained a bone of contention, and time limits on interventions and rules governing expropriations were not resolved. Another by-election in Coquimbo province was also coming up, which did not help matters. So this effort also failed.[16] On 16 September 1973, after the coup, the *New York Times* editorialized: "If Dr. Allende had moved more deliberately; if he had paused for consolidation after nationalizing Chile's basic industries and had delineated reasonable boundaries for his socialist program, he probably would have completed his term with considerable measure of success." Paul Sigmund has asserted that the June negotiations between Tapia and Fuentealba were probably "the last chance to prevent the polarization which terminated in the 1973 coup." The June 1972 negotiations were undoubtedly a turning point.[17]

Posturing and intermittent negotiating over the proposed Hamilton-Fuentealba "Three Areas" amendment continued without decisive result until 15 May 1973, when Allende finally signed a decree promulgating those parts of the amendment he agreed with.[18] That did not end the dispute, of course, and maneuvering went on right up to 11 September. Nationalization policy remained a festering sore, and each requisition or intervention, and each renewed wave of workers' plant seizures, produced new crises, renewed frustration, and heightened outrage in opposition ranks.

## Revelations in Washington

Most of the news on Chile which came out of Washington between December 1971 and May 1972 proved unsettling in Santiago. In late November 1971 a senior White House official, Herbert G. Klein, said in an interview with reporters that Salvador Allende "would not last long." Klein and White House counsellor Robert H. Finch had recently toured Latin America and had heard second-hand reports from diplomats, journalists, and officials that Allende was in trouble. Although Klein was apparently only passing on this talk, the impression created was that the Nixon White House had reason to know that Allende would be toppled.[19]

I had first heard of Klein's prediction when listening to a speech by Clodomiro Almeyda at the Foreign Ministry's anniversary celebration of 1 December 1971—the day of the march of the empty pots. Almeyda expressed his understandable indignation that a government which maintained full relations with Chile's constitutionally elected administration would openly forecast its demise.

As luck would have it, my wife and I found ourselves at dinner with the Almeydas later in the same evening; they were courteous, if visibly resentful. Next morning I found myself in Almeyda's ornate, brocaded office in the Moneda Palace, receiving a stiff formal protest.

That was only the beginning. On 21 March 1972 Jack Anderson published the first in a series of columns about anti-Allende plotting carried on by ITT. Day after day the columns appeared, with excerpts from highly confidential internal ITT memoranda and messages back and forth to ITT's Chilean representatives. In his columns Jack Anderson revealed much of what I have recounted about the ITT "track" in chapter 1. U.S. government complicity was not established, but ITT representatives Harold V. Hendrix and Robert Berrellez had been in frequent touch with Ambassador Korry and provided colorful quotations of what he allegedly told them. Supposedly the ambassador characterized the Chilean military as a "bunch of toy soldiers" and asserted that President Frei had to be told to "put his pants on." The memos treated the ambassador himself no more kindly, characterizing him as having become "a sort of male Martha Mitchell." As for Assistant Secretary Meyer, Hendrix accused him of being the weakest assistant secretary in at least twenty-two years and someone who should return to his former employment at Sears Roebuck.[20]

Columnist Georgie Anne Geyer reported from Santiago on 23 March 1972 that Anderson's accusations, "if they are true, . . . largely destroy the Nixon policy" of a mature partnership with Latin America. She might have exaggerated, but the revelations certainly dented the official U.S. image in Chile.[21]

In spite of the uproar, some caution should be exercised before concluding that the course of U.S.-Chilean relations, or even the fate of ITT's investments in Chile, were determined by Anderson's columns. Before turning to this question, however, it might be useful to describe another story that Anderson broke exactly a week after the first ITT bombshell. This story referred to me personally.

Anderson's headline in his 28 March 1972 story was: "ITT Hope of Ousting Allende Remote." The text, in part, but with all quotations from me included, follows:

> Any hope International Telephone and Telegraph may have
> of ousting Chile's President Salvador Allende, in the view of

American Ambassador Nathaniel Davis, is unrealistic.

In a secret cable to the State Department, Davis reported that "prospects of military intervention for the foreseeable future are extremely small.

"It is held that military will turn blind eye to virtually any constitutional abuse, and Allende is smart enough to avoid abuse so flagrant as to force open that blind eye." . . .

Before we published the incriminating ITT memos, he [Davis] summarized the situation in Chile for the State Department.

He reported "growing conviction in opposition parties, private sector and others that opposition is possible." He cited intelligence reports that "discontent and plotting in the military services have been substantially greater."

But he concluded: "It is not our impression that Chile is yet on brink of showdown. In fact, there is some reason to believe that new opposition spirit could prove transitory. . . .

"My colleagues continue to warn me that events move slowly in Chile, or perhaps better said, Chileans have great ability to rush to the brink, embrace each other and back off.

"With Russian and East European help . . . and with some breaks, Chile just might be able to rock along for some time to come."

In his secret summary, however, the new American Ambassador suggested that "Allende's course is working less well. If this trend continues, it will increase pressures on Allende to move toward radical solutions or in other directions.

"Allende's decisions may, in turn, sharpen the choices of his opposition and also of the military." Davis pointed out that "there is considerable variety in ways military might intervene."

Before ITT is likely to get its military coup, however, Davis suggested that public opposition to Allende would have to become "so overwhelming, and discontent so great, that military intervention is overwhelmingly invited.

"It is held that military will wait for this public repudiation to become more clear and more open than it is likely ever to be."[22]
[Reprinted by permission © 1972 United Feature Syndicate, Inc.]

I was told after the Anderson story hit the press in Santiago that President Allende was "amused" by my leaked message. He may also have been reassured that I, at least, did not regard his demise as imminent.

My telegram 6008 of 7 December 1971, from which Anderson

quoted, floated in and out of the press for some years. Its checkered history illustrates some issues in the interrelationship between journalism and diplomacy. According to investigative journalists' accounts, the cable leaked when a navy yeoman working for the National Security Council staff, Charles E. Radford, took it and a number of others and gave them to his friend and fellow Mormon parishioner Jack Anderson.[23] Radford and Anderson have demurred at this explanation, but Anderson certainly obtained the cable one way or another. Anderson kept regurgitating one or another part of my telegram, a little the way a cow brings up its cud for a ruminative chew. The language, however, seemed to change in Anderson's recycling.

In his 28 March 1972 column Anderson directly linked the "ITT Hope of Ousting Allende" and my telegram, which, he implied, characterized that hope as unrealistic. My telegram had been written several months earlier in compliance with a State Department request, and I was not privy to the interaction between ITT and the U.S. government when I wrote it. I had never met Hendrix or Berrellez, as they had departed Chile before my arrival; it was Jack Anderson who had himself introduced ITT and its hopes. I should add, nevertheless, that the specific quotations Anderson chose to publish gave a reasonably balanced impression of the telegram's message.

In Santiago the Communist daily *El Siglo* and the Socialist-leaning newspaper *El Clarín* both reported Anderson's column and headlined his lead sentence to the effect that ITT's hope for a coup "does not correspond to reality!" *L'Humanité* in Paris appears to have been more calculating, however, as it immediately put a twist on the story. According to *L'Humanité*, the U.S. ambassador had "informed the Department of State of all his conversations with . . . active-duty officers and of the fact that these conversations were fruitless. . . . According to this curious diplomat [Nathaniel Davis], it would be necessary first to create conditions for a very great discontent in order that a military intervention might be carried out, and this would mean sabotage of industrial and agricultural production, of the supply of raw materials, and of stocks of food and clothing." The *L'Humanité* story was pure invention, but it purveyed the line leftists throughout the world would subsequently take.[24]

On 12 September 1973, the day after the coup in Chile, Jack

Anderson was interviewed by Maury Povich on TV station WTTG in Washington. The Chilean press reported the interview as follows: Anderson: ". . . 'I have a document here. It was written by our Ambassador [in Santiago] . . . a few months ago [actually, almost two years previously]. . . . It carries the notation: "Eyes Only, Exdis and Secret." There is nothing really secret in it.' " (If intelligence reports on coup plotting are not secret, what is?) As the Povich interview went on, Anderson added the following, previously unrevealed, quotations from my telegram:

> " 'The attitudes of the military are the great unknown of Chilean politics. . . . They are still far from taking direct immediate action, but it has been galling to military and civilians to have men in uniform tear-gassing women. Some officers' own women folk were in the procession protesting shortages [the reference is to the march of the empty pots on 2 December 1971]. . . . It is galling to have it implied women are braver than they.' "
> [Povich] "This means, Jack, that you think that this is really an internal situation in Chile and there wasn't outside help?"
> [Anderson] "I believe that's the case."[25]

On 17 September 1973 Jack Anderson published still another column, which carried the quotations he had used with Povich. His lead was: "Simple Latin American machismo, or manhood, may have been a factor in the dramatic overthrow of President Salvador Allende." I thought he was stretching things to use my 1971 telegram to describe Chilean officers' macho resentment in September 1973![26] But on 22 September he and his colleague Les Whitten wrote still another column using the same 1971 telegram. By then, my 6–9 September trip to Washington to meet Henry Kissinger— which will be described in Chapter 13—had hit the news and had become controversial. Anderson and Whitten absolved me of complicity in the coup, however, suggesting that I had left Santiago thinking that things would be quiet. To illustrate my purported confidence in Chilean tranquillity, the columnists quoted me as saying that "events move slowly in Chile, or perhaps better said, Chileans have great ability to rush to the brink, embrace each other and back off." It was, of course, the same passage Anderson had quoted a year and a half earlier, used in this later instance to suggest that I did not appreciate the depth of the Chilean political crisis in September 1973.[27]

Another year passed, and investigative reporter Seymour Hersh was in full cry over U.S. covert action in Chile. On 3 November 1974 Anderson quoted from my 1971 cable still another time, as always with no acknowledgment that he was recycling material. This time, however, he turned the meaning around in the way *L'Humanité* had twisted it in March 1972. He said that "at first" I thought prospects of military intervention small, and my "secret cables" (in the plural) "stressed" that public opposition would have to become so overwhelming and discontent so great "that military intervention is overwhelmingly invited." Then he quoted me as saying that the "military will wait for this public repudiation to become more clear. . . ." He cut off the remainder of the sentence, which was: "and more open than it is likely ever to be." Anderson's next sentence completed the alteration of meaning: "The U.S. then began to create the 'discontent' that Davis had advised would be necessary." So a telegram of 7 December 1971, which Anderson correctly described in 1972 as reporting the unlikelihood at that time of a military coup became, through journalistic transmogrification, a recommendation to *create* the conditions necessary for a coup. He thus embraced the interpretation long since adopted by the world's leftists.[28]

Anderson regurgitated that same 7 December 1971 telegram still another time. In a column on 24 April 1975 he wrote: "It has been our lot to chronicle the tragedy of Chile," including quoting from "secret U.S. Embassy cables. . . ." Anderson then requoted my "rush to the brink" passage and my estimate that the likelihood of a coup was small—leaving the implication that my estimate had been cabled to Washington shortly before the 1973 coup. Anderson went on: "The Embassy was wrong. The generals moved against Allende. . . ."[29]

I suppose I should be grateful. In this column Anderson seemed to have backed off from the indictment that we deliberately fomented the coup and to have embraced the more benign allegation that our crystal ball was cracked. But how many times can you milk the same old cow?

To keep matters in perspective, I should note that Anderson's use of my 1971 telegram was relatively harmless and probably motivated more by the desire to impress his readers with his continuing inside sources than by any driving ideological bias. There are those who have ground much larger axes than he has in reporting on Chile. Indeed, I even have reason to be grateful to Anderson's sense of responsibility. Once in 1975, when I was the object of some deliberate communist disinformation (unrelated to Chile), Anderson had the grace to call me and check it. I convinced him the charge was false, and he killed the story.

Nevertheless, it is disingenuous to pretend that public servants and even nations are never harmed by journalistic revelations. For example, in the batch of cables slipped to Anderson in December 1971 there was a telegram from Phnom Penh, from Emory Coblentz Swank. In the cable Ambassador Swank made frank and penetrating comments about the moral and political weaknesses of President Lon Nol and his intimates. Anderson's publication of Ambassador Swank's honest assessment must have undermined the ambassador's effectiveness. It may also have made other ambassadors wonder about the risks of fearless reporting to a leak-prone U.S. government. Do smart ambassadors pull their punches and send Washington mush that can be revealed without damage? Phnom Penh was Swank's last ambassadorial responsibility, and he retired from the U.S. Foreign Service in 1975 at the age of 53 for reasons that reflect poorly on the moral courage of the Department of State's leadership and America's commitment to a professional diplomatic service. It is hard to know how much Anderson's revelations contributed to this misfortune, but some of Anderson's exposés have without question damaged the U.S. national interest. Although I do not reproach Mr. Anderson for his muckraking, or for his having obtained purloined documents and having printed them, he must have known that he was dealing loosely with the truth when he manipulated the text of that 1971 Santiago cable half a dozen times over more than three years, reinterpreting its meaning each time.

## The International Telephone and Telegraph Corp.

ITT's interest in Allende and the fortunes of his government did not stop with the Chilean president's inauguration. Curious episodes continued to occur. For example, Russ Tagliarini, ITT's deputy director of security, and John Ragan, part-time security director for the Republican National Committee in Washington, apparently traveled together to Chile in mid-1971 and spent eleven days there, ostensibly teaching antibugging procedures to officials

of the UP government. Ragan reportedly met Allende and conducted an electronic sweep of his summer residence and, by one
account, also of his Moneda office. Ragan has said that he only
swept for bugs and did not plant them. Nevertheless, it was a
strange incident, both from ITT's and from Allende's point of
view.[30] ITT had a peculiar, mixed relationship with Allende and, if
Ambassador Korry is to be believed, money changed hands.[31] It is
conceivable that ITT was prepared to do favors for Allende, and it
is possible that Allende was willing to accept them.

Korry has asserted that a Chilean named Jacobo Schaulsohn
Numhauser was a link between ITT and Allende. Schaulsohn, a
round, bearded, incisively intelligent friend of Allende's whom the
president appointed a member of Chile's Constitutional Tribunal,
was associated with the Santiago law firm that handled ITT's business in Chile. I particularly remember encountering the man on one
occasion coming out of the president's study at Tomás Moro, at the
moment before I was scheduled to go into it to discuss ITT
nationalization questions with the president. So the private links
between ITT and the president were not always implacably hostile.[32]

By mid-September 1971 Harold Geneen of ITT had seen the writing on the wall. He lunched with Alexander M. Haig, Kissinger's
deputy, and Peter G. Peterson, President Nixon's assistant for international economic affairs. He warned his White House contacts
that the Chilean Telephone Company (Chiltelco) would soon be
expropriated.[33] He was almost right. While not actually expropriating Chiltelco, as formal expropriation would have required a constitutional amendment in Chile, the Allende government did seize
operational control of the company and named an intervenor a
week or two later.[34]

On 28 September 1971 ITT representatives called on Assistant
Secretary Meyer at the State Department and urged that the U.S.
government embargo Chilean copper and cut off AID and IDB loans
to Chile. They received what they took to be vague answers.[35] Then
on 1 October the head of ITT's Washington office, William R. Merriam, submitted an eighteen-point plan to Peterson designed to
prevent Allende from getting through the "crucial" next six
months. Specifically, ITT wanted an immediate shutdown of new
AID assistance, a crackdown on credit, blockage of the use of IDB
funds for earthquake assistance, the closing off of Chilean exports

to the United States, including copper, and a delay or embargo of key U.S. exports to Chile—perhaps including fuel deliveries to the Chilean armed forces. The plan also recommended developing contacts with the Chilean armed forces, the judiciary, the civil service, the news media, and opposition congressmen. In addition, it proposed efforts to block Allende's diplomatic initiatives, and consultations with foreign governments on ways to put pressure on Chile. Among these latter ideas was a suggestion to disrupt Chile's plans for the third UN Conference on Trade and Development, scheduled to convene in Santiago the following April.[36]

Peterson later testified that he did not take the ITT program seriously. He said that he had received Merriam's letter but had not read the accompanying action memorandum. No word of Merriam's proposals reached me at the time, either from U.S. officials or from ITT's Washington representatives (whom I had met in early October 1971 at about the time Merriam was submitting his eighteen-point proposal to the White House.)[37]

On 21 October 1971, after I had arrived in Chile, Secretary of State Rogers met with the main U.S. companies with investments in Chile. ITT then submitted what it described as a Chile White Paper. This seven-point proposal was quite similar to the eighteen-point, economic warfare plan submitted to Peterson. Reaction to the ITT proposals was mixed, both on the part of Secretary Rogers and on the part of other company representatives at the meeting. The subsequent ITT memo summarizing the discussion concluded that Rogers was "pretty much going along with the . . . soft-line, low profile policy for Latin America" of Assistant Secretary Meyer.[38]

ITT's Latin American chief, John Guilfoyle, traveled to Santiago in February 1972 and talked with President Allende about possible formulas for settling the Chiltelco question. Talks also were held in the United States between ITT officials and the Chilean ambassador, Orlando Letelier del Solar. None of these talks had much result, and the two sides remained widely separated. The Chileans asserted that ITT's 70 percent ownership of Chiltelco was worth only about $24 million, while ITT was claiming $153 million. The Chileans proposed that the discrepancy be resolved by experts from the International Telecommunications Union who would evaluate Chiltelco's plant, lines, and facilities. ITT proposed that an international auditing firm examine the company's books. The Chileans wanted to assess the current quality of service, which they alleged was terrible. ITT claimed that the Chilean intervenor was running the company into the ground and that the only fair way to assess value was to go through past expenditures and note the large investments recently made. ITT also pointed out that the Chilean government had had representatives on Chiltelco's Board of Directors and that any board decision required their concurrence. In the past these government representatives had examined and approved Chiltelco's accounts. The Chileans countered that by law Chiltelco's profits could not exceed 10 percent of investment, so investment figures had been inflated for years to permit ITT to milk Chiltelco. They also alleged that ITT was stalling because it had OPIC insurance and would prefer to collect quickly from the U.S. government rather than wait up to fifteen years for Chilean compensation even if adequate payment were agreed upon. ITT was quick to point out that the U.S. government would inherit ITT's interest if the insurance were paid, and Chile would then be dealing with America's full power. The negotiations were a kind of ping-pong match of arguments and counterclaims.[39]

On 17 March 1972 Ambassador Letelier, who had returned from Washington to Santiago for consultations, told me that the Chilean government was willing to accept ITT's most recent proposal. ITT had suggested that the two sides name technical experts who would work toward an agreement on Chiltelco's monetary worth. The Chileans found the suggestion acceptable on the condition that the technical talks last no more than two to three weeks. The Chilean government still feared that ITT would stall.[40]

Jack Anderson's columns on ITT began appearing four days later, on 21 March. Two days after Anderson's first column on the subject appeared, the Foreign Relations Committee of the U.S. Senate met in closed session to discuss the allegations. Although Secretary of State Rogers assured the committee that the administration had not acted "in a wrongful manner," the senators' concerns resulted in the establishment of Senator Frank Church's investigative subcommittee on multinational corporations.[41]

On 18 April 1972 President Allende announced plans to expropriate Chiltelco by means of a constitutional amendment, which would be submitted to the Chilean Congress. On 12 May he submitted that amendment.[42] Many scholars and reporters have concluded that Allende's decision to expropriate Chiltelco was the direct result of Jack Anderson's revelations of ITT wrongdoing. The forthcoming nature of Ambassador Letelier's 17 March conversation with me, which the ambassador subsequently told the Washington press about, strengthened the impression. Moreover, President Allende himself explained his expropriation decision to me in these terms, as will be discussed below.

It is true that the ITT revelations were the trigger for Allende's decision, but they were probably not the cause. Even if the Chileans had gone ahead with the technical experts' meeting Letelier proposed, a meeting of minds remained unlikely. The Chilean government had no intention of paying anywhere near $153 million, and ITT had no interest in accepting compensation remotely close to $24 million—particularly as ITT had OPIC insurance and could hope eventually to collect a sum in the neighborhood of $100 million from the U.S. government. So the realistic view, I believe, is that the Anderson stories provided a public justification for Allende's move toward expropriation, but they were not the cause.

This conclusion is strengthened by the fact that Chile's indignation over ITT perfidy did not move the Chilean government to expropriate ITT's new San Cristóbal Hotel and the Hotel Carrera, both of which were a convenience to the Chileans in terms of foreign-exchange earnings and prestige. In order to continue their access to communications technology and spare parts, the Chileans also refrained from expropriating Standard Electric, ITT's equipment subsidiary in Chile.

Years later, in Washington, ITT and OPIC arbitrated their differences, including the clause in ITT's insurance contract that invalidated OPIC coverage if it could be shown that expropriation was the result of provocation by the investor. I testified on these treacherous issues before the three distinguished retired judges who formed the arbitral panel. The judges decided in favor of ITT, and the OPIC insurance was not invalidated.

ITT's activities in Chile had raised other interesting issues. Anthony Sampson, in his book about ITT, calls it a "sovereign state": in Chile it had a foreign policy, a foreign service, a clandestine branch, an information service, and much of the other paraphernalia of nations. Moreover, ITT's operations involved more than the gross national product of most of the world's countries. ITT's embarrassing public failure in Chile will probably shape American and world attitudes toward the foreign activities of businesses for years to come.

**The Paris Club**

The so-called Paris Club conjoins representatives of the world's great industrial lending and trading nations. When a developing country gets over its head in intergovernmental debt, it usually owes the debt to countries in the Paris Club, and to this informal club the debtor must come to negotiate rollover, partial postponement of debt servicing, or some other measure to forestall total default.

In November 1971—as already described—the depletion of Chile's foreign-exchange reserves forced the country to declare a partial moratorium on servicing of its foreign debt, and it soon took the initiative to renegotiate payments. Paris Club talks with Chile's eleven principal creditor governments were scheduled for February 1972. Out of almost two billion dollars owed worldwide, Chile owed close to a billion dollars to the United States. From the November 1971 moratorium on debt servicing to the end of 1972, Chile faced worldwide payment obligations amounting to about $260 million, of which about $145 million would be due to the United States.[43] These figures concern intergovernmental debt; Chile had already reached agreement with private U.S. banks on 9 February 1972 to refinance about $300 million in debts to the private sector.[44] Private bankers, incidentally, find it generally easier than governments do to renegotiate developing countries' debts. The bankers have little choice but to make an arrangement or lose their money. Governments, on the other hand, worry about politics, policy, precedent, and the protection of the rights of their citizens and business interests. Governments also have great power to resist, defer a settlement, or be unalterably stiff-necked.

The Chileans held that it would be improper for the renegotiation to address the question of compensation to the copper companies, as that question had been settled by Chilean constitutional action and a new constitutional amendment would be required to modify the outcome. The Nixon administration would have none of this view, however, and was determined from the start to link debt renegotiation with compensation for expropriated properties.

On 19 January 1972 President Nixon issued a policy statement on aid and expropriation throughout the world that resulted directly from Chilean copper nationalizations. The president's statement reiterated the U.S. view of international law: owners of expropriated properties had a right to "prompt, adequate and effective" compensation. Failing a reasonable provision for payment, "we will presume that the U.S. will not extend new bilateral economic benefits" unless "there are major factors affecting U.S. interests which require continuance" of such benefits. Without reasonable provision for compensation, there would also be "a presumption against U.S. support" for loans from multilateral development banks. The U.S. government promised to consult within the international community on these questions. A willingness on the part of the nationalizing country to refer a dispute to international adjudication or arbitration would be regarded as a "reasonable provision for compensation."[45] The intent and the threat were clear enough, although the statement was less categorical than it might have been.

At the initiative of Representative Henry B. González, the U.S. Congress promptly amended an appropriation bill to require U.S. representatives to multinational lending institutions to vote against loans to countries that expropriated U.S. companies without compensation. The González Amendment thereupon took its place as law beside the already famous Hickenlooper Amendment, which directed the U.S. president to suspend all foreign aid to a country that had expropriated U.S. property without compensation or had not taken steps within six months to move toward arbitration or other means of discharging its obligations under international law.[46]

The U.S. government avoided any formal application of the González and Hickenlooper amendments to Chile. Neither amendment was invoked during Allende's presidency, although multinational loans to Chile were blocked in informal ways. So far as the Hickenlooper Amendment was concerned, there was always some appeal, further step, discussion of arbitration, or other recourse available in the various cases at hand, including those of Anaconda, Kennecott, and ITT. I was glad of it, because when we had threatened to invoke the Hickenlooper Amendment in other Latin American countries, the situation created generally had not helped the United States.

While there had been some negotiated purchases of U.S. firms by the Chilean government,[47] the copper companies' plight and the threat to ITT continued to dominate policy thinking in Washington. Expropriation merged with debt renegotiation as preparations for the Paris Club meeting picked up momentum—although the meeting would eventually slip from February to early April. In his memoirs Henry Kissinger graphically depicts Treasury Secretary John Connally's attainment of bureaucratic supremacy. By January 1972, as Kissinger describes it, Connally had overpowered Peter Peterson, "and was ready to take on the State Department." Kissinger continues:

> [Connally] personally brought to Nixon's attention a memorandum implying that his opponents in State were prepared to reschedule Chile's debt payments . . . and that this in turn would stampede other creditor countries into the same cowardly course. Connally argued that the real purpose of the Paris meeting should be to isolate Chile.
>
> All this was grist for Nixon's mill. It sounded tough. It confirmed his worst suspicions about the effete State Department. It had an anti-Allende thrust. He did not concern himself with the central contradiction of Connally's position: If the objective was to isolate Chile, we would have to overcome European reluctance about confrontation. . . . If we insisted on . . . opposing rescheduling, the chances were that it was the United States that would end up isolated.
>
> Connally was aware of this, of course. His real point was to ensure that the Treasury Department would be in charge. . . . Nixon covered the memorandum with marginalia that any agreement to reschedule Chilean debt was "*totally* [Nixon's underlining] against my instruction." . . . In short order . . . a memorandum emerged from the Oval Office. . . .
>
> "I hereby appoint Treasury to head the United States Delegation to Paris. . . . Any suggestion, expressed or implied, that I favor US support of an agreement to renegotiate the Chilean loan is in total contradiction to the views I have expressed."[48]

Some months later I was in Washington on consultation, and friends at the State Department showed me a copy of this memorandum in great confidence. It was still regarded as a kind of guilty secret, and even then my colleagues at the Bureau of Inter-American Affairs were mystified as to why they had been so inexplicably and gratuitously maligned. In any case, the assistant secretary of the treasury for international affairs, John M. Hennessy, was appointed chairman of the U.S. delegation to the Paris talks. Hennessy was a young, cocky, hard-line banker from New York who had married a Latin American, spoke Spanish, and knew the hemisphere well.

At the end of February 1972 I sent a long telegram to Washington responding to a request for my views in preparation for the forthcoming Paris Club meeting. I had no knowledge at the time of Connally's power-grab or of President Nixon's memorandum. I warned my superiors that Allende might be able to build a national consensus in Chile against a "foreign threat" from the United States if we moved to destroy what the Chileans regarded as their economic rights: the right to own the copper companies without the need for massive equity compensation and the right to obtain relief from a massive foreign-debt burden. My colleagues and I believed, I said, that while Chilean relations with the East Bloc would become progressively stronger, Allende would not freely choose irrevocable ties to the communist world. As for reciprocal Soviet attitudes, I noted that the Soviets, like Castro, probably did not believe that Unidad Popular could achieve socialism in a consumption economy, and the Soviet ambassador and his Eastern European colleagues were privately complaining that "Chileans don't like to work." Only in a situation of considerably greater austerity or a staggering economic crisis, with a nationalistic confrontation or a Chilean break with the United States, did I think the Soviets would overcome their reluctance to extend truly large-scale aid. I therefore urged that our delegation in Paris stay close to our European allies, as a rift between the United States and Europe would give the Chileans their best chance of turning the meeting to their own purposes. Lastly, I noted that the Chilean government would be willing to make concessions only as long as it believed there was a chance for beneficial relations with us.

An ambassador can never be sure what impact a message of this sort will have in Washington. In this case, as might have been expected, my colleagues in the Inter-American Bureau were delighted with the telegram. They agreed with me, and the message strengthened their hand against officials in the Treasury Department whose instincts were to "clobber Allende's Marxist crowd" in any way they could. An embassy view has the advantage of reality as seen by the people on the spot, and it has the additional strength, when the issue is controversial, of striking a divided group of policy makers in Washington. In this particular instance my view fitted the objective expressed in NSDM 93, which warned against giving Allende a foreign target to help him rally domestic loyalties and mobilize international support. I suspected that we could count on a sophisticated U.S. posture in Paris if Henry Kissinger were focusing on the issues. As later became clear, he was.[49]

In the Paris talks Hennessy did maintain solidarity with the other important creditors and agreed to a rescheduling of the Chilean debt. The "fig leaf" for this somewhat conciliatory position was an ambiguous passage which Hennessy successfully inserted into the agreement as Article Four. In it, Chile expressed a willingness to pay "just" compensation for nationalized properties in accordance with Chilean legislation, international law, and UN Resolution 1803. These three governing criteria were mutually inconsistent, of course, as the recently enacted nationalization amendment to the Chilean Constitution did not provide the prompt, adequate, and effective compensation which the U.S. interpretation of international law required. UN Resolution 1803 provided support to the Chilean position that a developing country had a right to ownership and control of nonrenewable natural resources.[50]

On 18 April 1972, just as Hennessy was about to sign the Paris Club agreement he had negotiated, Salvador Allende dropped his bombshell. The Chilean president had summoned me on that day to talk about copper compensation and had made some conciliatory statements about the possibility of working something out. He went on to inform me, however, that the Chilean government was changing its position on ITT. After the revelations in Washington of ITT's intervention in Chilean affairs, Chilean dignity and self-respect required an end to negotiations with that corporation. I reported this development immediately to Washington and Paris, and the reaction in the U.S. delegation in Paris was one of consternation. That evening (early the following morning, Paris time) Allende told a massive workers' rally in Santiago of his plans to expropriate Chiltelco.

Allende, I suspect, had not thought through the impact of his public announcement on the Paris Club talks; it would have been relatively easy, with planning, to hold up the Chiltelco decision until the agreement had been signed. By the morning of 19 April, however, Hennessy was threatening in Paris that he would refuse to sign the final agreement in light of Allende's announcement. Somebody on the Chilean delegation in Paris no doubt put in a quick trans-Atlantic telephone call to Allende. It was then early morning in Santiago, and I suddenly found both Allende and Almeyda phoning me at home in separate, repeated calls, with long, conciliatory explanations of the Chiltelco nationalization plans and promises that the experience of the copper companies would not be repeated with respect to ITT. Allende gave me his full "flexible wrist" treatment, in his most disarming fashion.

We all needed a way to get off the hook. Even Hennessy was looking for a way out that would enable him to avoid being isolated from our allies. Besides, Jack Anderson's revelations had not left ITT very popular. I sent off an immediate telegram reporting Allende's and Almeyda's assurances. They fooled nobody, but it was what all parties needed.

On 20 April, Hennessy signed the Paris agreement. Chile could defer payment on 70 percent of its debts maturing between November 1971 and December 1972, pushing these obligations back three years. A new rescheduling session was scheduled for the end of 1972, to consider debts coming due in 1973. In actuality, these talks did convene, after several postponements, in mid-1973; they were still going on at the time of the September coup.[51]

The agreement of 20 April gave Chile almost $200 million in relief from her creditors, most importantly the United States. It provided that individual creditor nations should subsequently negotiate bilateral implementing understandings with the Chileans. The United States never did so—not the result of kindness but rather of the conviction in the U.S. government, particularly in the White House and the Treasury Department, that we should not negotiate the debt bilaterally until the expropriation issue had been resolved. The paradoxical result was that Chile negotiated bilateral understandings with her other creditors, and paid 30 percent of the monies due to them, but paid nothing to the United States. The International Monetary Fund later estimated that de facto relief to Chile in 1972 reached a total of some $243 million. The American contribution to that figure, although not wholly intended, was considerable. Chile was earning a billion dollars a year from exports, so the renegotiation increased the foreign exchange availability to the UP government by one-third. Things may have worked out for the best. Chile probably could not have paid the United States substantial sums, and a great American effort to squeeze blood out of the turnip might have made matters worse. Connally, Kissinger, and Hennessy understood these realities pefectly well.

To conclude, Jack Anderson's revelations, the ITT problem, the broader question of expropriation, and the Chilean debt negotiation came together between March and May 1972. Partly through chance, but also because of favorable political instincts on both the Chilean and the American sides, the resulting policy mess did not translate itself into a total break. It was a good thing that the entanglement did not become a decisive confrontation.

# Chapter 4

# Left Extremists, Miners, and Truckers

BY June 1972 conditions in the economy had gotten so out of hand that Allende felt compelled to dismiss his firebrand minister of economy, Pedro Vuskovic. The president did not turn his back on the political extremists, however, and Altamirano still rode high. The Cubans shipped in arms and agents; workers, shanty dwellers, and rural agitators began to organize paramilitary forces; and the leftists were seen as having "cooked" the tally in national trade union elections.

More trouble was reported from Washington: burglars with suspected connections in U.S. official circles rifled the Chilean Embassy's offices. Still, U.S.-Chilean military cooperation proceeded undisturbed. The question of copper nationalization bumped along without resolution; meanwhile Kennecott tried to block the sale of Chilean copper all over the world.

With the post-Vuskovic economic program working no better than its predecessor, demonstrations and strikes broke out in August and September. They culminated in the first great truckers' strike, which came close to bringing the UP government to its knees.

**Dropping the Economic Pilot**

A surefire way to pump up the blood pressure of Chilean conservatives was to mention the "ECLA crowd" in the UP government. The Economic Commission for Latin America and several other UN technical offices lie clustered around a little Tower of Babel on Santiago's outskirts. During the Alessandri and Frei time Marxist economists had found jobs there, and anti-Marxist Chileans and their American friends could recite a litany of UP luminaries who had passed from that alleged sinecure to Allende's halls of power. Among them were Gonzalo Martner, head of planning (ODEPLAN), Alfonso Inostroza, president of the Central Bank, and—most important of all—Pedro Vuskovic, the minister of economy.

Vuskovic became a symbol of the ultra leftists' ambition to build socialism through the destruction of private enterprise. Shortly after Allende took office, Vuskovic had said with candor: "State control is designed to destroy the economic bases of imperialism and the ruling class by putting an end to the private ownership of the means of production."[1] Believing that reform could come only through the institutional transformation of the country's economic life, he urged that nationalization of industry should be pushed forward even if it caused economic disorder and declining production. In fact, the shattering of the bourgeois economy could be seen as the first step in remaking the social and economic order. Although Vuskovic called himself an independent, his views coincided with those of Carlos Altamirano and the dominant left wing of the Socialist party.

Vuskovic's nationalization drive was not limited to interventions and direct-action plant seizures; he also used the government's control over prices and credit to force enterprises into the nationalized sector. The Directorate of Industry and Commerce (DIRINCO), a dependency of the Ministry of Economy, had the authority to approve or disapprove price increases. State-run firms easily obtained price hikes from DIRINCO and promptly passed them on to the public, and often to harassed entrepreneurs who were not so favored, in the form of higher prices for component parts and higher costs for raw materials. Government-mandated wage increases contributed to the squeeze; DIRINCO could thus bring disfavored businesses near to bankruptcy, and then the state authorities could buy the enterprise cheaply or assume control. DIRINCO's first director under the UP government was Alberto Martínez, a veteran of Castro's bureaucracy in Cuba and a man who well knew the power of state regulation. Anti-UP observers asserted, moreover, that DIRINCO established a secret committee in 1971 to monitor the selective political application of pricing policy. And certainly the progressive nationalization of the banks enabled the government increasingly to deny credit to politically targeted enterprises.[2]

Vuskovic's rapidly advancing program of nationalization had important economic and political effects, not least because of notably bad management of expropriated industries and generally ineffective state planning. Alberto Baltra, the Left Radical party leader and a distinguished economist, comments: "Even though it appears incredible, under the government of Unidad Popular the social area [that is, nationalized enterprises] did not work in a planned fashion. There were planning and planners, but the plan remained on paper. The firms of the social area . . . functioned according to the knowledge and understanding of the intervenors [the goverment appointed managers], who lacked . . . experience."[3]

Government-appointed managers were usually named on the basis of a political patronage system that would have put Tammany Hall to shame. For political and other reasons (some laudable), the Chilean government recruited few planning experts from Eastern Europe. Those experts and technicians they did bring to Chile did not generally work out well, because of professional weaknesses, cultural differences, and lack of fluency in Spanish. The result was an extraordinary crudity in Chilean economic forecasting. To illustrate, it was said that Chilean government planners made up their 1972 models and production targets by straight-line projection through 1972 of gains in output achieved in 1971, when idle capacity was being absorbed.[4]

The economic costs of Vuskovic's nationalization drive skyrocketed, and the fiscal and monetary effects of his policies became increasingly evident. The stimulative and ultimately inflationary impact of "pump priming" in Allende's first year, including wage and salary increases and widespread new hiring, had resulted in immense budget deficits for the government and floods of red ink on the books of nationalized firms. The government met these proliferating obligations by printing money and extending Central

Bank credits. At the same time the Central Bank was financing the purchase of enterprises from private owners through credits to the Chilean Development Corporation. These costs were also monetized. On the income side of the government's ledger, the tax base was shrinking as private enterprises were nationalized or went out of business and as wealthy taxpayers went abroad.[5]

The regular government's deficit increased from 13 percent of all governmental expenditures during 1970 to 34 percent during 1971 and 40 percent in 1972. The money supply increased by 116 percent in 1971, and in the next year it increased 171 percent over that. Currency in circulation increased from 8 billion escudos in 1970 to 21 billion in 1971 and 57 billion in 1972. The losses of state corporations alone were estimated at 50 billion escudos in 1972.[6] The result was runaway inflation. The rise in the cost of living, as reflected by *official* prices, reached 163 percent for the year 1972; a factoring in of black-market prices would have pushed the figure even higher. Consumers were, of course, turning increasingly to the black market as shortages increased.[7]

In March 1972, with accelerating inflation still in its incipient stages, Orlando Millas of the Communist party was already cautioning that the cost of living had increased 10 percent in January and February while it had gone up only 22 percent in all of 1971.[8] One did not have to be a Communist to discern the trend of events. At the end of February I had reported to Washington that economics would largely determine the future of Chilean politics and that the magnitude of Chile's problems would inexorably increase while the Chilean government's ability to cope with them would diminish. My colleagues and I saw no sign of governmental self-discipline in fiscal and monetary policy and foresaw massive inflation, ever higher effective demand, and greater shortages.

For some months the government had ignored the evident danger signals and resisted policy changes—although it did not remain totally inactive. The escudo was devalued in December 1971 for some products, though not for food and petroleum. The government had hoped this move would spur exports and check imports, but the devaluation was late and half-hearted. In February 1972 Vuskovic announced a sharp change in economic policy and the end of the large government subsidy on basic foodstuffs. Prices were increased by more than the cost-of-living wage increases given throughout 1971. Vuskovic explained that consumption would have to be cut back to achieve a higher level of investment.[9]

Far from increasing, however, investment slid further. Even in 1971, when industrial production had increased by 12 percent, the flow of capital into the economy had been dwindling, threatening to curtail future growth. Private entrepreneurs were mostly unwilling to reinvest their earnings for fear of being nationalized. As an additional disincentive, they also found their profits dwindling as they were obliged to pay higher and higher wages. So they used available liquid funds to buy dollars, for use if they left Chile. There were reports of massive smuggling, as Chileans spirited medicines and other valuable commodities out of Chile to be sold for dollars in Argentina, Bolivia, and Peru. Even the nationalized sector failed to invest heavily. Vuskovic used his resources for further nationalizations rather than for new capital equipment and expanded capacity. He recognized that industrial expansion was needed but felt that it had to be postponed until ownership of the means of production had been transformed.[10]

Production continued to increase moderately until mid-1972, although the rate of increase progressively slackened, and by the September-to-December 1972 period it was actually below the level of a year before.[11] The Communists, particularly Millas and Party Secretary Luis Corvalán Lepe, became increasingly critical of Vuskovic and his economic management. Believing it was unwise simply to go on "provoking our enemies," they proposed "consolidating what we have." Millas argued that it was necessary to restore the confidence of what was left of the private sector in order to boost production.[12] But that was exactly what Vuskovic and his ultra-leftist allies did not want.

In June, UP leaders met at Lo Curro in a conclave much like the earlier El Arrayán conference. Economic policy was thrashed out, and the communist position more or less won. Vuskovic was forced out, and he was missing from a new all-civilian cabinet announced on 17 June. While Vuskovic was given other high positions and retained the president's ear, he never again directed the Chilean economy. In the cabinet shuffle Millas was brought in to assume the key portfolio of finance. Carlos Matus Romo, less commanding but virtually a twin of Vuskovic in policy, was appointed minister of economy in Vuskovic's place (Matus was to last all of five months).[13]

In July 1972 President Allende announced a new economic plan.

It would rely on loans, mostly from Eastern Europe, to increase investment. Taxes would be increased for the wealthy and upper middle classes. Price adjustments would enable nationalized industries to become "self-financing," small and medium enterprises would be encouraged to earn "reasonable" profits, and larger industries would be allowed "enough to operate."[14]

In mid-August the government authorized price increases of 50 percent to over 100 percent on basic items. The inflation rate doubled in that single month and jumped another 50 percent in September, bringing the official increase in the consumer price index to 100 percent for the first nine months of 1972. The government tried to soften the blow by promising a congressional bill mandating bonuses to all Chileans on 18 September (Chilean Independence Day), wage and salary adjustments to counteract the inflation, and a market basket of fixed-price items for the poor. The opposition, while denouncing the "market basket," went along with the bonuses and adjustments. Nobody had any real idea of how to pay for them, however, except by printing more money. The dog was chasing its tail.[15]

The Communists may have won victories in the factional struggle within Unidad Popular, but they did not succeed in taming the economy itself. Things had degenerated too far. No party in the divided government had a solution short of a level of austerity that carried an intolerable political price.

On political strategy it was the Socialist party that was scoring gains in the intra-UP struggle. The Socialists had already blocked Allende's efforts to broaden his political base. The president's desire to lure prestigious independents into the government had borne no fruit; after a brief time in the cabinet the PIR had gone into opposition; and repeated efforts to negotiate an accommodation with the Christian Democrats had failed. Millas's economic strategy of restoring private-sector confidence might have worked had it been matched by a political strategy non-UP circles could trust, but that was not to be. On the other hand, Vuskovic and the left-wing Socialists understood that retreat from headlong expropriation would leave residual centers of economic power in the hands of Unidad Popular's enemies, and there is no question that these enemies made use of what economic power remained to them. As so often happens, policy compromises denied both government factions their best shot at success.

## The Left Extremists, the Cubans, Arms, and More Polarization

The ideological affinity between the dominant Altamirano wing of the Socialist party and the MIR has already been indicated; so, too, has the attitude of President Allende, who was ever reluctant to repress even the most unruly extremists of the left. The MIRistas themselves had their origins among the socialist students at the University of Concepción. A number of socialist leaders broke with or were expelled from the Socialist party in the 1961–64 period, and they formed the Marxist Revolutionary Vanguard. The vanguard became the MIR in 1965. The movement spawned four action groups to mobilize university students, industrial workers, farmworkers, and shantytown squatters. The Movement of the University Leftist (MUI) was always the most important of these groupings, and even land seizures in the central valley between Santiago and Puerto Montt were mostly led by students rather than farmworkers. Students also played leading roles in recruiting shantytown dwellers and workers in the industrial belts (*cordones*) around Santiago.[16]

MIR agitation, power, and influence reached a high during the last year or two of the Frei administration and the first year-and-a-half of Unidad Popular. In January 1972, however, the MIR narrowly lost the student elections at the University of Concepción to a rival UP candidate. As 1972 progressed, the Communists prodded the UP government into sporadic but nevertheless increasingly determined measures to curb the MIRistas' disruptions and excesses. The Communists detested the MIR, with communist ideologue Volodia Teitelboim describing them in a September 1972 interview as "these individuals [who] flow out of the people's party like excrement. . . ." In the same interview Teitelboim lamented that MIR-organized farm occupations were stripping "the government's expropriation plan of legality."[17]

Three ultra-leftist groups other than the MIR also deserve to be mentioned. As may be recalled, Edmundo Pérez Zujovic of the Christian Democratic party was assassinated in June 1971 by members of the Vanguardia Organizada del Pueblo. The VOP had split off from the MIR in 1969 over the question of terrorism and political assassination, with the VOP taking an ultra-extremist position a little like the Narodniki's in 19th-century Russia. The killing of the VOP's leaders in the shootout which followed the Pérez Zujovic murder virtually destroyed the organization, but it did participate in a few violent demonstrations and occupations of farms, factories, and government buildings at various times during the Allende years.[18]

A second violence-prone organization had also split off from the MIR. Like the VOP, it declined and then had a modest revival under the UP government. It was the Manuel Rodríguez Revolutionary Movement (MR-2). It never became an important actor on the scene, but it did carry out a few small terrorist acts that complicated the lives of the carabineros and order-minded governmental authorities.[19]

The third group was a Trotskyite-Maoist organization, which called itself the Revolutionary Communist Party (PCR). While small, it had some influence. A lawyer-journalist, Robinson Rojas Sandford, edited a periodical that generally expressed PCR views and scorned the UP as a "reformist bourgeois" regime. The PCR believed that victory would come only through prolonged violent struggle, and it worked to arouse the Mapuche Indians and factory workers in SUMAR and other large plants.[20] Led by a student leader named Emiliano Campos, PCR militants took advantage of the UNCTAD conference in Santiago in April 1972 to organize a demonstration of approximately three hundred extremists outside the UNCTAD meeting place, at which time they burned a U.S. flag and denounced the alleged detention, and torture in some cases, of two hundred ultra-leftists.[21]

Other extremist groups agitated, demonstrated, seized farms and factories, and battled carabineros. Yet it may be that the leftists who maneuvered ambiguously in the no-man's-land between the MIR and Unidad Popular were more important than extremists who operated openly against the government. Besides the Altamirano wing of the Socialist party, two such "Christian" political forces participated in the cabinet while sometimes surreptitiously opposing Allende.

The first was the Movement for Unified Popular Action (MAPU), whose leaders had split from the Christian Democratic party in 1969 over the party's nominee for the 1970 presidential elections. The Christian Democratic party had developed factions, with the "Rebels" (*rebeldes*) on the left, the Frei-government faction (*oficialistas*) on the center-right, and the Third Force (*terceristas*) in between. At a 1 May 1969 meeting of the Christian Democratic

Assembly, an *oficialista* resolution on electoral strategy barely defeated a *tercerista-rebelde* one, and the *rebelde* leaders resigned
from the party. Among the politicians who bolted were two
senators, a deputy, and the former head of the Institute of Agricultural and Livestock Development (INDAP), Jacques Chonchol
Chait. Most of the CD youth division and some peasant and trade
union leaders also resigned. On 18 May 1969 the dissidents formed
the MAPU, with Chonchol as its first secretary general.[22]

As time went on, the MAPU drifted further left, declaring itself
Marxist in 1971. In late July of that year six Christian Democratic
deputies and most of the new leaders of the CD youth division
defected from the mother party, much the way the MAPU people
had done two years earlier. They formed a new grouping called the
Christian Left (Izquierda Cristiana). These left-wingers were reacting against the party's new links to the "reactionary" National party
and to the Radical Democrats in the recently concluded Valparaíso
by-election. The most prominent of the original founders of the
MAPU, including Chonchol, who was the minister of agriculture,
thereupon left the MAPU, citing its un-Christian embrace of Marxism, and joined Izquierda Cristiana.[23]

Both the MAPU and the Christian Left had ties to the MIR. Chonchol was sympathetic to the MIRistas' farm seizures, and some
officials of the land reform agency CORA cooperated with the
MIRistas, including helping them to get arms. In early 1972 Izquierda Cristiana and the MIR joined forces to contest elections in
the Chilean trade union confederation, and soon thereafter representatives of the MIR, Izquierda Cristiana, the MAPU, and some
Socialists and Radicals held a "popular assembly" in Concepción,
denouncing the Chilean Congress and advocating "direct action."[24]

The MAPU continued to drift leftward, and in-fighting became
sharper, with Jaime Gazmuri and Minister of Finance Fernando
Flores Labra heading the more centrist, government-oriented
grouping and Oscar Guillermo Garretón Purcell, Vuskovic's subsecretary of economy in 1971–72, heading the ultra-leftist one.
Only the prospect of congressional elections in March 1973 kept
the two factions within the MAPU, as the more extremist leaders
realized that they needed to run as MAPU candidates if they hoped
to win seats in the Congress. After the 1973 elections the MAPU did
indeed split.[25]

There were yet other groups. In July 1972 Chilean military intelligence uncovered what it said was an extreme leftist plot to attack the president's residence on Tomás Moro Avenue and identified the plotters as the "July 16th Command of the National Liberation Army." Presumably the attack was intended to bring things to a head and radicalize the revolution. According to the military, the group included a former member of the president's guard (GAP) and some Socialist party militants, among them Arturo Hoffman, a former private secretary to the president's sister, Laura Allende.[26]

In early 1972 the GAP was alleged to have lent a small truck to the MIRistas, who in turn used it to transport weapons stolen from the army. This truck apparently was intercepted in the town of Curimón, causing much speculation in the press about GAP-MIR links.[27]

The "left frontier" of Unidad Popular was not a sharply defined boundary. It was a mutually permeating and interacting mass of personalities and groups, some inside the government, some outside it, and some variously inside and outside depending on occasions, opportunities, and overlapping loyalties and convictions. The ambiguity on Unidad Popular's left fringe complicated the government's task enormously. It meant that Allende and the Communist party never quite knew what was going on in the left wing of the governing coalition. It also meant that the carabineros never knew if they were on solid ground in upholding order.[28] It left military leaders frustrated and fearful for their "monopoly of force" in the face of leftist groups bearing arms under some degree of UP protection. It left some otherwise cooperative Christian Democrats and centrist opposition politicians feeling that Allende was unreliable and that his people were disloyal to the country's democratic institutions. In this sense the uncertain affiliation and loyalty of the UP left wing, which was never clarified, contributed to the government's ultimate demise.

Another development in 1972 complicated the situation still further. That was the establishment of the *focos*, the *campamentos*, and the *cordones*. The *focos* resembled the Viet Cong–controlled areas in the Vietnam countryside in the 1960s; in a few places the MIR rather than the government held effective control. The most famous of the *focos* was the wooded, hilly stretch of land close to the Argentinian border about 500 miles south of Santiago where "Comandante Pepe" held sway and where carabineros did not venture.[29]

The *campamentos* were shantytowns, filled with families living in little prefabricated or jerry-built wooden houses. They were mostly in the suburbs of Santiago and other large towns, and the MIRistas and other left extremists organized them into militarized hamlets. The first were the Lenin and the 26th of January encampments, organized in mid-1970, even before Allende's election. My family and I witnessed the establishment of a new *campamento* in early 1973 at the edge of the wealthy Santiago suburb of Las Condes, as it was on our fourteen-year-old daughter Margaret's way to school. The encampment was staked out under cover of darkness in a single night, and its establishment came as a shock to its affluent neighbors. Margaret told her diary:

> At first the Campamento Fidel-Ernesto was a mess of Chilean flags and cheap wooden tent-like things, made of old wood or cardboard, and only high enough to sit in. Within a week there were pre-fab houses in orderly lines, all facing each other. During the next week there were clotheslines, with clothes drying, to be seen here and there. At the end of that week there were fences all along the street, between the houses and the street we took to school. Outhouses, children—it really looked lived in. Clean, too. The people wrote pro-U.P. signs all over the street and signed them all with Fidel-Ernesto. They're pro-Altamirano.
>
> They've just finished putting in pipes. At the moment they're building a big wooden wall, and with good wood, planks with straight sides and of the same length—and yellow, not grey or brown. . . .

In other places around Santiago the encampment dwellers protected their settlements with barbed wire and had sentries, strong internal organization and, in some cases, impressive discipline. There were even some encampments where drinking was controlled, and a few were reminiscent, in their evident dedication, of religious communes.[30]

The first of the *cordones*, or worker-controlled industrial belts, was the Cordón de Los Cerrillos, along the avenue out to Los Cerrillos airport. Workers in the local factories organized themselves in June 1972 to press for state takeovers of several still-private firms in the area. Left Socialists and MIRistas seized leadership of the workers' organization, and their vigilante squads became formidable. Later, in a dispute between Allende and his senior army generals in

January 1973, it is alleged that Allende threatened to take refuge in the Cordón de Los Cerrillos, boasting that "you will never get me out."[31]

Workers in the factories of the *cordones*, and in neighboring living areas, organized what they called "communal commands" *(comandos comunales)*, faintly reminiscent of the *soviets*, or workers' councils, in the Russia of 1917. These commands became nucleus organizations for the effort to establish a parallel, nongovernmental mobilization of the workers, which became known as "People's Power."[32] The next requirement was arms. At first, weapons were hand-forged and hand-tooled in the factories themselves. Apparently, the workers also manufactured a few "people's tanks," built around forklift trucks to which metal plating was attached.[33]

By mid-1973 a dozen *cordones* ringed the heart of Santiago, stretching out along the principal avenues. They had their sentries, and slogans slashed in garish colors across the pastel walls and factory entries.[34]

All three ganglia of revolutionary organization—the *focos*, the *campamentos*, and the *cordones*—would have greatly aided a Viet Cong struggling against a hostile Saigon regime. Yet the workers' own representative was sitting in the Moneda Palace. Allende never quite made it clear whether he was on the side of the mobilized workers or his own governmental authorities, and the workers of the revolutionary vanguard never made it clear whether they supported the government or were trying to organize for their own revolution.

Crossed signals proliferated. In early 1973 Allende made the symbolic gesture of setting up his presidential office temporarily in the nationalized Sumar textile plant. He apparently passed some of his time talking to workers about various subjects, including the problem of alcoholism, its effect on production, and the need for factory discipline. A few days later Carlos Altamirano went out to the Cordón Vicuña Mackenna and instigated the construction of barricades when it was feared that then minister of economy Millas intended to return some illegally seized factories to their owners. The result was neither the left extremists' prescription for action, although it was a beginning, nor was it Allende's Chilean Way, which it undermined.[35]

Did the Cubans provide arms to the left extremists? During late

1971 it was said that unmarked planes from Cuba arrived each Saturday night at Pudahuel airport outside Santiago. Reportedly the planes taxied to a little-used part of the field, and cargoes were transferred to trucks without passing through customs. It was never proved that these deliveries contained weapons, but when the opposition press publicized the flights, they stopped.[36] One purported arms delivery, on 11 March 1972, exploded into a major governmental crisis. That day a Cuban Airlines plane landed at Pudahuel, and thirteen crates, supposedly containing works of art and gifts to Allende, were rushed onto trucks without passing through customs—a transfer said to have been under the supervision of Minister of Interior del Canto. The press reported that men unloading the crates dropped one and that automatic weapons spilled out onto the ground. Mostly as a result of this incident, del Canto was impeached in the Congress and removed from office on 27 July. After the 1973 coup the military government would publish documents inventorying over a ton of armaments, which it said were the contents of these crates.[37]

There is little question that the Cubans were highly active in Santiago, and publicity about their activities further polarized Chilean political life. It did not help that Allende's daughter Beatriz was married to Luis Fernández Oña, a diplomat in the Cuban Embassy. The opposition press avidly described Fernández's supposed Cuban nickname, "Quick on the Trigger," his help to Che Guevara when Guevara was fomenting insurrection in Bolivia, his alleged training of the GAP, his Cuban intelligence ties, and his office in the Moneda Palace. Jack Anderson made a further contribution to anti-Cuban sentiment when he claimed on 30 March 1972 that Cuban subversive activity against all of Latin America was based in Santiago.[38]

Two other events in 1972 further polarized the country's political forces: the elections in the Central Workers' Confederation (the CUT or CUTCH) and the long crisis at the University of Chile. A congress of the CUT had met in December 1971 and decided to hold nationwide union elections for the first time ever; CUT leaders had previously been elected by delegates to CUT congresses.[39] The three main contesting forces were the Communists, the Socialists, and the Christian Democrats. Ernesto Vogel of the Christian Democrats was very popular, and the Christian unions were strong. The ballots were cast on the last days of May and the first days of June.

A month and a half then passed. Rumors circulated that Vogel clearly led, but ballot counting went on at a snail's pace. The official results were announced on 15 July 1972: the Communists got 170,000 votes, the Socialists 145,000, the Christian Democrats 144,000, the MIR-Izquierda Cristiana slate 10,000, and other minor slates a few votes. About half of the million members the CUT claimed were not recorded as having voted.[40]

The reaction of the Christian Democrats can be imagined. They screamed that the results had been cooked. Not only did they believe the communist victory was fraudulent, but they also thought their total had been deliberately reduced to a thousand votes less than the Socialists' figure. In the Santiago voting the Communists got about 300 votes more than the Socialists did, and even most Socialists thought the Communists had altered those results. Taken overall, the CUT elections increased the bad blood among the political parties in Chile and fed the Christian Democrats' growing resentment.

Meanwhile, the rolling crisis in the universities, a continuing feature of political life in the Allende years, produced several critical developments. As always, events in Santiago were of crucial importance, and the immense establishment of the University of Chile was the bellwether. The rector of the University of Chile was elected by weighted voting where faculty votes counted 65 percent, student votes 25 percent, and the ballots of nonacademic employees 10 percent. A Christian Democrat, Edgardo Boeninger, had been elected rector before Allende took office. The university's governing board had a Marxist majority, however, and the Marxists developed a plan to restructure the university's twelve professional schools and faculties in such a way as to consolidate Marxist dominance.[41] In late October 1971 anticommunist students at the Law School seized that building, which overlooked a main thoroughfare, and festooning the edifice with flags, they urged every passing car to honk in solidarity. The din became a source of pleasure to Santiago's middle-class commuters for months to follow. In due course anti-Marxist students occupied other faculty premises, interrupted half the university's classes, and demanded a university plebiscite on reorganization. On 17 November 1971 leftist students countered by occupying the main offices of the university and holding Boeninger prisoner for several hours. Boeninger then led two hundred students and professors in a march on the Moneda Palace. The march was broken up by police, using tear gas; Allende threatened Boeninger with criminal prosecution; the Communists called on "democratic forces" to defend the government. More student clashes on 22 November involved over two thousand students of both the Catholic University and the University of Chile, and student rioting spread to campuses in Valparaíso and Concepción.[42]

After weeks of uproar and maneuver, a compromise was worked out in January 1972. Boeninger agreed to resign and stand for reelection in university-wide voting on 27 April. The university's governing council also agreed to withdraw from office, to be replaced by an interim governing board. At the end of February Allende announced that the leftists' candidate for rector would be the widely admired Felipe Herrera. Boeninger nevertheless won the election, with 52 percent of the votes, and anti-Marxists also won a slim majority in the governing council. Nearly 70,000 professors, students, and employees had voted.[43]

In September 1972 candidates from the CD-National party slate won a majority of department chairmanships at the University of Chile in closely contested elections. Opposition candidates won the elections in November for rector and vice rector at the University of Concepción, the MIR student stronghold. Reportedly the two winning candidates had barely escaped assassination one week earlier, when they were fired on by alleged left extremists.[44]

The Marxists used their continuing control of student organizations at the University of Chile to press their campaign for restructuring and for the dismissal of "reactionary" professors. They also resorted to direct action. In January 1973 they seized the university's TV station and operated it illegally for eight months, while government authorities "postponed" the execution of several court orders mandating eviction. Three days before the 1973 coup carabineros, with still another court order, finally ejected the occupiers.[45]

Two things are clear. First, anti-Marxists slowly gained ground in university voting. Second, the increasing polarization of political life found its reflection on the campuses, and campus developments in turn fed the polarization they reflected.

### The Chilean Embassy Break-in and Orlando Letelier

A rash of break-ins spread through the Chilean official community in the United States during 1971 and 1972. Between 5 April

1971 and 8 May 1972 the Chileans reported six incidents, including several cases where would-be intruders were surprised and frightened off.[46] Then, during the weekend of 13–15 May 1972, the Washington offices of the Chilean Embassy itself were rifled. In his own third-floor office the ambassador found a filing cabinet pried open and drawers jimmied. Files and papers covered the floor. Upstairs, according to the ambassador's report, "Embassy First Secretary Fernando Bachelet found a similar scene. The burglars had not removed cash and expensive office equipment but had taken four small radios and one electric razor." Andrés Rojas's passport was stolen from his desk.[47]

Subsequent revelations by the Watergate burglars and their U.S. government associates leave little doubt that the embassy break-in was the work of the "plumbers," the same group who broke into the democratic party's offices in the Watergate building a month later. James McCord would testify to the Senate Watergate Committe that the U.S. government had also tapped the telephones of the Chilean Embassy.[48] David Wise, author of *The American Police State*, also describes an operation to bug the Chilean Embassy in 1971, about a year before the embassy was entered. While Wise is unfriendly to U.S. officialdom, he is a diligent investigator whose revelations have often proved accurate:

> The CIA privately admitted to [Church Committee investigators] . . . that there had been an electronic eavesdropping operation directed at the Chilean embassy, involving both the CIA and the FBI.
>
> By the CIA's account, it first proposed that the FBI bug the embassy in April, 1971, but Hoover refused. On April 23 Helms wrote Attorney General Mitchell requesting that he reverse Hoover's decision, which Mitchell did. The CIA delivered sophisticated bugging equipment to the FBI three days later, and between April 27 and mid-May the FBI got into the embassy and installed several mikes.
>
> The bugs worked, and for more than eight months the government listened to conversations taking place inside the embassy. But in February, 1972, Hoover, still smarting over being reversed by Mitchell, threatened to tell Congress that the FBI was bugging the embassy at the CIA's request. The CIA hastily asked that the eavesdropping be stopped, and the FBI either went in and pulled out the miniature transmitters or turned them off by remote control.

> Again by the CIA's account, it asked the FBI to "reinstitute
> coverage" of the embassy on December 8 [1972]. . . . By the day
> after Christmas the bugs were broadcasting again, although
> there is some evidence they may have been turned off or re-
> moved again in February, 1973.[49]

As evidence corroborating the February removal, David A. Phillips, who became chief of the Western Hemisphere Division of the
CIA in June 1973, has told me that the CIA was not eavesdropping
by means of microphones in the Chilean Embassy when he took
over and that "bugs" were not used against it between June 1973
and the time of the coup.[50] Wise suggests that the embassy break-in
might have been an effort by the White House "plumbers" to fill the
gap in coverage left when J. Edgar Hoover got the electronic eavesdropping stopped. This interpretation would fit the pattern of the
plumbers' other operations and would also reflect the intensity of
White House interest in matters Chilean.

I first learned about possible U.S. official complicity in the Embassy break-in years later, from published sources. My involvement
in these matters began and ended on 16 May 1972, when Aníbal
Palma, Chilean subsecretary of foreign relations, called me into his
office, described the Chilean Embassy break-in to me, and expressed his government's concern for the security of its diplomatic
mission. I expressed regret that the incident had occurred, as did
the Department of State in Washington.

I wondered whether the incident would trigger retaliation
against our embassy in Santiago. An Eastern European country
would surely have struck back, but there was no such move. Was
this a desire not to exacerbate things? Did whatever "dirty tricks"
organizations the Chilean authorities maintained lack follow-
through? Was the UP government preoccupied with other crises?
Perhaps all these possibilities contain elements of truth.

Orlando Letelier played a central role in all U.S.-Chilean relations during Allende's time. Wise offers this word-picture of the
Chilean ambassador:

> Letelier, a distinguished and aristocratic diplomat, had red hair,
> a trim mustache, warm brown eyes, and a long rather sad but
> friendly face; there was a hint of Fernandel in his expres-

sion. . . . A lawyer and an economist from an old Chilean family—although the name is originally French—Letelier came to Washington in 1960 with the Inter-American Development Bank. After a decade in Washington with the bank, he resigned to become ambassador to the United States. Of his four children, all boys, one was born in America.[51]

On the whole, Wise captures Letelier pretty well, although "trim" is not the word I would have chosen to characterize the flaming brush Letelier sported under his nose. Wise is right that there was a hint of the great French actor Fernandel in him.

Orlando Letelier was an extraordinarily effective ambassador, one of that small band who knew how to work the U.S. capital with consummate skill. He knew everybody, most particularly the representatives of the press. He could drop tidbits of news and explanation which would promptly find their way into the *Washington Post*. He was straight with me in our many dealings, even though we spoke to each other across an ideological divide and upheld different interests. He had weaknesses, of course,[52] but I truly admired Orlando Letelier.

### U.S.-Chilean Military Cooperation

Considerable controversy has arisen over the continuance of U.S. military assistance and loans to Chile between 1971 and 1973, a period during which new economic aid was being curtailed or obstructed. Some critics even allege that military aid was greatly increased from the levels of the Frei period, but the value of military assistance was actually lower on average during the Allende time.[53] Nevertheless, it was substantial.

In 1971 the U.S. Department of Defense reported $700,000 in programmed military assistance to Chile, including the training of 146 Chileans in the Panama Canal Zone. U.S. military sales to Chile that year amounted to $3 million. In May 1972 an additional $10 million loan to the Chilean military was approved in Washington, mostly for additional C-130 aircraft but with a possibility of Chilean purchases of tanks, armored personnel carriers, and trucks. Overall figures for military assistance in 1972 were $900,000 programmed and $2.2 million provided, with 197 Chileans trained in the Canal Zone. So far as military sales in 1972 were concerned, about $6 million in new orders were placed and about $4.6 million in arms were delivered.[54]

While it is getting ahead of the story, here are the rough 1973 figures. Programmed military assistance ($940,000) was slightly higher than in 1972; delivered military assistance ($900,000) was less than half the 1972 figure; arms orders were sharply up ($15 million, which drew down considerably on earlier loan extensions), and deliveries ($2.2 million) were down; Panama training (257 persons) was up by about 30 percent. In June 1973 the United States agreed to sell F-5E fighter aircraft to Chile, and that year Chile purchased, among other items, three Landing Ship–Tanks, eight T-37 trainer aircraft, and spare parts.[55]

Military relationships always involve visits, and we had several of them. U.S. Air Force chief of staff John Ryan visited Chile in March 1972; Chilean Air Force commander-in-chief César Ruiz Danyau returned the visit in October; and General Prats, Admiral Montero, and Rear Adm. Sergio Huidobro, head of the Chilean Marines, all visited the United States. Such military visits always seem to produce new weapons procurement plans, just as high noon follows the morning sun.

For General Ryan's visit, the Chileans did their best to put on the dog. The high point of the military display was an air show at El Bosque field outside Santiago, commemorating the forty-second anniversary of the Chilean Air Force. The ceremonies, as always, started with President Allende and his defense minister reviewing the troops. Allende was a short man; José Tohá stood 6′ 3″.[56] With his thick glasses and bristling little mustache, the president thrust out his chest and marched forward with great determination in his own middle-aged version of a martial posture. We all sensed the psychic effort he expended in upholding the dignity of the Chilean presidency. Tohá marched, if one could call it marching, beside the president. Not only was he very tall, he was also very, very thin. With his pointed beard and sharply etched face, he looked like one of those old woodcut drawings of Don Quixote, though he was thinner. Connected to the turf by a bit of shoe leather far beneath him, he would progress forward in a gently swaying motion next to the president, a grave and thoughtful expression on his long face. They made an almost successful effort to keep in step. Every once in a while the president would make a little trot to catch up, and turning corners presented their own problems.

Tohá was a man of delightful warmth and immense personal charm. But this is not to say that he was a towering intellectual figure or a terribly hard worker. He was finally eased out of the

Ministry of Defense, it was rumored, because Allende and his advisers had the feeling that the country's senior military officers did not quite take Pepe Tohá seriously. A fellow Socialist, Tohá was one of Allende's closest personal and political friends, and his ironic wit was legend.

During the air show at El Bosque the Chileans displayed their mastery of precision maneuver in gliders. The denouement came when the perfect "V" formation of air force gliders swooped silently down to about twenty feet above the ground, directly in front of the grandstands. Then they did a loop-the-loop in formation, and set down one after the other on the strip. Minister Tohá turned to me with a smile as the gliders rolled by and said: "Just think, Mr. Ambassador, what our Air Force could do if you would only consent to sell us motors!"

A few hours later I took General Ryan by Tohá's office in the Ministry of Defense for a courtesy call. The minister had assembled all the generals and admirals in town. He fell to talking about his earlier job as minister of interior, responsible for internal security and the police. He had felt, he said, as if he were going up and down the great chain of his country's volcanoes, trying to snuff out each erupting disorder. It was as if, by sitting on each volcano, he was trying to quench its fire. Tohá then looked around; his present job was "much easier." As minister of defense he knew that if the volcano he currently minded were to erupt, "it would only erupt once." In the ensuing silence a few sheepish smiles passed over the faces of the assembled generals and admirals.

Besides the visits of individual senior officers, there was the Unitas task force visit to Chile in October 1972. Unitas was, and is, an annual cooperative naval exercise in which a U.S. force, usually four ships, circumnavigates South America and conducts maneuvers at sea with each friendly navy along the route. I took Rear Adm. John Shanahan, the task force commander, to call on Allende. The president was unfailingly courteous, animated, and charming during visits of this kind, and he seemed to enjoy them.

The Unitas task force came equipped with a complete band and musical comedy troupe, and they put on a show for the Chilean military establishment at the embassy residence. I could have done without the sailor dressed in a grass skirt and padded bra who did bumps and grinds in front of the Chilean admirals' ladies, but the Chilean military were so pleased to have U.S. military cooperation, they would have applauded anybody we might have sent.

The Chilean armed forces valued the continuation of these military ties with the United States, but the ties' significance should be kept in context. For a time the assurance of American military assistance and credit enabled the military to fend off pressure from Allende and other UP leaders to accept incomparably more generous Russian and Eastern European offers of help. These pressures continued to mount, however, and by 1973 they were beginning to unseal the Western-oriented arrangements of the military. The military and naval visits, while psychologically supportive, were of limited importance. The central drama was always the unfolding relationships between the Chilean military and the top UP leaders. Moreover, it is worth noting that nothing in the area of U.S.-Chilean military cooperation drifted past the notice of Allende and his intimate advisers. Minister of Defense Tohá countersigned every contract, every agreement, every arms purchase, and every training arrangement with the United States.

### More Copper—or Less

We left the copper expropriation problem with the comptroller general of Chile upholding President Allende's determination about excess profits on 11 October 1971. Technically, the great copper companies had the right to appeal this decision to a five-member copper tribunal on which Allende's appointees were in the majority. To exhaust their legal remedies, Anaconda and Kennecott did appeal, but they were not optimistic about their chances.[57]

The Chilean government claimed it was making some conciliatory moves. President Allende announced in November 1971 that Chile would assume the copper companies' debt. This debt, about $700 million, covered the obligations undertaken by the Copper Corporation (CODELCO) when the Chilean government had bought 51 percent of the American copper companies' assets. The Chileans argued that assumption of this debt represented a form of compensation, as about a third of it was owed to American companies and agencies. For their part, however, the copper companies argued that Chile had purchased its interest at book value, which underestimated the worth of their Chilean assets. Chilean government spokesmen countered that Anaconda and Kennecott had sold copper at much less than world-market prices to the United States during World War II, in the Korean War, and in the Vietnam hostilities up to 1966. By allowing U.S. companies to conform to U.S. wartime price-freezing arrangements, Chile had lost hundreds of millions of dollars. The Chileans argued that this practice had in itself been a form of "compensation," and historical justice required that the factor be taken into account.[58]

Then, on 30 December 1971, President Allende announced that Chile would not pay the first $6 million payment on the debt to Kennecott.[59] Nobody who knew President Milliken of Kennecott expected him to take the announcement lying down. A smallish, craggy, broad-faced man, he confronted the world. On 4 February 1972, while still pursuing the copper tribunal appeal, Kennecott sued Chile in the Southern District Court of New York. The court duly moved to block the New York bank accounts of nine Chilean agencies. The accounts were not large, perhaps $250,000 in total, but the threat was clear. The Chilean national airline, LAN-Chile, temporarily suspended flights to New York for fear that its planes would be attached. Three weeks later the Chilean government paid the $6 million, although it suspended payments again in early 1973. Anaconda, which had followed Kennecott's lead in bringing suit in New York, had a similar experience, but Chile paid only one installment in 1972 before again suspending payment.[60]

Anaconda's and Kennecott's appeals to the copper tribunal had the expected outcome. On 11 August 1972 the tribunal upheld the Chilean government's position by four to one. On 7 September Kennecott announced that it was withdrawing from legal proceedings in Chile and that it would write off its equity in El Teniente. Anaconda had already written off its equity in its main Chilean mines.[61]

In late September, Kennecott initiated a new round of suits to attach Chilean copper shipments, this time mostly in Europe. Kennecott claimed the shipments were stolen property.[62] Kennecott also appealed to the American and international business community not to buy Chilean copper, an effort that came to be known as Kennecott's copper boycott. Legal battles raged in French, German, Swedish, Italian, Canadian, and Dutch courts through October and November 1972, although copper shipments themselves were generally not attached. Canadian and Dutch banks suspended lines of credit to Chile pending resolution of the suits. French and Swedish courts determined that payment for two copper shipments should be placed in escrow. On 22 January 1973 a West German court decided in favor of the Chileans, saying that it could not rule on the legality of nationalizations in Chile. The results of the other suits were also mixed. Although customers and shipping routes had to be changed from time to time, Chile continued by and large to market its copper at world prices. A decline in sales to Western Europe and the United States was balanced by increased shipments to Japan, Latin America, and communist states.[63]

Lawsuits were not the only difficulties the Chileans faced. Production was not increasing as planned. Figures were slightly higher in 1971 than in 1970, and about 4 percent higher in 1972 than in 1971, but overall production had begun to decline by mid-1973. In the Chilean context this record was a serious failure. The Frei nationalization agreements had provided for a massive increase in capacity, so slight gains represented a large deficiency in the yield from investment. Two newly opened mines, Anaconda's Exótica and Cerro's *Andina,* had just come into production in 1970–71, and without them Chile's total output would have declined by about 9 percent in 1971. Copper output at El Teniente had dropped by more than 17 percent in that year. In 1972 production at El Teniente recovered, but production at Chuquicamata, El Salvador, and Exótica declined.[64]

Highly technical problems contributed to these production difficulties, and the mass departure of American experts and many of their American-trained Chilean colleagues had left the Chilean mining industry short of skilled technicians who could solve them. Theodore H. Moran lays considerable added blame on featherbedding, labor indiscipline, and quarrels among communist, socialist, and other leftist leaders at the mines. Norman Gall of the American Universities Field Staff visited Chuquicamata in February 1972 and noted that "the professional or supervisory payroll was swollen by swarms of new nontechnical personnel . . . who plunged into political work on behalf of the *Unidad Popular* or infantile rivalries among themselves." David Silberman, the communist manager of Chuquicamata, is quoted as saying: "There are few people who know about copper and have the government's confidence." In May 1972 three-dozen senior technicians at Chuquicamata resigned in protest over what they claimed was "chaotic administration." Every few months *El Mercurio* would run exposés of mismanagement in the mines, sometimes narrated by Chilean mining technicians who had quit their jobs.[65]

The copper workers were quick to strike when disputes arose, partly because Allende declined to employ force against strikers, and partly because some were led by Christian Democrats and others in the opposition. The president was driven in October 1972 to report no fewer than thirty smaller work stoppages in Chuquicamata under UP rule, and there were several one- and two-day minewide strikes between January 1972 and January 1973. As Chuquicamata miners had not called a major formal strike across the previous five years, their attitude struck Allende as pointedly disloyal to a workers' government.[66]

UP authorities initially tried to blame foreigners rather than workers for production problems in the mines. They attributed bottlenecks to the indifferent performance of U.S. technical personnel still on the scene, even accusing some of them of sabotage. Later they blamed Kennecott's and Anaconda's suits and those companies' efforts to disrupt the supply of spare parts to the nationalized mines. Although the American companies' boycotts did produce dislocations and misadapted equipment, the spare-parts problem was aggravated by the Chilean government's inefficient procurement and lack of credit and foreign exchange. It was usually possible to obtain parts when the Chilean government was in a position to pay for them.[67]

The copper issue moved along a track parallel with the ongoing official dialogue between the U.S. and Chilean governments. On 15 September 1972 the United States proposed intergovernmental talks, as luck would have it just before Kennecott filed its suits against Chile in Europe.

On 18 October the Chilean subsecretary for foreign affairs, Luis Orlandini, called me into the Moneda Palace to hand me a long, accusatory note identifying the U.S. government with the actions of the copper companies. Asserting that the United States was engaged in "true economic aggression," the note said that the U.S. government was intervening directly in Chilean affairs. I read the note quickly and appealed to Orlandini to reconsider it. I pointed out that Kennecott's lawsuits in Europe were not actions of the U.S. government and that the note's accusations could not help matters. Orlandini, a moderate in the Radical party and a great gentleman, agreed to treat the note as undelivered and to review it. Six days later Foreign Minister Almeyda summoned me to the Moneda

Palace again and handed me a revised note. Saying that I could react as I had to Orlandini only once, I put the note in my pocket without looking at it; I read it back at the embassy. Changed in tone, the note still reflected resentment at Kennecott's lawsuits. More important, however, was the clear distinction it now made between the acts of a private U.S. company and the official acts of the U.S. government. It also expressed interest in bilateral talks on the governmental level, though indicating that economic actions directed against Chile should be discussed as well as the issue of compensation.

The distinction I made between U.S. government acts and those of private companies was real, as Kennecott had acted on its own initiative when it filed its suits in Europe. This is not to claim that Washington disapproved of Kennecott's move. It is to say only that the Chilean and American governments' willingness to observe the distinction facilitated dialogue and made official relationships easier.

The ensuing talks began in Washington on 20 December 1972 and lasted three days. Assistant Secretary Meyer chaired the U.S. team, and Ambassador Letelier headed the Chilean one, supported by several socialist and communist subsecretaries. The closing communiqué noted the "positive climate" of the talks, but no solutions were reached. A second round was scheduled for early 1973.[68]

Soon after the December 1972 talks Charles Meyer left the State Department, to be replaced several months later by Jack Kubisch. Partly as a result of the change in leadership at the Inter-American Bureau, talks did not resume until 22–23 March 1973, once again in Washington. The U.S. team was headed by Acting Assistant Secretary John Crimmins for the Bureau of Inter-American Affairs and Assistant Secretary Hennessy for Treasury, while Ambassador Letelier once again headed a mixed UP delegation. At the time the American press was headlining testimony before the Senate Foreign Relations Committee, in which Geneen, McCone, Merriam, and other ITT officials acknowledged their activities in 1970 aimed at preventing Allende's assumption of power. It is hard to say how much these revelations affected the official talks, but the atmosphere was considerably less cordial than in December.

The Chileans proposed activating a 1914 treaty of conciliation and arbitration between the two countries. The treaty had established a standing five-member commission; two members were appointed by each country and the fifth, the presiding officer and presumed tie breaker, was appointed by agreement. During the Kennedy administration a distinguished professor of international law in Paris, Suzanne Bastid, had been appointed to the key fifth position. Treaty procedures provided for study, conciliation, recommendations for solution, and finally arbitration for referred disputes, although there were reservations about questions affecting sovereignty.[69]

From late 1972 onward I had been urging Washington to keep the door open to the employment of this treaty option. It was not a hopeful resource as it stood, for the procedures allowed for substantial delay and the binding arbitration provision was doubtful. Nevertheless, I believed that the treaty might open the way to a bargain that would provide for consideration of both our copper compensation interests and Chilean grievances over credit blockages, concerns over debt, and other issues. The fact that the treaty was already long in force made it politically easier for both sides to accept than the negotiation and ratification of a new agreement. For what it was worth, Jacobo Schaulsohn of the Chilean Constitutional Tribunal had told me—probably after consulting Allende—that a new constitutional amendment might not be necessary for an agreement to arbitrate the copper dispute under the treaty.

Sure enough, the Chilean delegation to the March 1973 talks proposed invoking the 1914 treaty and asked that the commission examine all pending disputes. The U.S. counterproposed bilateral negotiations under Article 4 of the April 1972 Paris Club agreement. The negotiations became tense and difficult. In particular, Letelier later told me of a post-coffee-break session on Friday, 23 March, that struck the Chilean delegation as "threatening."

It was clear that the U.S.-Chilean relationship was deteriorating rapidly. According to the press in both countries, the talks had ended in an impasse. Armando Uribe, a senior diplomat of the Allende government who was in Santiago during March and April 1973, later charged that the U.S. government had assumed a new "hard line" toward Chile, the result of a high-level decision made just before the talks. Crimmins, Uribe wrote, threatened a rupture, or what would effectively be "war," and he quotes a Chilean Foreign Ministry analysis written the following month to the effect that the U.S. decision before the talks must have been to "destroy" the UP government by "more varied, less cautious, and more aggressive" means than had previously been envisaged. Uribe characterized this American "decision" as the most important shift in U.S. policy since 1970.[70]

In fact, U.S. policy had not changed. There had been clashes of personality at the talks and some genuine misunderstanding of intentions on both sides. My colleagues in Washington, suspecting the Chileans were deliberately trying to provoke a confrontation, sent me a telegram asking me what I thought. I told Washington I believed this suspicion unfounded, and I requested and received authorization to reassure Foreign Minister Almeyda that there had been no U.S. "policy reversal" nor any U.S. decision to reject the 1914 treaty procedure. In our ensuing talk I urged Almeyda not to overload the treaty, a "small, leaky craft," with great, unwieldy pieces of freight. In Uribe's later account, he makes an indirect reference to my reassurances, alleging that we Americans were simply trying to deceive the Chileans.[71]

During the following two months, both sides worked at avoiding an irreconcilable break. Secretary of State Rogers called on Allende on 25 May: both were in Buenos Aires for Héctor Cámpora's inauguration, and a cordial talk eased the tension. A couple of weeks later Allende felt me out about a possible solution to the copper dispute. His idea was an agreement that would have enabled the Chileans to pay compensation over quite a few years while receiving substantial credits "up front." He was obviously casting around for some way to relieve Chile's pressing credit squeeze. Both sides began to consider a third round of bilateral talks in late June.

This time the Chileans began to complain about always having to come to Washington. Besides pride, their reaction may have reflected Orlando Letelier's return to Chile in May to become minister of foreign affairs, with the result that he was no longer available in Washington to lead the Chilean side.

Jack Kubisch telegraphed me in mid-June to say that Washington had decided that the talks should be held in Santiago and that he and Hennessy would be the U.S. delegation. I could see my effectiveness in Chile being undone if the American delegation to Santiago did not even include the U.S. ambassador, in obvious contrast to the confidence the Chileans had placed in their own ambassador for the Washington sessions. Although I was not well informed about it at the time, the fight between State and Treasury over control of Chilean policy was obviously continuing. In a telegram answering Kubisch's message, I offered my resignation. I also pointed out that the situation in Santiago was getting dicey. The arrival of Kubisch and Hennessy in the Chilean capital would, I suggested, cause a maelstrom of political speculation in the Chilean press.[72] Noting that Letelier would be at an international conference in Lima within two weeks and that Kubisch wanted minimum publicity, I suggested a discreet meeting in Peru.

Friends later told me that this telegram captured the attention of my Washington superiors. Fortunately, my warning about the political situation in Santiago and the suggestion of the Lima alternative presented a way out for everybody. Jack Kubisch phoned me and authorized me to try out the Lima possibility on Letelier. The foreign minister was agreeable to my proposal and did not insist on Santiago as reciprocity for Washington.

The third round of talks was held in Lima from 23 to 26 June 1973. The Chileans pushed even more strongly for the employment of the 1914 treaty. The U.S. delegation expressed cautious interest. Little was achieved but the atmosphere was more friendly than in March, and both sides agreed to meet again soon. In early August my colleagues at the State Department pushed within the U.S. government to loosen the tie between copper compensation and debt rescheduling under the Paris Club agreement. The idea was to make possible the collection of the $44 million Chile had agreed at Paris to pay the United States. I supported the initiative but the Treasury Department opposed it, and it did not get anywhere.

The fourth round of bilateral talks was held in Washington on 16–17 August, with Kubisch and Hennessy on the U.S. side and José Tohá, by then former minister of interior and of defense, heading the Chileans. According to Letelier's subsequent account, Chilean governmental approval to engage in this round had not been easy to secure. Apparently Altamirano and his left-wing socialist colleagues opposed negotiations with a country they believed was seeking to overthrow the UP government. Neverthless, Allende went ahead, partly as a concession to the Chilean armed forces, whose leaders were pressing for U.S.-Chilean reconciliation. He did so at the last moment: the Chilean delegation, including Tohá himself, did not apply for visas until the eve of the talks. So far as substance was concerned, a bit of progress was made with the 1914 treaty idea but the overall results were inconclusive.[73]

An effort was made to maintain the strictest of confidentiality about these August talks, to the point that Chilean opposition leaders, including Frei, heard only rumors about them. Fearing serious consequences in Santiago, I gave a very private rundown to one of Frei's intimates, reported my action to State, and received a reprimand, later withdrawn, for my action.

In what proved to be a last gasp in the copper negotiations with the UP government, the Department of State sent me a very long telegram on 10 September, giving me pages of questions to put to Tohá as a follow-up to the August meetings in Washington. By the time I received the telegram, it had been overtaken by the coup.

There are many views, and as many interpretations, of the overall significance of copper in U.S.-Chilean relations during Allende's time. Left-wing observers assert that the U.S. government and the copper companies sabotaged production, disrupted marketing, dried up credit, blocked spare parts, made copper earnings plunge, and spearheaded the relentless economic blockade which brought Chile down. Right-wing observers assert that Allende trampled on international law, stole the proceeds of productive enterprise, contributed to the disintegration of the international order, compromised worldwide possibilities for technology and capital transfers essential for development, and promoted irresponsibility everywhere. Both views contain elements of truth, although neither is altogether correct. The real significance of the copper issue, I believe, lies in what did *not* happen. The issue never really came to a head. The endless litigation, appeals, and talks prevented copper from becoming the ultimate determinant in Chilean politics or the U.S.-Chilean relationship. Copper diplomacy thus served one useful purpose. It purchased time and enabled both sides to avoid a total confrontation.

### Strikes

It is time to return to the events of mid-1972. After Vuskovic's dismissal, the new economic leadership failed in its turn to provide an effective solution for the country's problems, and the mid-August price increases, soon to be followed by wage adjustments and a nationwide bonus, only steepened the inflationary spiral. The price increases also brought political trouble.

Within days resentment at the mid-August price hikes merged

with anger at an incident in the extreme south of Chile. A super-market owner in Punta Arenas died of a heart attack on 17 August after authorities had tried to force open his store, which he had closed to protest the government's policies.[74] Protest demonstra-tions, strikes, shop closings, and the declaration of a state of emergency in Magallanes province followed. The national Confed-eration of Shopkeepers, with 125,000 members throughout the country, declared a one-day solidarity strike for 21 August. The confederation's president, Rafael Cumsille, explained that the strike was also a protest against inflation, scarcities, and price con-trols. It was the first nationwide strike of small entrepreneurs since Allende had taken office. On the morning of the strike government inspectors tried to force open shops in Santiago, and clashes en-sued. Opposition youths erected and set fire to barricades along Providencia Avenue, the main route from the center of Santiago to the wealthy suburbs. Others, probably members of Patria y Liber-tad, tried to break into a construction site downtown, and pro-government workers hurled bricks at them from nearby scaffolding. Carabineros had to break up fighting in many places, and one re-porter described downtown Santiago as looking like a "battlefield." Shortly before midnight on 21 August a state of emergency was declared in Santiago province.[75]

Several weeks of intermittent street violence and flash strikes followed. On 30 August the focus of trouble was Concepción, where both pro- and anti-UP youths held illegal demonstrations. A carabinero was killed in the subsequent fracas, and a state of emergency was declared in that province. Roving gangs of leftist and rightist students battled each other two nights later in Santiago, setting bonfires and blocking traffic. The upcoming 4 September anniversary of Allende's election stimulated more demonstrations and clashes.[76]

UP supporters marched in strength on the anniversary. Two days later street fighting forced the police to seal off the center of the capital, and a youth was killed by a teargas canister which hit him on the head. On 11 September there were more clashes, between high-school students of opposing political loyalties. On the four-teenth the opposition held a march to counter Unidad Popular's of ten days earlier, and LAN-Chile airline mechanics struck.[77]

While things were quieter during the latter half of September, the country did not return to normal. Then a government initiative in the remote southern province of Aysén triggered worse trouble. The Aysén provincial office of the Chilean Development Corporation announced that it planned to establish a state enterprise to run land, water, and air transport in the extreme southern provinces. By 1 October truckers in the town of Coyhaique in Aysén were on strike, and the alarm sounded that the Aysén initiatve was a pilot plan to prepare for the nationalization of trucking throughout the country. Chilean truckers were fiercely independent-minded entrepreneurs. Most owned a single truck or, at most, two or three. They were organized in the National Confederation of Truck Owners, headed by León Vilarín. In a country shaped like a string bean, the 47,000 trucks that carried goods up and down the land were of vital importance.[78]

On 9 October 1972 a partial national truckers' strike began. Vilarín was demanding higher trucking rates, the abandonment of the Aysén initiative, and measures to overcome the worsening shortage of spare parts. The next day Vilarín and three other leaders of the truckers were arrested, and on the eleventh the strike went nationwide. One day later Rafael Cumsille of the shopkeepers declared his organization's solidarity with the truckers and called for a shopkeepers' strike of indefinite duration. Within a few days the Federation of Taxi Drivers' Unions, the Confederation of Production and Commerce, and the Sole National Confederation of Small Industry and Artisanry joined the strike. These were the guilds, or *gremios*, of Chile, and their strike was essentially a middle-class movement. Before long, lawyers, engineers, ship captains, bank employees, anti-UP secondary-school students, and some doctors, dentists, druggists, teachers, pilots, and farmworkers were adhering to the strike. They formed a National Command of Guild Defense and submitted a "Petition of Chile" to the president. The petition went beyond immediate bread-and-butter issues to demand promulgation of the Three Areas amendment, strict conformity with judicial decisions, free entry and exit from the country for all Chileans, and other political demands.[79]

The government responded vigorously. Several hundred trucks were requisitioned. The CUT mobilized workers to move people to and from work in trucks, to distribute food directly in the poorer districts, and to escort and protect strike breakers. The military escorted trucks carrying essential supplies. The government declared a state of emergency in most provinces and imposed a midnight to 6 A.M. curfew in Santiago during the two weeks after 17 October. The curfew was of considerable use to the government, not only because it forced demonstrators and gangs off the streets but also because it gave the government's authorized agents an exclusive opportunity to move about during those hours.[80] The government also declared a national broadcasting network, locking radio transmitters into one government-supervised program. Some of the opposition broadcasters soon broke out of the network. In response the government closed down their facilities; the broadcasters appealed to the comptroller general and the courts, and they were upheld on the basis that a compulsory network violated the Statute of Democratic Guarantees. The courts had also freed arrested leaders of the Truck Owners' Confederation. In the meantime, CD party president Fuentealba denounced the government for "trampling upon the constitutional guarantees it promised to respect" and for violating workers' rights.[81]

The truckers remained the core of the strikers movement, and their struggle had great drama. Thousands of them collected their trucks in immense pasture-land parking lots in the countryside with the trucks clustered together, protected by owners armed with clubs, sticks, rocks, and a few guns. The truckers lived with their trucks, and farmers gave or sold them food. The women of the wealthier suburbs of Santiago also collected supplies from house to house and streamed out to the truckers' parks in their cars and station wagons. The opposition press published numerous photographs of the truckers, shawled in blankets in the early spring mornings, standing around steaming pots.[82] Other thousands drove their vehicles deep into the woods and covered them with boughs. I remember walking with my wife up a little country track during this time when we came upon an ancient, battered vehicle pulled off and parked among the trees. Next to it stood a solitary figure, smoking a crudely-rolled cigarette, waiting, apparently, not for the day to end but for the whole threatening time to pass. As we later came back amid the lengthening shadows, he was still there in the same place, alone. Clearly he was ready to spill blood before relinquishing his truck.

*Miguelitos*, bent nails welded together and sharpened at both ends, were strewn by the millions over Chile's highways. Some truckers who had arms fired on strike-breakers as they drove along in the countryside. Filling stations in Santiago ran out of gas, and people waited for hours in long lines for thimblefuls of gasoline. There was a brisk black market in government-issued gas coupons, which were supposedly for official vehicles. Bakeries closed for lack of flour. Long lines of women could be seen throughout the poorer residential districts, waiting for food. These women tended to buy supplies every day, and the shortages hit them particularly hard. Violence erupted periodically, especially when government personnel smashed locks and tried to force open the stores of striking shopkeepers. The main rail line between Santiago and Valparaíso was dynamited more than once.

Downtown Santiago had a somber look even in better times, although animated figures and flashing dresses normally brightened the scene. In these days, however, the melancholy avenues revealed no such movement. Midday Santiago looked like Manhattan in the postdawn hours of a holiday morning, with steel shutters down, the ubiquitous gratings drawn across every aperture, and empty streets.

Twice in October 1972 the government seemed on the point of turning things around. On the seventeenth President Allende managed an agreement with the country's bus and taxi owners and successfully dissuaded them from joining the strike movement. The next day, however, the government requisitioned CENADI, the last large, private, wholesale products distribution company. On 19 October the Shopkeepers' Confederation added the derequisitioning of this company to its list of demands and vowed to continue to strike. Were it not for the requisitioning of CENADI, the dynamic of confrontation might possibly have been changed.[83]

The second moment of near-success for the government was on 25 October, when Allende seemed to be on the point of reaching agreement to end the strike with a delegation of truck owners. The negotiations broke down at the last moment, however, and army tanks were called out two days later, for the first time, to maintain order in Santiago.[84]

On the last day of the month Allende's cabinet resigned, to give the president a free hand. It was reported that Allende was already negotiating with the top military leaders to bring them into the government.[85]

There is a poignant sidelight on the great October 1972 truckers' strike. According to Gonzalo Martner, Alende's chief of planning, the president suffered a heart attack during this time. Martner is quoted as describing the episode as follows:

> [It] was kept secret lest word of his illness spark a move to have him retire from the presidency. For ten days Allende remained bedded down in his private office in the presidential palace under the care of his cardiologist, Dr. Soto. Despite severe chest pains and a high fever, Allende insisted on being involved in the day-to-day proceedings concerning the strike. Since he was unavailable for interviews, the press was told that the President was too busy drafting a solution to the strike. Soon after the strike came to an end, Allende snapped back to normal. It was a near-miraculous recovery.[86]

One theory among commentators sympathetic to Allende holds that the October strikes caused the economic difficulties which ultimately brought the president down. The time sequence is wrong, however. Chile's economy began unraveling before the October strike movement, and the economic crisis of August 1972 was an immediate forerunner. This is not to deny that the October strikes severely damaged the Chilean economy. Estimates made at the time indicated that Chile lost $150 to $200 million in productive activity forgone during those three weeks. Nevertheless, the strikers did not cause the Chilean economic distress.

There has also been a continuing argument whether grievances caused the strikes or were pretexts for a subversive political effort to bring on a coup d'etat. Motives were mixed. There were genuine economic grievances and compelling fears, but political factors were also clearly present. Despite the strikers' jumble of motives, one issue was ever present: expropriation. The truckers' decision was triggered by the announced nationalization of transport in Aysén. The first shopkeepers' strike was set off by the seizure of a supermarket in Punta Arenas. The requisitioning of the CENADI on 18 October made things worse. Even before these particular incidents occurred, the fear of losing trucks, shops, and livelihoods was becoming a consuming passion.

The Christian Democrats may have been right that only a clear definition of the rules, expressed in the Three Areas constitutional amendment or in some equivalent way, could have provided the reassurance needed to normalize economic and political life. Millas saw this necessity, but Vuskovic and Altamirano profoundly believed that bourgeois power could not be appeased. They insisted that radicalization and the smashing of the economic bastions of reaction were the Chilean revolution's only hope. So nationalization was the issue for truckers, shopkeepers, professionals, and guild members, and also for politicians of every ideological hue.

*Chapter 5*

# Military Officers Join the Government

It was surprising how quickly the situation quieted down after 2 November 1972, when Allende brought senior military officers into his cabinet. Not everyone supported the move, of course, and Jacques Chonchol, until then minister of agriculture, left the government over the issue. Nevertheless, the general situation soon improved to the point where Allende felt able to leave the country for a two-week, whirlwind tour of New York, Moscow, Algiers, Havana, and other places. In New York he delivered his famous indictment of American imperialism and what he described as its insidious, bland-faced, financial aggression. In Moscow he walked a red carpet but received no commitment to a full-scale, hard-currency bailout. At home his troubles multiplied.

## Prats to the Rescue

Carlos Prats González was a central actor in the Chilean drama throughout the Allende time. Of medium height and a bit jowly, he was crisp, self-confident, and straightforward. The Germans had furnished inspiration to the Chilean Army before World War I, and the Chileans still goose-stepped and affected the great military capes of the Prussians. Prats wore his cape comfortably enough, though he did not look the part of a Junker.

Prats's intelligence and sophistication were reflected in his diary, published in Mexico City after his death, under the title *A Life for Legality*. The title is apt, because Prats really did give his life for Chilean constitutionality. Some have questioned the authenticity of the book, but it has the ring of truth, even if a few entries may have been excised. Prats's political insight seems utterly genuine in these writings.[1]

Prats was the leader for the moment. By 31 October, as already noted, rumor was already annointing high military officers in cabinet office. Prats had been discreetly active for some days trying to mediate the national crisis. On 19 October he had talked about the truckers' strike with leaders of the Christian Democratic party, and a day or two later he had let it be known that he favored accommodation (including some substantive concessions to the strikers). For about a week Prats had also been negotiating with Allende—at Allende's initiative—about military participation in the government. Finally, on 2 November 1972, Allende announced his new cabinet, with Prats named minister of interior, the highest ranking cabinet officer and the constitutional vice president. In addition to Prats, Brig. Gen. Claudio Sepúlveda Donoso of the Chilean Air Force was named minister of mines, and Rear Adm. Ismael Huerta Díaz was named minister of public works and transportation.[2]

Prats vowed publicly that he would restore normality in the country by 6 November. His tactic was to offer substantive conciliation to the strike leaders in private talks, while publicly threatening drastic action if the strikes did not end. On 5 November the strike leaders called on their supporters to go back to work. For the government, Prats promised that trucking would not be nationalized, that legislation would be introduced to protect small businessmen and artisans, that all legal action against the strikers would be dropped and reprisals against either strikers or strike-breakers barred, that requisitioned trucks and other property, including the wholesale distributing company CENADI, would be returned, and that committees would be formed to consider trucking rates, the supply of spare parts, and the strikers' other complaints.[3]

Altamirano and some other left-wing leaders opposed Prats's agreement, but Allende backed the general. The curfew was lifted, and the twenty-one provinces being administered by the military under the state of emergency were returned to civilian rule. Strike leaders publicly asserted their confidence that the military men in the cabinet would assure that Prats's pledges would be upheld.[4]

While the agreement looked like a considerable victory for the strikers, it was not entirely one-sided. The strikers' overtly political demands were rejected. Although the government complied for a time with most of its pledges, nothing much came of the legislation to protect small businessmen, nor of the committees to consider grievances. Nevertheless, truckers kept their trucks and trucking was not nationalized. Even more significantly, normality really did return to the country, more or less, and the political parties turned their attention to the forthcoming elections. The political atmosphere was transformed.

The participation of military officers in the government had several practical effects. Even before Prats and his colleagues entered the cabinet, Allende had been so concerned about the strike crisis and the need for military support that he had promulgated an arms control law virtually as presented by the Congress. It was said that Prats had been centrally involved in pushing the measure through.[5] Heavier arms, such as submachine guns, large-caliber, high-penetration automatic weapons, grenades, and teargas launchers and bombs were to be reserved to the armed forces, carabineros, investigative police, and prison guards. The law also gave the courts, other authorities, and the armed forces themselves the right to authorize military searches and inspections for proscribed arms. Moreover, it gave the armed forces the authority to license smaller weapons by permit and to try violators of the law in military courts. Lastly, it outlawed private militias and unofficial armed groups. Strictly applied, it would have curbed even the president's own force of approximately 200 personal bodyguards, the GAP.[6] The military authorities would make increasing use of the authority to carry out arms searches.

Brigadier General Palacios, minister of mining between April and June 6 1972, had left the cabinet at military insistence. One of the generals' reasons had been the demands placed upon Palacios as a minister to cosign decrees of insistence. These decrees, which had to be signed by all members of the cabinet, were an expedient the government used to circumvent legal objections to the requisitioning of businesses. When the military entered the cabinet in

November, they made it clear that they would not sign decrees of insistence, and they did not do so. They put a brake on expropriations.[7]

Controversy over the great pulp and paper company, the Papelera, had remained unresolved. Notwithstanding the impassioned loyalty of Papelera stockholders, the government's squeeze on the company was severely affecting it by October 1972. That month the Inter-American Press Association held its annual convention in Santiago, and the associations' Committee on Freedom of the Press reported on the Papelera's predicament:

> Allende's Government concentrated its offensive on . . . rejecting the readjustment of prices on those products that the [Papelera] Company delivers to consumers. . . . The local increase in the value of the US dollar for its imports, plus increases in many other cost production factors, represent today nearly a 100% increase in the cost of final products. Wages and salaries have been constantly readjusted. . . . After long . . . delay . . . the government had decided to increase the price of newsprint by [only] 19.6%. . . . Faced with this deliberate economic warfare, the [Papelera] Company has made a public announcement that it will be forced into bankruptcy within 60 days.[8]

Military representatives, once they had entered the government, insisted that the Papelera be authorized to raise prices sufficiently to relieve the company of its current operating deficits. As a result, the Papelera was allowed in December 1972 to raise its prices by 45 percent—and by 300 percent or more in some lines.[9]

The Statute of Democratic Guarantees, it will be recalled, protected the traditional, "nondeliberative" role of the armed forces. As Prats put it in October 1971, "the tradition of command which has guided my endeavors has been . . . apolitical and law-upholding professionalism . . . which makes the army an exclusive and indispensable instrument of force, which does not deliberate." Prats had then expressed concern at "constant attempts of extremists to involve the institution or its members in political affairs."[10] Obviously, by November 1972 Prats's apolitical and nondeliberative stance was shifting. Moreover, it was Allende himself who drew military officers into cabinet responsibility. The military joined the government hesitantly, after Allende had pressed them.

This vitiation of the military commitment to noninvolvement in politics ultimately weakened the barriers to a coup.[11]

The fault was not entirely Allende's. From the start, and in spite of the constitutional prohibition of military "deliberation," generals and admirals regularly convened to discuss the unfolding political and economic situation. They also met frequently with the president to talk about these subjects, both at his initiative and at theirs. It is said that Allende had such discussions with the military on an average of once every two weeks during his early months in office. In May 1972 the generals warned the president in pointed and specific terms that inflation and production declines were dangerous for the country, a position they justified taking because they were responsible for the defense of Chile against possible attack. Economic chaos would jeopardize Chile's ability to survive.[12]

In July 1972 the Council of Army Generals asked Prats to convey its view to the president that copper production should be put into military hands, that an effort should be made to work out the compensation problem with the United States, that U.S. and Western economic help should be sought, and that agrarian, banking, and other policies should be modified.[13] These proposals amounted to a self-insertion into policy making, and Allende understandably resisted them.

The knife cut closer to the bone for everybody in Chile. With wives standing in endless lines and children hurling rocks in the streets, the Chilean military worried, talked, and deliberated. Notwithstanding these observations, however, it remains true that Salvador Allende pulled an essentially reluctant military into progressively more intimate political collaboration. The tensions created in this process undermined the generals' and admirals' constitutionalist resolve.

### Chonchol Abandons Ship

The entry of military officers into the government in November 1972 had an additional direct consequence. Izquierda Cristiana's Jacques Chonchol, the minister of agriculture, so deeply opposed the move that he resigned.

In his two-year incumbency Chonchol had shaped Allende's agricultural policies and profoundly changed earlier patterns of land tenure and agricultural production. Unlike the situation in some parts of Latin America, where farming was conducted in small, intensely cultivated plots, in Chile almost feudal agricultural barons had established large estates. In 1965, shortly after Frei had taken office, three-quarters of the cultivated land in the country was in the hands of 1.3 percent of the farmers. The Alessandri administration had already passed a modest agricultural reform, but Frei managed to push a more ambitious law through Congress in 1967. It provided for expropriation in the case of farms with more than 80 "basic" productive hectares, some 200 acres.[14]

Frei's land reform was administered by left-wingers in the Christian Democratic party, one of whom was Chonchol. Until late 1968 Chonchol had headed one of the two principal organizations involved in the transformation of the countryside.[15] Nevertheless, the reform had been administered judiciously. With U.S. financial aid, the government had ensured systematic training of farmers who would receive land and substantial investment in machinery, livestock, buildings, and organizational support. As a result, agricultural production did not suffer great transitional disturbance.[16]

If one important advantage of the Frei reform was rational execution, its disadvantages were several. First, the social transformation of the countryside was slow. Only about fourteen hundred large farms were expropriated during Frei's presidency, while two-and-a-half times that number were expropriated in Allende's first two years. By the end of 1972, it was estimated, nearly three-quarters of Chilean cultivated land had been brought within the "reformed area."[17] Another disadvantage of the Frei reform was its cost, and a third was the reform's failure to benefit agricultural day laborers and tenant farmers on unexpropriated lands. Indeed, some small farmers who received land in the Frei era had the look of the Russian kulaks—rich peasants who hired and exploited their neighbors.[18]

Chonchol had studied the Russian experience and had served as a UN-employed adviser in Castro's Cuba. Unlike the Bolsheviks, who had consolidated their power for a decade before attempting their bloody collectivization drive, Chonchol was a man in a hurry. With the Chilean Congress in opposition hands, however, he had to make do with Frei's law and reform. His people resorted to the same expedients Vuskovic was using in industry. Loopholes were exploited; administrative discretion was used to stretch the law; and collusion with the MIR grew, as the MIRistas seized more and more farms through direct action.[19] Alongside the Frei reform's cooperative farms, Chonchol started "centers of agrarian reform," in which day laborers, tenant farmers, and the wives and children of beneficiaries had membership.[20] Instead of buying machinery for each farm, Chonchol set up machinery stations, patterned on the machine tractor stations of the USSR. Thereby he tried to stretch available resources as the expropriation drive hurtled forward.[21]

Chonchol's "centers of agrarian reform" were regarded as transitional. Chonchol ultimately envisaged collectivizing agriculture by establishing Chilean counterparts of Soviet collective and state farms. "Assigned cooperatives" would fill the role of the former, and "centers of production" would be like the Soviets' "factories in the countryside." Nobody would own land. A few immense, cattle-grazing "centers of production" were established in Tierra del Fuego, and agricultural officials had plans in 1973—which even UP peasant organizations resisted—to convert large vineyards into state farms. The "assigned cooperatives," or collective farms, were also highly unpopular, and only a few were successfully established. UP reform officials fell back on the transitional "centers of agrarian reform," informally converting these into rudimentary collective farms by not awarding promised titles to land. These centers soon became just as unpopular as the "more advanced" types of farms, and the UP authorities were able to set up only about fifty of them. In practice, reform officials usually bowed to the farmers' pressure and established Frei-type cooperative farms despite the government's ideological distaste.[22]   Chonchol was open about his intentions; ideology vanquished guile. One must respect Chonchol's straightforwardness, but his program resulted in almost immediate declines in agricultural production. Farmers and landowners who had not yet suffered expropriation slaughtered their animals, invested nothing, milked their farms of liquid assets, and awaited the worst. Many newly benefited farmers thrashed about in disorganization, and work discipline was poor. A report of the Socialist party, which leaked to the press in 1972, admitted that almost half of the land expropriated since 1970 was not under cultivation.[23]

In fairness to Chonchol, he understood what would happen. During the early months of Unidad Popular Chonchol wrote that it is a mistake, when people are trying to "bring about basic changes," to expect "social improvement and economic growth at the same time."[24] Like Vuskovic and Altamirano, Chonchol was prepared to pay the price in loss of production. Luis Corvalán, Orlando Millas, and other communist economists were, as with Vuskovic's industrial policies, less enthusiastic.

Chonchol and his colleagues suffered from an additional difficulty: the Christian Democrats had stolen the march in organizing the farmworkers. Even before Frei's election, Catholic leaders in rural Chile had been active in social development initiatives. When I was in Chile with the Peace Corps in 1962, our U.S. volunteers were already working with the Catholic-supported Institute of Rural Education (IER), which sought out very poor boys and girls in the countryside, taught them productive skills, educated them in basic school subjects, and gave them leadership training. Alumni of these IER programs had an important role in organizing Christian federations in the countryside when the Frei administration succeeded in legalizing agricultural trade unions in 1967.[25] During the Allende time the rural trade union movement was split into six significant organizations; two favored the government and four the Christian Democrats.[26] UP militants tried to best the CD forces in various ways, including witholding the check-off dues which the 1967 law had mandated, but they had limited success.

My wife and I inevitably had a fair amount of contact with the wealthier landowners. Santiago matrons would tell my wife how their husbands and sons went to their country places to keep vigil, often alone, watching for the MIRista-led gangs to come in the night and seize their estates. Landowners were prepared to fight for their holdings, and some of them organized vigilante groups.[27]

The Chilean countryside became the scene of mounting violence as the MIR-led farm occupations spread. It did not become another rural Vietnam, however, or even another Colombia of the days of "La Violencia." People were killed, but such deaths in the Allende period were counted in scores, not in thousands.[28] The opposition press denounced and dramatized killing on an individual scale. Single acts still brought political responses, reflecting the fact that the social fabric was still largely intact.

The 1971 harvest, gathered during the first months of the year, was mostly unaffected by Chonchol's program and was good. The 1972 harvest was variously reported as being 4 to 12 percent below 1971's; 7 percent might be a reasonable figure. The October 1972 strikes, however, affected Chilean spring planting and the winter wheat, and the 1973 harvest was estimated at 16 to 25 percent below 1971's. As many private landowners slaughtered their herds and did not replace them, beef production suffered badly, with some 1972 estimates running at less than half of normal. Wheat production was also reported as down by almost a half between 1971 and 1972—from a 1971 harvest of 1.36 million metric tons down to approximately 700,000 metric tons. The 1973 harvest was worse still, estimated to have been only about 550,000 metric tons.[29]

Diversions to the black market aggravated the situation, and the government's own policies actually stimulated black-market sales. The government aimed to become sole buyer of agricultural products, but it also imposed price controls and for many months tried to check inflation by maintaining artificially low prices for food. Consequently, farmers who offered their products through legal channels were paid only a fraction of the price they could get through black-market sales.[30] Even state-run enterprises found that their workers diverted production into the black market, pocketing the proceeds.[31]

The black market came to dominate food distribution. To buy a chicken legally, one would have to wait hours in line and then receive only one bird, regardless of the number of mouths to feed. In contrast, women of the affluent suburbs, government employees with access to a car, and countless others would drive into the countryside for black-market shopping, for their own needs or for resale.

Supply and demand were still further skewed by increases in purchasing power. The poor had more money and were eating better, and food consumption except for meat actually rose by as much as 25 percent during Allende's first two years in power.[32] To bridge the widening gap between declining production and rising demand, the UP government sharply increased imports and paid a skyrocketing foreign-exchange bill to do so. Food imports rose from $168 million in 1970, to $260 million in 1971, to $383 million in 1972, to $619 million in 1973—almost four times the 1970 bill. The 1973 bill matched the total earnings of Chile's recently nationalized copper mines during that year, and it represented well over half of Chile's foreign-exchange income. Things got to the point where Chile's port facilities and internal transportation could hardly move the food which was being imported.[33]

Clearly, the 1973 coup was not incubated in the countryside, and rural violence did not trigger it. Urban food shortages and marketing dislocations were crucially important, however, and the political fallout was ultimately devastating. Starting with the march of the empty pots in December 1971, food and supply problems intruded on the country's economic and political life through countless encounters and confrontations. Shortfalls in agricultural production brought more black marketing and inflation. The foreign-exchange problem created by the staggering volume of food imports foreclosed alternative economic initiatives which might have improved the government's prospects. Although agricultural policy was not the sole cause of Chile's economic crisis, it was a central element in it. The economic crisis, in turn, was not the only cause of the coup, but it was a prime factor.

### Allende Travels to New York

On 30 November 1972, three-and-a-half weeks after the truckers had gone back to work, Allende left Chile for a two-week intercontinental tour. The president's decision to take the trip demonstrated his confidence in Prats's loyalty, and Prats minded the store efficiently until Allende's return.

Allende's first stop was the Lima airport, where he met briefly with President Velasco of Peru. He then flew north to Mexico City, where President Echeverría and a tumultuous crowd of his countrymen greeted Allende enthusiastically. Allende addressed the Mexican Congress on 1 December, accusing ITT of having brought Chile to the brink of civil war.[34]

The Chilean president then traveled north. In the land of Goliath the welcome was considerably cooler. Ambassador Letelier had been in Santiago shortly before Allende's trip and had suggested to me that Allende would welcome an invitation to Washington— implying a meeting with President Nixon—or a courtesy call on him in New York by Secretary Rogers or Henry Kissinger. Letelier believed matters were at a turning point—he had pressed so hard, in fact, that I had visions of Castro's 1959 visit to Washington and its subsequent political legacy of lost opportunity. I expressed these concerns to Washington. Knowing, however, that a Nixon-Allende meeting had no chance of acceptance, I urged that Secretary Rogers call on Allende in New York.[35]

Reports of my cables to Washington seemed by then to be acquiring a propensity to appear in Jack Anderson's column, and sure enough, I soon read his version of the Chilean initiative:

> President Nixon studiously snubbed Chile's embattled President. . . . The President based his action on the secret reports of U.S. Ambassador Nathaniel Davis, who cabled from Santiago that Allende wanted an audience with Mr. Nixon. . . . As Allende headed for the United States, he radioed a friendly greeting to President Nixon. But the President, not wishing to help the Marxist leader stay in power, pointedly ignored the hint. Allende received no invitation to visit the White House but had to settle for an audience with Nixon's United Nations ambassador, George Bush.[36]

President Allende gave one of the more memorable speeches ever heard in the great hall of the UN General Assembly.[37] He accused ITT of trying to prevent his own accession to office—which was true. He accused ITT and Kennecott of having "buried their fangs" in his country. He went on:

> The power of [all these multinational] corporations is so great that it transcends all borders. . . . We are facing a . . . collision between the great . . . corporations and sovereign states. . . . [But the corporations] do not have to answer to anyone and are not accountable to . . . any parliament. . . .

Allende dramatized the developing nations' sense of having been victimized, and his story inspired investigation of the issue throughout the world. He charged aggression:

> We are the victims of a new form of imperialism, one that is more subtle, more cunning, and for that reason, more terrifyingly effective [than in the past]. . . . External pressure . . . has tried to cut us off from the world, to strangle our economy. . . . The financial-economic blockade against us . . . is oblique, subterranean, and indirect. . . . We find ourselves facing forces operating in the twilight, without a flag, with powerful weapons. . . . We are the victims of almost imperceptible ac-

tions, generally disguised in phrases and declarations that extol respect for the sovereignty and dignity of our country.

It was almost as if Allende had read NSDM 93, the secret policy paper of November 1970 that had advocated covert measures against the Allende government under a "correct outward posture." The recognizable kernel of truth in what Allende said gave his speech its importance.

However, the whole truth was, as usual, more complicated. Allende listed "equipment, spare parts . . . food and medicine" as casualties of the insidious blockade. Except for Kennecott's "copper boycott," however, there were no embargoes. The real question, as Allende acknowledged, was credit. He talked of efforts to deprive Chile of access to international financing. He explained that his predecessors had undertaken development projects on the understanding that credit would be continuing. He conceded that "the United States, in its exercise of sovereignty, may grant or withhold loans with respect to any country it chooses"; but he denounced the use of international organizations to further the "policies of individual member states . . . no matter how powerful," and said that such use was "legally and morally unacceptable."

Allende said that Chile, potentially rich, lives in poverty. "We go from place to place seeking credits and aid; and yet—a true paradox of the capitalist economic system—we are major exporters of capital." He explained that the great corporations had repatriated their investment many times over, while developing countries pay out more every year than they receive. Latin America, he said, had contributed a net of $9 billion to "the rich world" in the decade just past.

President Allende asserted as a principle of international law that "a country's natural resources—particularly when they are its very lifeblood—belong to it." He cited UN Resolution 1803, saying that nationalization is an expression of sovereignty and the settlement of disputes falls within the jurisdiction of domestic courts.

It was a powerful speech, and it struck a chord of response which reverberates to this day. It was an expression of deeply felt Third World values. To the developed world, however, matters were less clear. Has the international law which has served capitalism for so long been decisively repudiated? Did the government in Chile have a right to new loans?[38] In the decision making of international bankers, what was the balance between official U.S. malevolence and Chile's credit rating?

U.S. private banks described their policies in subsequent testimony to congressional investigators. The Bank of America maintained short-term credit at about its 1970 level until Chile declared its moratorium on debt servicing at the end of 1971. After suspending credits at that time, a few cautious lines of credit were later reopened. Chase Manhattan gradually reduced its lines of credit thoughout 1971, from slightly over $30 million to about $5 million; Manufacturers Hanover followed a similar course. American banks, taken together, apparently reduced their lines of credit from over $200 million in 1970 to about $30 million in 1972, evidently responding to their own estimation of risk. An additional factor in some bank decisions was the nationalization of their branches in Chile, with which they terminated the lines of credit they had customarily made available to their Chilean affiliates. The last U.S. bank with a branch in Chile, First National City Bank, reluctantly withdrew its representation at the end of 1971.[39] These considerations are not to deny that private bankers maintained informal contact with U.S. officials in Washington, particularly representatives of the Treasury Department. They no doubt did, and they surely became aware of the Nixon administration's sentiments about the Allende government.

The Export-Import Bank's downgrading of Chile's credit rating at the beginning of 1971 and its ambiguous and no doubt politically motivated handling of the LAN-Chile loan have already been described. After Chile's moratorium Ex-Im followed what it stated were long-standing policies with respect to defaulting creditors and indefinitely deferred all new loans and guarantees to Chile. Disbursements under existing loans continued until June 1972, with approximately $1.6 million obligated.[40]

AID had sharply reduced assistance to Chile even before Allende came to power, largely as the result of high copper prices and Chile's decreased need for outside help. There is no question, however, that U.S. assistance was cut back for political reasons after Allende's election. NSDM 93 was implemented, and new projects were not undertaken. Joel Biller, the U.S. AID director, recalls flying to Washington from Santiago in May 1971. He was shown the relevant portions of NSDM 93 and was instructed to curtail bilateral economic assistance as much as was possible without giving the Chilean government an issue it could exploit. As a result, an education loan that was ready for signature was left unsigned, and disbursements under a construction loan for the improvement of the port of San Vicente were delayed. This was prior to Chile's default on AID loan payments, of course, and I remember that we were still stringing the Chileans along in connection with the San Vicente project when I arrived in October.

Nevertheless, AID did continue to provide dried milk and milk substitutes, as already described, at a cost to the U.S. government of about $15 million. Technical assistance grants at a level of about $1 million a year were maintained—although the recipients were nongovernmental cooperatives, independent farmers, private social welfare groups, and other organizations that adhered to values the United States supported. Five-and-a-half million dollars in disbursements on existing AID loans were made in 1971 and 1972, although the Allende government had repaid more than this amount in debt servicing for AID loans before the November 1971 moratorium.[41]

In late 1972 the Commodity Credit Corporation extended a $4 million supplier line of credit to Chile to buy U.S. surplus agricultural products. The move was an unvarnished mistake. The Department of Agriculture, or that corner of it, had not gotten the word that such credits were against U.S. policy. In the State Department the officials concerned had to explain to the White House and Treasury why the loan had not been prevented, and they were instructed to make sure such things did not happen again. After the coup some U.S. government spokesmen tried to take credit for U.S. benevolence, but U.S. generosity at the policy-making level was not the cause of the action.[42]

The Chilean government was receiving a steady stream of credit from other Western countries, not only from Latin American nations but also from Western Europe, Canada, and Australia. By the end of 1972 these loans totaled over $500 million.[43] Argentina and Brazil extended $400 million in new credits to Chile during Allende's last months in office, with the principal motivation in both cases having been to promote the sale of those countries' products. Western European credit lines were also extended mostly to facilitate exports. Political attitudes in Europe ranged from sympathy for the UP government to skepticism and considerable detachment. Later, as the Chileans progressively nationalized European-owned

companies, the governments whose citizens' interests were affected became less friendly to Chile.[44]

The Inter-American Development Bank approved two university
loans, totaling $12 million, in January 1971. Between December
1970 and December 1972, $54 million from previously approved
loans were disbursed while Chile's repayments on debt to the IDB
totaled about $10 million less. A total of slightly more than $70
million was disbursed from previously approved loans during Allende's three years. No new loans were approved after January
1971, and it would be fair to say that the U.S. government induced
the IDB management to pigeonhole Chilean loan proposals, at least
in 1971 and 1972. In mid-1973 pressures were mounting for the
IDB to approve something for Chile, largely because Santiago was
scheduled to host the IDB's annual meeting in 1974. It was an old
tradition to sweeten the pot for the country hosting the annual
meeting, and IDB officials were clearly becoming embarrassed at
the prospect of going to Santiago empty-handed.[45]

The International Bank for Reconstruction and Development—
the World Bank—approved no new loans to Chile during the Allende time. It processed an application for a fruit and vineyard loan
in 1971 but advised Chile in late September of that year that it had
questions about Chile's credit-worthiness. The World Bank had a
long-standing policy requiring "reasonable progress" toward the
settlement of nationalization disputes. At the 1972 annual meeting
bank president Robert S. McNamara defended the bank's overall
record of approving loans despite nationalization disputes but asserted that Chile was too much of a credit risk to receive more
loans. The bank did pay Chile about $46 million in drawdowns on
previously approved loans between mid-1970 and mid-1973.[46] The
International Monetary Fund, consonant with its past policies, extended two loans of about $40 million each in December 1971 and
December 1972, to help Chile overcome the effects of falling copper
prices.[47]

Clearly, the reactions of the international banking institutions
were unhelpful to the Allende government. Still, Chile received
more in disbursements from public international sources during
the UP government than in any other comparable period in Chilean
history.

Chile had a foreign debt of about $2.5 billion when President

Allende took office, and positive exchange-reserve balances of over $350 million. The country's foreign debt had grown by $1 billion by September 1973—almost the highest per capita debt of any country in the world—and an exchange reserve *deficit* of about $400 million. These figures represent an increase in indebtedness of almost $2 billion. Allende had almost $600 million in short-term credits available to him on 30 August 1973, which was almost twice the figure available to him in 1970. Alberto Baltra calculated after the 1973 coup that the Allende government had received over $800 million in foreign short-term credits, three-quarters of which came from noncommunist countries. In fact, the Allende government received more economic help and promises of help than any previous Chilean government in any three-year period. Of course, most of these credits were tied to the lending country's export sales, but in many cases this condition—a long-established practice—was not onerous, as the Chileans would have spent hard currency for Argentinian beef, for butter from New Zealand, for wheat, and for other foodstuffs and vital equipment and machinery. Other loans were less fungible. Romanian tractors could not substitute for American copper-mining machinery, and the UP government's credits did not eliminate its pressing need for cash.[48]

If Richard Nixon and Henry Kissinger really wanted to run the Chilean economy into the ground by means of a credit squeeze, they were not very efficient at it. Part of the reason may have been the U.S. desire to maintain a "correct outward posture" and not to be caught in the appearance of economic warfare. The result was ambivalence, even within the U.S. government, and a certain conspiratorial quality in actions taken at the White House.

Salvador Allende won the argument over "economic strangulation" in the forum of world opinion. The counterarguments, valid or not, have never quite caught up with his eloquent indictment.

## Allende's Chile and the Communist World

The second grand destination of Allende's intercontinental tour was Moscow. On his way from New York he stopped for part of a day and night in Algiers, where he conferred with President Boumedienne and declared his support for the Palestine Liberation Organization. He flew on to Moscow, where what he wanted was economic help. He was reported to be seeking half-a-billion dollars in hard currency. Our best indications in Santiago were that he went to Moscow with doubts about the Soviets' response.[49]

The Soviet leaders extended all honors to Allende. The big three, Brezhnev, Podgorny, and Kosygin, met him at the airport. He was lavishly entertained, and his three-day visit, mainly around Moscow and in Kiev, was extensively reported in the Soviet press. It appeared, however, that the Soviets were reluctant to add a major commitment to Chile onto their already burdensome one to Cuba, and they did not furnish Allende with the half-billion dollars he wanted. It was reliably reported that the Soviets advised Allende shortly after his visit that he might do well to seek a degree of accommodation with the United States, perhaps even showing some flexibility on copper compensation. The advice was not realistic, however, as the U.S. government was manifestly unwilling to bail out Allende.[50]

The Soviets did give Chile $30 to $50 million in short-to-medium term credits and $180 million in longer-term credit lines for the purchase of industrial equipment and capital goods. They also agreed to renegotiate payment of Chile's $103 million bilateral debt.[51] These new Soviet commitments were in addition to a $50 million balance-of-payments loan extended in early 1972, a $27 million supplier credit, and roughly $240 million in long-term loans for the purchase of Soviet machinery, tractors, equipment, and new plants. These earlier loans had brought total Soviet credits to $300 to $400 million in June 1972. The December commitments increased the total to the neighborhood of $500 to $600 million.[52]

The word got back to Santiago even before President Allende did that he had not received big money. On 11 December 1972 Jorge Godoy, president of the CUT, was explaining to pro-UP radio listeners that Allende's visit in Moscow would have positive results, "despite the fact that the Socialist countries have a system which keeps them from giving technical and economic aid without previous planning." The opposition press soon reported that Allende's appeal to Moscow had "failed."[53]

On his way back from Moscow, Allende stopped briefly in Morocco. From there he flew to Havana for a visit of two or three days, returning Castro's 1971 visit to Chile. As a goodwill gesture, Castro shipped Chile some free sugar.[54] After a brief additional stopover in Caracas, Allende returned to Santiago on 14 December 1972.

During Allende's first year in office the Soviets were already making clear in private statements that they did not want Chile to become another Cuba. Nevertheless, Politburo member Andrei P. Kirilenko visited Chile about one year after Allende took power, and a Soviet state planning team paid a follow-up visit in January 1972. A substantial infusion of credits and assistance followed these visits, as the timing of the $50 million balance-of-payment loan indicates. Even so, in February 1972 Allende was still saying that Chile had to be careful of its relations with the United States because it "could not depend on the Communist countries" for all of its needs.[55] In June 1972 Soviet ambassador Aleksandr Basov finally returned my initial protocol call, after a delay of approximately six months. What Basov wanted to talk about was U.S. conditions for an economic settlement with Chile. His inquiry foreshadowed the Soviets' advice after the Moscow trip to make an accommodation with the United States.

The Soviets' interest in an easing of the U.S.-Chilean economic relationship continued right up to the time of the coup. A CIA officer testified after the coup on the Soviet attitude in August 1973: "We did have some quite reliable reporting . . . indicating that the Russians were advising Allende to put his relations with the United States in order, if not to settle compensation, at least to reach some sort of accommodation which would ease the strain between the two countries. There were reports indicating that . . . they were in effect trying to move Allende toward a compromise agreement. . . ."[56]

The smaller Warsaw Pact countries made additional loans to Chile. In early 1972 the loans totaled about $150 million, practically all long-term investment financing. By the end of 1972 the overall figure for smaller East bloc countries had climbed to roughly $250 million, about half the Soviet figure.[57]

Economic assistance was not the only thing Allende talked about in Moscow. Military aid was also discussed. Apparently the Soviets offered $50 million in fifty-year credits at 1 percent interest for military equipment.[58] After he returned to Chile, Allende repeatedly pressed his commanders-in-chief to take advantage of the Soviets' offer.[59] The Russians even increased their enticements—

hardly surprising, as the Soviet Union almost always finds it easier to sell arms on easy credit terms than to extend regular economic assistance or provide hard currency. As Soviet top-of-the-line weapons become obsolete, the Soviets move these items into their foreign military sales.[60]

The discomfited Chilean military chiefs dragged their feet for months, but Allende finally prevailed on Prats to travel to the USSR in May 1973. Prats came to see me about the matter and expressed his reluctance to become deeply involved with the Soviets. I believe his reluctance was genuine. Moreover, he was most anxious to "balance" his Soviet visit with one to Washington, which was quickly arranged.[61]

On 6 May 1973 Prats said publicly from Washington that he was not ruling out buying arms from the USSR, as Chile did not want to depend on only "one line of supply." Prats then flew to London and on to Moscow, where he was received by Kosygin and Defense Minister Grechko. Prats was given a glittering tour, and on 18 May the Chilean Army commander-in-chief signed a military cooperation agreement. Prats reportedly later described the agreement, more modest than the Soviets would have welcomed, as providing "logistical equipment, but not tanks, as the latter would require further study."[62] Nevertheless, the agreement began a definite shift toward Soviet arms supply. Had other events not intervened in Chile, that shift would surely have gone further.[63]

Events in Chile did intervene, however, and the first was the refusal of the comptroller general to register Prats's 18 May agreement, due to technical and legal objections. At the end of July 1973 the Chilean decree was still unregistered, and Prats was forced to tell the Soviet ambassador that it would be "difficult" to begin practical implementation of Chilean-Soviet military cooperation plans. Behind the technicalities there was a game of political poker going on, with Allende, the comptroller general, Prats, and Prats's anti-Soviet opponents in the Chilean high command playing for high stakes.[64]

Chile and the People's Republic of China had established relations in January of 1971—although the Chinese ambassador who came to Santiago did not speak Spanish and wandered around diplomatic receptions in the company of a colleague who acted, with modest competence, as his Spanish-Chinese interpreter. Chile's foreign minister, Clodomiro Almeyda, the Maoist in the top

UP leadership, was sent off on a visit to the People's Republic of China in January 1973. Like Allende, Almeyda was soliciting economic help.[65] The Chinese did what they could. They gave the Chileans a $65 to $80 million loan for developing small and medium-sized industry, under easy terms, in January 1972. An additional $55 to $65 million interest-free loan followed in June 1972, and they extended a supplier credit of $62 million for food, medicines, machinery, and equipment at the turn of the 1972–73 year.[66] Shipments of Chinese pork, the notorious *chancho chino*, also began arriving in Chile. The word spread like wildfire through the affluent suburbs of Santiago that the pork was carrying trichinosis, though for all I know it was perfectly safe.

To sum up, the communist world's assistance to Allende was relatively modest if measured against Chile's predicament. Not only were the Soviets worried about another drain like the Cuban one, but they resented "socialism with red wine and meat pies," lazy workers, interparty UP squabbling, disregard of their own and the Chilean Communist party's advice, and Allende's pointed dissociation of the Chilean Way from the blood, sacrifice, and "social cost" of their own history. Should the Russians ante up a hard-gained half-billion dollars for this? These undisguised sentiments did not mean, however, that the Soviet leaders were indifferent to Allende's fate. They were rocked and disoriented by his overthrow. The cautious Soviet reaction to Allende's appeal for help in 1972 was probably a miscalculation. I do not believe that the Soviets made a considered decision to cut their losses and let the UP government perish. More probably, they tried to save money and muddle through, and they failed as a result to take measures that might have produced a different outcome.

## Military Participation Was Not a Panacea

While military participation in Allende's cabinet was a moderating influence, it did not solve the country's problems. Neither did it successfully control the activists in Unidad Popular or prevent them from taking initiatives which churned the waters. Two such moves caused particular trouble: the introduction of "rationing" and the educational reform. Both initiatives came from minor-party representatives in the cabinet, and it is probable that neither was carefully coordinated as UP policy before being launched.

Fernando Flores of the Movement for Unified Popular Action

(MAPU) had been named minister of economy when the military entered the cabinet in November 1972. On 11 January 1973 he was due to change places with Orlando Millas, the communist minister of finance, because the Congress was about to dismiss Millas after impeachment proceedings. On the day before the switch, 10 January, Flores announced a government monopoly in the distribution and marketing of thirty basic food items then in short supply. A National Secretariat of Distribution would be set up within the Ministry of Economy, and it was soon announced that the secretariat would be headed by Brig. Gen. Alberto Bachelet Martínez, a progressive air force officer sympathetic to the UP government. The secretariat would funnel basic necessities through the already existing Councils of Supply and Prices (JAPS), and supplies would be distributed according to "family quotas." Ration cards were never issued, and the government stoutly maintained that the new system was not rationing, but this explanation was not generally believed.[67]

The government's trouble was aggravated by the JAPs' already bad reputation. A unit of the Ministry of Economy's Directorate of Industry and Commerce had organized JAPs in order to ensure "adequate supplies and the enforcement of price controls and fighting against speculation and monopoly." The opposition believed these JAPs were patterned on the Councils of Supply in Cuba, which Castro had used to impose political controls, mobilize support at the neighborhood level, and freeze out the opposition.[68]

Rear Admiral Huerta resigned as minister of public works and transportation when Flores made his 10 January speech on food distribution. He was soon forced into retirement from the navy. Although another rear admiral, Daniel Arellano, assumed Huerta's ministerial responsibility, most naval officers sympathized with Huerta and reacted with smouldering anger.[69]

In actuality, the distribution of food through the JAPs never worked well enough to enable Unidad Popular to consolidate its control at the neighborhood level. The JAPs' monopoly was undermined by the black market, opposition-controlled distribution channels, and uncontrolled commercial supply, which continued to provide a large proportion of the food available, even in the poorer neighborhoods. In any case, the "rationing" controversy deepened suspicions and further enraged the opposition and the military.[70]

The second unsettling minor-party initiative, educational reform, was launched by Jorge Tapia, a member of the anticlerical Radical party, who had been named minister of education in the November 1972 cabinet shakeup. On 30 January 1973 Tapia announced a plan to create a unified national school (ENU). A proclaimed objective of the plan was to inculcate "values of socialist humanism" in achieving a "harmonious development of young people's personalities." Tapia went on to stipulate that private schools, including parochial schools, would be "obliged to adopt the content and curriculum of the ENU" and proposed that all secondary-school students should work in nationalized, state-owned enterprises as part of their regular program of instruction. The plan was to be implemented on an experimental basis with ninth-grade students on 1 June 1973.[71]

The Catholic church and the Christian Democrats reacted instantly. This was just the kind of program the Statute of Democratic Guarantees had been constitutionally adopted to prevent. The ENU stirred up the darkest fears of Christian Chileans about the upbringing and teaching of their children. For the first time the Catholic heirarchy in Chile spoke out in thundering public opposition to government policy.[72] A large segment of the military was also outraged. Rear Admiral Huerta, just retired, led about one-hundred-fifty officers in a confrontational meeting with Tapia. At one point in the stormy session Tapia reportedly admitted that the school system of East Germany had served as a model in drawing up his plan.[73]

On 12 April, Tapia advised Raúl Cardinal Silva Henríquez in a public letter that implementation of the ENU would be postponed—in effect, his surrender. The aftertaste did not disappear, however, nor did the protest demonstrations immediately die down.[74] Over a month later Prats commented on the episode in his diary:

> The times demand that the armed forces remain united. But, within them, a process of polarization becomes clearer every day. For the first time since the accession to power of Unidad Popular, many members of the armed services frankly and sometimes rudely express their disagreement with government policy. If this is not so, how can one interpret the strong statements of Rear Admiral Huerta concerning the Unified National School? . . .

The majority of the officers attending the meeting demonstrated their enthusiastic support of his words. Such conduct is a symptom of a growing tendency to lose respect for the constitutionally established government, and this loss of respect increases in direct proportion to the government's errors, such as the ENU proposal, in the case of which the government had to retreat, with a consequent loss of authority.[75]

A last sidelight on the difficulties Allende had while the military participated in his government comes from an incident that occurred in Valparaíso on 16 December 1972. The graduation ceremony of the Chilean naval cadet school took place on that day, with President Allende attending. Captain Davis of the U.S. Military Group and I were both scheduled to present U.S.-donated prizes. When Allende stepped forward to present a prize named for the president of the Chilean Republic, he was greeted with a chorus of derisory whistles from the families and friends of the graduating cadets. When Ray Davis and I stepped forward to discharge our responsibilities, we were greeted with wild clapping and cheers. Far from being pleased by this display, I was embarrassed, and I found it ironic that the occasion in Valparaíso was only two days after Salvador Allende had returned from the world's center stages, the great hall of the UN General Assembly and the reception rooms of the Kremlin. It must have galled him to have been treated so shabbily by his own countrymen.[76]

While military participation in the cabinet was no panacea, and while it did not halt the drift toward polarization in Chile, it did provide a respite. Passions quieted. More important, the country turned its energies and attention to the upcoming elections. Chile had a glorious democratic tradition, and its people prepared to go to the voting places on 4 March 1973.

*Chapter 6*

# The Time of the
# March Elections

THE Chileans conducted their 1973 congressional election campaign in their own inimitable fashion as January and February slipped past. I visited the extreme south of Chile, deliberately out of sight and mind. There was relatively little violence, and the voting was peacefully conducted on 4 March.

Although the opposition parties registered a clear majority of 56 percent, the outcome was a disappointment to them, as it did not change the political balance. Predictably, the anti-UP coalition failed to reach the two-thirds majority that would have made possible the impeachment and removal of Allende. Political divisions sharpened, and frustration magnified the animosity on both sides. Eduardo Frei stepped back into the center ring of Chilean politics, assuming the presidency of the Senate.

## The Congressional Election Campaign

In some ways the Chilean campaign was like political contests fought the world over. Supporters organized mass meetings, candidates addressed them and pressed the flesh, and newspapers made guesses about comparative turnout or made exaggerated claims.

Funds were solicited; debts piled higher. Trucks, buses, and cars were at a premium as they were used to transport people to swell crowds. Dedicated party workers were always needed.

Yet in significant ways the Chilean election campaign differed from the North American variety. In 1973 radio was more important in Chile than in the United States, and television less so. Jingles had an importance in the Chilean campaign that campaign songs have never had in the United States. Every candidate had his song, and in the final weeks these theme songs were played on the radio day and night. Gustavo Alessandri of the National party had a cheerful, lilting ditty that ended ". . . Gustavo Alessandri, poop-poop!" Former president Frei, running for the Senate, had a haunting melody that I thought surprisingly characteristic of the man. Other jingles were strident; still others were cloying; and a few were close to repellent. Perhaps, even in 1973, the Chileans had taken a step ahead of the United States toward subliminal campaigning. The jingles may have had trivial lyrics, but they did convey moods.

In Chile, as in much of the world, campaign posters were slapped on every wall, and at night men and teenagers, armed with glue pots, pasted their own posters over their opponents'. There was much less direct mail in Chile than there is in the United States, and fewer telephone banks.

Party labels were more important than in the United States, because Chile elected its congress by a system of modified proportional representation. It was imperative for a candidate to be strategically placed on his party's list to get elected. Chile's parties also represented fundamental political, religious, and ideological positions to an extent never seen in the United States. Moreover, two-and-a-half years of UP government had polarized Chileans' loyalties and had convinced the entire population that it was voting on the future of the nation.

As the campaign progressed, the opposition reported with indignation that the government was using official vehicles in large numbers to transport voters to rallies. Toward the end of the campaign, food supplies improved, particularly in the poorer neighborhoods. Anti-UP leaders predicted hungry mouths once the election was over. The government denied all charges. Unofficially, sources close to the government shrugged, pointing out that all governments trying to stay in power do the same things. In spite of the straitened circumstances in the nation, everybody seemed to have enough money to inundate the electorate.

There was some violence. Deputy Arturo Frei Bolívar, the former president's nephew, was shot at after a rally in Concepción. Left Radical candidate Eugenio Velasco was stabbed in Talca. Five persons were killed in political violence between 6 January and 19 February, the last of them a teenaged Christian Democrat shot in the heart as he was putting up campaign posters.[1]

On the day the sixteen-year-old was shot, Prats met with the leaders of all the parties and extracted a pledge from them to take measures to control their militants. A sixth person was killed later in the campaign, but the violence was said to be more or less "normal" for a crucial national election.[2]

Sergio Onofre Jarpa, the head of the National party, launched a campaign theme that came to dominate the opposition's electoral stance. He appealed passionately for a two-thirds majority in both houses of the Congress. Jarpa presented the constitutional majority required to impeach and convict the president, as well as to veto legislation, as the way out of Chile's stalemated political crisis. He left the impression that such a victory could be achieved.[3]

The trouble with Jarpa's theme was that such an outcome was impossible. Our calculations at the embassy showed that the opposition would have to win 67 to 70 percent of the total vote to emerge with two-thirds majorities in both houses.[4] While the opposition lacked only two seats for a two-thirds majority in the Senate, with the upper chamber divided 32 to 18, those two extra seats were beyond reach. The senators up for reelection had been chosen six months after Frei's 1964 triumph, at the height of his popularity. So far as the Chamber of Deputies was concerned, a two-thirds majority would have been even harder and would have required a gain of eight seats.

The polls tended to produce results consistent with the desires of those paying the pollsters. Some polling results seemed more believable than others, however, and they showed the opposition falling short of their goals. For example, a poll commissioned by the Christian Democrats and taken two or three weeks before the elections in the cities of Santiago, Valparaíso, and Concepción (where about half the electorate lived) showed a 60–40 split in votes.[5]

The Radicals' situation made opposition gains even more unlikely. Senator Julio Durán and his anti-leftist followers had been expelled from the Radical party in 1969, it may be remembered, and Senators Baltra, Bossay, and other non-Marxists had split off in 1971. The rank-and-file Radical loyalists had tended to remain in the historic party despite its leftward drift. As a result, the two opposition Radical parties were long on leaders and short on voters. The leaders' congressional terms ran out in 1973, and the elections were likely to bring a reckoning. Indeed, there had not been an election in a generation where as many as two-thirds of Chilean voters had cast their ballots against the left. The vision of two-thirds majorities was a chimera.

Jarpa's drive for the magic two-thirds created a psychology where anything short of that result would seem to be failure. Unidad Popular, on the other hand, downplayed the significance of the voting and predicted only that it would do better than the 36 percent received in the presidential elections of 1970.

### The March Election Results

When the polls closed on Sunday night, 4 March 1973, the country waited breathlessly as the counting progressed. The five UP parties had banded together in a "federated" UP party, and the five opposition parties had done more or less the same thing. The difference was that the opposition parties had actually formed a two-tiered "confederation," because the Christian Democrats were ever reluctant to appear too closely tied to the National party or to Julio Durán's Radicals. The opposition's united Democratic Confederation came to be known as CODE. Only Raúl Ampuero's tiny Popular Socialist Union (USOPO) ran alone, as the direct-action groups on the left and right fringes did not present lists.[6]

The election results dismayed the opposition. The CODE received 54.7 percent to the UP's 43.4 percent in the elections for the Chamber of Deputies. Eliminating blanks, nulls, and splinters, the split was 56 to 44. The UP gained six seats, to elect 63 deputies out of a total of 150. In the Senate voting, where senators were up for election in half the districts, the UP gained two seats, bringing its total up to twenty, or 40 percent of the upper chamber.[7]

Unidad Popular compared the results to the presidential elections of 1970, noting with public satisfaction that the government had increased its support seven percentage points.[8] The assertion was of questionable validity, since in 1970 Tomic and Alessandri had been running against each other in separate opposition slates, and Tomic had undoubtedly received the votes of quite a few leftists. In a three-way race, two of the parties' votes summed together will almost always exceed the vote they could draw as a coalition, when they aggregate their enemies. The combined leftist vote of the Socialists, the Communists, and the Radicals in the last congressional elections, those of 1969, had totaled 43 percent—almost exactly the same as the percentage the UP won in 1973.[9] Nevertheless, Allende pointed out that a Chilean administration in power almost never did better in midterm congressional elections than in the original presidential ones, and the UP had confounded that old rule.

Opposition leaders also picked the past election that best suited their purposes for comparison. Of course, the results would not have been nearly so bad for them had they not created such ambitious expectations. After all, they won an absolute majority. If one compares the results to the 1971 municipal elections, the results reflected a gain of about seven points.[10] CODE's highest percentages were among the German-Chileans and other hard-working farmers of the south-central valley above Puerto Montt, where the opposition parties got well over 60 percent of the vote, and in Santiago province, where Frei pulled up the ticket. CODE's greatest relative gains over 1971 were in the north, where the great Chuquicamata copper mine is situated, and in the southernmost province of Magallanes, where independent-minded sheep and cattle farmers railed against a distant, oppressive socialist bureaucracy. It is also possible that anti-UP military commanders in these places had some influence on the outcome.

So far as the individual parties were concerned—compared with 1971—the Socialists dropped from 23 to 19 percent but were nevertheless relatively satisfied. Earlier, in 1969, they had drawn only 12 percent of the vote. They remained the largest vote-getter in the UP coalition, and they doubled their representation in the Chamber of Deputies, going from 14 to 28 seats.

The Communists slipped from 17 percent in 1971 to 16 percent, about what they had received in 1969. Like the Socialists, however, they gained seats in the Chamber, picking up three. Compared to

1971, the historical Radical party lost half its strength, falling from 8 to 4 percent, and it lost seven of its twelve seats in the Chamber. The once-proud Radical party was in the process of dissolution.

In the opposition camp the Christian Democratic party—compared to 1971—rose from 26 to 29 percent, widening its lead as the country's greatest political force. The Christian Democrats gained three Chamber seats but lost one Senate seat. The National party went up from 18 percent in 1971 to 21 percent in 1973, gaining one Chamber and three Senate seats. Durán's Democratic Radicals (PDR) slipped from 4 to 2.3 percent, and the Left Radicals (PIR) captured only 1.8 percent of the vote. In Chilean political life the four great parties, the Socialists and Communists on the left and the Christian Democrats and Nationals on the center and right, were consolidating their own positions and squeezing out all the smaller groups, most notably the three splinters of the Radical party.[11]

For the opposition there was another, bleaker way of looking at things. If one extended the trend of ebbing government popularity registered in the three by-elections held after July 1971, one would get a projected split close to 60-40, rather than the actual 56-44. Why did the trend of rising opposition strength seem to reverse itself? There were several explanations given for this outcome, some based on demographics and changed voter eligibility and some alleging fraud by the UP.

In the two years between 1971 and 1973, as always, young voters turned 21 while old voters died. The expanding population tipped the numbers in favor of the younger, presumably more leftist, voters. Moreover, the voting age had been lowered from 21 to 18 since the last nationwide elections, and illiterates had been given the vote. It was reported that among illiterate, deaf, and blind voters, the UP had an absolute majority. About one in six of the four-and-a-half million eligible voters were newly enfranchised.[12]

Then there is the question of fraud. In actuality there is some fraud in virtually every large election, whether it be in the United States or in Chile. The real questions are almost always: "How much?" and "Did the cheating make any significant difference?" Opposition politicians lost no time before they charged dirty counting. The first controversy surrounded the "women's vote." When women's suffrage in national elections had been introduced in Chile in 1949, women's polling places were simply added onto the existing ones for men, so one could tell how each sex voted. In 1973 the men split almost 50-50, with a very slim CODE majority, while over 60 percent of the women—many of them obviously loyal churchgoers—voted in favor of CODE. As early as mid-morning of election day Agence France Presse was describing large turnouts of women at the polls. It was, therefore, suspicious when returns from the women's polling places began to lag behind those of the men in the counting. Reporting of these results even stopped altogether at one point.

There was a second suspicious delay. The results from Santiago province continued to be unreported, as returns from most of the rest of the country poured forth. The story soon spread that the UP was desperately trying to cook the results to prevent the defeat of Volodia Teitelboim, the Communists' ideological guru. It was clear that Frei, Jarpa, Altamirano, and a second Christian Democrat, the highly popular José Musalém, were assured of election. It was whispered that the National party's candidate, retired colonel Alberto Labbé, was leading Teitelboim. (Labbé was the commander of cadets who was retired after his troops refused to honor Fidel Castro in December 1971.) To make matters even more humiliating for the Communists, Teitelboim's defeat would have left them as the only major party failing to elect a senator from the lustrous Santiago district. It may never be known for sure whether the results were cooked. When the ballots were all counted, however, Volodia Teitelboim was declared elected.[13]

In the meantime Christian Democratic leaders issued an enraged public statement charging that the 1973 elections were the first time in modern Chilean history when national election results were not known within twenty-four hours of the closing of the polls. Prats defended the integrity of the counters, asserting that the complicated system of federations and confederations made it necessary to make double counts. The Nationalists' Radio Agricultura charged on 6 March that sacks full of opposition-marked ballots, notably ballots from women's polling places, had been found under a bridge and at some polling places. The Christian Democrat who presided over the Senate, Ignacio Palma Vicuña, brought reports of discrepancies in southern provinces to Prats's attention. Nothing much came of these charges, however, and some of the purveyors, such as Radio Agricultura, were not famed for reliability.[14]

In July 1973 a new round of fraud charges agitated the politicians and the public. Jaime del Valle, dean of the law school at the Catholic University of Santiago, published a study purporting to show that at least 200,000 fraudulent UP votes had been cast in the March elections. He cited multiple registrations on the literate and illiterate rolls and registrations of deceased persons. He also reported higher new registrations in districts where there were key senatorial races. One district showed a 37 percent increase over the old rolls, while registrations in a nearby district where there was no senatorial race increased by only 18 percent. In addition, he found that some identity cards used for registration were fraudulent and that the vote tallies in communities where registrations had jumped showed lopsided pro-UP strength. Lastly, del Valle asserted that the increase of 750,000 registrants since the 1971 municipal elections could not be accounted for—although his critics alleged his methodology was faulty and failed to take into account young people turning twenty-one between 1971 and 1973 (although the new 18- to 21-year-old voters were taken into account). The Congress appointed a special committee to investigate del Valle's charges, but it did not succeed in clarifying matters.[15]

One must conclude that there was fraud, but less than del Valle charged and not enough to make a significant difference. Demographics, the lowering of the voting age, and the enfranchisement of illiterates probably accounted for most of Unidad Popular's relatively strong showing.

### The Post-Election Reality

A reality that was discouraging to both sides came out of the 1973 congressional elections. Unidad Popular found itself a continuing minority for the foreseeable future, and the opposition found its majority insufficient to force legitimate change. The situation resembled the one after the 1971 elections, in that both popular consultations had resulted in a closed door. In 1971 the door to a successful plebiscite and Allende-sponsored institutional change had closed, even though Allende never quite accepted the fact. In 1973 the door to constitutional resolution had slammed in the face of the opposition. The political deadlock continued.

The polarization of opinion—or intensification of the class struggle—had two additional consequences. One was the virtual elimination of uncommitted onlookers and swing voters. The other was a solidfication of loyalties on both sides. This hardening of lines did not serve Allende. Unidad Popular had needed to extend its reach into the urban lower middle class and small farmers. Unfortunately for the government, the hard core of "workers and peasants" was not a majority. Chile had a larger politically aware middle class than most Latin American countries, and what was even worse for Unidad Popular, substantial numbers of Chilean working-class people, particularly women, had a middle-class mentality. In the cities the shopkeepers and artisans had come to fear nationalization and had found solidarity and purpose in the October 1972 strike movement. They had become a rock-hard element of opposition. In the countryside, while the government won some expansion of support among farmers on confiscated lands, the small independent farmers lived with the same fear as the shopkeepers of losing their property.

So Allende got what he did not want. He wanted greater numbers and deepening commitment among his own followers, and shrinking numbers and evaporating commitment in his opponents' ranks. The sharpening ideological confrontation solidified both camps, but it probably hardened his opposition more than it consolidated his own forces. The numbers did not change much.

The politicians reacted to the postelection reality with a sense of letdown. The campaign had been, in a peculiar way, an escape for both sides, an opportunity for the politically active to throw their energies into the task at hand and let tomorrow take care of itself. Tomorrow came, and the election that was to have resolved Chile's political dilemma had resolved nothing.

Allende urged the nation to get down to work. He edged closer to open polemics against the left-wing Socialists and their encouragement of violent confrontation. He talked of the "lunatic fringe" of his own forces, but he did not force a showdown. He maneuvered several personal allies into the Socialist party leadership, replacing two wild-eyed left extremists, but he did not push Altamirano out. In May 1973 Allende induced Clodomiro Ameyda to leave the Foreign Ministry in order to devote his efforts to the Socialist party, the consolidation of Unidad Popular, and domestic policy. It was a sensible step, but it came too late. Had Allende made the move a year or two earlier, the history of Unidad Popular might have been different.[16]

The Christian Democrats wondered what to do next. Eduardo

Frei and his party colleagues renewed their effort to define nationalization policy through the Three Areas constitutional amendment. Prats's 8 March entry in his diary, written only four days after the election, noted that Allende had already met with several leaders of the opposition, including Patricio Aylwin of the Christian Democrats, about the proposed amendment. In that meeting, according to Prats, the opposition representatives warned the president that the congressional majority would proclaim the country in a "state of illegality" if the amendment were not promulgated.[17]

The top military leaders decided that their choice was either to remain in the government with increased powers or to withdraw altogether. They presented fourteen conditions if Allende wished them to remain in the cabinet. Among these were promulgation of the Three Areas amendment; more orderly public administration, in which government decisions would be executed and enforced uniformly; the disarming of paramilitary groups; and an effort to resolve outstanding problems with the United States. Inconclusive discussions continued between the generals and the president, but the military leadership left the cabinet on 27 March. Altamirano and his left-wing Socialists regarded the officers' departure as a victory.[18]

### Eduardo Frei Montalva

Elected in 1973 with the highest number of votes of any candidate in the nation, Frei was voted in as president of the Senate. He presided over the democratic opposition in Chile, its uncontested leader.

Frei's personal characteristics had long been familiar to all Chileans. A tall, lean, reflective-looking man with a rather large nose, Frei could not be described as handsome. His visage could be presented as evidence, however, that qualities of character ultimately find their expression in a person's face. Frei was a practicing Christian, known by all to be devoted to his wife María who, like her husband, was more worthy than pretty. The Freis lived modestly in a smallish house on Hindenburg Street.

Throughout my stay in Chile I met Frei about once every month or two for tea at the home of a mutual friend, for we wanted to meet discreetly but not furtively. The Freis very occasionally came to the U.S. Embassy Residence for a dinner or a reception, but it seemed inappropriate that we should be in frequent public contact. I developed great admiration for Eduardo Frei. He had breadth of view and nobility of purpose.

Our relationship was not crisis-free. On 6 April 1973 Laurence Stern of the *Washington Post* published an exposé of U.S. covert help to the Christian Democrats in the period leading up to the 1964 elections. Stern laid out the facts that were published in 1975 by the Church Committee, with a few embellishments and some fuzzing of the line between covert funding and overt assistance given with a political purpose. Stern quoted a U.S. intelligence source as having said that U.S. intervention had been "blatant and almost obscene." Frei was deeply upset. Christian Democratic party president Renán Fuentealba manfully denied that the U.S. had contributed $20 million to Frei's 1964 campaign—which was technically true. Fuentealba also asserted that Christian Democratic political campaigns were "fundamentally" funded by party dues, although CD sources did acknowledge some income from abroad and from companies doing business in Chile. Fuentealba challenged the *Washington Post* to examine the funding of the Marxist parties' campaigns.[19]

We at the embassy were pressured by people close to Frei to have the U.S. government deny the Stern exposé. I knew we could not do so, as the story was essentially true, and I telegraphed Washington recommending against any U.S. statement. Frei himself never raised the matter, although he unquestionably found the episode painful. The issue did blow over in Santiago, and it proved less damaging to the Christian Democrats than I believe they feared.

By the time of the coup it had become clear that Frei and his party had concluded that a military solution was the only possible way out of the crisis. The Christian Democratic party stated so publicly after the coup.[20] Frei never advocated a coup to me in our talks, however, and I never supported the idea in talking to him.

Eduardo Frei lived quietly in Santiago for eight years after 1973, occasionally traveling abroad and intermittently appearing in the news columns of the world's press as he indicated measured disapproval of the junta government's failure to restore constitutional rule. Complications followed a hernia operation and resulted in the

former president's death on 22 January 1982. To my mind it has
been one of history's tragedies that Eduardo Frei never had a renewed opportunity to lead his country. He was 71 when he died,
which is not so old, and had he lived a few more years, changing
circumstances might have given him a role in helping to restore
democracy in Chile.

# Chapter 7

# To the Tancazo

IT was a peculiar period between the March elections and the Tancazo of 29 June 1973. Everybody knew that the situation could not go on without some clearing of the air. Renewed labor troubles were building, while the political parties of the left, center, and right were busying themselves with increasingly sterile political maneuvers. The parties were becoming less relevant as other actors moved to the center of the stage.

Among the emerging forces was a conglomerate of groups that had been involved in the October 1972 strikes. The previously inchoate "guild movement" was transforming itself into an independent political entity, operating in coordinated fashion both in tense periods and also in quieter times. In addition, coup plotting was increasing within the three armed services. These various developments were more in the nature of sea changes than of sharply defined political events.

## More Troubles for Allende

The copper miners at El Teniente were not reactionaries, and their grievances were over bread-and-butter issues. Their quarrel with the government revolved around the relatively favorable contract the miners had negotiated before the general wage readjustment of October 1972. Now, in 1973, the government wanted to subtract these previously negotiated wage increases from the benefits given under the nationwide readjustment, and the miners, who saw themselves as Chilean Knights of Labor, would have none of it.[1] On 19 April 1973 the miners struck, and the work stoppage at El Teniente cost Chile a million dollars a day in lost foreign-exchange earnings. Allende was reported to have been greatly upset by this workers' "betrayal."[2]

Violence erupted in Rancagua, the capital of O'Higgins province, where the mine lay. About a hundred and twenty miners clashed with police, and the government declared a state of emergency in the province. It did not end the dispute, however, and the copper miners at Chuquicamata declared a two-day sympathy strike on 11–12 May. On the fifteenth the professional employees at El Teniente walked out, and on the twenty-third even more violent clashes occurred in Rancagua after workers at a strike meeting were fired upon. The police blamed the Socialists and raided their local headquarters, seizing arms. The commander of the city garrison, known to be strongly anti-UP, was relieved of his post for having ordered the raid.[3]

Some Chuquicamata miners renewed their solidarity strike on 1 June but voted by a narrow margin on the sixth to return to work. In the meantime, on 5 June, the government had suspended copper shipments abroad. The violence in Rancagua flared up again in the first days of June, sparked by the death and funeral of a miner shot by a military patrol on 30 May. Strikers set fire to barricades and hurled dynamite, reportedly blowing up offices of progovernment parties.[4]

On 14 June the violence spread to Santiago. Approximately 5,000 miners marched on the capital and were met on the outskirts by police. The marchers were dispersed with tear gas, but later about two thousand of them filtered into the city. The next day Allende received a delegation of them, but the Socialist and Communist party leadership publicly disavowed the president's action. While the president was conferring, prostriker school and university students clashed with pro-UP paramilitary groups, and the students took refuge inside the buildings of the Catholic University and the University of Chile. The next day, 16 June, miners were fired upon from the National Telecommunications Company building, and they retreated to the headquarters of the Christian Democratic party, where volunteers bandaged their wounds. As the miners had no place to sleep, the universities and the opposition-led Congress extended the hospitality of their premises.[5]

On 19 June the violence in Santiago picked up again, as police and demonstrators battled each other amid tear gas and flying rocks. Meanwhile, in O'Higgins province the government offered productivity bonuses and a lump-sum payment to the unskilled workers at El Teniente, and many of these laborers joined UP miners in returning to work. But most of the skilled workers continued to strike. They virtually occupied Rancagua and were sustained by food from farmers in the Central Valley, brought up by truckers who had struck the previous October. On 20 June teachers, students, physicians, nurses, dentists, druggists, and other professionals walked out in sympathy. On the same day President Allende flew to El Teniente to assess the situation. On the twenty-first the communist-led Central Workers' Confederation called a one-day general strike in the capital to demonstrate pro-UP labor's power. The day ended in shootings, bombings, and clashes.[6]

During the last week in June other events moved to center stage. The tancazo, soon to be described, riveted the attention of the capital. In the mysterous way things sometimes happen, with events influencing each other but not quite causing the result, conditions were created to end the strike. El Teniente workers received a retroactive "productivity bonus," effective 1 April. It was really a wage increase—all workers received it—and not a productivity bonus at all. The government's face was more or less saved, however, and the miners returned to work on 2 July 1973.[7]

The Gremialists, or guild forces, had played a crucial role in the October 1972 strikes but had not then coalesced into a continuing political force. During the ensuing months, however, the Gremialists emerged as a power center with impressive direct-action capability, independent of the party system.

The leaders were the heads of the great business associations: Jorge Fontaine Aldunate, president of the Confederation of Production and Commerce, and his brother Arturo, subdirector of the newspaper El Mercurio. Other key figures were Hernán Cubillos Sallato, number one on the business side at El Mercurio, and Orlando Sáenz, head of the Society for Manufacturing Development (SOFOFA). The presidents of the National Society of Agriculture were also leaders: first Benjamín Matte Guzmán and then Alfonso Márquez de la Plata. There were also the heads of the powerful confederations so much involved in October: Rafael Cumsille of the shopkeepers; León Vilarín of the truckers; Juan Jara Cruz of the National Confederation of Land Transport; Ernesto Cisternas of the microbus and taxi owners; and Julio Bazán of the professionals (CUPROCH). Lastly, there was Jaime Guzmán.[8]

Guzmán provided the Gremialists with much of their ideology. This man had led anti-UP students to victory in campus elections at the Catholic University, outflanking both the leftists and the regular opposition. He believed in the corporativist state. While he admired post-1964 Brazil more than fascist Italy, the corporativist ideology has a whiff of fascism, no matter where it comes from. Guzmán was a highly articulate spokesman, a television star on the Santiago talk shows, and a man ready for bigger things.[9]

Between March and June 1973 the gremialist conglomerate systematically developed its organizational resources. Its leaders also became increasingly convinced that party-based democratic institutionalism was a blind alley. The stalemated March elections had disappointed their last hopes for a constitutionalist escape from Chile's political crisis. During these months they seem to have become systematic coup plotters. They developed contacts with key military officers, and they pursued their contacts abroad, particularly in Brazil and Argentina.

Only four days after the elections, on 8 March, Prats was writing in his diary: "The outcome of the elections, it would seem, has not so far brought any improvement in things. On the contrary, it appears that the pro-coup sector is taking the initiative in the opposition." Two months later he was telling his diary: "Many industrialists who had not earlier set out on the road to sedition, now gradually are beginning to assume this orientation."[10]

My wife and I were invited to a dinner at the house of Orlando Sáenz on 15 March 1973. Jorge Fontaine was there, as well as other senior business leaders. It was all very decorous, and nobody suggested directly that the United States should support a coup, but the talk turned to politics and I was given every opening to encourage such thinking. The conversation became an amiable but pointed verbal fencing match. I kept indicating institutional and political avenues to improve the situation, in disregard of what those distinguished Chilean business leaders felt to be stark realities.

Many such conversations were going on in Santiago during those months, I am convinced, some of them no doubt with other foreign ambassadors.

Another force was becoming increasingly important during these months: Patria y Libertad, the Fatherland and Liberty Nationalist Front. Indeed, this period was the organization's meridian—at least during the time I was in Chile—and it later declined in power and importance. Its swastika-like spider was appearing more frequently on Santiago walls. So was a scrawled warning, "Djakarta," a menacing reminder to leftist Chileans of the failed communist coup attempt in 1965 against Sukarno's leftist government in Indonesia, after which anticommunists had killed some 300,000 leftists in Java.

Patria y Libertad also painted the walls with the inscription, "SACO Is Coming!" Prats described SACO, "System for Action by Civilians who are Organized," in his 7 April 1973 diary entry as a program to conceal a portion of production and distribute it to opponents of the regime. Factory owners were also supposed to make up lists of pro-UP workers and find pretexts to discharge them. In the countryside sympathizers would falsify agricultural production figures, divert food supplies, create self-defense groups, and make lists of pro-UP activists. Shopkeepers would hold back merchandise from leftists, and other activists would scout out ways to cut electric power. Women would spread intimidating rumors. Prats realized that Patria y Libertad was incapable of doing all these things, but the right extremists still worried him.[11]

If truth be told, provocative wall slogans and grandiose schemes were probably Patria y Libertad's long suit—along with efforts to subvert rightist military officers. Patria y Libertad also encouraged the organization of vigilante squads in the wealthy suburbs of Santiago and maintained gangs of youths who appeared on the streets whenever violence was the order of the day.

On 4 May 1973 Mario Aguilar Rogel of Patria y Libertad was killed in a violent protest demonstration in the center of Santiago. On 6 May Pablo Rodríguez Grez, the head of Patria y Libertad, speaking at Aguilar's funeral, called for a new government. The next day the second man in the organization, Walter Roberto Thieme Scheires, surfaced with a fellow militant in Mendoza, Argentina, where they had flown in a private plane. Thieme had been believed dead, but the "accident" in which he had "perished" in early 1973 had been staged. It was said that Thieme and his collaborator had fled to Argentina when an alleged coup plot they were leading was discovered by the authorities. In any case, the police rounded up about fifty Patria y Libertad militants on 11 May, although they released most of them shortly thereafter.[12]

According to subsequent accounts, Patria y Libertad organized a clandestine northern route of arms supply into Chile from Argentina in the early months of 1973. Allegedly, the arms trafficking was carried out with the collusion of military officers in the Atacama district. Collaborative ties were also alleged between Pablo Rodríguez, retired major Arturo Marshall Marchesse—who had taken refuge in Bolivia after having plotted against both Frei and Allende—and Brazilian anticommunists. Arms running decreased in volume with the apprehension or exiling of a number of Patria y Libertad leaders in mid-1973, but the activity continued on a reduced scale right up to the coup.[13]

On 4 June the provincial governor of Valparaíso, Carlos González Márquez, ordered the arrest of Patria y Libertad's chief in Valparaíso and other militants. Apparently even the Christian Democrats, not usually sympathetic to Patria y Libertad, regarded these arrests as arbitrary, and they and the National party's deputies impeached the governor.[14] Late that same month, with Patria y Libertad the suspected perpetrator, bombs exploded in Santiago outside a Socialist party office, a government office, a TV installation, and a Cuban diplomat's home.[15]

Patria y Libertad and the MIR were, effectively if unwittingly, allies in disruption and violence. The right and left extremist fringes effectively joined each other coming around the dark side of the Chilean political world. They shared the conviction that force was the only way to get what they wanted. Both helped to sink the chances of institutional democracy, an objective they had in common.

A strange incident on 27 June 1973 may have brought Allende more trouble than all his other difficulties during this time. The episode dramatized the tension and frustration that had become a part of army commander-in-chief Prats's life. A motorist named

Alejandrina Cox pulled up beside General Prats's car in rush-hour traffic crawling toward the center of Santiago. Mrs. Cox stuck out her tongue at the general, made an ugly face, and perhaps made an obscene gesture. Something inside the general snapped, and he gave chase to Mrs. Cox, firing a shot into the lower portion of her car. Catching up with her, Prats allegedly aimed a gun at her head and demanded an apology. A crowd gathered; Prats jumped into a nearby taxi and sped away; the crowd assaulted the official car and its hapless driver, scrawling antigovernment slogans on it and deflating the tires. It took three busloads of riot police, firing off tear gas, to quiet things down.

UP spokesmen alleged a deliberate plot. Ungallantly, they described Mrs. Cox as a masculine-looking woman whom Prats mistook for a man. (In a Latin society it was painful to acknowledge that Prats would have knowingly conducted himself in the way he did toward a woman. Knowing Prats's chivalry, I was prepared to believe that he might have thought Cox a man, at least in the beginning.) Prats submitted his resignation to the president, but Allende declined it and declared a state of emergency in Santiago province, calling it "a necessary measure to confront the excesses of fascism."[16]

The Prats-Cox incident did not disappear from Chilean minds, and it damaged Prats, who became a markedly less effective and commanding public figure. Allende's strongest supporting oak in the Chilean military establishment had been struck by lightning. It still stood, but not as before.

## The Leftists Move toward Confrontation

Two leftist initiatives gained momentum between March and June 1973. They were the organizing and arming of paramilitary forces, and the infiltration of left extremists into the armed services.

Both activities had commenced before March 1973, of course; the president's GAP bodyguards had long trained at El Arrayán, and "Comandante Pepe" defended his rural stronghold with guerrillas. The MIRistas and other extreme leftist groups trained their armed bands;[17] both the Communists and the Socialists had paramilitary units in the Ramona Parra and Elmo Catalán brigades; and the MAPU had reportedly begun training with arms at the end of December 1972.[18]

The importation of Cuban weapons was already being reported in 1971, and primitive weapons and "tanks" were being manufactured in factories in 1972. As for the infiltration of the armed forces, the MIR and left-extremist elements in the Socialist party had been engaged in small-scale efforts along these lines for a year or more. As early as 1 March 1972 *El Mercurio* also published a story on infiltration of the services by the Communists. They were by then making systematic efforts to suborn inductees.[19]

What happened in the second quarter of 1973 was a quantum jump in these activities. In addition to Comandante Pepe's fiefdom, at least eight rural guerrilla centers were reported to have been established. Significant paramilitary training facilities were developed in factories in the Santiago industrial belts. Chilean military intelligence reportedly began discovering Cuban, Czech, and East German military instructors visiting the Cordón de Los Cerrillos. A paramilitary training center was also said to have been established in a prefabricated-housing plant near Valparaíso which the Soviets had financed.[20]

The Communists began systematic efforts to arm the Ramona Parra brigade between March and June. The leftists stepped up the crude manufacture of weapons, including plastic-encased bombs, in the factories. Foreign-manufactured arms, including weapons from the USSR and Czechoslovakia, began to appear at about the same time.[21]

On 9 June 1973 there was an exchange of gunfire between members of the Ramona Parra brigade and an air force unit at Los Cerrillos airport. It appears to have been the first open military clash between organized leftist paramilitary units and the armed forces, and the psychological impact of the event was considerable.[22]

Reports of leftist infiltration of the armed forces increased markedly during the second quarter of 1973. Leftist-oriented propaganda began appearing in barracks and on recruiting-station walls. Handbills were also passed around at military bases. Some of these materials openly promoted insubordination, particularly when arms searches against leftist strongholds were being ordered.[23]

The military began to make larger-scale use of the arms control law. Between April and June they carried out an average of three searches a week, almost all of them against leftists. After June the average was even higher.[24] The harder the military searched, the more arms they found; the more this went on, the louder the left-wing Socialists and their allies screamed in public protest—and the harder the leftists worked to distribute and conceal more arms in the industrial belts. The efforts of the searchers, and the responses of those searched, built a mutually reinforcing sense of anger, frustration, and distrust.

The president was aware of the arming for confrontation. In late July Castro sent Allende a letter in which the Cuban prime minister referred to Allende's desire "to gain time, in order to improve the correlation of forces for the eventuality that fighting should break out." Three weeks later the president's garrulous friend Régis Debray spent a Sunday with him at El Arrayán. According to Debray, Allende described the "chess game" he was playing with the Chilean military. Debray went on to say that "everyone knew" that this game was only to secure time to organize, to arm, and to coordinate the military forces of the UP parties—"a race against the clock which had to go on week after week."[25]

Allende seems to have had ambivalent feelings. At a rally on 21 June the president had urged his listeners to "create more popular organizations to counter the proliferation of rightist and ultrightist ones . . . more popular cordones. . . . Create People's Power . . . but not independently from the government."[26] It was a somewhat equivocal declaration.

Joan Garcés, the president's Spanish aide and confidant, wrote in early June that there was a need to organize the people "to resist a confrontation beginning in three to four months." President Allende also seems to have told UP leaders on 6 June that a rightist insurrection would take place within three months unless he called a plebiscite. Both Garcés and Allende proved to have had a good sense of timing.[27]

The Communist party had always been the force supporting caution and relative moderation during the Allende time. By May and June 1973, however, there were signs that even the Communist party was changing its orientation. On 16 May party secretary Luis Corvalán told his party's plenum that he feared confrontation was inevitable. By 15 June, as already noted, the Communist party had joined the Socialists in disavowing Allende's negotiations with El Teniente copper miners.[28] The next day Prats commented in his diary: "The Communists and Socialists have committed an unpardonable error in repudiating the president's conversations. . . . The Socialist stand is nothing new. They believe that confrontation is inevitable and, through that, want to sharpen tensions, but I cannot understand the Communist position. Are they not the ones who support dialogue and the avoidance of civil war?"[29] The communist declarations in June 1973 had a new tone of militancy and psychological preparation for violent confrontation.[30]

Characteristic of so many situations in Allende's Chile, maneuvering within Unidad Popular on the issue produced vacillation in policy. The workers were being organized for violence and possible civil war, but they were not being trained or armed fast enough to enable them to stand against the country's military forces. At the same time the mobilization of workers produced a sharp reaction among armed service leaders. After 11 September Patricio Aylwin of the Christian Democratic party said flatly that it was the arming of "People's Power" which caused the coup. An oversimplification, Aylwin's remark nevertheless indicates the importance both of the leftists' paramilitary effort and of the military's reaction to it.[31]

## Coup Plotting

While coup plotting had ebbed after Schneider's murder and during Allende's first year or so in power, it had never ceased. Considerable information is now available about abortive plots, and we know outlines of the discussions among the military officers who overthrew Allende.

By the time I arrived in Santiago in October 1971, and for two or three months thereafter, unrest among Chilean officers was increasing. Bad economic news and Chile's debt moratorium were changing the atmosphere. Chilean officers were outraged at Castro's visit and the Cuban dictator's antics. They were also goaded and shamed by the women's march of 2 December 1971. The correlation between the level of political and economic crisis and the intensity of coup plotting was close. In Chile, as in most countries, military attitudes responded to the national mood and changed with it. By 8 December 1971 I was informing Washington—as Jack Anderson subsequently reported—that "discontent and plotting in the military services" had been "substantially greater."[32]

Three incipient coup attempts were revealed in 1972 and early 1973. Then minister of interior Hernán del Canto announced the discovery of a plot to overthrow Allende during the week of 19–25 March 1972. Large landowners, militants of Patria y Libertad, and retired military officers were involved. Subsequent reports indicated that several active-duty officers may also have been implicated, including Brig. Gen. Hernán Hiriart Laval, head of the Valdivia Cavalry Division, Col. Julio Canessa Robert in Temuco, and Brig Gen. Alfredo Canales Márquez, the commander of the crucially important Santiago garrison. The government either did not obtain proof of active-duty officers' involvement, however, or did not regard it as politic to accuse them.[33]

Later in 1972 a "September Plan" was exposed. September was classic coup-plotting time in Chile because army units were regularly moved into Santiago to participate in the Independence Day parade on the nineteenth, and subversive troop movements might be masked by normal deployments into the city. On 2 September 1972 Allende publicly denounced this new plot. The Socialist party followed up three days later with its own public revelation, and Allende asserted on the fourteenth that the plans had included interception of food-bearing ships, blockage of highways, and sabotage of railroad lines. Retired major Arturo Marshall was involved from his Bolivian sanctuary. So was Brigadier General Canales in Santiago. Reportedly the plot was revealed when Canales got drunk and confided his plans to Rear Adm. Horacio Justiniano Aguirre. Justiniano talked to Prats, and the army commander-in-chief convened the Generals' Board and decreed Canales's retirement.[34]

I was in an open-air box just behind the Chilean generals at the Independence Day parade. Canales was by then the talk of Santiago. Resplendent in uniform, he passed up and down the line of seated generals, talking, shaking hands, and looking for all the world as if he were running for office. His retirement became effective on 21 September, and such was the civilized way in which the government seemed to have handled things that he remained in Santiago, no doubt still plotting, throughout the ensuing year. In early August 1973 Prats wrote in his diary that Canales had just told him that he, Canales, had visited Viaux in prison, that they were in agreement, but that they had "not yet" talked with active-duty officers. Prats characterized Canales's remarks as "pure and simple sedition." There is no indication that Prats actually did anything at that point, however, except to write in his diary.[35]

The third coup threat surfaced in May 1973. Apparently the commander of an air force base in Santiago threatened to carry out his own coup, but a loyalist army colonel who commanded a neighboring infantry regiment forced his air force colleague to back down by threatening to attack the air base with infantry.[36]

The plot that actually succeeded seems to have grown slowly, watered by the storms and squalls of political strife, paramilitary violence, strikes, and economic decline. The contacts and associations among officers who ultimately carried out the September coup seem also to have developed slowly, as events and chance encounters drew these men together.

A year after the coup, Arturo Fontaine of *El Mercurio* published an account of early meetings among key officers. According to Fontaine, the Schneider assassination had forced the postponement of the regularly scheduled 1970 session of Chile's interservice National Defense High Command course. The result was that a double contingent of 42 officers and civilian functionaries attended the 1971 session. Most of these men were soon to become Chile's generals and admirals, and officers who became key figures in the plotting were among them. UP cabinet ministers who addressed the students either irritated them with "absurd" and overoptimistic economic projections, as Planning Chief Gonzalo Martner reportedly did, or frightened them with candid explanations of the economic disaster in prospect, as Pedro Vuskovic reportedly did. The questioning of UP speakers was unremitting, and the officers' appreciation of the social, political, and economic trouble ahead became focused and informed. The long hours of common study also created ties of mutual confidence among these officers.[37]

Over the years the practice had grown up of each military service maintaining emergency plans, designed for use in the case of earthquakes or other natural disasters, or in cases of civil disorder or insurrection. A National Defense General Staff was charged with overall planning for emergencies. This interservice general staff was a consultative and coordinating office that reported to the commanders-in-chief of the armed forces. In times of emergency it also worked with the commanders of nine Jurisdictional Zones of Internal Security. These commanders headed the six army divisions, the two main naval districts, and the air force brigade at Puerto Montt, and they reported to the minister of interior through the commanders-in-chief and the minister of defense.[38] Plans and mechanisms to deal with emergencies could be adapted to a military seizure of power. All that stood between a counterinsurgency capability and a subversive one was the military's intent.

In January 1972 Lt. Gen. Augusto Pinochet became chief of staff of the army, Commander-in-Chief Prats's deputy. Early in April Pinochet ordered the Directorate of Intelligence to draft a study of the developing internal security situation and its implications. This document was submitted to Pinochet on the thirteenth of the month, and it concentrated particularly on dangers from the MIR and other extreme-left activists. It also addressed the possibility of violence or civil war growing out of a standoff between President Allende and the Congress, the possibility of a rightist or opposition-led coup, and the possibility of an *autogolpe,* a left-extremist coup mounted against the leftists' own government.[39]

Recalling this April study in a March 1974 interview, Pinochet said that "on April 13, 1972, . . . we concluded that the insuperable conflict between the executive and legislative branches did not allow for a constitutional solution." In the interview Pinochet was also quoted as saying that, in the April study, he and his colleagues had begun "analyzing the possibilities of carrying out a coup." He added, however, that "we always wanted to keep ourselves apart from coup plotting" even as late as in mid-1973. Pinochet went on to describe his state of mind when he became commander-in-chief in August 1973. At that time, sixteen months after the April study, Pinochet said his ideas were "beginning" to coincide with those of his restive officers.[40]

It is worth noting Pinochet's statements that he was reluctant, well after the April study, to enter into coup plotting because some commentators have seized on his assertion in the same interview that coup possibilities were analyzed in April 1972 as proof that Pinochet and his colleagues made the decision to plot Allende's overthrow at that time. The full text of the interview does not support this interpretation. Moreover, excerpts of the April study were published after the coup by army officers close to Pinochet, and they indicate that in his interview Pinochet sharpened the study's gloomy description of trends and dangers. Quotations from the study do not support Pinochet's assertion that it said constitutional government was doomed. They also do not describe an analysis of "possibilities of carrying out a coup." The postcoup apologia in which the quotations appear was disseminated in order to burnish Pinochet's image as a coup leader. It was trying to hawk his involvement, not conceal it, so its inconsistency with his exaggeration is significant.[41]

Why did the army make the April study at the time it did? Political events in the country provide an explanation. PIR minister of justice Sanhueza had just been repudiated by the president as a result of Sanhueza's agreement with the Christian Democrats to regulate expropriation policy. Altamirano and the left-wing Socialists had carried the day against Sanhueza, and the Left Radical ministers had departed from the cabinet, feeling themselves betrayed. All this had happened about a week before the army's analysis of 13 April. If supporting evidence were needed to show that nationalization policy was crucially important in Allende's Chile, this sequence of events provides it.

In June 1972 the general staff updated its national security plans and carried out further studies of the national situation. These studies envisaged confrontations between increasingly polarized political forces. The next month Pinochet ordered officers subordinate to the army general staff to revise the internal security plan, reorienting it to be "more offensive or preventive, in order that coercive measures already organized and provided for might anticipate events." Other documents were prepared in July and August. After the coup Pinochet showed reporters some of these memoranda, which "suggested the possibility of taking control of the nation."[42]

So far as the political context was concerned, June 1972 was the month when the economic crisis was coming to a head and producing the decisions of the conference at Lo Curro, and when the workers began to organize themselves in the Cordón de Los Cerrillos. In his postcoup interviews Pinochet explicitly noted that the army was beginning to prepare units at this time "to face extremist groups around the capital," including those in the industrial belts and in the squatters' shantytowns.[43]

The army was not the only service analyzing the national situation, updating emergency plans, and thinking about contingencies. The other branches were doing the same thing, and the Chilean Navy was revising plans with at least as much energy as the army was. The army's conspicuous effort after the coup to publicize its early planning was motivated, at least in part, by Pinochet's and some of his colleagues' vulnerability to accusations of having been "laggards" in the plotting, with the navy having been in the fore-front. Pinochet and the generals ended up dominating the Junta, and they used their postcoup leverage to "rectify" their image after the fact.[44]

In mid-1972 Vice Adm. Patricio Carvajal Prado took over leader-ship of the National Defense General Staff, and he subsequently emerged as a central figure in coup planning. His deputy was an air force brigadier general, Nicanor Díaz Estrada, one of the students at the 1971 National Defense High Command course and also a key personality in later plotting. The secretary of the National Defense General Staff was Col. Pedro Ewing Hodar, later secretary general of the Junta government.[45] Between June and September 1972 another National Defense High Command course was carried out, with 27 colonels, captains, and Foreign Ministry civilians in attendance. Many of these men would also play important roles in the coup.[46]

The August 1972 price hikes led to the disorders and violence of September and the October truckers' strike. After the coup Chilean Army colonels told Jonathan Kandell of the *New York Times* that October 1972 was when they had decided that military interven-tion could not be avoided. Kandell writes:

> The first attempts to coordinate action in the army, navy and air force . . . grew out of a 26-day . . . strike . . . in October, 1972. The strike ended when Dr. Allende invited . . . Prats . . . into the Cabinet. [The officers said:]
> "Just about everybody in the armed forces welcomed this. . . . because at the time we considered Prats a traditional military man who would put a brake on Allende.
> "But almost immediately, General Prats came to be viewed as favorable to the Allende Government. By late November, army and air force colonels and navy commanders began to map out the possibilities of a coup. They also contacted leaders of the truck owners, shopkeepers, and professional associations, as well as key businessmen, who had backed the October strike.
> "We left the generals and admirals out of the plotting, . . . because we felt that some of them like Prats would refuse to go along." . . .
> The plotting subsided somewhat in the weeks of political campaigning leading to the March legislative elections.[47]

It was said to have been in October and November 1972 that "hit lists" of leftists to be neutralized or eliminated began to be drawn up. The intelligence services of the three military branches also became active. Recalling his own impressions of the time in a post-coup interview, Pinochet said that subordinate officers did not talk to him directly about their thoughts and fears in very late 1972 and early 1973, but he sensed them.[48]

According to Gen. Arturo Yovane Zúñiga of the carabineros, he and Gen. Cesar Mendoza Durán (later the carabinero member of the Junta government) decided to support the idea of a coup at the beginning of 1973. Fontaine describes how their disaffection came about: General Mendoza was police chief of Santiago in December 1972, when a judge ordered the police to clear a Peñalolén market of leftists who were occupying it. After vain efforts to consult the UP governor of Santiago and Subsecretary of Interior Daniel Vergara, Mendoza executed the judge's order. Allende called Mendoza: "General, between an order of your President and one of the Judicial Authority, which will you carry out?" Mendoza gave the president a response that Allende found unsatisfactory and lost his job. He was reassigned to head the Welfare Office at carabinero headquarters, with four employees reporting to him. Yovane had also lost his job as police chief of Valparaíso for political reasons and had also been reassigned to insignificant duties at carabinero headquarters. The two men shared their resentment.[49]

According to the postcoup apologia written by Pinochet's army colleagues, Pinochet consistently cautioned his more activist fellow officers not to anticipate popular opinion, and he continued to hope that public pressure would force Allende to change. Reportedly a U.S. intelligence officer from Panama talked with Pinochet in February 1973 and (foolishly) said to him: "You are on a sinking ship. When are you going to act?" Reportedly Pinochet replied: "Not until our legs are wet," explaining that the armed forces could not move until the people poured into the streets and begged them to. "If we act too soon, the people from all sides would unite against us."[50]

Coup plotting picked up with a vengeance in March 1973, when it became clear that the elections had solved nothing. In the middle of March, according to Kandell, the plotting colonels invited several generals and admirals to join them.[51] According to General Pinochet, he and seven or eight other generals reached the conclusion on 20 March 1973 that a constitutional solution was "now impossible." They also revised and updated the army's emergency plan for internal security. After the coup Pinochet gave the following reasons for the military decision to consider intervention: the electoral stalemate, the fact that economic chaos in the country would leave Chile defenseless against hostile assault, and the growth and arming of leftist paramilitary groups.[52]

Brig. Gen. Sergio Arellano Stark of the army recalled after the coup that he had entered into conversations in March 1973 with Juan Soler of the air force and captains Hugo Castro and Arturo Troncoso of the navy. Arellano and Castro had been students together at the 1971 National Defense High Command course; Troncoso had attended the 1972 session. A bit later Arellano held conversations with Lt. Gen. Gustavo Leigh Guzmán of the air force and Vice Adm. José Toribio Merino Castro, both of them later members of the four-man ruling Junta.[53]

The colonels Kandell interviewed told him that the government "somehow found out that we were plotting" in April 1973 and "started to consider ways of stopping us."[54] Pinochet subsequently reported that he had been outraged by a left-extremist instruction manual for "armed subversion" which began appearing that month in the workers' settlements.[55] In May 1973 there was a sharp increase in coup-related planning. Pinochet mentioned after the coup that he and his colleagues analyzed the possibilities "once again" in May and updated the internal security plan.[56] In another interview Pinochet cited 28 May as the first time "active planning" commenced. According to Pinochet, the army then began to work out a "Dawn Plan," which included an outline for suppressing progovernment radios and other UP communications facilities. This subsection came to be known as the "Silence Plan." May 1973 was also the month that Miguel Enríquez of the MIR later identified as the time when "the revolution's enemies" commenced systematic coup planning.[57]

According to Joan Garcés, air force coup planning started in serious fashion in June 1973; in a postcoup interview Lt. Gen. Germán Stuardo de la Torre of the air force confirmed the June timing.[58]

This description brings the story up to the eve of the tancazo. That episode affected everybody profoundly, and coup plotting increased greatly after 29 June. But the generals and admirals did not rush to their task of overthrowing the president. They had not simply decided in secret—sometime in 1972—that things were falling apart and turned to planning their seizure of power. They went to the president again and again, mostly through their commanders-in-chief but sometimes collegially, and asked the president to reconsider his policies and to control the extremists. They squirmed, temporized, and looked for ways out, and it was a reluctant, uncertain, inconclusive process. The distinction was not always clear between seditious plotting and troubled consultation.

Again and again the record indicates that "serious planning" commenced, that conclusions were reached, or that judgments were made. In actuality there were ebbs and flows of planning and activity which followed the successive pulls of national crisis and subsided when the nation's politics moved in quieter ways. Each flowing tide of plotting reached farther than the last, and ebbed less far, but it was not a continuous advance.

A military officer regards contingency planning as a professional function, and planning is supposed to precede decision and not preempt it. The senior Chilean officers' passage from planning and talk to decision and action was made slowly. It was late—only days before the coup—when the armed forces moved collectively beyond the point of no return.

### Americans in Chile

Thornton Wilder lived in Newport, Rhode Island, in the interwar years, and he wrote a novel which described the "nine cities" of that town, "one on top of the other . . . some superimposed, some having very little relation with the others—variously beautiful, impressive, absurd, commonplace, and one very nearly squalid."[59] All of the cities Wilder described contained Americans, living in the same place, all passing each other, day by day, in their habitual rounds. The American communities in Santiago were a little like Wilder's cities, deposited one on top of another. For some, Nixon's official community was the squalid city, but others had different candidates for that distinction. Politics and conviction divided Americans in Santiago.

Starting from the political left, a few hundred North Americans admired Allende's political experiment and wanted to have some part in it, or at least to be present for it. Most of these Americans were young and essentially indistinguishable from hundreds of thousands of others seeking adventure in scores of countries.

Most of these Americans assiduously avoided the U.S. Embassy.

Very few registered as U.S. citizens at the consulate, and they would have regarded U.S. official interest in them as malevolent. So far as I know, we did leave these Americans alone. I was prepared to meet and talk with any U.S. citizen inclined to meet with me, but there were not many in this group who sought the opportunity.

One example of the public activities in Santiago of a few members of this group was the following invitation, which appeared in the press on 31 August 1972: "The North American Community in Chile invites Ambassador and Mrs. Davis, representatives of the present administration in Washington, D.C., to view the current exhibit at the National Museum of Fine Arts, NORTH AMERICAN POSTERS OF PROTEST, revealing the sentiments of the people of North America." The news column went on: "For obvious reasons the names of those subscribing to the invitation are not published."[60] I did go to the exhibit on opening day but found the North Vietnamese flag fluttering atop the building. As Americans were in combat in Vietnam, I passed on by.

The activities of a very different group of North Americans was reported in the Chilean and American press a day or two after the poster exhibit story. Led by Ira Leitel, a young American lawyer working with the Catholic University in Santiago, a McGovern for President Committee started work in Santiago. The committee held a fund-raiser cocktail party or two, mailed literature to twelve hundred local American residents, and predicted confidently that the Democrats would easily carry the American absentee vote from Chile.[61] Somebody in Richard Nixon's White House must have read about the committee's work. I soon received a telegram asking for names and data on those active on the committee as well as other information about the involvement of private Americans. This was the only direct contact I had with the type of White House activities which ultimately led to President Nixon's resignation. In my answering cable I simply reported what had appeared in the press. Fortunately, I knew no more, and I did not try to find out more.

There was a considerable American academic community in Chile. It included students writing dissertations and professors at the Catholic University, the University of Chile, and the Latin American Faculty of the Social Sciences (FLACSO). The natural scientists tended to be apolitical, and the social scientists more liberal. Notable private American visitors included Robert F. X.

Kennedy, Jr., who came to Chile in June 1973 for a skiing vacation at Portillo. One day he climbed up on skis with friends to the Christ of the Andes statue on the Chilean-Argentine mountain border—and was shot at by a border guard.[62] Luckily, the guard missed.

The Missioners' Committee on International Awareness called on me in April 1972, reflecting the views of still another North American group. Six of the Catholic missioners on the committee expressed their indignation at the ITT revelations and asked for any explanation I could give them of U.S. official involvement. They also asked about the current presence and activities of the CIA in Chile and expressed concern over the "unjust" influence big business had over the U.S. government. Though I had to decline to answer some of their questions, it was a constructive exchange. Unfortunately, Father Albert Buckwalter, one of the six, died less than a month later in a motorcycle accident as he was traveling back to town from doing voluntary work in a poor settlement outside Santiago.[63]

Other institutional connections brought a considerable group of Americans to Chile. Peter Bell headed a Ford Foundation office. William Lowenthal, an AID professional and a longtime colleague of Raúl Prebisch, had a key leadership role in the UN Latin American Institute for Economic and Social Planning (ILPES). Lowenthal also ably directed the governing board of the U.S.-oriented international school in Santiago, which employed some American teachers. The school bore the highly sophisticated name of "The Eagles' Nest."

The U.S. press corps covering the southern cone of Latin America was mostly based in Buenos Aires and shuttled back and forth across the Andes. The group included some highly experienced and sophisticated reporters. Juan de Onís and later Jonathan Kandell represented the *New York Times*, and Lewis H. Diuguid wrote for the *Washington Post*. There were also some who visited from farther away, including William Montalbano of the *Miami Herald*, David F. Belnap of the *Los Angeles Times*, James N. Goodsell of the *Christian Science Monitor*, and Everett Martin of the *Wall Street Journal*. As luck would have it, news stories in both Argentina and Chile reached incandescent heat simultaneously in the middle months of 1973, leaving America's news organizations with the disagreeable task of deciding where their crack journalists should concentrate their efforts. Most left the old hands in Buenos

Aires and sent new, relatively junior correspondents to Santiago, charged with familiarizing themselves in a hurry with local events. Some of these younger people went on to achieve notable distinction, but reporting from Santiago before and immediately after the 1973 coup sometimes reflected inexperience. A few, including a local stringer or two, captured American attention with reporting that verged on the sensational.

The U.S. business community almost disappeared as Allende's nationalizations progressed. Since time immemorial U.S. businessmen in Chile had held monthly meetings with the U.S. ambassador, and attendance was a measure of the community's dwindling size. In 1970, as the magazine *Business Week* duly reported, about "fifty executives" were regularly in attendance. By August 1972 there were nine. In August 1973, five businessmen were present, representing four firms.[64] The businessmen I knew in Chile had a shrewd view of the realities and a sensible attitude.

Still another community of Americans in Chile consisted of retired people, American women who had married local nationals, and a few American men who had married Chilean women. Allende's political upheaval put great strains on these families. Sometimes the American women, seeing what was happening, wanted to go home; occasionally it was the other way around. I remember one American woman of distinguished background, an able and much admired leader in the Santiago community, who was married to a Chilean physician. The doctor-husband decided to go abroad and reestablish himself, counting on his highly transferable medical skills for a new start. The American wife had made her life in Chile, however, and the two of them ended in divorce.

Then there were retired Americans, sometimes old and alone, and children of U.S. citizens working in Chile. They held every possible political view. Michael Vernon Townley, later to become notorious in the assassination of Orlando Letelier, and his "career" illustrate the complications that resulted from private Americans' involvement in Chilean politics.

Two weeks after the March 1973 congressional elections a peculiar story surfaced in the Chilean press. In the early morning of 19 March a five-man brigade, connected to the rightist *Patria y Libertad*, reportedly broke into a power station to destroy some equipment which was jamming an opposition TV station outside Concepción. The intruders entered through the house next door, where they aroused the occupant, a house painter. Presumably by mistake, they bound and gagged this man so tightly that he suffocated and died.[65] In early June the director of the investigative police, Alfredo Joignant, told news reporters that Townley had been one of the five-man brigade (although later U.S. accounts indicated that Townley had reconnoitered the station but had not actually been present at the break-in).[66] Townley managed to elude the police and escape to Argentina, according to Joignant, five days after the dead house painter was found.

Townley was the son of a Ford Company executive. He had been known to U.S. Embassy officers before the Concepción incident, but simply as a young American of obviously rightist sympathies who had stayed in Chile after his parents were transfered to Venezuela and had married a Chilean woman. It appears that Townley had tried unsuccessfully to establish a connection with the CIA in Miami in late 1970, and he tried again in the spring of 1973 after making his way from Argentina to Florida. These approaches are described in various books, but none of the accounts presents any evidence that the CIA—or the U.S. Embassy— sponsored Townley. So far as I know, the U.S. government did not have anything to do with Townley's anti-UP activities.[67]

Private U.S. citizens were not the only Americans who threatened to get the United States into difficulty. We had some narrow escapes in the official community. On one occasion an American associated with an agency involved in technical, non-political work imported hundreds of copies of a book, by Frederick C. Schwarz of the Christian Anti-Communist Crusade, entitled *You Can Trust the Communists* (to be Communists).[68] Naively, the American official began distributing these copies to Chilean friends. The importation had been illegal, and the American did not have diplomatic immunity. Fortunately, we discovered what was happening before the Chilean authorities did and took steps to have the American transferred for his own protection.

On another occasion Chilean employees at the NASA satellite tracking station began slipping surplus and outmoded technical parts to friends at Chilean opposition radio and TV stations. These activities could have jeopardized the entire NASA facility, and we stopped them in a hurry.

Even more significant than the hazards of this sort of "private enterprise" in Chilean politics was the degree to which Allende's

Chile was "wide open." All kinds of people were "doing their thing"—leftists, rightists, and centrists. Chile was not a police state, let alone an effective one, and it was still a largely untrammeled society.

## The Tank Insurrection—or the Tancazo

During the latter days of June 1973 leaders of Patria y Libertad and restive military officers at the Santiago-based Second Armored Regiment entered into a plot to mount a coup or kidnap Allende on 27 June. The plans leaked, and a Patria y Libertad leader, learning that the plot had been discovered, warned an officer in the Second Armored Regiment of this fact. The coup attempt was canceled. Military intelligence was not deterred from reporting the plot up the chain of command in the evening of 26 June, however, and the wheels of military justice began to turn. On the following day Capt. Sergio Rocha Aros of the Second Armored Regiment was arrested, having been identified as a prime organizer of the sedition. He was held in a cell in the basement of the Ministry of Defense, which lay diagonally across Morandé Street from the Moneda Palace. Under questioning Rocha was said to have implicated Lt. Col. Roberto Souper, his regimental commander, although other reporters claim Souper was not party to the plot. In any case, the army's generals decided to relieve Souper of his command and so informed him. Before the ceremony of relief could take place, however, Souper and his fellow officers at the regiment decided to act.[69]

Shortly after 8:30 on the morning of 29 June three combat groups of tanks and armored cars, with about one hundred troops, left their barracks and made for the center of the city. The revolt had its comic aspects: the column obeyed all the traffic lights and at least one tank stopped to fill up at a commercial gas station.[70] At about 8:55 the attack started. The insurgents successfully assaulted the Ministry of Defense and freed Rocha. They also surrounded the Moneda Palace, firing in all directions, but did not succeed in overwhelming the palace guard of carabineros.[71]

President Allende was not in the Moneda but at his Tomás Moro residence. He went on the air over Radio Corporación, calling on the workers of the industrial belts to mobilize. He said: "I call upon the people to take over the industries, all the firms, to be alert, to pour into the center of the city, but not to become victims; the people should come out into the streets, but not to be machine-gunned; do it with prudence, using whatever resources may be at hand. If the hour comes, the people will have arms."[72] As he had done at other times, the president blew a strangely ambiguous trumpet call.

General Prats was in touch with the president as soon as he learned of the uprising and pledged his loyalty and support, as did the other service chiefs. Prats and his senior generals then fanned out to key military installations across the capital in order to prevent other units from adhering to the uprising. By 9:45 A.M. Prats was at the Noncommissioned Officers' School—a suspect institution commanded by Col. Julio Canessa, who had been a suspect in the incipient coup attempt of March 1972. Pinochet went to the Buin Regiment, headed by a colonel believed to be a "constitutionalist." Another senior general, Oscar Bonilla Bradanovic, went to the Second Armored Regiment to convince those still in barracks to put down their arms. After visiting several units, Prats went to the scene of battle at the Moneda. Submachine gun in hand, striding up and down the square with no protection from rebel bullets, he demanded that one tank after another surrender. He quelled the insurrection, mostly by the force of his authority. It was a dramatic and impressive performance, and the last of the rebels surrendered at about 11:30 in the morning. Twenty-two persons, mostly civilian passersby, were reportedly killed.[73]

If the tancazo caught the Chilean government by surprise, it caught me in the same condition. My wife and I were in Portillo, having taken that Friday to go skiing. An instructor slid up in some agitation, at about 9 A.M., with his transistor radio at his ear. My wife listened beside him to the crackle of gunfire coming over the radio waves as I made for Santiago. In the city center I walked the last several blocks to the embassy offices, past barricades and debris, hearing the sniper fire and smelling the acrid odor of tear gas. Clouds of smoke and fumes billowed through the streets.

Late in the afternoon Pablo Rodríguez, the head of Patria y Libertad, Benjamín Matte, head of the National Society of Agriculture and until then a "closet" member of Patria y Libertad, and three other leaders of the movement received asylum in the Ecuadoran Embassy, acknowledging that they had tried to overthrow the government "together with a heroic unit of our army." They complained of the lack of support from other units which "had previously manifested their support."[74]

Workers from the industrial belts did not march to the center of the city in response to the president's appeal. The ambiguity of the president's call may have been the reason; possibly the workers had not done the planning necessary for so decisive a maneuver. Maybe they felt more confident on their own turf and hestitated to face the army's tanks; perhaps the UP leadership failed to mobilize them in time. Whatever the reason, the workers did not march.

Instead, the workers seized factories. The number of companies reported taken over by the government nearly doubled, rising from 282 to 526.[75] The Central Workers' Confederation and the Communist party collaborated in the factory seizures to a degree previously unseen, and for three reasons. First, the Communist party's position was shifting as the party began to see that confrontation was inevitable. Second, the Communists wanted to be seen as leading the workers and not following the Left Socialists and the MIR. And third, Allende himself had called for the seizures. This last fact made it difficult for Allende later to undo the occupations. A week after the tancazo, in a talk to some foreign journalists, he spoke of these factories: "I am a supporter of the return of many of them . . . but in a moment in which legality was broken, I told them to do what they did."[76] Most of the seized factories remained in workers' hands, and opposition political forces felt confirmed in their belief that Allende was unwilling to curb the lawless destruction of private rights.

After the tancazo the workers extended their control over industrial-belt neighborhoods, organizing sentries and militias, assuming internal police functions, and excluding or impeding the entry of uniformed carabineros. They also expelled Christian Democratic and other opposition-oriented workers from their industrial-belt redoubts.[77] This change in the political organization of the industrial belts complicated matters for the government. Production in the seized factories fell as paramilitary activism interfered with labor discipline. The industrial belts increasingly competed for power with the government rather than following it. Allende appreciated the problem on the day of the tancazo itself, and went on the air that evening to exhort the workers to "organize and create popular power, but not against the government or independent from it. . . ."[78] He was talking into the wind.

The tancazo gravely damaged the military leaders' relations with Allende, and his with them. The president had revealed by his actions on 29 June that his response to military revolt on any scale would be to mobilize illegal paramilitary forces. This he had been threatening all along, of course, but on the twenty-ninth he actually did so. Even worse from the military point of view, the president had acted in this fashion at the very moment when the service commanders were discharging their duty unflinchingly. Allende had gone off half-cocked and had encouraged an illegitimate and unnecessary challenge to the military leaders' "monopoly of force" and their ultimate responsibility for order. This challenge was what the military most feared and most deeply opposed.

It is easy to appreciate emotions on both sides. Allende counted on the workers for support against a military establishment he knew he could not trust. Yet his manifest distrust undermined the military loyalty he had tried so long to foster. Military leaders, who had demonstrated their reliability in full measure, saw themselves repaid in what they regarded as the coin of subversion. Resentments on both sides fed the mutual sense of unease and the fear of ultimate betrayal.

There was a last consequence of the tancazo. The military had noted with great interest the failure of the workers to pour into the center of the city, weapons in hand, to defend their president and the revolution. After the 11 September coup General Yovane of the carabineros commented: "The tancazo was not just a dramatic episode. It was the chance to see how the pro-government elements acted. I carefully noted what they did—the buildings they occupied, the sectors the industrial-belt workers sealed off, the number of people they mobilized, and everything else. The eleventh of September was very easy as a result, because they repeated exactly the same moves."[79] Pinochet also noted the failure of the workers to come to the center of the city. He later said that in July and August he modified his contingency planning accordingly.[80]

The international press drew the same conclusion. David Belnap of the *Los Angeles Times* reported a week after the tancazo, for example, that "Administration spokesmen from Allende downward endlessly brandish admonitions of impending civil war before a citizenry whose vast majority of whatever persuasion not only does not want such a conflict but would not fight if one somehow got started. The public dramatically showed its repugnance for armed conflict during and after the June 29th uprising."[81] Even authors sympathetic to the UP government, like John Dinges and Saul Landau, later noted that the "civilian mobilization" in support of the president, which "the right wing had anticipated, had not occurred."[82] Regardless of one's sympathies, the failure of the workers of the industrial belts to march to the heart of Santiago became a deeply significant political fact.

In conclusion, the tancazo was an insurrection ill-conceived, ill-coordinated, and ill-executed. The intention had even been to abort the plans when they were discovered, and Colonel Souper would doubtless not have launched his quixotic foray at all had his own removal from command not been imminent. The insurrection did not have the backing of the military establishment, nor even the support of flag officers who were already plotting. No general wants to follow a colonel into a revolution, particularly as a victorious colonel's first act will probably be to remove the generals from command.

These considerations expose a larger reality. They help explain why, after Allende was overthrown, the Junta leaders insisted on calling their military action a "pronouncement" rather than a coup. What ultimately happened was no sergeants' revolt. Within the armed services the institutional chain of command was maintained intact, because of the cohesion and discipline of the Chilean armed forces.

Allende had been punctilious in his relations with the military. He had worked very hard at wooing top officers, and he had never made the Frei administration's mistake of whittling away officers' pay and perquisites. The president vacillated, however, both before the tancazo and after it. He never quite decided whether he would put his money on the loyalty of the military or purge those he distrusted. Total faith and reliance might have inspired greater fidelity in the hearts of honorable officers and might have avoided the provocation of Allende's call on the workers to begin the seizure of power. A purge and promotion of favorites might have garnered supporters among the generals, or at least protected the disintegrating authority of the loyal service chiefs. By vacillating, the president harvested the disadvantages of both trust and mistrust, and ultimately the whole military institution would move against him, essentially undivided.

# Chapter 8

# The July–August Crisis

THE two-month period that followed the tancazo was a time of unbroken political, economic, and military crisis. The revolving door of Allende's cabinet whirled ever faster. Several eleventh-hour attempts were made to negotiate agreement between the government and the Christian Democrats. The truckers went back on strike, and their allies of October 1972 joined them. The effects were both economically and politically catastrophic. A rolling institutional crisis raged through the three military services, ultimately resulting in the decapitation of each of them.[1]

The tancazo precipitated a cabinet reshuffle, and that government lasted five weeks. The 9 August cabinet lasted less than three weeks. The 28 August cabinet served three days before the month ended—and ten days after that.

## The Formation and Time of the 5 July Cabinet

By the end of June 1973—even without the tancazo—it had become necessary for Allende to form a new government. His cabinet of March 1973 was falling apart. Four cabinet ministers had been

dismissed by the Congress or were in various stages of impeachment. The Senate had dismissed the Communist labor minister,
Luis Figueroa, and the Christian Left mining minister, Sergio Bitar
Chacra, on charges of having precipitated the copper strike at El
Teniente. The Communist economy minister, Orlando Millas, had
been impeached for a second time, for alleged discrimination in the
distribution of food through the JAPs. The Socialist interior minister and vice president, Gerardo Espinoza Carrillo, was the object of
impeachment charges for violating university autonomy in a police
raid on 19 June against the University of Chile's TV Channel 6 (the
opposition-controlled university station set up after the leftists had
seized the regular one). These four proceedings were the largest
number in the history of UP rule; only Tohá, del Canto, and Millas
had earlier been impeached by the Congress.[2]

The tancazo insurrection had intervened on 29 June, momentar-
ily pushing the cabinet crisis aside. Even before the gunsmoke had
cleared, however, Allende was asking the Congress to authorize a
State of Siege. That initiative reopened the question of ministerial
responsibility, as a State of Siege would place extraordinary powers in the hands of cabinet ministers. The Christian Democrats
answered Allende on Saturday, 30 June; they would support congressional authorization of a State of Siege if the president would
agree to appoint a military cabinet—to guarantee that siege powers
would not be used for partisan ends.[3] So the issue of military participation in the government was renewed.

What were the country's military leaders doing? A group of air
force generals assembled in General Ruiz's office at the Defense
Ministry on the day of the tancazo, according to Arturo Fontaine's
account. Ruiz was soon summoned to the Moneda by the president,
where he appeared with the other commanders-in-chief in a public
balcony scene. Meanwhile the generals talked on in the Defense
Ministry. Ruiz, accompanied by Admiral Montero, returned at
about 10 P.M. The generals told Ruiz that they had found the display of military solidarity with Allende on the balcony "humiliating."

Montero went up to his office but soon reappeared to say that
some admirals had assembled and wanted to talk to their air force
colleagues. Half-a-dozen generals went up and conferred with the

admirals, discussing Prats's support of Allende and the disunity in the armed forces. Virtually round-the-clock consultations and meetings continued the next day, the thirtieth.[4]

According to other reports, the Council of Army Generals also met on Friday afternoon, 29 June, and again on Saturday. Prats attended briefly but soon withdrew. There is some indication that part of the meeting was a rump session, with neither Prats nor Pinochet present.[5]

The result of these meetings was the creation of a joint committee of fifteen officers, with the commander-in-chief and four senior flag officers representing each military service.[6] A meeting of this committee was set for 6:30 P.M. on the same day, Saturday. Learning of it, Allende summoned the three commanders-in-chief to his Tomás Moro residence at 6 P.M., hoping to preempt the committee session. The other generals and admirals decided to await the commanders' return, however, and the meeting finally started at about 10 P.M.

As both a navy representative and head of the National Defense General Staff, Admiral Carvajal opened the discussion, saying that improved interservice coordination was imperative. As Fontaine relates, Pinochet suggested that political questions be laid aside, although the country's economic predicament clearly had to be addressed. He obviously was trying to walk a narrow line between loyalty to Prats and responsiveness to the assembled officers' convictions. The committee reacted that the crisis was both political and economic, and discussion of only one aspect was impossible. Ruiz and Montero reported that they had told Allende that the institutional loyalty of the armed forces had just been manifested *in spite of* the services' reservations about UP policy. Prats, noting the danger of civil war, urged that a bloodbath be avoided; Ruiz said he would step aside rather than lead a coup d'etat. Prats asserted that the opposition bore much of the blame for the economic situation, because the Congress had blocked necessary financing for the recent nationwide salary readjustments. The generals and admirals demurred. After talking through much of the night, the committee members agreed to draft a memorandum to the president on Monday, making policy recommendations for overcoming the national crisis. They believed Allende wanted to bring some officers back into his cabinet, and the memorandum would lay down their conditions.

The memorandum of the committee of fifteen was completed on

Monday, 2 July, largely on the basis of air force and navy suggestions. Its 29 points were an effort to redirect government policy into
"constitutional channels." Substantive proposals included respect
for the prerogatives of the judiciary, the comptroller, and the Congress; promulgation of the Three Areas constitutional reform; the
curbing of illegal factory and land occupations; the suppression of
illegal armed groups; the enforcement of court decisions; and the
cessation of musical chairs when a cabinet officer was impeached—the "castling" of ministerial chessmen. Ruiz and Montero objected to this last point, saying that such a demand would
infringe on presidential prerogatives. That point and one other
were dropped.[7] In the meantime the generals and admirals continued to meet. Reportedly, their antipathy to political "games"
was expressed with great depth of feeling, and the idea of military
intervention was whispered, although most subsequent reports—
even from some leftists—indicate that these ideas were still nebu-
lous.[8]

Fontaine describes how Ruiz and Montero then took their copies
of the committee's memorandum to the Moneda, expecting to meet
Prats there so all three could deliver it to the president. They found
Allende, Defense Minister Tohá, and Prats already closeted. Allende, forewarned and shaking with indignation, admitted the air
force and navy commanders-in-chief to his office. The memorandum was then presented. In the ensuing discussion Tohá mentioned that he never would have accepted the defense portfolio in
1972 if he had realized the depth of the services' antipathy to
"castling." His statement disturbed Ruiz and Montero greatly, as it
revealed that Prats not only had unilaterally showed Allende and
Tohá the memorandum but had also discussed points that had been
cut from it.[9]

By Tuesday, 3 July, the cabinet negotiations between Allende
and the military leaders had failed. On that day the president announced that he would form an all-civilian cabinet.[10] The positions
on both sides were clear. Even before the cabinet crisis that played
itself out between 29 June and 3 July, the president had wanted
generals and admirals in his cabinet—but essentially on the terms
under which they had served after the 1972 truckers' strike. He did
not want a dominant contingent of military ministers, backed up by
military undersecretaries and officers in subordinate posts. He
would not accept military determination of policy. In fact, the

president never made a substantive response to the policy memorandum presented to him in the first days of July.[11]

The view of the military leaders was also clear, although their position of formal subordination restricted their ability to make demands. Even before the Alejandrina Cox incident on 27 June, Prats had tried to convince the army generals' council to rejoin the government without extensive policy conditions, but he had been voted down by eighteen to six.[12] As neither Allende nor the military chiefs obtained their terms, there was no deal.

The cabinet that emerged on 5 July was much like its predecessor. Carlos Briones Olivos, an old-line Socialist and close friend of the president's, was named minister of interior and vice president. Briones enjoyed the respect and goodwill of opposition leaders—and the considerable ill will of Carlos Altamirano. José Tohá was dropped from defense, and he temporarily receded to a less active role in UP affairs. Clodomiro Almeyda was brought back into the government to take Tohá's place at defense, which cut short Almeyda's assignment to straighten out domestic policy and curb the left extremists in the Socialist party. Millas stepped out of the government, and his fellow Communist, José Cademártori Invernizzi, took over at the Ministry of Economy. The venerable Radical, Edgardo Enríquez Froedden, became minister of education. His sons, Miguel and Edgardo, led the MIR, but that did not mean that their father shared their extremism. Letelier remained foreign minister, a position he had held since May, when Almeyda had been shifted over to domestic party work.[13]

These changes portended no new policy line nor image of unity. It was a patched-together cabinet, a touch more moderate in its personalities than the outgoing lineup but not different enough to change expectations. The polemical, extremist fringe was not eliminated from the councils of government, and incompatible points of view meshed no better than before. The only aspect of the new cabinet that was truly significant was the absence of the military leadership.

Consultations within the military establishment continued. The committee of fifteen frequently met at the National Defense General Staff headquarters or the Navy General Staff offices in Santiago.

The commanders-in-chief were sometimes present, sometimes not.[14]

The Army General Staff, under Pinochet's direction, further developed the emergency plans that had been drafted in April 1972 and successively redrafted. With a "cover" designation (labeled "Internal Security War Game"), a new draft was made on 4 July 1973, and the transition from a "defensive" contingency plan to a "defensive-offensive" one was unmistakable. According to Pinochet's later account, he decided on the fourth "to prepare air-mobile units to be moved by helicopter, for use in urban combat." The events of the tancazo morning guided his thinking. Pinochet, according to Fontaine, turned to Brig. Gen. Hermán Brady, at the Academy of War, to develop this urban plan for Santiago, with provisions for neutralizing the encampments and shantytowns, for preparing photographs of leftist leaders and groups, and for studies of the city's communications, public services, and terrain. Responding to some disparaging comments Allende reportedly had made on 29 June about the army's "little tanks," Pinochet ordered the rehabilitation of some old Sherman tanks.[15]

In the course of July additional operational plans were drawn up, fleshing out the overall arrangements. For example, Col. Julio Polloni, director of army intelligence, asked Sergio Moller, an electronic engineer at the Military Polytechnic Academy, to prepare a plan to control and link the country's radio stations "in case of emergency." The navy had been working since 1970 on acquiring secure communications. This net tied together "green phones" on all bases and ships. Fontaine describes how the three military services worked out parallel operational plans, with Capt. Ramón Aragay heading the navy effort and Col. Francisco Herrera carrying out the air force project. Apparently Vice Admiral Carvajal managed to get Prats to approve and sign the army's plan, in spite of his known misgivings. It is not certain whether Prats failed to grasp the full import of what was going on, or whether Carvajal convinced him that such precautions were necessary for antisubversive purposes.[16]

On 17 July two incidents reminded Chileans that extremists of both sides were traveling on parallel tracks. The publicity mouthpiece for the MIR, *Punto Final*, called for the "dictatorship of the people." On the same day Roberto Thieme, acting head of Patria y

Libertad, called on the radio for a "total armed offensive" in a broadcast-and-run transmission.[17] Neither event was of great importance, neither appeal met with mass response, and neither statement reflected a decisive change in the orientation of these extremist groups. But the two calls did signify that the MIR and Patria y Libertad were still augmenting each other's efforts in furtherance of the same goal—the destruction of the last, fragile chance for Chilean institutional democracy.

Perhaps these extremist calls to action did not matter, but eight days later, on 25 July, the truckers announced a new stoppage, and that *did* matter. Trucker resentment had been growing for months as, the truckers believed, the authorities reneged on promises made in 1972 to address the problem of trucking rates, the lack of spare parts, and the unavailability of new trucks.[18] It is difficult to be sure how political motives also influenced the truckers' decision. The truckers' president, León Vilarín, was active in the guild movement, which was increasingly orienting itself toward fomenting a coup. On the other hand, the truckers' economic grievances were genuine, as was their visceral understanding that the UP government would destroy their independent way of life as soon as it felt strong enough to do so. No UP leadership could leave this kind of economic power indefinitely in the hands of such intractable entrepreneurs. Each side understood the other's imperatives and knew that peaceful coexistence between government and truckers was impossible.

The subsecretary for transportation in the Ministry of Public Works and Transportation, Jaime Faivovich, was appointed intervenor and was told to force a settlement. Truckers gathered once again in fields outside the cities or hid their trucks in the woods. Shortages of gasoline, kerosene, food, and cooking oil soon afflicted the Chilean people. As before, *miguelitos*, bent nails, were strewn far and wide on streets and highways.

If anything differed from October 1972, it was the immediacy of the government's effort to break the strike. Faivovich led carabineros to the truck parks, where confrontations occurred and forcible seizures were made. Violence ensued; hundreds of truckers and carabineros were injured in clashes. About one thousand of the truckers' 50,000 vehicles were requisitioned during the first several days. Many of these trucks were put back into service, with pro-UP workers driving them. Striking truckers pelted scab drivers with rocks and occasionally shot at them. Most strikers soon removed and hid vital parts of their truck engines. Efforts were also made to sabotage rail transport, and several railway bridges were dynamited. Probably militants of Patria y Libertad were at least as active as truckers in carrying out these last acts.[19]

For those who know the outcome, there was a sense of inevitability in the strikers' ultimate triumph, but things were not so clear at the time. The government did not lose every battle, and the forces of the left often successfully rode shotgun as convoys of goods moved across the countryside. There were days when it looked as if the government might seize enough trucks to prevail. Faivovich came close to breaking the strike and was poisonously detested by anti-UP Chileans as a result. He did not succeed, however, and the government's efforts began to lose momentum after about ten days. Apparently, Allende was not prepared for even bloodier battles at the truck parks, and it would have come to that.

On 27 July a peculiar incident involving the Chilean Navy agitated Santiago. President Allende's naval aide, Arturo Araya Peters, was gunned down in the early hours of the morning on the balcony of his house. He had had an automatic weapon in his hand, and the opposition press soon began to allege, scurrilously perhaps, that a member of the Cuban Embassy had been in the street below and that the imbroglio was over a woman. Some even suggested that the woman was Allende's daughter and that Araya had been cuckolding her husband, Luis Fernández Oña of the Cuban Embassy.[20]

Government leaders responded by charging Patria y Libertad with complicity in the shooting. Their rationale was that rightists were trying to remove Araya because he had been an effective link between the president and the navy. The Communist party head, Luis Corvalán, declared that opposition sectors "that seek the overthrow of the government" had killed the president's naval aide.[21]

Reacting to the government's charges, the acting head of Patria y Libertad, Roberto Thieme, furiously denied that his organization had been involved in Araya's death and offered to surrender to the navy in order to prove his movement's innocence. This offer was close to the last thing the admirals would have wanted to cope with, but—fortunately for them—nothing came of Thieme's grandstanding.[22]

The plot, from the opposition's point of view, thickened when Castro's vice prime minister, Carlos Rafael Rodríguez, turned up in Santiago on 30 July accompanied by the Cuban secret police chief, Manuel Piñeiro Losada. The Cuban visit triggered a call for a congressional investigation. The suspicion was that Rodríguez and Piñeiro had come to advise the government on ways to defang the political and military opposition. After five days in Santiago the Cuban visitors departed—after making some private recommendations to Allende which subsequently proved to have been along the lines the opposition feared. The official explanation of the Cubans' mission, consultations over an upcoming international nonaligned conference, convinced no one.[23]

In the meantime, with the encouragement of Cardinal Silva, Allende had renewed his effort to negotiate with the Christian Democrats. On 27 July Allende proposed new talks to Patricio Aylwin, who had by then succeeded to the presidency of the CD party. Senator Aylwin was from the party's center, close to Frei, and a great gentleman.

The two delegations began their talks on the thirtieth. The next day the Christian Democrats presented a letter with five points as a basis of settlement: reestablishment of constitutional norms; promulgation of the Three Areas amendment to regulate expropriation policy, plus Senator Moreno's companion amendment on agricultural expropriation rules; the return to their owners of factories seized during and in the wake of the tancazo; intensified efforts to disarm civilians; and the appointment of military representatives to the cabinet to guarantee the first four points.[24] The similarity of these points to the armed services' memorandum presented a month earlier was not coincidental. The generals and the opposition politicians knew what the crucial issues were and consulted closely in mid-1973.

Allende, as before, did not oppose military participation in the cabinet. He still wanted to incorporate a few key generals and admirals, preferably the commanders-in-chief themselves. Allende's position on the Christian Democrats' policy demands was that "study commissions" should be established so that the two sides could work toward a reconciliation of views. The Christian Democrats correctly interpreted this position as a delaying tactic, and on 3 August they declared the talks ended.[25]

The private microbus and taxi owners joined the striking truckers on the day the talks ended, and the pattern of October 1972 began to repeat itself. Associations of professional people followed soon thereafter, although their adherence was intermittent during August.[26]

Developments in two of the armed services soon agitated the scene still more. On 4 August units of the Chilean Air Force carried out a search for arms at a wool-processing plant in Punta Arenas, and a worker was shot and killed. Leftist congressional and trade union leaders almost immediately demanded the removal of Brig. Gen. Manuel Torres de la Cruz, who was both governor and army commander in the extreme south of Chile. Feisty and strong-willed, Torres de la Cruz was a particular target of the leftists, but the general flew up to Santiago and won Prats's somewhat reluctant support. Rumors flew in Santiago that Allende would nonetheless force out Torres de la Cruz and a half dozen other generals and admirals, but the president did not do so.[27]

Two air force generals did lose their jobs. On 6 August 1973 Allende retired Lt. Gen. Germán Stuardo, second in seniority in the air force, and Lt. Gen. Agustín Rodríguez Pulgar, fourth in seniority. Air force officers suspected that Allende was preparing the way to get rid of air force commander-in-chief Ruiz and wanted to open the line of succession to Lt. Gen. Gabriel van Schouwen, who was fifth in seniority and thought to favor Unidad Popular (perhaps in part because his nephew was a leader of the MIR). It was also reported that the recent Cuban visitors, Rodríguez and Piñeiro, had put Allende up to firing the two generals.[28]

Relations between Allende and General Ruiz received an added setback when Ruiz appeared on a popular TV program, "The Ad Lib Hour," and hardly concealed his resentment at the forced retirements in the air force. Prats later described Ruiz's public conduct as a "striptease," as the veils that concealed Ruiz's disaffection successively fell away. Allende's dissatisfaction with air force leaderhip, meanwhile, was aggravated by his belief that the air force was overassiduous in searching leftist strongholds for weapons.[29]

On 7 August the office of the commander-in-chief of the navy announced the discovery of a mutinous plot that was supposed to have been executed on the eleventh in Valparaíso and Talcahuano, the naval base outside Concepción. Twenty-three sailors were arrested. The navy soon accused Altamirano, MAPU deputy Oscar

Garretón, and MIR secretary general Miguel Enríquez with being
involved. In Valparaíso, it was reported, small cells of sailors on
board the cruiser *Almirante Latorre* and the destroyer *Blanco En-
calada* were conspiring to murder their officers and to bombard
marine and navy barracks near the Naval Academy.[30]

General Prats commented on the navy plot in his diary entry of 7
August. He speculated that anti-UP people, or perhaps naval intelligence, had trapped Altamirano and Garretón and had induced
them to believe that an antigovernment coup was being prepared,
and that the senator and the deputy had foolishly allowed themselves to become implicated in the sailors' counterplot. According
to Prats, the leftist politicians' action had opened the way for coup-
minded admirals to discredit Admiral Montero, who was still loyal
to Allende. Prats concluded that Montero was being held virtually
a prisoner and noted gloomily that the politicians' folly had permitted coup-minded admirals to gauge loyalties and political orientation of noncommissioned officers. He concluded that the
position of the "constitutionalists" in the navy had suffered a rude
blow.[31]

Allende continued to want military officers in the cabinet, but
only on his own terms. He publicly ruled out military participation
on 3 August but almost immediately began pressuring the commanders-in-chief to accept ministerial portfolios. On Monday the
sixth Allende met with the three service chiefs and indicated he
was disposed to accept most of the policies they wanted in return
for their entry into a cabinet of national security. Whether Allende
was prepared to make a hard commitment in this regard, and stick
to it, was problematical. Fontaine describes what happened next.
In discussions after meeting with the president, Prats said he was
prepared to accept; Montero vacillated; and Ruiz was opposed. The
Army Council of Generals met and voted against Prats entering the
cabinet. Prats said that three generals—Urbina, Pickering, and
Bonilla—should go to the president and tell him the council's decision to his face.[32]

The three generals did call on Allende the same day. They told
the president that the army most particularly could not accept a
renewed appointment of Prats as minister of the interior and vice
president, because such an appointment would tear the army apart.
According to a postcoup interview with Brig. Gen. Sergio Arellano,

the president responded: "Gentlemen, if you take this position, it means that we shall find ourselves on opposite sides of the barricades."[33]

Allende met with the three service chiefs again later in the day, reiterating his willingness to accept most of the military's policy requests. Ruiz was alone in resisting cabinet office, as Prats was representing the army at this meeting and following his own convictions in supporting the president. Ruiz explained to his generals the next day how difficult it would be for him to continue holding out in isolation, and in the end all the commanders-in-chief agreed to serve.[34]

The six weeks between the tancazo and the military's entry into the government might be regarded as the first phase of the final crisis. The indicators of national health were turning downward. The chances of political accommodation seemed at a dead end, and the strikes were worsening the country's economic plight. The killing of Araya, the "mutinous plot" on the coast, and the forced retirement of the air force generals, with the prospect of more dismissals, threatened to end the modus vivendi with the armed services' leadership which was reflected in the Statute of Democratic Guarantees. In his adversity the president had turned once again, as he had in late 1972, to military representation in the cabinet and the hope that the commanders-in-chief could restore political confidence, economic normality, and a measure of domestic tranquillity to the Chilean nation.

### The Military Back in the Government

On 9 August the president announced his new cabinet. Prats was named minister of defense—which met the generals' minimum condition that he not be appointed minister of interor and vice president. According to Prats's diary entry, defense was the post he had wanted. Navy commander-in-chief Montero was appointed minister of finance, a key post but an incongruous assignment for the old sailor. Air force commander-in-chief Ruiz was named minister of public works and transport, acquiring the difficult and distasteful responsibility of finding a way to end the truckers' strike. The director general of the carabineros, Gen. José María Sepúlveda Galindo, was named to the relatively unimportant portfolio of lands and colonization. At Altamirano's insistence, Allende's old Socialist friend Carlos Briones was dismissed as minister of interior, and Orlando Letelier, vacating foreign affairs, was named in his place. Almeyda vacated defense in favor of Prats and moved back to foreign affairs.[35]

Prats called the new cabinet "the last chance for Chile." He went on in his diary: "The task is great. The truckers' strike continues, as does that of the owners and the professionals' guilds; terrorism is spreading; the crisis in the navy weighs on all the armed forces and on the carabineros; the dialogue between the government and the Christian Democratic party has, for the moment, failed. The country is tired."

If November 1972 had repeated itself, the entry of the armed forces into the government would have produced a quick turnaround. It did not. In the first place, the situation in the country was worse than in 1972, when upcoming elections had provided an avenue of hope. In August 1973 there was only the continuing winter of Chile's frustration. Allende wanted to call his famous plebiscite in order to change the psychological atmosphere to a more hopeful and future-oriented one. UP party chiefs, particularly Altamirano, knew Allende would lose a plebiscite and kept dissuading him. All Altamirano proposed, however, was domestic violence and possible civil war.

César Ruiz, as minister of public works and transport, was cast in the role Carlos Prats had played in November 1972. There were those in Santiago who said pointedly that Ruiz was no Prats in terms of loyalty to constitutionalism and force of personality. It was also true that Ruiz had considerable sympathy for the truckers and did not want to go down in Chilean history as the man who betrayed them. Prats wrote in his diary on 10 August:

> I am concerned at the incomprehensible attitude of General César Ruiz Danyau, minister of public works, who seems more a spokesman of the strikers than the representative of the government. If the problem preventing resolution of the conflict is Jaime Faivovich's continuance in office as subsecretary of transport, then Ruiz should replace him and energetically assume the responsibility personally of obliging the truckers to return to work.

On the day after the new cabinet was sworn in, Jaime Faivovich and five hundred Chilean police advanced on a truckers' park near

Santiago in an attempt to requisition a thousand additional trucks. They managed to move three trucks from the compound before the operation was temporarily suspended to avoid further bloodshed and violence.

Allende and his ministers then gave the truckers a 48-hour ultimatum: return to work by the twelfth or face arrest and the forcible seizure of vehicles. Prats saw the difficulty: "I told the president I agreed with the ultimatum to the truckers, but always on the indispensable condition of every ultimatum—that when the time runs out, the corresponding measures are taken against those who do not comply, without any vacillation, with the greatest energy, and without retreat. The president said he agreed. Would that it were so!" On the twelfth the president declared a state of emergency in all the provinces of the country, with military commanders in charge, but he did not resort to mass arrests and wholesale seizures. On the thirteenth Prats wrote in his diary: "As I feared, the vacillations came."

The next day the president's confidential advisor, Joan E. Garcés, wrote Allende a private letter that was discovered after the coup. He had seen the problem as clearly as Prats had: "A military-civilian cabinet created with sufficent authority to give the striking truckers 48 hours to return to work cannot give the painful impression of letting the designated time pass and not doing anything. If this is a political error for any government, it is much more so if the armed forces are directly in the ultimatum. . . ." The declaration of a state of emergency only worsened the problem, Garcés wrote, as it put the armed forces in a good position to suppress the militant workers who were emerging as the UP government's last defense. He noted that the workers found themselves "disconcerted and uncertain."[36]

In the meantime the plotting went on. Air force general Gustavo Leigh had lunched with navy captain Arturo Troncoso when he had gone to Valparaíso at the end of July as part of President Allende's delegation at Captain Araya's funeral. Out of that meeting, according to Fontaine, came interservice efforts to ensure that the navy's marines would be available to protect and defend the air force's planes. Shortly thereafter the air force's Hawker Hunters were redeployed from Los Cerrillos, where they were vulnerable to leftist attack, to Punta Arenas, Puerto Montt, Antofagasta, and Concepción.[37]

After the coup General Arellano described an ongoing series of meetings in Santiago:

> The secret meetings were initiated in the house of Jorge Gamboa, a lawyer [and cousin of Arellano's wife]. . . . We went in two autos, not more than a dozen of us. Gustavo Leigh drove one car and I drove the other. . . . We drove a block apart. We returned at two or three in the morning. Only once did patrols surprise us to check licenses, but there were no apparent repercussions. Among those who participated in these meetings were people like Generals . . . Javier Palacios, Sergio Nuño, Arturo Viveros, Francisco Herrera, Nicanor Díaz, and myself, and Admirals Patricio Carvajal and Ismael Huerta, representing Admiral Merino.[38]

It was a strange time. All the Chilean generals and admirals knew they faced a choice. They could not stand on a safe shore, as there was none, nor find refuge in the swamp of indecision. They could, with Prats, march on to a lonely destination called honor; or they could step down, in their gleaming uniforms and brightly polished boots, and wade through dark waters toward what they might hope was higher ground, and a destination called power. A few followed Prats, but not many.

A series of episodes involving the U.S. Embassy blipped across the Santiago political screen in mid-August. First, the Socialist newspaper *Ultima Hora* suggested on 13 August that the U.S. Embassy, at my personal direction, had financed the 1972 truckers' strike, was financing the new wave of strikes then in progress, and was supporting Patria y Libertad's criminal hit squads. These accusations were untrue.[39] Former minister of interior Hernán del Canto published a signed article in the same edition of *Ultima Hora* defending the Cuban Embassy in Santiago, then under attack in connection with the shooting of Araya and the Rodríguez-Piñeiro visit. Del Canto suggested that the CIA and the U.S. Embassy were instigating congressional attacks against the Cubans, repeating an accusation printed in the communist newspaper, *El Siglo*, ten days previously.[40] The next day, the fourteenth, *Ultima Hora* published a list of seven U.S. Embassy officers who allegedly were CIA agents. The names were taken from the East Berlin publication *Who's Who in the CIA*, misspellings and all, and included people who had been transferred from Santiago before my arrival almost two years previously.

The following day "bombs" were discovered in the gardens of three embassy officials. U.S. correspondents in Santiago—and later Henry Kissinger in his memoirs—speculated that the episodes were the beginning of a campaign against the U.S. Mission.[41]

While Allende often used a touch of the "foreign-devil" theme in his speeches, I doubt that the speculation about a basic shift in strategy was on the mark. The incidents took place on the very eve of José Tohá's departure for Washington to negotiate on copper compensation and other important issues. Allende and Almeyda cared about these talks, and it would not have made sense for the president to have launched an anti-American campaign at that particular moment.

The *Ultima Hora* attacks were, moreover, clearly reacting to the opposition's agitation for an investigation of the Cuban Embassy's activities. The newspaper was an Altamirano-wing Socialist mouthpiece, in spite of Almeyda's and Tohá's history of partial ownership in it. *Ultima Hora*'s editors often embarrassed Allende with ill-coordinated sallies, and there was every reason to believe that the attack on the U.S. Embassy was a foray of this sort.

Lastly, the "bombs" in the embassy gardens were dummies, pieces of pipe filled with sand. In considerable likelihood, they were planted by extreme rightists, or possibly the MIR. Allende himself had warned me a couple of months earlier of a report he had received that Patria y Libertad militants were planning to kidnap me. While Allende's motives for his "warning" were suspect,[42] the idea of staging a kidnapping to trigger a coup lingered in the minds of rightists and leftists alike.

The episodes in mid-August highlighted a more general phenomenon that characterized the U.S. Embassy's experience. If anything was surprising during those last months, it was how little—not how much—Allende's government harried the U.S. Embassy. We were left alone, and embassy officers were working as they would elsewhere in the West. Part of the reason was that the country was, as already noted, a free society until the very end. Also, Allende and his colleagues did want to maintain a tolerable relationship with the United States. We at the embassy made an effort to keep a low profile, which probably helped. Chileans were bound up in domestic politics and internecine struggles, and they hardly had time for concerted harassment of an American Embassy that did not force itself upon them as an immediate challenge or a large-scale public embarrassment. Deliberate Chilean official bullying was largely absent.

Investigaciones, the investigative service and the closest thing the Chileans had to secret police, was quite ineffective. Its operatives were certainly not always benign, as brutality and torture were practiced in its cellars, but the organization was consumed by personal squabbles between the Socialists and the Communists.

Having served in several Communist-ruled countries, I was interested in the contrast between Eastern Europe and Chile. In Eastern Europe everything happens according to plan—including anti-U.S. demonstrations, surveillance, and harassment. In contrast, leftist actions in Chile were unpredictable and less organized, even on the part of private citizens. While leftists in other free-world countries feel a compulsion to harry their own governments through demonstrations against the Americans, this need was absent in Chile as the leftists were themselves in power. The majority of Chileans, who were in opposition to the UP government, tended to be sympathetic to the United States—as is also true in Eastern Europe, where repressed citizens display what friendly feeling toward America they dare. The U.S. official community in Chile benefited on all counts, receiving considerable official tolerance and little harassment and also enjoying considerable popular goodwill.

It thus appears that Allende did not turn to a deliberate and concerted "foreign-diversion" strategy in mid-August 1973 to save his regime. The incidents involving the U.S. Embassy were hardly more than foam blowing across the storming billows of Chilean political life.

Chile's political storms were getting rougher. President Allende's address to the nation on the evening of 13 August was blacked out. The culprit had apparently been Patria y Libertad, which had successfully dynamited a key power-line tower outside the city.[43]

The government declared a second ultimatum for the truckers to return to work, with a deadline of 16 August; this demand was also ignored. The next day the government announced that it would commence requisitioning trucks on a mass basis and simultaneously relieved Faivovich of his responsibilities in connection with the truckers' strike, appointing Brig. Gen. Hermán Brady in

his place. Brady had already been acting in this capacity in Santiago province since the twelfth and had proved no more anxious to
provoke a bloody showdown than Ruiz had been in early August.
On the same day the Christian Democrats declared their support of
the truckers.[44] Prats commented in his diary:

> Frei has spoken publicly once again, and has done so in order to
> attack the government at a raw nerve—the armed forces. He says
> the government is "using" us to save itself from "disaster."
> I think the problem is different. It is that we are not being used
> to our full capacity, or in accordance with the appropriate forms
> of military procedure. The vacillation of the government has
> translated itself into posturing on the part of the armed forces in
> front of the truckers; and that is fatal.[45]

In anticipation of the fourth round of U.S.–Chilean copper
nationalization talks, I had been asked to assess the current atmosphere in Chile. On the fifteenth I reported to Washington that
Allende was clearly losing ground on both the left and the right and
that his 9 August cabinet would last at most a few weeks. A source
very close to Allende had just told me that the president had broken down emotionally in meetings on several occasions during the
two or three weeks past. The death from cancer of his beloved sister
Inés had affected him deeply, and his sister Laura was said to have
health problems, perhaps also cancer. The rumored implication of
his Cuban son-in-law in Araya's death also bothered him.

In my telegram I mentioned the conviction of the military that an
accommodation with the United States was the only way out of
Chile's trouble. The ultra leftists were, however, furiously attacking
the presence of service chiefs in the government. Altamirano believed, as always, that compromise with the political reactionaries
and the military would bring the revolution to disaster. For their
part, the Christian Democrats were uncomfortable about a military
presence in the cabinet which provided the semblance of policy
accommodation without its substance. The military knew that they
were being used. I concluded that the generals and admirals probably figured that they had only two, three, or four weeks to make up
their minds about what to do. In the meantime the officers were
continuing to talk, plan, worry, and squirm. The choice they faced
was not between acting and waiting; it was to act or to be the object
of a purge, and the leaders of Unidad Popular were coming to see

their choice as a purge of the military or acceptance of the consequences of failing to defang them.

U.S. correspondents in Santiago and their editors in the United States were also aware that the body politic was sliding toward the destruction of the Chilean Way. As early as 25 June the *New York Times* had been editorializing: "Genuine dialogue with his opponents . . . would inevitably mean that Dr. Allende would have to forego much of the pervasive socialist program . . . but it might save Chile from either a military takeover or the civil war that the President rightly fears."[46] On 18 August the same newspaper editorialized: "Now the country is again lurching toward chaos, with the statesmanship, restraint and goodwill necessary for averting civil war not yet in evidence."[47] On 27 August the *Washington Star-News* commented: "The worsening violence . . . and the hardening attitudes . . . raise new doubt that the Marxist government of Salvador Allende can long continue on the path it mapped out. . . . Allende . . . should understand by now that he cannot make willing marchers-to-socialism of enough Chileans to complete the trip. . . . If he tries, Chilean democracy could perish along the way."[48]

On Friday 17 August, the air force entered an institutional crisis that almost became a coup attempt. Obviously at odds with government policy on the truckers' strike, Ruiz called on the president that morning and tried to resign as minister of public works and transport and return to his duties as commander-in-chief of the air force. Allende told Ruiz that he would have to resign as head of the air force if he wished to leave the cabinet and gave him until 5 P.M. to think things over. Outraged pilots at El Bosque, the main air base in Santiago area, commenced a kind of "sit-in." Other air force officers appealed to army commander-in-chief Prats to declare solidarity with Ruiz, but Prats refused to do so. Before the end of the day Prats was comparing the situation to the tancazo. The crisis went on through the night and into the next day.[49]

On Saturday morning, Allende offered Ruiz's job to his deputy, Gen. Gustavo Leigh Guzmán, knowing that Leigh would be acceptable to the air force. Leigh declined, saying he was not a politician, and offered to retire. Allende also sounded out General van Schouwen, who also demurred. The officers corps of the air force was becoming ever more restive. As Jonathan Kandell later reported, jet aircraft streaked out of Santiago to fly to Concepción, apparently preparing to come northward again in a combat role for a coup. In the meantime Ruiz and Leigh went out together to El Bosque and talked with the officers at the air base. Ruiz agreed to step down in favor of Leigh, and open mutiny was averted. At 2 P.M. Leigh informed Allende that he was prepared to accept appointment as commander-in-chief, but he proposed a colleague, Brig. Gen. Humberto Magliocchetti Barahona, for the ministerial portfolio.[50]

Late Saturday the president announced that Ruiz had resigned his cabinet post, to be replaced by Magliocchetti, that Faivovich—already relieved of his responsibility to deal with the truckers—was also dismissed as subsecretary, to be replaced by General Brady, and that Ruiz had laid down his command, to be replaced by Leigh. The air force change-of-command ceremony did not materialize, however, and Ruiz went on "The Ad Lib Hour" in the evening of Sunday the nineteenth and explained his position quite candidly. Gremialist leader Jaime Guzmán commented pithily on the inappropriateness of a president dismissing a commander-in-chief for trying to withdraw from a political responsibility.[51]

The twentieth was another agitated day in the air force, with rumors flying and Ruiz and Leigh returning to El Bosque. Reportedly Ruiz met with 120 air force officers at the base at noon and changed his position, asserting that he would resist forced retirement. In the meantime Allende and several other high government officials had flown to Chillán to commemorate the anniversary of the birth of Bernardo O'Higgins. A kind of incipient coup attempt, or "emergency in the air force" as Prats described it, occurred while Allende was on the trip. Allegedly, air force officers tried to enlist the support of several army regiments in Santiago, the junior officers' school, and naval forces in Valparaíso. That afternoon Air Force wives demonstrated in support of Ruiz, but Prats threatened as minister of defense to assume personal command of the air force. Finally Ruiz yielded, and at 7 P.M. that evening the change-of-command ceremony was carried out. The first of the armed services had been decapitated.[52]

The result, according to Prats, was that a "sluggish, ambitious, mediocre coup plotter has been replaced with another coup plotter, who is intelligent, astute, and ten times more ambitious." Leigh, moreover, had succeeded in obtaining the arrangement Ruiz had asked for in the first place: the air force commander-in-chief being relieved of the ministerial job. Ruiz was bitter about Allende's willingness to concede to Leigh what he was unwilling to give Ruiz.[53]

Allende's determination had apparently faltered between his dismissal of Ruiz and naming of Leigh because of the intervening development: the air force's threat of an uprising. Had Allende appointed a more compliant officer than Leigh, he might have faced a full-blown coup attempt. Such, at least, may have been the president's calculation. Allende did not lack courage; but his instinct was to manage today's problem even at the cost of tomorrow's trouble. With Leigh, that cost was high.

Meanwhile the truckers' strike was continuing. The lines of people waiting to buy at shops were getting longer, and supplies were more often running out before the long-suffering standees could make their way to the head of the queues. Gone was the spring weather of October 1972. It was winter, and the cold from lack of fuel bit sharply. Strike-breaking UP truck drivers were hard pressed to maintain even minimal supplies for industry and the people's essential needs. The shortage of fertilizer for the coming spring planting caused much worry in the countryside. About half of the country's medical doctors were either on strike by 19 August, or declaring flash 24- or 48-hour stoppages. While the doctors explained their strikes on the basis of professional grievances, their true motivations were largely political.

On the nineteenth seventy trucks were burned in a truck park in Puente Alto, fifteen miles south of Santiago, in the course of a government attempt to requisition the vehicles. Two days later the shopkeepers, the airline pilots, the engineers, technical and professional people, and some Christian Democratic–led unions went on strike, some for 48 hours and some joining the truckers in an indefinite walkout.[54]

On 21 August, the second great institutional crisis in the armed forces came to a head. As so often in modern Chilean history, it was the women who triggered it—although their husbands had clearly instigated the action of some of them. A group of several hundred army wives, including the wives of some generals, gathererd outside Prats's house in the afternoon. Prats was at home with a heavy cold. The women shouted "Maricón!" ("Homosexual!") and they threw corn on the sidewalk ("Chicken!"). Youths of the opposition parties and of Patria y Libertad accompanied them and allegedly roughed up passersby and smashed the windows of parked cars. Minister of Interior Orlando Letelier was with Prats and called the carabineros, who ultimately broke up the demonstration with tear gas.[55] According to Letelier, General Prats, "his cheeks burning red, stood rigidly throughout the ordeal." Letelier's account continues: "Later, Prats sat erect in his living room chair, his ironed Prussian-style tunic with polished epaulets tailored to fit his middle-aged body. 'I never thought,' he said . . . 'that generals and colonels whom I have known since childhood would hide behind the skirts of their wives. I am sad for Chile because I have seen not only treason but a kind of cowardice that I did not conceive as possible.' "[56]

Gen. Oscar Bonilla came to see Prats after the women had been dispersed. Bonilla, according to a diary entry Prats wrote that night, said: "I think you have to go, and I intend to present this question at tomorrow's meeting of the Council of Generals. You are leading the army to compromise itself in favor of Marxism." Prats shot back: "You mean commit itself to the Constitution!"[57]

The president also came by early that evening. He and Prats agreed that Prats would send General Urbina to the president's house at 11 P.M. "to adopt measures in light of the indication that a coup d'etat was in progress." Pinochet and Urbina came by Prats's house before Urbina was to go to Tomás Moro. Apparently Urbina had talked with the president, perhaps by phone. Prats ordered Pinochet and Urbina to go to the president's house together, by then in the early morning of Wednesday, the twenty-second.[58]

Pinochet informed the president that the meeting of the Council of Generals had been called off, or at least suspended for the moment. Pinochet sought to reassure the president of the army's continuing loyalty, as well as of his own.[59]

Before going to bed Prats recorded his sentiments about the day's events. He asked himself: "What should I have done? Give the generals the pleasure of seeing me descend to bicker with their wives? Confront them, those who sent their wives to lead the demonstration? One thing is clear. Unity in the army will not be possible if I remain in the army together with the generals who sent their wives to the door of my house, the house of the commander-in-chief."

Prats went to his office the next morning. According to Prats, all the generals came by, one by one, first to Pinochet and then to Prats, and declared their loyalty to Prats as their commander-in-chief. After the generals' visits Pinochet commented to Prats: "The army, as a single man, stands with you. We only have to worry about Bonilla and the little group around him who are conspiring with Frei."[60]

Notwithstanding Pinochet's assurance to the president, the Council of Generals convened that afternoon, 22 August. The generals voted 12 to 6 against Prats.[61] It is not clear whether the generals had been dissembling, hedging their bets, in their professions of loyalty in the morning or whether some wave of anti-UP, anti-Prats sentiment swept over them in the intervening hours. Probably both things were true. Prats told his diary that night: "In the afternoon came the dramatic meeting in which the same men who had sworn loyalty to me in the morning knifed me in the back. I informed the president at the Moneda: 'Mr. President, I have been left in a minority in the corps of generals.' The generals are very, very disturbed. Their spirit of discipline and their loyalty to the Constitution have been undermined."[62]

After the meeting of the generals' council two among the six pro-Prats generals, Mario Sepúlveda Squella and Guillermo Pickering Vásquez, told Prats that they had decided to retire, as they were clearly at odds with most of their colleagues.[63] Prats also decided to resign. He wrote in his diary on Wednesday night: "Only one road remains to me, to resign. It is the best and supreme service I can render to my country's armed forces. I do not wish to be either the motive or the pretext for the holocaust."[64]

His "irrevocable" letter of resignation was published on the twenty-third. The next day Pinochet was elevated to commander-in-chief, but he did not assume a ministerial portfolio. On the same day navy commander-in-chief Montero quietly returned to his navy office and duties, leaving the Ministry of Finance for others to cope with. He had also submitted his resignation as commander-in-chief of the navy on that same day, but Allende had declined it.[65]

On the day of Prats's humiliation by the generals' council, 22 August, the Chamber of Deputies had passed a resolution declaring the Allende government outside the law and the Constitution. This declaration, reminiscent of congressional action in 1891 that ended in President Balmaceda's suicide, was the culmination of several earlier pronouncements. The most significant had been the Chilean

Supreme Court's pronouncement on government illegalities of 26 May 1973, and its second such declaration a month later; the comptroller general's refusal on 2 July 1973 to register President Allende's partial veto of the Three Areas amendment; and the joint condemnation of governmental lawlessness by the presidents of the Chilean Senate and Chamber of Deputies of 8 July 1973.

In May the governor of O'Higgins province had directed the carabineros to disregard court instructions to clear a building of illegal occupiers. In the unanimous view of the Supreme Court, expressed in its letter of 26 May to the president, this executive-branch defiance of judicial orders was producing a "peremptory or imminent breakdown of juridical legality in the country." Allende replied on 12 June with a general indictment of the higher courts, accusing them of failing "to understand the process of transformation" through which the country was passing, and on the twenty-first he publicly asserted that "the judicial branch must realize that it cannot . . . apply laws dating back a century and reflecting another reality, because the course of history cannot be stopped by outmoded codes."[66]

The Supreme Court, outraged, sent a second letter to the president. The justices denounced a "rebellion" of the administrative branch against the rule of law and complained that the president, who was supposed to provide the highest guarantee of the judicial institution's ability to function, was siding with partisan militants who were in contempt of it.

The comptroller general's letter of 2 July rejected the president's claim that he could promulgate a constitutional amendment while vetoing clauses he did not like. In the inflamed political atmosphere Comptroller General Humeres's action was interpreted as adherence to the Supreme Court's pronouncement of the previous week. Actually, Humeres was quite circumspect in his formulation, and his expressed intent was narrow and specific.

Six days after the comptroller general's letter the Christian Democratic presidents of the two chambers of Congress, Eduardo Frei and Luis Pareto, issued a joint declaration calling for the reestablishment of "legality" in the country. The declaration demanded the promulgation of the Three Areas amendment, a crackdown on "parallel" armies, an end to illegal occupations of factories, and a more vigorous search for arms.

The Chamber's culminating resolution of 22 August passed by 81 votes to 45. The Allende government, it said, was seeking to assume total power. Listing violations of congressional prerogatives, the powers of the Supreme Court, and the functions of the comptroller general, it said the rights of citizens had been violated and freedom of the press had been curtailed. It charged that university autonomy had been breached; the right of assembly had been curtailed; freedom of education had been attacked; property rights had been assaulted; persons illegally arrested had been tortured; opposition trade unions had been denied their rights and workers had been denied the benefits of wage settlements; state farming had been forced on rural workers contrary to the agricultural reform law; and the right of emigration had been curtailed through illegally imposed restrictions. The resolution went on to denounce the establishment of illegal organizations, under official protection, designed to create People's Power outside the law and ultimately to create a totalitarian dictatorship. Lastly, it decried the misuse of the armed forces to accomplish partisan and improper policy objectives.

In its operational paragraphs the resolution called on the president and the military officers in the cabinet, in light of their oath to the Constitution and laws, to put an immediate end to illegalities and to redirect the government's actions into legal and constitutional channels. Should military cabinet officers not do so, the resolution stated, they would gravely compromise the national and professional character of their services, directly violate the Constitution, and damage the prestige of their institutions.

The resolution did not invite military intervention, although the military later used it to justify their action. It was an indictment of the legitimacy of the Allende government. An unbridgeable chasm now lay between government and opposition.

### Allende's Last Cabinet

By 24 August it was clear that Allende's second cabinet since the tancazo was in dissolution. No commander-in-chief remained in the government. General Magliocchetti, not Leigh, was minister of public works and transport, and Prats and Montero were gone. Other ministers were covering for them, wearing two hats until the president decided what to do. Allende announced a new cabinet on the twenty-eighth.

Allende's eighth cabinet had one portfolio for each service. Allende was able, once again, to override Altamirano's objections on one side and the reluctance of the military on the other. It had not been easy. In fact, the announcement of the new cabinet slipped a day while the military argued among themselves over a possible refusal to participate.[67] Allende had had to resist additional pressure from CD president Patricio Aylwin, who had called publicly on the twenty-fifth for at least six military ministers, additional military undersecretaries, and still more military agency heads, all of them appointed to guarantee a return to legality—what came to be known as Aylwin's demand for a "white coup."[68]

Rear Adm. Daniel Arellano took Montero's place at Finance; army brigadier general Rolando González assumed the mining portfolio; Magliocchetti remained at public works and transport; and Carabinero chief Sepúlveda remained at lands and colonization. Among the civilians, Letelier moved over to defense. To the further annoyance of Altamirano and his left-wing Socialists, Allende reappointed Briones to the Ministry of Interior and the Vice Presidency. Almeyda remained at foreign affairs. José Tohá's brother Jaime became minister of agriculture, and the Communist José Cademártori continued to run economy.[69] The formation of Allende's new cabinet, far from being a cause for hope, confirmed the continuing impasse.

The military had pressed Allende hard to try again for an understanding with the Christian Democrats. They had reassured him, in the delicate way such things are done, that such an agreement, including a settlement of the strikes, could forestall a coup. Other powerful leaders were also pressing for talks, most notably the Catholic primate.[70]

I had come to admire Cardinal Silva and I maintained informal contact with him. Dressed in black suit and clerical collar, he was hardly distinguishable from the parish priests he led and served. He was a progressive, deeply committed to the underprivileged of his land, and indefatigable in his efforts to find a constitutional solution to Chile's agony.

In the latter days of August the cardinal offered his good offices and his archbishop's palace as a site for a last-ditch attempt to bridge the abyss between government and opposition.

After a private meeting between the president and Aylwin at the archbishop's palace, Allende designated Interior Minister Briones to continue the discussions. "Informal" talks started on the twenty-eighth. Apparently Briones, at Allende's behest, asked for a draft of an amendment Aylwin had tentatively offered which would protect the president from impeachment. The Christian Democrats, for their part, wanted concrete governmental action without delay to promulgate the Three Areas amendment, and to "restore legal and constitutional normalcy," particularly with respect to El Teniente copper workers, who had not gotten their jobs back, and Channel 9, the University of Chile's TV station under leftist occupation. They also talked about ways to end the truckers' strike.[71]

In the "informal" Aylwin-Briones talks Unidad Popular perceived an effort by the Christian Democrats to seize control of governmental policy. In reality, government by loophole and fait accompli had become so much a part of the UP program that a return to "legality" would have required a virtual counterrevolution. This Allende was understandably unwilling to concede.

The Christian Democrats perceived the talks as yet another demonstration of Allende's famous *muñeca*, his "flexible wrist." He was prepared to talk, to clarify, to hint at real concessions, and to show beguiling willingness to compromise. If he was really prepared to promulgate the Three Areas bill, however, why did he not do so? Each side was accurate in its assessment of the other's position. As a result the talks went nowhere.

By the time the cabinet of 28 August was sworn in, moreover, the truckers' strike had entered its thirty-third day. It had already lasted a week longer than the October 1972 strike, and the economic damage even then exceeded the earlier toll. Shortages were more acute, more railroad bridges had been dynamited, more train tracks had been torn up, and more scabs had been shot at.[72] The strike of private microbus and taxi owners was entering its twenty-fifth day, and doctors, dentists, nurses, auxiliary medical personnel, and some postal workers struck indefinitely on the twenty-eighth. The shopkeepers also closed down their stores that day, although in Santiago compliance with the strike call was incomplete. Solidarity among strikers was higher in the south than in the capital, amounting in some places to an almost total paralysis of commercial activity.[73]

On 29 August Carlos Prats, by then former commander-in-chief of the army, wrote in his diary that he had met with leaders of the Communist party and had shared concerns with them about "open" coup preparations in the armed forces. He wrote that the Communists seemed convinced that a coup was "inevitable."[74] The vignette is revealing. Prats's consultation with the Communists about his own military colleagues' plotting would seem out of keeping with the transcending institutional loyalty that had impelled his resignation six days earlier. Such consultations would have outraged Prats's fellow officers, and one is led to wonder whether bitterness had not been eating away at Prats in the intervening days of retirement. A more generous interpretation would be that Prats was trying to perform one last-ditch service to his president and the constitutional order.

On 28 and 29 August the Council of Army Generals met in around-the-clock sessions to "review the international and national situation" and its possible impact on Chile's security. The council had before it a memorandum prepared by the operations directorate of the army. Excerpts were published after the coup, and the language reflected considerable influence from the guild movement. Government parties were described as rent by division and the opposition parties as swayed by rancor. Workers were not working; farmers were idle; students were not learning; production was declining; no one was investing; foreign debts and domestic inflation were spiraling; and politics dominated everything. Chile was isolating itself from countries that could help it, particularly the United States. The armed forces remained a bastion of moral authority and national support, anti-Marxist and constitutionalist but undermined by subversion and penetration. The memorandum suggested that a military intervention—if one finally came— would have to be maintained until the country could recover, which would require some years.[75] The operations directorate's memorandum was obviously not given to the president, but some document was presented to him.[76] It was no doubt much like the memorandum the military had given Allende after the tancazo.

On the twenty-ninth an incident occurred that further inflamed military emotions. A second lieutenant, Héctor Lacrampette Calderón, was shot and killed during an arms search at the Indugás compressed cooking-gas factory in Santiago. Apparently a Mexican extremist, Jorge Albino Sosa Gil, had been working and agitating at the plant. His involvement in the shooting increased the military's fears that an international extremist network was helping to push

Chile into revolutionary chaos.[77] The day after Lacrampette's death an air force unit searching for arms near Nahuentué in Temuco province occupied a MIR guerrilla camp and detained twenty-eight militants. Air force spokesmen later announced that the camp had contained a hand-grenade factory and that the MIRistas had pressed surrounding farmers into service without compensation, achieving what the officers described as "slavery" through intimidation.[78]

By late August military arms searches were approaching a rate of one a day. Leftists correctly believed that the military were looking more assiduously for leftist-held arms than they were for the rightist groups' weapons. The military, on the other hand, saw the leftists pushing systematically to arm a "parallel army" based in the industrial belts, in the squatter settlements, and in rural paramilitary training centers. Both sides' perceptions were accurate, and each resented what the other was doing.

Other events connected with the navy intensified the military services' agitation. On 27 and 29 August the leftist press carried the text of a Socialist party declaration expressing "fullest solidarity" with navy personnel arrested for alleged mutinous plotting in Valparaíso and Talcahuano and asserting that they had been tortured in detention. Vice Adm. José Merino, head of the first naval district in Valparaíso and number two in the navy, and Rear Adm. Sergio Huidobro, who was head of the Chilean Marines, came up to Santiago to tell Montero that the Council of Navy Commanders had decided he should step down. Reportedly, the two admirals made a midnight visit to the president at his Tomás Moro residence and told Allende that Montero no longer had the navy's confidence. They also reported the results of the navy's investigation into the Valparaíso-Talcahuano affair. Allegedly Allende reacted in anger, saying: "What you discovered at Valparaíso is only one-tenth of what the Communists and the MIRistas are doing. I have declared war on the navy." Allende reportedly cooled down later in the meeting and adopted a more conciliatory stance. That was Allende's way.[79]

On the following day, the thirtieth, Montero drove down to Valparaíso, met with the admirals' council, and agreed to resign. The same day Admiral Merino formally presented a request to the Valparaíso Court of Appeals for the lifting of Altamirano's and Garretón's parliamentary immunity, so they could be held accountable for alleged incitement to mutiny. Merino's request triggered protest demonstrations in Valparaíso on the thirty-first, in the course of which carabineros were fired on from some university buildings. Clashes between leftist and opposition students were finally quelled by police and naval units, but only after battles in the streets.[80]

On the same day Admiral Montero once again put his own incumbency as naval commander-in-chief at the president's disposition. This renewed offer to resign immediately became known, even though its submission was not officially acknowledged for several days. The raging crisis within the navy was soon headlined in the press.[81]

As August ended, the avenues of possible accommodation between Allende and the non-UP power centers in the country were becoming impassable. Resignations, removals, or the discrediting of leadership had ruptured Allende's modus vivendi with all the military services and had undermined his control. For Allende, the result was a substitution of less trustworthy military commanders for the more reliable ones who had previously held office.

The dialogue with the Christian Democrats was over. It had represented the last chance for a political solution to the country's dilemma. The Congress, the Supreme Court, and other spokesmen for institutional legitimacy had repudiated Unidad Popular's claim to legality. Strikes, sabotage, violence, and the struggle over paramilitary forces had brought economic havoc and political hatred. The lights of hope were darkening everywhere.

*Chapter 9*

# Ten Days That Shook Chile

THE first ten days of September 1973 did not have the impact of the days in 1917 that John Reed recorded in *Ten Days that Shook the World*, but they did echo throughout Chile and around the globe. Spring was returning to Santiago. The sun was beginning to warm the Chileans gathering along the banks of the Mapocho and on the walks of the San Cristóbal and Santa Lucía hills. The great, gleaming white Andean curtain was beginning to rise above the haze and smoking chimneys of the city, revealing below the snow-covered peaks a band of brown-green mountain sides. One could look up at skies often blue and no longer leaden-gray.

### Saturday, 1 September: The Admirals and Letelier

The truckers' strike entered its thirty-seventh day. The doctors and other medical workers finished almost a week of continuous striking. The doctors were becoming increasingly uncomfortable, however, in the face of reproaches on moral grounds. The Socialist newspaper *Ultima Hora's* headline proclaimed that six children had died because doctors were not properly manning the country's public clinics, and accusations abounded that they were continuing to examine affluent patients in their private offices while leaving the poor unattended. It was estimated on the first that almost half of the doctors were once again meeting their obligations at public assistance centers and general hospitals.[1]

The shopowners were in a quandary. They had struck for four days the week before but had ended the strike when it became clear that many stores were opening for business, particularly in Santiago's poorer neighborhoods. In the south, where opposition to the government was solid, pressure was on to renew the strike.[2]

In the navy the members of the admirals' council met in the morning with Defense Minister Letelier. They talked about Admiral Montero's letter to the president tendering his resignation and urged that Admiral Merino be appointed in Montero's place. Letelier promised to pass the admirals' views on to the president.[3]

Rightist sabotage continued against railroad lines and trucks carrying fuel and cargo. The leaders of Women's Power, an organization of conservative opposition women activists, called on the president to resign "in order to save the fatherland's destiny."[4] The women rightly sensed that Chile's frail craft was being impelled ever faster toward the rapids ahead.

### Sunday, 2 September: A Day of Strikes and Little Rest

The admirals' council met again with Defense Minister Letelier. At the end of the meeting Admiral Montero confirmed publicly that he had placed his "post as commander-in-chief of the navy at the disposal" of the president.[5]

There were reports of a "military uprising over the weekend" in Cautín province, but the subsecretary of interior, Daniel Vergara, soon asserted that "the reactionary press has magnified and distorted" the facts.[6] Vergara was right; the "military uprising" was a false alarm. Everybody in Santiago was nervous, however, and ready to believe almost any report.

### Monday, 3 September: Allende's Promise to Replace Montero

The government devalued Chile's currency by 40 percent but retained its multitiered system of varying rates for different commodities and purposes. A Chilean buying foreign currency, even with official permission, would have to pay 1300 escudos for a dollar compared with 890 escudos previously.[7] The black market remained the principal recourse of Chileans scrambling to acquire dollars, however, and the change in the official rate caused hardly a ripple in terms of public reaction.

Radomiro Tomic, the Christian Democrats' presidential candidate in 1970, appealed for an accord between the government and his party, warning that, if some measure of agreement could not be achieved, the ensuing crisis would threaten the constitutional order.[8] He was right, of course, but by then he was largely without influence, except as government people might try to exploit his disaffection with his own party's leadership.

The great event of the day was the crisis in the navy. Still outraged by the Valparaíso and Talcahuano plots and determined to get rid of Montero, the admirals were fast becoming the most restive and openly defiant of the service hierarchs. Arriving at the Moneda on Monday morning, President Allende informed waiting reporters that he had declined Admiral Montero's resignation. As Fontaine describes the scene in the Ministry of Defense, Letelier invited Montero and his senior colleagues into his office, told them that he had consulted with the president, and said that Allende disagreed with the admirals' view that Montero should step down. Clearly in bad health, Montero had a fainting spell and was assisted back to his own office. Talking with Huidobro there, he criticized a number of admirals, including Merino, for their ambitions. Huidobro defended Merino, asserting that Merino had defended Montero loyally when Merino and Huidobro had recently spoken with the president.

Fontaine continues his account of Montero's and Huidobro's conversation:

> The dialogue was tense, hard and emotional. Huidobro . . . said he had the duty to say that he could not remain in the navy under such conditions. "Throw me out, admiral—but I shall not go before I know that you are going, too. . . ." And the stout and vigorous Huidobro broke into tears.
>
> Finally, they agreed that Huidobro would go up to Letelier—where Huidobro had been summoned—secure in the knowledge that Montero would step down. In the meantime, they both went up to the hall where the other admirals were meeting.
>
> The commander-in-chief reassumed the chair at the meeting and calmly turned to unrelated institutional matters. As the

meeting was coming to a close, he told the group that Huidobro had been summoned by the minister and would go up and talk with him "no doubt about problems related to the most recent arms searches."

Admiral Huidobro could contain himself no longer. He banged his fist on the table and recounted his previous conversation with Montero. Then Huidobro, the operational commanders, and the chief of the general staff of the navy went up to see the minister.

Letelier listened to them and suggested they talk directly to Allende. Montero, Merino, Weber, Huidobro, and Minister Letelier went to the Moneda.[9]

Two hours later Allende agreed to replace Montero with Merino by Friday the seventh. He also accepted the admirals' demands for legal action against Altamirano—that is, lifting the Socialist secretary general's senatorial immunity—in return for a promise by the navy to investigate the charges that the enlisted men under detention had been tortured. As Fontaine describes it, at the end of the meeting Allende started to shake hands with everybody, but when he came to Huidobro, he clasped his hands behind his back and said: " 'We shall see each other Tuesday of next week—September 11th—as we have many things to talk about.' "[10] None of the foregoing was made public, although it was relayed widely to the naval officer corps and soon leaked. As for the government's public position, Montero announced at the end of the day, after a long meeting with the president and Defense Minister Letelier, that he himself would continue in office.[11]

### Tuesday, 4 September: The Anniversary of Victory

On this, the third anniversary of Salvador Allende's victory at the polls, Unidad Popular assembled a crowd estimated variously as 300,000 to "over a million" in Constitution Square to hear Allende reassert his faith that the truckers would be defeated, that a higher world price for copper would enable the government to import more goods for factories and homes, and that the land would bear greater fruit. In the Congress, he charged, the opposition deputies were solemnly promoting a coup d'etat. He concluded that "we must not lose our composure. We must keep our heads high and our hearts strong."[12]

The strikes went on—truckers, bus and taxi owners, doctors, nurses, pharmacists, dentists, and some pilots. Santiago and Valparaíso continued to feel less of a pinch than the south. On this day the Confederation of Chilean Professionals (CUPROCH), with some 120,000 members, began a nationwide strike of indefinite duration, expressing solidarity with the truckers and demanding that the government change its policies. While a thin veneer of work-related grievances remained part of the rhetoric, the strike was openly political in intent. The merchant marine also began to strike.[13]

In the town of Leyda carabineros exchanged fire with truckers who had barricaded a highway and killed one trucker. In the community of Río Claro a railroad bridge was dynamited, forcing that major rail line out of service for a predicted two weeks to a month.[14]

The Executive Committee of the UP parties formally declared its solidarity with the navy enlisted men charged with plotting in Valparaíso and Talcahuano, and expressed support for Altamirano, Garretón, and Enríquez. This action caused such an uproar that Allende was obliged to disavow it. In the meantime the National party's Radio Agricultura charged that Marxists had tried to seize a navy helicopter near Valparaíso, and MIRistas threatened to dynamite the Valparaíso Palace of Justice, where the lifting of Altamirano's and Garretón's congressional immunity was to be adjudicated.[15]

The national council of the Christian Democratic party resolved to impeach *all* government ministers responsible for the continuing violation of the Constitution and of the laws. Up until this day the Christian Democrats had resisted National party pressure and had shied away from taking this drastic measure. Charges were to be introduced in Congress early in the week of the tenth.[16]

Radio Agricultura announced that Admiral Merino had held a lengthy closed-door session in Valparaíso with all the commanders of the first naval district. In Santiago the air force raided the MADECO and MADEMSA factories and found quite a few weapons. UP spokesmen denounced the raids, expressing particular indignation at the fact that they were carried out just as the workers were marching downtown to the president's anniversary rally.[17] In an ironic remembrance of the past Gen. Roberto Viaux was sent abroad to exile on this day, after having served a prison sentence for plotting to kidnap General Schneider in 1970. The history of Track II still lay hidden in CIA and White House files in Washington. Some two hundred chanting supporters waved small flags and white handkerchiefs as Viaux flew off from Santiago, his destination Asunción, Paraguay.[18]

At the U.S. Embassy activity went on as usual. The handful of U.S. businessmen still in Santiago came to me in the morning for their regularly scheduled monthly meeting. In the evening we had a welcoming reception for my new deputy, Herbert B. Thompson, and his wife, who had arrived in Chile the previous Wednesday. Fewer UP officials than usual attended; no doubt they were otherwise occupied. Looking back, it was surprising that so many of them did come by. Christian Democratic, National party and various Radical senators and deputies appeared in considerable force, and I was interested to note the intensity of the dialogue across the UP-opposition divide.

The original guest list for this party—in honor of a civilian diplomat—had included no Chilean military officers. The embassy attachés and Military Group officers advised me, however, that the omission of Chilean service representatives at that tense moment would be misunderstood, and of course they were right. So we invited a few generals, admirals, colonels, and captains. Most of them came and could be seen conferring gravely with Chilean civilian politicians in various corners of the embassy's reception rooms. The impression may have been only a retrospective one, but the air seemed to be crackling with electricity.

### Wednesday, 5 September: Chile's Shopkeepers Strike

On the fifth Chile's 125,000 shopkeepers went on strike in solidarity with the truckers and other strikers. The backbone of the strike movement during July, August, and September 1973 had been four confederations: the truckers, the private microbus and taxi owners, the professionals, and the shopkeepers. Each had its strengths and weaknesses. The truckers were disciplined and determined, and they had the greatest power to bring the government to its knees. Their vulnerability lay in their trucks, which might be seized by a resolute government prepared to enter the truck parks and pay the price in blood.

The microbus and taxi owners were small entrepreneurs, like the truckers, and also vulnerable to seizure. They were not so united as the truckers, however, and they performed a service less vital to Chile's economic well-being.

The professionals' guild (CUPROCH) was more of an umbrella organization, which relied on constituent professional groups for its clout. Some professions were more important to the life of the country than others. If physicians, druggists, and commercial pilots struck, it made a lot of difference, but (as already described) the doctors and pharamacists were vulnerable to charges that they were disregarding the demands of their humanitarian calling.

The shopkeepers were in a difficult position because a retail grocer in a poor section—serving families who bought food every day—could not easily close his doors. Such small shopkeepers also felt nakedly vulnerable to gangs of thugs who could smash their closed-up shops and destroy their livelihood forever.

The truckers had persevered through six violent, confrontational weeks. The private microbus and taxi owners had held out for five, with lesser discipline and lesser effect. The professionals, after fits and starts, had made their move to strike all out on Tuesday the fourth. Now, on Wednesday, after hesitations of their own, the shopkeepers completed the alignment.[19]

Most of the Chilean people were still going to work. Employees in public administration were generally on the job. The schools were open. Offices of most kinds were populated. Industrial managers and workers were generally functioning, although production was affected by the lack of supplies. Farm workers were tilling the soil—or failing to—as before.

On the fifth, rival groups of women demonstrated in downtown Santiago in a scene reminiscent of the December 1971 march of the empty pots. Middle-class women gathered in front of the Catholic University building banging pots and tin cans, waving white handkerchiefs, and shouting for Allende to resign or kill himself. Estimates of their numbers ranged from 15,000 to 30,000 and more, while one observer characterized it as "the largest assembly of women in Chilean history." In response, pro-Allende women assembled in Constitution Square, in front of the Moneda Palace, and carabinero brigades moved between the two groups, hurling teargas bombs to disperse the rioters. Young men on both sides began throwing stones and erecting barricades, and President Allende assembled his cabinet-level operations committee to deal with the situation. The disorder and violence lasted for more than three hours, and the chief doctor at the Catholic University hospital reported "many wounded," including some suffering from bullet wounds.[20]

Outside Santiago, strikers blocked access to the provincial capital of Los Angeles while the strikers' wives occupied bank offices inside that city. There were disturbances in another provincial capital, Linares. Subsecretary of Interior Vergara later reported that a student was killed in Linares during an attack by National party militants on the UP-dominated investigative police headquarters. In the melee rioters had also attacked the office of the provincial governor and had wounded a carabinero officer when they overturned his car and tried to burn it. Vergara also announced on the sixth that thirty "terrorist attacks" in various parts of the country had erupted during the preceding 24 hours.[21]

On this Wednesday, Pinochet told Letelier that the rehearsal for the grand parade of 19 September would be carried out on the fourteenth, mobilizing only troops from units stationed in Santiago. Pinochet's excuse for not bringing troops into the city for the rehearsal was to save gasoline, but Pinochet said after the coup that his real reason was that he intended to mount a coup on the fourteenth. Concerned that the workers in the industrial belts would trap his units in the center of the city, Pinochet wanted to maintain an outer, concentric ring of forces that could move against the *cordones* from outside Santiago.[22]

It is not clear how candid Pinochet was with his fellow generals, and the apologia written by Pinochet's army collaborators indicates that Pinochet, Carvajal, and other high officers were communicating in delphic phrases.[23] Nevertheless, the idea of using the rehearsal as cover for a coup was talked about among the generals. Prats seems to have gotten wind of these discussions and reported them to the president and Letelier two days later. Allegedly, Prats suggested that Allende remove five or six generals, thereby disrupting the plotters and pushing off their plans.[24]

For the second day in a row Admiral Merino held a lengthy closed-door session in Valparaíso with all the navy commanders in the first naval district. The time of the annual U.S.-Chilean Unitas naval exercises was approaching, and on this day—5 September— the Chilean fleet was due to weigh anchor and sail out toward the U.S. squadron, then off Peru. The Chilean fleet did not sail, and

Defense Minister Orlando Letelier explained publicly on the tenth, when the fleet finally did get under way, that the difficulties had been of a "technical" nature. The real reason, of course, was the crisis raging within the navy.[25]

As was later revealed, General Torres de la Cruz flew up to Santiago from Punta Arenas on this Wednesday to confer about the possibility of a coup with his fellow army generals and key leaders of the other services.

### Thursday, 6 September: Enough Flour for Three or Four Days

In a speech to the Chilean national women's secretariat, Salvador Allende told his listeners that there was enough flour in stock for only three or four days. He laid the blame on difficulties in agricultural production, clogged ports, railway congestion, sabotage of internal transport, and the truckers' strike.[26]

The strikes continued, although many shops in poorer neighborhoods opened. The doctors announced that they would continue striking, but only through Friday. Their decision came after shantytown dwellers, led by a priest, demonstrated in front of the Medical Association headquarters. The priest told reporters that "the poor are dying like dogs," while the rich "get excellent attention" in private clinics. National Electric Company workers decreed a two-day strike at power stations—although emergency crews would maintain a "normal supply of power." CUPROCH claimed new adherents to its strike, including savings and loans people, public works professionals, agricultural and livestock service personnel, and the pilots of the national airline, LAN-Chile.[27]

The National Party leadership called on its militants to desert their jobs "until the president resigns." This call did not have much effect, however, as the constituency of the National party was sparse among workers and others not already striking.[28]

On Thursday evening I flew north from Santiago in order to confer with Henry Kissinger in Washington. That trip engendered considerable subsequent comment about the alleged U.S. role in the Chilean coup, and it will be addressed in chapter 13.

Meanwhile, Chilean army generals met in around-the-clock secret sessions in Santiago. The emerging consensus appears to have been that a coup should be mounted and that the action should start on Monday the tenth.[29] General Torres de la Cruz, who had

strongly supported the idea of a coup in these meetings, flew south
to his command in Punta Arenas late in the day.

Pinochet's orientation toward these talks remains obscure. There
are those who believe that he did not agree at this time to take part
in the coup and told the other generals that he would not do so if
they went ahead with one. The postcoup apologia written by
Pinochet's colleagues, which Pinochet no doubt edited in large part
himself, is notably silent about what went on among the generals
between Thursday and Sunday—a silence all the more interesting
in light of the frenetic consultation and activity that was actually
going on.[30]

Gen. Sergio Arellano recalls that "we realized the end was approaching when Allende announced that there was only bread
enough for three days. I believe that was the decisive moment when
we decided to intervene, although we had not yet set a date."[31] It
should be remembered, of course, that bread is still the staff of life
in Chile. If the president's reference to the shortage was really the
decisive influence on the generals' thinking, the turn of events was
ironic. Allende had been under no compulsion to make the con-
fession and probably did not foresee its impact. The president's
remark about bread was actually an aside in a long and earnest
exhortation to the women of Chile to participate in the betterment
of the country's social and economic life. Allende had gone on to
indulge in a bit of self-congratulation for having solved much of the
immediate bread problem by convincing the Argentinian president
to load 45,000 tons of wheat onto three Chilean ships—in spite of
Argentina's domestic shortages. In his speech Allende had not been
crying out in desperation. Like so many other statesmen dealing
with a press they cannot control, he found that the opposition
media instantly inflated his passing bit of puffery to the magnitude
of shocking and ominous news. The resulting psychological impact
was shattering, both to the generals and to the nation.[32]

It was also on this day, Thursday, that carabinero generals were
said to have entered actively into the interservice discussions about
a possible coup. According to a postcoup interview with General
Yovane, he and General Mendoza had already made private "commitments of honor" to several generals and admirals from other
services in early 1973. By 6 September coup talk was spreading
among the senior carabinero commanders, and Director General
Sepúlveda reportedly was saying that he would have no part in any

coup plotting but would step aside if the military services and his fellow police generals repudiated his loyalist stand.[33]

Yovane describes his meeting on the sixth with Col. Nilo Floody of the Military School:

> Shortly before the 11th of September, then Colonel Floody ex-pressed a desire to talk with me privately. I went to the Military School, in civilian clothes. Greatly to my surprise, when I en-tered the hall, I found about two hundred army officers as-sembled. [This meeting appears to have been called to discuss reports that President Allende intended to retire Generals Palacios, Viveros, and Arellano from active duty.] In his office Nilo Floody told me of his decision to act. In that meeting we talked for the first time in depth about the forces we could count on. It became clear that the army, the air force, and the navy were equally ready.[34]

So far as the air force was concerned, its commander-in-chief, Gus-tavo Leigh, was fully engaged in the interservice discussions. The navy remained in institutional crisis, with Admiral Montero isolated and repudiated by his fellow officers.[35]

### Friday, 7 September: Coup Plotting at White Heat

The strikes continued. A relay tower near Rancagua, south of Santiago, was blown up by right-wing terrorists, severing wireless communications to the southern part of the country and forcing the suspension for a few hours of national television transmissions. Violent clashes occurred in the countryside between striking truck-ers and government supporters moving goods and people in con-voy. Santiago drugstores started a two-day strike.[36]

The president invited Admiral Merino to lunch with him in pri-vate. The two men talked for six tense hours. According to later accounts by the military, Allende reneged on his agreement to ac-cept Montero's resignation on that day and to appoint Merino in his place. Allende attributed his decision to a headline published in *La Tribuna* that morning, which proclaimed: "Today the Ultimatum the Navy Gave the President Runs out!" He reproached Merino for the leak, but Merino answered that the leak must have come from the Moneda. Allende told Merino that, in any case, he could not be put in the position of buckling under insolent public pressure, and he asked the admiral and his navy colleagues for a little more time. Allende allegedly made several efforts to draw Merino into compromising deals. Merino later said he had had to excuse himself twice to phone his colleagues in Valparaíso and reassure them that he was still all right. Otherwise, he believed, there might have been some sort of violent move on the coast. Merino and the president parted without an understanding, and Merino returned to Valparaíso at about midnight.[37] While Merino had not received his expected appointment as commander-in-chief, he was by then the de facto head of the navy. Raúl Montero, the last true loyalist among the three services' commanders-in-chief, was a broken figure.

Allende reportedly had another stormy meeting, with the commanders-in-chief of the army and the air force. Leigh, supported by Pinochet, was said to have described the president to his face as "surrounded by thieves and liars," referring no doubt to politicians like Altamirano and Garretón and intimates like Augusto Olivares Becerra and Régis Debray.[38]

Within the government and Unidad Popular, meetings continued around the clock. On Friday evening UP leaders met to consider Allende's proposal to hold a plebiscite on the president's continuation in office, which would either confirm or repudiate Allende and his program. Altamirano opposed the idea because the government would probably lose, and he advocated the alternative of armed confrontation. The Communists gave Allende qualified support, apparently because a fresh focus on nationwide voting might defuse the crisis and give the government a renewed chance to ameliorate the economic and political situation. Allende decided to speak to the people in a nationwide address on Monday the tenth and formally announce his decision to call the plebiscite.[39]

Discussions continued among representatives of the three services. The admirals still favored a coup on 10 September, as that was the day the Chilean fleet was due to sail from Valparaíso to meet the Unitas task force. The army generals requested a postponement of at least one day to allow officers and troops scheduled to be away over the weekend to return to their bases. Other reports have it that the postponement from the tenth to the eleventh was not agreed to until Saturday or Sunday and that it was caused not by logistics but by Pinochet's own ambivalence about overthrowing the president. General Yovane of the carabineros recalled that it was Sunday the ninth when Admiral Carvajal told him that the coup would be postponed from Monday to Tuesday because, Carvajal said, the forces had to be mobilized in their barracks.[40]

Several postcoup first-person accounts give Friday morning as the time when most of the army generals—but perhaps not Pinochet—reached a consensus on the eleventh as the day to act and resolved to tell the navy that the date should definitely be pushed off from Monday to Tuesday. The admirals then seem to have thought of having the fleet sail out of Valparaíso on the tenth and return the same night under cover of darkness. While the admirals apparently still preferred the tenth, they began working on plans to occupy Valparaíso at 6 A.M. on the eleventh, with the coup starting in Santiago two-and-a-half hours later. Mobilized marines and sailors would be confined to barracks on Monday in Valparaíso. The public explanation would be the danger of riots on Tuesday following the scheduled court action in Valparaíso on Altamirano's and Garretón's parliamentary immunity.[41]

On Friday evening the air force, which had been consistently aggressive in enforcing the arms control law, carried out a search around the great Sumar textile plant on the outskirts of Santiago. Workers offered armed resistance, and a two-hour shoot-out ensued. According to the air force, the troops had originally been searching a private house in the neighborhood. They had found hard hats, steel-tipped lances, plastic bottles for Molotov cocktails, and Socialist propaganda. Sumar workers, they said, opened fire on the searchers, and some five hundred men dressed in dark clothing and sneakers dropped from the walls of surrounding houses and attacked. The air force troops withdrew, taking some twenty-three workers with them under arrest.[42]

### Saturday, 8 September: A Plebiscite on UP Government

The ongoing strikes resulted in longer lines and emptier shelves. Some bakeries ran out of flour for bread. Tensions grew, and rumors abounded. Soldiers of the Tucapel Regiment discovered a "guerrilla training camp" in Cautín province. Allende met all day with representatives of the six parties of Unidad Popular, encountering further resistance to his idea of holding a plebiscite.[43]

The MIRistas and elements of the Socialist party, the MAPU, and the Christian Left held an independent meeting and decided to break with the government and the Central Workers' Confederation (CUT), in order to organize the industrial belts for combat and promote resistance by troops against coup-minded officers. These left extremists denounced the "double-dealing" of the Communist party and of the "reformist" Socialists, most notably Minister of Interior Briones.[44]

There were reports that Pinochet continued to show signs of cold feet. General Arellano recalls that "Saturday was a day of intense agitation in the Ministry of Defense. In all the military institutions, it was a time of great excitement. The Defense General Staff organized inter-service liaison and coordination with the carabineros, through Generals Yovane and Mendoza." Apparently those two carabinero generals were still the only top police commanders on whom the coup planners could count for support.[45]

In Valparaíso the admirals conferred secretly all day and through the night, with some carefully selected navy captains joining the deliberations. Fontaine reports that Admiral Merino had convened a meeting of all naval officers of the rank of lieutenant, senior grade, and above for 11 A.M. Saturday. In clipped tones Merino emphasized the importance of strict obedience to orders and assured his fellow officers that "those who want action will have it." He inveighed against leaks, pointing out the damage done by *La Tribuna*'s story about the navy's ultimatum to Allende.[46]

At 5 P.M. some fifteen of the navy's most senior officers met with Merino at the Academy of War in Valparaíso. Admiral Carvajal had come from Santiago for the meeting. It appears that Admiral Merino made his final decision on this day, the eighth, to carry out Operation Seaweed, the code name for action on the coast. The disastrous encounter with Allende the day before, it was said, weighed heavily on him.[47]

### Sunday, 9 September: The Coup Pact

Sunday was not a day of rest for anybody. The shopowners announced that they would not open their stores until Wednesday. Engineers and lawyers joined the strike movement.[48]

For their part, the Christian Democrats had called provincial leaders from the entire country to a meeting with the party's officers in Santiago. The assemblage proposed that President Allende and the membership of the Congress resign and that a plebiscite and new elections be held.[49]

Orlando Millas, expressing the Communist party's position, called on all democrats, including specifically the Christian Democratic party, to reach an understanding and "minimum consensus" against a fascist coup. It was a conciliatory statement.[50] The secretary general of the Socialist party took a very different position. At a midday party meeting in the Chile Stadium Altamirano harangued the crowd, stating openly that he had indeed met with the sailors involved in the Valparaíso affair. These enlisted men, he explained, had assembled to condemn the subversive plans of their superiors. He went on to say: "I shall be present anytime they invite me in order to denounce actions against the constitutional government." He added that "the Right can only be defeated with the invincible force of the people, enlisted men, noncoms, and officers united with the constituted government."

Altamirano declared himself and the Socialist party against any compromise with the opposition: the Socialist party "has said that there can be no dialogue with terrorists." The Socialists would struggle in combat at the government's side, he said, so the government could carry out its program—the program to create People's Power and give it to the workers and the peasants. He also asserted that "the reactionaries' coup must be stopped by striking back, not by conciliating the forces of sedition. You do not fight insurrection through dialogues, but with the force of the people, their industrial commands, their peasant councils, their organization. Civil war should be combated by the creation of a genuine people's power. . . . In these three years we have aroused a combative force which nothing and nobody can contain."[51]

Allende heard Altamirano's speech at home on his radio. Reportedly, his reaction was: "That madman is sabotaging me."[52]

The president discussed alternative courses of action with various colleagues until about midnight, and his colleagues went on talking in his house until about 2 A.M. Some of Allende's advisers urged him to break openly with Altamirano, even if it meant splitting the Socialist party. There was also some discussion of Allende's resigning, but the president stuck to his resolve to call the not-yet-announced plebiscite.[53]

It is difficult to judge how important Altamirano's speech was in fortifying military determination to go through with the coup. Certainly, the military would not easily have accepted Altamirano's affirmation that he met with the naval "mutineers" and his appeal to the workers to resort to combat. On the other hand, the military's coup plans were already far advanced when Altamirano spoke. His speech may have had its greatest influence on the carabinero generals, most of whom apparently had been prepared to defend the president until they heard Altamirano's call to illegal action.[54]

Early Sunday afternoon I returned to Chile from Washington. Herbert Thompson met me and filled me in on the developing situation as we knew it. I then went home.

A Chilean who had been abroad surfaced Sunday evening. Having returned to the country secretly, Pablo Rodríguez of Patria y Libertad gave an interview in the rural town of Cactín to reporters from the National party's Radio Agricultura. He announced that he was reassuming leadership of his organization and, operating from a secret hiding place, would work to "liberate" Chile.[55]

The generals and admirals were not resting either. According to postcoup accounts, the ninth was the day the decision to mount a coup was sealed. As Fontaine describes events in Valparaíso, the navy chiefs "met Sunday, after attending mass, in the house of Admiral Weber, who expressed doubts about the decision the other services would take." Apparently, the date on which to act was still not settled, and a definitive commitment to go ahead was still lacking. At about midday on Sunday Admiral Merino sent two representatives, Admiral Huidobro and Capt. Ariel González, up the long hill from Valparaíso to Santiago to obtain Pinochet's irrevocable commitment to the coup. According to an anecdote I heard later, the two officers were originally commissioned as oral messengers, without any paper or document to carry with them. When they got to the toll plaza on the expressway, however, they discovered to their consternation that they had failed to bring the small sum in escudos necessary to pay the toll. So they had to return to Valparaíso. Ashamed to confess the problem, they hit on the thought—believing it a good idea in any event—that Admiral Merino should give them a written instrument for Pinochet and Leigh to countersign. At their request, Merino gave the emissaries such a letter on a little piece of lined notepaper, and Huidobro carried it to Pinochet's house that Sunday afternoon.[56] The text was:

Gustavo and Augusto: By my word of honor, D-day will be the eleventh at 6 A.M. If you cannot carry this out with all the forces you command in Santiago, explain on the back. Admiral Huidobro is authorized to negotiate and discuss any aspect. I salute you with hope and understanding. Merino. [And on the back]: Gustavo: this is the last chance. J.T. Augusto: If you do not commit all the force of Santiago from the first moment, we shall not live for the future. Pepe.[57]

Augusto Pinochet was at his house, a birthday party for his younger daughter in progress. Huidobro got hold of Admiral Carvajal, who called Leigh and asked him to meet the navy's representatives at Pinochet's home. In the ensuing talks Pinochet reportedly still leaned to the Independence Day rehearsal, 14 September, as the best time to act. According to Pinochet's later apologia, he came around to the navy's position because of the navy's determination to act, alone if need be, the eleventh and because such a move would be "suicidal" or could result in splitting the army, with some units joining the navy's uprising and some not. The result would be a "bloodier repetition" of the tancazo, and civil war.[58]

It is a tantalizing question whether Pinochet's reservations were simply over the alternative dates or whether he had deeper hesitations about the coup itself. The apologia says Pinochet "thought for a few moments about the import of the navy's acting alone."[59] This description has the air of something more basic than a disagreement over dates. In any case, Pinochet did accede to the timetable Merino was now proposing.

In agreeing to the navy's date, Pinochet observed to Leigh and the navy's emissaries that Altamirano's speech could be cited as a justification for confining troops to barracks in Santiago on Monday night.[60] Leigh signed his name, and the word "Agreed," on the back of Merino's little note. Pinochet then signed his own name and affixed his seal.[61] In this way the decision was made final that the military services would overthrow the president of Chile.

### Monday, 10 September: A Brief Excursion by the Chilean Fleet

Another trucker was shot and killed when a strikebreaking driver tried to ram a roadblock. The doctors extended their walkout. Striking LAN-Chile pilots taxied their planes to the air force sections of various air fields, so that the planes could not be seized and flown by strikebreakers. Most supermarkets, bars, and vegetable stands were closed.[62]

About two hundred women from the opposition gathered in front of the Defense Ministry shouting for the military to seize power. A few blocks away the head of the truckers, León Vilarín, rallied his people in a noisy demonstration.[63]

In government circles it was a day of intense activity. Mrs. Letelier describes her husband's day: "Letelier went to his office. It was his thirteenth day as defense minister. In and around his office men in uniform bowed and greeted him. He had solid information that some of them were plotting, suspected others, and believed that a core of the top brass remained loyal."[64] She continues: "On the morning of September 10th, Letelier received several of Pinochet's orders authorizing military operations under the arms control law. When Letelier confronted him, Pinochet became vague and refused to admit that he had authorized the raids."[65]

Letelier soon went to a two-hour cabinet meeting with the president. According to Isabel Letelier, "the cabinet ministers reported sabotage, violence, army raids against UP villages and factories. . . . Letelier remained optimistic: 'If they don't overthrow us this week, we'll never fall. Everything they have set up is ready to explode now.' The ministers planned countermeasures, relying on the mobilization of workers' defense units [and] using supposedly loyal elements inside the armed forces." Letelier, the president, and several others lunched together and continued talking until about 3 P.M., when Allende sent Letelier back to the Ministry of Defense, instructing him to "make sure the air force is obeying my order to suspend all raids."[66]

On Monday, in the early evening, the Bulgarians held their National Day reception, and I encountered many UP bigwigs there. Even Communist party chief Corvalán was present. It was a strange feeling to be talking normally with these men during that time of palpable crisis. In particular Mario Valenzuela, number three at the Foreign Ministry, expressed the hope that my conversations in Washington might have helped ease the troubles between our countries.

That same evening Letelier gave a press conference in which he reported that the fleet had sailed to the *Unitas* exercise, appealed for respect for the institutional character of the armed forces, and spoke of the need to take measures to avoid civil war. The news of the fleet's sailing had been a relief to Letelier, and also to the president.[67]

After his press conference Letelier went to the president's house at Tomás Moro, where he found Allende's family and a number of the president's intimates assembled at dinner.[68] After the meal Allende and his political advisers continued discussions. The president was making last-minute changes in his speech draft about the plebiscite, but the themes of the speech were still not sharply defined. Sometime during the day just passed, probably at lunchtime, the time of the speech had been pushed off from Monday to noon on Tuesday. Minister of Interior Briones—who had been with the president that evening—later explained that Allende, "overwhelmed by the innumerable problems he had," could not get the speech ready in time.[69] Allende's daughter Isabel said after the coup that her father already knew before midnight that "something extremely serious was being prepared, . . . but he did not imagine that the action could come so quickly."[70]

Late Monday night the communist leaders at party headquarters learned from their people in Valparaíso that the fleet had not sailed north but had returned. The Communists understood the ominous nature of the news, but it is not clear when they informed the president. The Political Committee of the Communist party convened in emergency session.[71]

Pinochet, according to Fontaine's account and Pinochet's post-coup apologia, informed the defense minister at 10:15 A.M., soon after Letelier had arrived in the office, that he, Pinochet, had decided to restrict troops to barracks in anticipation of disturbances connected with Altamirano's speech and the Valparaíso court action. Letelier made a wry comment about the Socialist party chief's conduct but said nothing more.[72]

Later in the morning Pinochet received a group of retired generals. At 12:30 the army commander-in-chief summoned generals Bonilla, Brady, Benavides, Arellano, Palacios, and Colonel Geiger. Some of these officers subsequently lunched together, and air force generals Leigh and Viveros also joined the group. At the prelunch meeting Pinochet took his saber and asked his colleagues to give him their soldier's oath of secrecy. He then described Sunday's coup agreement and made assignments of responsibility for troop command among the officers present.[73]

At 3:30 P.M. General Brady, the Santiago garrison commander, convened a meeting of unit commanders to review dispositions under the "internal security plan" and pass on orders for the confinement of troops to barracks.[74] General Arellano describes his own activities:

> Monday was filled with anxious activity and almost unbroken meetings. In the morning the generals met at the Defense Ministry, and in the afternoon there were final coordination meetings with the air force, the navy, and the carabineros. In that way there was contact with all the commands. We called a meeting of all the troop commanders of the army [no doubt the meeting Brady convened], telling them what was planned for the next day. Naturally, we asked them to observe absolute discretion, because otherwise everything would have been lost. I gave instructions that the Commander of Communications prepare to receive General Pinochet at Peñalolén [the Army Telecommunications School on the outskirts of Santiago, which was to serve as Pinochet's command post], and I advised my officers that they should make sure their families were in safe places. That meeting, like those the other commanders convened, was memorable. Not a fly buzzed. There was a sense of relief from the tension endured over so many months. We all now knew that the decision was made and, most importantly, that the armed forces were locked in a unity of steel, headed by our commanders-in-chief.
>
> The War Academy, at General Pinochet's direction, had worked out an emergency plan (which we always have for catastrophes, subversive situations, and strikes), and there was another such plan worked out at the Staff Office of the army's second division, under Colonel Orlando Ibáñez. These were the basic plans. But the operational orders for September 11 were worked out in my Staff Office that Monday.[75]

There is a discrepancy between Pinochet's and Arellano's accounts. Pinochet leaves the impression that the organization of the coup started after his own secret luncheon session. Arellano makes it clear that planning sessions were going on all morning. What may have happened was that the generals met without Pinochet in the morning, as they had been meeting on previous days. After noon—with Pinochet having told his generals he was committed to the coup—the army chain of command was reasserted at the top.

As already described, Army Intelligence Director Polloni had asked Sergio Moller in July to work out a way of linking the country's radio stations. A key element in this arrangement was a cable

channel between the joint staff headquarters and Radio Agricultura, the National party's station, which was chosen as leading
facility in the integrated network. On the tenth Polloni asked Moller to double this cable link.[76]

At 6:30 P.M. Pinochet called generals Lutz, Baeza, and one other
general into his office and assigned them intelligence and staff
functions.[77] Apparently he also sent a few trusted officers quietly
by plane to the cities of Antofagasta, Iquique, Concepción, and
Valdivia, with final instructions to be delivered at about 6 P.M. on
Monday. Pinochet also had coded messages prepared, to be radioed
to all army garrisons in Chile at 6 A.M. the next morning, ordering
them to occupy provincial governors' offices immediately.[78] It was
later reported that some fifty progovernment military officers were
arrested and detained incommunicado on Monday and in the early
hours of Tuesday. Several flag officers were said to have been
among them, but the operation was carried out with such quiet
efficiency that the government and UP parties apparently did not
learn of it.[79]

Down in Valparaíso, Admiral Merino seized control of the country's principal naval units, arresting Montero some time on Monday and holding him incommunicado. Merino told me several
weeks after the coup that he had hidden the signed pact of 9 September in his shoe and had walked around on it all day long on
Monday. Apparently he carried the note around in his wallet after
the eleventh as a momento.[80] Between 8 and 9 P.M. on Monday
Admiral Merino sent all navy commanders a message directing
them, at 6 A.M. the next morning, to follow the orders of the internal
security plan drawn up in early July.[81]

The fleet, which had sailed that afternoon, ostensibly to rendezvous with the Unitas task force, waited below the horizon and
steamed back into port at about 10 P.M. Admiral Merino recounted
after the coup that he told his wife at about that same hour: "Take
some money and leave the house as soon as you can. Take the
children. I can tell you no more." The money he shoved in her hand
was the equivalent in Chilean currency of about $135.[82]

General Mendoza went to see Admiral Carvajal at National Defense Staff headquarters and gave his and General Yovane's formal
commitment to the coup. The topmost carabinero generals never
did adhere to the plan. Apparently Mendoza signed the Junta's
joint declaration on the seizure of power late that evening.[83]

The events of this chapter end at midnight on Monday, 10 September. They end not because the day ended at midnight for the principal actors in Chile's drama; there was no hour of that night when they were all in their beds. So, like a gothic children's tale, the action stops as the clock strikes twelve, to be resumed in the next chapter, which is devoted to the long day of the coup, 11 September 1973.

## An Added Word about Pinochet

Almost nobody would now be prepared to depict Augusto Pinochet as a constitutional loyalist until shortly before the coup. Such an interpretation does not currently serve Pinochet's interest, and the world's leftists are, of course, unwilling to view Pinochet as anything less than a beast who concealed his traitorous designs during those August and September weeks.[84] But I am not so sure.

What opinions have those on the scene expressed about Pinochet's attitudes? General Prats, describing the crisis leading up to his own resignation as commander-in-chief, records that on 22 August Pinochet said that he had told Allende: "Mr. President, please know that I am ready to give my life in defense of the Constitutional Government of which you are the embodiment."[85] Allende later asked Prats what he thought of Pinochet. Prats replied: "I do not have any reason to advise against naming General Pinochet as commander-in-chief. I am confident that he will know how to support you with the same loyalty I have shown." Prats comments: "It is my conviction that he only climbed aboard the chariot of the coup-makers at the last minute. . . ."[86]

During a phone conversation on 7 September, Pinochet was reported to have reiterated to Allende that the president would always have the general's "unconditional loyalty." Isabel Letelier reported that Pinochet and Orlando Letelier had several conversations after Letelier's appointment as defense minister on 28 August, one in the presence of Allende. "Pinochet assured both men that he was, like his predecessor, loyal to the Constitution and to President Allende." Moreover, it appeared that Pinochet's professions of loyalty were believed.[87] In describing the extended cabinet meeting on 10 September, Orlando Letelier commented that "Pinochet was one of the generals on whom most of the assembled officials counted."[88] Civilian plotters in touch with the military had not believed

Pinochet was committed to a coup until right up to the eleventh itself, as they later indicated.

After the fact Pinochet himself claimed that he had prepared the coup "virtually alone over a long period," taking hardly anyone into his confidence.[89] On another occasion he claimed that he had started "to create the conditions to enable the army to respond to such a necessity" in March 1973 and had "entered into contact with eight generals to accomplish the necessary basic preparations."[90] According to Fontaine, Pinochet said that it was after the tancazo when "the scales fell from his eyes and he saw the road ahead clearly."[91] Fontaine goes on to say that an admiral who worked very closely with Pinochet during the months before the coup found that Pinochet had remained loyal to Prats throughout July and most of August: "He did not accept anything that was insubordinate to his commander-in-chief or disloyal to the chain of command in the army. So long as Prats remained in office, General Pinochet worked with him in disciplined fashion, keeping his concerns and hopes to himself."[92]

It is known that Pinochet was in the minority of six supporting Prats in the Council of Army Generals' meeting of 22 August, when Prats was repudiated.[93] It is notable how unclear the timing of Pinochet's decision to plot Allende's overthrow was, even in his later descriptions of his earlier thinking.

The mark left on Pinochet by his participation in the coup is also difficult to gauge. A few indications suggest that Pinochet might have suffered some inner turmoil. For example, several of the wives of Allende's cabinet ministers talked with Pinochet after the coup, appealing to him on behalf of their husbands. Isabel Letelier is quoted as describing the meeting in the following terms: "Pinochet became quite abusive and shouted at us for about twenty minutes. The veins on his neck swelled, his face alternately turned red and purple. There was obviously guilt and embarrassment which he tried to mask. . . ."[94]

Much earlier, in December 1971, General Pinochet had threatened to start judicial proceedings against *La Tribuna* for "insulting the armed forces" by criticizing them for continuing to support the Allende government. Pinochet had added: "Coups do not occur in Chile."[95] At the time his statement had a ring of conviction.

Several episodes in the days before 11 September indicate that

Pinochet might not have been on the side of the plotters at crucial moments. One intriguing episode, which occurred in the morning of the eleventh, will soon be described. It raises the same question. None of these incidents is conclusive, but, taken together, they are enough to make an observer wonder.

Pinochet was said to be a serious and believing Christian, and I have no basis for denigrating that judgment.[96] I believe one should not let one's disagreement with a person's later public policies become the exclusive measure of his character at an earlier time. Necessity presents hard choices, and who is to say that Pinochet's choice was perforce venal? In contrast, his policies and actions once he acquired supreme power as the head of Chile's government are subject to examination under different standards.

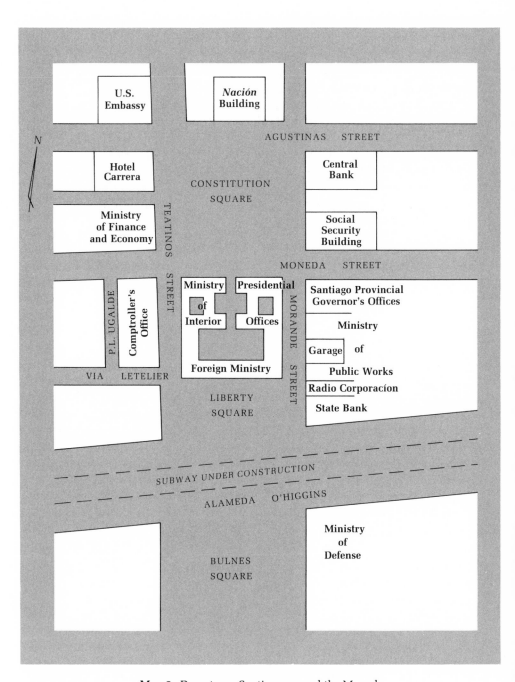

**Map 2.** Downtown Santiago around the Moneda

## Chapter 10

# The Longest Day

ON the night of 10 September the air was dry and crisp in Santiago.[1] Soon what many Chileans were to call "the longest day" began, and on that verge of the Latin American continent it did have the significance of the Normandy landing. The riddle was which side in Chile matched which force on the beaches of France. For some it was a day of national liberation from impending tyranny and a foreign yoke. For others it was the beginning of fascist rule and the end of a shining dream.

**Midnight to 6 A.M.: Things Done and Not Done**

President Allende was still meeting with his intimate advisors at his Tomás Moro residence when René Largo Farías, the head of the Office of Information and Broadcasting (OIR) at the Moneda Palace, phoned with disturbing news. It was twenty-eight minutes after midnight when the call came. Three minutes earlier the provincial governor of Aconcagua province had reported that trucks with soldiers from the Old Guard Regiment in Los Andes and the Yungay Regiment in San Felipe had been observed moving south toward Santiago by night laborers on the highways. Personnel at the air force base in Los Andes were also on the move, and troops were quartered in suspicious locations in Santiago.[2]

A presidential GAP bodyguard had taken the call from the Moneda Palace and had passed the information on to presidential confidant Augusto Olivares, who interrupted the president with the news. Allende directed Defense Minister Letelier to phone Gen. Hermán Brady, the commander of the Santiago garrison, and find out what was happening. Brady told Letelier he knew nothing. Letelier gave Brady fifteen minutes to check and then called again. Brady told the minister that he was taking charge of the situation and that the troops were in barracks. He apparently added that a few reinforcements were being brought into the city to handle any disturbances that might occur.[3]

Allende was at least a bit reassured by the response from Brady, a fellow Mason in whom Allende had special confidence. Neither Allende nor Letelier appears to have taken further substantive action, although Letelier phoned around in an effort to check on the disturbing reports. According to Isabel Letelier's account, Letelier also made several suggestions to the president about ways to deal with the coup threat. Allende liked the one Prats had earlier proposed, which was to force six or seven generals into retirement, thereby disorienting the plotters. Allende reportedly decided that he would inform the Chilean people of the forced retirements in his radio speech at noon.[4] After these discussions Allende went to bed, remarking that the coming day would be long and hard. Briones and Letelier went home. Olivares and Joan Garcés stayed the night at Tomás Moro.[5]

The Communist party's Political Committee, it may be recalled, had convened shortly before midnight on the tenth, when party leaders discovered that the Chilean fleet was back in port. In the very early hours of the eleventh committee members ordered the headline for that morning's edition of *El Siglo* to be changed from "The Plebiscite Will Take Place!" to "Everyone to His Combat Post!" In the front-page article the party directed the "workers of city and countryside" to take combat positions, "ready to repel the rash attempt of the reactionaries who are determined to bring down the Constitutional Government in the course of the next few days." The party also began to round up communist plant managers and transport them to their factories, so they could mobilize the workers of the industrial belts. Lastly, communist leaders began to move to underground locations.[6]

A young Socialist at Radio Corporación reported after the coup that he and his colleagues had been called from another UP radio station with the news that officers were advising their families not to go into the center of the city on the eleventh. Colonel Souper's brother, a militant in Patria y Libertad in Concepción, was also in town and "up to something." The source of the report was a low-ranking officer, and the Socialists tried to check out the information with trusted, senior military officers, including some generals. All their military friends and "great contacts" told them that there was nothing to worry about and that they should go to sleep. At about 2 A.M. they did so.[7]

Back at the Moneda, Largo Farías was still uneasy. At eight minutes before 2 A.M. a call had been received with information that there had been some shooting near the Buin Regiment's barracks in Santiago, apparently directed at a passing vehicle. At 2:30 A.M. Largo Farías shared his concerns with Alfredo Joignant, the director of the investigative police, but Joignant did not give great credence to the reports. Largo Farías left the Moneda to go home at about 2:35 and was made still more uneasy by the unusual level of actvity he observed still going on at the Ministry of Defense, across the square.[8]

Shortly after midnight carabinero generals Mendoza and Yovane went to the School for Noncommissioned Officers of the police forces, apparently the only remaining carabinero unit in Santiago where loyalties were still unclear. The two carabinero generals revealed the coup plan to the school's officers and received their adherence. This school was crucially important, as the Moneda Palace guard was organizationally a part of it.[9]

By his own subsequent account, General Pinochet returned home just in time to allow himself to be observed there when the UP surveillance car, which passed by his house every night, made its customary midnight check. He walked for a few minutes alone on the sidewalk, came home, turned out the lights, and went to bed, but not to sleep.[10]

Down in the navy's Academy of War in Valparaíso, Admiral Merino had coffee with his most intimate collaborators shortly after midnight. The admiral observed that even the sailors, who had been told nothing of the plan of the day, were feeling the tension and sense of anticipation—"like just before the Guadalcanal landing in World War II."[11]

Minister of Interior Briones did not sleep. He telephoned one place after another throughout the country, trying to inform himself of developments. The reports he got seemed neither reassuring enough to put his mind to rest nor alarming enough to confirm his fears.[12] Minister of Defense Letelier arrived home at about 3:00 A.M. Isabel Letelier told authors Dinges and Landau what happened:

> He said goodnight to his bodyguard, smoked a last cigarette— was it his fourth or fifth pack?—and let the reports from intelligence officers about coup plots run through his mind as he undressed.
>
> "How was your meeting?" Isabel murmured as he climbed into bed beside her.
>
> "Excellent. Salvador will announce later today that he will have a referendum. I am certain we will win it, and that will reduce the chances of a coup."
>
> Isabel came fully awake. "We were waiting for the coup," she later explained. "Each day we kind of expected it, so when Orlando told me that plans had been made for the national vote of confidence, we both went to sleep happy."[13]

There is some evidence that the military made arrangements before 2:00 A.M. to have an aircraft ready to fly Allende out of Chile. An emergency staff office manned by professors and students at the Academy of War and the army's general staff office, headed by General Arellano, worked throughout the night, perfecting and clarifying the plans. Arellano went home at 3 A.M. It was also 3 A.M. when a number of the carabinero commanders in Valparaíso reportedly agreed to participate in the coup.[14]

At 4 A.M. someone, presumably a Communist party representative, called or went to the house of Luis Fernández Oña of the Cuban Embassy (Beatriz Allende's husband), with the warning that a coup would break out at 7:45 A.M..[15] I myself was awakened a couple of times during the early morning hours by embassy officers who drove by to bring me ominous reports.

According to subsequent accounts, at 4 A.M. all Chilean Army personnel not already in barracks were ordered to report for action.[16] A military reserve doctor later told my wife that he had been called at 5 A.M. on the eleventh and had been told to be at a local hospital by eight, ready to meet any medical needs that might arise.

General Arellano arose at five, after a fitful hour or two of sleep, and showered and dressed. He then took his wife to the house of some friends, where she might be safer if things went badly, and told his married daughter not to remain in her own home. At five o'clock or shortly thereafter other leaders of the coup were also getting up: Nicanor Díaz of the air force, Javier Palacios of the army, Mendoza and Yovane of the carabineros, and Admiral Merino down at the Academy of War in Valparaíso. Pinochet described afterward how he rose at his usual hour of 5:30 A.M., doing nothing to vary his routine and thereby raise suspicion. He did his setting-up exercises until six o'clock, as always.[17]

In Valparaíso reveille sounded at 5 A.M., at which time sailors and other troops stationed there were mobilized on the pretext of an early-morning arms search. It was only then that most navy officers learned of the plan. Sailors on shipboard were told of it at 5:30 A.M.[18]

At 5:45 A.M., under Admiral Merino's orders, Captain Arturo Troncoso executed "Operation Silence." His men seized the telephone company's Recreo plant and cut all possible telephone lines. One line was retained for the navy's own use, perhaps to talk to Allende. Radio transmitters were confiscated or put out of commission. According to Captain Troncoso, the operaton was carried out by 150 navy men trained as commandos.[19]

What seems notable about the first six hours of the eleventh is how much the leaders of Unidad Popular were in a position to know and how little any of them did. The Communist party was obviously better informed than the president, but the Communists seem to have largely failed to communicate with him or their UP allies and failed to coordinate action. Where were the independent communications facilities of the leftists? Where was their intelligence capability? Where were the leaders and workers of the industrial belts, the leftist settlements and encampments, the paramilitary forces, and the rural guerrilla camps? In the days after the coup the leftists fought with determination and courage, holed up in their redoubts, until they were picked off one by one in one-sided military operations. This same determination might have brought better results for them had they used the first six hours of 11 September more effectively.

Part of the reason so little was done may be found in the bickering, backbiting, and lack of cooperation that were by then endemic within Unidad Popular. Moreover, Unidad Popular's dilemma had not been resolved. The expedients necessary to counter a coup—systematic parallel communications, intelligence, and organization—were the very measures that would have pushed the military to mount one. Allende had never made his choice.

So far as the president and his entourage were concerned, pure exhaustion, physical and psychic, may have been a large part of the problem. There had always been a certain air of improvisation in the way Allende and his colleagues ran things; Régis Debray remarked after the coup that "Allende never planned anything more than forty-eight hours in advance."[20] In the end it seemed as if Allende was living off his nerves and relying on little more than style, personality, and flair. To the luster of Allende's memory, these last qualities never deserted him.

### Six to Seven A.M.: A Bit Late to Post Number One

Down in Valparaíso, sailors, marines, and supporting troops seized the city and the rest of the province, starting their sweeps at about 6 A.M.. Within forty-five minutes or so the occupation was established. Naval units fanned out to the factories, the shantytowns overlooking the port, the workers' districts below, the universities, and government offices. A pro-Allende scholar, Samuel Chavkin, comments: "To everybody's great amazement . . . a fight which had been expected to go on for at least three days had ended within one hour. In the ports of Valparaíso and Viña del Mar the inhabitants had sought refuge in their homes and given up any thought of resistance. All eyes were now turned to the capital city."[21]

There was one radio-telephone in Valparaíso that the navy did not silence. It belonged to the carabineros. Shortly after six o'clock a carabinero officer at the port called headquarters in Santiago, reaching the deputy director general of the national police, Jorge Urrutia. The officer advised Urrutia that the navy had seized Valparaíso and the surrounding area and that trucks with navy troops were moving toward Santiago.[22] General Urrutia telephoned the news to Allende sometime between 6:10 and 6:20 A.M.[23]

Allende ordered one of his GAP bodyguards to wake the other guards "discreetly" and to prepare to defend Tomás Moro. The president then quickly dressed. The sleepy GAP bodyguards, it was said, thought it was all a joke, and a considerable alarm had to be sounded in order to get them up and going. Allende did not wake his wife. He phoned Briones, who later reported that the president had told him: "Very grave events are taking place. I am going to the Moneda." Allende and Olivares then tried to phone the service chiefs, but only the carabinero generals responded with any impression of normality. In his postcoup apologia Pinochet describes how his home phone rang at 6:30A.M. It was the Tomás Moro telephone operator. Pinochet tried to sound sleepy and was told that he would be called again a bit later. He probably did not answer the second call. According to UP accounts, the only senior commander who could be reached was General Brady, who gave the president vague answers.[24]

Allende got through to Isabel Letelier, who answered the phone at about 6:30A.M.. Mrs. Letelier later recounted what happened:

> "It's Salvador," she said [to her husband, who thereupon came to the phone]. Allende, calm, firm, clear, told Orlando, "The navy has revolted. Six truckloads of navy troops are on the way to Santiago from Valparaíso. The Carabineros are the only units that respond. The other commanders in chief don't answer the phone. Pinochet doesn't answer. Find out what you can."
>
> Orlando asked Isabel to call Admiral Montero and General Prats. He would use the other telephone to call Investigaciones . . . and the Ministry of the Interior.
>
> Isabel dialed and waited and waited. No answer at the Prats or Montero houses or offices. Orlando's calls confirmed Allende's reports.
>
> Letelier phoned his own office. To his surprise, Vice Admiral Patricio Carvajal answered.[25]

According to another account, Carvajal then "airily explained that he had arrived at his office early to deal with an inordinate amount of paperwork that had piled up on his desk. And he happened to be walking by Letelier's office, he said, when he heard the phone ring; so he picked it up."[26]

Isabel Letelier continues: "'Your information is wrong, Señor Minister,' Carvajal told Letelier. 'It's some kind of a raid, nothing more. We're trying to get through to Valparaíso now. I'm looking into it.' Letelier phoned Allende. 'Go, Orlando, and take control of the Defense Ministry if you can get there.'"[27]

Professor Enrique Kirberg, a leftist and the rector of a bastion of Unidad Popular in Santiago, the State Technical University, got a call at 6:45 A.M. The university custodian was on the phone, and he informed Kirberg that five men in civilian clothes, armed with machine guns, had overpowered the security guard and smashed the transmitters of the university radio station. "It was a quick, hit-and-run operation, obviously the work of technically trained marauders. . . . As they left, with some of the university night staff screaming and pushing toward them, they fired several rounds to intimidate the few pursuers."[28]

The incident Kirberg relates was part of the same Operation Silence that Merino had been engaged in on the coast. It was later revealed that a contingent of marines had carried out the action. Some of the leftist transmitters in Santiago were silenced by cutting their power. Still others were later physically seized.[29] Unlike the situation in Valparaíso, however, some pro-UP radio stations did stay on the air.

Army troops were on the move. Among their first tasks was a coordinated takeover of electricity, oil, water, gas, telephone, and other means of communication. Ostensible arms searches provided the cover for much of this activity. The objective was not to interrupt service but to safeguard its continuance. Unlike the situation the previous June, when the tancazo left much of Santiago without electricity, public utilities in the capital functioned without interruption on the day of the coup.[30]

Admiral Carvajal was in charge at the Ministry of Defense from 6 A.M. onward. He was "serene, courteous, imperturbable, and in impeccable uniform," as his colleagues described him. Brig. Gen. Sergio Nuño of the army and Brig. Gen. Nicanor Díaz of the air force were with Carvajal at the ministry.[31]

General Arellano came to the army's Second Division headquarters (the Santiago garrison) at 6 A.M. and by 6:30 was holding a meeting of all commanders of units in the "central zone" of the city. General Brady was in command of Santiago operations.[32] Brig. Gen. Raúl César Benavides commanded the "east-southeast zone," which included the industrial belts of Los Cerrillos and Vicuña Mackenna. The core of his force was the Old Guard Regiment of Los Andes, the one that had been reported to Allende shortly after midnight as moving toward Santiago. Colonel Geiger commanded the "northern zone" of the city; Gen. Javier Palacios commanded the reserve troops and, as it turned out, the strike force against the Moneda itself. This strike force consisted of the Second Armored Regiment (of tancazo fame), part of the troops of the Infantry and Noncommissioned Officers' Schools, and elements of the Tacna Regiment.[33] In light of their experience in the tancazo the officers of the Second Armored were initially reluctant to follow Palacios in another uprising. According to Chavkin, "without hesitation, General Palacios climbed up on a tank and shouted to the surprised regiment, 'This is now under my command!' As one man, the regiment fell in behind him."[34]

At 6 A.M. Sergio Moller of the Military Polytechnical Academy started to activate the radio network centered on Radio Agricultura.[35] Generals Mendoza and Yovane arrived at police headquarters in the Norambuena building by 6:45. The plan was that at seven o'clock the two generals would arrest any senior carabinero colleagues who still supported Allende, but a "mysterious" call from Valparaíso had intervened (no doubt the call that had caused Urrutia to alert Allende), and Director General Sepúlveda, Urrutia, and Alvarez, a third senior carabinero commander, had gone off to the Moneda. Mendoza and Yovane took off for the Moneda as well, no doubt to counter the other generals' loyalist efforts.

Mendoza and Yovane soon returned to Norambuena, but there was a further hitch in their plans. The arrangement had been that Carvajal and Pinochet would consult from their command posts, after which a plane would be sent over the city to give the signal to various commanders, including Mendoza and Yovane, to move into action. Mendoza and Yovane waited at carabinero headquarters, but the plane did not appear overhead.[36]

Where was Pinochet? Between 6 and 7 A.M. he deviated little from his normal routine. He bathed, dressed, breakfasted, and left the house sometime between 6:50 and 7:10. He had the army driver take him to his daughter's house and remained there some minutes, looking down at his sleeping grandchilden.[37]

It is difficult to know whether Pinochet was feeling some lingering reluctance to be on the cutting edge of sedition. He had known for at least half an hour before he left his house that Allende was trying desperately to reach him, so the rationale for maintaining a "normal" routine had already been shattered. The hitch in signals that the carabinero generals talked about is also puzzling, as Pinochet was obviously expected to be at his action post and able to consult with Carvajal before 7:40 A.M.—which is the time his post-coup apologia says he arrived.[38] He seems to have been the last of the principal actors to assume his place.

Post Number One, Pinochet's command headquarters, was in the red headquarters building of the Army Telecommunications School at Peñalolén on the outskirts of Santiago. Post Number Two was Leigh's, and the air force commander-in-chief established himself at Group Ten headquarters, located at the Academy of Air War in Las Condes suburb, at 6A.M. At the Ministry of Defense Carvajal coordinated communications among the posts and maintained contact with Admiral Merino in Valparaíso. Short-wave and VHF radio nets were in service, some manned by sympathetic ham-radio operators.[39]

### Seven to Eight A.M.: Why Not to Los Cerrillos?

At 7:10 A.M. Joan Garcés entered President Allende's study at Tomás Moro and found the president still immersed in his frustrating round of telephone calls. The president told Garcés: "The navy has revolted—including the ships *Simpson* and *Latorre*. The naval infantry is coming toward Santiago. The carabineros stand with me. As for the others, I don't know anything. . . ."[40]

The president left his residence between 7:15 and 7:20, traveling at 50 to 60 miles an hour in a motorcade of five bulletproof Fiat-125s, a light truck, and two armored personnel carriers filled with carabineros. Allende, Olivares, and Garcés went in the cars, accompanied by 23 members of the GAP, each armed with an automatic weapon. The group was armed in addition with two machine guns and three bazookas. The presidential party drew up at the main doors of the Moneda between 7:30 and 7:40 A.M. According to military observers, the president grabbed an AK rifle, seated a bullet in the chamber so it was ready to fire, and entered the Moneda. There were police armored personnel carriers drawn up outside the palace, and about three hundred carabineros were on hand. Inside the Moneda the carabinero palace guard appeared alert and ready to protect the president.[41]

Allende, apparently somewhat reassured, met with his GAP guards in the "security room." Then he counted available arms, began to organize the defense of the palace, and continued his efforts to reach key people by phone. He called his wife at Tomás Moro at 7:40, telling her that "the situation has turned serious; the navy has revolted. I shall remain here. You must remain in Tomás Moro." Allende also called Altamirano and CUT leaders Rolando Calderón and Luis Figueroa, urging them to mobilize the workers.[42]

General Brady had apparently been embarrassed by the president's call to him at 6:30 or so. According to subsequent reports, Brady complained to Carvajal at the Ministry of Defense, saying that the president was "bothering" him. Carvajal thereupon amiably ordered that the direct presidential phone line to Brady be cut.[43]

Isabel Letelier subsequently described her husband's movements. Apparently Orlando Letelier left his house at seven or a little after and found his driver, but not his bodyguard, in the street. Dinges and Landau recount what happened:

> Letelier inquired about the absence of his bodyguard. Jiménez, the driver, a giant of a young man, appeared vague and confused. . . .
> As the car drove through the Santiago streets Letelier noticed troops in small patrol-size units. . . . There was no traffic other than army trucks and vehicles. Letelier leaped from his car as it pulled up in front of the Defense Ministry. . . . Troops in battle dress guarded the door. Letelier approached, and the troops pointed automatic weapons at him. "I'm sorry, I have orders that you cannot enter. . . ."
> Then a voice from inside the ministry doors said, "Let the minister come inside." The doors opened. Letelier forced his spine erect, stuck his chin forward, and marched inside with his best military bearing. Just inside the door, "I [Letelier] felt a sharp poke in my back and some ten to twelve men moved to surround me, aiming submachine guns at me. They wore combat uniforms and seemed excited. . . ." [Letelier] was shoved

downstairs in the basement. "They took my tie, my belt, my jacket. They searched me, threw me against the wall."[44]

Foreign Minister Almeyda has also described his experience. Still feeling jet lag from his flight from a nonaligned conference in Algiers the day before, Almeyda was called by the president from Tomás Moro at about 7 A.M. Allende told him about the Valparaíso naval uprising and summoned him to the Moneda. Almeyda took leave of his family and drove to his mother's house for another hasty farewell. "We'd become very realistic . . . so when we said goodbye to each other, we didn't embellish it. . . ."[45]

At 7:20 A.M. the National party's Radio Agricultura broke into its regular programming for a flash: "A few moments ago an unusual police movement was observed. Armed personnel carriers carrying carabineros with revolvers in their hands passed in the direction of the Presidential Palace. Moreover, it has been learned that communications with the port of Valparaíso have been interrupted."[46]

A few moments after the Radio Agricultura flash Adrian Schreiber, the U.S. assistant naval attaché, called me at home and reported what the radio was saying. I was having breakfast. I had seen the intelligence reporting of the day before and, as already noted, had been visited in the early morning hours by colleagues bearing reports. I had been determined, however, not to vary my schedule unless or until overt developments occurred. I did not want the press reporting that the U.S. ambassador had spent the night in the office waiting for a coup. The day before, Herbert Thompson had pointed out that M.Sgt. Isidro Benavides of our embassy lived on my same ridge, and Thompson urged me to ride with Benavides in case of need. Herb had also seen to it that George Frangullie and Charlie Cecil of the U.S. Drug Enforcement Agency would be on hand, as they were good men to have around in moments of possible danger. Herb, I am sure, was anxious to avoid any necessity to explain later to Washington that I had been waylaid coming to the office.

After Adrian Schreiber's telephone call I phoned Benavides, and he cheerily told me that he, George, and Charlie would be along shortly. Soon the ancient, wheezing bus of the Nido de Aguilas international school lumbered up the driveway to our door, coming to pick up our children. My wife told the driver to turn around and take everyone back home. The driver would have none of the idea, but my wife continued to insist—much to the embarrassment of our own offspring. Finally, since my wife lacked the needed authority in the bus driver's eyes, an uneasy compromise was reached, and one of the girls on the bus, Samira Atala, called her father, a trustee of the school. Only he had the authority to tell that loyal driver to turn his bus around and take the children home, which he then did.

Why did Allende not do what he had repeatedly said he would and take refuge among the armed workers in the industrial belts? Would it not have been better to have made for Los Cerrillos? As it turned out, some of the workers in the factories would hold out for days. With Allende in their midst, appealing to all for support and invoking legitimacy, who knows how the situation might have developed? It is true that a dash from Tomás Moro to Los Cerrillos would have required crossing Santiago, but once the presidential motorcade was hurtling across the city, it probably could have kept right on going. Allende's carabinero guards might have peeled off and made for their own headquarters, but judging from their other actions, they would probably not have battled the GAP in order to detain the president.

On the other hand, there were several arguments in favor of going to the Moneda. Allende still trusted the carabineros, and he must have been attracted to the radio-communications facilities and other services available at the Palace. Moreover, the symbolic importance of the Moneda as the historic seat of Chilean presidents made it natural and fitting for Allende to face his crisis there. Frei had dealt with the Tacna Regiment's revolt from the Moneda; other presidents had met national challenges from the same place. Allende might have calculated that the dignity of the presidential palace would strengthen his hand.

Allende's psychological makeup might also help explain his decision. While he had briefly set up offices in the industrial belt early in 1973, he had not been at ease during that episode, nor fully in control of his environment. He may not have trusted the left extremists who were leading the militant workers. He probably felt more secure continuing to act "presidential," relying on his great office and calling on the workers to come to him.

There are also those who think Allende shrank from provoking a civil war and the bloodshed that a sacrificial stand would have inflicted on his people. Laura Allende was quoted after the coup as recounting a conversation she had with her brother just before the eleventh: Allende: " 'Laurita, you must understand me. . . . I don't want a civil war. I cannot allow an armed confrontation to break out. Chile is divided. Our own family, for example, our own nephew is with the opposition. Just think of all those workers who might die in a civil war. No Laurita, I am not irresponsible.' "[47]

Talking with Régis Debray and other friends in August, Allende had expressed a similar idea. When he was urged to mobilize the working masses into action, his retort was: "How many of the masses are needed to stop a tank?" Debray commented that Allende had "a visceral rejection of a civil war, which he judged as lost, given the power differential in the contending forces. . . . He did not wish to assume responsibility for thousands of useless deaths. Other people's bloodshed horrified him."[48] To his credit, Allende was not Che Guevara, nor Joseph Stalin. His dream had been the Chilean Way, not bloody revolution and a dictatorship of the proletariat established in death and blood. Had the latter been his predilection, he might have made straight for Los Cerrillos.

While threatening repeatedly to hole up in the industrial belt, Allende had remained ambivalent to the very end. He had also repeatedly asserted that he would depart the Moneda during his constitutional term only in a wooden box.[49] A last stand at the palace fitted his psyche better than resistance in the industrial belts. On that morning of 11 September it was probably instinct which ruled.

My experience in the U.S. Foreign Service left me with an ironic parallel. My first post was Prague, Czechoslovakia, where I witnessed the Czech coup in 1948. There, President Beneš's unwillingness to bring on civil war crucially immobilized him, and the Communists' triumph ensued. Allende was motivated by similar compassion for his countrymen, and the overthrow of Marxist rule was the result. Humanistic presidential impulses played roles that were complementary in a perverse, cosmic sense in those two countries and at those two times.

### Eight to Nine A.M.: Out in the Open

At eight o'clock, at Tomás Moro, the following little drama is said to have taken place. As on all mornings, the bus carrying troops of the relief watch of carabineros drew up. The troops of the relieving unit got out of the bus; the troops of the night watch climbed in; the troops of the relieving unit climbed back in behind them; and the bus departed, leaving Tomás Moro devoid of police guards. Allegedly, the GAP guards did not realize they were being deceived until the bus was gone. This story typifies the response of many carabineros. They neither fought with the president nor against him; they simply shied away from the action. It should be added, however, that a considerable number of special service carabineros obeyed Mendoza and Yovane and fought actively alongside army troops.[50]

At the Moneda, Allende stepped out on an open balcony a little after 8 A.M. and was photographed in a picture later published throughout the world.[51] In the center of the city, troops had not yet appeared and the carabineros around the Moneda gave every outward sign of being deployed to protect the president.[52]

At about the same time Allende made an effort to get in touch with Letelier and find out whether he had taken charge at the Ministry of Defense. He sent Colonel Valenzuela, a member of his military entourage, to check on the situation there.[53] He then turned to the preparation of an appeal to the Chilean people. In his first transmission, at about 8 A.M., Allende told the workers to mobilize, gather at their factories, and prepare to defend UP power. He called for calm vigilance and urged his supporters to avoid provocations and to stand ready for further instructions. He said that part of the navy in Valparaíso had rebelled but that Santiago was quiet, and went on to state that the head of the Santiago garrison (General Brady) had told him that army troops were in their barracks.[54]

At about 8:15 the UP radios that were still functioning broadcast another appeal by Allende, much like the first.[55] Within the next five minutes, however, two developments shook the president's hopes that the insurrection was confined to the navy on the coast. Dinges and Landau pick up the story of Colonel Valenzuela's return to the Moneda: "'I've just come from the Defense Ministry,' shouted the colonel whom Allende had sent to check on Letelier. 'I tried to get in, but they wouldn't let me. The army controls it.'"[56]

A moment later, the president is reported to have received a telephone call from his air force aide, Col. Roberto Sánchez, whom Allende trusted as a friend. Sánchez was speaking for General van Schouwen, whom Allende had also regarded as sympathetic. It must have been a shock when Sánchez, speaking in the name of van Schouwen, urged the president to resign and said that a plane was standing by to fly him out of the country. Allende is reported to have replied: "Tell General van Schouwen that the president does not flee by plane. The general should know how to act like a soldier, just as I know how to carry out my sworn duty as president of the republic." Reputedly, Allende's muttered comment was: "The traitors, the traitors. . . . They don't even have enough guts to tell me this directly. . . ." Other accounts describe the president shouting into the phone: "As traitorous generals, you are incapable of knowing what honorable men are like."[57]

It appears that Allende made his next broadcast to the people almost immediately after talking with Sánchez. In it, he told his listeners:

> I shall not leave the Moneda. I shall not resign. I call on the workers to remain at their stations in factory or plant. I am at this moment anticipating expressions of support from soldiers determined to defend their government. I renew my determination to continue to defend Chile and the authority the Chilean people has placed in me. I shall pay with my life to defend the rights of Chileans. The future belongs to the workers. I am ready to resist by any means whatever, so that this may serve as a lesson in the ignominious history of those who use force, not reason.[58]

The last phrase was an allusion to Chile's motto: "By reason or by force." Allende also observed in his broadcast that air force planes were flying above the Moneda and were about to open fire. The president said that this action would "mark the infamy of those who have betrayed the fatherland and the people."

Allende's several statements were broadcast at different times by one or another of the pro-UP stations and became somewhat intermingled. Some opposition radios also carried one or two of the president's appeals. In each of these messages Allende seemed uncertain about the scope of the uprising and the degree of support it was attracting in the various services.[59]

Other governmental leaders also went on the air, asserting that the armed forces were "divided." They alleged that "some" officers were participating in the rebellion, but other officers were not and most noncommissioned officers and troops remained loyal. Altamirano addressed the people by radio urging them to mobilize against the "fascist uprising."[60] Pro-UP radios were transmitting "alert" and mobilization messages to leftist paramilitary formations, with some of the broadcast signals consisting of cryptic or coded phrases.[61]

CUT leaders continued their efforts to mobilize the workers. For example, a union official at the Sumar textile plant recounted after the coup that CUT headquarters had phoned him at about 8 A.M. saying that there had been a navy rebellion in Valparaíso and that he and his fellow workers should remain at the plant and await instructions on how to defend themselves. At the plant, "men and women were congregating in small groups, talking, questioning each other, all quite dazed."[62]

Most indications were that the UP cadres were somewhat ill-organized. A young woman who was a communist militant and party functionary commented after the coup:

> . . . Like the other day when you had to be up early to stand watch, or when you stayed all night in your place of work because of the situation. That is where you would find us; we were always standing by. . . .
>
> Then came the moment of real confrontation, and our organization didn't budge. We didn't know how to get communications going in spite of all our security measures. . . . We had no point of contact because the compañeros had all been rounded up. . . . We were not organized. The machinery did not work.[63]

One by one, colleagues, family members, and friends of Allende made their way to the Moneda. Half a dozen leftist police detectives turned up and joined the GAP defenders. Minister of Interior Briones appeared at about 8:20 A.M. Describing the scene as he arrived, he later said "there was already a great movement of troops" in the center of the city. Of the remaining members of the cabinet, Foreign Minister Almeyda, Minister of Agriculture Jaime Tohá, Finance Minister Fernando Flores, and Government Secretary General Aníbal Palma also joined the president. Minister of Education Enríquez appears to have turned up briefly but then decided to go on to his office and "get some work done." Daniel Vergara, the subsecretary of interior, and Hernán del Canto also appeared. The president's secretary and mistress, Miriam Contreras, better known as "La Payita," joined him at about 8:35 A.M.

Beatriz Allende de Fernández, pistol in hand, turned up at 8:50 after running a police barrier; José Tohá arrived ten minutes later; Isabel Allende then came, as did Frida Modak, the president's press secretary. Former investigative police chief Eduardo ("Coco") Paredes, Radical party leaders Hugo Miranda and Orlando Cantuarias, and some others, including half a dozen physicians, soon appeared.[64] Some were unable to make their way through to the president. For example, a group of about fifteen members of the GAP, heavily armed, tried to reach the Moneda but were apprehended by special service carabineros.

In the early hours of the morning pro-UP militants had holed up in the upper stories of buildings surrounding the Moneda. Many were leftist foreigners who had come to Chile in the Allende years, and some had received paramilitary training in their home countries, including experience in urban guerrilla warfare. It was probably about eight o'clock when they began firing down on special service carabineros, or perhaps the carabineros tried to clear some of these buildings. Seesaw gun battles ensued. For example, the lower floors of the Santiago provincial governor's offices, just east of the Moneda Palace, were successfully occupied by special service carabineros, but the upper floors remained in the hands of pro-UP snipers.[65] The carabineros found themselves in an unenviable predicament. The carabinero palace guard was still deployed to protect the constitutional president, while other carabineros were battling Allende's supporters.

Regular army units, led by General Palacios and the Second Armored Regiment, arrived outside the Moneda at about 8:30 A.M. They did not attack the palace right away, but soon there were exchanges of fire with the leftist snipers and skirmishing in the streets.[66]

At the embassy residence Sergeant Benavides, Frangullie, and Cecil turned up at about 8 o'clock, and we drove into town. The sun was warm. By then there was more traffic and bustle than Orlando Letelier had seen from his car an hour earlier. As we approached the downtown area, perhaps twenty blocks from the Moneda and the embassy, we saw carabineros systematically blocking off streets leading to the center with orange traffic cones. We raced along parallel to the line of barriers and managed to find a section that was not yet blocked. In we went. We got to within three or four blocks of the embassy before we had to park the car because of the fighting and proceed on foot. By then it was about 8:30 A.M., and the army was moving into action in the center of the city. We heard the crack of rifles, the chugging of teargas guns, and the burping of automatic weapons a block or two away. It was the second time in ten weeks I had walked through smoke and the acrid smell of violence in order to reach the embassy offices.

At about 8:30 A.M. Orlando Letelier was brought out of the Ministry of Defense in custody.[67] Chilean television broadcast this scene, and my wife viewed it. She recalls that Letelier had always been positive and upbeat, his faith in the future manifest. He looked very changed. Except for newspaper photos, that was the last time my wife or I saw him.

Between eight and nine A.M. armed troops were progressively occupying the progovernment radios. My wife described what happened in a letter written shortly after the coup:

> Before the takeovers, the radio played music very normally, almost with an eerie calm and detachment. After a radio was seized, there were marches. . . . We turned on three radios. One had the chain of stations that were formerly "opposition," which quickly linked into the military forces' network. Another radio had a pro-government station; and on the third radio we "cruised" the dial. One by one we heard the pro-government stations go off the air.

My daughter Margaret described one of these takeovers: "We heard gunshots and screams; then there was a short silence; then there was the ubiquitous martial music."

The Junta's "pronouncement" of military rule, "Edict No. 1," was broadcast at about half past eight in the morning. At 8:28 A.M., as the Chilean magazine Qué Pasa described it, "Gabito" Hernández of Radio Agricultura ordered the station to play the national anthem. It was to have been followed by the Junta's message, but the link to military headquarters had been severed. So the radio played the national anthem a second time, in an atmosphere of great tension. The air force, it turned out, had bombed some of the pro-UP radio antennae and had broken the Junta's own cable link in doing so. The cable was fixed before the end of the second rendition of the national anthem, however, and the Junta's announcement then came on the air. Apparently, Allende himself had not heard it but was immediately told of it by Largo Farías, who had by then returned to the Moneda.[68]

The Junta's proclamation cited Chile's grave social and moral crisis, the government's inability to prevent chaos, and the constant increase in paramilitary groups, which were leading the country "to an inevitable civil war." The message then demanded the president's resignation and proclaimed the Junta's determination to liberate the country from the Marxist yoke and to restore order and "institutionality." The declaration promised workers that they would not be deprived of their "economic and social gains," ordered progovernment media to close down immediately or be attacked, and advised the public to stay at home. According to subsequently published transcripts of Pinochet-Leigh conversations, the reassurance to workers and advice to the public were added at Pinochet's request.[69]

The Junta's message was signed by Pinochet, Merino, Leigh, and Mendoza, and it appears to have been the first confirmation the president received that Pinochet had joined the coup. It was also the first public evidence, and probably the first indication to Allende, that Merino had displaced navy commander-in-chief Montero and that Mendoza and some carabineros had joined the uprising. When the president heard the names of the Junta leaders, he reportedly "looked out of the window," and said: "Traitors."[70] Qué Pasa picks up the account: "Allende was in his office, surrounded by about twenty people. He had taken off his jacket and put on an olive-green helmet. He had exchanged his AK rifle for the submachine gun of Soviet manufacture which Castro had given him. . . . At the military proclamation, . . . his spirits sank considerably."[71]

The Junta's pronouncement and Pinochet's defection appear to have hardened Allende's attitude toward all the military. The president's naval aide, Capt. Jorge Grez, drove up to the Moneda at about 8:35. Allende did not want to let him inside. Grez saw La Payita arriving at the same time, however, and managed to enter the building with her.[72] Samuel Chavkin describes the scene:

> Inside the building, confusion reigned. Most of the security personnel [GAP] carried submachine guns and had assumed battle positions in front of strategic doors and windows.

> Grez found the President in his office surrounded by approximately thirty people: GAP, ministers of state, advisors, secretaries, and people from the office of Information and Broadcasting (OIR).
>
> Allende was trying to contact Radio Magallanes. . . . When he saw Captain Grez, he [looked up and remarked dryly]: "Once again, problems in your fleet, captain."[73]

Air force planes made low passes over the city and continued to hit selected targets, most of them pro-UP radio facilities. By 9 o'clock, of the pro-government stations in the capital only Radio Corporación, Radio La Candelaria, and Radio Magallanes appeared still to be in service. Radio Magallanes was a mobile, independently powered station, and it survived for an extra hour or two.[74]

Chavkin describes the anomalous position of the carabinero leadership at about 8:30 A.M. Director General Sepúlveda "had reinforced the guard outside the palace. . . . But the general director had a nasty shock; his subordinates lacked their usual respect and hesitated at his orders."[75] At about quarter to nine the three hundred carabineros outside the Moneda quietly withdrew, ceding their positions to Palacios's troops and tanks. Subsequent accounts indicate that the carabineros were obeying Mendoza and Yovane, but it is possible, too, that they were reluctant to confront the army's heavy weapons. Coming so shortly after the Junta's pronouncement, the carabineros' silent withdrawal was said to have been a sore blow to the president.[76]

At 8:55 A.M. Allende seems to have met with Sepúlveda and the other senior carabinero commanders still inside the palace. They informed him that carabinero headquarters had been seized and they could not communicate with Mendoza.[77] A GAP eyewitness reports that "there was division among the upper commands which led to chaos in the Moneda. Nothing came out well. . . ."[78] Other accounts allege that the senior carabinero generals declined to defend Allende out of cowardice.[79] It is more likely, however, that they knew their troops would no longer follow them.

While the coup had started in Valparaíso, and Santiago was the key, important actions were also going on in the rest of the country. In most places the military moved smoothly and efficiently to seize control. Concepción, the country's largest city after Santiago and Valparaíso, fell by 8:50 A.M. "without a shot." Brig. Gen. Washington Carrasco Fernández, allegedly with the help of only one engineer and three telephone company experts, had seen to it that 1,800 telephones of UP and MIR leaders were disconnected in the very early hours of the morning. He then had these leaders arrested, as well as the UP civil and administrative authorities. Lastly, he subdued the industrial belts and the university, detaining UP leaders in those places as well.[80]

### Nine to Ten A.M.: Allende's Last Appeal

At 9 o'clock the Moneda was surrounded by army tanks. The Junta broadcast an edict over the radio warning that sabotage of businesses, factories, communications, or transport would meet with summary justice, and citizens were urged to report any subversive elements they observed in action.[81] Sniper fire from pro-UP militants in the buildings around the Moneda increased. Special service carabinero units continued their efforts to subdue the snipers and clear out resistance in the downtown buildings and even in some factories.[82]

Within the Moneda there was animated consideration whether Allende should submit. The president was surrounded by members of the GAP, however, who were determined to fight to the end. Minister of Interior Briones later commented: "The presence of the guards made it impossible for us to speak alone with the president and to try to convince him to negotiate his surrender."[83]

The president ordered his staff to burn documents and rosters of the names of supporters. A friend of mine at the Foreign Ministry—which was located in the south wing of the Moneda—told me a few days after the coup that he found his office ransacked, with the safes forced open and papers strewn in heaps on the floor. Other staff members inventoried weapons and ammunition in the palace arsenal, and the doctors prepared a makeshift clinic and infirmary.[84]

Admiral Carvajal talked with the president by phone at about 9:25, asking him to surrender, guaranteeing his physical safety, and again offering a plane to take him and his family out of the country. According to Carvajal, the president's response was a stream of profanities. Captain Grez, on whose "green telephone" the call had come in, heard the president's end of the conversation and later quoted Allende as saying to Carvajal: "You have been conspiring for a long time, you vulture! And I won't forget it. You are mistaken if you think that I am going to allow this to go on." Allende—or Carvajal—then slammed down the phone.[85]

It was close to 9:30 A.M. when the armed forces broadcast an ultimatum to the president and his supporters to leave the Moneda before eleven o'clock or be attacked by land and air. Inside the Moneda Palace Allende reportedly did not believe that air force pilots would actually carry out the attack, because their superiors would be afraid of hitting the surrounding buildings, including the U.S. Embassy. The president may also have thought that respect for the historic palace would deter the attackers. Allende decisively rejected the idea of giving up. Subsequently, the ultimatum from the armed forces was repeated at intervals over the radio, as tension in the city mounted.[86]

At about 9:30 the president broadcast his last declaration to the Chilean people. By then, only the Communists' Radio Magallanes was functioning reliably in progovernment hands.[87] The president said:

> Surely this will be my last opportunity to address you. . . . My words are not spoken in bitterness, but in disappointment. They will be a moral judgment on those who have betrayed the oath they took as soldiers of Chile, as legitimately designated commanders-in-chief. . . .
>
> I shall pay with my life for the loyalty of the people. . . . The seed we have planted in the worthy consciousness of thousands upon thousands of Chileans cannot forever remain unharvested. . . . They have the might and they can enslave us, but they cannot halt the world's social processes, not with crimes, nor with guns. History is ours, and the people of the world will determine it.
>
> Workers of my fatherland . . . I wish to thank you for the loyalty you have always demonstrated, and the trust you extended to a man who was but the interpreter of your deep yearnings for justice. I gave my word that I would respect the Constitution and the law, and I have done so. In this final moment before my voice is silenced, I want you to learn this lesson: foreign capital and imperialism, united with reaction, created the climate for the armed forces' break with their tradition—the tradition taught by General Schneider and reaffirmed by Captain Araya, victims of the same social forces which even now wait in their houses to reconquer power, through the hands of others, in order to preserve their privileges and gains.

I address myself above all to the modest woman of our land, to the woman of the soil who believed in us, to the working woman who redoubled her labors, to the mother who recognized our concern for her children. I address myself . . . to the professional people of the land . . . to the youth, to those who sang and gave their joy and fighting spirit to the struggle . . . to the laborer, the farmworker, the intellectual, to those who will be persecuted because fascism has already been present in our country for many hours in the acts of terrorists who blew up bridges, who cut railway lines, who destroyed oil and gas pipelines, while those with the responsibility to counter these acts remained silent. They were accomplices. History will judge them.

Surely Radio Magallanes will soon be silenced, and the calm timbre of my voice will not reach you. It does not matter. You will continue to hear me. I shall always stand with you. My legacy will remain that of a worthy man, a man who was loyal to his country.

The people should defend themselves, but not sacrifice themselves. The people should not let themselves be riddled with bullets nor cut down, but they should not let themselves be humiliated either.

Workers of my fatherland! I have faith in Chile and in its destiny. Other men will overcome this dark and bitter moment, when treason strains to conquer. May you go forward in the knowledge that, sooner rather than later, the great avenues will open once again along which free citizens will march in order to build a better society.

Long live Chile! Long live the People! Long live the Workers! These are my last words, and I am sure that my sacrifice will not be in vain. I am sure that this sacrifice will constitute a moral lesson which will punish cowardice, perfidy and treason.[88]

The army's guns opened up on the Moneda at about 9:30 A.M., and the tanks surrounding the building started firing about twenty minutes later. Infantry advanced under cover of these volleys, and the GAP responded with small arms and bazookas. It is said that the president himself participated in the counterfire.[89]

The president's army and navy aides appear to have waited for their air force colleague, Colonel Sánchez, to join them before asking to talk to the president alone. They had been consulting with the senior military commanders besieging the palace. When Sánchez arrived, some minutes after 9:30 A.M., the three aides requested a private audience. Allende agreed, but his GAP bodyguards refused to leave the room. Allende had to insist very energetically before they would obey him. During the talk, which lasted less than ten minutes, the aides pointed to the futility of resistance and urged surrender as the only way of saving the president's life. Allende declined to negotiate with the military under the conditions presented—although reportedly he did say he would treat personally with the Junta members if they would come to the Moneda. Allegedly he also tried to get the military to promise that the National party would not be included in a future cabinet. Finally Allende declared: "I shall defend myself to the end, and the last bullet of this submachine gun I shall shoot here"; and the president indicated his own jaw. Allende told the three aides to leave the palace. The aides ordered subordinate military personnel to withdraw as well, and they left the Moneda by the door on 80 Morandé Street.[90]

Across Constitution Square from the Moneda, we in the U.S. Embassy discharged our responsibility to report events to Washington as best we could. Communications with Washington were no problem. The defense attaché's office, for example, had put in a long-distance telephone call to the Defense Intelligence Agency and kept the line open for hours, until the connection was finally cut off sometime in the afternoon, probably by a telephone operator in Peru. The local telephones were also working without interruption, and we could both make and receive calls. Snipers shot out the glass in virtually every window of the ninth floor, the topmost of the embassy's three floors of offices. Probably because of the angle, the seventh and eighth floors received considerably less fire. The file room, a large, mostly interior space, became a kind of headquarters, which the embassy's communicators, archivists, and marines secured by propping mattresses against its two or three windows.

The president's last address was the most memorable event of this hour. Apparently he delivered it without a single note,[91] and it will go down in Chilean history as a moving statement of the aspiration of the Chilean left. It also contains a kind of postscript to the president's decision to avoid a bloodbath. Allende made an explicit appeal to the people not to "sacrifice themselves." Freed and

Landis comment: "In his final address . . . Allende changed course. He no longer urged the workers to take a stand. Instead he pleaded with them not to become needless victims." Freed and Landis then quote a supporter of Allende, Fernando Alegría, talking about the president's last statement: "Allende displayed his fundamental humanitarian quality. He knew that since there was no hope for his supporters to get arms, there was no point in getting themselves killed. In my opinion Allende will not emerge in history as a revolutionary fighter, although he died fighting as a revolutionary."[92]

There may be truth in what Alegría says. Does one define Allende's impulse as humanitarianism and compassion or as ambivalence? There were elements in Salvador Allende's psyche to confirm both judgments.

### Ten to Eleven A.M.: Only the GAP to Defend Him

The carabinero palace guards hesitated and conferred among themselves for over an hour, until about 10 A.M.. At that time the Junta commanders gave them a thirteen-minute ultimatum to abandon the Moneda or suffer bombardment. Director General Sepúlveda advised the president of the ultimatum, and the carabinero troops then abandoned the palace. Before they left the building, they destroyed some weapons they were unable to take with them, and they had a rapid exchange of fire with the GAP forces as they departed. Allende was left with only his own entourage, a few investigative police, and the GAP defending him in the palace— two- to three-score fighters against the massed tanks and troops of the Chilean military. The snipers in the encircling buildings were also supporting the president, of course, and the battle was intensifying on all sides.[93]

At about 10:30 Allende called a meeting of those still in the Moneda, except for the men at battle stations near windows and doors. Frida Modak later described what went on:

> Allende was serious but unruffled. He seemed almost relieved that his mind was made up; that there were no options; that the only honorable alternative was to show Chile and the world that anti-Fascists would not surrender without a fight.
>
> The meeting took place in Sala Toesca, the largest conference hall at La Moneda. A huge chandelier lit up the unadorned, pale-yellow walls of this ceremonial chamber. . . . Allende sat

down behind a huge table on the platform, at the head of the hall. . . . The President . . . spoke of his decision to fight it out. . . . But, he explained, this was to be a political action, and should not be viewed in terms of personal martyrdom. Dispassionately he went on to declare that the battle of La Moneda was only the beginning. "That is how we write the first page of history," he said. "The next page will be written by the Chilean people and by all Latin Americans." And once again he called on those in the palace who had no experience with firearms to get out, and help develop the resistance against the Junta on the outside. . . . "The struggle against fascism need not result in useless deaths; there will be plenty to do. . . ."[94]

Some of Allende's political collaborators did take his advice, shook his hand, and escaped through side doors.

By 10:30 Radio Magallanes was silent, although Radio Corporación continued some intermittent broadcasting.[95] According to a young Socialist who was at Radio Corporación, burst-type FM and short-wave transmissions were maintained until midafternoon. Here is his account:

Between 9:00 and 10:00 A.M. the transmission plant was being bombed and the frequencies were cut off. . . .

We had electronic equipment inside that allowed us to transmit on FM and short wave. So we formed a pool of people and called up different industries to tell them what wavelengths we would broadcast on. Every half hour we broadcast for five minutes; the political director spoke in the name of the Socialist Party and called on the workers to organize themselves for the struggle and told how the resistance should be oriented. The technicians explained that we could broadcast only five minutes every half hour so that the military would not be able to locate where we were broadcasting from. This transmission was maintained until around 4:30 in the afternoon, when the political director said that it was insane to stay inside because the radio station would obviously be visited by the military and there would be blood and fire.[96]

At about 10:30 A.M. José Tohá talked by phone with Admiral Carvajal. In his usual calm, tranquil voice Tohá requested a ten-minute cease-fire in order to convince Allende to surrender. The admiral answered that he would be unable to accomplish such a cease-fire, as a veritable army of snipers was firing down at the troops surrounding the Moneda. Nobody, Carvajal said, could get these snipers to stop firing. Chilean authors Florencia Varas and José Manuel Vergara continue the account of the conversation:

> [Carvajal] ". . . Time is running out. The Air Force has already been given its orders. The planes may arrive at any moment—"
>
> [Tohá] "I have tried everything in my power to try to convince the president, but—"
>
> [Carvajal] "Well then, throw him out by force."
>
> [Tohá] "Ah, but he is armed with a submachine gun. Why don't you try talking to him, admiral? Perhaps your arguments shall be more—convincing than mine."
>
> [Carvajal] "What? I, talk with Allende? You can't ever talk with that man. All he does is insult you."
>
> [Tohá] "Well, then, I'll see what I can do. . . ."[97]

The satellite communications link between Santiago and Buenos Aires was severed by the Chileans at about 10:30, as was air service between the two countries.[98] At about this time the Junta broadcast a fourteen-point declaration justifying the coup. This proclamation, Edict No. 5, denounced violations of the law, the Constitution, and Chilean freedoms and cited the fomenting of class struggle, executive-branch usurpations of power, the imposition of ideas foreign to the Chilean way of life, and policies leading to runaway inflation, economic decline, anarchy, and vulnerability to attack. The proclamation concluded that these abuses justified military intervention in order to prevent greater evils and to reestablish social and economic normality. Reportedly the editors of this message borrowed heavily from the Resolution of the Chamber of Deputies of 22 August 1973 and the memorandum prepared by the directorate of operations of the army in late August.[99]

At almost the same moment when the Junta was broadcasting its fourteen-point declaration, Allende and Carvajal talked again by phone. According to Carvajal, the president was more restrained in this conversation than he had been in their first one. Allende requested a brief truce to allow the women to leave the Moneda. The president noted that his pregnant daughter Beatriz was among them. Varas and Vergara report the ensuing conversation:

> [Carvajal] "I understand perfectly. We'll let them leave."
>
> [Allende] "I want a vehicle with an officer to give them protection."

[Carvajal] "Fine. I will send a vehicle with an officer."

[Allende] "I want you to give me your word of honor that you are not going to shoot them."

[Carvajal] "How can they be shot?"

[Allende] "There are some who might do it, some Fascists."

[Carvajal] "What Fascists are you talking about?"

[Allende] "I am not referring to you personally, admiral, but there are some people who may shoot."[100]

At about the same time Brig. Gen. Ernesto Baeza, who was acting as Pinochet's liaison at the Ministry of Defense, telephoned the president, perhaps through Colonel Badiola, the President's army aide who was by then at the ministry. Baeza repeated the military's guarantees of Allende's life and a plane for him and his family, and urged him to surrender. The president responded by reiterating that the Junta members should come to the Moneda, treat with him, and receive what he suggested would be his resignation. He declined, however, to leave the palace in surrender, and no agreement was reached. Allende then asked Baeza—as he had Carvajal—for a truce to allow the women to leave the palace and for a jeep to take them to safety. Allende got assurances similar to those Carvajal had given him.[101]

In a few moments the proclamation of a state of siege and a curfew came over the military radio network. Planes and helicopters passed overhead. From Post Number One at Peñalolén, Pinochet told Carvajal at the Defense Ministry that the troops around the Moneda should pull back at 10:50 A.M. and find cover, in order to avoid injury during the air force's rocket attacks. The soldiers were also ordered to wear white handkerchiefs on their shoulders to mark their positions for the aerial bombardiers. Carvajal reported that the carabinero headquarters had been "neutralized" and that the police troops were obeying Mendoza. Carvajal and Pinochet discussed the president's demand that the Junta leaders come to the Moneda. Pinochet commented that Allende would shove the commanders-in-chief of the services into some basement if they did and that Allende should come to the Ministry of Defense instead, and meet the Junta there.[102] Allende was maneuvering desperately to save his power, and the military were clearly unwilling to place themselves in his hands.

Elsewhere in the city and the country there were numerous developments. At about 10:15 A.M. anti-UP civilians blocked the street leading to the Cuban Embassy in Santiago. Embassy personnel sallied out, shooting automatic weapons into the air, and knocked down the barricade. At about the same time leftist militants attacked the National party's headquarters. Eight hundred miles to the north, at Chuquicamata, the communist head of the copper mine, David Silberman, and a hundred armed supporters barricaded the entrances—although later *Qué Pasa* asserted that Silberman and about twenty followers escaped into the mountains before any engagement actually took place.[103] Comandante Pepe and his guerrillas besieged a carabinero reserve station, defended by two carabineros and the carabinero sergeant's wife. The wife of a NATO ambassador told my wife that the MIR had established roadblocks in the hills around Santiago. This woman had made her way back to the capital from the coastal summer community of Zapallar on the eleventh, and she talked and bribed her way past a MIR barricade by giving the guerrillas five liters of gasoline. By the following day, when the woman's daughter drove the route, only military checkpoints were in evidence.[104]

Leftist sources claim that resistance to the takeover among loyalist troops was considerably more serious than the Junta government has ever acknowledged. These sources claim, in particular, that soldiers in a number of regiments defied their seditious commanders and rose up in defense of the president. According to the leftists, some troops did so in all the following units: the Infantry Regiment of San Bernardo; a detachment of the Buin Regiment in the Conchalí section of Santiago; the Noncommissioned Officers' School of the carabineros; the Cuirassiers of Viña del Mar; and the Infantry of San Felipe, where the troops were said to have killed their commander, Colonel Cantuarias. Hand-to-hand fighting was said to have taken place at El Bosque, the air force base south of Santiago. Some accounts also describe loyalist troop actions in the provinces of Concepción and Valdivia and a rising of the Railroaders Regiment at Puente Alto. Carabineros at the Vitacura police station in the Barrio Alto of Santiago and at the Fifteenth Precinct in the center of the city were also said to have battled procoup forces. In the northern province of Antofagasta a carabinero sergeant, Eduardo Schmidt Godoy, reportedly shot two of his chiefs before being gunned down himself.[105]

While it is difficult to judge the accuracy of these claims, resist ance to the Junta forces in some of these units, particularly at the carabinero Noncommissioned Officers' School and among some troops of the Buin Regiment, was widely reported, and the reports were probably true. Nevertheless, it was the cohesion and solidarity of the armed forces, not the scattered loyalist actions, that became the significant reality of 11 September.

### Eleven A.M. to One P.M.: Bombing the Moneda

Eleven o'clock came and went, and the aerial bombardment did not start. Throughout the city, people waited by radios, or looked at the sky. My wife and children went to the garden of the embassy residence and watched for the planes, but none appeared. Apparently, the negotiations to allow the women to leave the Moneda were continuing. According to René Largo Farías, Allende had started urging the women to leave at about 10 A.M.[106]

The Junta's radios soon broadcast that the women would be given a few minutes to abandon the palace. Half a dozen women, and a few men, soon marched out of the Moneda. La Payita hid herself to avoid leaving. There was something affecting in this, with Allende's wife in Tomás Moro, far from the husband she still loved and supported, and La Payita, who also loved Salvador Allende, at his side at the end.[107]

Frida Modak tells what happened to the women who marched out:

> We suddenly found ourselves out on the street, with the door shut behind us. But there was no jeep at the door, nor any soldiers in view. Nor was there any shooting. . . . What had happened was that the military had already been pulled back to a safe enough distance to be out of range of the air attacks. . . . There were only two drunkards. . . . The two men would stagger about on rubbery legs, throw their arms about in all directions as though directing traffic, and mindlessly keep lurching on.
>     . . . We walked a bit farther but saw no jeep nor any human being. . . . There was an eerie silence as we neared the vacant broad avenues. . . . Beatriz . . . ran back toward the Morandé Street door.
>     Beatriz knocked frantically but only the small lookout window was opened. Dr. Bartolín was at the door. Beatriz told him there was no jeep. . . . She begged him to let us back in. But Bartolín handed her his car keys . . . and said he was sorry but the president's order was not to let us reenter. . . .[108]

According to Mrs. Allende, her pregnant daughter Beatriz began to have uterine contractions. The women sought shelter first in *La Prensa*'s building and then in a nearby hotel. Ultimately, they managed to reach the homes of relations and friends.[109]

The president, reportedly in a state of considerable excitement,[110] inspected the defensive arrangements, had the carabineros' small-arms magazines opened, and had some gas masks distributed. He received an added blow when Alfredo Joignant telephoned to report that investigative police headquarters had been seized by troops.[111] It is alleged that alcohol flowed freely within the Moneda, and well it might have, for alcohol helps dull anguish—as the president had long known. According to Allende's daughter Isabel, the president never lost his human touch: "The last picture I have of my father in my mind's eye is as a combatant, going from window to window, raising the spirits of his guards, joking with them. . . ."[112]

At about 11:30 A.M., Socialist deputy Erich Schnake broadcast a dramatic but fruitless appeal to the Chilean people to march to the center of Santiago. He was at Radio Corporación, which was still broadcasting in bursts over the FM band. Apparently there was also a direct telephone hookup between Radio Corporación and the president's office, and Schnake and Allende had talked briefly by phone before Schnake went on the air.[113]

Outside the Moneda the action resumed. Tanks of the Second Armored Regiment were drawn up north of the palace across Constitution Square. Soldiers of the Infantry School were on Teatinos Street, between the Hotel Carrera and the U.S. Embassy offices. Troops of the army's Noncommissioned Officers' School were on Morandé Street, east of the Moneda.[114] The Tacna Regiment was to the south, on the Alameda O'Higgins. All these troops were exchanging fire with the GAP in the Moneda and with the snipers on the higher floors of surrounding buildings. To the south of the palace the great excavation ditch for the Santiago subway formed a moat. There was a bridge of boards across it, but any soldier who stepped on the bridge was exposed to fire from the Moneda. Some troops attempting to advance were subjected to withering fire from high scaffolding on the ENTEL building tower. After a sergeant was killed, General Palacios—enraged—ordered a tank to open fire on the tower, demolishing the scaffolding.[115]

The Junta's renewed demands that Allende and his people surrender were met by the president's continued refusal to do so. Pinochet urged that the air bombardment commence without further delay, as he feared that Allende was trying to gain time for the workers of the industrial belts to come to the center of the city. The impending Hawker Hunter attacks were delayed again, however, because the planes were low on fuel after their earlier operations against radio installations, and the pilots had to fly to Concepción, almost 300 miles to the south, to refuel. It may be recalled that the Hawker Hunters had been moved from the Santiago area in August because they were vulnerable to left-extremist attack from Los Cerrillos.[116]

Employees and guests at the Hotel Carrera, including over thirty foreign journalists, were shooed downstairs to the safety of the cellars. As might be expected, however, many of the journalists continued watching and photographing the scene from the hotel windows, risking the fire of the soldiers below, who were ready to shoot at any moving curtain. The carabineros herded journalists from the streets into the subterranean garages under Constitution Square.[117]

Finally the aerial attack commenced. The first pass came at 11:52, followed by six more in the ensuing twenty-one minutes. The planes turned behind San Cristóbal hill, went into a very steep dive, and launched their rockets when they were over the Mapocho railroad station. Their aim was perfect. The rockets went straight into the doors and windows of the north side of the Moneda Palace.[118]

Those of us in the embassy felt the tremor of the explosions beneath our feet. In a letter a day or two later my wife described the scene as it looked from four miles away, on the crest of the ridge on which the embassy residence sat:

> Shortly before noon we heard the jets. It was an eerily beautiful sight as they came in from nowhere. The sun glinted on their wings. There were only two. Still in formation, they swung gracefully through the sky in a great circle, and then they tipped and dove . . . one bomb each . . . then, a gentle curve upwards.
>
> Sun glistened on the wings again, and there was another run. Nathaniel called to say that the Embassy and surrounding buildings had not been hit. I passed the word to other wives and families. . . .
>
> Margaret [aged fifteen] was fascinated, and understood every-

thing throughout the morning. Helen [almost twelve] was not much interested, until the bombing. Even then, she watched until it was done, asked no questions, and went back inside to play. Jim [almost ten] didn't really know what a revolution was, but he understood every movement of the planes, every sound of explosion, and reproduced it all later for his father—with sound effects. Of course, Tom was only four.

My daughter Margaret also described the bombing to her diary:

I now know what the sound of a bomb dropping is like. A whistle, high at first, then lower, lower, lower. . . . Two planes and nothing else. The helicopters all went home for lunch. . . . I've started to come in at least five times when the planes' noise died down but every time I got to my room they came back and I rushed outside to watch. . . .

Some houses are putting out their Chilean flags.

12:18. A mad rush of cars coming from the downtown section . . . except for an ambulance. We saw a big bus go by, jam-packed. . . . The Moneda or someplace near is sending up smoke. . . . The carabineros at the front gate withdrew a while ago. . . .

A kite just came down into our garden. A blue and red one. Shows how much some are worried. Heck, I'm just barely excited. It passes after a while. . . .

Victor called the Embassy, and it's true. The Moneda is actually on fire. The radio's got soupy music on. Wow! That was some boom! Another! A call for the firemen to stand by. . . . If I keep on recording the booms I'll never get to write this. . . . I've heard . . . sixteen. . . .

Dad called from the office. He said they're not in hardly any danger there because they stopped bombing already and it all is at street level with the tanks. . . .

Allende sure does have courage. Earlier this morning he said he wouldn't resign and it seems to me he'll stick to it. . . . Poor Allende! He didn't deserve all this. . . . And the opposition thinks Allende's making a mess of the country!

The president and his entourage had taken refuge in the side cellars of the Moneda, on the theory that the pilots would hit only the central portion of the palace in order to avoid damaging surrounding buildings. Allende was under the Ministry of Interior wing and reportedly suffered some injuries caused by flying glass. Briones, the Tohá brothers, and Almeyda had taken refuge in a storeroom under the Ministry of Foreign Affairs, on the south side of the Moneda. After the attack they went up to a ground-floor office, and José Tohá telephoned his wife. Apparently they remained there until the resistance ended, at which time they were taken into custody.[119]

The bombardment set fires in the Moneda, and the conflagration soon spread, filling much of the north side of the building with smoke, flames, and gases. The defenders' gas masks apparently were not effective. Part of the roof caved in, and pieces of plaster, splintered furniture, curtains, and office materials were strewn about.[120]

One is led to wonder why the Junta waited so long for the aerial attack. The tanks, after all, could have blasted through the Moneda's doors at any time. It was said that the air force was permitted to bombard first in order to give it its part in the common effort. The coup's leaders apparently also calculated that a bombing would intimidate workers in the industrial belts. In a postcoup interview Admiral Carvajal said that the Junta wanted to warn those who might fight back and that the speed and precision of the operation would save lives by discouraging further resistance. Pinochet is quoted as having said essentially the same thing just before the coup: "If there is armed resistance, we shall strike hard. . . . The more drastic the action, the more saving of lives there will be."[121]

Sometime after the aerial bombardment, perhaps at about 1 P.M., four persons emerged from the Moneda under a flag of truce. They were Minister of Finance Flores, Subsecretary of Interior Vergara, Osvaldo Puccio, Allende's executive secretary, and Puccio's nineteen-year-old son who had insisted on accompanying his father.[122] The three delegates and Puccio's son went to the Ministry of Defense and discussed possible surrender terms. According to Briones's subsequent account, Allende had instructed his representatives to ask for a cease-fire, a commitment that the working-class areas of the city would not be attacked, agreement that a civilian be named to the Junta, and an agreement from the Junta to begin conversations with him, Allende. Allegedly the president also wanted a promise that his companions in the Moneda would be allowed to leave the country with him. Apparently Allende offered to send a letter with his proposals. According to later reports, Pinochet exploded at Allende's offer. "Let him leave first! We shall read his letter when he's in the air. . . ."[123] The talks led nowhere.

The leaders of the air force advised their colleagues that the DC-6 waiting to take the president and his family out of the country would have to take off by about 4 P.M. or be delayed until the next day. The air force did not want to risk escorting a night departure. Leigh and his colleagues also indicated that the destination should be a South American country, or Mexico at the farthest.[124]

At approximately ten minutes before one, General Palacios and his troops began their advance toward the Moneda.[125]

At Tomás Moro the army and the GAP engaged in combat almost as furious as the action around the Moneda. At 12:30 P.M. Hawker Hunters bombarded Tomás Moro. As in the bombing of the Moneda, the army pulled back from the target prior to the aerial attack. Both the president's wife and the GAP guards seem to have taken adavantage of this withdrawal to leave the premises.[126] Mrs. Allende described the scene to Mexican journalists in a telephone interview several days after the coup:

> The planes came, fired their rockets, and returned to their base to reload. Between each attack there was wildly intense firing. The residence became a mass of smoke, gunpowder fumes, and destruction. [Allende's widow affirmed that she had given orders to the guards not to fire against the army, but her desires were disregarded after the bombardment had begun.]
>
> I made my last calls to the Moneda Palace on the floor, sometimes on my knees and sometimes prone. While I was reduced to this situation, my chauffeur, Carlos Tello, came to find me. He had succeeded in bringing a car to the back patio of the house. We took advantage of a moment in which the planes had returned to their bases . . . and departed. . . .
>
> I decided to go to Felipe Herrera's house [Allende's old friend and the former head of the Inter-American Development Bank]. Luckily, nobody followed us. I stayed there all day. . . .[127]

Reportedly, English nuns who ran a school at the neighboring Convent of the Sacred Heart opened their grounds in order to let the president's wife drive through. Later, the Mexican ambassador sent his car to bring Mrs. Allende to refuge in his embassy.

### One to Three P.M.: The Surrender and Allende's Death

The fires in the Moneda burned on unextinguished, ultimately spreading to gut large parts of the north wing. Southeast of the palace General Palacios and his troops continued their slow advance under intense sniper and GAP counterfire.[128] The magazine *Qué Pasa* describes what happened next: "At 1:30 P.M., in the middle of devouring flames, the attackers entered the ground floor. The GAP guards defended themselves ferociously. They died, gunned down or casualties of the fire. In order to suppress the resistance, carabineros fired off countless teargas bombs inside the Moneda. The smoke and the gases made the air asphyxiating. More or less at the same hour . . . Augusto Olivares committed suicide. . . ."[129]

Varas and Vergara give a description of the death of Allende's friend and adviser. Apparently Olivares informed the president at about 1:30 P.M. that there were no indications of support from any branch of the armed forces, and Allende decided that there was no choice but to surrender. Allende suggested that Olivares call the Ministry of Defense. Olivares reached Carvajal's office on the telephone intercom, and spoke with Col. Pedro Ewing. He asked Ewing if Allende's three delegates had reached any agreement and was told that there was nothing to discuss except unconditional surrender. Olivares then asked whether the delegates would return to the Moneda; he was told that they would not.

> Olivares . . . told Allende about the failure of the three delegates, then went down to a bathroom under the staircase which led to the kitchen. Without bothering to close the door, he started to urinate. At that moment Oscar Soto was passing. Bitter jokes were exchanged. Then Dr. Soto continued upstairs. A few minutes later he heard a shot. He ran back to the bathroom. Olivares had shot himself with a revolver.
> Carlos Jorquera, the presidential attaché, when he saw the body of his friend and colleague, started to cry bitterly.
> For Salvador Allende the suicide of his closest collaborator represented a heavy blow.[130]

At about 1:50 P.M., according to the military, Allende asked for a five-minute cease-fire in order to surrender. According to other accounts, it was the military who gave the defenders a four-minute ultimatum to capitulate. Allende's three delegates were reported to have been involved in these surrender negotiations, even though they were essentially in custody at the Ministry of Defense.

It was also reported that an armored vehicle was dispatched from the Ministry of Defense to bring the president out unharmed, but sniper fire obliged it to turn back. One of Allende's companions recounted that the president, who was defending the palace from the second floor, said: "Surrender? This is a massacre. La Payita should leave first. I will go at the end."[131]

La Payita then led a procession of the Moneda's defenders down from the second floor to the Morandé 80 door.[132]

General Palacios was approaching the Morandé 80 door from the outside, and subsequently described the scene to Varas and Vergara. Dr. Soto apparently gave the two authors his account as experienced from the inside. The combined description follows:

> The noise was deafening. . . . General Palacios saw a white doctor's coat hung from one of the balconies of the Moneda as a sign of surrender. At that very instant, inside . . . a group of about thirty people including members of the GAP, the National Bureau of Investigations, and doctors was approaching the same door that the general was trying to break down.
>
> . . . The door . . . suddenly collapsed and a platoon of soldiers . . . charged in. . . .
>
> Dr. Soto heard the general saying to him, "Go up to the second floor and tell Allende that he has ten minutes left to surrender. . . ."
>
> Dr. Soto obeyed and went up to the second floor.
>
> There he found Allende . . . dispensing orders. . . . Allende seemed not to hear him.
>
> . . . At last he said, as if from another world, "Go down, go down all of you. I shall go down last of all. . . ."
>
> The ten minutes . . . expired. . . . The general went up, accompanied by a few men.
>
> He searched the presidential Gallery. . . . Seven or eight GAPs were still putting up a proud and desperate resistance. As the fire advanced upon them from the rear with devastating rapidity, these GAPs either fell, riddled with bullets, or perished in the fire, but those who remained alive would not surrender.
>
> . . . The GAPs were just a few yards away, darting from room to room, poking their heads around the doorways as they fired, continuously shouting to each other to keep their courage up. References to the soldiers' parentage, genitals, and rear ends reverberated with the bullet shots from one side to the other.
>
> When the general reached the O'Higgins Hall it was already in flames. . . .

> Explosions could be heard when a crate of ammunition caught fire. . . . The general calculated . . . there can be no more than four or five [defenders] left. . . .
>
> The roof began to cave in and was gradually enveloped in the flames. General Palacios' group was joined by the other soldiers who had been advancing from the other end of La Moneda. . . .
>
> An officer shouted, "Over here, General! In Independence Hall!"[133]

The magazine *Qué Pasa* picks up the story of what happened at the back end of the procession that La Payita had led down the stairs. The account is based on the recollections of Patricio Guijón Klein, one of the doctors in Allende's entourage:

> The president was last in the line. Passing the Independence Salon, he slipped out of the procession and—without being observed—entered it. He sat down on a sofa, took off his gas mask, his helmet, and his glasses. As he had threatened to do, he placed the muzzle of Fidel's gift automatic rifle under his chin. The rifle was set on "automatic," and there were two shots left. He pressed the trigger. The two bullets blew out his cranial chamber. There was not much blood; only brain matter propelled in all directions.
>
> Doctor Guijón heard the shots, went into the Salon and—in an instinctive professional reaction—tried to help the chief magistrate. In doing so, he changed the position of the automatic rifle.[134]

Guijón was later quoted as saying that he stayed with the body for eight or ten minutes, as the rest of the defenders had already left. He then saw three or four soldiers enter, led by General Palacios.[135] Varas and Vergara resume the account from an interview with Palacios:

> General Palacios . . . found himself in a room that was almost intact, furnished in red plush. . . . Leaning back in the center of the red sofa, his head slightly tilted over his shoulder, was a man whose face at first sight was unrecognizable.
>
> His hands were swollen and covered in dust. Around him . . . were empty submachine gun shells. On the sofa were a steel helmet and a gas mask. He was wearing reddish brown trousers, a gray pullover, and a tweed jacket. Strangely enough, his shoes were clean.
>
> . . . There was not a single spot of blood, just his brains

spattered all over him. A bullet hole could be seen in the tapestry covering the wall. . . . Leaning against the body was the
submachine gun received from Fidel Castro as a gift.

The general turned toward the other man. . . . "And who are
you, young man?"

". . . Patricio Guijón. . . ."

"I was going downstairs," said the doctor, "deathly afraid. . . .
I suddenly heard two shots, turned around, opened the door,
and saw President Allende's body slumped on the sofa. . . .

"The first thing that occurred to me was to attend to his injuries, but right away I realized there was no point. I took the
submachine gun and stood it up again."[136]

Apparently Allende died between 1:50 P.M. and 2:20 P.M.; accounts
differ as to the exact time. Within minutes the last of the GAP
guards also perished.[137]

Leftist descriptions of Allende's death differ drastically from
those quoted above. Their versions have Chilean soldiers gunning
the president down in a firefight. These conflicting accounts of the
president's death will be examined in chapter 11. Suffice it to say
here—pending undiscovered evidence to the contrary—that Salvador Allende probably did die in the Independence Salon from
bullets from Fidel Castro's gift submachine gun, fired up through
his head, and did not die gunned down by soldiers in a firefight in
another location. That conclusion does not diminish Allende's real
courage in his last hours, or in many earlier ones, nor does it negate
his sacrifice for his political beliefs.

### Three P.M. to Day's End—and a Little Beyond

The Moneda continued to burn. The radios of Chile went on
broadcasting martial music, interspersed with announcements to
the populace from the Junta's representatives. The Communist and
Socialist party headquarters were attacked, and the Socialist party
building burned like a torch for hours in downtown Santiago. The
destruction may have been a blessing for the leftists: many of their
records were consumed in the flames.[138]

The military patrolled the downtown area and controlled all
movement. Clusters of half-a-dozen soldiers were stationed on the
sidewalks and streets, block by block, as other troops pressed on
with the slow process of eliminating snipers. Helicopters swept the

high roofs of office complexes as soldiers and carabineros slowly moved up through them, floor by floor.[139]

Besides the fighting downtown and at Tomás Moro, the main pitched battles were fought at the factories, at the State Technical University, and in a few workers' residential districts. In the INDUMET factory special paramilitary forces of the Socialist party carried on a gunfight with carabinero troops until about 3:30 P.M. One group then sallied out and made for the nearby Sumar plant to join another fighting contingent. After a bloody battle the carabineros overwhelmed the subgroup left in the INDUMET factory, but the fight went on at Sumar.[140] One of the plant's defenders describes the action:

> By 1:30 P.M. it was evident that the likelihood of getting armament or getting word from our union was most remote. . . . Only about forty men—mostly union officers—remained. . . . At about 2:00 P.M., a mini-bus dashed up the driveway and hastily unloaded about thirty rifles and a few machine guns. The two drivers were in a great hurry to get on to their next destination and all they could tell us was that a few of the shantytowns were putting up a stiff fight.
> . . . An army helicopter began buzzing our plant . . . spraying the area with machine-gun bursts. We returned the fire and a few of us actually scored direct hits.[141]

Other accounts assert that the Sumar workers disabled the helicopter at about 3:45. Nevertheless, the socialist fighting squads and armed factory workers were finally forced to abandon the Sumar factory and retreat to the neighboring workers' residential district of La Legua.[142] The failing light of the late afternoon gave the fleeing leftists some cover:

> From a distance the noise from La Legua sounded like ominous thunderclaps, but as we neared the town, we could distinguish the sound of cannon and machine guns. We took a circuitous route and presently were in the battle zone. . . . The entire population seemed to be on the firing line. Men, children and even women, some obviously pregnant, were rushing about with machine guns, rifles and pistols, firing away at the military who seemed to be stuck at the entry gates of town. . . . Some of us took up positions in the firehouse. Others were in the small church rectory.

> It was a ferocious battle with many, many casualties. . . . The
> streets began to look like an open grave. . . . [Ultimately, days
> later,] the Junta soldiers broke through.[143]

The State Technical University survived the night under siege and
was occupied by the military on the following day, in a bloody
operation that leftists later called a "massacre." The Junta announced that about six hundred militants, many of them foreigners, finally surrendered; large quantities of arms were found on
university premises.[144]

Resistance at the Pedagogical Institute and at the enterprises of
Pizarreño, Viña Santa Carolina, and Cristalerías Chile also led to
bloodshed. Some factories were finally reduced through hunger,
exhaustion, and depleted ammunition.[145] Regarding these operations, General Arellano made the following somewhat deprecatory
comment: "We thought the resistance would have been greater. The
people in the industrial belts had arms, but fortunately they were
not very confident in their leaders, even though Allende used to say
that he counted on a million workers ready to fight. The foreign
extremists were those who acted with the greatest decisiveness.
There were about 15,000 of them in the country."[146]

Arellano was obviously commenting with his own purposes in
mind, but he was probably right in saying that the military expected more organized resistance than they actually encountered.
Leftist sources reported "furious battles" in Valparaíso during the
days after the coup, and the leftist militants seem to have been
slaughtered. Some leftist resistance was also said to have continued
in Linares province.[147]


In the late afternoon of the eleventh the Junta declared a period of
free transit and urged all those who had spent the day in downtown
offices to proceed to their homes. The center of the city appeared
largely pacified—although intense sniper fire resumed that night
and flared up after dark for several nights thereafter. We sent most
of the embassy personnel home at this time.

My deputy, Herb Thompson, urged me to return home as well,
suggesting that we alternate nights at the embassy offices. I realized
that the three Junta principals were headquartered outside the center of the city, and had I been directed from Washington to talk with
any of them, my being holed up in the embassy offices until the

curfew ended might have complicated matters. With mixed emotions, I made my way toward the embassy residence.

My daughter Margaret recorded my description of my transit through the city:

> After six P.M. *no one* can move on the streets. . . . Dad came home at seven to six. I remember looking to see whether he had made it. He said the streets were so quiet it was eerie. No cars, no people—only police barricades . . . frisking. . . . It was raining a bit. . . . He said they were still shooting down there. I asked him what had happened to Allende. He said he didn't have the faintest idea, but that there had been rumors. One was that he had taken asylum in the Mexican Embassy; another was that he had been seen taken out of the Moneda with his hands tied; another was that he was dead. . . .

The embassy residence stands at the top of a shrub-covered ridge, several hundred yards above a front gate normally guarded by two or three carabineros. Behind the house there was only a low concrete wall, which my children regularly scaled to wander in the empty woods rolling down to the then abandoned greens of Los Leones golf club. The MIR could not have realized how easy a target we were. I later learned that I occupied the number one spot on their postcoup hit list.

The evening was silent and almost tranquil on that ridgetop. An occasional military helicopter passed overhead, and we heard some exchanges of fire around us. We could also hear some of the military sweep operations in the distance and see flares and detonations reflected against the sky. Fires lighted the night in various parts of the city, including the area of the Moneda, although we could not see the building itself.

It was later reported that the Forensic Division of the Homicide Squad was admitted to the Moneda Palace at about 4:20 P.M. By 6:10 the division had examined the president's body, made sketches, taken 27 police photographs, certified the death, and done whatever else such squads do.[148] The report concluded:

> An external examination by the police revealed in the chin a star-shaped erosive-contused wound, representing the point of entry of the projectile, and on the borders of which was an appreciable amount of carbonaceous dust. In the right

superficial zygomatic arch, another wound, apparently the point of exit of the projectile or of a bone splinter. In the left parietal region, a wound marking the bullet's point of exit producing the shattering of the cranial vault. There are fractures in the upper jaw, maxillary, the lower maxillary, the nose, and the forehead. Lividity developing in the corresponding areas. Incipient rigidity at the maxillary level. Probable cause of death: cranial-encephalic trauma from a bullet wound of a suicidal nature.[149]

According to the report, no wound was noted other than those mentioned. None of the 27 photographs has ever been published.

General Palacios apparently covered the president's remains with a Bolivian poncho he found in the Independence Salon and had the body taken to the military hospital for an autopsy by military, police, and forensic doctors. The president was buried the next day, shortly after noon, in a family vault in the Santa Inés Cemetery close to the Allendes' house in Viña del Mar. The air force had flown the remains down to the coast that morning, accompanied by the president's widow, his sister Laura, nephews Eduardo Grove Allende and Patricio López, and the president's air force aide, Colonel Sánchez. Apparently the military did not permit Allende's own name to be chiseled on the stonework of the crypt, perhaps in hopes that the grave would not become a shrine. Nor was the president's widow allowed to have the coffin unsealed and touch the remains, although the military officer in charge, Commander Contreras, had the lid raised so she could look for a moment through a glass panel and see either the bandages around her husband's head or a cloth covering the remains.[150] According to Varas and Vergara, Contreras explained his refusal to open the coffin by the fact that he did not have the authority and that the coffin's seals could not be resoldered. The account continues:

> Hortensia Bussi de Allende apparently decided not to press the point, and the casket was placed in the tomb of the Grove family.
>
> Laura watched the faces of the six men who were lowering the coffin into the crypt and concluded from their expressions that they were unaware of whom they were burying.
>
> "Here lies comrade Allende," she said to them. "The people will not forget him."

> Then, according to Commander Contreras, the widow plucked a wild flower and dropped it on the coffin.[151]

According to other reports, the president's widow then declared, with her voice raised so the gravediggers could hear: "Salvador Allende cannot be interred in so anonymous a way. I want you, at least, to know the name of the person you are burying. . . . Here we leave Salvador Allende, who is President of the Republic. . . ."[152] Varas and Vergara continue: "Laura Allende also plucked a wild flower and cast it on the coffin, but it did not hit its mark. One of the workmen went down into the crypt, picked it up, and laid it in its intended place. Laura noticed the eyes of one of the workmen were filled with tears."[153]

Learning with reasonable certainty on Thursday that the president was dead, I sent a handwritten letter of condolence to Mrs. Allende at the Mexican Embassy. I meant what I wrote, although I doubt that Mrs. Allende either welcomed my letter or believed me. I did not report the dispatch of my personal note to the Department of State until the U.S. government subsequently came under fire for having made no expression of condolence to Mrs. Allende.[154] At that time I sent a telegram informing Washington of what I had done.

The Junta, Pinochet, Merino, Leigh, and Mendoza, formally constituted itself at 4 P.M. on the afternoon of the coup, with Admiral Carvajal signing the act for Admiral Merino, who arrived in Santiago by helicopter at six o'clock. At 7:10 P.M., at the Military School, the Junta held its first formal session, and later in the evening the members of the Junta took their oaths of office.[155]

Almost exactly at midnight on 11 September there was an exchange of fire between the Junta's troops and personnel of the Cuban Embassy. Ambassador García Incháustegui was wounded superficially in one hand.[156]

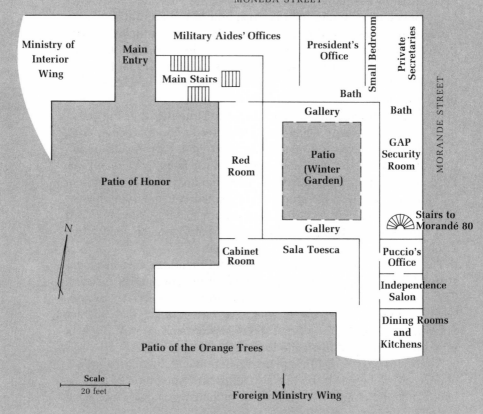

**Map 3.** Second floor of the Moneda, north

# Chapter 11

# Assassination or Suicide?

As high-school English teachers have pointed out over the years, a Shakespearean tragedy has its climax, and the climax is followed by the denouement, which clarifies the outcome but inevitably brings a letdown. So it must be with this story. The narrative must now give way to analysis. The historical impact of Allende's death and the destruction of *Unidad Popular* was searing and the United States assumed a central role in the Chilean morality play.

This chapter and the two that follow examine questions on the U.S.-Chilean relationship. This chapter inquires into the manner of Allende's death; chapter 12 will examine U.S. covert action in Chile during Allende's last two years; and chapter 13 will consider allegations that the U.S. government masterminded the 1973 coup. Does the manner of Allende's death matter? The meaning of contemporary Chilean history is the same no matter whether the president killed himself or was killed. The debate affects Americans, however, as U.S. moral complicity in Allende's murder is widely charged.

Unfortunately, the analysis requires an almost clinical examination of the condition of the deceased president's remains. It would have been more respectful to Salvador Allende's memory to have avoided this forensic examination, but the controversy over his death will not go away. The truth, moreover, must be pursued by sifting through seemingly minor facts and circumstantial details, but there is no real way around this necessity.

The military version is that Allende committed suicide. Five contrary accounts of Allende's death have created the basis for the hypothesis that he was murdered. They are the testimony of a young GAP fighter in the Moneda; a version disseminated by Fidel Castro; a narrative written by Gabriel García Márquez; an account published by a Chilean journalist named Robinson Rojas Sandford; and a report published by Taylor Branch and Eugene M. Propper in their book *Labyrinth*. The military version and the five opposing descriptions will all be examined.

### The Military Version

The Junta's version is essentially the one recounted in the previous chapter. In brief, the president decided at about 1:50 P.M. to end the armed resistance and surrender. Allende ordered his companions to march down the stairs to the Morandé 80 door of the Moneda, with La Payita at the front of the procession and the president himself bringing up the rear. Unbeknownst to the others, Allende ducked into the Independence Salon. He placed his submachine gun between his knees, put the end of the barrel under his chin, and pulled the trigger. Dr. Guijón heard the shots and rushed back to find the dead president; he maintained a terrified vigil over the body for eight to ten minutes. Then a group of military led by General Palacios burst into the Independence Salon. They found that the top of the president's head had been blown off and brain matter had spattered the ceiling and a tapestry on the wall behind the president.

Nobody questions Guijón's presence in the Moneda, and numerous witnesses confirm that he was in the procession. General Palacios and his military did not see the president die, of course, but the general's testimony, if truthful, would confirm the scene in the Independence Salon and Guijón's presence there. Palacios was probably also in a position to know whether or not soldiers obedient to the Junta had gunned Allende down.

Yet the military version can be assailed. In *The Murder of Allende* Robinson Rojas Sandford presents a detailed, point-by-point refutation of the official suicide account.[1] He attacks the description of the location and condition of the president's body, the plausibility of the surrender and procession downstairs, and the validity of Guijón's and Palacios's eyewitness testimony. Regarding Allende's body, Rojas claims flaws in pro-Junta descriptions of the position of the corpse, the seat on which the dead president was situated, and the place where Castro's submachine gun was found. He decides that the suicide was staged, as described below. An examination of this argumentation will accompany my analysis of Rojas's "staged suicide" hypothesis.

Regarding the surrender procession, Rojas begins his book by describing a furious military engagement inside the burning palace and Allende being gunned down without ordering any surrender. Rojas talks of "defenders who had no intention of surrendering" and continues: "As has been established, the defenders in the Palacio de La Moneda never expressed any desire to surrender. . . ."[2] It is indeed true that a number of GAP guards fought to the end, but there is little question that Allende ordered his companions down the stairs to surrender. He did say that he would go last, and some GAP guards, doctors, and others did file down. These events are confirmed by so many witnesses including leftist companions of the president, and by so many photographs, TV films, and contemporaneous reports over Chilean radio stations, as to make their reality certain.[3] A surrender procession that some GAP guards joined is not inconsistent with other GAP guards battling on, and continuing resistance by some GAP defenders is no proof that the surrender and procession were invented.

Rojas questions the consistency and credibility of eyewitnesses. Dr. Guijón is quoted in most versions of his story as having heard shots and as having rushed back to find the dead president in the Independence Salon. Rojas quotes Brig. Gen. Ernesto Baeza, the Junta's director of investigative police, however, as announcing a different version to reporters on 20 September 1973. Rojas says that Baeza quoted a deposition made by Guijón as follows:

> As we were going down to the Morandé Street door to give ourselves up, I remembered that I had left my gas mask behind. . . . And just as I went to look for it, I passed in front of the door to the next room. Just in front of me, to the right, sitting on a sofa, I saw President Allende at the precise moment when he shot himself with a gun between his legs.

I could see his body shake and his head explode upward in smithereens. . . .[4]

Curiously, *El Mercurio* of 21 September 1973 quotes Baeza as having said something quite different in the press conference. The newspaper says: "According to the testimony of Dr. Patricio Guijón Klein . . . the last in the procession was Allende. Passing by the 'Independence Salon,' the former Chief Magistrate dropped behind, and when he had closed the salon's double door, which left him alone, he sat down on a sofa and shot himself with his submachine gun."[5] This account, published at the time, would seem to be more reliable than Rojas's description written several years later, particularly as Rojas cites no source. But the answer is not that simple. Other reporters, publishing in the past year or two, have described interviews with Guijón in which the doctor seems to have said roughly what Rojas quoted him as saying. For example, a Spanish journalist, Pedro Pascual, published articles in September 1983 in which he said Guijón told him a few months after the coup that he had actually seen Allende shoot himself. A French journalist, Philippe Chesnay, published an article at about the same time saying he had just interviewed Guijón in Santiago and had been told that Guijón had looked through a half-open door and had seen the president in that very instant "pulling the trigger of his submachine gun which he had between his knees. . . . He saw the jolt, the jump of the president's body resulting from the impact, and the explosion of the cranial chamber."[6]

What could be the explanation? Guijón, one might think, would have a clear recollection of so transcending an event. One might speculate that the military authorities talked Guijón into changing his story in order to make it more vivid or credible. Or Guijón might have come to exaggerate the immediacy of what he had witnessed for reasons of self-importance. Another possible explanation is less flattering to Allende and to Guijón, but it would provide Guijón with a compelling motive for changing his story. Mario Arnello, a leader of the National party, made the following comment about Allende's last act: "He hesitated. . . . Some say that he even asked the doctor to pull the trigger."[7] Guijón, if he did in fact pull the trigger at the president's behest, would have had good reason to falsify elements of his later testimony.

Rojas quotes a statement by General Palacios on 22 September that he came upon Guijón when the doctor was either beside the president "or in a corner" of the Independence Salon. Rojas suggests that Palacios's uncertainty about Guijón's location discredits the general's veracity. Moreover, says Rojas, Palacios on the 22nd asserted that Guijón "was shaking and could hardly speak." This description, according to Rojas, contradicts Palacios's later, more matter-of-fact statement that Guijón had identified himself and attested that the president had committed suicide. Rojas claims that Guijón "'shaking' and babbling . . . is replaced by a Guijón with aplomb." The contrast is overdrawn, however; the two statements are not contradictory.[8]

Guijón's account is supported by Carlos Briones. In a newspaper interview Briones said that Guijón, on the very day of the coup, had related to him how he had gone back from the procession and had come upon Allende in the Independence Salon. The military would not have had much time to concoct a fable and suborn the doctor if Guijón was already telling Briones, a loyal friend of Allende's, about his experiences within a few hours of their having taken place.[9]

Moreover, as Chesnay points out, Guijón was not set free but sent to Dawson Island, together with other important UP prisoners. Had Guijón really betrayed Allende by testifying for the Junta's big lie, his position vis-á-vis his fellow UP detainees would have been highly precarious. One would have expected the military at least to have isolated him for his own protection.[10]

Rojas attacks additional inaccuracies in the official version. He makes a point, for example, of a discrepancy in the police report fixing the time of the president's death. The report says death occurred six hours previous to the completion of the Homicide Squad's examination at 18:10—while, in fact, the president died at about 2 P.M.[11] It would not have been surprising, however, if the police had substracted 6 from 18 and inadvertently got 2 P.M.. Such an error may seem unlikely, but the police were operating under great pressure. In any case, Rojas gives no rationale to show that the discrepancy served a purpose of concealment or deceit. Rojas also conjectures a deliberate mixing-up of the Homicide Squad's examination of the remains in the Independence Salon and the military-led autopsy later in the evening. There was some confusion between references to the two examinations, but Rojas gives no rationale for the mix-up.[12]

Palacios and Guijón both had strong incentives to conform to the Junta's public position. Palacios would presumably follow orders, and Guijón, in captivity, would have felt himself under pressure to say what his captors wanted in order to save his own skin. Rojas notes that Guijón was "freed unconditionally" in December 1973.[13] Perhaps release was his payoff for false witness, but Guijón was actually freed during the same period as were most of the other surviving doctors.

To conclude this discussion of the Junta's version, Rojas points out real discrepancies. But were they innocent reflections of the confusion of the moment or the result of a sinister fabrication? By far the most serious inconsistency is between Guijón hearing shots and Guijón seeing Allende shoot himself—or having helped him do the deed. With these considerations in mind, it is time to examine the five leftist accounts of assassination.

### The González Version

Luis Renato González Córdoba was a 17-year-old GAP member who, from refuge in the Mexican Embassy a week or so after the event, taperecorded an account of what he had experienced on the day of the coup. Apparently, González had acted as a steward at Tomás Moro and was, he claimed, the one who woke the president every morning. After fighting in the Moneda battle, González eluded the military and made his way to safety with the Mexicans.[14] He reports Allende's combat death in the following excerpt:

> We encountered a group of fascists under the command of Captain Mayor, in the halls near the Red Room. He shouted: "Surrender, Señor Allende." Our compañero said, "Never. It is better to leave dead than surrender." When he finished we heard a shot from the military. It hit the Doctor [Allende]. They opened machine gun fire, and we fired against them. Twelve of our compañeros fell dead at the side of President Salvador Allende. Our firing became more intense. The officer and six soldiers fell. We approached the President's body. He was mortally wounded. He told us, "A leader may fall, but still there is a cause. America will be free." It was 1:50 P.M. when compañero Allende fell, assassinated by the bullets of the fascists and traitors. He had been hit by about six bullets; four in the neck and two in the thorax.
> . . . We picked up his martyred body and took it to its place,

the Presidential Office. We sat him in his seat, put his Presidential banner on, his gun in his arms, and embraced him. We found the flag . . . and covered his body in it.[15]

There is evidence, however, that González was in no position to know how Allende died. Manuel Mejido, a reporter for the Mexican newspaper *Excelsior*, managed to interview several of the asylees in the Mexican Embassy, including González, and wrote a story about these interviews on 18 September, only a week after the coup. Mejido quoted González at that time as follows:

> "On leaving thru the door into Morandé Street, I threw myself to the ground and pretended to be having an attack. One of the president's doctors . . . told the carabineros that I was suffering from an attack of hepatitis. They believed him and I went to the military hospital as a detainee.
>    "Another doctor from the Popular Unity helped me to escape [from the military hospital in disguise as an orderly]."[16]

In this early interview González seems to be saying that he himself left the Moneda in the procession led by La Payita. If he did, he could not have been back in the Moneda watching Allende being gunned down, carrying the president to his office, embracing the remains, and covering them with a flag.

González's taped account of Allende's murder is, moreover, inconsistent with generally established facts. "Captain Mayor" appears in no other known report. It is not entirely clear, in fact, whether "Mayor" was a name or a rank—the Spanish for major. Moreover, four bullets in the president's neck and two in the thorax would have been difficult to conceal from later witnesses and would have left a considerable trail of blood.

The locations in the Moneda that González mentions are also inconsistent with other evidence. The Red Room, the president's office, and the Independence Salon were three separate rooms in the Moneda Palace, and some distance removed from one another. If the president died in a hall near the Red Room, how does one account for the cranial matter that most witnesses described on the wall and ceiling of the Independence Salon?

The entire text of González's taped account has misstatements of fact.[17] For example, González describes how the military killed a number of Allende's prominent colleagues who either did not actually perish or are known to have died in other ways. He pictures Flores and Vergara returning to the Moneda from their surrender negotiations at the Ministry of Defense and being shot in the back outside Morandé 80, with Vergara "assassinated." According to other accounts, the emissaries were detained at the ministry, and Vergara was actually sent to Dawson Island.[18] González says he witnessed Olivares falling dead in a fire fight. Other accounts have Olivares committing suicide. González also has Palma coming out of the Public Works Ministry with his hands up and being "riddled with bullets." Other accounts—and publicly viewed TV footage—place Palma inside the Moneda and show him arrested and led off in custody. Palma, like Vergara, was later detained on Dawson Island.[19]

González seems to have changed his line sometime after being interviewed by Mejido. The Mexican journalist explicitly reports that Allende "died by his own hand." Nowhere in the news story does Mejido indicate that González told him anything at variance with the suicide account or that González had been an eyewitness to assassination. In the same news story Mejido reports interviews with René Largo Farías and his deputy, Jorge Uribe. Mejido quotes Uribe as saying: "I was also beside President Allende at the last moment." None of the three men who had been in the Moneda gave Mejido reason to believe that Allende's death was anything but suicide.[20]

A few conjectures suggest how and why González might have shifted his story. The Buenos Aires newspaper *El Mundo* reported on 12 September 1973 that the Chilean Socialist party was accusing the military of having murdered Allende, Vergara, Olivares, Palma, and Briones.[21] Except for Briones, these are the same people González said were gunned down—a striking coincidence.

González's narrative became the account to which the world's leftists first pointed in saying that Allende was assassinated. It later transpired, however, that González's description of events had too many inaccuracies to hold up, and other assassination accounts gradually replaced it.

The second significant event in the suicide-or-murder controversy was Mrs. Allende's own shift in position. It should probably be discussed together with the González version because Mrs.

Allende may have been referring to González's taped account when she changed her public stance.

In a 15 September 1973 long-distance telephone interview with a Mexican TV reporter from her refuge in the Mexican Embassy in Santiago, the president's widow confirmed that Allende had shot himself. Reuters from Mexico City reported her statement: "Asked if she believed her husband had committed suicide, she said, 'Yes, he did it with a submachine gun given to him by his friend, Fidel Castro.' "[22]

Mrs. Allende did not herself witness the events in the Moneda, of course, but she had moved about Santiago to some degree after the coup, had flown to and from Valparaíso for her husband's interment, and had talked to her daughters and others by telephone. How much contact she had had with other asylees in the Mexican Embassy is not clear. González had been in the Mexican Embassy for three days and Largo Farías and Uribe had been there for two days when Mrs. Allende made her statement of the fifteenth.

When Mrs. Allende arrived in Mexico City on the sixteenth, she reiterated that President Allende had committed suicide. She told newsmen at the airport: "My husband preferred to kill himself rather than be betrayed alive."[23] On the nineteenth, however, she announced that "on the basis of new information" she had changed her mind. She had learned, she said, that there were "several bullet wounds" in her husband's stomach and chest in addition to the one bullet hole through the mouth that the Junta reported. "I think he was murdered because of the bullet wounds he received," she said; and she cited "eyewitnesses," including her daughters and doctors and reporters whom she said she could not identify for fear of jeopardizing their safety.[24]

Mrs. Allende's daughters had left the Moneda two hours or so before the president's death and could not have been eyewitnesses. Nor were the doctors present, unless Mrs. Allende meant Dr. Guijón. Both the "eyewitness" reference and the "several bullet wounds" in her husband's stomach and chest sound like González's "eyewitness" report of bullets in the president's neck and thorax.

Mrs. Allende changed her position three days after her arrival in Mexico. It is noteworthy that a spokesman for the UP-appointed Chilean ambassador in Mexico City said publicly on the day after the coup that President Allende had not committed suicide but had died fighting a platoon of soldiers in the Moneda Palace.[25] González must have taped his account in the Mexican Embassy in Santiago sometime after the Mejido interviews, which were conducted on or just before the eighteenth. The timing fits closely. One could deduce that UP leaders in Mexico City and others in refuge at the Mexican Embassy in Santiago were in communication with each other, and that those in Mexico City advised Mrs. Allende to change her position at about the same time their colleagues in the Mexican Embassy in Chile, four thousand miles away, were helping González tape his "eyewitness account."

### The Fidel Castro Version

On 28 September 1973 Fidel Castro addressed a great crowd in Havana and gave his version of Salvador Allende's death:

> At about 2 P.M. they [the fascists] succeeded in occupying a corner of the second floor. The President stood backed up for defense, together with some of his companions, in a corner of the Red Room. Advancing toward the place where the fascists were, he was shot in the stomach and doubled up in pain. But he did not stop fighting. Leaning on a chair, he continued firing against the fascists at short range, until a second shot in the chest brought him down, and—already dying—he was riddled with bullets.
>
> Seeing the President fall, members of his personal guard counterattacked vigorously, and again pushed the fascists back to the main stairway. There followed, in the middle of the combat, a gesture of unusual dignity. Taking the inert body of the President, they carried it to his office; they sat him in his presidential chair; they placed his presidential sash on him; and they wrapped him in the Chilean flag.
>
> Even after the death of their heroic president, the deathless fighters in the palace resisted the savage, attacking fascists for two more hours. Only at four in the afternoon . . . was the last resistance extinguished.[26]

Castro had a number of knowledgeable sources. The Cuban ambassador, his staff, and embassy dependents, including Allende's daughter Beatriz, had flown to Havana after the coup. Apparently Castro also relied heavily on Jorge Timossi, chief correspondent in

Santiago of Prensa Latina, the Cuban news agency. Timossi had been in contact by phone with the defenders inside the Moneda during the day of the coup and was well informed about the events of the eleventh.[27] It is unlikely, however, that Castro had access to people who might have seen President Allende die.

Castro's account is not compatible with verified facts. Even the excerpt just quoted contains inaccuracies. For example, most contemporary accounts indicate that the battle ended considerably earlier than at 4 P.M. So far as Castro's description of Allende's death and the subsequent ceremony is concerned, it is essentially the same as González's and is subject to the same objections. Additional evidence, in fact, tends to refute the assertion that the president's body was moved to his office for the "gesture of unusual dignity." There was a direct telephone hookup, already noted, between the president's office and Radio Corporación, which was maintained, with an open microphone in the Moneda, until the military seized the office. As a result, people at Radio Corporación could hear what was happening. The young Socialist whose experiences at Radio Corporación were later published gives the following account:

> We . . . listened to what was going on in the president's office over the microphone. . . .
> We kept in contact with President Allende until approximately 2 P.M. At this time the person in the president's office who was attending the microphone said that everything was very difficult and that we shouldn't call because they could not distract anyone in order to answer. He left the microphone on, however, on top of a table, so we could continue hearing what went on inside. We recorded this and the tape is now outside Chile. There were more than eighteen of us inside the station and we heard how the president gave orders to fight and resist, how they took out cases of munitions, how they gave out some arms (which belonged to the palace guard and had all been there before), and later we heard a long silence. After ten minutes of profound silence we heard intense firing, and later a new silence. No more than three or five minutes passed when we heard the voices of military officials saying, "Lieutenant, here is a case; give me something to open this desk with," but not once did they speak about President Allende. Later we learned that the Junta was saying that the president had committed suicide in his office. We were listening to everything that went on inside his office and at no time did they speak about President

Allende. This, of course, is very curious and makes us imagine a
series of things with respect to the way the president died.[28]

The young Socialist was mistaken when he said the Junta placed
Allende's death in his office, where the microphone stood. The
Junta has always reported the president's death as having taken
place in the Independence Salon. The significance of this testimony is that it contradicts González and Castro. It is conceivable
that the moving of the body, the vesting of the president with his
sash, and the placing of the flag around him could have been carried out without a sound or a word, but it is highly unlikely.

As the young Socialist describes later in his reminiscence, most
of the eighteen at Radio Corporación were captured and then released before 6 P.M. on the day of the coup. They probably became
active in the Socialist underground, which was organized immediately. Within twenty-four hours the Socialists were disseminating a report of President Allende's assassination. The dark
apprehensions of these young Socialists may have had some role in
producing the charges of murder that have spread around the
world.

The young Socialist's account does bear a sign of editing. It passes from the vivid description of the scene at 2 P.M. to a word
picture of the distribution of arms from the palace guard's stocks,
implying that these two events followed each other. Yet the opening of the small-arms magazine and subsequent distribution of
arms took place earlier.[29] It is also interesting that the tape recording, which the young Socialist said is "outside Chile," presumably
in leftist hands, has never surfaced.

Castro himself, in his speech of 28 September, expressed doubts
about the murder theory:

> The fascists . . . have tried to emphasize the suicide version.
>     But even if Allende, gravely wounded, in order not to fall
> prisoner to the enemy, should have shot himself, this would not
> be to his discredit, but would have constituted a gesture of
> extraordinary valor.
>     Calixto García, one of the most glorious figures in our history,
> was taken prisoner by the enemy. When they told his mother
> that her son was a prisoner, she said: That cannot be my son!
> But when they told her: Before being taken prisoner, he fired a
> shot in order to take his own life, she said: Ah! Then yes. That is
> my son![30]

If Castro, after an investigation that allegedly was extensive, produced so equivocal a conclusion,[31] his comments could almost be regarded as backhanded support for the suicide theory—as well as a testimonial to Castro's candor.

### The García Márquez Version

A third description of Allende's death scene was written by Gabriel García Márquez, the Colombian Nobel Prize–winning novelist. It clearly postdates the González and Castro accounts:

> Around four o'clock in the afternoon, Major Gen. Javier Palacios managed to reach the second floor with his adjutant, Captain Gallardo, and a group of officers. There, in the midst of the fake Louis XV chairs, the Chinese dragon vases, and the Rugendas paintings in the red parlor, Salvador Allende was waiting for them. He was in shirtsleeves, wearing a miner's helmet and no tie, his clothing stained with blood. . . .
> Allende knew General Palacios well. . . . a dangerous man with close connections to the American Embassy. As soon as he saw him appear on the stairs, Allende shouted at him: "Traitor!" and shot him in the hand.
> . . . According to the story of a witness who asked me not to give his name, the President died in an exchange of shots with that gang. Then all the other officers, in a caste-bound ritual, fired on the body. Finally, a noncommissioned officer smashed in his face with the butt of his rifle. . . .[32]

García Márquez differs considerably from González and Castro. Unlike earlier versions, García Márquez's takes into account the fact that the president's skull was found broken open. He also does not repeat the discrepancies associated with the surrender procession down the stairs.

The observer has no way of knowing whether García Márquez was in a position to know the facts. García Márquez explains that his story had to be "pasted together from many sources, some reliable, some not,"[33] and he identifies none of them. But his account does contain many factual errors. He says Palacios reached the second floor of the Moneda "around four o'clock." While Castro has the GAP fighting on till then, no observer besides García Márquez fixes the president's death as later than a few minutes after 2 P.M. García Márquez has Palacios reaching the second floor with his "adjutant, Captain Gallardo." The name Gallardo or Garrido will be discussed below, but it does not appear that Palacios had an adjutant with such a name.[34] García Márquez shows Allende personally wounding Palacios in the hand. It is true that Palacios was wounded in the hand, but not by the president.[35] García Márquez has Allende knowing Palacios well; Palacios said afterward that he had met the president only a few times.[36] With respect to Palacios's "close connections to the American Embassy," the general had been abroad and had no particular familiarity with U.S. Embassy people. García Márquez is alone in describing the "caste-bound ritual," nor is there any history in Chilean military tradition of such a ritual.

In a crucial revelation García Márquez says Allende's clothing was stained with blood, whereas nonleftist accounts have Allende's clothing essentially unstained and the president free of body wounds even in death. This difference has become a major point of controversy, since González's and Castro's accounts—and García Márquez's version—have the president receiving multiple body wounds, and since Mrs. Allende explained her shift to the assassination theory on the basis of reports of such wounds.

García Márquez concludes his description of Allende's death scene by saying that a noncom "smashed in his face with the butt of his rifle." Other accounts report that the top of the president's head had been blown off but that his face was largely undestroyed. García Márquez also does not explain the brain matter observed by witnesses on the wall in the Independence Salon. According to García Márquez, Allende died and his remains were defiled in or just outside the Red Room. The Red Room, as García Márquez describes it, was a room with "Rugendas paintings," but there were no Rugendas paintings in that chamber in 1973.[37] Could García Márquez have been mixed up in his locations altogether?

Three key points of controversy emerge: the location of the president's death, the extent of his bodily wounds, and the nature of the damage to his head. These questions will be examined further as the fourth and fifth accounts of Allende's death are addressed.

### The Rojas Version

The fourth account on which the assassination theory rests is contained in Robinson Rojas Sandford's *The Murder of Allende*. The following excerpts give the essentials according to Rojas of President Allende's last moments:

Six or seven minutes past 2 P.M. . . . an infiltration patrol of the
San Bernardo Infantry School commanded by Captain Roberto
Garrido . . . advanced to the entrance of the Salón Rojo [the Red
Room], the state reception hall. Inside, through dense smoke . . .
the patrol captain saw a band of civilians braced to defend
themselves with submachine guns. In a reflex action, Captain
Garrido loosed a short burst from his weapon. One of his three
bullets struck a civilian in the stomach. A soldier in Garrido's
patrol imitated his commander, wounding the same man in the
abdomen. As the man writhed on the floor in agony, Garrido
suddenly realized who he was: Salvador Allende. "We shit on
the President!" he shouted. There was more machine-gun fire
from Garrido's patrol. Allende was riddled with bullets.

According to Rojas, civilian defenders drove Garrido and his
patrol back down the main staircase to the first floor. Several of the
civilians then returned to the Red Room, where Dr. Enrique París,
the president's personal doctor, examined Allende.

The body . . . showed the points of impact of at least six shots in
the abdomen and lower stomach region. After taking Allende's
pulse, he signaled that the President was dead. Someone, out of
nowhere, appeared with a Chilean flag, and Enrique París cov-
ered the body with it. . . .
Around quarter to three in the afternoon, the civilian de-
fenders were overcome. . . . Palacios . . . followed by Captain
Garrido and his patrol, marched into the Salón Rojo. . . . General
Palacios ordered: "We must seal off this room. . . . Put me
through to headquarters, to General Pinochet in person. . . ."
"Mission accomplished. . . ."
"How is the body?" the Army's commander in chief asked.
"Destroyed."
"Don't let anyone see it. Wait for instructions."

Rojas breaks off his account at this point and resumes some pages
later to describe the staging of the "suicide."

The body had to be moved to another, more appropriate location, since the Salón Rojo was half destroyed. They chose the
Salón Independencia. . . . There, SIM men [military intelli-
gence], under the command of General Javier Palacios
Ruhmann, divested Allende's body of the bloodied turtleneck
sweater he had been wearing throughout the siege. They also
removed his blue trousers, which were perforated and had
blood stains around the abdomen. They dressed him in dark

gray pants, scavenged from one of the cadavers inside La Moneda, and Allende's own gray turtleneck, the stains on which they covered by putting him into his gray tweed jacket and fastening the bottom button (the President had removed the jacket during the battle and left it on his work table). Then the SIM men seated him on the red velvet sofa against the wall that faces Morandé Street, propped him against the back of the sofa, placed in his hands the machine gun he had been using almost an hour and a half earlier, and pressed the trigger just once. Allende's head split in two; part of the brain, blood, and pieces of hair flew upward and stuck to a tapestry more than three yards above on the wall behind the sofa. . . . Because the body was already stiff from rigor mortis, it had not been easy to arrange on the sofa; the SIM men had to use force to straighten the President's legs, leaving them wide apart to stabilize the body. The arms were left hanging slightly apart from the torso.

It was 3:30 P.M. . . .[38]

While Rojas's narrative was not the cause of the worldwide impression that Allende was murdered, his description has become the one most widely quoted and believed in current times. His text was completed after the three other versions were published, and Rojas clearly takes the deficiencies of the three earlier versions into account.[39] He explains the condition of the president's head and the presence of brain matter on the walls and ceilings of the Independence Salon. He accounts for the fact that the body was viewed in the Independence Salon, not in the Red Room or in the president's office. He reconciles the assertion of leftists that the president suffered multiple body wounds with the observations of newsmen, Chilean firefighters, and others, who reported seeing no such wounds.

Rojas claims to have talked with "eyewitnesses," but he provides no indication of his sources. Although the English version of Rojas's book has over 40 pages of endnotes for 220 pages of exposition—a full page of notes for every six pages of text—the crucial discussion of the staged "suicide" and the "contradictions" in the Junta version carries no endnote or citation of any kind. These twenty pages of text include extensive quotations from purported press interviews with generals Palacios and Baeza, Guijón's deposition read to newsmen, and so on,[40] so there could hardly have been a need to protect vulnerable informants in connection with all of these materials.

Rojas's version is not entirely consistent with known facts. As already indicated, for example, Rojas asserts that the surrender and procession did not happen. In addition, Rojas seems to have the description of some of Allende's clothing wrong, including the color of his trousers.[41] Other accounts contradict Rojas's contention that the military were forced back downstairs at shortly after two and kept there for three-quarters of an hour.[42] The role of Dr. Enrique París also remains unconfirmed by other sources.[43]

After his version of the repulse of Garrido's patrol and the Enrique París episode, Rojas describes how General Palacios arrived on the scene (in his version about half an hour later than contemporaneous radio, TV, and eyewitness reports indicate). According to Rojas, Palacios then reported Allende's death directly to Pinochet by voice communication. Elsewhere in his account, however, Rojas says that Palacios informed Pinochet by means of a written "classified" message sent by jeep.[44] In actuality, Palacios was reporting to General Brady or Admiral Carvajal by voice communication, but not to Pinochet directly. It was Carvajal who informed Pinochet of the president's death, by short-wave, VHF radio-telephone. Conversations among top Junta leaders over these facilities were recorded, and transcripts were later published.[45] The 11 September recordings were also played to Spanish-speaking U.S. newspapermen after the coup. One of these Americans confirms that the published transcript of the Carvajal-Pinochet conversation is authentic. He adds that Pinochet sounded dismayed when he reacted to Carvajal's report of Allende's death.[46] Rojas was aware of these recordings when he wrote his book, and he postulates a second, rehearsed conversation in which Carvajal playacts as he notifies Pinochet of Allende's death. Rojas alleges that the fake notification was arranged to fool foreign journalists into reporting Allende's suicide to the world.[47]

What about the "staged suicide"? Rojas presents no evidence that it occurred, and he quotes no witness who might have seen the proceedings. His rationale is built entirely on a critical examination of the Junta's description of the position of Allende's body when found, the seat Allende was on, and the moving of the submachine gun. Nobody disputes the moving of the gun, by the way, as Guijón acknowledged from the start that he had done so.[48] First, Rojas observes that General Palacios reported the dead president "lean-

ing back in the center of the red sofa, his head slightly tilted. . . ."
Rojas asserts that shots from so powerful a weapon as Castro's gift
submachine gun would have thrown Allende to the floor. According to Rojas, the lack of support on either side of the president
made it even more unlikely that Allende could have remained
seated upright. Lastly, Rojas asserts that Allende would have had to
lean forward to shoot himself up through the chin, sitting in an
"unstable equilibrium" frontward.[49]

Rojas goes on to say—sarcastically, when describing the Junta
version—that Allende's "body became *rigid immediately after the
shots.*" What really happened, he suggests, was that the president's
legs were positioned apart as props when they were "already
rigid," in order to keep Allende from "falling off the sofa. . . ."
Otherwise, he claims, rigor mortis would have *had* to have set in
instantly or the president would have toppled over.[50]

The logical counterargument is that the top of the president's
head was blown off with such force and rapidity that the body was
left largely as it was. The "tremendous fire power"[51] of Allende's
submachine gun might actually have increased the chances that
inertia would leave the mass of the body on the sofa. The bullets
might have impelled his head up and his upper body back, against
the backrest behind him—which is what happened according to
the Junta account. So far as instant rigor mortis is concerned, Rojas's only real evidence is that Allende's legs were somewhat
spread, which proves little one way or the other, and his claim that
the president's body—in the absence of rigor mortis—would have
fallen off the sofa.

I have checked Rojas's description of the position of Allende's
body and his conclusion with two medical examiners with national
reputations in the field of forensic medicine. Their reactions to the
supposition that Allende's body must have been thrown to the floor
were: "Possibly, but not necessarily." From the facts presented, the
remains could have been found either on the floor or on the sofa in
the position described. They believe that a definite answer is not
possible.[52]

Rojas's account has a quality that is not characteristic of real-life
situations. There is the moving of the body from room to room, the
grave-robbing aspect of taking trousers from a nearby cadaver, the
changing of the dead president's clothes, the forcing of his remains
into a sitting position, and the discharging of Castro's gift to blow

the corpse's brains out. I find it difficult to picture the military carrying out these lugubrious procedures in guilty, lonely moments among the roaring flames of the Moneda. It would also be peculiar for the generals to stage so elaborate a tableau—and then fail to publicize it.[53] The president's remains were carried out of the Moneda under a poncho. Brutal acts were performed on the day of the coup, but such acts were generally more straightforward than the ones Rojas describes.

The murder of Allende by "Captain Roberto Garrido" (or "Gallardo") remains to be considered. Rojas reports that at 4 P.M. on the eleventh a short-wave radio located at the Ministry of Defense broadcast a report that Garrido had "executed the Communist tyrant in his own palace." The broadcasters called themselves the "Association of Free Chileans" and identified their station as Santiago 33.[54]

Civilian ham-radio operators sympathetic to the military were certainly broadcasting on the eleventh, disseminating both reliable and highly unreliable reports.[55] Moreover, the "Garrido" story was circulating within several days among foreign correspondents trying to enter Chile across the Argentinian border west of Mendoza. One of these correspondents, Juan Gossaín, published the story in the Colombian magazine *Cromos* on 24 September 1973. His description of the "Santiago 33" broadcast is clearly the same story Rojas picked up. According to Gossaín, an Argentinian ham-radio operator, Emilio Benochet, received the report and passed it on to the foreign correspondents assembled in Mendoza. Gossaín also claims that a ham operator in "Estchborn," Germany, heard the same broadcast.[56]

None of the foregoing explains Rojas's vivid description of the scene inside the Moneda, however, where Garrido guns Allende down. Both Gossaín and Rojas quote the same essential text for the "Santiago 33" broadcast, and it has only the bare announcement of Garrido having "executed" the president.

Gossaín recounts how the description of the death scene supposedly reached the outside world. He says that he heard a clandestine radio broadcast which related the following:

> The young officer who commanded the battalion went up the flight of stairs. It was Captain Roberto Garrido. With his auto-

matic pistol in his right hand, and a radio transmitter in his left one, he entered the President's office. Allende stood with his back to the door.

Garrido addressed him: "Surrender!" he said.

Allende, who had left his submachine gun on the table, answered: "You'll have to come get me." And he took a step toward the table.

Captain Garrido fired two shots. The first wounded Miriam Rupert Contreras [La Payita] in the chest. The second wounded the President below the chin. The captain must have fired low.

It was 2:10 in the afternoon.

Allende fell to the floor. There, stretched out on the rug with nobody to help him, he was finished off by the submachine guns of the troops which entered the palace.

The secretary, Contreras, was taken to a military hospital. In the afternoon of the following day, after the interment of the President, Allende's wife spoke with her. The secretary related how the last moments of the Chief Magistrate had been—up to the time Captain Garrido entered and she fell wounded. A little later, that same Wednesday, the clandestine radio broadcast the secretary's account, given from her hospital room to Hortensia Bussi [Mrs. Allende].[57]

This description cannot be true. If it were true—if one believes the young Socialist at Radio Corporación—eighteen people would have heard the action over the open mike. La Payita was not wounded and has given no substantiating eyewitness reports along the lines of Gossaín's report. Until 19 September, as already noted, Mrs. Allende was saying that her husband had committed suicide, and even then she did not say that La Payita had called her. It is probably safe to conclude that this particular "Garrido" story was simply one of the many unsubstantiated reports circulating at the time. It is more difficult to say whether Rojas's "Garrido" version was like the foregoing report or was based on something more substantial.

There are significant differences between Rojas's original 1974 Spanish text and his 1976 English version. The following example of an excision is one of many. The conspiring generals "were searching for an 'eyewitness,' and found one who filled that role under threat of being accused, by the very insurrectionary high commanders, of being the 'murderer of the President of the Republic.' "[58] The statement at least implies that the military found Guijón vulnerable, isolated, and close to the place where the president died—hence the effective threat. In fact, a Junta representative explicitly stated in a press conference on 20 September 1973 that the military had suspected Guijón of having been the "possible perpetrator of the killing of the Chief Magistrate."[59] In another passage in the Spanish text Rojas describes how Guijón was found by soldiers a few meters from the Independence Salon, huddled against a wall, shouting hysterically: "I haven't done anything." Rojas goes on to describe intelligence officers bringing Guijón to the Independence Salon and threatening to shoot him, so his own dead body would bear witness that he was the president's killer.[60] Of course the military could have found Guijón anywhere and threatened anything, but all in all it is perhaps not surprising that Rojas eliminated these tantalizing passages from the revised 1976 version of his text.

Does the rest of Rojas's book hold up in terms of reliability and seriousness of scholarship? The answer is a clear "No." The book contains a rich profusion of fanciful tales. I am mentioned exactly once, and though my own testimony about what happened in my house cannot be proved, the passage helped frame my judgment of the book. In describing the scene two nights before the coup, Rojas writes:

> What is most important is that at 4 A.M. on the tenth . . . a Chilean Army colonel in civilian clothes arrived at the house of Nathaniel Davis, the U.S. Ambassador, where there were also two members of the U.S. military mission in Santiago.
>
> After this meeting there occurred a strange event: the radio counter-intelligence services intercepted a coded message originating from the American radio transmitters in the Defense Ministry. It instructed the Operation Unitas task force. . . . Two of the destroyers were to remain more than 200 miles outside Valparaíso on the high seas. One destroyer and the submarine were to stay more than 200 miles outside Talcahuano.[61]

I know what I was doing at 4 A.M. on the tenth. I was in bed, asleep. No members of the U.S. military mission were at my house. No Chilean Army colonel came. There was no meeting. The U.S. military mission sent no coded messages from American radio transmitters in the Defense Ministry. Moreover, Rojas does not explain how he knows what the U.S. "coded message" contained. Is he claiming to have cracked U.S. military codes? As for the Unitas task force, its ships were a thousand miles, and three full days' steaming time, from Valparaíso and farther than that from Talcahuano. They never did come much closer, as will be discussed in chapter 13. The locations of the Unitas ships are fully verifiable.

One other example of Rojas's unreliability is worth mentioning: his surprising allegation of villainy on the part of Gen. René Schneider in 1970 juxtaposed against a proconstitutionalist intervention on the part of U.S. representatives. Rojas asserts that high Chilean military officers plotted a coup in September 1970; that René Schneider was "agreeable"; that the U.S. military mission in Santiago was consulted and informed the Pentagon, but the Pentagon *opposed* a coup; that the U.S. military mission informed Schneider of this position in early October 1970; and that only then did Schneider assume a constitutionalist position.[62] Rojas concludes: "What had happened in the first week of October 1970 was that the Pentagon had said *no* [his emphasis] to a military coup in Chile. The Chilean generals were left with the awkward task of dismantling the already functioning coup machinery."[63]

While this account reflects well, in a way, on the Pentagon, it is unflattering to Schneider's memory and is inconsistent with everything we now know about Track II. Of course, Rojas lacked the Church Committee's later revelations when he was writing his book in Spain. He did have Seymour Hersh's story about U.S. covert action in Chile before he published, however, and wrote an appendix, dated 6 October 1974, on the subject. Rojas concluded that the CIA and Henry Kissinger had been offered up as sacrificial lambs by the Pentagon chiefs in order to conceal the U.S. military's masterminding of the coup.[64]

### The Labyrinth Version

The last of the five murder versions appeared publicly in 1982. Eugene M. Propper was the prosecuting investigator of the U.S. Department of Justice who was principally responsible for solving the Letelier assassination case, and the *Labyrinth* account is unlike previous ones in that responsible U.S. officials disseminated it. Not only did Propper associate his name with the veracity of the story in *Labyrinth* but his coauthor Taylor Branch's source for two key assertions in the account proved to be the U.S. legal attaché in

Buenos Aires who covered Chile for the FBI, Robert W. Scherrer. Scherrer's sources—as will be explained below—were two Chilean officials of the investigative police under the Junta. The Branch and Propper version cannot be labeled as simply a leftist invention.

Branch and Propper describe Allende's death and its aftermath as follows:

> From his command post at Peñalolén, General Pinochet consults by radiophone with General Baeza and Admiral Carvajal. Baeza orders a renewed assault by his elite infantry school regiment, supported by eight Sherman tanks. . . .
>
> Infantry companies force their way into La Moneda. Small groups of them run upstairs through the smoke, covering themselves with bursts of submachine gun fire. A blond Chilean lieutenant, René Riveros, suddenly finds himself confronting an armed civilian dressed in a turtleneck sweater. Riveros empties half a clip of ammunition into the President of Chile, killing him instantly with a string of wounds from the groin to the throat.
>
> . . . General Baeza instructs regular police detectives to enter La Moneda to conduct a standard investigation of Allende's death. This move provokes the first major controversy among the new ruling generals, most of whom violently oppose any forensic examination by professionals. They want to present Allende's demise as a suicide. General Baeza objects that this is unmanly and that no such story can be maintained convincingly. The next day he will resign over this question, and only Pinochet will be able to persuade him to remain as the military government's new chief of Investigations.
>
> Baeza is overruled on the afternoon of the coup. Inside La Moneda there is great confusion over what to do with Allende's body. In the end, it is placed in a metal coffin, which is then welded shut and flown to Viña del Mar for burial. Army, navy, air force, and *carabinero* doctors have already certified that his death was a suicide.[65]

This version looks as if it were taken in large part from Rojas's book. There are striking similarities in language and description.[66] Branch did have Rojas's book at hand when he wrote the *Labyrinth* account,[67] and Branch and Propper conform to Rojas's idiosyncrasies of interpretation in some controversial areas. For example, the description of Baeza calling in the Homicide Squad and causing a "major controversy among the new ruling generals" is very much

Rojas's version of what happened. Branch and Propper also garble
the roles generals Palacios, Brady, and Baeza played in the assault
on the Moneda, saying that Baeza commanded the Santiago garrison and was in charge of the infantry school regiment in the attack.[68] Rojas had written the same thing—that Baeza commanded
the troops invading the center of Santiago. In point of fact, Baeza
was Pinochet's liaison at the Ministry of Defense, while the line of
command went from Brady, in charge of Santiago operations, down
to Palacios, in charge of the assault.[69]

Like Branch and Propper, Rojas also describes Baeza's offer to
resign on the twelfth, but Rojas gives different reasons for it. Rojas
writes that "the discrepancies even at the time were so serious that
on Wednesday afternoon, September 12, General Baeza . . . offered
his resignation to General Pinochet, shouting: 'It serves us right for
working with such dumb sonafabitches!' What had aggravated
Baeza was a press release on Allende's suicide . . . full of inaccuracies which could later cause problems. . . ."[70]

Baeza, according to Rojas, shouted that " 'this kind of declaration
[the official press release] . . . thrusts back on us precisely the
suspicions that we want to avert': the suspicions that Salvador
Allende had been assassinated."[71]

Assuming the resignation incident happened at all, two issues
arise in connection with it. First, did the official press release have
discrepancies so glaring as to put the official suicide version into
serious doubt? Second, did Baeza offer to resign as a matter of
honor or in anger over the foul-up?

The discrepancy Rojas quotes is a statement in the press release
that "at 13:09 Salvador Allende offered to surrender. . . ." Rojas
interprets the meaning as that the press release "placed Allende's
'suicide' shortly after 13:00 hours," unquestionably the better part
of an hour earlier than it could have occurred. The error probably
belongs to Rojas, however, not to the Junta. The version of the 12
September press release Rojas published was recorded from the
radio, and he seems to have misheard the time given. The regular
media, including both radio and press, that carried the press release on the twelfth and the thirteenth, recorded the Junta's version
of the surrender hour as 13:50, which is consistent with known
events on that day.[72]

Nevertheless, there was one undeniable inaccuracy in the Junta's
press release, and it just might have triggered Baeza's frustration

and anger. The release stated that the patrol sent to conduct Allende to safety, which was impeded by sniper fire, was the same one that found the president's body. Rojas did not mention this discrepancy, but it was a clear and probably embarrassing mistake.

Then there is the second question, whether Baeza resigned in honorable protest over a cover-up of Allende's murder or in frustration at the inaccuracy of the press release and perhaps of previous public statements. To sort out this question, it is necessary to describe the information Branch and Propper obtained from Robert W. Scherrer, the U.S. legal attaché from Buenos Aires. Scherrer contributed two elements to the *Labyrinth* version: first, corroboration from sources besides Rojas that Baeza offered to resign on the twelfth, and second, an identification of Allende's "killer" as a then lieutenant in the Chilean Army named René Riveros. Apparently Scherrer was told these things by investigative police officials shortly after meeting Riveros on a trip Scherrer made to Chile in 1977. Branch and Propper describe the episode as folows:

> At Pudahuel Airport, Scherrer was standing somewhat nervously in the immigration line when a blond man in civilian clothes approached him, looking official. He paid his compliments and said he was there to provide assistance. At his direction, subordinates fell into escort behind Scherrer, and they all marched around the immigration and customs lines. . . .
>
> Scherrer . . . knew—from the way Riveros had treated the flunkies around him at the airport—that the captain was a man of some influence. . . . After spending nearly two days over coffee or drinks with various Chilean confidants, Scherrer found out what he wanted to know. Captain René Riveros was a private hero to certain members of the Chilean army; it was he who had killed President Allende during the 1973 coup.[73]

Robert Scherrer was a colleague of mine when he was traveling back and forth to Santiago during the Allende time. He tells me that his sources were two senior subordinates of General Baeza in the investigative police. It was from them that Scherrer—and later Branch and Propper—got the idea that Baeza's motive was outrage at the Junta's dissembling. The interpretation that Baeza tried to resign over a cover-up is important, for it would mean that a murder must have occurred.

Scherrer notes that his sources were intensely loyal to Baeza and were trying to put their chief in the best light possible to an American official who did not sympathize with cover-ups. They would have had strong motives for gilding Baeza's reasons for his resignation on the twelfth, representing them as honor rather than frustration.

It is also somewhat unlikely that Pinochet would have maintained Baeza in the highly sensitive postion of investigative police chief if, as Branch recounts, Baeza had tried to resign over an "unmanly" act Pinochet himself was perpetrating. Pinochet would more likely have wanted someone who would support him through thick and thin—someone without too great a propensity for moral protest. In addition, Baeza soon became the chief spokesman of the Junta government on the suicide itself; it was he who described the circumstances of President Allende's death to the press on 20 September 1973.[74] If Baeza considered lying about the death to be dishonorable, it is difficult to believe that he would have been willing to become the chief disseminator of the falsehood.

What did happen? Did Baeza offer his resignation at all? If the Junta was innocent of gunning Allende down and the discrepancies in the 12 September press release were not so serious after all, why did Baeza get so excited? I accept that there might have been some sort of resignation crisis on the twelfth; Rojas and the two officials are very disparate sources to have independently furnished the same bit of fiction. I can imagine Baeza flaring up under the immense tensions of the time and threatening to quit. But I do not know what happened and the answer to this particular riddle awaits more information.

Next is the question of Riveros's identity as the killer. Scherrer tells me his two informants frankly acknowledged that their information abvout Riveros was hearsay. Moreover they were talking to Scherrer some three years after the coup. There is no question that Captain René Riveros was real, and met Scherrer that day at the airport (and had had various involvements in the Letelier case).[75] Riveros never indicated to Scherrer, however, that he had shot Allende; only Scherrer's two contacts made that allegation.

Scherrer subsequently talked with Michael Vernon Townley, the young American who had worked for the Chilean political police (DINA) and who had played a key role in Orlando Letelier's assassination. Townley had been very well connected in Junta circles before he turned U.S. state's witness in the Letelier case. Townley had known Riveros slightly but told Scherrer he had never heard it said that Riveros had killed Allende. Townley knew Riveros had carried out some "heavy contracts" for Pinochet immediately after the coup, and Townley claimed that Riveros was feared and respected by DINA agents and army colleagues for that reason. Townley told Scherrer he had heard nothing from fellow DINA agents about Allende having been shot by Chilean military personnel.[76]

Finally, there is the matter of the overall credibility of the *Labyrinth* account. Following the main outlines of the Rojas version, Branch and Propper's narrative suffers the same problems as Rojas's reasoning does. One would have to accept Rojas's staged tableau in the Independence Salon, the firing of bullets up through the dead president's head, the changing of his clothes to conceal the wounds, and so forth. Branch and Propper mention none of these things, perhaps because they found them as difficult to credit as other observers have. If they do not credit them, however, they are left with the unanswered questions that make the three pre-Rojas murder versions implausible and that Rojas "solved."

It is surprising that so little corroboration has surfaced over the past decade if either the Branch and Propper or the Rojas account is true. If one accepts the "staged tableau"—which the plausibility of both versions requires—considerable numbers of army intelligence personnel and others would have been involved. Augusto Pinochet has accumulated quite a number of enemies over the years, even within the Chilean military and police establishments, and Branch and Propper themselves give vivid descriptions of the infighting which has gone on. Is it not likely that some disgruntled officers or officials would have added corroboration by now? Perhaps not, but the secret of Allende's murder, if such a secret exists, has been better kept than most such secrets in our time.

### Allende's Wounds

One element common to all five murder accounts distinguishes them sharply from the official version of Allende's death. They all describe the president's torso as riddled with bullets. If evidence could determine the existence, or the absence, of chest and abdomen wounds, we would be closer to solving the larger riddle of the president's death.

A number of people besides Guijón, Palacios, and Palacios's

troops saw Allende's body in the Independence Salon. Rojas describes how Palacios admitted newsmen from the Catholic University TV station and El Mercurio to the salon at about 6:30 P.M.[77] El Mercurio's photographer, Juan Enrique Lira, had a phone conversation on the same day with the editor of a newspaper in Mendoza, Argentina, and Lira told the editor that he had seen Allende's body with "a bullet wound in his mouth."[78] Then there were the firemen fighting the flames in the ruined palace. Robert J. Alexander visited Santiago in 1974 and talked to the first fireman to enter the Moneda. The fireman said he had seen Allende's body and that a gun discharged under the president's chin had destroyed a good part of the president's head. Alexander's account mentions no other wounds.[79]

Rojas could say with some justification, of course, that it was precisely to create these false impressions that the military had changed the dead president's clothes and arranged the scene. One has to wonder, however, how easy it would have been to conceal Allende's body wounds if they were as extensive as Rojas and others indicate.[80]

Some eyewitnesses actually examined the body. Judd L. Kessler, a U.S. Embassy officer in Santiago, had been in the habit of playing basketball with Héctor Henríquez, the principal fingerprint expert of the Homicide Squad. It was Henríquez who took the president's fingerprints in the Independence Salon.[81] When he and Kessler met at the Santiago YMCA shortly after the coup, Henríquez confirmed the suicide account, including the head wound and the absence of body wounds. The Homicide Squad had examined the body carefully, and it is difficult to imagine Henríquez not having learned of multiple fatal wounds in the torso if they had existed. Kessler is convinced that his friend was not lying to him.

I can add from my own recollection that U.S. Embassy intelligence reporting after the coup indicated suicide. Our sources of information included some that, we could be quite sure, were not intended for American ears. There was no intimation of a staged suicide from any intelligence source.

## Other Indications and Speculations

What were former colleagues of Allende saying? Carlos Briones, Allende's last minister of interior, was still talking in early November 1973 about Allende's "suicide," without any indication that he had come to believe it was murder.[82] Carlos Prats mentioned in his diary a few days after the coup that Vice Admiral Carvajal told him "that they found the president dead." Even in the privacy of his diary Prats gives no indication that he doubts this particular statement—although he is bitterly unbelieving of other things Carvajal told him in the same conversation.[83] Even Régis Debray wrote from France on 15 September 1973 that "assassination or immolation—it doesn't much matter."[84] In context, Debray's "immolation" clearly meant suicide.

So far as centrist political circles were concerned, the 27 September 1973 statement of the Governing Council of the Christian Democratic party explicitly says that the president "committed suicide."[85] At that time the Christian Democrats were becoming increasingly disinclined to give the Junta gratuitous support. Nevertheless, they, opposition Radicals, and other displaced politicians on the Santiago scene accepted the Junta's description of Allende's death in private talks with my colleagues and me. If strong evidence of murder had been circulating in the capital's clandestine leftist subculture, centrist politicians would probably have known about it.

Jonathan Kandell of the *New York Times* interviewed middle-ranking officers who had been involved in the coup plotting and heard some highly revealing accounts of their secret conspiracies. Regarding the suicide or assassination question, however, these officers "denied that President Allende was killed, insisting that he had committed suicide rather than surrender."[86]

Did Allende contemplate suicide before the event? It may be recalled that, shortly before 10 A.M. on the day of the coup, Allende was reported to have told his service aides that he would use his last bullet to take his own life. In her 15 September telephone interview the president's widow asserted much the same thing: "Mrs. Allende said that her husband . . . had talked of suicide before. 'He always said he would never abandon the Moneda as president and he would kill himself rather than betray all his ideals.' "[87]

Paul Sigmund reports that Allende talked of suicide in his 7 September 1973 meeting with UP parties, that he had often talked about suicide, and that he had "even been known to point to a statue of a former president [Balmaceda], who had shot himself, and to assert, 'That's the way I'll go if I do not finish my term.' "[88] Germán Picó, head of a center-left newspaper in Santiago and an old friend of Allende's, told *Qué Pasa* in 1977:

> Allende told me: "Look, Germán, I swear to you before the memory of my mother that I have been tempted twenty times to take a revolver and put a shot into myself." I know he told the French Socialist, François Mitterrand, the same thing. . . . I say that the president was under very great pressure—or under very great nervous depression. I found him spiritually spent . . . the idea of suicide obsessed him a bit. For this reason, when the coup of 11 September materialized, I was left without any doubt at all that his death was a suicide.[89]

The motive for the dead president's political heirs to claim that he was murdered was strong. Fidel Castro's comments notwithstanding, suicide has a bad aura in Latin America—a more negative one than in Protestant, northern climes. It offends "machismo" and conveys a sense of weakness—besides being regarded by Catholics as a grave sin. Allende's leftist heirs would have wanted to say to the world that Salvador Allende had died with his guns blazing. They could then identify villains and exhalt the martyred hero.

When an event is this controversial, it is always difficult to know what can surely be regarded as fact. Still, all historical writing involves judgment, and the weight of evidence in this case is strong. Pending undiscovered evidence to the contrary, it would appear that the Junta version is true in its essentials, and the five opposing versions are not.

# Chapter 12

# The Covert U.S. Role, 1971–1973

CHARGES of U.S. involvement in Chile's internal affairs were pandemic throughout the Allende presidency. The ITT revelations, the copper suits and boycotts, and the "invisible blockade" were high blips in the incidence charts, but the accusations never dropped to the zero line. These allegations have been discussed in earlier chapters, and the arguments will not be repeated here— although they formed part of the indictment of the United States when Unidad Popular fell. What we are concerned with now is the question of CIA covert action of a more direct kind.

U.S. culpability in the undermining and ultimate destruction of the Chilean Way by means of covert financing and direct action is widely believed, and the facts established by the Church Committee have provided fertile ground for an ever more luxuriant undergrowth of speculation. This chapter examines CIA programs conducted between 1971 and 1973; the next will consider allegations that the U.S. government secretly masterminded the coup of 11 September 1973.

These are difficult subjects. One must thread one's way between justifications of wrongdoing and indiscriminate scandalmongering. As Flora Lewis of the *New York Times* has commented, "everything that comes out makes skepticism look nearer the mark on public affairs these days than credence, though there is also the danger of what David Reisman wisely calls 'the gullibility of the cynical.' "[1]

## U.S. Covert Action between 1971 and 1973

Whatever else is in dispute, all commentators would no doubt agree that U.S. covert action after 1970 concentrated on the funding of opposition parties and media in Chile. As described in chapter 1, almost $2.6 million in covert expenditures were approved by the U.S. Forty Committee during Allende's first year in power. Between 3 November 1971 and 11 September 1973 the additional disbursement of about $4.7 million was approved, although the last million dollars of this sum—authorized on 20 August 1973—had not been spent when the coup intervened. The U.S. government spent, in rough figures, a little more than $6 million for covert action in Chile during Allende's three years in power, about $2 million a year.[2]

Covert expenditures during the last two years of UP government essentially continued programs undertaken during the 1970–71 period, and most of the money went to the Christian Democrats, the National party, and smaller Radical splinters. An expenditure of $815,000 was approved on 5 November 1971 with almost all of the money earmarked for sustaining the organization, press organs, political activity, and publicity of these opposition parties. Another $1.8 million was approved to help finance opposition campaigns in the 1972 by-elections and in the March 1973 congressional voting, bringing the total to some $2.6 million.[3]

The sky was never the limit on these expenditures. For example, the CIA station asked in February 1973 that I support a recommendation for supplemental funds to aid opposition parties in the March elections. I opposed it, based on my conviction that the specific proposals were going beyond reasonable limits. The additional moneys were not approved.

Ongoing support of the newspaper *El Mercurio* totaled $965,000 between November 1971 and September 1973. This sum was in addition to the $700,000 authorized in early September 1971, bringing total expenditures to sustain *El Mercurio* to approximately $1.7 million during Allende's three years in power.[4]

Between November 1971 and September 1973, $50,000 were approved on 24 April 1972 for "an effort to splinter" the UP coalition, and $24,000 were approved on 21 September 1972 for support to "an anti-Allende businessmen's organization." The "effort to splinter" the UP coalition sounds more grandiose than the reality was, as the original idea had been to attract UP Radicals over to the ranks of the opposition Radicals. The funds ended up supporting the opposition Radical parties in their struggles to stay in business. A small part of the $815,000 for the opposition parties that the Forty Committee had approved on 5 November 1971 had been used for similar assistance to the opposition Radicals' efforts. I think it is fair to say that no historic Radical leaders were suborned, and the PIR departure from the UP government in April 1972 was inspired by no CIA actions that I know of.

The Church Committee staff report, from which these figures come, is somewhat ambiguous about the $24,000 that went to an anti-Allende business organization. In one context it calls the $24,000 "emergency support," and in another context it talks about funding "an opposition research organization."[5] U.S. press and scholarly accounts later identified the organization in question as the Society for Manufacturing Development (SOFOFA).[6] It was public knowledge that SOFOFA was under heavy financial pressure in mid-1972. The society established a small economic research organization and transferred over some staff economic analysts, thereby reducing its own financial liabilities. As the staff report explains, "The CIA also funded progressively a greater portion—over 75 percent in 1973—of an oppositionist research organization. A steady flow of economic and technical material went to opposition parties and private sector groups. Many of the bills prepared by opposition parliamentarians were actually drafted by personnel of the research organization."[7]

When the $24,000 for the "businessmen's organization" had been approved on 21 September 1972, the Forty Committee—on my recommendation—decided against financial support to other private-sector organizations "because of their possible involvement in anti-Government strikes."[8] While the first truckers' strike had not yet been called, the striking shopkeepers and others had already created a highly turbulent situation. The rationale of U.S. covert policy, as the Church Committee staff report explained, was to sustain opposition forces but not to foment strikes, nor to promote disruptive physical action against the UP government, nor to encourage coup plotting.[9]

Somewhat later in the year, $100,000 of funds approved for the March 1973 election campaigns went to SOFOFA, CAP (the Confederation of Private Associations), and FRENAP (the National Front of Private Activity). The staff report continues: "According to CIA testimony, this limited financial support to the private sector was confined to specific activities in support of the opposition electoral campaign, such as voter registration drives and a get-out-the-vote campaign." Had U.S. policy changed in the interim? No. By then the focus of opposition activity had shifted to the election campaign, and the danger of private-sector groups attempting to subvert the government through strikes had lessened. After the March elections had failed to end the political impasse, the U.S. policy dilemma reappeared—and with it, strong arguments for restraint on the part of the U.S. government.[10]

Although the level of funding made available to the three private-sector groups was relatively low, these were conceptually the most controversial CIA programs carried on during Allende's last two years in power. These groups, and right-wing elements in the National party, were becoming increasingly convinced that a coup was the only possible solution to the Chilean crisis. Nevertheless, as the Church Committee staff correctly described it, American policy makers attempted to maintain a "clear" and "careful" distinction "between supporting the opposition parties and funding private sector groups trying to bring about a military coup."[11]

### Did the U.S. Ambassador Know the Facts?

Edward Korry found out about Track II only long after he had left Chile. Was I in a similar position? For ten years I have made it my business to discover whether such activities were also carried on behind my back. Pending some future disclosure, I believe I knew the essentials of what was transpiring.

"The essentials" is a slippery phrase, the meaning of which the revelations of the Church Committee help clarify. For example, the staff report says that the station "suggested" in a private operational message sent to Washington in November 1971 "that the ultimate objective of the military penetration program was a military coup." Headquarters in Washington "responded by rejecting that formulation of the objective, cautioning that the CIA did not have 40 Committee approval to become involved in a coup."[12] Elsewhere, the staff report makes another reference to what seems to be this same Washington message, saying that "the Station was instructed to put the US government in a position to take future advantage of either a political or a military solution to the Chilean dilemma, depending on developments. . . ."[13] I was not informed of this exchange. The CIA station chief has since explained to me that he dispatched the message as an informal request for guidance, necessitated by his own CIA officers' differing interpretations of Washington's standing instructions.

In the same time period, according to the staff report, the CIA station increased its military contacts, "including a short-lived effort to subsidize a small anti-government news pamphlet directed at the armed services, its compilation of arrest lists and other operational data, and its deception operation."[14]

With respect to the "news pamphlet," it is not clear from the staff report whether this short-lived action occurred before or after my arrival. It appears to have been approved before I was on the scene. In any case, I was not told of it.

As for the "compilation of arrest lists," this effort was "operational intelligence necessary in the event of a coup—arrest lists, key civilian installations and personnel that needed protection, key government installations which need to be taken over, and government contingency plans which would be used in case of a military uprising." The report goes on: "According to the CIA, the data was collected only against the contingency of future Headquarters requests and was never passed to the Chilean military."[15] Internal "homework" that had no operational expression was not something the rules of the game required that the ambassador be told about. In any case, I was not consulted.

The "deception operation" was a project CIA officers in Santiago had proposed to Washington in September 1971, prior to my arrival in Chile. The idea was to provide military contacts with information—some of it fabricated by the CIA—to stir them up by insinuating that Chilean investigative police officers were conspiring with the Cubans and were digging up dirt about the Chilean Army high command. CIA headquarters in Washington rejected the deception proposal in favor of passing "verifiable" information to a military leader who was plotting against the Allende government. CIA officers in Santiago reproposed the "deception operation," however, and Washington did agree to it, "with the objective of educating senior Chilean officers and keeping them on alert." A month or two later the operation was undertaken: "In December 1971 a packet of material, including a fabricated letter, was passed to a Chilean officer outside Chile. The CIA did not receive any subsequent reports on the effect, if any, this 'information' had on the Chilean military. While the initial conception of the operation had included a series of such packages, no further packets were passed."[16]

I was not informed of these efforts. A technicality in White House–established rules may have relieved the CIA of the obligation to inform the ambassador. The agency was supposed to consult the ambassador concerning operations inside the country where the ambassador was accredited but did not have to tell him about actions in other countries, relevant or not. This "third-country" loophole was cumbersome, however, and its awkwardness may have been a reason for phasing the operation out after passing only one packet.

An added comment should be made about "third-country" CIA operations. When the CIA covert program in Chile came under public scrutiny in September 1974, press stories asserted that funds were provided to Chileans through European or neighboring Latin American conduits. For example, Laurence Stern reported on the eighth of the month that "funding was provided to individuals, political parties and media outlets in Chile, through channels in other countries in both Latin America and Europe."[17] In a similar story published the same day Seymour M. Hersh wrote: "At a closed hearing on Chile . . . [CIA director] Colby refused to rule out the possibility that some anti-Allende demonstrations in Chile may have been assisted through subsidiaries of United States corporations in Brazil or other Latin American countries."[18] *Time* asserted three weeks later that "laundered CIA money, reportedly channeled to Santiago by way of Christian Democratic parties in Europe, helped finance the Chilean truckers' 45-day strike [in 1973]." William Colby himself, in *Honorable Men*, said that "aid to the center parties, support for free and opposition journals and radios, and assistance to student and syndical groups were all funneled through third-country intermediaries to keep them alive. . . ."[19]

The common thread in these reports is the channeling of funds through third-country intermediaries. In this case, however, the station chief in Santiago did inform me of some contacts made and moneys passed outside of Chile in conformity with Forty Committee policy decisions. Colby, former CIA Western Hemisphere operations chief David A. Phillips, and other CIA executives have since told me that—apart from the examples cited from the Church Committee staff report—the third-country loophole was not employed to carry out programs of which I was ignorant. The two senior committee staff investigators for Chile, Gregory F. Treverton and Karl F. Inderfurth, confirm their statements. In this regard, it is significant that the investigative reporters who broke the 1974 stories recounted that operations went forward under explicit Forty Committee approval. If this is true, third-country operations could not have gone beyond programs of which both the Church Committee investigators and I were informed.

The foregoing does not mean, however, that Washington willingly supported the ambassador's right to know. Senior former CIA officials have told me that they resisted attempts by Henry Kissinger and his deputy, Brent Scowcroft, to deny me access to information about sensitive covert activities in Chile. Kissinger's reported attitude was: "Don't tell anybody!" Apparently, Kissinger—no doubt reflecting President Nixon's preference—would have liked to have indefinitely perpetuated the Track II arrangement, where neither the ambassador nor the secretaries of state and defense were informed.

There is still the murky question as to when Track II stopped. It may be recalled that Thomas Karamessines, head of CIA clandestine operations between 1970 and early 1973, testified that, so far as he was concerned, "Track II was really never ended." Karamessines is no longer living; David A. Phillips has explained the background to me as he views it, however, and Phillips is in an excellent position to know the facts. Not only was he the head of the CIA's task force on Chilean operations during the Track II period, but he was chief of the CIA's Latin American clandestine operations between June 1973 and the time of the Chilean coup. Phillips has also consulted his former deputy, who discharged that responsibility in the Western Hemisphere division of the CIA through all of the Allende time. In his published memoirs Phillips has used the pseudonym "Abe" for this man, and Abe does not even now wish to be identified. According to Phillips and Abe, Karamessines was right that the White House never canceled Track II. Abe was Phillips's source for the following description, as Phillips himself had returned to his overseas assignment in Brazil in late 1970, and tells me he did not until much later hear what happened to Track II after his task force was dismantled and he went back to post:

> It just faded into oblivion as new crises demanded Kissinger's attention. We did not think Track II was workable in the first place, and were quite content, as the White House chiefs turned to other matters and relaxed the pressure on Karamessines, and he on us, to put it on the back burner. This is not to say that we forgot Track II. Chile was still a concern in 1971, and something could happen that would set off a spasm of renewed interest and requirements for status reports on our Track II progress.
>
> In fact, Track II really expired in November 1971 or shortly thereafter. Abe was in charge between two chiefs of the division. He sent a written despatch—not a telegram—to Santiago, gently suggesting, almost, that it was time to forget about a coup and concentrate on intelligence reporting. It was not an order, but rather a philosophical exposition. A telegram would have been flagged for Karamessines' attention and would have put him on the spot. Karamessines, who did things by the book, would surely have felt he had to check back with Kissinger. So Abe did not discuss the despatch with Karamessines, who probably never saw it.[20]

This statement explains a lot. It explains Ambassador Korry's feeling—mentioned in chapter 1—that some CIA activities were going on without his knowledge in 1971. It explains my discovery in the Church Committee report, to my discomfiture, that operations were going on without my knowledge in the weeks after my arrival. There evidently was continuing authority under Track II, even without the third-country loophole, for these activities.

Phillips, Abe, and other former CIA officers have helped me piece together what seems to have happened. After the failure of the Track II operation in 1970, as the Church Committee reports, "the CIA rebuilt its network of contacts and remained close to Chilean military officers in order to monitor developments within the armed forces."[21] The station was under explicit orders from Washington headquarters to expand its ability to collect military intelligence and build a capability to push for a military coup if and when directed to do so. By late 1971, the station had gotten to the point where further enhancement of military sources would in its view make the U.S. "a bit pregnant" and convey encouragement to plotters. Besides, as already noted, the officers of the station were not of one mind in interpreting Washington's standing instructions. So the station sent Washington the November 1971 message referred to by the Church Committee report, in which it was suggested that the U.S. objective was a coup. Apparently the Washington reply described in the Church Committee report was Abe's "philosophical" despatch. Abe admonished the station at one point in his message to "report" history, not "make" it. He also expressed his conviction that the Chilean military commanders could not be pushed into a coup action unless or until they made that decision on their own. Still more important, Abe's caution that the Forty Committee had not approved involvement in a coup—and therefore the CIA should not act in anticipation of a go-ahead—must have put the station on notice that the Track II mandate to work behind the backs of Forty Committee members and the ambassador was no longer in force.

An ambassador must continually strive to exercise vigilance. One episode was probably the tensest moment in my relationship with the Santiago chief of station. In one of its financing operations the station had shifted from one Chilean party official to another as a conduit. The station chief was reluctant to tell me who the new "bag man" was. In a highly charged discussion I said that I did not care if the contact man was below a rank and importance that I specified, but if he was more senior than that, I would be dealing with him, and I would not tolerate doing so blind-sided. I suggested that the station chief think about the matter, and the next day, the station chief identified his contact to me.

Even had he refused to do so, virtually all covert operations can sooner or later come to an ambassador's attention. In another country where I served as chief of mission a local friend of mine once told me that a man he knew had recounted how a purported CIA representative had attempted a recruitment. But the recruitee wanted to satisfy himself that the recruiter was not an impostor. The recruiter told him to stand in front of the U.S. Embassy at high noon and watch Old Glory fluttering from its staff. The flag would be dipped three times. Sure enough, at high noon the next day the flag was dipped three times. I took a dim view of this use of the embassy's American flag. When I made my feelings known to the station chief, he sheepishly acknowledged that the incident had occurred. In Chile, to conclude, I am reasonably confident that nothing was done to me like the Track II deception of Ambassador Korry.

## More Charges and How They Came About

It is widely believed that the United States "destabilized" the Chilean government in order to bring it down, fomented and financed demonstrations and strikes, and made common cause with right-extremist subversives. Are these allegations true? How did they come about? For those that are not true, how can one show that they are not?[22]

It is difficult to prove a nothing—like Sherlock Holmes's case which was solved because a dog did not bark in the night. It is worse, in fact, because Holmes ultimately discovered a series of acts—not non-acts.[23] In the case of false allegations, one must try to show that no deed was done at all. In Chile's case, there is an additional order of difficulty. The "nothings" are intermixed with genuine revelations. So the task is to sift out the wheat from the chaff of accusation in a context where truthful disclosure shocked U.S. opinon.

The story begins with a secret briefing which CIA director William E. Colby gave on 22 April 1974 to the Intelligence Oversight Subcommittee of the House Armed Service Committee, about CIA operations in Chile. This subcommittee, chaired by Congressman Lucien N. Nedzi, was charged with monitoring CIA covert action throughout the world, and it was the only House committee that the CIA felt had the right to be fully informed. Colby, Kissinger, and others had previously testified in executive session about Chile to members of the House Foreign Affairs and Senate Foreign Relations committees and had acknowledged some U.S. covert financial support to the Chilean opposition, but these other intimations had not leaked. Colby's report to the Nedzi Committee was later described as complete, detailed, and downright clinical in tone.

Congressman Michael J. Harrington, an outspoken critic of U.S. policies toward Chile and a member of the House Foreign Affairs Committee, had been pressuring Nedzi to hold the hearing and asked to see the transcript.[24] Groundrules in the House gave him this right, and twice he was allowed to read it but not to take notes.

He then tried to convince colleagues in both the House and the Senate to initiate a full-scale investigation of CIA actions in Chile. One letter he wrote in this regard, dated 18 July 1974, was to House Foreign Affairs Committee chairman Thomas E. Morgan, and it described U.S. covert actions in Chile in detail, citing the Colby testimony. A copy came into the hands of Seymour M. Hersh, an investigative reporter of the *New York Times*, and Laurence Stern of the *Washington Post*.

Hersh and Stern published news stories about the Harrington letter on 8 September; other reporters followed suit; and a public furor ensued.[25] The controversy, and Hersh's later revelations about domestic intelligence, led the Senate to establish a select committee under Frank Church's chairmanship to look into the facts. After an investigation which lasted the better part of a year, the Church Committee published its celebrated report.

A comparison between Hersh's and Stern's original revelations, taken from Harrington's letter, and the Church Committee staff report reveals three interesting points: first, Harrington was ignorant of Track II, which surfaced only later; second, Harrington's letter, except for Track II, was comprehensive; and third, subsequently disputed questions concerned not so much the actions of the U.S. government as its purposes.

Did Colby withhold information about Track II from the Nedzi Committee on 22 April? Colby explains what happened in his memoirs:

> I was in something of a dilemma. I had no problem testifying and answering questions on all of the CIA's covert political-action operations up to Allende's election and since his installation in office—our so-called Track I activities. But there was Track II. . . . Although it lasted only six weeks and was cut off after Allende was inaugurated, in Track II we had indeed looked for a coup. But President Nixon had ordered Helms and the Agency to keep that activity in the strictest confidence, reporting it to absolutely no one.
>
> After I had completed my testimony on Track I and answered all the Congressmen's questions on it in full detail, however, I felt I could not in good conscience leave it at that. . . . So, once . . . the session was adjourned (and the transcript closed), I approached Nedzi, who had only the committee counsel still with him, and in a quiet voice . . . I gave him a summary of Track II in a very few words. He listened, asked how this related to the

Track I story I had testified on and then sternly demanded my assurance that Track II had been cut off in 1970 and that I had been accurate in my testimony that CIA had not been associated with the military coup in 1973. I gave these assurances, and we let the matter drop.[26]

At whatever cost to his relationship to the White House, Colby did tell Nedzi about Track II. Acts like this one ultimately cost Colby his job. Track II was not cut off in six weeks, however, and I have asked Colby and Phillips about this discrepancy. Both men say that they themselves were not aware in 1974 that Track II had lingered on beyond 1970. Neither of them had been personally connected with Chilean matters in the 1971–1972 period, as Phillips was in Brazil and Venezuela and Colby was working on and in Vietnam. This explanation may not quiet the reader's doubts, but—ingenuous or not—I am prepared to believe it. The pressures of high office can get in the way of determined research into the historical record, and—knowing Colby—I think he would have been more careful in talking to Nedzi and in his memoirs, had he known the full history.

The second aspect of the comparison between the Hersh-Stern revelations and the Church report is the confirmation that Harrington had what was essentially the complete story on Track I. Even the "Rube Goldberg" gambit was alluded to, including the idea of bribing Chilean congressmen.[27] While the Church report is more extensive, coherent, and penetrating than the September 1974 disclosures, the facts did not change—except for Track II. Seymour Hersh has subsequently published a stream of amplifying details and vignettes, some new revelations of secondary importance, some interesting first-person testimony, intriguing speculation, provocative suggestions, and a few false reports. The overall result of his work, however, has been to present new facets of the original basic story and of the Church Committee's revelations connected with Track II. The Church Committee had access to CIA documents of the highest classification, Forty Committee records, and other highly sensitive materials and files. In sum, what happened was that Colby testified accurately about Track I in April 1974; his testimony leaked and was published in September 1974; and the Church Committee investigators unearthed Track II and published those facts in 1975. Since then the outlines of the Chilean story have not changed.

The main elements of CIA activity after Track II faded were confirmed by President Gerald R. Ford eight days after the reporting bombshell of 8 September 1974. Asked about the revelations at a press conference, the president said: "In a period of time, three or four years ago, there was an effort being made by the Allende government to destroy opposition news media, both the writing press as well as the electronic press. And to destroy opposition political parties. And the effort that was made in this case was to help and assist the preservation of opposition newspapers and electronic media [i.e., some of the parties' radio stations] and to preserve opposition political parties."[28]

The statement was artfully worded. It has stood up pretty well under subsequent investigation. Regarding Track II, President Ford avoided the issue. He put his statement in the context of the Allende government's effort to run the opposition into the ground when in office. So the Track II period in 1970—the crucial effort—was excluded from the context of the president's statement. Also not mentioned were CIA support to private-sector groups and the splintering of the Radicals, but the former effort was mostly in connection with the opposition parties' March 1973 election campaign and the splintering effort had little practical consequence.

The third aspect of the comparison between the Hersh-Stern revelations and the Church Committee findings involves U.S. government motivation, and it is here that real and substantial discrepancies are found. U.S. government spokesmen have consistently asserted that CIA covert action was intended to enable the Chilean democratic opposition to survive until the 1976 elections. Harrington, on the other hand, described Colby's testimony as an effort to "destabilize" Allende's government and bring it down. That is quite a difference. Did the United States want to preserve a democratic system or destroy a democratically elected government?

U.S. administration spokesmen were interpreting official desires as "preservation" rather than destabilization within a week of the coup. For example, Jack Kubisch, assistant secretary of state for Inter-American affairs, told professors who came to his office on 18 September 1973 that the U.S. government would have preferred to see Allende complete his term and see Unidad Popular voted out of office through the constitutional decision of the Chilean people.[29]

Colby took issue with Congressman Harrington's leaked letter and its characterization of U.S. policy as destabilization. On 18 September 1974 Colby sent a letter to the *New York Times* about the allegation: "I reexamined the transcript of the testimony and determined that the word 'destabilize' in whatever grammatical form, does not appear. . . . I so stated publicly on September 13 at a public meeting, attended by Representative Harrington. . . . To insure that no mere difference in semantics is involved, I added that 'this term especially is not a fair description of our national policy from 1971 on of encouraging the continued existence of democratic forces looking toward future elections.' "[30]

Colby's letter directly states that the purpose of U.S. policy was to encourage "the continued existence of democratic forces" rather than the overthrow of Allende. Second, Colby is careful to distinguish between U.S. policy earlier and policy "from 1971 on." Colby's letter—like President Ford's statement—was sent before Track II was known, even before the Church Committee had been established, and Colby must have thought twice before he inserted a qualification that might have drawn attention to CIA activities in 1970. Lastly, Colby's statement that he never used the word "destabilize" is categorical, and it is unlikely that he would have gone public in order to grasp at the chance to perpetrate a falsehood.

Congressman Nedzi later confirmed his impression that Colby had not used the word "destabilization."[31] The probability is that Michael Harrington, who had deep convictions about the Chilean question, did coin the word and characerized U.S. policy and objectives through the prism of his own beliefs. The word "destabilization," which has entered the English language, is his, as is the policy perception it expresses.

The etymology of "destabilization," although it bears on the case, does not in itself elucidate the U.S. government's true purpose. Additional clarification comes from an episode involving Ray S. Cline, head of intelligence and research during William Rogers's time as secretary of state; Lawrence S. Eagleburger, Henry Kissinger's confidant and executive assistant; Daniel Schorr, an investigative newsman and TV reporter who rivals Seymour Hersh in his record of successful exposés; and Hersh himself. Schorr got the scoop, as will be revealed shortly. After broadcasting it on CBS news, Schorr passed on his information for Hersh to use in the *New York Times*, so the initial written record appears there. Schorr's own description of the episode is in his *Clearing the Air*.

Ray Cline, who had left the State Department in late 1973, was reported by Hersh on 16 October 1974 as having asserted that he personally had been "dubious" of the wisdom of covert U.S. operations in Chile. As Hersh reported the matter, Cline added that the State Department and the CIA "went along, because the White House—either Nixon [or] Dr. Kissinger, or both—decided to push the program."[32] Enraged, Kissinger was said to have instructed Eagleburger to show Schorr documents that would demonstrate Cline to have been, on the contrary, among the most hawkish advocates of aggressive covert action in Chile. Exactly what happened then is disputed, perhaps because the passing of top secret documents on CIA clandestine operations to a newsman in order to expose the pretensions of a former official, or to get even with him, is a dubious tactic.

All accounts agree, however, that Eagleburger called in Schorr a few days after Hersh's story about Cline and gave him enough information to indicate that Cline had been a hawk and not a dove. Schorr broadcast his story, and Hersh published his version on 21 October 1974 after rechecking the facts with Eagleburger. Eagleburger, according to Hersh, was by then denying that he had shown Schorr any documents at all, saying that "all I provided was a general broad statement" dealing with Cline's role. Eagleburger additionally insisted that he had made the decision to brief Schorr personally, without any instructions from Secretary Kissinger. While quoting Eagleburger's disclaimers, Hersh gave a detailed description of the three documents Eagleburger reportedly had let Schorr read. In the first, dated 30 August 1970, the State Department urged caution in expending covert funds in the 1970 electoral campaign; Cline, in a handwritten comment, urged major financial support for anti-Allende forces if it could "make a difference." In the second document, dated 4 September 1970, the day of Allende's narrow victory at the polls, the question of bribing Chilean congressmen to prevent Allende's congressional confirmation was discussed. Hersh reported that Wymberley Coerr, a professional diplomat responsible for coordinating Forty Committee staff recommendations, had opposed the suborning of Chilean congressmen; Cline, in another handwritten comment, depicted Coerr as "hung up" on subornation and reluctant to recognize the world of "realpolitik." The third document, dated 25 July 1973, included a discussion by Jack Kubisch of CIA proposals that later became the 20

August 1973 approval of $1 million to support opposition parties and private-sector organizations.[33]

Schorr himself wrote later that "each of the documents [Eagleburger showed him] . . . bore hand written remarks by Cline, generally supporting strong action and scoffing at the doubters." According to Schorr the documents also discussed "working with the Chilean military."[34]

Cline acknowledges the authenticity of the three documents, although he claims that his handwritten comments were not as hawkish as Eagleburger, Schorr, and Hersh made them sound. Schorr has since reviewed his notes taken when examining the top secret papers and has written me that recommendations regarding 1973 were for a "sustaining operation to keep opposition going until 1976 elections." He adds that nothing in the recommendations after 1970 went beyond this general framework and intent.[35]

What does all this mean? The Eagleburger-to-Schorr disclosures support the original Hersh-Stern revelations, additionally confirming that Colby testified comprehensively on 22 April 1974 about covert action (except for Track II); that Harrington recorded the facts accurately in his 18 July 1974 letter to Chairman Morgan (although he got "destabilization" wrong as an expression of purpose); and that subsequent revelations have mostly added details to Colby's report. Except for Track II, what is notable is not how much the picture has changed since the September 1974 revelations, but how little.

Seymour Hersh then published a story on 24 September 1974 asserting that U.S. covert operatives in Chile organized anti-UP demonstrations, starting with the march of the empty pots. Hersh wrote:

> The Nixon Administration, in what amounted to a change of its clandestine policies . . . officially authorized the Central Intelligence Agency to begin supplying financial and other aid to anti-Allende factions in mid-October, 1971, highly reliable intelligence sources said today.
>
> The administration directive, characterized by one insider as an order to "get a little rougher," resulted in direct CIA involvement six weeks later in the first large-scale, middle class demonstrations against the Allende regime, . . . the "march of the empty pots" . . . .

> According to an administration source with first-hand knowledge, the change in American clandestine policies toward the Allende Government was communicated to Mr. Davis shortly after his arrival in Chile on October 13, 1971. Mr. Davis, who was reassigned to the State Department late last year, refused to comment today. . . .
>
> One administration official with first-hand knowledge of the events in Chile summarized the message sent to Ambassador Davis as saying, in effect, "from now on you may aid the opposition by any means possible." Another source said simply that the ambassador had been told to "get a little rougher." . . .
>
> Another source confirmed Ambassador Davis' direct involvement. . . .[36]

I received no such message or order. So far as I know, the CIA did not conceive or foment the march of the empty pots. In fact, at the time the station chief expressed chagrin to me that his organization had not had better and earlier intelligence about the initial planning of it. His contacts knew about it when it was being organized, of course, but so did many of the matrons of Santiago's wealthy suburbs. Hersh did call me before publishing his story. I was not authorized to make comments for the record on clandestine operations and told him so. At the same time I told him on personal background that the story was not true.

I have wondered how the story could have originated. There is no reflection of anything like this in the Church Committee staff report. The report makes clear, in fact, that there was no mid-October shift in U.S. clandestine policies to "begin" financial aid to anti-Allende factions. The only place I have seen a similar allegation was in the testimony of Edward Korry, my predecessor, to the Senate Foreign Relations Committee on 11 January 1977, in which he said that only after September 1971 did "any appreciable money . . . begin to flow into Chile through the CIA" to anti-UP parties and press outlets.[37] I do not know whether Ambassador Korry was one of Hersh's sources, but I do know a person who was. Judd Kessler has told me that he had perceived my views toward Unidad Popular as being tougher than Korry's in 1971 and told Hersh just before he wrote his 24 September 1974 story that this had been his impression. What Kessler had seen in fact was the copper nationalization crisis coming to a head at the time I arrived—as described in chapter 1. This event caused much resentment in Washington, and I felt fortunate at the time to have helped keep the keel as even as it remained. I believe Hersh himself has subsequently learned that his 24 September story was not accurate.

Four days before his story on demonstrations Seymour Hersh published a piece purporting to show that the CIA financed the 1972 truckers' strike and other strike movements in 1973. Hersh wrote that intelligence sources had revealed to him that the CIA had used "the majority of more than $7 million authorized for clandestine CIA activities in Chile . . . in 1972 and 1973 to provide strike benefits and other means of support for anti-Allende strikers and workers. . . ." Hersh continues: "Among those heavily subsidized, the sources said, were the organizers of a nationwide truck strike that lasted 26 days in the fall of 1972. . . . Direct subsidies, the sources said, also were provided for a strike of middle class shopkeepers and a taxi strike, among others, that disrupted the capital city of Santiago in . . . 1973. . . ."[38]

Church Committee investigations disprove Hersh's allegation that "the majority" of the $7 million for covert action was spent on strike benefits, as the figure refers to the entire CIA program authorized between 1970 and 1973. Most of the money, as already described, went to the political parties, their electoral campaigns, and *El Mercurio*. The Church report is also explicit that "the Forty Committee did not approve any funds to be given directly to the strikers." Nevertheless, one unauthorized diversion of $2,800 to the truckers did occur at the time of the 1972 truckers' strike.[39]

The CIA station in Santiago favored U.S. financial support to the truckers in 1973 and I opposed it. In light of our policy difference, we agreed to refer the matter to Washington. A specific proposal for $25,000 of support to the truckers was forwarded, with my opposition made a part of the record. The Church Committee staff report says that "it is unclear whether or not that proposal came before the Forty Committee. On August 25—16 days before the coup— Headquarters advised the Station that soundings were being taken, but the CIA Station's proposal was never approved."[40]

In Senate testimony Karl F. Inderfurth of the Church Committee staff amplified the staff report: "Nathaniel Davis, US Ambassador to Chile, and the State Department, had strenuously objected to any funding of the strikers. . . . There's no question that the strikers were creating a climate in which a military coup appeared to be inevitable. So any direct assistance to the strikers would be directly heating up, building up, tension in Chile, which eventually did lead to the coup."[41]

Former senior CIA officials declare to a man that funds to support the truckers were not approved.[42] Even Congressman Harrington's leaked letter of 18 July 1974 states that the Forty Committee rejected support for the truckers.

One important source for Seymour Hersh's 20 September 1974 article has been identified. On 17 October 1974 Hersh quoted Ray Cline as "the first high official to permit his name to be used" as saying the CIA bankrolled the truckers.[43] Cline told me in 1978, however, that his comments were misinterpreted by Hersh. In any case, after the publication of the *New York Times* articles Cline, who had been out of government for about a year, requested and received the opportunity to review his own classified intelligence files and refresh his memory. Having done so, he objected strongly to Hersh's stories. On 22 October the *New York Times* published a "correction" quoting Cline as actually having said only that trade groups and labor unions, including truckers, "had benefitted indirectly from CIA financial aid to political parties."[44]

The *New York Times*'s "corrected" version raised a new substantive question: was there a large-scale seepage of CIA funds to the truckers through the political parties and private-sector groups in Chile? The Church Committee investigators had suspicions in this regard, although they found no evidence beyond the $2,800 already mentioned.[45] I am not aware of more such leakage. Obviously, if one gives a political party money to meet its needs, somebody or some group which otherwise might have contributed to those needs could contribute to the truckers; but that is not the same thing as the party acting as a conduit. It is not difficult to tell if money given to a political party for electoral posters or advertisements, for example, is being used for that purpose. The CIA has developed techniques for determining whether its moneys are being used for the activities authorized and intended. The CIA did discover the $2,800 diversion, after all. As for the private-sector groups which received CIA money, they were given relatively small sums and their own needs were pressing.[46]

Ray Cline took issue with the *Times*'s "correction" of 22 October, which said that the truckers "benefitted indirectly from CIA financial aid to political parties." In October 1978 he wrote me: "What I really said throughout was that CIA support to the Frei political group and to the press (mostly *El Mercurio*) helped these groups encourage the strikes. I did not say money was passed."[47]

Colby and I, separately, tried to correct the record on the truckers and empty pots stories when Hersh published them. Press statements by each of us were telexed up to Secretary Kissinger in New York on 24 September, but he never gave his assent to their release. My guess is that knowing about Track II as he did, he miscalculated, hoping that the whole Chilean mess would drift away. Even now, I believe that immediate, strong, explicit statements would have reduced American public credence in falsities. Perhaps not, but the lost moment never returns.[48]

A number of commentators, many of them liberals sympathetic to the UP experiment, have put forward a fourth set of allegations.[49] They charge that U.S. covert funds went to private-sector groups in the guild movement (the *gremios*) and to extreme rightist groups such as Patria y Libertad.

Private-sector groups in the guild movement received some support that I have already discussed, mostly for the 1973 congressional campaign. It is also true that the CIA had earlier provided Patria y Libertad with $38,500 through a third party during the Track II period in 1970 and approximately $7,000 more in small sums until disbursements ended sometime during 1971.[50] The real issue with respect to Allende's last two years in power, however, is whether the CIA continued to provide support to these groups as their activities became more coup-oriented, and particularly whether the CIA supported the powerful antigovernment movements of October 1972 and August–September 1973. The Church Committee staff examined these questions and drew the following conclusions, which I believe are accurate:

> Various proposals for supporting private sector groups were examined . . . but the Ambassador and the Department of State remained opposed to any such support because of the increasingly high level of tension in Chile, and because the groups were known to hope for military intervention.
>
> Nevertheless, on August 20, the Forty Committee approved a proposal granting $1 million to opposition parties and private sector groups, with passage of the funds contingent on the concurrence of the Ambassador, Nathaniel Davis, and the Department of State. . . .[51]
>
> That agreement was not forthcoming. . . .[52]

None of these funds were passed to private sector groups before the military coup three weeks later. . . .

The pattern of US deliberations suggests a careful distinction between supporting the opposition parties and funding private sector groups trying to bring about a military coup. However, given turbulent conditions in Chile, the interconnections among the CIA-supported political parties, the various militant trade associations *(gremios)* and paramilitary groups prone to terrorism and violent disruption were many. The CIA was aware that links between these groups and the political parties made clear distinctions difficult.[53]

To conclude, I am confident that no element of the U.S. Mission in Chile extended financial support to the strike movements of October 1972 and August–September 1973. Insofar as I know, no moneys or support of any kind were passed to Patria y Libertad at any time during my incumbency. I avoided opportunities to meet or know Cumsille of the shopkeepers, Bazán of the professionals (CUPROCH), Jara of the land transport confederation, and Vilarín of the truckers.

I did fight off some questionable proposals. For example, a highly placed visitor from Washington pushed me hard at one point to support a covert bailout of the Papelera. I would not do so, and I still shudder to think how much money could have been absorbed in that operation.

I am reasonably confident that it was not U.S. policy during my time in Chile to "destabilize" Allende and bring him down. I cannot say with the same confidence, however, that all personalities in Washington were of the same mind. Seymour Hersh has explicitly charged that there were sharp differences within the Nixon administration. On 8 September 1974, quoting Colby indirectly and other reliable U.S. officials as his sources, he described the lineup as follows: "The agency's operations from 1970 to 1973 . . . were considered a test of the technique of using heavy cash payments to bring down a government viewed as antagonistic toward the United States. . . . 'The State Department . . . wanted to stretch out any clandestine activities to permit the regime to come to a political end. The argument was between those who wanted to use force and end it quickly rather than to play it out. Henry [Kissinger] was on the side of the former—he was for considerable obstruction.' "[54]

Hersh's description of a kind of laboratory test of a technique seems implausible. From everything we know about their feelings, both Richard Nixon and Henry Kissinger had deeply held emotions and convictions about Chile. Besides, that is not really the way the world works. But the differences and tensions between the White House and the State Department were real enough. Jack Kubisch has told me that he was informed that Kissinger did favor giving money to the truckers in August 1973. Kubisch was strongly against it, as was I. At one point William J. Jorden, Kissinger's senior staffer for Latin American matters, asked Kubisch whether his convictions were so strong that he was prepared to resign as assistant secretary rather than support subventions to the truckers. Kubisch said they were, and his answer may help explain why the proposal to aid the strikers drifted off into the bureaucratic haze in Washington.[55]

I was not explicitly informed of State Department–NSC policy differences at the time, either in messages to Santiago or in the consultations that occasionally brought me back to Washington. I did have a good idea of the predilections of various personalities on the Washington scene, however, and subsequent revelations of their attitudes contained few surprises.

Washington's views shifted as the situation in Chile changed. U.S. policy in 1970 had been "destabilization," if one should choose to give Track II that name, with a vengeance. Unfriendly sentiments in the White House toward Salvador Allende no doubt continued. Elsewhere in Washington, however, enthusiasm for covert activism ebbed, and Washington policy makers focused increasingly on the importance of avoiding compromising acts. There was also progressively less Chilean institutional viability to "destabilize." If Hersh was right, and Kissinger wanted to precipitate decisive action while the State Department wanted to play things out, then the pace of events in Chile played to Kissinger's interest while the State Department was winning hands down on a low U.S. profile.

In Santiago the gap between the desires of the Chilean opposition and the inclinations of our embassy widened. As 1973 progressed, anti-UP forces were coming to favor a coup, and even the Christian Democrats were despairing of a constitutional outcome. The U.S. government could have done little to prevent or slow this trend, and seeing this, we tried to avoid bankrolling the plotters and to keep away from the plotting. As procoup sentiment spread, the effort became more and more difficult, but it was honestly sustained.

The U.S. government wished success to opposition forces, a position intrinsically counter to the governing coalition's interest. Is that "destabilization"? March 1973 was probably the last time when covert financial aid to the opposition parties was relevant. In later months party electoral strength was no longer the decisive element. By mid-1973 it was becoming clear to responsible U.S. officials in Washington as well as in Santiago that the U.S. record of abstention from coup plotting was going to be more important than any resort to increasingly superfluous covert intervention.

Other actions taken and not taken had lesser impact on world opinion than the controversies just discussed, but they are worth a mention. In his book Seymour Hersh correctly notes that two men from the Australian Secret Intelligence Service (ASIS) were stationed at their embassy in Chile. He reports that they monitored and controlled three Chilean agents on behalf of the CIA and relayed their information to Washington. Sandwiching this report between the CIA's compilation of arrest lists and its 1971 disinformation program, he implies that the Australians might have been involved in some particularly sensitive, still undisclosed, operation. He concludes: "Just what the ASIS operatives were doing in Chile on behalf of the United States was not made public."[56]

The episode caused a furor in Australia, and the record there is quite explicit. According to Australian disclosures, the American request for help was made in November 1970, when the CIA station in Santiago feared that its ability to collect intelligence might be terminated by a break in U.S.-Chilean relations. ASIS personnel assumed the monitoring of three long-standing Chilean informants, who were providing regular intelligence information—and not conducting any covert action program. In due course the Australian government changed. Gough Whitlam became prime minister, and he ordered the ASIS activity in Chile stopped. The three agents were handed back to the CIA station some months before the 1973 coup. The station chief kept me informed of the ASIS officers' activities and their termination. I understand why Prime Minister Whitlam might not have wished to continue this activity, but it did not represent any unique or especially sensitive CIA operations in Chile.[57]

Some observers have also questioned whether any U.S. agency besides the CIA might have been engaging in clandestine action in Chile. The most pointed suggestion in this regard came from Diane LaVoy, one of the Church Committee staff investigators. LaVoy was quoted in 1978 by an investigative author, Thomas Hauser, as follows:

> "The major line that I was looking for . . . was a Track III—that is, a line of orders occurring not so much through the CIA, perhaps originating at the White House, being implemented in large measure through military channels. . . . That's what we were digging for towards the tail end of our investigation when the question of the military track became more and more disturbing to those of us who were working on it. We didn't get beyond a preliminary stage for a combination of reasons that included, at root, timing within the Committee."[58]

In the spring of 1982 I called on Diane LaVoy to see if she would give me any indication of the basis for her suspicion. She pled that the seven intervening years had driven any sharp recollection from her mind, but she did say that I should look into Task Force 157, the naval unit established in 1967 to carry out special intelligence operations worldwide.

I checked with U.S. MILGROUP officers, defense attachés, and the CIA station chief in Chile at the time. They all told me that, to their knowledge, Task Force 157 was not operating in Chile. Senior CIA officers in Washington, including Colby and Phillips, confirmed what they said. According to everyone I asked, the U.S. military was conducting only normal intelligence activity in Chile during the 1971–73 period. Clandestine military action programs would have been contrary to operating instructions and interagency groundrules, and the Church Committee staff report gives no indication of such programs. LaVoy told me that her concerns about a "military track" were in the nature of suspicions, not facts, and every "special operations" military officer I have asked denies knowing of any military special operations in Allende's Chile.[59]

The preceding pages may have the flavor of personal apologia. Let me end, then, with Senator Church's general conclusion about my role.

As Chairman of the Senate Committee which investigated the Chilean affair, I wish to state for the record that Nathaniel Davis never appeared to have actively engaged in covert efforts to subvert the elected government of Chile. Rather, the available evidence suggested that Davis opposed such a conspiracy and sought to maintain a correct relationship with the Chilean regime.[60]

### The Brazil Connection and Other Ties

Many observers have suspected that people outside Chile advised and bankrolled the guild movement and the anti-Allende strikers, particularly in 1973. The United States was not the only possible source of such support, however, and Brazil is an obvious additional possibility. Marlise Simons of the *Washington Post* interviewed leading figures in the Institute of Research and Social Studies, a private anticommunist thinktank in Rio de Janeiro, in 1974. They affirmed that they had coached Chilean opponents of Allende and that São Paulo magnates gave money, "a lot of it." Paramilitary couriers delivered the funds to Chilean opposition groups, including Patria y Libertad. The Brazilians' "recipe" involved "creating political and economic chaos" and "fomenting discontent." Simons continues:

> The coup that brought Brazil's armed forces to power in March, 1964, appears to have been used as a model for the Chilean military coup. The private sector played a crucial role in the preparation of both interventions, and the Brazilian businessmen who plotted the overthrow of the left-leaning administration of President João Goulart in 1964 were the same people who advised the Chilean right on how to deal with Marxist President Allende.[61]

The idea that the Chileans actually "copied" the Brazilian coup of 1964 is a particularly Brazilian viewpoint. Nevertheless, the Brazilian connection has been confirmed by many sources. In his congressional testimony former ambassador Korry asked, for example, "Was there not an almost mirror image of what occurred in the overthrow of Goulart in Brazil in 1964 and what occurred in Chile in 1973 when Allende was ousted? . . . I have good reason to believe that Brazilians and other Latin Americans were advising the Chilean generals. . . ."[62] He has since written even more explicitly that "the actual technical and psychological support" for the coup "came from the military government of Brazil."[63]

In congressional testimony Frederick D. Davis of the CIA said:

> There is some evidence of cooperation between business groups in Brazil and Chile. However, this is a small share of the financial support. Most of the support was internal. . . . [There was] some funding and cooperation [with the Chilean anti-Allende forces from] groups with similar outlooks in other Latin American countries. . . . I was not thinking so much of companies or firms [as of] groups, organizations of businessmen, Chambers of Commerce, and that kind of thing in a country such as Brazil.[64]

Leftist authors such as Camilo Taufic also note the parallel between Chile and Brazil in 1964. MIR secretary general Miguel Enríquez accused the Brazilians of complicity—as well as the Americans, of course. Raúl Ampuero, the dissident Socialist, alleged that "Chilean generals were the recipients of . . . Brazilian know-how. . . ."[65]

The Brazilian ambassador in Santiago, Antonio Castro da Cámara Canto, was a great horseman, much admired by the Chilean military. At lunch with me in late March 1973 he made a series of leading suggestions (which I turned aside), trying to draw me into cooperative planning, interembassy coordination, and joint efforts looking toward the Allende government's demise. Later I noticed that the reminiscences of leading coup planners like General Arellano reflected a special tie of consideration for the Brazilian ambassador, manifested even in the frenetic days before 11 September.[66] All in all there is no real doubt in my mind that allegations of a Brazilian connection are true.

The next question is whether the Brazilians were acting as CIA agents when they supported Patria y Libertad and the other plotters. Colby and Phillips have assured me categorically that the CIA did not use Brazilians or Brazil to conduct programs in Chile. Presumably the Church Committee staff would have come across traces of Forty Committee consideration or approval of covert financial aid to Patria y Libertad or the truckers, channeled through Brazil, had the U.S. government resorted to such a practice. They were certainly looking for that sort of thing, but Inderfurth and Treverton of the committee staff have also told me they found no evidence of CIA support given through third-country conduits to any activities beyond those noted in the staff report.

While Brazil was the most obvious source of Latin American support to the rightist opposition in Chile, there were other possibilities. In her article about Brazilian-Chilean anti-Allende ties Simons also noted that Chilean activists against Allende raised money in Argentina and Venezuela and that there were ties to Major Arturo Marshall, the inveterate plotter against Allende living in Bolivia.[67] Other reports could be cited. For example, Jonathan Kandall of the New York Times reported on 16 October 1974:

> The widespread strikes that set the stage for the military coup that overthrew the late President Salvador Allende Gossens were partly financed by funds provided by companies based in Mexico, Venezuela and Peru, according to leading Chilean businessmen.
>
> The businessmen, ranking members of the SOFOFA . . . said that they had personally channeled these funds—amounting to $200,000—to striking truck owners, shopkeepers and professional groups in the weeks preceding the fall of the Allende Government on September 11, 1973. . . .
>
> The Chilean business sources did not link the money they received to the CIA. . . .
>
> The sources said that the money from the Mexican, Venezuelan and Peruvian companies suddenly started to arrive during the first half of 1973. . . .
>
> SOFOFA officials said the money was distributed to strikers weekly in July, August and September of 1973. The dollars were converted on the black market at up to 500 per cent the official exchange rate.
>
> "We were giving the truckers about $2000 a week," said one businessman. . . .[68]

The reference to converting dollars on the black market should be noted; Simons makes the same point, quoting a Brazilian businessman as saying that "the money we sent would go a long way on the black market." Even Robinson Rojas, hardly an observer sympathetic to the United States, identifies industrial groups in Brazil, Argentina, and Venezuela as helping virtually to halve the value of the escudo against the dollar on the black market during the October 1972 strike. In short, actors from a variety of countries were buying Chilean currency on the black market at various times. Fluctuations in the dollar-escudo black-market rate have been cited by critics of the U.S. government as evidence of CIA support for the truckers' strikes in 1972 and 1973, but third-country black-market operations could have induced fluctuations.[69]

European support for anti-Allende forces is also alleged. In particular, the Chilean Christian Democrats were said to have received support from the German and Italian Christian Democratic movements, during the presidencies of both Frei and Allende.[70] *Time* magazine goes further, alleging that "laundered CIA money, reportedly channeled to Santiago by way of Christian Democratic parties in Europe, helped finance" the Chilean truckers' strike of 1973.[71] Colby and Phillips tell me, however, that these allegations are untrue, and Church Committee staffers take the same position. There is no record of Forty Committee approval for such funding. Pending new evidence, I believe that the CIA supported neither the extreme rightists nor the truckers through foreign conduits. Not everything done in support of Salvador Allende's opposition had its origin in Langley, Virginia, or in the West Wing of the White House.

### Can U.S. Covert Actions Be Justified?

Few public officials of any country have the luxury of entering into virgin territory in another place, and U.S. officials in Chile were no exception. In October 1971 my colleagues in Santiago and I could not start afresh and give covert support to nobody. The question for us became: Would it have been better in October 1971 to have cut off ongoing CIA covert action rather than continue it? Personally, I did not have authority to make that choice, of course. I was informed of ongoing programs in Chile during Washington consultations in September 1971. I did have the option of resigning over the issue (as I later would do over covert intervention in Angola in 1975).[72] So I shared the responsibility for U.S. covert actions from that time forward.

Moreover, a suspension of ongoing covert support can have profound consequences. For example, it has been asserted that the abrupt termination of CIA payoffs to the mullahs in Iran during the Carter administration contributed to the unraveling of the shah's power and "set up" the Khomeini revolution.[73] As Ray Cline put it, "intentionally or unintentionally, the United States influences foreign events by its action or by its inaction. It is too powerful to be neutral. . . ."[74]

Americans have a great ambivalence about covert action. We still have not, as a society, thought through the practical and ethical implications of this kind of activity. Nor is the problem new. Former assistant secretary Charles A. Meyer, justifying his actions when he presided over Chilean covert action, told the Church Committee some nineteenth-century history:

> In Washington, Eaton, the US Consul in Tunis, laid before Jefferson a scheme. . . . The Bashaw of Tripoli was a usurper, having stolen the throne from an older brother who was now wandering forlornly somewhere in Africa. Eaton proposed to find the brother, give him sympathy and support, and install him as rightful head of state. Jefferson approved the idea and thus was launched the first, although not the last, American effort to overthrow an objectionable foreign ruler and put a cooperative one in his place. Jefferson also chose to have that plot proceed quietly, in twilight. He would send the would-be bashaw, through Eaton, a few artillery pieces and 1,000 small arms. . . .[75]

In more recent times critics of U.S. covert action have taken contradictory positions. For example, some who condemned covert support to Allende's opposition in Chile would applaud secret help to the Marxists' opponents in Portugal two years later. Yet ethical considerations in the two cases are similar—until, with hindsight, one looks at the two successor regimes. William V. Shannon, then of the *New York Times* editorial board, explains his conviction in an editorial of 3 August 1975:

> If the United States over the last year had possessed competent leadership in foreign affairs, it would have provided Portuguese democrats with money and political support to help them offset the advantages of the Portuguese Communists in propaganda and organization. The Swedish and German Social Democrats have helped their counterparts in Lisbon but the flow of money from them has been trivial compared to the heavy subsidies to the Portuguese Communists by the Soviet Union.[76]

Shannon wrote these words shortly before it was revealed that the CIA was, in fact, taking the very action he advocated.[77] Shannon, moreover, joined in the general condemnation of covert action in Chile. He later became President Carter's ambassador to Ireland. The *Washington Post* took a position similar to Shannon's.[78]

On the more general question of covert action *Time* commented on 29 September 1975: "The CIA must also be able to carry out non-military clandestine actions, such as the funding of pro-American political forces in countries where the Soviets are backing their own candidates, as they did in Portugal earlier this year."[79]

The Soviets backed Allende, just as they did the Portuguese leftists. Perhaps Americans regard leftist inroads within a NATO-allied government as more threatening than leftist control of a distant Rio Pact ally. The principle, however, is the same.

Part of our conceptual difficulty with covert action may be America's historical predilection for ideological pronouncements and abstract expressions of principle in foreign policy. Until the turn of the century we could afford this luxury because we were both safe and removed from—even irrelevant to—most of the great international struggles of the world. So we were free to preach, even posture. We fought World War I under the leadership of Woodrow Wilson, whose rhetoric was in our self-righteous tradition. World War II was an ethically clear struggle, and the Cold War at its height was perceived in the United States as a similar pitting of right against wrong. Covert action—including "dirty tricks"— was more acceptable in these contexts. Since Kennedy's presidency, however, the United States has found itself embroiled in increasingly ambiguous situations. This ambiguity has interfused the issue of covert action and its use as an instrument of national policy. We have never truly decided which we are against: covert action as such, or involvement in disagreeable situations that seem to have no "good" solution.

A judgment about U.S. covert financial intervention has to take some account of what others were doing. In Chile, as in most democracies, the continuation of constitutional government depended on the survival of a constitutional opposition, and the UP government was attempting to asphyxiate its adversaries.

The UP campaign against the opposition media was deliberate and persistent. It ranged from direct political action through legal harassment to an economic squeeze. Among the newspapers, *El Mercurio* was a particular and early target. Its editor, René Silva

Espejo, wrote an impassioned description of UP assaults on the viability of his newspaper in the first pages of El Mercurio's Brief History of Unidad Popular.[80] The troubles started almost immediately after Allende's victory, when a small minority of pro-UP employees tried unsuccessfully to whip up a labor dispute and break the editors' control. Later the same tactic was tried against other newspapers, mostly outside Santiago. For example, striking workers closed two anti-UP newspapers in Concepción in October 1971 and again in the following spring. Opposition newspapers were generally returned to their owners relatively quickly under court orders, but workers ignored court action on occasion.[81]

Frequently, UP officials were the ones who forced newspaper shutdowns or harassed opposition editors with legal action. The Committee on Freedom of the Press of the Inter-American Press Association (IAPA) condemned the actions of the government, which kept "the responsible editors of newspapers under constant and hostile attack." They particularly decried "a tactic [which] has been introduced by which jail sentence is applied to journalists before they appear in court and before the judge can rule on the case before him."[82]

By the end of 1972, forty-seven suits had been brought against the National party's La Tribuna and its editor, who had also been briefly jailed several times. Brief government-ordered suspensions of publication for violations of Chile's internal security law also occurred.[83] As the IAPA report noted, the courts almost always sided with the press, ordering that the editor be released or that the newspaper be permitted to resume publication. While government representatives harassed opposition journalists and editors, they did not effectively curtail their work.

Blatant financial and economic pressures were more serious than the direct actions of the government. In this area, too, El Mercurio was among the first to be affected. Its books were examined for months in 1970–71, allegedly because the newspaper was suspected of evading taxes. On another occasion the government ordered La Tribuna's building sold at auction, supposedly because the newspaper had not paid social security contributions. After a crowd of demonstrators physically prevented the auction, the government backed down and a settlement was worked out. In other cases ancient fire codes were exhumed, and bills for back taxes were presented under new interpretations of the law.

Credit was withheld.[84] Former ambassador Korry has commented that Allende, after he had nationalized the banks, controlled all the opposition newspapers' credits, "and he was not going to give them credit unless they gave him political support. We knew that for a fact."[85] The importation of necessary equipment and supplies was also affected. The IAPA report said that the Central Bank was "creating difficulties even to the point of refusing authorizations to buy foreign currency needed for indispensable imports and remittances abroad."[86]

Some publishing enterprises were driven into bankruptcy. One such example is Zig-Zag, the largest publishing conglomerate in Chile before 1970. In the months immediately after Unidad Popular took over in 1970, a tripartite arbitration panel on which a communist Labor Ministry official had the swing vote gave Zig-Zag's workers a 67 percent wage readjustment, more than twice the rise in the cost of living during the previous year. The firm was told to pay 25 million escudos to its employees, a sum of money Zig-Zag did not have. These actions pushed the firm under. The government bought the plant, the machinery, and some of the firm's copyrights, and reorganized the properties into the national enterprise Quimantú. Subsequently, Quimantú denied normal-quality paper supplies to the anti-UP news magazine *Ercilla*, disregarding contractual arrangements.[87]

In the case of newspapers, radios, TV stations, and other opposition enterprises the government had substantial control over both the income and the outlay sides of the enterprises' ledgers. On the income side the government controlled and sometimes blocked increases in the prices at which newspapers, magazines, and newsprint were sold. On the outlay side—as already illustrated in the Zig-Zag case—inflation became the justification for officially decreed wage and salary hikes. The best-known example of this squeeze, of course, was the experience of the Papelera, Chile's great supplier of newsprint.

For the newspapers themselves, the critical problem was the drying up of advertising income. As the IAPA report put it, the Allende government carried out "a deliberate policy of economic warfare by discriminating in the handing out of fiscal advertising [that is, advertising by the government and its dependencies] and by eliminating advertising coming from industry and commercial companies that were being nationalized . . . [thereby] weakening many publications."[88] Other advertising inexorably declined as well, as the private sector shrank with every nationalization. *El Mercurio* grew thinner as advertisements disappeared. By the end of 1972 an estimated 80 percent of industrial production was state-controlled, and private advertising was largely gone.[89] Such practices were not invented by the UP, of course, and one can argue that the channeling of official advertising to friendly media seems to be a perquisite of power in quite a few countries. Nevertheless, the effects were real and part of a pattern.

The radios were hit harder than the newspapers, particularly outside Santiago. In March 1972 the head of the National Radio Association reported that wages for radio employees had risen by 75 percent since November 1970 and income from advertising had fallen by 42 percent. Conditions worsened. More small provincial radio stations than newspapers went under, to be bought by the parties of the government. By September 1972 UP parties had added twenty of the country's 170 radio stations to their share of the total and had been licensed to establish five more. UP and MIR activists had seized thirteen additional stations for varying times. Over half a dozen physical attacks had also put anti-UP radios out of business for brief periods.[90] The opposition remained fully able to compete with the UP over the country's airwaves, but pressures were mounting and the balance was shifting.

Opposition television was still more beleaguered than radio, although less important in terms of its impact on the Chilean public. The principal television outlets were those of the government (which had a nationwide network of transmitters), the University of Chile, and the Catholic University. The UP government promptly took control of the national channel when it came into power.[91]

Channel 9, the University of Chile station, remained under the control of UP militants until the police finally enforced a court order to evict the occupiers on 8 September 1973. Channel 6, a second University of Chile station set up by the Christian Democratic university leadership, was raided in June 1973 by police acting on government orders (as the station was pronounced illegal), and the equipment was smashed.[92] The Catholic University channel in Santiago was the only TV station regularly airing non-UP views.[93]

The leftists were candid about their fight against opposition media outlets. The communist trade union chief, Luis Figueroa, had stated publicly that all mass media should be placed under state ownership. Even the official UP platform of December 1969 asserted that an "educational orientation" to help in the formation of "a new culture and a new man" should be stamped upon the media, with measures to put them at the disposal of "social organizations" eliminating the "unfortunate presence of the monopolies" and the media's "commercial character."[94] To his credit, Salvador Allende never completely endorsed these views.

The opposition parties' press and radio expenses had mostly been funded by businessmen and individuals and from bank loans. Financial support for the opposition parties themselves—for salaries, posters, printing costs, transport, and other operational costs—had also been defrayed from private donations and loans, and it was wasting away as donors emigrated or found their businesses nationalized. Very soon after coming to power, Unidad Popular made clear that it intended to choke off enough of the opposing parties' funding to disable them and to force the closure of the opposition parties' media. What did the CIA do? The United States stepped in—with money—to counter UP efforts to squeeze off the opposition's financial lifelines. Both the UP strategists and the U.S. government recognized that this was a critical struggle.

There were all too many thumbs pushing to unbalance the Chilean political scales. Not only did the Allende government try to cripple the opposition, but UP leaders and their foreign backers also financed progrovernment parties. Government-controlled transport, communications equipment, supplies of paper, and printing facilities were made available to UP political operatives. Such practices were not new in Chile, but the UP's partisan diversions were very large and very systematic. It was reliably reported that government offices kept secret ledgers alongside the official ones. Allegedly the Chilean Foreign Ministry disposed of more than a million dollars a month in clandestine funds, and state-run enterprises—notably the publishing house Quimantú—helped finance UP political work.[95]

UP parties skimmed a percentage off the top of some import-export operations. The Radical party was known to treasure its control over key government offices regulating foreign trade. Reportedly, the Communist party in Chile—as in other Western countries, among them Italy—collected a percentage of the proceeds from commercial transactions with Eastern European states.[96]

Food imports give an illustration of what happened. A Communist named Leonardo Fonseca was vice president of the state Enterprise for Agricultural Commerce (ECA). The general manager of the Central Bank, Pedro Bosch, was an activist in the Altamirano wing of the Socialist party. Guillermo Castillo, Communist party secretary Corvalán's brother-in-law, ran one of the national corporations dealing in the import of cereals. In August 1972 ECA converted its purchasing system from public bids to private negotiation, and its budget jumped sharply at about the same time. It was reported that ECA, using interlocking arrangements with the Central Bank and with Castillo's corporation, was able to skim millions of dollars, much of which was converted to escudos at black-market rates. With this money, the Communist party was reported to have bought four radio stations in southern Chile. It should be noted that the Communists were not suspected of personal defalcation, but rather they were charged with diverting official assets to party purposes.[97]

National party congressman Hermógenes Pérez de Arce wrote in his newspaper column on 11 June 1973 that the Fiat automobile company had sold cars to the MAPU party at unrealistic prices at the time of the 1973 congressional elections, effectively subsidizing the MAPU and buying influence. Paul Sigmund supports Pérez de Arce's charge:

> It was already known that MAPU had made huge sums . . . by reselling on the black market cars which it had obtained at official prices. [After the coup] a search of one of the two houses owned by Luis Guastavino, a Communist deputy from Valparaíso, produced $145,000 and bundles of new escudos— including packets of 5,000 escudo notes which had not been put into circulation. A member of the Christian Left who headed the Valparaíso Development Corporation was reported to have fled with $80,000 and 7 million escudos in his bags.[98]

The Church Committee reported CIA estimates that "the Cubans provided about $350,000 to Allende's campaign" in 1970, "with the Soviets adding an additional undetermined amount."[99] Other sources assert that Soviet funding of Allende's 1970 campaign climbed to as much as $20 million. Although this figure may not be reliable, there is little doubt that from 1970 to 1973 the UP parties and candidates went into their electoral campaigns well financed.[100]

Allegedly, under-the-table payments also swelled UP coffers. Former ambassador Edward Korry has asserted that "the government of Salvador Allende accepted bribes from such companies as International Telephone and Telegraph, General Tire, Cerro Copper, and Anglo-Lautaro Nitrate Mines to prevent expropriation." After the coup a Junta spokesman alleged that the Mafia had paid Allende's police authorities $30,000 a month.[101] It should be added, of course, that not everything Junta spokesmen asserted was true.

Two facts nevertheless emerge as incontrovertible. First, the UP government systematically undermined the financial resources of the opposition. Second, it augmented the resources of its own parties and media by diversions from official transactions and by subventions from leftist sources abroad. The choice facing U.S. policy makers was not between CIA intervention and a hands-off posture that would leave the Chilean political process to function undisturbed. It was between covert action and abstention in a skewed political struggle.

Looking back on the Chilean experience, some commentators have engaged in circular argument. They have noted that most newspapers, radios, and TV stations of the opposition survived; and they have concluded that Americans therefore need not have helped them. For example, Georgie Anne Geyer writes: "Richard Helms . . . should be called to account for the utter and incongruous stupidity of involving us and our national integrity in a situation like Allende's Chile, which was already self-destructing. . . ."[102] Aside from getting her villain wrong, Geyer seems to be saying that the Chilean opposition did not die and ultimately prevailed over Allende; therefore, the opposition had not needed the medicine given it to stay alive. The real question, of course, is whether the opposition could have survived without American help.

Church Committee staffers affirmed in congressional testimony that the UP government "was moving forcefully to stifle some of the opposition press," including El Mercurio.[103] They seemed less convinced that UP strategists would have moved on to stifle the rest of the opposition press after demolishing their initial targets, but I think they would have. From exile, after the coup, UP leaders made this clear.[104]

The political parties had an acute problem. As Ambassador Korry explained, the Christian Democratic party, in particular, ended the 1970 presidential campaign owing "large amounts of money to banks the Allende government would quickly nationalize; we reckoned that the Allende government would exploit bank nationalization to blackmail, to coerce and to starve financially . . . numerous and influential members of the party." Moreover, the Christian Democrats "owned no national newspaper, had no TV outlet and influenced few of Santiago's many radio stations at the time of Allende's election."[105] However the Christian Democrats had gotten into this predicament, the party's trouble was real. The Church Committee staff report, viewing this problem, simply reports that "the US government judged that without its support parties of the center and right might not survive either as opposition elements or as contestants in elections several years away."[106]

Some critics assert that covert aid to political friends in electoral campaigns is actually damaging—counterproductive. For example, Thomas Powers comments: "Are the Chileans too poor to finance their own campaigns, or too foolish to direct them? It is sheer presumption to assume . . . that they can't get along without us. Events suggest that our help is a mixed blessing."[107] I have some sympathy for this point of view.[108] Subventions do create dependencies. But the short term sometimes does not permit us the luxury of the longer perspective. Take U.S. covert support to the Christian Democrats in Italy in the 1948 elections. The dependencies this support created no doubt weakened the CD party, but during the election campaign the Communists had been pointing out the lampposts from which their enemies would be hanging if they won. Italian Christian Democrats might have been in no condition to worry about long-term dependencies after a communist victory. Democrats in Czechoslovakia—not so far away, and in the same year—were deprived of the opportunity for such concerns.

Powers voices an additional criticism of U.S. covert action in the sentences quoted above. Not only does he ask whether the Chileans were too poor to finance their own campaigns, he also inquires whether U.S. officials thought they were "too foolish to direct them." But the U.S. government did not try to use covert financial support to seize control of the opposition's policy making. Robert Alexander correctly comments that "the staff report of the Church Committee makes no suggestion" that the CIA influenced "the decision making of opposition groups during the Allende period."[109] The U.S. government had influence, of course, but U.S. representatives did not direct or determine opposition parties' positions nor *El Mercurio's* editorial line. Most opposition party leaders were not aware that CIA subventions were being made. So far as I know not even the editor of *El Mercurio*, René Silva, was informed of U.S. financial support to his newspaper—an ignorance that led him furiously to deny, after the Hersh-Stern revelations, that payments had been made to *El Mercurio*.

The foregoing argument is double-edged, of course, as some hoped we would exert greater influence on opposition policies, to push them toward conciliation with the UP government. Interventionist acts are always more palatable if they coincide with one's political preferences. Nevertheless, former assistant secretary Meyer made the point in his testimony before the Church Committee that the United States did not attempt to subjugate the Chilean opposition. Senator Church had asked him how he could square U.S. covert financing with a claim that U.S. policy was to leave Chilean affairs to the Chileans. Meyer replied:

> Chile has prided itself on [its democratic pluralism] . . . as the unique quality of Chilean democracy in this hemisphere. . . . I did not feel . . . [that a free political and journalistic policy] was in any way other than a Chilean posture. We did not . . . say to so-and-so, whom we found somewhere in the woodwork, here's a lot of money, do something. . . . We did not create newspapers. To my knowledge, we did not create radio stations. . . . [We used U.S. money] to assure a continuity in Chile of pluralistic democracy and freedom of the press.[110]

It may have been unfair to René Silva to have supported his newspaper without his knowledge, but it did leave his editorial autonomy intact. There is a real difference between covert financing that facilitates the continuation of a country's free political processes and covert financing that corrupts them. My colleagues and I in the Santiago embassy did not abandon hope that Chilean institutional democracy might survive.

*Chapter 13*

# U.S. Actions and the Coup

CAN it be said with confidence that the United States did not plot the Chilean coup? What were the charges of U.S. complicity and why did they arise? Did the U.S. government know of plans for the coup before 11 September? If so, why did we not warn Allende?

**Did the United States Plot the Coup?**

In his news conference of 16 September 1974 President Ford said: "As I understand it, and there's no doubt in my mind, our government had no involvement in any way whatsoever in the coup itself."[1] The Church Committee, after examining top-secret CIA, State Department, Pentagon, and White House documents, concluded: "Was the United States *directly* involved, covertly, in the 1973 coup in Chile? The Committee has found no evidence that it was."[2]

The qualification "directly" might appear to mean the U.S. government was indirectly involved. Gregory Treverton, the senior Church Committee staff member concerned with this section of the report, has explained. He told me the staff believed that U.S. actions during the 1970 Track II period must have had an afterlife in the consciousness of Chilean military officers who were aware of CIA and U.S. attaché contacts with Generals Valenzuela and Viaux. Treverton also cites the ill-disguised hostility to Allende of top Washington figures, which the plotters must have sensed. Lastly, he reasons that the CIA must have faced difficulty in monitoring the plotting without signaling encouragement. All of these reservations are reflected in the staff report, which, after stating there was "no evidence" of direct involvement, goes on: "However, the United States sought in 1970 to foment a military coup in Chile; after 1970 it adopted a policy both overt and covert, of opposition to Allende; and it remained in intelligence contact with the Chilean military, including officers who were participating in coup plotting."[3]

Treverton has some highly placed support for his contention that Track II may have influenced the Chilean military leaders' expectations vis-à-vis U.S. policy. William Colby says in his memoirs: "I am not trying to whitewash CIA's activities in Chile. . . . Certainly in Track II in 1970 it sought a military coup. . . . Certainly, having launched such an attempt, CIA was responsible to some degree for the final outcome, no matter that it tried to 'distance' itself and turn away well before 1973."[4]

I am not convinced, however, that the memory of Track II played an important role in forming military views in 1973. Viaux was sitting in jail until a week before the coup and went directly into exile. Valenzuela had been exiled in 1971. I know of no evidence that the attitudes of such people as Pinochet, Leigh, and Merino were influenced by a knowledge of Track II.

Regarding Treverton's second point, Richard Nixon's and Henry Kissinger's antipathy to Allende was no secret, but animosity in itself is not complicity. Many statesmen dislike each other. If antipathy were guilt, culpability in international politics could be found everywhere.

As for Treverton's third point, the Church Committee staff report explains:

> Although the purpose was information-gathering, the United States maintained links to the group most likely to overthrow the new president. To do so was to walk a tightrope; the distinction between collecting information and exercising influence was inherently hard to maintain. Since the Chilean military

perceived its actions to be contingent to some degree on the attitude of the U.S. government, those possibilities for exercising influence scarcely would have had to be consciously manipulated.

A few pages later, the report elaborates: "The United States—by . . . the nature of its contacts with the Chilean military—probably gave the impression that it would not look with disfavor on a military coup. And U.S. officials in the years before 1973 may not always have succeeded in walking the thin line between monitoring indigenous coup plotting and actually stimulating it."[5]

The foregoing comments pose the fundamental question whether intelligence gathering inherently carries with it the transmission of signals to those being monitored. This question will be examined below. Suffice it to note here that the staff report's qualification that there is no hard evidence of *direct* U.S. assistance to the coup refers to the three reservations Treverton expressed to me and not to some secret the staff refrained from disclosing. The staff report presented the evidence that the investigation uncovered. Treverton and Inderfurth have assured me of that, and I believe them.

As with the covert activities discussed in the preceding chapter, the full story in its essentials was described by the press in September 1974, and the facts remain as they were reported then. In Seymour Hersh's original article of 8 September 1974 he stated explicitly: "All of the officials interviewed emphasized that the Central Intelligence Agency was not authorized to play any direct role in the coup that overthrew Dr. Allende."[6]

Chilean military leaders have expressed contempt for the idea that they might have launched the coup with American inspiration. For example, Pinochet said on a number of occasions that the United States did not have "anything to do with it."[7] C. L. Sulzberger, after a visit to Chile, quoted General Pinochet as follows: "I never had any kind of contact with anyone from the CIA or with any ambassador, US or otherwise. I wanted to be free of any obligation to anybody. And of course I wanted to protect my intentions by total discretion. Why, afterward, even my family asked what kind of help I received from the United States. I told them: 'Not even good will.' "[8] There is reason to think that Pinochet involved himself in coup plotting late in the game, of course. So Pinochet's denials, even assuming his sincerity, are not conclusive. Nevertheless, the reminiscences of the other generals, while they reflect a Brazilian connection, do not reveal any equivalent involvement with Americans.

I should, perhaps, add for the record that I did not engage in coup plotting and am unaware of any of my U.S. colleagues having done so, including the personnel of the CIA station, the attaché offices, and the Military Advisory Group. I gave instructions to the U.S. Mission staff that no one was to involve himself in coup plotting or in conversations on the subject that could be construed as encouragement.

The memoirs of former responsible officials of the CIA are categorical and consistent. Colby reports his solemn assurances to his congressional oversight committee chairman, Lucien Nedzi, "that CIA had not been associated with the military coup in 1973."[9] He has taken the same position in numerous public speeches.[10]

David Phillips, head of the CIA's Western Hemisphere division in September 1973, is equally explicit. At one point he went so far as to write a public letter to Mrs. Allende: "You have been led to believe that evidence exists which makes the CIA accountable for the circumstances which brought your husband to his untimely end. Because I supervised that component of CIA concerned with Chile and its neighbors, the accusation bothers me personally. The claim, I assure you, is untrue and the evidence tainted."[11]

But was some lingering ghost of Track II still haunting the scene? Or even apart from Track II, was there some residual conviction in the minds of CIA officers in Washington or Santiago that President Nixon wanted Allende out and that there was therefore some authority to encourage or engage in plotting? In May 1973 "Abe" was once again in charge of the CIA's Western Hemisphere division, in the hiatus before David Phillips assumed direction in June. Karamessines had retired in February, and Abe himself was planning to retire before long, and he appears to have acted out of his own conviction, without checking with anybody. He sent out a formal telegram on 8 May, instructing the Santiago station to steer clear of coup plotting and military plotters.[12] Phillips later described the cable in his memoirs, saying that the message represented "a rather abrupt departure" from CIA custom, as "these instructions pointed out the probability of an opposition move against Allende and the inevitability that CIA would be blamed as the instigator of any coup." Phillips goes on:

The station response to the first message reminded headquarters that CIA continued to have the responsibility of predicting a coup—ringing the gong—and the station could hardly be expected to do that unless its agents penetrated all conspiracies. The second headquarters cable [despatched on 23 May, as Phillips informed a Washington press conference on his retirement] countered this valid argument saying that, this time, keeping CIA's record clean was more important than predicting a coup. In short, the CIA Station Chief was ordered to do the best he could on forecasting a coup from the margin of any plotting and to avoid contacts or actions which might later be construed as supporting or encouraging those who planned to overthrow Allende.[13]

In recent correspondence with me Phillips has added the following comment: "Of one thing I am morally certain. We did not promote or assist that coup, and we did everything we could possibly do to avoid any inference of involvement, short of closing down the Station and leaving Chile."[14]

Colby mentions the same episode in his memoirs. He writes: "CIA sent clear instructions to its station in Santiago in May and June, 1973, [early and late May] to separate itself from any contact with the Chilean military so that it could not be misunderstood to have been involved in any coup action the military might undertake."[15] Cord Meyer, another retired CIA executive, comments: "When the Chilean officers finally moved to overthrow Allende in September, 1973, they did so on their own initiative and for their own reasons and without consultation or coordination with either the US Embassy or the CIA station in Santiago."[16]

Accusations of U.S. military complicity have been less widespread than those in connection with the CIA, and the denials have been less frequent. Moreover, armed service intelligence officers who in 1973 were overseeing Latin American operations have not written memoirs. Military officers I have questioned have assured me, as I have already noted, that they did not engage in coup plotting, and I have found no evidence that they did so.[17]

The Church Committee staff report has been influential in bringing some of the informed U.S. press to accept U.S. official denials of complicity in the coup. Commenting at the time of the publication of the Church Committee report, the *New York Times* editorialized as follows: "The United States was not basically responsible for the overthrow of the Chilean government of President Salvador Allende. . . . The coup was actually conceived and carried out by Chileans, acting for reasons of their own."[18]

## Accusations of American Complicity

Hundreds of allegations of U.S. involvement in the coup have been put forward, and some of them have come to be widely believed.

The charge that U.S. pilots bombed the Moneda came from Gladys Marín, a communist deputy who was questioned by an Italian journalist in a Santiago hideout two or three weeks after the coup:

> The US Air Force gave the Chilean Air Force the rockets to bomb La Moneda Palace on 11 September. . . . Gladys Marín added that perhaps it was the US acrobatic pilots who bombed the government palace during the coup. . . . The Communist Party member said that the participation of the expert US acrobatic pilots in the bombing of the palace is confirmed by the fact that none of the rockets missed the target. "It was a job done by professionals," she emphasized. . . . The precision of the attack was extraordinary.[19]

Marín's evidence for American participation is the somewhat insulting suggestion that Chilean pilots were not professionally competent to perform the task, and the scheduled visit to Chile of the "Thunderbirds," the U.S. Air Force acrobatic flying team. The "Thunderbirds" were on a Latin American tour and were scheduled to perform in Chile between 24 and 27 September 1973. The coup intervened, however, and their visit was canceled before the pilots arrived. The prospective visit had been public knowledge in Santiago; Marín probably picked up a garbled version of the planned exhibition and jumped to the conclusion that the pilots had entered the country. So far as I know, the rockets used were part of the regular Chilean Air Force inventory.

Miguel Enríquez, secretary general of the MIR, probably first made the allegation that U.S. intelligence officers were aboard the Chilean Navy's ships. He gave an interview from hiding shortly after the coup, saying that he had publicly revealed, a month before the coup, that there had been a meeting between a member of the

U.S. Embassy and Chilean Navy commanders and northern Chilean
Army chiefs on board a Chilean cruiser in Arica on 20 May 1973.
He also said that officers of U.S. Naval Intelligence had accom-
panied every ship of the Chilean fleet in June and July.[20]

I first heard of these allegations in the published interview. I have
since checked with Capt. Ray E. Davis, the head of the U.S. Military
and Naval Advisory Group. He assures me that none of these allegations is true. There was no 1 A.M. meeting with a member of the U.S.
Embassy in Arica. From what Captain Davis remembers of the
movements of Chilean ships that month, it is unlikely that there
was a Chilean cruiser in Arica at that time. U.S. naval officers did
not accompany Chilean ships in June and July, as Enríquez
charged. The U.S. Naval Advisory Group did send an officer to
prospective Unitas ports of call shortly in advance of the Unitas
ship's scheduled arrival, but such visits would not have been made
in May for September exercises.

Mrs. Allende, Robinson Rojas Sandford, Thomas Hauser, and
many others have made or reported the allegation that Unitas warships were standing off Valparaíso and Talcahuano.[21] The facts are
that the Unitas task force never got much south of Chile's border
with Peru, a thousand miles north of Valparaíso. The Unitas exercises had been regularly conducted for a dozen years, and the 1973
itinerary had been established many months in advance. The ships
spent the night of 8–19 September in Callao, the port that serves
Lima. Chilean liaison officers boarded two of the U.S. ships there.
The task force got underway to Ilo Bay, Peru, on the 9th—in full
view of the citizens of Callao—and steamed south. The ships had
proceeded to a point off Arica, Chile's northernmost city, by the
morning of the eleventh, when word was received that the coup
was in progress. A Chilean oiler, the Araucano, was close by and
the task force refueled in the afternoon. It then proceeded north,
having received orders to reverse course, and docked in Rodman in
Panama, where the Chilean liaison officers were disembarked.[22]

Suggestions that U.S. Naval Advisory Group officers stationed in
Valparaíso were plotting appear in several published works, in-
cluding Thomas Hauser's Missing and Gary MacEoin's No Peaceful
Way.[23] A typical example is a statement by Godfrey Hodgson and
William Shawcross in the London Times: In planning for the coup

d'etat, Admiral José Toribio Merino maintained "close personal touch" with Lt. Col. Patrick J. Ryan, USMC, of the US Navy Mission in Valparaíso, Chile.[24] Colonel Ryan comments:

> Although I found the London Times reporting of my daily and personal liaison with Admiral Merino most flattering, I also found it completely untrue! During the eight months in Chile preceding the coup, my desk calendar reveals only two appointments with Admiral Merino, and they dealt with strictly mundane matters. These appointments were typical vice admiral-lieutenant colonel contacts. He talked, I listened and then carried out his orders. The London Times' report of my liaison duties with Merino in connection with the coup was absolutely false and typified the misinformation and fabricated "facts" that were disseminated to the world regarding the coup in Chile.[25]

I do not believe U.S. officers in Valparaíso were implicated in the coup plotting, and I have seen no credible evidence indicating that they were. More recent allegations of coup plotting by U.S. officers, including Ryan, in Valparaíso have been subsumed into the controversy surrounding the death of Charles Horman.

A young American named Charles E. Horman and a friend, Terry Simon, found themselves in Viña del Mar, the seaside resort next to Valparaíso, on the day of the coup. They had an encounter on the twelfth with a third American, Arthur P. Creter, and that conversation has given rise to allegations that Creter was a coconspirator in the Chilean Navy's plotting on the coast. In particular, Thomas Hauser published a book in 1978 asserting that Creter told Horman and Simon at that meeting: "I'm here with the United States Navy. We came down to do a job and it's done [Hauser's emphasis]." According to Hauser, Creter also volunteered that he had been on a ship in the harbor for about a week and was in Chile at military invitation. Later in his account Hauser says that "the Department of State . . . fails to explain who came with Creter—the 'we' of his remarks; and . . . why . . . he said the job he had come to perform was 'done.'" Hauser goes on to recount theories that Creter might have been in Chile to coordinate communications for the U.S. National Security Agency or that he was a CIA agent responsible for funneling supplies to the Chilean military.[26]

Hauser's speculations rest on the alleged remark that "we came to do a job. . . ." Terry Simon must have been Hauser's source, as Charles Horman tragically died a few days after the coup, and Creter—the only other participant in the encounter—does not support Hauser's account. Simon described the encounter herself in notes she typed up on 23 September 1973, in an article published in December 1973, and in a notarized statement made on 11 April 1974. All three accounts, written within seven months of the meeting in question, sound less suggestive than Hauser's version, and none of them talks about the "we" Hauser points to. In her notes Simon writes: "Been here long? No, just down here to do a job." In her article she has it: " 'Have you been here long?' we asked. 'No. I'm just down to do a job.' " In the notarized statement Simon says that "Creter explained that he was in Chile to do a job with the Navy."[27]

Creter was a retired U.S. naval engineering technician working as a civilian employee of the U.S. government, installing, inspecting, and repairing machinery. Creter had been sent to Chile to work on equipment to produce carbon dioxide for recharging shipboard fire extinguishers, a device to measure $CO_2$ in extinguisher bottles, a portable fire pump, and several similar pieces of gear.[28]

Creter explained in documents available to all parties that the "job" he told Horman and Simon he was in Chile to do was the technical engineering assignment just described, and he had told them so.[29] As Simon herself observed in her notes of 23 September 1973, Creter "couldn't really speak Spanish."[30] It would seem implausible that the CIA would have given a coup-plotting assignment to an operative who could not speak to the Chileans in their own language; it is far-fetched to think of Creter as a master spy; and it is still more unlikely that, if he were one, he would have spilled out his guilty secret to two total strangers.

U.S. spy planes handled the plotters' communications, according to allegations publicized by Mrs. Allende, Camilo Taufic, Gary MacEoin, and others.[31] Mrs. Allende charged that 32 U.S. observation and battle planes landed in Mendoza on 7 September, that one of them became a "flying electronic control station, serving to coordinate the communications of the putschists" on the day of the coup, and that 15 of the 32 planes left Mendoza forty-eight hours after the coup.[32] Various of the accounts assert that the plane active on the day of the coup was a WB57 weather plane, license number

631-3298, flown by majors V. Dueñas and T. Schull or Shull, both of the U.S. Air Force.[33] The interview with Gladys Marín about Americans allegedly bombing the Moneda also seems to have gotten mixed up with the Mendoza-based flying control station in these accounts.

Max V. Krebs was deputy chief of mission in Buenos Aires at the time in question, and—at my request—he has checked further with responsible U.S. military personnel. The United States did bring aircraft to the Argentinian Air Force base in Mendoza to carry out an ongoing, long-established, unclassified, high-altitude meteorological program. Argentinian officers and civilians participated in the group's open scientific work. The Chilean leftist accounts are in fact referring to a plane engaged in this work.[34]

There is no evidence that the Chilean armed forces coordinated their efforts using any foreign aircraft, nor did they need to. Extensive and detailed descriptions of the Chilean military's communications arrangements were published after the coup, and none of them makes the U.S. "flying electronic control station" remotely believable. Interestingly, postcoup accounts leave the impression that much communication among the coup leaders was by plain telephone. The Chileans also had—as already described—the Chilean Navy's "green" secure phone net and VHF radio phones.

The other principal story of direct U.S. involvement in the coup involves my trip to Washington from 6 to 9 September 1973.

### A Precoup Trip to Washington

A widely circulated story has it that I met with Henry Kissinger in Washington just before the coup in order to plan the deed. I did fly up to Washington; that much is true. What is not true is that my trip was for the purpose of coup plotting.

Former secretary Kissinger gives his version of my trip in his memoirs, a version I find accurate in many respects but not altogether so. Kissinger's insistence that he and I knew of no "specific plan," "time frame," or "date" for the coup when we met claims a greater lack of information than was true.[35] That the United States had considerable intelligence on the coup plotting soon leaked, and the result was that the credibility of Kissinger's account suffered, even though his central assertion that we did not participate in the coup was correct.

Kissinger describes the sequence:

> Seventy-two hours before the explosion—on Saturday, September 8—I met Nathaniel Davis for the first time. . . . The truth is that my appointment with Davis had nothing to do with Chile at all. After I was nominated as Secretary of State on August 22, I asked for a list of the ablest senior State Department officers for possible elevation to key positions. Davis's name appeared on that list. Since I had never met him, I asked the State Department to invite him for an interview. I suggested the weekend of September 8–9 because it was the first free moment after my return to Washington from San Clemente. Davis was told to pick another date if that proved inconvenient or if his presence was required in Santiago.[36]

The genesis of the trip to Washington looked to me much as described, although the weekend of 8–9 September was not the time originally suggested. Nor was it my first meeting with Kissinger, as I had accompanied him to a dinner honoring Chilean foreign minister Almeyda at Ambassador Letelier's Washington embassy in 1971.[37] But the great are better known than knowing, and Kissinger's impression on me was more memorable, I am sure, than mine on him.

By 27 August 1973 Bernard Gwertzman of the *New York Times* had already learned of Kissinger's "talent search."[38] On the twenty-ninth the State Department cabled me to make plans for a quick trip. The secretary-designate suggested that he would not wish me to come if I thought the trip imprudent in light of the situation in Chile. The proposed time frame was the week of 10–16 September. I replied that the Chilean situation was indeed "unstable" and suggested that I should fly up very shortly before the scheduled meeting, when Kissinger had decided on which day he wished to see me. One does not lightly tell the secretary of state–designate that an interview with him is inconvenient, and I knew of no hard facts to justify a demur. Had the schedule held firm, 11 September would have come before or during my trip.

On 31 August another cable proposed the appointment at 6 P.M. on Thursday the sixth. On the day after that a third cable said the White House wished to reschedule the appointment for 10 A.M. on Saturday the eighth. These shifts were more than understandable in light of the pressures on Kissinger's schedule. At his 6 September press briefing the State Department's spokesman, Paul J. Hare, mentioned Kissinger's impending appointment with me; there was no secret about it.[39] Chilean defense minister Letelier and I talked by telephone in the evening of the fifth, and I let him know that I was flying up to Washington on the following day.[40]

I flew from Santiago on Thursday evening, 6 September, still without reason to believe that a coup would be coming when it did. In retrospect, it now appears that the Chilean generals reached their consensus to act on the very day I flew north, and agreed with the admirals on the 11 September coup date when I was in Washington (see chapter 9).

I arrived in Washington slightly before noon on Friday. During that afternoon and early on Saturday morning Deputy Assistant Secretary Harry Shlaudeman and I went through the proliferating intelligence reports about Chile in Harry's office on the sixth floor of the State Department. I was surprised by the change in the Chilean situation revealed in intelligence received since my departure on Thursday. This was because events in Chile were moving very fast and also, in part, because the State Department in Washington had quick access to current intelligence obtained on a worldwide basis. Prospects were becoming more ominous by the hour. It was with this ominous intelligence very much on my mind that I went on Saturday to the West Wing of the White House for my 10 A.M. appointment with Kissinger. Lawrence S. Eagleburger greeted me and found me a place to sit. After two or three hours, with frenetic activity underway in Kissinger's office, Eagleburger suggested I go to lunch. When I returned, he said that my appointment might have to slip, perhaps to the next day, perhaps longer. I could see myself sitting in Washington as a military coup transformed Chilean history, and I explained the developing situation to Eagleburger in sharp colors. I urged that we stick to schedule—at least to a degree that would enable me to fly back to Chile that evening. Eagleburger conferred with Kissinger, and the secretary-designate made time for our talk.

Kissinger's memoirs continue the story: "The subject of our meeting was internal State Department organization and personnel. It resulted in my appointing Davis Director General of the Foreign Service. Before turning to my principal concern, however, I asked him to bring me up to date about Chile. . . ."[41]

[Davis] Well, I certainly haven't improved the situation. The economy continues to go downhill, polarization of the political forces continues, and each of the three armed forces has at one point or another faced an internal crisis. As a result, the anti-Allende forces are stronger in each of the three services. As you know, General Prats has resigned. . . .

[Kissinger] Will there be a coup?

[Davis] In Chile you can never count on anything, but the odds are in favor of a coup, though I can't give you a time frame.

[Kissinger] We are going to stay out of that, I assume.

[Davis] Yes. My firm instructions to everybody on the staff are that we are not to involve ourselves in any way.

[Kissinger] Do the Chileans ever ask us for our view?

[Davis] Yes, on occasion they'll sidle up and ask what we think about the situation. But as I said, my strong instructions to the staff are that they are not to get drawn into any conversation on the subject. . . .

[Kissinger] What should we do there [in Chile]?

[Davis] Things are moving fast enough. Our biggest problem is to keep from getting caught in the middle. We must leave the Chileans to decide their future for themselves.

[Kissinger] What's your bet on an Allende overthrow?

[Davis] I would think that Allende has about a 25 percent chance of finishing out his term in 1976. I think there's a 35 to 40 percent chance that there will be a golpe [coup]. I think there is perhaps a 20 to 25 percent chance that the military will enter the government but in such a role that it really runs the government. I think there is a very small percentage chance that Chile will become a Cuba-type situation.[42]

When Secretary Kissinger's second volume of memoirs was published in 1982, it rather startled me to read the foregoing as a "transcript" of what was said in that 1973 meeting. I wondered if Kissinger had been bugging himself, but Eagleburger later informed me that what Kissinger called a "transcript" was actually a write-up of the notes that he, Eagleburger, had jotted down during the conversation. That explains why the language in the "transcript" was so crisp. It also means that approximations, or even inaccuracies, might have been set down. It was certainly not a verbatim record. For example, I was surprised to see myself quoted as giving a "very small percentage chance" that Chile would become a Cuba-type situation. I thought at the time that this danger was considerable.

There is a more serious problem with the "transcript." It does not start at the beginning of the conversation about Chile. As I entered the room, Kissinger said: "So there's going to be a coup in Chile!" As memory fades, I am not sure these words are exactly reproduced, but I am certain that they convey the meaning of Kissinger's sardonic remark. Eagleburger disputes my recollection, but I am sure. I answered Dr. Kissinger's sally with a remark that one could not surely predict these things, and the conversation proceeded from there, with Kissinger than asking me a more general question about the political situation. Eagleburger was doing a lot of rushing in and out—as was his wont—and it may well have been that he was not in the room when Kissinger greeted me.

Given the state of our knowledge on the afternoon of the eighth, it is simply unbelievable that I told Kissinger I could not give him "any time frame" for a coup.[43] I had just finished appealing for the interview to be held on the day scheduled so I could be back in Santiago as soon as possible.

Some commentators allege that the decision to overthrow Allende was made first, with my knowledge or even instigation, and that I then flew to Washington to discuss the plans with Kissinger. Rojas, for example, reports that the generals agreed "on the morning of September 7" to overthrow the government and then "US Ambassador to Chile Nathaniel Davis traveled to the United States on Friday, Sept. 7. . . ."[44] By giving the wrong date of my departure from Santiago, Rojas creates a conspiratorial cause-and-effect sequence.

To conclude, Kissinger's recollections in his memoirs and his "transcript" are correct in their main point. The secretary-designate and I were both centrally concerned at the time of our meeting with the avoidance of U.S. involvement in Chilean coup plotting. On the eighth I got no intimation of the interventionist enthusiasm Kissinger has been accused of in other quarters at other times.

### The Extent of U.S. Foreknowledge

How much *did* the U.S. government know on Saturday, 8 September—or on Sunday, or Monday? As described, we were better informed than Henry Kissinger acknowledges in his memoirs.[45] According to leaked reports, Kissinger expressed himself in even vaguer terms in his executive-session testimony to Congress on 17

September 1973. Reportedly, he said that in our conversation on the eighth he told me to keep embassy personnel away from the plotters, "if there are plotters," and that "there was no talk between us about the coup except the rumors that had been around for weeks and months."[46] Various other U.S. officials talked about "rumors" and reports of the "possibility" of a coup.[47]

It is difficult even now to discuss the full extent of U.S. foreknowledge. There are still valid reasons for keeping some secrets; the "protection of sources and methods," as the CIA puts it, may still be important. Nevertheless, the public record is by now quite extensive, and much of the information emanated from high Washington sources.

Ex-CIA director William Colby has testified: "We obviously had some intelligence coverage over the various moves being made. . . ."[48] Ex-CIA Latin American operations chief David A. Phillips has written:

> In late August of 1973 it became increasingly evident that a coup was imminent in Chile. Following the abortive effort of the tank commanders in June [the tancazo], resentment and discontent festered among the military. . . . The Chilean Air Force conspired with the Chilean Navy. . . . The missing element was the army, vital to any coup endeavor. There were several false starts and postponements. Then a report said that the army was about to join the other conspirators.[49]

The Church Committee staff report says that the volume of intelligence reporting reached a peak at the end of August and during the first part of September. The report goes on: "It is clear the CIA received intelligence reports on the coup planning of the group which carried out the successful September 11 coup throughout the months of July, August and September 1973."[50] The description of the quality of U.S. intelligence during those weeks is clear, although it should be remembered that the Chilean plotters themselves came to their determination to proceed only a very few days before the coup.

So far as those last days were concerned, the *New York Times* reported leaked testimony by Assistant Secretary Kubisch in Congress on 12 September to the effect that "a Chilean officer" had told the U.S. Embassy on Sunday that there would be a coup on Monday, and an officer had told the embassy on Monday that it had

been pushed off and would be on Tuesday (see chapter 9).[51] James
Goodsell of the *Christian Science Monitor* reported that Washington had known "48 hours" before the coup began.[52] Reuters said the
U.S. government knew "at least 40 hours in advance."[53] For myself,
I went to bed Sunday night thinking that a coup might be coming
the next morning but was told on Monday of the intelligence that it
had been pushed off until Tuesday.

Phillips of the CIA writes that "on the night of September 10" he
telephoned Assistant Secretary Kubisch and William Jorden of
Kissinger's NSC staff, "saying that this time it looked real."[54] State
Department spokesman Paul Hare stated on the thirteenth that the
U.S. Embassy in Santiago received reports "around midnight on
September 10 . . . that September 11 was to be the date."[55]

Communications to the Unitas naval task force give an additional
public reflection of the state of U.S. foreknowledge. A "State Department official" was reported by Bernard Gwertzman to have said
on the thirteenth that the U.S. task force of four ships was advised
on the tenth of "rumors of a coup that day."[56] The reports were of a
coup scheduled for Monday morning, 10 September. As no
confirmation of the report was received, the task force left port as
scheduled.

The Washington Special Action Group met on the eleventh while
the coup was in progress. Kissinger reportedly testified later that he
was confronted at that meeting with "total confusion."[57] I have
since been told that there were inter- and intra-agency dis-
agreements in the Washington intelligence community, not only
about the facts but also about their import. During the week or so
before the weekend of 8-9 September it appears that the Defense
Intelligence Agency analysts and those in covert operations at the
CIA were more inclined to believe that a coup was imminent than
were the CIA's current intelligence analysts.[58]

In conclusion, the U.S. government had intelligence on the coup
plotting through the months of July and August and the first days of
September. By 9:30 A.M. on 8 September, when I left the State
Department to meet Kissinger at the White House, we had indications of the Chilean generals' and admirals' deliberations about
mounting a coup on Monday the tenth. Over the weekend the coup
was pushed off until Tuesday, and we had intimations of this
change on Monday, with increasingly reliable confirming intelligence coming in through the night. My own recollection conforms

to this sequence, and published reporting is essentially consistent with it.

### Does Foreknowledge Indicate Complicity?

Many commentators say the fact that the U.S. government had good intelligence on the coup means that the plotters and U.S. agents must have been in cahoots. They evidently believe that the intelligence needed to monitor coup plotting must perforce have sent back signals of encouragement to the conspirators. Can one conclude, then, that the monitoring must have made the United States a party to Allende's overthrow?

This line of reasoning may take incomplete account of the different ways in which intelligence can be obtained. There are at least four such ways: collection from open sources; passive collection; espionage conducted through "cut-outs"; and direct agent contact. The first activity, open collection, is how the United States acquires, by volume, most of its intelligence. Most CIA employees spend their lives piecing together press items, published material, public statements, and open political information. When a Chilean politician reveals the latest coup report to a political officer of the U.S. Embassy over lunch, that is not espionage. It is overt collection. Journalists in Santiago were privy to rumors of plotting that were circulating there, but that knowledge did not make them parties to conspiracy. Santiago was awash with such reports during August and September 1973.

The second category, passive collection, includes everything from troop movements observed by a U.S. official through a train window to any of the more esoteric, technical means of eavesdropping. For example, on the night before the coup night laborers on highways north of Santiago observed trucks with soldiers moving south, and this information was reported to President Allende. The intelligence was passive; Allende did not inevitably send signals of discovery to the convoy commanders or the plotters. Most of the intelligence acquired by technical methods is also passive. Communications intelligence of all kinds, including international radio transmissions and radio-relayed telephone traffic, has figured in every political crisis in recent times, and there is no reason to suppose that Chile was an exception. Such intelligence does not send a signal of encouragement back to those being monitored. It is possible to receive without transmitting and to hear without speaking.

The third category, "cut-outs," involves foreign agents who collect and transmit reports without knowing for whom the information is intended. If a Chilean plotter confides in another Chilean who is a controlled agent of U.S. intelligence, or if the chain involves more than one intermediate "cut-out," feedback may be avoided. In fact, David Phillips and his deputy tell me that the station, under Washington instructions, relied more heavily on cut-outs, avoiding direct contacts, than even the Church Committee investigators quite realized.[59]

Third-country citizens may also become part of the chain. The "Brazilian connection," discussed in chapter 12, provides an example. Marlise Simons notes that, before the coup, Brazil's minister of war, Gen. Orlando Geisel, told the Paraguayan ambassador to Brazil that Chile would soon be "in military hands." Simons also recounts how Argentina's interim president, Raúl Lastiri, was also tipped off that a coup "was being prepared."[60] I have no information indicating that these particular reports were passed on to the U.S. government, but they might have been. Such information could have reached us without any return signal being given.

It is in the fourth category, direct, knowing contact between a Chilean plotter and an identified American official or agent, where the acquisiton of information may become consultation or encouragement. This possibility concerned the Church Committee staff, but the authors of the report acknowledged that the concerns they expressed were based on supposition rather than evidence.

The issue affects U.S. intelligence collection throughout the world. In recent years U.S. commentators on intelligence policy have sometimes made a significant distinction between intelligence collection—which is regarded as necessary and justifiable—and clandestine operations—which are regarded as counterproductive and inconsistent with American principles. If we cannot have one without the other, and the arrangements the CIA has worked out over the years to maintain the distinction cannot be trusted, then the conclusions are far-reaching. Is anybody prepared to advocate the cessation of intelligence collection in the world in order to ensure the avoidance of signaling? As the U.S. ambassador in Chile, I was in no position to tell the CIA station to stop collecting intelligence for fear of transmitting encouragement to plotters. I had to trust the CIA's ability to walk the line between intelligence collection and covert action.

The problem of learning without transmitting is one of the oldest in the intelligence business, and one of the most centrally important requirements of effective intelligence operations. I cannot be sure that the Santiago CIA station was effective in this regard. I have enough respect for the perspicacity and dedication of those professionals, however, to give them the benefit of the doubt. I shall not assume their failure unless or until confirming evidence of failure comes to light.

Separate from CIA penetration and monitoring of coup-plotting groups is the question whether the plotters took the initiative and approached the U.S. government. The range of possible contacts could go from Pinochet, Leigh, Merino, or Mendoza down to some low-level military officer or civilian "in the know" who might have approached the CIA station, an attaché, or a civilian embassy officer. Pinochet did not tell us, nor did he want us to be informed. So far as I know, the same can be said for the other men who later constituted the Junta.

Indications are that the top coup planners made a policy decision not to consult the Americans. David Binder of the *New York Times* reported on 14 September 1973 that the Junta had taken pains to explain to us within 48 hours of the coup that we had been deliberately left in the dark.

> Chile's ruling four-man junta has informed Washington that it deliberately kept its plans for a coup on Tuesday to itself to prevent any possibility of United States involvement in the overthrow of President Salvador Allende Gossens, according to a Cabinet-level official of the Nixon Administration [probably U.S. ambassador to the UN John Scali].
>
> A representative of the junta made this statement yesterday to Ambassador Nathaniel Davis. . . .[61]

Actually, the statement was made to a senior U.S. military advisory group officer rather than to me, but I do believe that the statement presented Junta policy. Later one member of the Junta apologized to me personally, saying he regretted that he and his colleagues felt they could not inform me of their decision to execute a coup.

Ambassador Scali, who evidently had obtained his information at a cabinet meeting at the White House, appears to have told Bin-

der that "tips that the coup was pending—a dozen such tips culminating in a warning Monday night—were made to United States
diplomats in Santiago by lower-level Chilean military officers who
were not directly involved in the plans."[62] What Ambassador Scali
presumably meant by the "warning" on Monday night was that a
Chilean officer advised one of our attachés on Monday night to
"stay off the streets" on Tuesday. His meaning was by then unmistakable, and the attaché reported the conversation to Washington
and then drove by my house and told me about it. In general, while
there were some direct contacts during the hours preceding the
coup, by then the die was cast and no conversations or signals
could have significantly encouraged or discouraged the overthrow,
which was already in train.

### Should the United States Have Forestalled the Coup?

Bernard Gwertzman wrote on 13 September that administration
officials said "that President Nixon had received numerous reports
in the last year of an impending military coup in Chile, and had
decided against taking any action that would encourage or discourage the overthrow of the Government of President Salvador Allende Gossens."[63] The State Department spokesman, Paul Hare,
soon elaborated, saying that official consideration had been given
to the possibility of warning Allende but that the idea had been
rejected. He explained that "the decision was made not to inform
Dr. Allende . . . because it might have been construed as intervention in Chile's internal affairs."[64] While this position seems hypo-
critical in light of what we now know, Hare was probably ignorant
of the history of U.S. actions in Chile when he spoke.

Nobody ever contacted me about the possibility of warning Allende; in fact, I received no instructions at all on the subject. Had I
proposed such an initiative, my Washington superiors would no
doubt have concluded that I had gone around the bend.

David Phillips felt the way I did. He comments:

> A decision to advise Salvador Allende's Marxist government
> would have had to be made at the highest levels of the United
> States government. I'm not sure what Henry Kissinger's posi-
> tions would have been, although I can make an educated guess.
> There was never a doubt in my mind what Richard Nixon's
> decision would have been had he been asked whether we

should forewarn Allende, and thus allow the Marxist to defend himself. It never even occurred to me that Nixon would have done otherwise than scotch the proposal. And that is the real reason no United States official even considered the idea. It would have been a waste of time to ask.[65]

What I think might have happened was that somebody raised the question of warning Allende in or with the White House in the hours immediately before the coup, and the idea was promptly rejected.[66] Then, when some "smart-aleck" reporter asked why we did not warn Allende, Hare gave the answer he did, somewhat magnifying the seriousness and duration of consideration given.

Even if one could imagine Nixon or Kissinger instructing me to go to Salvador Allende to tell him that his senior military commanders were planning to overthrow him, it is difficult to picture the reaction at the Moneda. President Allende might well have thought the U.S. government was trying to destroy whatever confidence remained between him and his senior military commanders. I do not think it is conceivable that Allende and his intimates would have believed our motives were benign.

Phillips addresses another possibility: "If the United States government were to warn the incumbent regime in Latin America each time there were reports of a coup it would soon become suspect, as most coups are planned but do not come off." Phillips calls this "crying coup-wolf." He goes on: "What happens should the Americans warn a regime that it is about to be overthrown and it is. Relations with the new government, when its leaders learned that the gringos had attempted to thwart their plans, would be sticky indeed."[67]

In warning Allende our government would have had to have been both credible and successful in saving him. Allende and his colleagues did in fact get considerable warning from elsewhere and did not take effective action.

To have had any chance at all of Allende's believing us and acting decisively himself, we would have had to give him detailed information about the plotters, including any officers who might have directly or indirectly passed on reports. Would that have been an honorable course of action in September 1973? There are many levels of betrayal in this world.

On a deeper level I am not sure the U.S. government *should* have acted to abort the coup. Institutional democracy in Chile was probably doomed by September 1973, and the United States—had we warned Allende convincingly and effectively—might have become the instrument of Chile's transformation into a leftist totalitarian regime. After all, the Chilean Supreme Court, the Chamber of Deputies, the comptroller, the Christian Democratic party, and other democratic and constitutional forces in the country had already declared that the Allende regime was acting outside the law. This argument is complicated, of course, as it involves fundamental judgments about the Pinochet regime and the nature of the leftist government that might have emerged from a foiled coup.

In any case, the military's decision to act came by stages in the days before the coup, and was not sealed until Sunday, 9 September. Even assuming complete and reliable U.S. intelligence at every stage of this process, the moment at which to go to Allende and provide him with a convincing and definitive warning before the coup was a fleeting one. If we had decided to try to forestall the coup, the practical thing to have done, no doubt, would have been to go to the plotters and tell them in the strongest terms of our opposition to their plotting, threatening dire consequences in their relations with the United States should they persist. The sensible time to have taken such action would probably have been in the formative stages of the plotting, perhaps in July or early August.

Of course, such a course of action would have encountered many of the problems mentioned in connection with warning Allende, starting with President Nixon's almost certain unwillingness to have had the United States act in this way. Moreover, one should bear in mind that the Chilean military were, and are, an immensely proud group of men, probably even more resistant to American guidance than their counterparts in other Latin American countries. The coup leaders were neither consulting nor advising us, by deliberate decision, and our ability to go to them, reveal our intelligence, and tell them what not to do would have been limited. They might also have calculated that—whatever we said—we would come to terms with them after we were presented with a fait accompli. Lastly, the task of picking the right moment to accuse the generals of sedition and force them to desist might have been as difficult as finding the moment to go to Allende.

*Chapter 14*

# Military Government

It is time to pick up the Chilean narrative once again—even though my own mission in Chile would last only fifty more days. The U.S. government wisely delayed for two weeks after the coup before establishing official diplomatic contact with the Junta government, and my transfer from Santiago was announced two-and-a-half weeks after that. That announcement made me a lame duck, and I left Chile on 1 November 1973.

Controversy over the U.S. role in Chile has continued to trouble Americans to the present day. In fact, introspection has so dominated the U.S. reaction as to obscure the lessons the Communists have drawn from the fall of the UP government. These leftist reactions over the past decade have significantly affected the Communists' global ideology and doctrine.

### The First Seven Weeks of Junta Rule

What was the fate of the UP leaders? Some died in the fighting, including Eduardo "Coco" Paredes, one-time head of the investigative police, and Arnaldo Comú, the Socialist party's paramilitary chief. The Junta announced that José Gregorio Liendo, "Comandante Pepe," was captured after having held out for a week or two in his redoubt. He was sentenced to death by a military court and executed on 3 October.[1]

Most of the president's high-level colleagues who had been in the Moneda and taken prisoner were held initially in the Ministry of Defense and ultimately detained on Dawson Island, south of Punta Arenas on the Straits of Magellan, where they suffered cold, privation, indignity, and physical abuse. Among them were Clodomiro Almeyda, Orlando Letelier, Aníbal Palma, Fernando Flores, Daniel Vergara, José Tohá, Luis Corvalán, and about thirty others. Tohá died in captivity in early 1974 of what was variously reported to have been cancer, suicide, or murder. Vergara survived, but he was said to have developed gangrene as the result of ill-attended wounds received on the eleventh.[2]

Still others took refuge in foreign embassies, including Oscar Garretón, Jaime Faivovich, Jacques Chonchol, Gonzalo Martner, Jaime Suárez, and hundreds of others.[3] Carlos Altamirano went into hiding and later escaped from Chile. He was probably spirited out of the country under the aegis of a Latin American embassy. The ambassador of that country approached me, in fact, asking my help in the operation, but I was not in a position to render this assistance. A last few, including Volodia Teitelboim, had found themselves abroad on the eleventh.

Estimates of the number of people killed during and immediately after the coup vary from a low of 2,500 to a high of 80,000. A range of 3,000 to 10,000 deaths covers the more reliable estimates. The Junta's figures clearly underestimate the loss of life. As late as 16 September 1973 the Junta was giving out a figure of 93 people killed.[4]

Some news reporters, on the other hand, clearly overestimated the loss of life. For example, John Barnes of Newsweek wrote on 8 October 1973 that the Santiago morgue alone processed 2,796 bodies in the first two weeks after the eleventh. Other journalists later corrected Barnes, noting that bodies in the morgue were numbered consecutively from the beginning of the year, and Barnes's number represented bodies processed since 1 January 1973.[5]

Two correct conclusions emerge from information available about the death toll in Chile during the coup and its aftermath. First, there was a tragic loss of life, which was particularly shocking in a country of Chile's democratic and law-abiding traditions. Second, the number of deaths was relatively limited compared to Chileans' precoup expectations.

The central question may be not how many died but *how* the victims died. Deaths in pitched battle alone would not support the accusation that atrocities occurred; but if even a few defenseless citizens were massacred, or if captives were lined up, shot, and dumped into the Mapocho River, it would be an uglier story. And indeed, quite a number of bodies in the Santiago morgue looked as if execution had been the manner of death. While I do not know how many Chileans were summarily shot, I do know that more such killings occurred than Chilean authorities have acknowledged.

In revolutionary situations the accustomed veneer of restrained and decent conduct which prevails in quieter times is ripped off, exposing the darker aspects of human passion and fear. Neighbors denounced neighbors in Santiago during these days. Extravagances of zeal, hatred, and vengeance brushed aside decency, law, and moderation; even when those in authority wanted to uphold justice, their orders sometimes went unheeded. Families—already split apart—found their ties of love weaker than the calls to violence, and events followed the logic of passion. It has been a long time since North America has been subjected to such a rending of the social fabric as Chile experienced before and after 11 September 1973.[6] I hope Americans would react differently, but I am not sure we would.

Junta leaders had asserted that the bombing of the Moneda would save lives. I was warned when I came to Chile in 1971 that the army enforced curfews with bullets, and a violator risked death if he failed to halt as ordered. At the time of the June 1973 tancazo General Pinochet, then army chief of staff, was asked why there had been so many casualties compared with earlier disorders, which had been handled by the carabineros. General Pinochet replied: "When the army comes out, it is to kill."[7]

Allende estimated before the coup that a civil war would cost a million lives.[8] Expectations of bloodshed remained high even after the coup. For example, Laurence Birns predicted—mistakenly, so far—that the workers and the poor would "bomb . . . kidnap, and . . . assassinate," and turn Chile into a Northern Ireland "at the very least. . . . No military force is large enough to prevent this."[9] However one judges the Junta's measures, the military was effective in cowing resistance, at least for a time.

"Plan Z" was the name Junta leaders gave to an alleged precoup plot to murder Chile's senior military commanders and to carry out a left-extremist *autogolpe*. This plan was used to justify the decision to seize power on the eleventh. Plan Z had several variants. According to a story that surfaced a few days after the coup, socialist, communist, MAPU, and leftist trade union leaders began on 22 August, the day when army wives demonstrated against Prats, to prepare a "defense plan" that would have involved a seizure of total power. Another story had the MIR working on a plan to overthrow Allende on 13 September. A third said that left extremists in Unidad Popular were preparing a coup for 17 September, which would have involved the murder of top military commanders and opposition leaders. On the sixteenth the Junta announced that it had discovered this third plan in Subsecretary of Interior Vergara's safe.[10] A week after that announcement a list of six hundred people marked for assassination—perhaps part of the third plan—was said to have been found in the notebook of a Socialist leader in Concepción.[11] Finally, in October, the Junta published its *White Book*, which contained documents purportedly constituting Plan Z (or Plan Zeta). These papers, dated 25 August 1973, called for Allende's GAP bodyguards to murder the "generals, admirals and other high officials" assembled at the official army day luncheon on 19 September.[12]

There was certainly some truth in the rightists' conviction that left extremists were plotting to seize total power. Altamirano said almost as much publicly, in his famous speech of 9 September.[13] But the authenticity of Plan Z is highly doubtful. Even members of the Junta were candid in saying that it had not motivated them in their decision to mount the coup. Pinochet was quoted on 18 September as merely having said: "It is quite possible that they [the leftists] really were preparing a coup. There were so many rumors. . . ."[14] In another interview, in March 1974, Pinochet was asked if the army had known about Plan Z before the coup. He answered: "We had some indications. We knew that they had arms, . . . and that something was being prepared, but we didn't know what."[15] Gen. Gustavo Leigh said at the end of October 1973 that the military leaders had not known "details of Plan Zeta until after the coup, when the documents were found in a cash box in the presidential palace [presumably in Vergara's safe]. Nevertheless, Military Intelligence had the outlines of the plan, thanks to monitoring of the Moneda telephones" (which is in itself an interesting acknowledgment).[16]

The Junta never produced supporting evidence for Plan Z.[17] Marlise Simons gives one possible explanation for the provenance of the plan: "After Chile's coup, a prominent Brazilian historian . . . said . . . 'Chile's military . . . allegations that the "Communists" had been preparing a massacre . . . were so scandalously identical to ours, one almost presumes they had the same author.' "[18]

In the days after the coup a story swept Santiago that retired general Carlos Prats had escaped to the south and was marching against the capital at the head of a mighty column of loyal troops. Prats was probably the only man with the military stature to make the generals uneasy. Troop movements north of Puerto Montt probably triggered the story, but these troops were reserve units moving under the Junta's command.[19] Prats wrote in his diary that he and Vice Admiral Carvajal talked, and Prats agreed to make a "brief declaration on television" disavowing reports that he was leading organized resistance.[20] Prats did go on the air and make these statements.

Probably as a consequence of Prats's willingness to make this broadcast, and also no doubt because his continued presence in Chile would have made Pinochet and his colleagues exceedingly uncomfortable, the retired commander-in-chief and his wife Sofía were permitted to drive to Argentina on 15 September and settle in Buenos Aires. The couple was assassinated a year later by persons widely believed to have been agents of the Pinochet regime.[21] So ended the life of Carlos Prats, a tragic, poignant, and affecting figure in contemporary Chilean history. If and when political progressives govern Chile again, Prats will be remembered.

Adm. Raúl Montero was allowed to retire to private life and was subsequently given a diplomatic appointment. He paid a call on me a few days after the coup, and I found it a sad experience. The old sea dog was much reduced in manner and appearance. I had the impression that the skin of his face was ashen and flaking. He was his usual courteous, courtly self, but the toll of those August and September days was etched in his countenance.

General Ruiz was appointed rector of the University of Chile. An odd compromise must have led to Ruiz assuming this dignified post, as only a month before Ruiz had been Leigh's commander-in-chief and—but for the vagaries of that August crisis—would have been a member of the Junta. When Ruiz went to the University of Chile, he displaced Edgardo Boeninger, the courageous and indomitable academician who had stood up against the machinations of the leftists at the university throughout the Allende time.

The Junta did not confine its institutional revolution to the academic world. The country's leftist parties were outlawed, the center and conservative parties were "recessed," and the Chilean Congress was dissolved. A cabinet almost exclusively composed of generals and admirals ran the government. Active or retired officers took over senior and middle-level administrative jobs throughout the country and filled the important diplomatic posts. Trade union offices were closed down. The leaders of all the religious communities, including Cardinal Silva, found themselves under suspicion, and foreign-born priests suspected of "progressive" sympathies were detained or expelled.

Representatives of the Junta displayed hostility or indifference to political and societal forces of almost every hue. It was as if the military leaders really thought they could run the country alone. This attitude came as a particular shock to leaders of the National party. Although the conservative politicians had a modest amount of influence, the attitude of Gen. Washington Carrasco seemed representative of the new government's view: "The politicians have already worked a lot in this country. Now it is only fair that they take a long rest."[22]

To the extent the generals assumed a political orientation, it was oriented toward the business and professional associations, or guilds. Orlando Saenz and Jorge Fontaine had access, jobs, and influence. So did Jaime Guzmán, with his corporativist ideas. There were also men close to Patria y Libertad who helped run the country.

Relations between the Junta leaders and the Christian Democrats were crucial to the prospects of the regime, but it appears that the generals did not understand the fact. Reportedly Leigh entertained the idea of turning power over to Frei after an interval of military rule (in spite of connections between Leigh's brother and the National party). It was said, however, that Pinochet would not countenance anything of the sort. By then, of course, Pinochet had assumed the dignity of chief of state.

For their part, the Christian Democrats had issued a statement immediately after the coup absolving the military of seeking power for themselves, expressing confidence that the military would "return power to the sovereign people," and asserting that the military's "proposals to establish institutional normalcy, peace and unity . . . merit the cooperation of all sectors."[23] This Christian Democratic overture was conspicuously rebuffed.

In his memoirs General Prats tells the story—which he admits may be apocryphal—or former president Frei going to call on the newly appointed vice president and minister of interior, Gen. Oscar Bonilla. According to the story, Frei was obliged to return home on foot after soldiers requisitioned the automobile he had had at his disposal as president of the Senate.[24] True or false, the anecdote reflects the atmosphere of the time, and the willingness of many in the military regime to denigrate the towering political figures of Chile's democratic era.

Bonilla was the member of the Junta leadership who most conspicuously tried to cooperate with the Christian Democrats. He had been Frei's military aide. Bonilla died in an air crash in March 1975, in circumstances that aroused suspicions in the press outside Chile and gave rise to reports of foul play.[25]

Former Christian Democratic party president Renán Fuentealba invited my wife and me to his daughter's wedding on 29 September. Former president Frei, Patricio Aylwin, Edgardo Boeninger, and most of the other distinguished figures of the CD party attended, and there was considerable joshing about the fact that everybody was an "ex-." There was also serious and rueful talk about the state of the country. In later, more private, conversations with Christian Democrats I heard even more melancholy reports.

The Junta paid a heavy price for its rejection of the Christian Democrats and other former opposition parties. The new government's alienation from the forces that had commanded the loyalties of the Chilean majority throughout Allende's time made inevitable the Junta's reliance on intimidation as the cement of domestic rule. In the international arena the Junta's decision made the ostracizing of the new government unavoidable. I doubt that the senior military leadership was psychologically prepared for the damage it did to itself when it turned its back on the nation's democratic political forces.

## Seven Weeks in U.S.-Chilean Relations

The first postcoup decision facing the U.S. government involved the question of official relations with the new regime. International practice concerning "recognition" has been in a state of flux in recent years. The trend has been away from public acts of recognition, which seem to convey a measure of approval. States now tend simply to deal with each other as ongoing entities. Still, the political symbolism in recognition persists, and I had vivid recollections of the outcry when the United States was perceived as hurrying to recognize the military government of Brazil within two or three days of the 1964 coup. Our precipitate act of establishing formal ties at that time had been interpreted as reflecting complicity in the generals' seizure of power. Apparently this danger was on Henry Kissinger's mind as well as mine. He testified at his congressional confirmation hearings in mid-September 1973 that his guidance at the White House Special Action Group meeting on the eleventh had been to say nothing that would indicate "either support or opposition—that we would avoid what we had done in Brazil . . . where we rushed out by recognizing the government."[26]

We had good reason to be careful. Reuters was reporting pointedly on the sixteenth that the first to recognize the Chilean regime were "two of Latin America's right-wing military governments." As the news agency's dispatch explained, "the right-wing military rulers of Brazil and Uruguay" had announced recognition of the Chilean military government on 13 September.[27] The United States waited eleven more days, and I presented the U.S. recognition note to Chilean foreign minister Huerta on 24 September 1973. By that day twenty-two countries had already taken similar action, including such staunch democracies as Venezuela, Switzerland, France, Austria, Denmark, and the United Kingdom. Even so, U.S. recognition was headlined in black boldface letters that dominated *El Mercurio*'s front page, with an accompanying picture of Richard Nixon.

The shooting in the center of the city persisted for about a week, particularly during the hours of darkness. On 19 September my wife wrote in a letter:

The curfew has gradually been lifting, 8 P.M. to 7 A.M. at this point. There is still sporadic shooting, but the center of the city is finally quiet. We had shots, including machine gun fire, last night, not far from our house—which caused a number of calls from friends to see if it was here, but it wasn't.

The greatest part of my contribution has been to stay near the telephone—a continuous series of urgent phone calls of one kind or another—how to get Rh Negative blood, how to get word to a family, how to get someone out of jail, could my husband see so-and-so, etc., etc., etc. Even at night the calls keep coming regularly.

We have four guards to feed, as otherwise they do not eat.[28]

On the twenty-fifth Elizabeth wrote that "we have heard no shooting for several nights." By 2 October she was writing: "For a week we had no shooting near here at all, but we did have some two nights ago. We had carabineros with big guns at our gate for a while, but now we have our friendly ones again—and no guns, just pistols. Embassy-hired guards have been added, and now patrol in the garden at night . . . and Nathaniel rides with a guard."

Each year, since time immemorial, the U.S. ambassador in Santiago had invited the embassy's Chilean employees to his house, either on the day preceding the Chileans' National Day holidays or on the first subsequent working day. The purpose of the occasion was to express American thanks to the Chilean staff for their help and dedicated work during the year. After some hesitation, and with an eye to the curfew, I decided to observe the custom with a 3-to-5 P.M. gathering on the twentieth. I thought a few words of thanks would be in order in light of the very heavy pressures under which the local staff had been laboring. I mention this gathering because of subsequent allegations that the embassy "celebrated" the coup.[29] There was no celebration, and my words expressed no pleasure at the death of Chile's constitutional president and institutional regime.

Henry Kissinger asked me to fly up to Washington a second time over the weekend of 22–23 September. He was still contemplating how to put his State Department team together and was considering me for two or three jobs. He later told Carl Rowan, who wrote it up in a newspaper column, that he wanted to appoint me as under secretary for political affairs.[30] I left Santiago in mid-afternoon on Friday, 21 September, and landed in Santiago again on Monday afternoon, the twenty-fourth. In Washington all I did was keep my appointment with Kissinger at the White House and talk with colleagues at the Bureau of Inter-American Affairs at the State Department. Kissinger hardly mentioned Chile. He clearly felt that it had become a second-rank problem, and his restless mind was already moving on to other crises. The press in the United States was also less interested in this trip than in my earlier one—much less.

In one interesting conversation with Assistant Secretary Kubisch the question of (up-to-then) ongoing covert support for the Christian Democrats and other democratic parties arose. Kubisch wanted to cut off subventions immediately, and he expressed his unease, as a matter of principle, about all such covert programs. I was concerned at the beleaguered state of the democratic parties in Chile, already facing the Junta's antipathy. Foolishly, perhaps, I expressed myself as less convinced than he was of the need to cut off support immediately, particularly to the Christian Democrats. Kubisch was probably right; in any case, we discontinued this support without delay.

A new kind of difficulty surfaced at the end of September. A senior Chilean businessman with excellent connections among the generals newly in power established a back-channel to powerful U.S. business leaders who had White House ties. For a few days it looked as if the Chileans would be able to use this link to short-circuit the embassy, the Department of State, and the U.S. policy process in their ongoing effort to achieve an unrestrained and unconditional U.S. embrace. Fortunately a Chilean businessman in the know told me about these activities, and I sent Washington a meticulous, deadpan account of the goings on and asked for guidance. My telegram was EXDIS (exclusive distribution), which ensured that fifty to a hundred copies were sprayed out to key Washington offices. I received a somewhat embarrassed reply, relayed from the White House, and these back-channel activities ceased.

The most controversial matters in the activity of the U.S. Embassy after the coup involved asylum for Chileans, human rights, and the welfare and protection of Americans. Concerning asylum for Chileans, the policy of the U.S. government was clear. Essentially, the granting of asylum was prohibited unless the person seeking refuge was being chased by a mob or in immediate physical peril. The United States had never signed the various Latin American conventions on asylum, and the U.S. asylum prohibition was generally known in political and informed circles throughout the hemisphere.

The fact that U.S. policy was long-standing did not, of course, make it right, as it deprived the United States of the ability to carry out acts of compassion, to affirm principle in the face of political wrongdoing, to express human solidarity, and to speak courageously to the world in times of a friendly nation's tragedy. There are also strong arguments, however, against U.S. adoption of Latin American asylum practices. As a nation we are so dominant in the hemisphere that any and all of our deeds are politically charged. Moreover, should the United States regularly grant asylum, we would seldom be in the position of giving shelter to beleaguered left-wing constitutionalists after a right-wing coup. More frequently we would be facing pressures to give refuge to rightist dictators. Even in Chile the United States was, I think, fortunate that Pablo Rodríguez and his colleagues in Patria y Libertad made for the embassy of Ecuador and not to us when the tancazo failed.

With respect to violations of human rights, I expressed profound U.S. concerns to the new Chilean government, as Assistant Secretary Kubisch testified to the U.S. Congress. These approaches were to various levels of the Chilean government, up to and including the foreign minister and members of the Junta. As State Department spokesman John King reported on 2 October 1973, the Chileans responded that they would "uphold all Chile's obligations in the field of human rights."[31] Neither my representations nor those of other ambassadors and international representatives were welcome. On 3 October United Press International reported the Junta's public statement that "attempts by foreign governments to intercede on behalf of Chileans imprisoned since the September 11 coup . . . will be rejected."[32] Junta leaders were convinced that they had "saved" Chile and that noncommunists in the world should be greeting them with support, not carping. They did not conceal their resentment at the criticism to which they were being subjected. Washington was clearly not prepared to institute Draconian reprisals, and I doubt that anything less would have produced a turnaround.

Then there was the question of the welfare and protection of U.S. citizens. Twenty-five Americans were swept up in the wave of arrests. Usually, people who were picked up were taken for initial screening to one or another of the carabinero or military stations around the city. Some were then transferred to the National Stadium, which had been converted into a detention center. There up to 7,000 prisoners were housed in the locker rooms and other spaces under the stands. Our consular officers and Chilean clerks, officers and Chilean staff from other embassy sections, and attachés and Military Group officers toured carabinero and military stations, the Santiago stadiums, the hospitals, the morgue, and other points in the city to locate and obtain the release of any U.S. citizens who had been detained. All Americans whom we were able to locate in detention were released—usually into our "custody." I remember signing one such custody document for U.S. citizens Adam and Patricia Garrett-Schesch, which made me take responsibility for their subsequent "good conduct"—presumably meaning that they would not later publicize their experiences in custody. I did not pass this "requirement" on to the two Americans in question. Upon landing in Miami, they told an improvised press conference that they had been eyewitnesses to 400–500 executions in the National Stadium, and they created just the kind of worldwide press furor I suppose the Junta authorities were trying to forestall. More searching interrogation by reporters soon revealed that they had not actually seen the executions but had heard shooting from what they believed were the guns of firing squads.[33] In any case, these and other detained Americans suffered harrowing experiences.

Two Americans were not found alive: Charles E. Horman and Frank Teruggi. The death of Charles Horman has received widespread publicity in the years since 1973, but Frank Teruggi's death was equally desolating. His remains were identified in the Santiago morgue on 2 October by Steven Volk, a friend who went there with two consular officers to doublecheck a body which another friend had failed to identify as Teruggi's. The Chilean government subsequently told the embassy that Teruggi had been arrested for curfew violation on 20 September, had been released the next day, and had later been found in the street, dead of bullet wounds. This explanation was not consistent with the known circumstances of Teruggi's arrest in his home, and the Chilean authorities never satisfactorily explained how he died.

I had not known nor heard of either Teruggi or Horman before the search for each of them started, and neither had registered with the consulate. From the evidence we now have, I believe that each of them was dead when we first were told that he was in trouble. I find it some consolation in terms of the embassy's efforts to think that we might have succeeded in saving them if we had known about their detention when they were still alive.

Regarding Charles Horman, it may be recalled that a conversation between Arthur Creter, Horman, and Terry Simon on 12 September resulted in allegations that Creter had been a coconspirator with Chilean Navy plotters on the coast.[34] The book by Thomas Hauser on the Horman case became the basis of a film released in 1982 directed by Costa-Gavras, entitled *Missing*. The movie, depicts Creter as blabbing about his involvement. In order to silence Horman— and perhaps also Simon, although the rationale is not altogether clear in this regard—colleagues and I at the U.S. Embassy supposedly "fingered" Horman to the Chilean military, who arrested and killed him.

In October 1977, even before Hauser's book was published, the Horman family and others filed a law suit against eleven defendants who had been U.S. officials in 1973, including me. The discovery of evidence lasted over three years, leaving a paper trail of thousands of pages. The plaintiffs discontinued the action in 1981. A new suit is now underway against those who made the movie, in which my defamed colleagues and I are the plaintiffs. We hope that this action will show conclusively that we were innocent of complicity in Charles Horman's death, and that it will help defend the integrity of U.S. public service.

As the movie *Missing* explicitly asserts that it is based on the "true story" of the Horman family's ordeal, some further commentary on it and on the underlying Hauser narrative seems warranted. Several days after the Creter episode, Capt. Ray E. Davis, head of the U.S. Military Group, gave Horman and Simon a lift up to Santiago. The two were reunited with Charles's wife, Joyce Horman, on the sixteenth, and the three of them went in to the center of Santiago on the morning of the seventeenth.[35]

Charles Horman returned home alone in the late afternoon, and is shown in the movie being taken off by troops a few minutes later. This is a good depiction of what appears to have happened. The troops then ransacked the Hormans' apartment. The movie shows Joyce being caught by the curfew [7 P.M. that night] and spending the night huddled in a stairwell watching in terror as scenes of brutality are enacted before her eyes and a white horse gallops riderless through the streets. This is a dramatic highpoint of the movie, but it may not be true. Marvine Howe of the *New York Times* interviewed Mrs. Horman about ten days after the coup and reported her saying that she had spent that night "in the home of a girl-friend."[36] Terry Simon's December 1973 article indicates—somewhat ambiguously—that Joyce Horman spent that night at home.[37] The movie followed the account in Hauser's book.[38]

The juxtaposition of times is highly controversial. Three events stand in key relationship to each other: first, when Joyce Horman learned her husband was in trouble; second, when the U.S. Embassy was told of this; and third, when Charles Horman died. The Hormans have charged that the embassy failed to act when it should have, and they have attributed malign motives to U.S. officials for this failure.

According to Simon's article, Joyce Horman was told by neighbors on the morning of the eighteenth that Charles had been taken away the previous afternoon.[39] Hauser writes that a neighbor told her when she returned home that morning that soldiers had been there, but did not tell her that Charles had been carried off. Joyce Horman then went to the house of Chilean friends and started calling around, trying to locate Charles. Only late that day, just before the curfew (at 8 P.M. that night) did the son of the house return from visiting other friends who had been afraid to talk on the phone and report that Charles had been apprehended.[40]

Joyce Horman's Chilean friends telephoned the embassy and passed on what had been learned. Another friend of the Hormans, Warwick Armstrong, also informed the embassy that he had been told that his film-maker friend (Charles) was being held at a nearby police station. The consulate's notation of that call was set down after the Chilean friends' call and identified as "another" report—so presumably it was later. Joyce Horman, impeded by the curfew from coming to the embassy on the eighteenth, reported her husband missing the following morning.[41]

When did Charles Horman die? According to the Chilean authorities, an autopsy was performed on 25 September, fixing the time of death at 9:45 A.M., 18 September.[42] How the autopsy could have established the time so precisely is not clear. The logbook of the Santiago morgue registered-in the remains later determined to be Charles Horman's at 1:35 P.M. on the eighteenth.[43] A man named Enríque Sandoval told an embassy officer on or about 30 September that he had learned that Horman had been executed in the National Stadium "about a week earlier."[44] Sandoval also told roughly the same thing to Canadian diplomat Marc Dolguin, who told Ford Foundation executive Lovell Jarvis, who passed on the report to Charles Horman's father Edmund on 17 October. Edmund Horman and Thomas Hauser have since asserted that Jarvis pinpointed the date as 20 September, but Joyce and Edmund Horman were both still saying publicly in November—well after Edmund Horman's interview with Jarvis—that Charles had died on the eighteenth.[45]

Was the embassy slow to act? Consular officers called police stations and checked with the investigative police the same day the calls were made, the eighteenth. The consul visited the National Stadium the next day and checked for Horman, and continuing efforts by consular officers, defense attaché personnel, and embassy officers, including me, were made in the days and weeks following.[46]

The central implication of the movie *Missing*, however, is not that U.S. official efforts were slow but that the embassy had had Horman killed. In a crucial scene the movie shows Charles Horman's father and widow going to the Italian Embassy, where a Chilean police officer had taken refuge. Edmund and Joyce Horman never went to the Italian Embassy; this is pure invention. In actuality, newspaper reporters and U.S. Embassy officials interviewed the police officer in 1976, three years later. The police officer, called "Paris" in the film and Rafael Agustín González in real life, said he saw Charles Horman in custody at the Chilean Defense Ministry shortly after the coup. Apparently Charles was sitting under guard in the anteroom of Chilean military intelligence chief Augusto Lutz. Summoned to General Lutz's private office, González entered the room to see Lutz, his deputy (Col. Victor Hugo Barría), and an "American" sitting there. He overheard Lutz saying that the prisoner "knew too much" and would have to "disappear." In the film González is asked in the Italian Embassy interview if the Chileans could have ordered an American to disappear like that without consulting the Americans first, and González is shown replying that they would not, as "they wouldn't dare."[47]

So far as the "American" was concerned, González said in a subsequent deposition that he did not recognize the man, who never spoke a word. González's only reason for thinking that he was American was the look of his clothing. An officer of the U.S. Embassy questioned González about this, and the following exchange took place:

> [Embassy officer] "And the unknown person who was in General Lutz' office?"
>
> [González] "I don't know anything about him. I don't know his name, who it was, nothing."
>
> [Embassy officer] "But it was your impression that he might be American?"
>
> [González] "Yes . . . you . . . that type of shoe is not found in Chile. You could be identified here in Chile as an American because of the shoes you are wearing."
>
> [Embassy officer] "But there are many Chileans who have been to the United States who wear shoes like that, aren't there?"
>
> [González] "Very few. But you know, in any case, that the person either was in the United States or is an American. These are small details."[48]

On González's testimony rests the entire "evidence" that the U.S. Embassy had Charles Horman killed. There is nothing else. Even if the "third man" in Lutz's office was an American, that does not in itself indicate that he was connected with the U.S. government. All U.S. agencies have been checked, and no trace of such a person has been found. Michael Vernon Townley has been deposed but has testified that he was not the "third man" and knows nothing about Charles Horman's death. There are obviously Chileans somewhere who know something, but the Chilean authorities, equally evidently, are not prepared to make them available to testify. I have heard that Lutz and Barría are no longer living. From looking at the film *Missing* it appears that the actor who plays Capt. Ray E. Davis comes on screen as the "third man" in Lutz's office. This Captain Davis understandably regards as part of the film's libel against him.

On 11 October 1973 the Department of State advised me that my appointment as director general of the U.S. Foreign Service and chief of personnel for the State Department would be announced the following day. I had mixed emotions about the news. The job in Washington was a crucial but very frustrating one, as the U.S. government makes its diplomatic appointments and assignments in ways that produce an inordinate amount of human suffering, including some on the part of the director general. Moreover, I knew that Jack Kubisch wanted me to remain in Santiago, at least for a while. I knew the Junta government's leaders, and the fact that we had experienced recent Chilean history together probably gave me some influence with them. I hoped it might be possible to encourage the military leadership in humane policies and constructive relationships with moderate forces in Chile. The self-interest of the Junta should have been an ever-present ally. I was probably indulging in wishful thinking, however, and I half knew it.

The remaining days of October were filled with meetings, demarches, representations, departure calls, packing, private leavetakings, official ones, and essential business. One of the more interesting occasions was a private supper arranged by a prominent member of the local Jewish community who was a friend of Admiral Merino, the navy member of the Junta. The admiral arrived at our friend's house riding in a tire-wheeled tank, which waited for him throughout the dinner. Merino spent much of the evening reminiscing about the dilemma he had struggled with in the days before the coup; he had some appreciation of the moral implications of what he had done.

Congressman Michael J. Harrington arrived in Santiago on 25 October for a three-day visit. He arrived, I believe, with many preconceptions about Chile, the U.S. Embassy, and what he would find. I could not meet him at the airport because I had to call on the Chilean minister of education in connection with a local crisis involving a U.S.-run Catholic secondary school. I suggested that he proceed from the airport to my house or office for a talk, and I also offered to go meet him at his convenience. None of these suggestions proved satisfactory. On his departure Harrington met with U.S. correspondents and "expressed regret that his only opportunity to talk with the United States Ambassador to Chile, Nathaniel Davis, was in the presence of 'three or four Chilean generals.' "[49] The generals were three of the four members of the Chilean Junta, an appointment Harrington had asked us to arrange for him. Harrington also demanded that I meet him in the early morning of 27 October at the entrance to the National Stadium, in order to inspect the detention facility. I agreed to do so, over objections from the embassy staff, but Harrington then withdrew the request. I was to hear many comments from Michael Harrington in the years that followed, none of them very friendly.

On 31 October, the day before we left, Elizabeth and I went to pay farewell calls on Isabel Letelier and Irma Almeyda. To our regret, Mrs. Almeyda was not at home, and I asked two embassy colleagues to find her later and convey our respects—which they did. Isabel Letelier was in her apartment under a sort of house arrest. She received us with dignity and style, and her first thought was for her husband. She urged me to do what I could. She, understandably, has not wished to be in touch with us in the years since she and her husband came to the United States after Orlando Letelier's release from Dawson Island.

My family and I left Santiago on Thursday afternoon, 1 November 1973. Just before my departure the newspaper *Las Ultimas Noticias,* in its column "From Pluto's Doghouse," published a little article entitled "Chao, Mister Davis." After describing me as "portly, of affable face and mannerisms, unruffled and sagacious in conversation," the article said that I looked and sounded much like my new boss, Henry Kissinger—a description that would probably not have charmed the new secretary of state. As violence in Allende's Chile had mounted, the article went on, "Mister Davis and his wife nevertheless followed a normal and serene life. . . . We have heard him speak with the greatest affection for the Chilean people. . . . We know him as a friend, a gringo who knows our world. . . . [And, in English] Good bye Mister Davis and good luck."[50]

### Subsequent Involvements with Chile

In Washington it was not long before the aftermath of the Chilean coup was demanding my attention. The Latin American Subcommittee of the Senate Committee on Foreign Relations asked me to testify in closed session on 9 November 1973, with Senator Gale W. McGee presiding. Critics of the U.S. role in Chile have singled out this testimony as concealing guilty secrets or as proof of perjury on my part. Neither was the case. Two aspects of the testimony, in particular, have lingered in controversy: first, my exchange with Senator Jacob Javits on the Horman case; and second, the question whether I lied about the U.S. covert role in Chile later revealed by the Church Committee.

On the Horman case Senator Javits questioned me sharply, asserting that Charles Horman's father, Edmund, had told him that embassy officers suspected Charles of having been a leftist agitator and consequently had a callous attitude about his fate. I described our efforts to find Charles Horman and answered the senator's questions as responsively as I could. I did not, however, confess egregious official wrongdoing, and I fear that only such a response would have satisfied the senator. Not only was Edmund Horman a constituent, but he was also a friend of the senator's. I have no evidence that Senator Javits subsequently engaged in a vendetta against me—although the assistant secretary for Inter-American affairs, Viron P. Vaky, later advised me that while looking for another assignment for me in Latin America, he had been told by his superiors that Chile and Javits's possible reaction precluded any such nomination. The Department of State's chiefs sometimes display preemptive cowardice.

I was given no information on previous testimony about U.S. covert action before I went to the Capitol. Apparently, Secretary Kissinger had already described U.S. covert action in Chile in executive session (except for Track II, which I did not know about). Senator McGee described what Kissinger had said about secret assistance to opposition groups looking toward the 1976 elections and asked me if that was correct. I affirmed that it was and said that we did not engage in coup plotting and did not finance the truckers' strikes. I also testified about the human rights situation, summary executions, events in Chilean universities, and the Junta's recessing of the Chilean Congress.[51]

Laurence R. Birns, professor at the New School for Social Research, later wrote that I had "probably perjured" myself in this testimony. Birns asserted that "it seems all but certain that Davis misled the Congress." I wrote Professor Birns to inquire what basis he had had for his allegation. The relevant portion of his answer follows: "After that session terminated, Senator Javits was heard to say that the US ambassador assured us that the US was not involved in the coup itself or events leading up to the coup." The senator's quoted remark could indeed be regarded as a rough paraphrase of my testimony—assuming that the coup plotting and the truckers' strike are interpreted as "events leading up to the coup."[52]

It was saddening to observe the plight of Chilean politicians and other leaders who were in trouble with the Junta. In the case of those outside Chile, I was able to recommend a few for academic and other jobs. Clodomiro Almeyda's and Orlando Letelier's situation on Dawson Island was of particular concern. I had made an appeal to Minister of Interior Oscar Bonilla for their release when I made my farewell call on 23 October. Bonilla had been polite but not responsive. I urged friends in the Bureau of Inter-American Affairs to intervene, and they tried. Deputy Assistant Secretary Harry Shlaudeman suggested to Ambassador David H. Popper on 4 March 1974 that he raise the possibility of Letelier's release with the Chilean government, and Popper did so.[53] We soon had a lucky break. McGeorge Bundy, then head of the Ford Foundation, urged Secretary Kissinger to intervene with the Chilean government on behalf of Almeyda. The secretary sent the letter to me for my opinion. I recommended that Kissinger intervene on behalf of both Almeyda and Letelier and—to the secretary's great credit—he did so, skillfully and effectively. I am confident that his action was a contributing factor in effecting these men's release in 1975. Considering Orlando Letelier's subsequent murder, the U.S. government's humanitarian intervention in 1974 takes on a bittersweet taste.

U.S. covert actions in Chile were important news in 1974. Chile received more than one-quarter of the total coverage of intelligence news by the major networks that year, exceeding domestic spying and the intelligence side of Watergate.[54]

A month or two after the uproar over Chile in September 1974, Kissinger asked President Ford to appoint me assistant secretary of state for African affairs. I had asked the secretary not to go forward with the appointment, but he was determined to do so. The nomination was announced on 8 January 1975, right before an African-American Institute meeting in Kinshasa, Zaire, convened. Some American participants apparently convinced President Mobutu of Zaire to tell the assemblage that he was "greatly surprised" to learn that "the former American Ambassador to Chile at the time of the death of President Allende" was being appointed. Congressman Charles C. Diggs, Jr., subsequently traveled in Africa encouraging further opposition. On 20 February the Ministerial Council of the

Organization of African Unity, meeting in Nairobi, passed a consensus resolution noting "with concern" the impending appointment of the "former ambassador to Guatemala and Chile" who was involved "with the US policy of 'political destabilization' in Latin America" that had culminated in "the overthrow and assassination of the progressive President Allende of Chile."[55] Far from being forced off course, however, Kissinger pushed ahead. I was confirmed in March 1975, and I then set out on the uphill road toward effective African relationships. Later a congressman of the House Black Caucus had the grace to say that he and his colleagues realized they had "overdone it" in their campaign.[56]

In July 1975 the Church Committee investigators got around to me. I appeared for questioning about Chile at the Senate offices of the committee staff on 16 July. Gregory Treverton headed the interrogating team, and he was assisted by Diane LaVoy and Peter Fenn. I was accompanied by J. J. Hitchcock, a friendly, bluff, retired intelligence officer, who represented the Department of State. It was during this meeting that Treverton first apprised me of Track II. He asked me if I knew anything about it; I said I did not. He also questioned me about other U.S. covert operations in Chile, which I was able to describe to him. Other than Track II, there were no surprises in what he asked me and what I told him.[57]

I appeared before the full committee in executive session, chaired by Senator Church, on 28 October 1975. Ralph A. Dungan, U.S. ambassador to Chile from 1964 to 1967, was present with me, but Edward Korry had not been invited. Much of the questioning was by staff. Assertions of U.S. official wrongdoing were thrown out as if they were fact to get my reaction and were later cheerily acknowledged as a bit of "fishing," to check some unverified allegation. I hope the senators who were present understood the technique, and I hope that future historians who review the transcript also do.

My testimony was uneventful. It revealed nothing beyond those facts covered in the Church Committee's staff report and did not conceal anything.

During the same month—July 1975—Secretary Kissinger and I had come to disagree profoundly on covert U.S. intervention in Angola.[58] As a result, I resigned as assistant secretary and offered to retire from the U.S. Foreign Service. The secretary called me into his office to convince me to reconsider. He directed the full strength of his formidable personality to the task, even suggesting that I would be an ingrate to repay his unwavering support with the coin of disloyalty.[59] I *had* been grateful for his support, but I found the secretary unresponsive to the idea that personal convictions could become overriding for me. Moreover, I knew I could not be an effective instrument, feeling as I did, to accomplish the covert action he was undertaking. Nevertheless, neither he nor I wished my clamorous departure from the foreign service to foreclose the secretary's and the president's chance of carrying out their covert program successfully. To my mind, the exposure of the clandestine effort in Angola as the direct result of my resignation would have constituted a subversion of the president's authority. The practical result was that I did not leave the foreign service but was posted to Bern.[60]

The Chilean controversy followed me inexorably to Switzerland. Even in that bastion of hospitality to all views I was greeted with occasional hostile comments in the press, a fair amount of misinformation about the U.S. role in Chile, and a few death-head-masked demonstrators. The Swiss authorities are resourceful and effective, however, and my "evil past" was not a serious problem.

Chile also followed me to Switzerland in a substantive way. In December 1976 it fell to me to make the final negotiations for the exchange of Luis Corvalán, the imprisoned secretary general of the Chilean Communist party, for Vladimir Bukovsky, a Soviet who had helped publicize the Soviet practice of committing political dissidents to psychiatric hospitals. The Chileans had shown considerable perspicacity in their willingness to make the trade. It may have been the first occasion in history where the Soviets exchanged "political prisoners" with a regime like Pinochet's and acknowledged by their actions that Bukovsky was such a prisoner and not a simple criminal or a psychiatrically disturbed patient.

A Soviet sub-cabinet-level officer came to Bern to talk through the arrangements. He acted a bit like the dowager in the famous *New Yorker* cartoon whose leashed poodle was relieving itself by a fire hydrant. She knew it had to happen but was trying to pretend that no connection existed between her and the dog. So it was with the Soviets. They insisted they would have to hide Bukovsky and his mother, with whom he would be traveling, behind the truck servicing their aircraft, while Corvalán would be received from my car with full honors and the inevitable bouquets. I would have to drive around behind the servicing truck after delivering Corvalán and pick up the Bukovskys. The Chileans had sent their UN ambassador at Geneva, Abelardo Silva, to Zurich to handle the exchange. He wanted the ceremony organized in such a way that he, representing Chile, would appear before the world delivering Corvalán personally and receiving Bukovsky. The Russians would never countenance such a procedure, but Ambassador Silva felt so strongly that I feared he might overturn the arrangements at the moment of the exchange and force his way to the ramp of the Soviet aircraft. Fortunately, the ambassador had to ride in my car, and I arranged matters so he would observe the exchange from an appropriate distance.

I was also uneasy about the possibility of driving around the servicing truck after having delivered Corvalán only to find no Bukovsky. Nevertheless, I decided to accept the risk, as the whole exchange seemed perilously close to falling apart.

It all worked out. Corvalán and his wife were surprised to find me at the bottom of the ramp when the Chilean aircraft arrived, but the conversation was pleasant. During the ride of a mile or two over to the parked Soviet plane, Corvalán made some pointed remarks about his treatment at the hands of the Pinochet regime. Ceremonies were then carried out as planned, with a Soviet delegation of about a dozen officials lined up to receive the Chilean party head. Bukovsky and his mother, an obviously indomitable woman, were waiting at the appointed spot (a grievously ill child in the family had already been driven off to a hospital). As we drove to the terminal, I explained to Bukovsky what awaited him: Ambassador Silva, hundreds of TV cameramen and print journalists, representatives of Amnesty International, and some fellow Russian dissidents. I felt good about having been able to speak Spanish to Corvalán, switch to Russian to talk to Bukovsky, and talk to the Swiss officials in German.

Ambassador Silva had his chance to greet Bukovsky in front of Chilean television cameras; Bukovsky's response to the ambassador was correct but chilly. The Russian had no intention of embracing Pinochet's regime, even though the Chileans' actions had resulted in his liberation. Bukovsky then went into the airport building to face the world's press. I was surprised to discover that his English, which he had taught himself in prison, was service-able, and his composure and assurance were impressive.

The Chileans had been smarter than the Russians in their treat-ment of their prisoner in the days and weeks before delivery. What-ever mistreatment Corvalán suffered during the years of his confinement, he looked pink-cheeked and well-nourished as he came down the ramp of the Chilean plane. Bukovsky's face, on the other hand, particularly his eye sockets, seemed to have the translucent quality of alabaster. Bukovsky told me that the Soviets had kept handcuffs of American manufacture on his wrists until the aircraft passed over the border of the Soviet Union. Only then had he been unmanacled. The Soviets' disdain for treating Bukovsky softly in preparation for release manifested the depth of Soviet officialdom's ideological conviction—at the disregard of subsequent repercussions.

The Soviet media tried to pretend at first that there had been no exchange and that pressure from the world's "democratic" forces had been the cause of Corvalán's release. When it did not wash, the Soviet line shifted to an assertion that Bukovsky was an expelled "criminal." Communist leaders in France, Britain, and Italy made clear, however, that even they regarded both Corvalán and Bukovsky as having been incarcerated for their political beliefs. Nevertheless, rescuing Corvalán had been important to the Soviets. He had been faithful to the Soviet-led communist international movement over a long and impressive career.[61]

With President Carter's accession to power in 1977, the memory of Chile became, in the eyes of the new administration, a legacy of official U.S. shame. In the election campaign debate of 6 October 1976 Jimmy Carter had said that the Nixon-Ford administration had destroyed "elected governments, like in Chile."[62] On 8 March 1977 Brady Tyson, U.S. delegate to the UN Human Rights Commis-sion meeting in Geneva, rose on behalf of the United States to express the "profoundest regrets" of the U.S. delegation for the "despicable . . . acts of subversion of the democratic institutions of Chile, taken by certain US officials, agencies and private groups." Tyson went on: "We recognize that the expression of regrets, how-ever profound, cannot contribute significantly to undoing the suf-fering and terror that the people of Chile have experienced. We can only say that . . . the policies and persons responsible for those acts have been rejected by the American people. . . ."[63] The press called Bern for my reaction, but there was not much I could say. Tyson subsequently proved to have been speaking without authorization, and President Carter characterized his official comments as "inappropriate."[64] Nevertheless, the episode did reflect widely held views in Washington and illustrated the "politicizing" of attitudes about U.S. professional diplomacy. In a month or two a real-estate magnate from Cincinnati, Marvin Warner, was appointed U.S. ambassador to Switzerland, and I was reassigned as State Department adviser at the U.S. Naval War College in Newport, Rhode Island.

## Reverberations on the Left

On a winter evening in 1978 my wife and I drove from Newport to Boston to see Patricio Guzmán's film *The Battle of Chile*. It was sponsored by the Angry Arts Bookstore of Cambridge. As we sat down in the hall, I wondered whether Guzmán's film would show a recognizable close-up of the face of the U.S. ambassador to Allende's Chile—the spider at the center of the web of imperialist villainy.

A young man introduced the progressive-minded luminaries who were present and gave an orientation lecture. He reminded the audience that the subtitle of the film was "A Revolution without Arms" and said that this was its lesson, that a revolution cannot be won without force of arms and without the total destruction of reaction. He went on to talk about the coming battle in the United States and the need to prepare for it—morally, intellectually, psychologically, and with concrete measures.

The cinematographic high point of the film for me was a series of shots taken from the top of a high building overlooking Constitution Square in Santiago during a rally where President Allende was scheduled to speak. The president was late, and a lesser speaker was warming up the crowd. At one point he started chanting: "Jump! If you are against fascism, jump!" The camera panned down on that sea of people jumping up and down, a great undulating wave of humanity. I sat there imagining the reaction of my colleague Aleksandr Basov, the Soviet ambassador in Santiago. I could almost hear him say: "Da, da. Yes. That is what was wrong with the Chilean Revolution. If you are against fascism, jump up and down!" The film whirred to its end, fortunately not showing my face. Workers in factories poignantly described their hopes and aspirations. There was good footage of Salvador Allende's eloquence. At the end Guzmán's camera faced a living-room television set in some Santiago hideaway, and the screen flickeringly revealed the faces of the four members of the Junta announcing their assumption of power.

Ambassador Basov, incidentally, had been a high political figure in the Russian Republic (RSFSR) before coming to Santiago and was a member of the Central Committee of the Communist party of the Soviet Union—a reflection both of his personal standing and of the importance of Allende's Chile to the USSR. After the coup Basov lost his membership on the Central Committee and was subsequently reassigned as Soviet envoy to Australia. One can guess that this assignment was a halfway measure, reflecting Moscow's disappointment in Basov's performance in Santiago, but its loyalty to him personally. As they demonstrated by the Corvalán exchange, the Russians normally support their people, even in adversity.

Moscow initially reacted to the coup by saying that Allende had failed to build upon the support of the middle classes and had fallen prey to the excesses of the ultra-leftist radicals. In effect, Moscow was upholding Corvalán's and the Communist party's line during the 1970–73 period.[65] By early 1974, however, the USSR party secretary responsible for relations with progressive forces in the developing world, Boris N. Ponomarev, had altered the Soviet line. Ponomarev stressed the importance of being able to shift from peaceful to armed struggle quickly and to "repel the counter-revolutionary violence of the bourgeoisie with revolutionary violence." He wrote that Allende should have neutralized the danger of a coup by infiltrating the army in order to "democratize" it. Additionally, Ponomarev opined, it would be crucial in future situations to deprive the class enemy of the levers of power embodied in the army and the media.[66] In May 1974 Ponomarev's colleague M. F. Kudachkin criticized Unidad Popular for failing to take "any decisive steps against Congress (carrying out a plebiscite, referendum, etc.) and the judiciary."[67]

Clearly, Allende's fall had been a severe blow to the Soviets. In 1976 Christopher S. Wren, a perceptive observer, wrote: "The Soviet Union still seems traumatized by the 1973 military overthrow, . . . possibly because the coup contradicted the Kremlin's ideological contention that détente favored the world revolutionary process."[68] Even later the wound had not healed. After the USSR's invasion of Afghanistan in 1979 Soviet ambassadors in Europe were explaining that the USSR "could not permit another Chile."[69]

By 1977 Chilean communist spokesmen were following the shift in line. In January of that year Volodia Teitelboim was calling for ideological indoctrination in the barracks to change the soldiers' "false social consciousness" and "false conception of public duty." He also said that Communists cannot be "Gullivers bound hand and foot by legality." The next month Orlando Millas wrote that "the primary duty of revolutionary forces . . . is to be firm in their resolve to deliver crippling blows to all who resort to counter-revolutionary violence. The effort to mobilize an active majority of the people must be supported by an appropriate mass organization which commands all requisite means and whose members have been properly educated and trained." In March a third communist leader, Rodrigo Rojas, criticized Allende for having allowed his opponents to stage demonstrations and for having failed to mobilize "the workers' sacred class hatred."[70]

At the end of 1977, about a year after Corvalán's release in the Bukovsky exchange, the Communist party of Chile held a central committee meeting in Prague. Corvalán reasserted that revolutionary change could be accomplished through nonviolent means and that the party's line had been correct. The party head also castigated the ultra-leftist forces that had weakened the government, implying that the MIR should be excluded from any future coalition. By December 1980, however, Corvalán had come around to the militant line and was calling for armed struggle to overthrow the Pinochet government. He asserted that unity, the key to victory, is molded by combat, as in Nicaragua. In January 1981 Corvalán expressed willingness to negotiate agreements with the MIR and commended their terrorist activities as "helpful." Shortly thereafter he signed a unification agreement with seven other Chilean leftist organizations, including the MIR. Volodia Teitelboim echoed Corvalán's action in a Moscow broadcast in January 1981, in which he said that the Chilean leftists' new line of action would consist of guerrilla warfare followed by mass resistance, terrorism, and a massive armed uprising.[71]

In short, communist advocacy of the Chilean Way and the peaceful road to socialism has effectively been replaced by the historically more orthodox Marxist-Leninist view that the dictatorship of the proletariat must normally be achieved through armed struggle and violent revolution. Carlos Altamirano must feel vindicated as he struggles in exile with Clodomiro Almeyda for control of the Chilean Socialist party.

Enrico Berlinguer, the head of the Communist party in Italy and the most prominent of the Eurocommunists, had felt "shock" after Allende fell, and the fading in the 1980s of Eurocommunism as a movement of the future has been linked by some observers to the "lesson" of Allende's fall. The Chilean experience has deeply influenced the thinking of Communists and other leftists in all parts of the globe.

# Chapter 15

# Reflections

HAS advocacy misshaped journalists', scholars', and politicians' judgments about Allende's Chile? Was U.S. policy all wrong? When and where did Salvador Allende go astray? Did he cross a Rubicon, take a wrong turn, or miss a crucial opportunity for success?

## Perceptions

It is the government's job to keep its secrets and almost always the journalists' job to ferret them out. It is not the press's obligation to suppress information leaked for reprehensible purposes, or to quash the publication of a purloined document, or to make its central business the weighing of the national interest in reporting the news. Advocacy journalism and muckraking are honored and public-spirited enterprises in our society, and they help make America more honest and more free. Yet the press has immense power, and great temptation always walks beside great power. To serve our society well, muckrakers and sectarian journalists should uphold responsible standards of accuracy in what they write. The advocate does not have the right to propagate falsehoods in order to further his cause or his case.

Commentators of all tendencies have committed transgressions against the truth in connection with Chile, and the lapses are equally reprehensible on either side of the political fence. The mid-1970s were years when conservatives were beleaguered, however, and liberal-oriented condemnation of wrongdoing was in vogue. America's great newspapers and foreign affairs magazines displayed some tendency to "paint their tails white and run with the antelopes," in Richard Nixon's sardonic phrase.

The press was not alone. Advocacy scholarship and a special kind of blindered politics followed the trail of advocacy journalism. Journalists, scholars, and politicians properly champion positions, of course, but the phenomenon of the mid-1970s carried elements that went beyond advocacy to embrace ad hominem attacks on opponents and efforts to deny adversaries a hearing.

All the public actors connected with U.S. policy toward Chile felt the impact of fashionable denunciation. Edward Korry, in particular, made a crusade of publicizing the phenomenon, at some cost to himself. He accused the Church Committee, with its Democratic chairman and majority, of engaging in a cover-up of the Kennedy and Johnson administrations' misdeeds in Chile in favor of concentrated fire against the Nixon administration's derelictions there during Korry's own assignment in Santiago. Korry accused Cyrus Vance of being part of this conspiracy, even testifying in congressional hearings that Vance told him his "trouble" was that he naively expected the Church Committee to uphold "legal" standards of fairness in a "political process." Korry went on:

> On Chile . . . I have been advised . . . that friends with standing in the Democratic party will not budge from partisanship for some unrewarding cause involving one individual's rights, that lawyers of national renown will let sleeping principles lie, that historians are not interested in the defense of issues which are not popular in academia, that corporate directors are concerned only to escape culpability for the actions of their own multinational, that foundation overseers are devoted to one or another theory for organizing society but avert their eyes from the reality of society. . . .

Korry additionally charged that a back-scratching network in the

U.S. liberal establishment had deliberately suborned the press. At the Vance nomination hearings he asserted:

> A very few . . . newsmen have, thanks to the protective silence of men such as the nominee, been able to engage in a most sinister form of bribery. . . . [Church Committee investigators] have indulged in [a CIA-type] "control process" by which an agent is recruited, molded and exploited. Newsmen such as Mr. Hersh and Mr. Larry Stern of the *Washington Post* could be fed a steady stream of official secrets . . . and in return, they would remain silent about evidence which might incriminate their informants or damage their political and other interests.[1]

Korry charged that one of Senator Church's staffers offered a deal to Korry himself, to have him testify selectively and falsely. He accused the *New York Times* of suppressing its own reporters' interviews with him about Chile. He testified that former U.S. Information Agency director Leonard H. Marks warned him: "I would know anguish beyond anything I had ever experienced if I persisted in my efforts to vindicate myself. He was correct."[2]

Edward Korry is not alone. Jean-François Revel has denounced the "indirect censorship" practiced by "fashionably left-wing media." He claimed that the conscience of the left and the longing for Marxist totalitarianism "is fed by subterfuge, deformation, selective memory, fear and even hatred of the truth."[3]

These harsh judgments are not entirely fair nor altogether right, but they carry germs of truth. Our national debate about America's role in the world needs more care about truth. We should be striving for a greater focus on issues and a lesser preoccupation with the imputation of motives. Such a change will not produce agreement, nor should it. But it might channel our contention into a more constructive course.

The Declaration of Independence speaks of "a decent respect to the opinions of mankind." Americans do care that divergent points of view should get a decent hearing. We must feel ashamed when rancor silences discourse. We must be concerned that public servants not be pilloried—whether they be Edward Korry, Charles Meyer, Richard Helms, William Colby, or our foreign service professionals. As the old saying has it, we must get about the task of raising our voices a little lower.

I am optimistic about America's potential for effective diplomacy. Our country stands for good purposes in the world, and I believe we shall sustain the power and influence to further them. Foreign problems and domestic frustrations have their seasons. With good leadership, luck, and time they may lose virulence and recede. Americans do not live comfortably with philosophic defeatism and Spenglerian senescence. The New World still turns its face to the future, and that future holds marvelous secrets for us all.

## Policy

The American notion that our works largely determine world events has led us to exaggerate our role in Chile's tragedy. While the indictment of our government was not created out of nothing, it has been amplified beyond reality. In addition, the explanation for U.S. help to the Chilean opposition has been glossed over. It is unlikely that the non-UP media and parties would have held up on their own, and institutional democracy in Chile could not have long survived their extinction.

Covert action was not the sum of our relations with Chile, and a few reflections about other aspects of our policy are in order. During the Allende time parallels with the Cuban situation of 1959–60 were haunting. The United States, after a brief period of attempting to maintain "correct" relations with Castro, imposed sanctions on oil and sugar and, as Philip W. Bonsal, the U.S. ambassador in Havana, described it, "confronted Castro."[4] Bonsal continues:

> The blow to Cuban-American relations was . . . grievous. . . .
>
> The United States government measures . . . went far beyond the retaliation warranted. . . . Measured American responses might have appeared well deserved to an increasing number of Cubans, thus strengthening Cuban opposition to the regime instead of, as was the case, greatly stimulating revolutionary fervor, leaving the Russians no choice but to give massive support to the Revolution. . . .
>
> Until July 1960 the Moscow bureaucrats advised Castro to proceed with moderation in his dealings with Washington.
>
> Now, however, the Russians were faced with the abandonment of the policy of restraint the United States had pursued toward Castro. The Soviet Union had the choice of furnishing the oil Cuba needed and buying the sugar Cuba had formerly sold to the United States or of letting the Cuban revolution perish. . . .
>
> The Soviet Union's assumption of responsibility for Cuba's

economic welfare gave the Russians a politico-military stake in Cuba. Increased arms shipments from the Soviet Union and Czechoslovakia enabled Castro to strengthen his rapidly expanding armed forces. . . .

Castro's goal was the elimination of the American presence. . . . Now suddenly the initiatives of the American government had created for him conditions . . . favorable for the rapid completion of his program. . . . The reluctant and cautious Russians had been forced into the Revolution's own warmly welcoming arms by the drastic actions of the Americans.[5]

Whatever the faults of U.S. policy toward Allende's Chile, the United States avoided repeating some of the mistakes Ambassador Bonsal describes with respect to Cuba. The U.S. government did not drive the Chileans into reluctant Soviet arms; it did not force the Soviets into a massive countercommitment; and it did not push the Chilean armed forces into dependence on Soviet military assistance and supply. The "cool and correct" U.S. public stance toward Chile was consciously designed to avoid giving Allende a foreign target which would help him rally domestic loyalties and mobilize international support. U.S. policy was largely successful in this regard. In contrast to what happened in Cuba, the United States did not become a Great Satan in the eyes of the Chilean people.

There is a problem, of course, in pursuing this line of argument. Since Chilean institutional democracy was swept away in the 1973 coup, an assumption that U.S. policy toward Allende's Chile was wiser than it was toward Cuba must rest upon a judgment that Chile under the Junta is preferable to a Castroite state. Jeane J. Kirkpatrick has become the high priestess of this belief, with her famous distinction between authoritarian and totalitarian regimes, and her reminders that Soviet backing of Marxist regimes makes leftist takeovers irreversible. Nevertheless, one does not have to be a friend of rightist tyrannies to prefer a nondemocratic regime in the Western Hemisphere that is not closely tied to the USSR to one that is. Cuba's current orientation matters to the United States because of the Soviet brigade there, the electronic marvels emplaced there, Cienfuegos, the MIGs, the submarines, the lingering memory of offensive missiles and the current presence of defensive ones, and because of all the other possibilities and dangers that Cuba and its exportation of revolution pose. It is not shameful for American foreign policy to be concerned about these things.

This is not to say that I agree with Ambassador Kirkpatrick. To me, she seems to elevate expediency to the level of principle and raise Hobson's choice to the plane of an ideological revelation. The world is full of tyrants with whom we must live and deal, and we move through a jungle of realities in the dark of night. At the same time, as Walter Lippmann once said, "the American conscience is a reality. It will make hesitant and ineffectual, even if it does not prevent, an un-American policy. . . ."[6] We need both *Realpolitik* and *Idealpolitik*. We require a foreign policy somewhere between Henry Kissinger's and Jimmy Carter's, as we have needed both elements of policy ever since the republic was founded. We also need a decent sense of the fitness of things, so we do not go around embracing dictators and congratulating oppressors on their occasional or nonexistent benevolent policies.

While Nixon and Kissinger have been rightly blamed for the dissembling that characterized our "correct outward posture" when we were pursuing inimical policies in secret, they also deserve the lion's share of the credit for successfully avoiding the follies that characterized our Cuban policy. Whatever his blind spots, Richard Nixon learned a lot in the years after his interview with Fidel Castro in April 1959.[7] Henry Kissinger also had a clear understanding of our need to avoid provocations that might enable Allende to rally domestic and international support. Additionally, I believe, a substantial part of the reason that our approach toward Chile had an element of genuine goodwill was the presence in the Bureau of Inter-American Affairs of Assistant Secretary Charles A. Meyer. He introduced courtesy and humanity into a policy that otherwise might have been more repellingly calculating than it was. It was also he who kept an ambassador in Santiago rather than resort to the empty gesture that resulted in the withdrawal of Ambassador Bonsal from Havana. Meyer's successor, Jack Kubisch, had similar instincts.

So far as my own contribution is concerned, I was reasonably low-key. At least I did not produce the type of confrontation we achieved with Perón in Argentina in 1945. My colleagues and I tried to maintain decent, friendly relations, on both the personal and the official levels. This effort required no spirit of deviousness on my part. I liked Salvador Allende, most of his colleagues, and the Chileans. My family and I were happy in Chile. I carried out my instructions, of course, and advised Washington straightforwardly and, I hope, professionally. At the same time I did not hope for

Allende's downfall. I tried to solve problems and reduce differences, not create them, and to bring about a better relationship between Allende's government and the United States.

As must be evident, I was a slightly incongruous "chosen instrument" for Richard Nixon's Chilean policy. I did not see the world as the president and his adviser saw it. Neither they nor I were as aware of this fact as we later became, although I had not deceived anybody. My record of service with Sargent Shriver in the Peace Corps, teaching at Howard University, and working in Lyndon Johnson's White House was unconcealed. By instinct and conviction, Meyer, Kubisch, and I, as well as John Fisher and many others in Washington and at the embassy, represented and upheld the openly declared nonhostile side of Richard Nixon's policy and worked in private, as well as in public, to achieve purposes consistent with it.

To end this discussion, a reminder should be given that the military regime's actions against the Christian Democrats and other moderates in Chile may be playing into the left extremists' hands. The possibility is real that the Junta's blows against Chile's democratic political forces may ultimately create a wasteland when Pinochet and his associates leave the scene, as sooner or later they must, into which the Marxists can advance all too easily. To illustrate this danger, I quote from a letter I recently received from a friend in Chile:

> Believe me, I would love to go to the United States to see my friends and breathe the winds of freedom. I was not born to live under a dictatorship, neither a red nor a white one. The situation for people who believe in peace based on justice and freedom is not very encouraging. I was jailed last [year] . . . and went through the Secret Police interrogation system. Luckily I did not suffer physical tortures. . . . What makes me feel pessimistic is that we all know how an extreme rightist dictatorship here will end. It will generate perfect conditions for an extreme leftist reaction. The Marxists will find a country with no solidly based political parties, free trade unions, student organizations, and community centers. These were the main obstacles to Marxist consolidation in 1970. The junta is destroying Chile's social fabric without putting anything in its place. Soon Chile's sense of community will be reduced to dust; and then the Communists will find perfect conditions to put their own organizations

in place. Rightist dictators hate the moderate center more than they do the Marxist left. They feel the need to eliminate the democratic forces in order to justify their own indispensability against the Communist threat. Both extremes need each other. This government is a kind of free gift to the Marxists.

If the present regime ends soon, things might come out all right; but the risks increase with every year. Milton Friedman's therapy is explosive medicine. The impoverishment of the middle class in favor of a small but very wealthy upper class is destroying the "mattress" between extremes. The middle class faced Allende long before the rich people did. The "proletarianization" of middle-class people will destroy their moderation, and frustration will radicalize them.

I hope next year will bring us more hope and freedom. . . .

My friend's name is not revealed here, for evident reasons. It does not matter. Millions of Chileans feel the way he does.

## Straying

When he assumed power, Allende had one great choice. He could select the path toward a showdown with the forces of reaction or he could follow the Chilean Way. Paul M. Sweezy, editor of the Marxist *Monthly Review* in New York, put the choice cogently in a piece he wrote only four days after Castro's celebrated departure speech of 2 December 1971. Noting that Allende's program during his first year had remained within the parameters of capitalism, Sweezy defined Allende's alternatives as to advance or to consolidate, to move forward to real socialism or to subside into social democracy of the Western European type. If he did the former, the army might well step in. If he did the latter, he could complete his term.[8]

Late in the game, on 29 July 1973, Castro wrote Allende a final letter reminiscent of his departure speech. Conceding the rationale of playing for time "in order to improve the correlation of forces in case the battle should break out," Castro admonished Allende not to forget for a second the "formidable strength of the Chilean working class" that "can, at your call, with the revolution in peril, paralyze the coup plotters, bind the vacillators to you," and decide Chile's destiny at a blow. "The enemy should know," Castro wrote, that the workers stand ready for action, and their "combat readiness can tip the balance. . . . Your decision" to pay "with your life if necessary" to maintain the advance toward socialism will "bring to your side" all forces "capable of combat." The key to the situation is "your courage, your calm and your audacity."[9]

It was probably too late in July 1973 for the workers to grasp total power by force of arms. Even early in Allende's regime Castro's prescription would have required a systematic purge of the Chilean officer corps, intensive infiltration of military ranks, sustained development of leftist paramilitary forces, and massive programs to arm them. All these measures were attempted, but belatedly and ambivalently. Allende never made up his mind, and he may not have realized when the last fork in the road had been passed, after which revolutionary battle was effectively foreclosed.

Then there was the second choice, true pursuit of the Chilean Way. It would have meant constitutional observance, careful adherence to democratic institutionalism, and bargains seriously entered into and consistently maintained. It would have necessitated compromises with the opposition and genuine political alliances outside Unidad Popular. As Sweezy feared, it might have resulted in "social democracy of the Western European type." On the other hand, while the march toward socialism would surely have slowed, it might not have stalled. Allende might have been able to hold to his original vision.

Allende did not decisively choose this path, either. His tragedy may have been that, beset by immediate imperatives and complications, he ended up meandering in the wilderness between his two great alternatives. The golden mean is sometimes not a good rule for a statesman; he may be better off making a decisive choice. It is sometimes true, in fact, that either one of two clear paths, if it is followed consistently, can lead to its own kind of success. Allende seemed perpetually to be turning left, turning right, doubling back, and marching forward as he came upon an endless succession of diverging paths. When his ultra-leftist allies challenged his fidelity to revolutionary ideals, his instinct led him to go left and prove himself. When he became convinced that accommodation of the opposition parties or the military was necessary to preserve his government and the Chilean Way, he turned right. His vacillation was all too often seen as dissembling, his reversals as betrayals, and his compromises as weaknesses.

There were half a dozen forks in the road where Allende, turning left, distanced himself from the Chilean Way, ultimately to find the terrain he would have to travel to rejoin that high road impassable. First, Allende's fingers had figuratively been crossed behind his back when he signed the Statute of Democratic Guarantees in October 1970. His action was probably not as cynical or frivolous as Régis Debray represented it to be, but the president did not assume a serious, continuing commitment to the statute's provisions, particularly when observance would be inexpedient, painful, and politically costly within his governing coalition. This attitude made the alienation of all political currents in the Christian Democratic party ultimately unavoidable.

Second, the Chilean economy had slid visibly out of control by October 1971, but Allende did not take effective countermeasures for many months, and he allowed Vuskovic to pursue the social restructuring of the economy at the cost of a downward economic slide. At the same time Allende allowed Chonchol to attempt the radical social transformation of the countryside, with similar negative economic results. Vuskovic was subsequently removed and Chonchol resigned, perhaps foreclosing the possibility that their extremist solutions might have "defanged" reactionary power. Allende did not take either road.

Third, Allende failed in his attempt in January 1972 to achieve an opening to the political center. He allowed the left extremists in his coalition to block the appointment to the cabinet of eminent political independents who were friendly to Unidad Popular and willing to serve. While he briefly succeeded in bringing the Left Radicals into the government, he let Altamirano push him into rejecting Left Radical minister of justice Sanhueza's compromise agreement with the Christian Democrats on nationalization policy and the Three Areas bill. As a result, the Left Radicals were driven into embittered opposition, and Allende was locked into a permanently closed, minority government.

Fourth, Allende and his ministers dallied with the Christian Democrats in post-Sanhueza negotiations on nationalization policy. The president remained unwilling to make the substantive concessions necessary for a bargain. In June 1972 the two sides came close to a negotiated agreement, but the Papelera issue and differences over rules to curb politically motivated factory interventions could not be surmounted. Even in mid-1973 spasmodic, last-ditch negotiations with the Christian Democrats found the president unready to define nationalization policy in ways that could lead to a settlement.

Fifth, at the same time that Allende pushed the military heirarchs into active politics and governmental responsibility he neutralized their influence and pressed forward with policies they could not support. While mutual suspicions grew and alienation increased, Allende surreptitiously but half-heartedly encouraged the arming of the workers, violating the armed forces' constitutional monopoly over the use and possession of arms. Allende then allowed the continuity of top military command to be broken and undermined the integrity of subordinate commands, without ensuring that the changes favored his governance. His ambivalence left him without the benefits of any clear military or paramilitary policy.

Finally, Allende failed throughout his presidency to impose discipline on his own coalition. He maneuvered Altamirano's election as secretary general of the Socialist party in January 1971; he tolerated and sometimes supported Altamirano's left extremism in the ensuing years; he briefly assigned Almeyda the task of curbing Socialist indiscipline in 1973, only to reverse course shortly thereafter; and he was finally toying with the idea of forcing a showdown with Altamirano when the coup intervened. Never did he face up to the problem of disarray in Unidad Popular. The left extremists pursued their own purposes without being effectively constrained. Militant UP officials and appointed governmental authorities systematically bent or broke the Constitution and the laws. Government by legerdemain and loophole ultimately made the repudiation of UP government by the Supreme Court, the Chamber of Deputies, the comptroller, and others an inevitability.

The fault was not all Allende's, of course. There was blame enough for everybody. Significant sectors of the opposition were also guilty of bad faith, subversive intent, destructive economic activity, dishonest use of the media, sabotage, terrorism, and the undermining of the social foundations of Chilean society.

A case can be made that Allende's Chilean experiment could not possibly have succeeded. We Americans have a tendency to think that problems do have solutions. In other societies less blessed than the United States, political philosophers may better understand that situations exist which have no possibility of a favorable outcome. After 1970 neither the achievement of socialism through institutional means nor its repudiation in 1976 through constitutional processes may have been possible. Chile's long-term alternatives may from the start have been a leftist tyranny on the Cuban model or military government of the Pinochet type.

I do not accept the foregoing diagnosis, perhaps because I instinctively reject such preordained afflictions and gloomy probabilities. It is true that the Chilean Way led across a sea of troubles. At first high and broad, the road was progressively eaten away by turbulent waters, with waves of leftist assault and UP folly undermining one bank as rightist attacks washed at the other. The causeway got narrower and more treacherous, and the prospect ahead more obscure. By the early months of 1973 thinking people could not help but see that the constitutional road to 1976 was crumbling. Nevertheless, Allende and his trusted collaborators could have made wiser decisions. Had they been more resolute, consistent, and farsighted, they could have faced the necessity of a clear choice of policy and made the commitments essential to it. It might have been painful, but it would not have been impossible.

All this matters, because it is important that hopes of social transformation through democracy and law be kept alive if possible, across the spectrum of the left. The Chilean Way was the highest expression we have yet seen of central-core Marxists trying to follow the peaceful road to socialism. Socialism may not be the best or even a good way to order a society's affairs, but the ability of free citizens to *choose* socialism, or capitalism, or some other economic system, is beyond price. Too many people in the world share Allende's socialist convictions for democrats to abandon that aspiration to men with guns who preach bloody revolution as the only road to social justice. Too many of the world's people live out their lives in the dust of poverty, hunger, sickness, ignorance, and oppression for democratic socialists to facilitate the task of the totalitarians of the left. It should not be necessary for those who shared Salvador Allende's dream to accept the secret policeman's boot on the stairs at night as a necessary price for the achievement of their economic and social values. If the possibility of a Chilean Way should be decisively ruled out for the world's leftists, we would all have reason to be sorry.

Chile is an extraordinary land occupied by an immensely talented people. I believe that democratic institutions will sooner or later return and a sound Constitution will again buttress a rule of law in that country. I nurture a faith that economic prosperity, equity, and justice will increase, that the Chilean armed forces will become, once again, the "nondeliberative" protectors of the political order, and that the sound of untrammeled politics will again be heard in that land. Salvador Allende will find his rightful place in Chilean history, honored for his spirit, his vision, and his aspiration. As he said on that fateful morning, his voice will again be heard. The great avenues will open along which free Chileans will march in order to achieve a better society.[10]

Augusto Pinochet and his military colleagues are also part of Chilean history, and patriots in the eyes of many of their countrymen. And Eduardo Frei's voice will also be heard, his path of Christian community followed, and his memory honored. So, too, will Chileans remember the integrity and strength of Jorge Alessandri. Chile's future is not altogether dark, nor is its light of hope extinguished.

# Acronyms

| | |
|---|---|
| AID | Agency for International Development |
| AIFLD | American Institute for Free Labor Development |
| API | Acción Popular Independiente (Independent Popular Action party) |
| ASIS | Australian Secret Intelligence Service |
| CD | Christian Democratic party |
| CEN | Consejo Ejecutivo Nacional (National Executive Council of the Radical party) |
| CODE | Confederación Democrática (Democratic Confederation) |
| CODELCO | Corporación del Cobre (Copper Corporation) |
| CORA | Corporación de la Reforma Agraria (Agricultural Reform Corporation) |
| CORFO | Corporación de Fomento de la Producción (Development Corporation) |
| CUPROCH | Confederación Unica de Profesionales de Chile (Sole Professional Confederation of Chile) |
| CUT | Central Unica de Trabajadores de Chile (Central Workers Confederation) |
| CUTCH | See CUT |
| DINA | Dirección de Investigaciones Nacionales (Directorate of National Investigations) |
| DIRINCO | Dirección de Industria y Comercio (Directorate of Industry and Commerce) |

| ECA | Empresa de Comercio Agrícola (Enterprise for Agricultural Commerce) |
| ECLA | Economic Commission for Latin America |
| ENTEL | Empresa Nacional de Telecomunicaciones (National Telecommunications Company) |
| ENU | Escuela Nacional Unificada (Unified National School) |
| FBI | Federal Bureau of Investigation |
| FLACSO | Facultad Latino Americana de Ciencias Sociales (Latin American Faculty of the Social Sciences) |
| FRAP | Frente de Acción Popular (Popular Action Front) |
| GAP | Grupo de Amigos Personales (Group of Personal Friends) |
| IAPA | Inter-American Press Association |
| IDB | Inter-American Development Bank |
| IER | Instituto de Educación Rural (Institute of Rural Education) |
| ILPES | Instituto Latinoamericano de Planificación Económica y Social (Latin American Institute for Economic and Social Planning) |
| ITT | International Telephone and Telegraph Corporation |
| JAPs | Juntas de Abastecimiento y Precios (Councils of Supply and Prices) |
| MAP | Military Assistance Program |
| MAPU | Movimiento de Acción Popular Unida (Movement for Unified Popular Action) |
| MILGROUP | Military Group, U.S. |
| MIR | Movimiento de Izquierda Revolucionaria (Movement of the Revolutionary Left) |
| MR-2 | Movimiento Revolucionario Manuel Rodríguez (Manuel Rodríguez Revolutionary Movement) |
| MUI | Movimiento del Universitario Izquierdista (Movement of the University Leftist) |
| NASA | National Aeronautics and Space Administration |
| NATO | North Atlantic Treaty Organization |
| NSC | National Security Council |
| NSDM | National Security Decision Memorandum |
| ODEPLAN | Oficina de Planeamiento (Office of Planning) |
| OIR | Oficina de Información y Radiodifusión de la Presidencia de la República (Presidential Office of Information and Broadcasting) |

| | |
|---|---|
| OPIC | Overseas Private Investment Corporation |
| PADENA | Partido Democrático Nacional (Democratic National party) |
| PCR | Partido Comunista Revolucionario (Revolutionary Communist party) |
| PDR | Partido de Democracia Radical (Party of Radical Democracy) |
| PIR | Partido Izquierda Radical (Radical Left party) |
| SACO | Sistema de Acciones Civiles Organizadas (System for Action by Civilians who are Organized) |
| SOFOFA | Sociedad de Fomento Fabril (Society for Manufacturing Development) |
| SRG | Senior Review Group |
| TFP | Tradition, Family, and Property |
| UNCTAD | United Nations Conference on Trade and Development |
| UP | Unidad Popular (Popular Unity) |
| USIS | United States Information Service |
| USOPO | Unión Socialista Popular (Popular Socialist Union) |
| VOP | Vanguardia Organizada del Pueblo (Organized Vanguard of the People) |

# Notes

All translations from Spanish sources are the author's unless otherwise specified.

### Preface

1. Salvador Allende, *Su pensamiento político* (Buenos Aires: Granica, 1973), p. 19. Speech of 5 November 1970.

2. As in the case of most such absolute claims, the historical record is ambiguous. The voters of tiny San Marino elected a Marxist government after World War II. It might also be said that Czechoslovakia installed a Communist prime minister after genuine elections in 1946.

3. Charles R. Foster, "Diplomatic Memoirs," *Foreign Service Journal*, March 1982, p. 6.

4. Mark Falcoff, "Reviews," *Orbis*, Summer 1977, p. 430.

5. *New York Times*, 8 July 1981, sec. 3, p. 27, reporting on a Bill D. Moyers interview with Dame Rebecca West.

6. John Le Carré, in a review by Anatole Broyard, *New York Times*, 29 August 1982, sec. 7, p. 23.

### Chapter 1. The 1970 Elections and Allende's First Year

1. Jerome Levinson and Juan de Onís, *The Alliance That Lost Its Way* (Chicago: Quadrangle, 1970), p. 204.

2. Unless otherwise indicated, percentages of the vote will exclude blank and invalid ballots.

3. Robert J. Alexander, *The Tragedy of Chile* (Westport: Greenwood, 1978), p. 46.

4. Ibid., pp. 49–50; César Caviedes, *The Politics of Chile: A Sociogeographical Assessment* (Boulder: Westview, 1979), pp. 57–59.

5. Robert Moss, *Chile's Marxist Experiment* (Newton Abbot, England: David & Charles, 1973), pp. 39–40. The main, or historic, Radical party was also called the CEN Radical party; CEN stands for the party's National Executive Council.

6. U.S. Congress, Senate, *Covert Action in Chile, 1963–1973*, Staff Report of the Select Committee to Study Governmental Operations with Respect to Intelligence Activities (Washington, D.C., 1975), p. 58; Thomas Powers, *The Man Who Kept the Secrets: Richard Helms and the CIA* (New York: Knopf, 1979), pp. 226–28.

7. Moss, p. 29. The sharp-eyed reader will note that these percentages add up to only about 99%, as ballots not cast for any of the three candidates have been left in the figure for the total votes cast. These 1970 percentages have received such wide dissemination that it seems best to use them here and avoid confusion.

8. Henry Kissinger, *White House Years* (Boston: Little, Brown, 1979), p. 671.

9. Powers, p. 230.

10. David Frost, *"I Gave Them a Sword"* (New York: Morrow, 1978), p. 161.

11. Richard Nixon, *RN: The Memoirs of Richard Nixon* (New York: Grosset & Dunlap, 1978), p. 490.

12. *Washington Post*, 10 September 1974, p. A12. Through a spokesman, Kissinger said that he had no recollection of having made such an observation. Powers discusses the quotation's authenticity on pp. 227 and 359, note 9, saying that Victor Marchetti and John Marks, in *The CIA and the Cult of Intelligence* (New York: Knopf, 1974), included this quotation but were obliged by CIA clearance authorities to delete it. Roger Morris, in *Uncertain Greatness* (New York: Harper & Row, 1977), p. 241, uses the quotation; so does Anthony Lewis, *New York Times*, 21 August 1980, p. A27.

13. Seymour M. Hersh, *The Price of Power: Kissinger in the Nixon White House* (New York: Summit, 1983), p. 270. Hersh goes on to suggest that Kissinger's real fear was that Allende *would* relinquish power democratically at the end of his term, which is a speculation I find unconvincing. Regarding Hersh's quotation of Roger Morris's views, it should be noted that Morris resigned from Kissinger's staff in policy disagreement and could not have been the recipient of Kissinger's confidences after the 4 September elections in Chile. Morris did stay in touch with other staffers close to Kissinger, however, and the quotation probably represents a secondhand report on Kissinger's attitude.

14. Quoted in *New York Times*, 20 September 1970, p. 24, and *Washington Post*, 10 September 1974, p. A12.

15. U.S. Congress, Senate, *Alleged Assassination Plots Involving Foreign Leaders*, Interim Report of the Select Committee to Study Governmental Operations with Respect to Intelligence Activities (Washington, D.C., 20 November [legis. day 18 November] 1975), pp. 227–28. See also Powers, pp. 234–35, and Hersh, pp. 273–74.

16. Powers, pp. 236–38; U.S. Senate, *Alleged Assassination Plots*, pp. 225, 229, 235–45; Hersh, pp. 273–96; U.S. Senate, *Covert Action*, pp. 10–11, 25–26, 36.

17. U.S. Senate, *Alleged Assassination Plots*, pp. 242–43, 246–53; Hersh, pp. 286–88.

18. U.S. Senate, *Alleged Assassination Plots*, pp. 226 and 239, note 2, and

pp. 244–46; U.S. Senate, *Covert Action,* p. 11; Moss, p. 32; Powers, p. 237; Hersh, pp. 289–92.

19. Hersh, pp. 258–59, 274–75, 292–93; U.S. Senate, *Alleged Assassination Plots,* pp. 228, 238, 241.

20. Hersh, p. 274; U.S. Senate, *Alleged Assassination Plots,* pp. 228, 244.

21. Powers, p. 229; Hersh, pp. 271–72; Paul E. Sigmund, *The Overthrow of Allende and the Politics of Chile, 1964–1976* (Pittsburgh: University of Pittsburgh Press, 1977), pp. 114–17; U.S. Senate, *Covert Action,* pp. 23–24; U.S. Senate, *Alleged Assassination Plots,* pp. 230–31, 234.

22. Edward M. Korry, letter dated 14 February 1981, in *New York Times,* 22 February 1981, sec. 4, p. 18; Hersh, pp. 271–72; U.S. Senate, *Alleged Assassination Plots,* pp. 230–31.

23. Hersh, pp. 272–73; Sigmund, p. 116; U.S. Senate, *Covert Action,* pp. 24–25; U.S. Senate, *Alleged Assassination Plots,* pp. 230–31.

24. Anthony Sampson, *The Sovereign State of ITT* (New York: Stein & Day, 1973), pp. 264–65, 276–77; Terry Sanford et al., "Report of the Special Review Committee of the Board of Directors," *International Telephone and Telegraph Corporation, Supplementary Report* (New York, n.d.), pp. 48–49; U.S. Senate, *Covert Action,* pp. 11–13, 21.

25. Sampson, p. 276; Hersh, p. 276; Sigmund, p. 113; U.S. Senate, *Covert Action,* p. 13.

26. U.S. Congress, Senate, *Multinational Corporations and United States Foreign Policy: The International Telephone and Telegraph Company and Chile, 1970–71* (Washington, D.C., 1973), pt. 2. pp. 624, 627, and 636. See also Sampson, pp. 278–80; Powers, p. 236; Sigmund, p. 117; and U.S. Senate, *Alleged Assassination Plots,* p. 231.

27. U.S. Senate, *Multinational Corporations,* Part 2, pp. 644, 646, and 659 in particular, but also pp. 608, 610, 612–13, 622, 625, 642, 645, 663–64, 675, 680, and 701–2. See also Powers, p. 227; Sampson, p. 281; and Henry Kissinger, *Years of Upheaval* (Boston: Little, Brown, 1982), p. 389.

28. Jack Anderson's revelations are treated extensively in U.S. Senate, *Multinational Corporations,* pts. 1 and 2. For an indication of a leftist's ability to guess the timing and nature of U.S. policy making in mid-September of 1970, see Armando Uribe, *The Black Book of American Intervention in Chile* (Boston: Beacon, 1975), pp. 51–52. The Forty Committee met on 14 September and President Nixon's meeting with Helms was on the fifteenth. ITT officials appear to have gained some indications of the results of both meetings.

29. Sigmund, p. 116.

30. Hersh, pp. 272–73; U.S. Senate, *Alleged Assassination Plots,* p. 234.

31. Sigmund, pp. 118–20.

32. From the Constitution of the Chilean Republic as amended by Law 17,398 of 9 January 1971. There were a few other provisions of lesser importance.

33. Régis Debray, *The Chilean Revolution: Conversations with Allende* (New York: Random, 1971), p. 119.

34. Salvador Allende Gossens, *Chile's Road to Socialism,* ed. Joan E. Garces (Harmondsworth, England: Penguin, 1973), pp. 101–2.

35. Sigmund, p. 123; Alexander, pp. 127–28.

36. Article 109 had been enacted during Frei's last year in power, on 23 January 1970. A majority of the valid vote was required to carry the issue.

37. Moss, p. 77–78.

38. *Economist*, 13 October 1973, p. 44.

39. Alexander, p. 174.

40. Ibid., p. 177.

41. Sigmund, p. 281.

42. Ibid., p. 143.

43. Juan de Onís, "Election Poses a New Test for Allende," *New York Times*, 18 July 1971, p. 12; de Onís, "Chilean Leftist Loses Key Election for a Deputy," *New York Times*, 19 July 1971, p. 3; Sigmund, pp. 149, 308.

44. Alexander, p. 169.

45. Everett G. Martin, "Dr. Allende Takes over Much of the Economy but Hits Some Snags," *Wall Street Journal*, 26 August 1971, p. 14.

46. Alexander, p. 207; Juan de Onís, "Strikes Adding to Allende Woes," *New York Times*, 12 August 1971, p. 3.

47. Carlos Prats, *Una vida por la legalidad* (Mexico: Fondo de Cultura Económica, 1976), p. 29; Alexander, p. 182.

48. Sigmund, p. 281.

49. Juan de Onís, "Christian Democrats in Chile Favor 'Communitarian Socialism,'" *New York Times*, 11 May 1971, p. 15.

50. Sigmund, pp. 99, 147–48; Alexander, p. 274.

51. Joseph Novitski, "Chilean Party Breaks off from Allende," *New York Times*, 26 September 1971, p. 22; *Foreign Broadcast Information Service, Daily Report, Latin America and Western Europe*, Santiago, PRENSA LATINA, 2330 GMT 22 Sept. 1971.

52. U.S. Senate, *Covert Action*, pp. 57–60; U.S. Senate, *Alleged Assassination Plots*, p. 229.

53. U.S. Senate, *Alleged Assassination Plots*, p. 254. For a full discussion of this statement, see chapters 12 and 13 below.

54. Seymour M. Hersh, "New Evidence Backs Ex-Envoy on His Role in Chile," *New York Times*, 9 February 1981, p. A12; Hersh, *The Price of Power*, pp. 292, 295.

55. Kissinger, *White House Years*, p. 681; Hersh, *The Price of Power*, p. 294.

56. Elmo R. Zumwalt, Jr., *On Watch* (New York: Quadrangle, 1976), p. 323; Sigmund, p. 308.

57. Kissinger, *White House Years*, p. 681; Zumwalt, p. 323.

58. Richard Nixon, "US Foreign Policy for the 1970's," *Building for Peace: A Report to the Congress*, 25 February 1971 (Washington, D.C., 1971), p. 54.

59. Zumwalt, pp. 323, 328.

60. Sigmund, pp. 152–55; Alexander, pp. 147–48; *New York Times*, 30 September 1971, p. 3.

61. A calculation of the real U.S. investment on which the $20 million annual profits were remitted would involve complicated judgments. For example, one would have to consider initial investment, additional moneys put in over the years, reinvested profits, loans, changing figures for estimated "book value," a dollar-escudo exchange rate set by the Chileans to increase dollars absorbed in local costs, intracompany and parent-to-subsidiary prices set by the North Americans to favor the U.S. side, and other arrangements that benefited one party or the other. Part of Kennecott's declared book value represented funds committed to the expansion program.

62. Sigmund, pp. 36–37; Alexander, pp. 100–103; *New York Times*, Business sec. stock price listings for August and December 1970 (which showed the 1970 high) and November 1971.

63. Edward M. Korry, "Statement," U.S. Congress, Senate, Select Committee to Study Governmental Operations with Respect to Intelligence Activities, Senate Resolution 21, vol. 7, *Covert Action*, 4 and 5 December 1975, Hearings (Washington, D.C., 1976), p. 33.

64. Benjamin Welles, "US Insuring Agency May Face Claims of $216 Million in Chile," *New York Times*, 6 March 1972, p. 5.

65. Ibid.; Sigmund, p. 194.

66. U.S. Senate, *Covert Action in Chile*, p. 26.

67. Hersh, p. 296.

68. Uribe, pp. 65–69.

69. Henry H. Schulte, Jr., ed., *Facts on File Yearbook, 1971* (New York: Facts on File, 1972), p. 980.

70. Zumwalt, p. 324.

71. Ibid., pp. 324–28.

72. New York Times, 30 June 1971, p. 1.

73. Drew Pearson and Jack Anderson, "Nixon Displays New Interest in Art," *Washington Star*, 28 November 1968, p. L19.

74. Jeremiah O'Leary, "US Guatemala Ambassador to Receive Chile Assignment," *Washington Post*, 5 April 1971; *Time*, 19 April 1971.

75. Juan de Onís, "US-Chilean Relations Running into Serious Snags," *New York Times*, 23 June 1971, p. 13.

76. *New York Times*, 30 July 1971, p. 6.

77. Theodore H. Moran, *Multinational Corporations and the Politics of Dependence: Copper in Chile* (Princeton: Princeton University Press, 1974), p. 252, note 7. The Almeyda-Rogers conversation was quite bland, essentially an exchange of courtesies.

78. See also David Atlee Phillips, *The Night Watch* (New York: Atheneum, 1977), p. 236.

79. John Dinges and Saul Landau, *Assassination on Embassy Row* (New York: Pantheon, 1980), pp. 47–49; Benjamin Welles, "US Export Bank Refuses Chile Loan to Buy 3 Airliners," *New York Times*, 12 August 1971, pp. 1, 11.

## 2. Castro and the Empty Pots

1. *La Segunda* ran its comical photo twice, first on 20 October 1971, p. 1, and again with the ration-card caption on 22 January 1973, p. 5.

2. *El Clarín*, 21 October 1971, p. 4; Gonzalo Cruz, "El, al trasluz; Las armas rusas le penaron al embajador de EE UU," *La Tribuna*, 21 October 1971.

3. Graham Greene, "Chile the Dangerous Edge," *Observer* (London), 8 January 1972, pp. 7–8.

4. David F. Belnap, "U.S. Envoy to Chile: He Wins Confidence," *Los Angeles Times*, 9 January 1972, Sunday sec. 1, Op-Ed page.

5. *La Nación*, 27 January 1972.

6. *El Clarín*, 29 March 1972, p. 24.

7. Juan de Onís, "American Colony in Chile Declines," *New York Times*, 5 July 1972, p. 7; Penny Lernoux, *Cry of the People* (Garden City, N.Y.: Doubleday, 1980), p. 203; Staff, North American Congress on Latin America, *United Fruit is not Chiquita* (New York and Berkeley, October 1971), p. 7.

8. Lernoux, pp. 211–13.

9. Robert J. Alexander, *The Tragedy of Chile* (Westport: Greenwood,

1978), p. 213; Paul E. Sigmund, *The Overthrow of Allende and the Politics of Chile, 1964–1976* (Pittsburgh: University of Pittsburgh Press, 1977), p. 162.

10. Alexander, p. 214.

11. Jack Anderson, "Aid Sought for Crusading Tenn. Editor," *Washington Post*, 8 September 1972, p. D19.

12. Salvador Allende, *Su pensamiento político* (Buenos Aires: Granica, 1973), pp. 112–13, 115, 117–21, 129. An English-language version appears in Salvador Allende, "First Message to the Congress by President Allende," in Régis Debray, *The Chilean Revolution: Conversations with Allende* (New York: Random, 1971), pp. 170–72, 177–82, 196.

13. Alexander, p. 215; Anderson, "Aid Sought. . . ."

14. Fidel Castro, "Acto de despedida," 2 December 1971 (F1776.3/C4C8/LAC), *Castro's Farewell Speech, Chile, Encuentro simbólico entre dos procesos históricos* (Havana: Comisión de Orientación Revolucionaria del Comité, n.d.), pp. 474–75, 477, 480, 483. An English-language version appears in Fidel Castro, "Who Has Learned the Most?" *Fidel in Chile* (New York: International, 1972), p. 200–201, 203–4, 208, 213–14, 219.

15. Karl Marx and Friedrich Engels, "The Communist Manifesto," in Arthur P. Mendel, ed., *Essential Works of Marxism* 2d ed. (New York: Bantam, 1971), p. 43.

16. Debray, p. 52.

17. Sigmund, p. 307.

18. Paul M. Sweezy and Harry Magdoff, *Revolution and Counter-Revolution in Chile* (New York: Monthly Review, 1974), pp. 14, 16, 79–93.

19. Interview with Miguel Enríquez, "The MIR Analyzes the Coup," *The End of Chilean Democracy*, Laurence Birns, ed. (New York: Seabury, 1973), pp. 100–101.

20. Juan de Onís, "Chilean Opposition Accuses Allende Aide," *New York Times*, 17 December 1971, p. 9.

21. Alexander, p. 294.

22. Juan de Onís, "Women's Protest Quelled in Chile," *New York Times*, 2 December 1971, p. 1.

23. The crammed-in car ride was at the inauguration of the Arauco cellulose plant on 12 February 1972, and Inés Allende de Grove's funeral was at the Santa Inés cematary, which serves Valparaíso and Viña del Mar, on 8 August 1973. The conversation at the funeral was the second-to-last time I talked with President Allende, the last time being at a reception in early September. The party at the Mexican Embassy was on 8 June 1973.

24. Pedro Ibáñez, "The Chilean Crisis and Its Outcome," 1974 mimeo, pp. 11–12, as quoted by Alexander, p. 140.

25. *Qué Pasa*, 8–14 September 1977, p. 29; Ibáñez, pp. 11–12; Gabriel García Márquez, "The Death of Salvador Allende," *Harper's*, March 1974, p. 53.

26. Florencia Varas and José Manuel Vergara, *Coup! Allende's Last Day* (New York: Stein & Day, 1975), p. 117; Ibáñez, pp. 11–12.

27. Anderson, "Aid Sought. . . ."

28. García Márquez, p. 53; Ibáñez, pp. 11–12; Charles Moritz, ed., *Current Biography Yearbook, 1971* (New York: Wilson, 1972), pp. 6–9.

29. Ibáñez, pp. 11–12.

30. Edward M. Korry, "Statements and Discussion," U.S. Congress, Senate, Committee on Foreign Relations, *Nomination of Hon. Cyrus R. Vance to be*

*Secretary of State,* 11 January 1977, Hearing (Washington, D.C., 1977), pp. 57, 67; *Newsweek,* 10 January 1977, p. 25 (or 17 January 1977, p. 22, depending on the edition); Sigmund, p. 263; *Wall Street Journal,* 12 January 1977, p. 14.

31. Ibáñez, pp. 11–12.

32. Hernán Millas and Emilio Filippi, *Chile '70–'73: Crónica de una experiencia* (Santiago: Zig-Zag, 1974), p. 16.

33. Paul E. Sigmund, in *Princeton Weekly Bulletin,* 13 February 1978, p. 1; Alexander, p. 141.

34. Allende defended the compatibility of Marxism and Freemasonry in a statement to the Masonic Grand Lodge in Bogotá, Colombia, on 28 August 1971. Apparently this statement was sent around the world, as I was given a mimeographed copy of it in Zürich, Switzerland, in 1976.

35. Carlos Prats, *Una vida por la legalidad* (México: Fondo de Cultura Económica, 1976), p. 94.

36. Quoted in Camilo Taufic, *Chile en la hoguera* (Buenos Aires: Corregidor, 1974), p. 88.

37. Robert Moss, *Chile's Marxist Experiment* (Newton Abbot, England: David & Charles, 1973), pp. 48, 105; Teresa Donoso Loero, ed., *Breve historia de la Unidad Popular: Documento de "El Mercurio"* (Santiago: El Mercurio, 1974), pp. 210–11; Alexander, pp. 274, 309.

38. Quoted in Taufic, p. 87.

39. Sigmund, *Princeton Weekly Bulletin,* p. 4.

40. Varas and Vergara, p. 171. Régis Debray also points out that Allende was a dreamer who refused to give up his dream. Taufic, p. 87.


**Chapter 3. Chilean Politics and Troubles to the North**

1. Paul E. Sigmund, *The Overthrow of Allende and the Politics of Chile, 1964–1976* (Pittsburgh: University of Pittsburgh Press, 1977), p. 165; Robert J. Alexander, *The Tragedy of Chile* (Westport: Greenwood, 1978), p. 286; Juan de Onís, "Allende Program Faces Test in Two Elections Sunday," *New York Times,* 13 January 1972, p. 2; and de Onís, "Chilean Opposition wins 2 Elections in Test of Allende's Socialist Program," *New York Times,* 17 January 1972, p. 14.

2. Sigmund, p. 282; David E. Clark, "The 'Power of Chaotization': The MIR's Chilean Radicalism" (unpublished research paper for the Post-Graduate Intelligence Course, Defense Intelligence School, PGIC 1–76, April 1976), p. 36.

3. Sigmund, p. 172; Alexander, p. 280.

4. Sigmund, p. 166; *New York Times,* 6 February 1972, p. 17.

5. Quoted in Robert Moss, *Chile's Marxist Experiment* (Newton Abbot, England: David & Charles, 1973), p. 59.

6. Sigmund, p. 166; Moss, pp. 21–22.

7. Sigmund, p. 164.

8. Alexander, p. 286; Camilo Taufic, *Chile en la hoguera* (Buenos Aires: Corregidor, 1974), pp. 15 and 18.

9. Sigmund, pp. 168–69; Alexander, p. 286; Teresa Donoso Loero, ed., *Breve historia de la Unidad Popular: Documento de "El Mercurio"* (Santiago: El Mercurio, 1974), pp. 174–75.

10. Sigmund, p. 159.

11. Alexander, pp. 16, 153–56.

12. Ibid., pp. 241–42; Sigmund, pp. 157–58.

13. New York Times, 20 February 1972, p. 7; Alexander, p. 253; Sigmund, p. 168; Moss, p. 129.

14. Articles 78, 108, and 109 of the Chilean Constitution, providing for a Constitutional Court, a new constitutional amendment procedure, and recourse to a plebiscite, were enacted by Law 17,284 of 23 January 1970.

15. Actually, the Constitutional Tribunal did not side with the president, deciding on 31 May 1973 that it lacked jurisdiction. See Sigmund, p. 207.

16. Sigmund, p. 170.

17. Ibid.; "The Chilean Tragedy," New York Times, 16 September 1973, sec. 4, p. 14.

18. Donoso, p. 338.

19. Herbert G. Klein, Making It Perfectly Clear (Garden City, N.Y.: Double-day, 1980), pp. 274–75; Jeremiah O'Leary in Washington Star, 5 December 1971; Puro Chile, 2 December 1971.

20. U.S. Congress, Senate, Multinational Corporations and United States Foreign Policy: The International Telephone and Telegraph Company and Chile, 1970–71 (Washington, D.C., 1973), pt. 2, pp. 609–10, 757, 745–46.

21. Georgie Anne Geyer, "ITT Memos Hurt New Latin Policy," Chicago Daily News, 23 March 1972.

22. Jack Anderson, "ITT Hope of Ousting Allende Remote," Washington Post, 28 March 1972, p. B11.

23. In actuality, I sent two telegrams to Washington, the first of which, Santiago 6008, described the situation, and the second of which made policy recommendations. Judging from Anderson's published excerpts, only the first of these two telegrams was passed to him. John Erlichman, Witness to Power (New York: Simon & Schuster, 1982), pp. 303–10; Seymour M. Hersh, The Price of Power: Kissinger in the Nixon White House (New York: Summit, 1983), pp. 258–59.

24. El Siglo, 29 March 1972; El Clarín, 29 March 1972. Quotations from L'Humanité are from a Prensa Latina dispatch carried in El Siglo, 30 March 1972.

25. El Mercurio, 4 October 1973, p. 24.

26. Jack Anderson, "The Washington Merry-Go-Round," Washington Post, 17 September 1973.

27. Jack Anderson and Les Whitten, "No Direct US Role Seen in Chile Coup," Washington Post, 22 September 1973, p. E6.

28. Jack Anderson, "The Economic War against Allende," Washington Post, 3 November 1974, p. C7. Sigmund, p. 309, notes more flagrant misconstruals of my 7 December 1971 telegram.

29. Jack Anderson and Les Whitten, "Chile's Junta Invades the Schools," Washington Post, 24 April 1975, p. G13.

30. David Wise, The American Police State (New York: Random, 1976), pp. 22–23. A J. W. Guilfoyle internal ITT memorandum describes an Allende request which may have been the genesis of the Tagliarini-Ragan trip. Multinational Corporations, pt. 2, p. 674.

31. Sigmund, pp. 103–4, 263; American-Chilean Council Report, 26 January 1977; Joseph Trento, Wilmington News Journal, 28 November 1976.

32. *American-Chilean Council Report*, p. 2.

33. Anthony Sampson, *The Sovereign State of ITT* (New York: Stein & Day, 1973), p. 285.

34. Ibid., p. 285; Donoso, pp. 88, 506.

35. Sigmund, p. 155.

36. Ibid.; U.S. Senate, *Multinational Corporations*, pp. 950–53; Sampson, p. 285.

37. Sampson, pp. 285–86.

38. U.S. Senate, *Multinational Corporations*, pp. 971–79; Paul E. Sigmund, "The 'Invisible Blockade' and the Overthrow of Allende," *Foreign Affairs*, January 1974, pp. 331–32.

39. Marilyn Berger, "ITT Refused Chile Offer for Holdings," *Washington Post*, 10 April 1972, pp. A1 and A4.

40. Ibid., p. A4.

41. Sampson, p. 266.

42. Taufic, p. 20.

43. Alexander, p. 223; Sigmund, *The Overthrow of Allende*, p. 175; Henry Kissinger, *Years of Upheaval* (Boston: Little, Brown, 1982), p. 391.

44. Kissinger, p. 385; Sigmund, "The 'Invisible Blockade,'" p. 335.

45. Official Text, *Nixon's Statement on Aid to Developing Nations*, 19 January 1972, 72/1, Cultural and Press Service, American Embassy, Chile, 82801. See also Laurence Birns, ed., *The End of Chilean Democracy* (New York: Seabury, 1973), p. 183.

46. Kissinger, p. 388; Sigmund, "The 'Invisible Blockade,'" p. 338.

47. For example, General Motors, First National City Bank, DuPont, and Coca Cola sold out their Chilean subsidiaries between January and June 1972.

48. Kissinger, pp. 386–87.

49. Ibid., p. 387.

50. Ibid., p. 391; Sigmund, *The Overthrow of Allende*, p. 175.

51. Alexander, p. 223; Sigmund, "The 'Invisible Blockade,'" pp. 335–36.

## Chapter 4. Left Extremists, Miners, and Truckers

1. Robert Moss, *Chile's Marxist Experiment* (Newton Abbot, England: David & Charles, 1973), pp. 59, 189.

2. Ibid., pp. 61, 63, 65, 77.

3. Alberto Baltra as quoted in Robert J. Alexander, *The Tragedy of Chile* (Westport: Greenwood, 1978), p. 190.

4. Alexander, pp. 150, 192.

5. Ibid., p. 187.

6. Paul E. Sigmund, *The Overthrow of Allende and the Politics of Chile, 1964–1976* (Pittsburgh: The University of Pittsburgh Press, 1977), p. 176; Moss, pp. 54, 76; Alexander, p. 188.

7. Robinson Rojas Sandford, *The Murder of Allende* (New York: Harper & Row, 1976), p. 171; Moss, p. 54; Alexander, pp. 187, 397. Some leftist observers have claimed that inflation was the fault of the Chilean Congress, which denied the government the resources to control it. For one such view, see Camilo Taufic, *Chile en la hoguera* (Buenos Aires: Corregidor, 1974), p. 23. There were times when the Congress did deny the government such resources and freedom

of action, but to explain the phenomenon in these terms is to ignore the thrust of Vuskovic's policies. See also Juan de Onís, "Allende Program Faces Test in Two Elections Sunday," *New York Times,* 13 January 1972, p. 2.

8. Rojas, p. 171.
9. Sigmund, p. 176.
10. Alexander, p. 159; Sigmund, pp. 177, 280.
11. Sigmund, p. 281; Alexander, p. 177.
12. Rojas, p. 110.
13. Moss, p. 22.
14. Sigmund, p. 177.
15. Ibid., p. 179.
16. David E. Clark, "The 'Power of Chaotization': The MIR's Chilean Radicalism" (unpublished research paper for the Post-Graduate Intelligence Course, Defense Intelligence School, PGIC 1-76, April 1976), particularly pp. 6, 27–39.
17. Ibid., p. 51.
18. Alexander, p. 274; Sigmund, pp. 99, 148.
19. Secretaría de Gobierno, *Libro blanco del cambio de gobierno en Chile: 11 sep. 1973* (Santiago: Empresa Editora Nacional Gabriela Mistral, n.d., 1973), p. 41; Alexander, p. 195.
20. Alain Labrousse, *L'expérience chilienne, réformisme ou révolution?* (Paris: Seuil, 1972), pp. 355 and 359–62.
21. Henry H. Schulte, Jr., ed., *Facts on File Yearbook, 1972* (New York: Facts on File, 1973), p. 311.
22. Sigmund, pp. 78–79; Alexander, pp. 63, 283.
23. Taufic, p. 15; *New York Times,* 29 July 1971, p. 7; 7 August 1971, p. 4; and 12 August 1971, p. 3; Sigmund, pp. 150–51; Alexander, p. 283.
24. Moss, pp. 22, 104.
25. Ibid., p. 104; Alexander, p. 256.
26. Moss, p. 104.
27. Moss, p. 111.
28. Alexander, p. 274.
29. Ibid., p. 275; *New York Times,* 21 September 1973, p. 12.
30. Moss, p. 113.
31. Ibid., pp. 99, 103; Alexander, p. 315; Sigmund, p. 215; Taufic, p. 22.
32. Teresa Donoso Loero, ed., *Breve historia de la Unidad Popular: Documento de "El Mercurio"* (Santiago: El Mercurio, 1974), pp. 248, 253, 279, 282, 289, 303, 307.
33. Moss, pp. 111–12; *Economist,* 13 October 1973, p. 44; Sigmund, p. 313, note 34; *Libro blanco,* pp. 42, 46, 70.
34. See Moss, p. 98.
35. Ibid., p. 100.
36. Ibid., p. 111.
37. *Libro blanco,* pp. 71, 99–108; *New York Times,* 29 July 1972, p. 8. The personal complicity of del Canto in the Cuban crates incident was not proved in the impeachment proceedings, notwithstanding the outcome.
38. Moss, p. 111; Jack Anderson in the *Washington Post,* 30 March 1972.
39. Alexander, pp. 195–96.
40. Ibid., pp. 196–97.
41. Schulte, *1971,* p. 915.

42. Ibid.

43. Taufic, pp. 19–20; Schulte, *1972*, pp. 10, 150, 330.

44. Schulte, *1972*, p. 960.

45. *Foreign Broadcast Information Service*, Daily Report, Latin America and Western Europe, Havana, PRELA, 1915 GMT 4 Sept. 1973; Santiago PRELA to Havana, 1254 GMT 6 Sept. 1973; 2246 GMT 8 Sept. 1973; 2247 GMT 8 Sept. 1973.

46. The six incidents referred to are listed in David Wise, *The American Police State* (New York: Random, 1976), p. 175.

47. The quotation and the facts cited are from John Dinges and Saul Landau, *Assassination on Embassy Row* (New York: Pantheon, 1980), p. 50. Dinges and Landau are not explicit in citing their source, but most such material in their book clearly was told them by Isabel Letelier, Orlando Letelier's widow. The same essential facts were given me by Chilean under-secretary of foreign affairs Aníbal Palma when he called me into the Foreign Office on 16 May 1972.

48. Lewis H. Diuguid, "Chilean Cites '71 Kissinger Assurances," *Washington Post*, 3 February 1975, pp. A1, A3; Vernon A. Walters, *Silent Missions* (Garden City, N.Y.: Doubleday, 1978), p. 591; Sigmund, p. 206.

49. Wise, p. 181.

50. Phillips adds that bugs were not in operation against the Chilean Embassy during his incumbency. Letter of David A. Phillips to author, 2 January 1984, quoted by permission.

51. Wise, p. 177.

52. See Edmundo del Solar, *Orlando Letelier* (New York: Vantage, 1978), pp. 32–34, 65–68; Taylor Branch and Eugene M. Propper, *Labyrinth* (New York: Viking, 1982), pp. 84–85, 170–73, 588.

53. U.S. Congress, Senate, *Covert Action in Chile, 1963–1973: Staff Report of the Select Committee to Study Governmental Operations with Respect to Intelligence Activities* (Washington, D.C.: 1975), pp. 37–38.

54. Ibid.; Tad Szulc, "U.S. Is Continuing Aid to the Chilean Armed Forces," *New York Times*, 9 December 1972, p. 12.

55. U.S. Senate, *Covert Action*, pp. 37–38.

56. Alejandro Witker V., *El compañero Toha: Esbozo biográfico, testimonios, documentos* (Mexico: Casa de Chile en Mexico, 1977), p. 34.

57. Taufic, pp. 15–17.

58. Penny Lernoux, *Cry of the People* (Garden City, N.Y.: Doubleday, 1980), p. 223.

59. Sigmund, p. 310, note 31.

60. Ibid.

61. *New York Times*, 8 September 1972, p. 45; Gerd Wilcke, "Bid by Anaconda Denied by Chile," *New York Times*, 9 September 1972, p. 29.

62. Taufic, p. 21.

63. Sigmund, pp. 191 and 310, note 31; "Chile Scores France on Copper Decision," *Washington Post*, 7 October 1972; Donoso, p. 228.

64. Moss, pp. 71, 74; Sigmund, p. 176; Alexander, p. 150.

65. Sigmund, p. 176; Alexander, pp. 149–50; Mark Falcoff, "Why Allende Fell," *Commentary*, July 1976, p. 45; Theodore H. Moran, *Multinational Corporations and the Politics of Dependence: Copper in Chile* (Princeton: Princeton

University Press, 1974), pp. 250–53; Norman Gall, "Copper Is the Wage of Chile," *West Coast South America Series, NG-4-72* (Hanover, N.H.: American Universities Field Staff, 1972), pp. 1–18, particularly pp. 6–7.

66. Alexander, p. 207; Gall, pp. 4–5. Gall correctly notes that Chuquicamata miners were often able to obtain concessions, even in the 1960s, by small, wildcat "partial stoppages" and sit-ins, so the pre-Allende record was not truly strike-free.

67. Moran lists the copper companies' retaliation as one of three reasons for Chilean production losses. He leans heavily on Gall's report in reaching this conclusion, however, and the Gall report taken as a whole explains the various causes of the spare-parts shortages more extensively and very objectively. Moran's book is adapted from a dissertation completed in June 1971 and Gall's report is dated August 1972, so neither work focuses on the later period of UP government.

68. "Mañana comenzarán las conversaciones con Estados Unidos," *La Prensa* (Santiago), 19 December 1972.

69. Treaty for the Advancement of Peace, signed at Washington 24 July 1914; proclaimed 22 January 1916. U.S. Congress, Senate, *Treaties, Conventions, International Acts, Protocols and Agreements between the United States of America and Other Powers, 1910–1923*, vol. 3 (Washington, 1923), pp. 2509–11. The reservations were with respect to "any question that may affect the independence, the honor or the vital interest of either or both of the countries, or the provisions of their respective Constitutions, or the interests of a third nation." As is evident, Chile could easily have invoked the reservation had it wished to do so.

70. Armando Uribe, *The Black Book of American Intervention in Chile* (Boston: Beacon, 1975), pp. ix, 51–52, 137–44. In note 1, chap. 10, p. 154, Uribe identifies his sources for the account of the Washington talks as Left Christian deputy Luis Maira and other members of the Chilean delegation.

71. Uribe, pp. 139 and 141. See also Moss, p. 70.

72. It was lucky that Kubisch and Hennessy did not come to Santiago. The rightist-inspired tank insurrection, or tancazo, occurred three days after they would have left the city.

73. Diuguid, p. A3.

74. Donoso, pp. 214–15; *New York Times*, 22 August 1972, p. 6.

75. *FBIS*, numerous entries in the "E" section of the report for 22 August 1972; *New York Times*, 23 August 1972, pp. 1–2.

76. *New York Times*, 1 September 1972, p. 30, and 2 September 1972, p. 2; Alexander, p. 207.

77. Joseph Novitski, "Allende and Foes Avoid Open Clash," *New York Times*, 7 September 1972, p. 11, and 10 September 1972, sec. 4, p. 3.

78. Sigmund, p. 184; Alexander, p. 303; Florencia Varas and José Manuel Vergara, *Coup! Allende's Last Day* (New York: Stein & Day, 1975), p. 139.

79. Rojas, pp. 115–16; Donoso, pp. 230–31, 235–37, 240–41. Cumsille's shopkeepers were united in the Confederación del Comercio Detallista y Pequeña Industria, hereafter called the Shopkeepers' Confederation.

80. Sigmund, p. 185; Donoso, pp. 231–35.

81. Alexander, p. 304; Sigmund, p. 187, Donoso, pp. 234, 236, 238–40.

82. Alexander, p. 230. For a discussion of alleged U.S. covert financing of the truckers, see chapter 12 below.

83. Donoso, p. 235.

84. Ibid., p. 240; Sigmund, p. 187.

85. *New York Times*, 1 November 1972, p. 7.

86. Samuel Chavkin, *The Murder of Chile* (New York: Everest, 1982), pp. 62, 67. The news agency United Press International might have got wind of this illness, or its aftereffects. See *FBIS*, PRELA, 1819 GMT 3 Dec. 1972.

### Chapter 5. Military Officers Join the Government

1. Carlos Prats, *Una vida por la legalidad* (México: Fondo de Cultura Económica, 1976). As an example of possible excisions, it may be worth noting that no trace appears of my many conversations with him, while his words with the Soviet ambassador are recorded.

2. Henry H. Schulte, Jr., ed., *Facts on File Yearbook, 1972* (New York: Facts on File, 1973), p. 851; *New York Times*, 22 October 1972, p. 18, 1 November 1972, p. 7, and 3 November 1972, p. 3.

3. *New York Times*, 4 November 1972, p. 10, 5 November 1972, p. 3, 5 November 1972, sec. 4, p. 3, 6 November 1972, p. 3, and 7 November 1972, p. 3.

4. *New York Times*, 9 November 1972, p. 5, 10 November 1972, p. 26 and 13 November 1972, p. 36.

5. "La acción del ejército en la liberación de Chile" (Santiago: historia inédita, circulated informally by senior Chilean Army officers, n.d.), p. 21.

6. Teresa Donoso Loero, ed., *Breve historia de la Unidad Popular: Documento de El Mercurio* (Santiago: El Mercurio, 1974), pp. 237–38.

7. Robert J. Alexander, *The Tragedy of Chile* (Westport: Greenwood, 1978), pp. 294, 311.

8. *Report on Freedom of the Press in Chile*, Committee on Freedom of the Press, presented to the General Assembly, Inter-American Press Association (IAPA), Santiago Meeting, 9–13 October 1972, documents presented at the meeting. In evaluating the IAPA as a disinterested or interested source, it should be noted that USIA director Charles Z. Wick acknowledged in 1983 that his agency had contributed, through third parties, "to various organizations, such as the Inter-American Press Association, which under its charter does not take government money but got $50,000 from the federals through an intermediate group." Mary McGrory, "Reagan's Pet Is Headed for Shredder," *Newport Daily News*, 4 March 1983, p. 4.

9. Robert Moss, *Chile's Marxist Experiment* (Newton Abbot, England: David & Charles, 1973), p. 140; Paul E. Sigmund, *The Overthrow of Allende and the Politics of Chile, 1964–1976* (Pittsburgh: University of Pittsburgh Press, 1977), p. 186.

10. Alexander, p. 296.

11. *Ercilla*, no. 1989, 29 August–4 September 1973, p. 7; Thomas G. Sanders, "Military Government in Chile, Part I: The Coup," *Fieldstaff Reports*, vol. 22, no. 1, West Coast South America Series (Hanover, N.H.: American Universities Field Staff, 1975), p. 9.

12. Alexander, p. 292.

13. Robinson Rojas Sandford, *The Murder of Allende* (New York: Harper & Row, 1976), pp. 85–87.

14. Moss, p. 17. As woodland, swamp, and unirrigated land counted as less

than a "basic" hectare, proprietors were left with considerably more than 80 hectares. On the other hand, nonadjustment for inflation and use of the proprietor's self-evaluation on the tax rolls resulted in undercompensation.

15. Sigmund, p. 72; Moss, p. 84. Chonchol headed the Institute for Agricultural Development (INDAP).

16. Alexander, p. 166.

17. Ibid., p. 161; Moss, p. 96.

18. Alexander, p. 163.

19. Ibid., p. 166; Moss, p. 89.

20. Alexander, pp. 161–62.

21. Ibid., p. 164.

22. This paragraph is based on Alexander, pp. 161–62, 165, 193.

23. Ibid., pp. 168, 171.

24. Moss, p. 91.

25. Alexander, pp. 87–89.

26. The six agricultural unions alluded to are La Confederación Campesina e Indígena Ranquil (UP—largely Mapuche); La Confederación Unitaria de Campesinos (UP—farm laborers); La Confederación Campesina El Triumfo Campesino (CD—tenants and laborers); La Confederación La Libertad (CD—tenants and laborers); La Confederación Nacional de Asentamientos (CD—cooperative farmers); and La Confederación Nacional de Pequeños Agricultores (CD—owners of small farms). Alexander, pp. 87–93, 169; Mark Falcoff, "Reviews," *Orbis*, Summer 1977, p. 437.

27. Alexander, p. 170.

28. A name-by-name list of people killed during the three years of UP government is given in chap. 4 of the Junta's White Book. Secretaría de Gobierno, *Libro blanco del cambio de gobierno en Chile: 11 sep. 1973* (Santiago: Empresa Editora Nacional Gabriela Mistral, n.d.), pp. 79ff.

29. Alexander, p. 171; Sigmund, pp. 140, 235; Moss, pp. 93–94.

30. Alexander, p. 164; Moss, pp. 94–95.

31. Moss, p. 94.

32. Moss, pp. 92–93.

33. Paul E. Sigmund, "The 'Invisible Blockade' and the Overthrow of Allende," *Foreign Affairs*, January 1974, p. 336; Sigmund, *The Overthrow of Allende*, p. 140; Moss, p. 93; Alexander, p. 170.

34. *Foreign Broadcast Information Service*, Daily Report, Latin America and Western Europe, Mexico City Domestic Service, 1856 GMT 1 Dec. 1972, L2 and L12.

35. *New York Times*, 4 December 1972, p. 2.

36. Jack Anderson, "A Hint Not Taken: Nixon Avoids Allende," *Washington Post*, 10 December 1972, p. C7. An erroneous description of my characterization of Allende's motives has been omitted. Clearly, Anderson did not read the telegram.

37. Naciones Unidas, Asamblea General, Vigésimo Séptimo Período de Sesiones, *Documentos Oficiales, 2096a Sesión Plenaria* (New York, 4 December 1972), pp. 1–9. For a translation into English, see Official Records of the General Assembly, 27th Session, *Plenary Meetings*, 2096th Plenary Meeting (New York, 4 December 1972), pp. 1–10.

38. For one comment, see Sigmund, "The 'Invisible Blockade,'" p. 340.

39. Alexander, pp. 151–52, 224–25.

40. Sigmund, "The 'Invisible Blockade,'" pp. 330–31.

41. Loans and Grants, Obligations and Loan Authorizations, 1 July 1970 to 30 June 1973. U.S. Congress, Senate, *Covert Action in Chile, 1963–1973, Staff Report of the Select Committee to Study Governmental Operations with Respect to Intelligence Activities* (Washington, D.C., 1975), p. 34; Sigmund, "The 'Invisible Blockade,'" p. 334.

42. Sigmund, *The Overthrow of Allende,* p. 284.

43. Sigmund, "The 'Invisible Blockade,'" p. 336; Sigmund, *The Overthrow of Allende,* p. 190; Alexander, pp. 212, 225–26; William Montalbano, "Allende Finding New Credit Sources," *Miami Herald,* 20 October 1972.

44. Sigmund, "The 'Invisible Blockade,'" p. 336; Alexander, p. 212.

45. Sigmund, "The 'Invisible Blockade,'" pp. 327; U.S. Senate, *Covert Action,* p. 33.

46. Sigmund, "The 'Invisible Blockade,'" pp. 327–29.

47. Ibid., pp. 329–30; Alexander, pp. 220–21.

48. Sigmund, "The 'Invisible Blockade,'" pp. 336–37; Sigmund, *The Overthrow of Allende,* p. 284; Alexander, pp. 219, 226.

49. Theodore Shabad, "Allende Arrives in Soviet, Seeks New Aid for Chile," *New York Times,* 7 December 1972, p. 10; Edward M. Korry, "Statements and Discussion," U.S. Congress, Senate, Committee on Foreign Relations, *Nomination of Hon. Cyrus R. Vance to Be Secretary of State,* 11 January 1977, Hearing (Washington, D.C. 1977), pp. 57, 71.

50. *New York Times,* 10 December 1972, p. 23; Korry, pp. 57, 71; Alexander, p. 212; Don Oberdorfer, "The U.S. and Chile: An Ex-Ambassador Speaks out," *Washington Post,* 19 December 1976, p. B3; Moss, p. 57.

51. Moss, p. 80; Sigmund, p. 194.

52. Benjamin Welles, "Debt-Ridden Chile Is Reported to Get Soviet Offer of $50 Million in Credits," *New York Times,* 16 January 1972, p. 20; Moss, pp. 57, 80; Sigmund, *The Overthrow of Allende,* p. 194; Cord Meyer, *Facing Reality* (New York: Harper & Row, 1980), p. 188.

53. *FBIS,* 0000 GMT 12 Dec. 1972; *La Prensa* (Santiago) 19 December 1972.

54. Sigmund, *The Overthrow of Allende,* p. 194.

55. Lewis H. Diuguid in the *Washington Post,* 17 October 1971; Schulte, *1972,* p. 131.

56. Tad Szulc, "The CIA and Chile," in Laurence Birns, ed., *The End of Chilean Democracy* (New York: Seabury, 1974), p. 161.

57. Montalbano, *Miami Herald,* 20 October 1972.

58. Sigmund, p. 194. Some say the Soviet offer was considerably higher than $50 million.

59. "La acción del ejército," p. 25.

60. Korry, p. 68.

61. Henry H. Schulte, Jr., ed., *Facts on File Yearbook, 1973* (New York: Facts on File, 1974), pp. 405–6.

62. "La acción del ejército," p. 25.

63. Ibid., p. 406; Prats, p. 65.

64. Prats, p. 65.

65. Schulte, *1973,* p. 36.

66. Schulte, *1972,* pp. 112, 470; Schulte, *1973,* p. 36.

67. Sigmund, p. 195; Donoso, pp. 278–79.

68. Moss, pp. 65–66.

69. Sigmund, *The Overthrow of Allende*, p. 195.

70. Ibid., p. 282.

71. Ibid., p. 203; Alexander, p. 307; Szulc, p. 26; Donoso, p. 289.

72. Szulc, p. 26; Schulte, *1973*, p. 341.

73. Sigmund, *The Overthrow of Allende*, p. 208.

74. Ibid., p. 204; Alexander, p. 311; Donoso, pp. 324–25.

75. Prats, p. 52.

76. *La Tribuna*, 19 December 1972, pp. 12–13; *La Segunda*, 21 December 1972.

## Chapter 6. The Time of the March Elections

1. Teresa Donoso Loero, ed., *Breve historia de la Unidad Popular: Documento de "El Mercurio"* (Santiago: El Mercurio, 1974), pp. 283, 296, 297.

2. Ibid., pp. 296–97; Jonathan Kandell, "The Chilean Military Sets Forth Its Position on March Elections," *New York Times*, 24 February 1973, p. 10.

3. Henry H. Schulte, Jr., ed., *Facts on File Yearbook, 1973* (New York: Facts on File, 1974), p. 195.

4. Arnold M. Isaacs of the embassy's political section had mastered the intricacies of Chilean voting patterns and was able to send Washington realistic appraisals of prospects and perceptive interpretations of the results.

5. Robinson Rojas Sandford, *The Murder of Allende* (New York: Harper & Row, 1976), p. 128.

6. The federated UP parties were the Communist party, the Socialist party, the historic or CEN Radical party, Izquierda Cristiana, the MAPU, and Senator Rafael Tarud's tiny Acción Popular Independiente (API). One CODE federation was composed of the Christian Democrats, the Left Radicals (PIR), and the little social democratic, pro-CD remnant, the Democratic National Party (PADENA). The other CODE federation was composed of the National party and Julio Duran's Party of Radical Democracy (PDR).

7. Voting figures are taken from *El Mercurio*, 9 March 1973, p. 19, and *Foreign Broadcast Information Service*, Daily Report, Latin America and Western Europe, 6 March 1973, pp. E1–E5.

8. Comparable figures would be 37% to 44% (major parties only) or 36.3% to 43.4% (total vote).

9. Paul E. Sigmund, *The Overthrow of Allende and the Politics of Chile, 1964–1976* (Pittsburgh: University of Pittsburgh Press, 1977), p. 199.

10. In the major-party split, the opposition rose from about 49% in 1971 to 56%.

11. The parties' percentages of the vote exclude blank and null votes. Comparisons with voting in earlier years draw on *El Mercurio*, 9 March 1975, p. 19; Robert J. Alexander, *The Tragedy of Chile* (Westport: Greenwood, 1978), pp. 269–70; and Sigmund, pp. 199–200.

12. Schulte, *1973*, p. 195. The voting preferences of recently enfranchised youthful and illiterate voters could be verified because, as for women, new, separate polling places had been established for these new voters.

13. *FBIS*, 6 March 1973, pp. E5–E7.

14. Ibid., pp. E5–E6.

15. Sigmund, p. 210.

16. Alexander, p. 272.

17. Carlos Prats, *Una vida por la legalidad* (Mexico: Fondo de Cultura Económica, 1976), p. 43.

18. New York Times, 28 March 1973, p. 2; Donoso, p. 313; Thomas G. Sanders, "Military Government in Chile, Part I: The Coup," *Fieldstaff Reports*, vol. 22, no. 1, West Coast South America Series (Hanover, N.H.: American Universities Field Staff, 1975), p. 4.

19. Schulte, *1973*, pp. 317–18.

20. Laurence Birns, ed., *The End of Chilean Democracy* (New York: Seabury, 1974), pp. 79–92.

### Chapter 7. To the Tancazo

1. Paul E. Sigmund, *The Overthrow of Allende and the Politics of Chile, 1964–1976* (Pittsburgh: University of Pittsburgh Press, 1977), p. 209.

2. Ibid., p. 311; Camilo Taufic, *Chile en la hoguera* (Buenos Aires: Corregidor, 1974), pp. 24, 26.

3. Henry H. Schulte, Jr., ed., *Facts on File Yearbook, 1973* (New York: Facts on File, 1974), p. 405.

4. Ibid., p. 475.

5. Ibid., p. 522; Robert J. Alexander, *The Tragedy of Chile* (Westport: Greenwood, 1978), p. 310; Robinson Rojas Sandford, *The Murder of Allende* (New York: Harper & Row, 1976), p. 158.

6. Schulte, p. 522.

7. Ibid., p. 564; Sigmund, p. 216.

8. Teresa Donoso Loero, ed., *Breve historia de la Unidad Popular, Documento de "El Mercurio"* (Santiago: El Mercurio, 1974), pp. 307, 331, 334, 356, 374.

9. Ibid., p. 416.

10. Carlos Prats, *Una vida por la legalidad* (Mexico: Fondo de Cultura Económica, 1976), pp. 43, 51.

11. Ibid., pp. 44–48.

12. Ibid., p. 50; Alexander, p. 311; Schulte, p. 405; Taufic, p. 24; *New York Times*, 6 May 1973, p. 7.

13. Rojas, pp. 112–13; Marlise Simons, "The Brazilian Connection," *Washington Post*, 6 January 1974, p. B3.

14. Schulte, p. 552.

15. Ibid.; *New York Times*, 22 June 1973, p. 3.

16. Rojas, p. 162; Donoso, p. 367; Jonathan Kandell, "Chile Declares Emergency in Capital after Disorders," *New York Times*, 28 June 1973, p. 18; *New York Times*, 29 June 1973, p. 28.

17. Secretaría de Gobierno, *Libro blanco del cambio de gobierno en Chile: 11 sep. 1973* (Santiago: Empresa Editora Nacional Gabriela Mistral, n.d.), p. 42. As described below, the document in the *Libro blanco* that describes Plan Z is probably a concoction. A number of other documents reproduced in the *Libro blanco* are almost surely genuine, however, and of interest.

18. Ibid., pp. 37ff., 41ff., 197.

19. Ibid., pp. 39ff.

20. Robert Moss, *Chile's Marxist Experiment* (Newton Abbot, England:

David & Charles, 1973), p. 101; *Libro blanco,* pp. 41, 43; *Foreign Broadcast Information Service,* Daily Report, Latin America and Western Europe, Paris AFP, 2031 GMT 23 Sept. 1973.

21. Moss, p. 101; Alexander, p. 264; *Libro blanco,* pp. 45ff.

22. Donoso, p. 362.

23. *Libro Blanco,* p. 25; Alexander, p. 229.

24. Rojas, p. 141; Sigmund, pp. 184, 227; Alexander, pp. 322–23.

25. For Castro's letter of 29 July 1973, see *Libro blanco,* pp. 73, 101–2; for Debray, see Taufic, p. 91.

26. *New York Times,* 22 June 1973, p. 3; Schulte, p. 552.

27. Sigmund, p. 211; according to Jorge Timossi, the Prensa Latina Bureau chief in Santiago, Garcés was a dual national of Spain and Chile.

28. See Alexander, pp. 309, 447.

29. Prats, p. 57.

30. The Junta's *Libro blanco,* p. 48, publishes a circular from Communist party regional headquarters for Santiago to its cells dated 30 June 1973, instructing each Communist to obtain a weapon and to take emergency supplies to the shantytowns. The purported instruction also says that specialized communist teams would eliminate opposition leaders and that water, electricity, and factories that could not be defended would be sabotaged. I do not know whether the circular can be regarded as authentic. In any case, the Communists' public line was hardening, as I reported to Washington at the time.

31. Florencia Varas and José Manuel Vergara, *Coup! Allende's Last Day* (New York: Stein & Day, 1975), p. 134.

32. Jack Anderson, "ITT Hope of Ousting Allende Remote," *Washington Post,* 28 March 1972, p. B11.

33. Juan de Onís, "Chile's Congress Sets CIA Inquiry," *New York Times,* 31 March 1972, p. 7; Rojas, pp. 49, 106. For another report of coup plotting in late 1971, see Thomas G. Sanders, "Military Government in Chile, Part I: The Coup," *Fieldstaff Reports,* vol. 22, no. 1, West Coast South America Series (Hanover, N.H.: American Universities Field Staff, 1975), p. 3.

34. Rojas, pp. 49, 114–15, 236, note 4; Sigmund, p. 181; Taufic, p. 21; Henry H. Schulte, Jr., ed., *Facts on File Yearbook, 1972* (New York: Facts on File, 1973), p. 706.

35. See also Jonathan Kandell, "Chilean Officers Tell How They Began to Plan the Take-Over Last November," *New York Times,* 27 September 1973, p. 3; Prats, p. 67.

36. Jonathan Kandell, "Plotting the Coup," in Laurence Birns, ed., *The End of Chilean Democracy* (New York: Seabury, 1974), p. 64.

37. Arturo Fontaine Aldunate and Cristián Zegers Ariztía, *Cómo llegaron las fuerzas armadas a la acción del 11 de septiembre de 1973?* (Santiago: El Mercurio, 11 September 1974), p. 4.

38. Ibid., p. 5.

39. "La acción del ejército en la liberación de Chile" (Santiago: historia inédita, circulated informally by senior Chilean army officers, n.d.), pp. 13–16; Sanders, p. 3; Sigmund, p. 170.

40. Interview with General Pinochet, *Ercilla,* 13–19 March, 1974, pp. 11, 14.

41. "La acción del ejército," pp. 13–16.

42. Fontaine and Zegers, p. 5; "La acción del ejército," pp. 17–20; John

Dinges and Saul Landau, *Assassination on Embassy Row* (New York: Pantheon, 1980), p. 52; interview with General Pinochet, *Ercilla*, pp. 11, 14. In the *Ercilla* interview Pinochet dates the shift in orientation to defensive-offensive operations as 28 May 1973, but his statement is somewhat ambiguous. "La acción del ejército," p. 6, says the shift from "defensive" to "offensive" planning was on 28 May 1973. The same publication, p. 17, says the shift proceeded, "step by step," starting in June, 1972, with the objective of "total planning" with an "absolutely offensive orientation."

43. "La acción del ejército," pp. 18–20.

44. Fontaine and Zegers, p. 5. For Pinochet's and the army's efforts to "rectify" their image, see "La acción del ejército"; *Ercilla*, 13–19 March 1974, pp. 11, 14; and other Pinochet postcoup interviews.

45. Fontaine and Zegers, pp. 4–5, 9–10.

46. Ibid., p. 4.

47. Kandell, "Chilean Officers Tell . . . ," p. 3.

48. Rojas, pp. 7, 195; *Ercilla*, 13–19 March 1974, p. 14.

49. Arturo Yovane, "From the Norambuena Building," *Qué Pasa*, 8–14 September, 1977, p. 34; Fontaine and Zegers, p. 7.

50. "La acción del ejército," p. 13; Douglas Edwards, CBS News, 3 P.M. EDT, 23 September 1974, Frank Manitzas interview with Col. Gerald Sills, U.S. Southern Command Intelligence Chief. I first learned of the purported Pinochet-Sills exchange after the CBS broadcast and do not have independent verification of its authenticity—nor any basis to dispute it.

51. Kandell, "Chilean Officers Tell . . . ," p. 3.

52. "The Eleventh, Hour by Hour," *Qué Pasa*, 10 September 1974; Sigmund, p. 312; Alexander, p. 334; "La acción del ejército," p. 22.

53. Sergio Arellano, "Preparations and Execution," *Qué Pasa*, 8–14 September 1977, p. 30.

54. Kandell, "Chilean Officers Tell . . . ," p. 3.

55. "La acción del ejército," p. 22.

56. Ibid., p. 23. Pinochet was still acting commander-in-chief, as Prats had not yet returned to his army duties.

57. Rojas, pp. 83–84; Miguel Enríquez, "The MIR Analyzes the Coup," in Birns, pp. 100ff.; interview with General Pinochet, *Ercilla*, pp. 11, 14; "La acción del ejército," p. 5–6.

58. Sigmund, p. 211; C. L. Sulzberger, "The Unmaking of a President," *New York Times*, 30 November 1975, sec. 4, p. 13. Pinochet claimed after the coup that he ordered the army's Academy of War to prepare a "game plan" for internal security in June but he probably gave this order the following month. See "La acción del ejército," pp. 27–28; Fontaine and Zegers, p. 12.

59. Thornton Wilder, *Theophilus North* (New York: Harper & Row, 1973), p. 14.

60. In Virginia Vidal's column, "No solo de pan" (Not by bread alone), *El Siglo*, 31 August 1972, p. 15.

61. *New York Times*, 4 September 1972, p. 16.

62. *Chicago Daily News*, 28–29 July 1973 (Associated Press report).

63. Missioners' Committee on International Awareness (Santiago, Chile), *Adentro Afuera*, no. 6 (May 1972), p. 3.

64. *Ultima Hora* quoted the *Business Week* figures in its issue of 2 November 1972. The August 1973 figure comes from my own records.

65. *El Mercurio*, 8 June 1973, p. 12; Rojas, p. 159. The TV station was an unlicensed subsidiary of Catholic University's Channel 13.

66. Taylor Branch and Eugene M. Propper, *Labyrinth* (New York: Viking 1982), p. 499.

67. Ibid., pp. 493, 500, and more generally 483–503. *El Siglo*, 8 June 1973, pp. 1, 9; *La Tercera de la Hora*, 8 June 1973, p. 35; *El Mercurio*, 8 June 1973, p. 12.

68. Frederick C. Schwarz, *You Can Trust the Communists* (Englewood Cliffs, N.J.: Prentice-Hall, 1960).

69. *New York Times*, 29 June 1973, p. 28; Jonathan Kandell, "Chilean Revolt Crushed as Army Backs Allende," *New York Times*, 30 June 1973, pp. 1, 17; Sigmund, p. 213; Fontaine and Zegers, pp. 7–8.

70. Patrick J. Ryan, *1000 Bungled Days* (New York: American-Chilean Council, November 1976), p. 7; Fontaine and Zegers, p. 7.

71. Alexander, p. 313.

72. Fontaine and Zegers, p. 9; Alexander, p. 313; Sigmund, p. 214; Kandell, "Chilean Revolt Crushed . . . ," pp. 1, 17. There is some dispute whether Allende told the workers to come out into the streets and to the center, or simply to mobilize in their factories. My daughter Margaret spent the morning listening to the radio, and she described what she heard to her diary as follows: "Allende said earlier for the workers to come out, but took it back. The Communist president of the CUT, Godoy, said for the workers to come out and go to the 'strategic places' of the city. I understand that is why the water and electricity was (and is) off for the Barrio Alto [Santiago's affluent suburb]." My own colleagues at the U.S. Embassy who had listened to the radio also told me when I arrived in the office that Allende had initially told the workers to come out in the streets and go to the center. This is also how Fontaine and Zegers and Alexander carry the text of Allende's appeal.

73. Prats, p. 59; Rojas, pp. 164–65; Fontaine and Zegers, p. 8.

74. Schulte, *1973*, p. 564; Sigmund, p. 216.

75. Sigmund, p. 215.

76. Alexander, pp. 314–15; Sigmund, p. 215.

77. Sigmund, p. 215; Alexander, p. 315.

78. Sigmund, p. 215.

79. Yovane, "From the Norambuena Building," p. 34.

80. *Ercilla*, 13–19 March 1974, p. 12. See also "La acción del ejército," pp. 25–27.

81. David F. Belnap, "2 Majorities Divide Chile against Itself," *Los Angeles Times*, 7 July 1973.

82. Dinges and Landau, p. 55.


**Chapter 8. The July–August Crisis**

1. The director general of the carabineros, José María Sepúlveda Galindo, was not removed, but his deputy was. President Allende took the opportunity presented by the absence from duty on the day of the tancazo of carabinero subdirector Arturo Viveros to remove him from that responsibility and appoint a more amenable carabinero general, Jorge Urrutia, as subdirector. Knowing

Viveros's views, Allende had delayed ten days before appointing him in early 1972.

2. Henry H. Schulte, Jr., ed., *Facts on File Yearbook, 1973* (New York: Facts on File, 1974), pp. 523, 552.

3. Teresa Donoso Loero, ed., *Breve historia de la Unidad Popular: Documento de "El Mercurio"* (Santiago: El Mercurio, 1974), p. 369.

4. Arturo Fontaine Aldunate and Cristián Zegers Ariztía, *Cómo llegaron las fuerzas armadas a la acción del 11 septiembre de 1973?* (Santiago: El Mercurio, 11 September 1974), p. 9.

5. Robinson Rojas Sandford, *The Murder of Allende* (New York: Harper & Row, 1976), pp. 166–167, 172; "La acción del ejército en la liberación de Chile" (Santiago: Historia inédita, circulated informally by senior Chilean army officers, n.d.), p. 26.

6. The carabineros were not technically a "military service" and not part of the formal national defense establishment. Chilean marines had considerably less autonomy from the navy than the U.S. Marine Corps enjoys.

7. Fontaine and Zegers, p. 10. See also Sergio Arellano, "Preparations and Execution," *Qué Pasa,* 8–14 September 1977, p. 30; and Arturo Valenzuela, *The Breakdown of Democratic Regimes: Chile* (Baltimore: Johns Hopkins University Press, 1978), p. 100.

8. See Rojas, pp. 166–67, 172.

9. Fontaine and Zegers, pp. 10–11, 14.

10. Schulte, p. 648.

11. Fontaine and Zegers, p. 11.

12. Thomas G. Sanders, "Military Government in Chile, Part I: The Coup," *Fieldstaff Reports,* vol. 22, no. 1, West Coast South America Series (Hanover, N.H.: American Universities Field Staff, 1975), p. 5.

13. Schulte, p. 648.

14. *Qué Pasa,* 8–14 September 1977, p. 30; Camilo Taufic, *Chile en la hoguera* (Buenos Aires: Corregidor, 1974), p. 114; Fontaine and Zegers, p. 11.

15. *Ercilla,* 13–19 March 1974, pp. 12, 14–15; Paul E. Sigmund, *The Overthrow of Allende and the Politics of Chile, 1964–1973* (Pittsburgh: University of Pittsburgh Press, 1977), p. 313, note 24; Florencia Varas and José Manuel Vergara, *Coup! Allende's Last Day* (New York: Stein & Day, 1975), p. 56.

16. *Qué Pasa,* 8–14 September 1977, p. 15; Fontaine and Zegers, p. 11.

17. Schulte, p. 648; Donoso, pp. 380, 382.

18. Robert J. Alexander, *The Tragedy of Chile* (Westport: Greenwood, 1978), p. 321.

19. Figures given for the number of trucks requisitioned in the first several days vary from approximately 900 to over 1200. Alexander, p. 322; *Foreign Broadcast Information Service,* Daily Report, Latin American and Western Europe, Madrid EFE, 0243 GMT 2 Aug. 1973.

20. Another allegation was that a member of the GAP by the name of Blanco, whose pseudonym was César, was implicated. *Qué Pasa,* 10 September 1974, p. 26. See also John Dinges and Saul Landau, *Assassination on Embassy Row* (New York: Pantheon, 1980), p. 56; Rojas, p. 174; Sigmund, pp. 222–23; Fontaine and Zegers, p. 13.

21. *FBIS,* Santiago PRELA, 1640 GMT 4 Aug. 1973; Havana Domestic Service, 1013 GMT 2 Aug. 1973; Santiago PRELA, 0035 GMT 5 Aug. 1973; Havana PRELA, 1843 GMT 4 Aug. 1973; Havana PRELA, 2253 GMT 7 Aug. 1973.

22. Schulte, p. 648.

23. Donoso, pp. 390–92, 398.

24. Ibid., pp. 389–90.

25. Donoso, pp. 392–93.

26. Ibid., p. 393.

27. Carlos Prats, *Una vida por la legalidad* (Mexico: Fondo de Cultura Económica, 1976), p. 68; Donoso, pp. 394–95.

28. *FBIS*, Santiago PRELA, 1324 GMT 6 Aug. 1973; 8 Aug., p. E12.

29. *La Segunda*, Santiago, 7 August 1973; *New York Times*, 8 August 1973, p. 10; Sigmund, p. 225; Secretaría de Gobierno, *Libro blanco del cambio de gobierno en Chile: 11 sep. 1973* (Santiago: Empresa Editora Nacional Gabriela Mistral, n.d.), p. 73; Prats, pp. 72–75.

30. Donoso, p. 395; Sigmund, p. 226; Alexander, pp. 276, 325–26; Taufic, pp. 27–28, 212–14; Fontaine and Zegers, p. 14.

31. Prats, pp. 68–70.

32. Ibid., p. 70; Marvine Howe, "Incidents in Chile Sharpening Allende-Armed Forces Conflict," *New York Times*, 8 August 1973, p. 10; Fontaine and Zegers, p. 14.

33. Arellano, p. 30.

34. Fontaine and Zegers, p. 14.

35. Prats, pp. 70–71. Quotations in the next six paragraphs are from ibid., pp. 71–73.

36. Quoted in Taufic, pp. 38–40.

37. Fontaine and Zegers, p. 13.

38. *Qué Pasa*, 8–14 September 1977, p. 30. Leigh, Herrera, Viveros, and Díaz were from the air force, and Arellano, Palacios, and Nuño were army men. This Arturo Viveros was not the carabinero subdirector mentioned in note 1.

39. These allegations are discussed in chapter 12.

40. *Ultima Hora*'s articles of 13 August 1973 were also repeating allegations made in the same newspaper on 7 August to the effect that the CIA was financing anti-UP plots.

41. Henry Kissinger, *Years of Upheaval* (Boston: Little, Brown, 1982), p. 402.

42. My suspicion at the time was that the Chilean government might want to assign agents to accompany me for my "protection"—with the real purpose of watching my movements and reporting on my activities. No such assignments were proposed, however, and the Chilean government took no further action that I know of in this regard.

43. Marvine Howe, "Allende Cabinet Orders Strong Steps to Curb Violence and End Truckers' Strike," *New York Times*, 15 August 1973, p. 10.

44. Donoso, pp. 402–4; Taufic, p. 29.

45. Prats, p. 73.

46. *New York Times*, 25 June 1973, p. 32.

47. Ibid., 18 August 1973, p. 20.

48. *Washington Star-News*, 27 August 1973, editorial page.

49. Donoso, pp. 404–5; Sanders, p. 5; Prats, p. 74; Sigmund, p. 229; Fontaine and Zegers, pp. 14–15.

50. Taufic, p. 29; Donoso, p. 404; Jonathan Kandell, "Chilean Officers Tell How They Began to Plan the Take-Over Last November," *New York Times*, 27 September 1973, p. 3; Fontaine and Zegers, p. 15; Sigmund, pp. 229, 231.

51. Sigmund, p. 229; Donoso, p. 405. This Sunday was the day on which Régis Debray spent some hours with the president relaxing at El Arrayán, a scene the French Marxist described a few days after the coup. Taufic, pp. 89–91.

52. Prats, pp. 74–75; Taufic, p. 90; Donoso, p. 405; Sigmund, p. 231; Rojas, pp. 14–15; Donald Freed and Fred Simon Landis, *Death in Washington* (Westport: Hill, 1980), p. 122.

53. Prats, pp. 75, 88–89; Sigmund, p. 229.

54. Donoso, p. 403.

55. Ibid., p. 407. It is alleged that the Christian Democrats' Corporation for Social, Economic and Cultural Studies planned the provocation of Prats. Marlise Simons, "The Brazilian Connection," *Washington Post*, 6 January 1974, p. 83.

56. As recounted to Isabel Letelier and recorded by Dinges and Landau, pp. 56–57.

57. Prats, pp. 76–77.

58. Ibid., p. 77.

59. Ibid. Pinochet's tactful euphemism for a coup attempt was "if normality in the country were broken."

60. Ibid., pp. 76, 77–78.

61. Sigmund, pp. 231, 237, 314; Kandell, p. 3.

62. Prats, p. 78.

63. According to "La acción del ejército," p. 31, they retired in anticipation of being relieved.

64. Prats, p. 78; Sanders, p. 5; *Ercilla*, 29 August–4 September 1973, p. 7.

65. Donoso, pp. 407–8.

66. *Libro blanco*, p. 215; Alexander, pp. 319–20. The next five paragraphs are based on *Libro blanco*, pp. 216–18, 231–34, 235–36, and 239–42.

67. *New York Times*, 28 August 1973, p. 9.

68. Ibid., 27 August 1973, p. 12.

69. Ibid., 29 August 1973, p. 12.

70. Kandell, p. 3. Kandell goes on to quote his military informants as having said that nothing could have stopped the coup after Prats's resignation, but I believe that the coup could probably have been stopped had the military leaders' conditions or those of the Christian Democrats been met. See also Prats, p. 80; *Ercilla*, 27–28 August 1973, pp. 7–8 (quoted in Sigmund, p. 312, note 1). Paul E. Sigmund holds a view similar to the one I express in this note; see his article in the *Princeton Weekly Bulletin*, 13 February 1978, p. 4. See also *New York Times* editorial, 31 August 1973, p. 24.

71. Sigmund, *The Overthrow of Allende*, p. 314; *FBIS*, Madrid EFE, 0236 GMT 31 Aug. 1973; and Santiago SOPESUR, 0110 GMT 1 Sept. 1973.

72. *FBIS*, Paris AFP 2106 GMT 6 Sept. 1973.

73. Donoso, p. 409; *New York Times*, 29 August 1973, p. 9.

74. Prats, p. 88; Kissinger, p. 410.

75. *FBIS*, Havana PRELA, 0154 GMT 31 Aug. 1973; "La acción del ejército," pp. 31–37.

76. "La acción del ejército," p. 39.

77. Donoso, p. 409; *New York Times*, 2 September 1973, p. 3; *Libro blanco*, p. 69.

78. Donoso, p. 412; *El Mercurio*, 9 September 1973, p. 11.

79. Genaro Arriagada Herrera, *De la "vía chilena" a la "vía insurreccional"* (Santiago: Editorial del Pacifico/Instituto de Estudios Políticos, 1974), p. 319; *Qué Pasa,* 10 September 1974, p. 20; *Economist,* 13 October 1973, p. 44; Sigmund, pp. 237–38 and 315, note 11; Rojas, p. 176.

80. Sigmund, p. 238; Donoso, pp. 410–11; *New York Times,* 2 September 1973, p. 3.

81. Donoso, p. 410; *FBIS,* Santiago PRELA, 1718 GMT 3 Sept. 1973.

### Chapter 9. Ten Days That Shook Chile

1. *Foreign Broadcast Information Service,* Daily Report, Latin America and Western Europe, Santiago PRELA, 2330 GMT 1 Sept. 1973.

2. Ibid.

3. Ibid., Santiago PRELA, 2206 GMT 1 Sept. 1973; Jonathan Kandell, "Chilean Officers Tell How They Began to Plan the Take-Over Last November," *New York Times,* 27 September 1973, p. 3; Arturo Fontaine Aldunate and Cristián Zegers Ariztía, *Cómo llegaron las fuerzas armadas a la acción del 11 de septiembre de 1973?* (Santiago: El Mercurio, 11 September 1974), p. 19.

4. *FBIS,* Santiago PRELA, 2229 GMT 4 Sept. 1973; Teresa Donoso Loero, ed., *Breve historia de la Unidad Popular: Documento de "El Mercurio"* (Santiago: El Mercurio, 1974), pp. 412–13.

5. *FBIS,* Paris AFP, 1511 GMT 2 Sept. 1973.

6. Ibid., Santiago PRELA, 2229 GMT 4 Sept. 1973.

7. Ibid., Madrid EFE, 1939 GMT 3 Sept. 1973.

8. Camilo Taufic, *Chile en la hoguera* (Buenos Aires: Corregidor, 1974), p. 32.

9. Fontaine and Zegers, p. 19.

10. Ibid.

11. *FBIS,* Santiago PRELA, 1718 GMT 3 Sept. 1973; and Paris AFP, 0231 GMT 4 Sept. 1973; Donoso, p. 413; Patrick J. Ryan, *1000 Bungled Days* (New York: American-Chilean Council, November 1976), p. 8; Carlos Prats, *Una vida por la legalidad* (Mexico: Fondo de Cultura Económica, 1976), p. 89.

12. *FBIS,* Santiago, Chile, Domestic Service, 0200 GMT 5 Sept. 1973; John Dinges and Saul Landau, *Assassination on Embassy Row* (New York: Pantheon, 1980), p. 58; Taufic, pp. 32, 41.

13. *FBIS,* Buenos Aires ANSA, 1533 GMT 4 Sept. 1973; and Buenos Aires LATIN, 0307 GMT 4 Sept. 1973.

14. Ibid., Santiago SOPESUR, 0104 GMT 6 Sept. 1973; Santiago PRELA, 0314 GMT 5 Sept. 1973; Santiago PRELA, 1932 GMT 5 Sept. 1973; Paris AFP, 2106 GMT 6 Sept. 1973; Santiago, Chile Domestic Service, 2314 GMT 6 Sept. 1973.

15. Ibid., Havana PRELA, 2350 GMT 5 Sept. 1973; Buenos Aires ANSA, 0504 GMT 5 Sept. 1973.

16. Ibid., Santiago PRELA, 0314 GMT 5 Sept. 1973; Donoso, p. 414; Genaro Arriagada Herrera, *De la "vía chilena" a la "vía insurreccional"* (Santiago: Editorial del Pacífico/Instituto de Estudios Políticos, 1974), pp. 319–20.

17. *FBIS,* Santiago PRELA, 0314 GMT 5 Sept. 1973; Santiago PRELA, 1957 GMT 5 Sept. 1973.

18. Ibid., Buenos Aires LATIN, 1835 GMT 4 Sept. 1973; Santiago PRELA, 0100 GMT 5 Sept. 1973; Prats, pp. 89–90.

19. *FBIS*, Buenos Aires ANSA, 1602 GMT 5 Sept. 1973.

20. Donoso, p. 414; Paul E. Sigmund, *The Overthrow of Allende and the Politics of Chile, 1964–1976* (Pittsburgh: University of Pittsburgh Press, 1977), p. 238; Laurence Birns, ed., *The End of Chilean Democracy* (New York: Seabury, 1974), pp. 206–7; *FBIS*, Buenos Aires LATIN, 0014 GMT 6 Sept. 1973; and Paris AFP, 0246 GMT 6 Sept. 1973; Secretaría de Gobierno, *Libro blanco del cambio de gobierno en Chile: 11 sep. 1973* (Santiago: Empresa Editora Nacional Gabriela Mistral, n.d.), p. 27.

21. *FBIS*, Havana PRELA, 2351 GMT 5 Sept. 1973; Paris AFP, 2106 GMT 6 Sept. 1973.

22. "La acción del ejército en la liberación de Chile" (Santiago: Historia inédita, circulated informally by senior Chilean army officers, n.d.), pp. 38–39.

23. Ibid., p. 39.

24. *Ercilla*, 13–19 March 1974, pp. 12, 15.

25. *FBIS*, 6 Sept. 1973, p. E5; Buenos Aires IPS, 2018 GMT 8 Sept. 1973; Santiago Radio Portales, 1100 GMT 10 Sept. 1973.

26. Ibid., Santiago, Chile Domestic Service, 2314 GMT 6 Sept. 1973; Santiago PRELA, 0005 GMT 7 Sept. 1973; Paris AFP, 0446 GMT 7 Sept. 1973.

27. Ibid., Santiago, Radio Balmaceda, 0025 GMT 6 Sept. 1973; Santiago SOPESUR, 0037 GMT 7 Sept. 1973; Buenos Aires LATIN, 0416 GMT 7 Sept. 1973.

28. Ibid., Santiago PRELA, 0244 GMT 8 Sept. 1973.

29. *Qué Pasa*, 10 September 1974, p. 21.

30. "La acción del ejército," pp. 39–40.

31. *Qué Pasa*, 8–14 September 1977, p. 30.

32. *FBIS*, Santiago, Chile Domestic Service, 2314 GMT 6 Sept. 1973.

33. *Qué Pasa*, 8–14 September 1977, p. 34; Sigmund, p. 239.

34. *Qué Pasa*, 10 September 1974, p. 21, and 8–14 September 1977, p. 34. The reason for the army officers' meeting, which appears in brackets, is given by the editors of *Qué Pasa* immediately following General Yovane's quoted statement. (This General Viveros should not be confused with the carabinero General Viveros.) Allende was correct in thinking that Palacios, Viveros, and Arellano were plotting.

35. *Qué Pasa*, 8–14 September 1977, p. 30.

36. *FBIS*, Santiago, Radio Corporación, 0205 GMT 8 Sept. 1973; Buenos Aires LATIN, 1600 GMT 7 Sept. 1973.

37. Ibid., Santiago PRELA, 0244 GMT 8 Sept. 1973; Ryan, p. 8; Sigmund, p. 240; Fontaine and Zegers, pp. 19–20.

38. Sigmund, p. 240.

39. Ibid., p. 239.

40. *Qué Pasa*, 10 September 1974, pp. 10ff.

41. Ibid.; Sigmund, pp. 239–40; Robinson Rojas Sandford, *The Murder of Allende* (New York: Harper & Row, 1976), pp. 191, 253.

42. Donoso, p. 415; *FBIS*, Santiago PRELA, 2025 GMT 8 Sept. 1973. According to Jorge Timossi, *Grandes alamedas: el combate del Presidente Allende* (Havana: Editorial de Ciencias Sociales, 1974), p. 28, the air force had provoked the encounter.

43. Donoso, p. 416; *FBIS*, Santiago PRELA, 2025 GMT 8 Sept. 1973; Buenos Aires LATIN, 0012 GMT 9 Sept. 1973.

44. *FBIS*, Santiago SOPESUR, 0102 GMT 9 Sept. 1973.

45. "La acción del ejército," p. 40, describes Pinochet passing Saturday and Sunday morning in his accustomed pursuits, implying that his objective was to avoid arousing UP government suspicions. The contrast between Pinochet's quietude and the agitation and excitement Arellano describes is close to incredible. For other hints of Pinochet's reservations about the plotting, see Taufic, p. 53, and Sigmund, p. 242. Interview with Gen. Sergio Arellano, *Qué Pasa*, 8–14 September 1977, p. 31.

46. Fontaine and Zegers, p. 20.

47. Ryan, p. 8 and back leaf; interview with Vice Adm. Arturo Troncoso, *Qué Pasa*, 8–14 September 1977, p. 29.

48. Donoso, p. 416; *FBIS*, Santiago PRELA, 1850 GMT 9 Sept. 1973.

49. *FBIS*, 10 Sept. 1973, pp. E4–E5.

50. *FBIS*, Santiago PRELA, 2346 GMT 7 Sept. 1973; Madrid EFE, 1658 GMT 9 Sept. 1973; Donoso, p. 416.

51. Ibid., Santiago PRELA, 1845 GMT 9 Sept. 1973; Arriagada, pp. 320–21; Sigmund, p. 241; Robert J. Alexander, *The Tragedy of Chile* (Westport: Greenwood, 1978), pp. 287, 326.

52. Alexander, pp. 327–28; Sigmund, p. 241.

53. Alexander, p. 328.

54. Ibid., p. 335. General Leigh said in an interview that Altamirano's speech crucially influenced the final decision by Pinochet, navy representatives, and himself to mount the coup. Leigh had the date of Altamirano's speech wrong by one day, however, and Merino's decision had already been made when Altamirano spoke. Nevertheless, the speech could have influenced the discussion at Pinochet's house on Sunday afternoon. Interview in the Brazilian magazine *Visão*, 25 February 1974, as quoted in Thomas G. Sanders, "Military Government in Chile, Part I: The Coup," *Fieldstaff Reports, vol. 22, no. 1, West Coast South America Series* (Hanover, N.H.: American Universities Field Staff, 1975), p. 9.

55. *FBIS*, Santiago PRELA, 0128 GMT 11 Sept. 1973.

56. Fontaine and Zegers, p. 20. The meeting at Weber's house is described here, and the anecdote about the toll booth is also reproduced here in its essentials.

57. *Qué Pasa*, 8–14 September 1977, p. 15; *Economist*, 13 October 1973, p. 48; Ryan, p. 9. "Gustavo" is Gustavo Leigh; "Augusto" is Augusto Pinochet; "J.T." is José Toribio Merino, as is "Pepe."

58. "La acción del ejército," p. 40–41.

59. Ibid., p. 40.

60. Fontaine and Zegers, p. 20. "La acción del ejército," p. 43, indicates that Pinochet came upon this rationale the following morning.

61. *Qué Pasa*, 8–14 September 1977, p. 15; *Ercilla*, 7–13 November 1973, pp. 14ff; Fontaine and Zegers, p. 20. In an interview on 22 September 1973 Leigh affirmed that the decision to overthrow Allende was "made" on the ninth and, as a result, on the eleventh the military leadership "had no plans for governing the country." *FBIS*, Buenos Aires LATIN, 2117 GMT 22 Sept. 1973.

62. Donoso, p. 416; *FBIS* Santiago PRELA, 1028 GMT 11 Sept. 1973; Buenos Aires ANSA, 0045 GMT 11 Sept. 1973.

63. *FBIS*, Santiago PRELA, 1838 GMT 10 Sept. 1973.

64. Dinges and Landau, p. 60.

65. Ibid., p. 59.

66. Dinges and Landau, pp. 59–60; *FBIS*, Santiago PRELA, 1900 GMT 10 Sept. 1973; Timossi, p. 25.

67. *Qué Pasa*, 8–14 September 1977, p. 32; Dinges and Landau, pp. 60–61; Rojas, p. 189.

68. Donald Freed and Fred Simon Landis, *Death in Washington* (Westport: Hill, 1980), p. 120; *Qué Pasa*, 10 September 1974, p. 21; Taufic, p. 67.

69. Florencia Varas, "Last Feverish Hours of Allende Regime," *Times* (London), 6 November 1973, p. 10; Sigmund, p. 241. Timossi, p. 29, describes the themes Allende planned to cover in his speech.

70. Taufic, p. 67.

71. Sigmund, p. 242.

72. Fontaine and Zegers, pp. 20–21; "La acción del ejército," pp. 43–44.

73. Fontaine and Zegers, p. 21; "La acción del ejército," pp. 44–46.

74. Fontaine and Zegers, p. 21.

75. *Qué Pasa*, 8–14 September 1977, p. 31.

76. Ibid., p. 15.

77. "La acción del ejército," p. 46.

78. *La Opinión* (Buenos Aires), 5 October 1973, as reported in Rojas, p. 253; *Economist*, 13 October 1973, p. 48; and "La acción del ejército," pp. 41–42, 46. Reportedly, General Torres de la Cruz was brought up again from Punta Arenas for last-minute consultations.

79. Kandell, p. 3.

80. Rojas, pp. 187, 191; Taufic, p. 109.

81. Sigmund, p. 241.

82. Florencia Varas and José Manuel Vergara, *Coup! Allende's Last Day* (New York: Stein & Day, 1975), p. 22; *Qué Pasa*, 10 September 1974, pp. 21ff.

83. Varas and Vergara, pp. 123, 125; Sigmund, pp. 239–41; Fontaine and Zegers, p. 21.

84. For example, see Freed and Landis, p. 22.

85. Prats, p. 77.

86. Ibid., p. 92.

87. Rojas, pp. 16, 139; Dinges and Landau, p. 57; Freed and Landis, p. 22.

88. Dinges and Landau, p. 60.

89. C. L. Sulzberger, "The Unmaking of a President," *New York Times*, 30 November 1975, sec. 4, p. 13.

90. *Qué Pasa*, 8–14 September 1977, p. 25.

91. Fontaine and Zegers, p. 11. "La acción del ejército," p. 27, carries the same statement but does not attribute the vision to Pinochet directly.

92. Ibid., p. 12.

93. Sigmund, pp. 231, 237, 314; Rojas, p. 178.

94. Freed and Landis, pp. 129–30.

95. Henry H. Schulte, Jr., ed., *Facts on File Yearbook, 1971* (New York: Facts on File, 1972), p. 980.

96. See *Ercilla*, 13–19 March 1974, pp. 14–15; "La acción del ejército," pp. 9, 31, 43.

**Chapter 10. The Longest Day**

1. Camilo Taufic, Chile en la hoguera (Buenos Aires: Corregidor, 1974), p. 65. That is also how I remember the weather.
2. Arturo Fontaine Aldunate and Cristián Zegers Ariztía, Cómo llegaron las fuerzas armadas a la acción del 11 de septiembre de 1973? (Santiago: El Mercurio, 11 September 1974), p. 21; Samuel Chavkin, The Murder of Chile (New York: Everest, 1982), pp. 17–19; Donald Freed and Fred Simon Landis, Death in Washington (Westport: Hill, 1980), p. 19; Paul E. Sigmund, The Overthrow of Allende and the Politics of Chile, 1964–1976 (Pittsburgh: University of Pittsburgh Press, 1977), p. 242; Marta Sánchez and Lillian Calm, "El once, hora por hora," Qué Pasa, 10 September 1974, p. 21; Florencia Varas, "Last Feverish Hours of Allende Regime," Times (London), 6 November 1973, p. 10; Philippe Chesnay, "La vérité sur la mort d'Allende," Paris Match, 30 September 1983, pp. 3–9. (A slightly more extended version appeared in Cosas (Santiago), October 1983, pts. 1–2, pp. 66–68, 56–59.) Chesnay says two army trucks loaded with troops jumped the gun and blocked the Chacabuco tunnel between Los Andes and Santiago.
3. John Dinges and Saul Landau, Assassination on Embassy Row (New York: Pantheon, 1980), p. 61; Freed and Landis, pp. 89–90; Chavkin, pp. 20–21.
4. Dinges and Landau, pp. 61–62.
5. Ibid., p. 61; Sánchez and Calm, p. 21.
6. El Siglo, 11 September 1973, p. 1; Sánchez and Calm, p. 25.
7. Judy White, ed., Chile's Days of Terror (New York: Pathfinder, 1974), p. 65.
8. Chavkin, p. 19; Sánchez and Calm, p. 21.
9. Qué Pasa, 8–14 September 1977, p. 34.
10. Ercilla, 13–19 March 1974, p. 15. See also Secretaría de Gobierno, Libro blanco del cambio de gobierno en Chile: 11 sep. 1973 (Santiago: Empresa Editora Nacional Gabriela Mistral, n.d.), p. 47, for surveillance of military officers.
11. Sánchez and Calm, p. 21.
12. Varas, p. 10.
13. Dinges and Landau, p. 62.
14. Sánchez and Calm. p. 21; Qué Pasa, 8–14 September 1977, p. 31; Sigmund, p. 241.
15. Sánchez and Calm, p. 21.
16. Sigmund, p. 242.
17. Sánchez and Calm, p. 20; Florencia Varas and José Manuel Vergara, Coup! Allende's Last Day (New York: Stein & Day, 1975), p. 125; Ercilla, 13–19 March 1974, p. 12.
18. Robinson Rojas Sandford, The Murder of Allende (New York: Harper & Row, 1976), p. 253; Varas and Vergara, p. 23; Qué Pasa, 8–14 September 1977, p. 29; Fontaine and Zegers, p. 21.
19. Sánchez and Calm, p. 20; Rojas, p. 253; Qué Pasa, 8–14 September 1977, p. 29; Fontaine and Zegers. p. 22.
20. Taufic, p. 90.
21. Chavkin, p. 30; Varas and Vergara, p. 50; Sánchez and Calm, p. 20;

Fontaine and Zegers, p. 22. Rojas, pp. 190–91, also describes the seizure of Valparaíso, but he seems to have the time wrong.

22. Varas and Vergara, p. 25; Chavkin, p. 19; Sánchez and Calm, p. 23; *Qué Pasa*, 8–14 September 1977, p. 29; Freed and Landis, p. 19; Fontaine and Zegers, pp. 21–22. Chesnay, p. 67, implies that Eugenio Sepúlveda was the carabinero officer who called Urrutia from Valparaíso.

23. Taufic, p. 69; Sánchez and Calm, p. 22; *Foreign Broadcast Information Service*, Daily Report, Latin America and Western Europe, Madrid EFE, 1345 GMT 11 Sept. 1973 (for Santiago local time, subtract four hours from Greenwich Mean Time, GMT).

24. Varas, p. 10; Taufic, p. 78; Chavkin, p. 118; Sánchez and Calm, p. 23; "La acción del ejército en la liberación de Chile" (Santiago: Historia inédita, circulated informally by senior Chilean Army officers, n.d.), p. 47; Chesnay, p. 68.

25. Dinges and Landau, pp. 62–63; Freed and Landis, pp. 19–20; Taylor Branch and Eugene M. Propper, *Labyrinth* (New York: Viking, 1982), pp. 63–64.

26. Freed and Landis, p. 90. See also *Qué Pasa*, 10 September 1974, p. 22; Fontaine and Zegers, p. 22.

27. Dinges and Landau, p. 63.

28. Freed and Landis, p. 94; Sánchez and Calm, p. 32.

29. Fontaine and Zegers, p. 22; Varas and Vergara, pp. 44–45; Sánchez and Calm, pp. 25, 27. The MIR-oriented station Radio Nacional, was seized by troops at 7:24 A.M.

30. Varas and Vergara, p. 45.

31. Sánchez and Calm. p. 23.

32. Ibid., p. 22; Fontaine and Zegers, p. 22.

33. Sánchez and Calm, p. 22; *Qué Pasa*, 8–14 September 1977, p. 31; Fontaine and Zegers, p. 22.

34. Chavkin, p. 30; see also Sánchez and Calm, p. 25, and Fontaine and Zegers, p. 22.

35. *Qué Pasa*, 8–14 September 1977, p. 15; Sánchez and Calm, pp. 27–28.

36. *Qué Pasa*, 8–14 September 1977, pp. 25, 34; Sánchez and Calm, p. 31; Varas and Vergara, p. 34.

37. *Ercilla*, 13–19 March 1974, pp. 12, 16; "La acción del ejército," p. 47.

38. "La acción del ejército," p. 47. See also Chesnay, p. 56.

39. Sánchez and Calm, p. 23; *Qué Pasa*, 8–14 September 1977, pp. 25–26; Fontaine and Zegers, p. 22.

40. Sánchez and Calm, p. 23; Freed and Landis, pp. 19–20; Chesnay, p. 68. The *Almirante Latorre* was the ship alleged to have been involved in the naval "mutiny."

41. Taufic, p. 69; Fontaine and Zegers, p. 22; Chavkin, pp. 30–31; Sánchez and Calm, p. 25; Varas, p. 10; Varas and Vergara, p. 40; Freed and Landis, p. 20; Chesnay, p. 68.

42. Taufic, pp. 70–78; Sánchez and Calm, pp. 25, 27; Chavkin, p. 37; Freed and Landis, pp. 21, 121. In an interview on 19 September 1973 in Mexico City, Mrs. Allende gave essentially the same account of the president's call to her as appears in the text. See *New York Times*, 20 September 1973, p. 3. According to Chesnay, p. 68, Allende also told Calderón to shut down *El Mercurio* and the

opposition's radios, but Chesnay's sources were military officers who would have had an interest in putting the president in a bad light.

43. Sánchez and Calm, p. 23; Fontaine and Zegers, p. 22.

44. Dinges and Landau, pp. 63–64. See also Freed and Landis, p. 90.

45. Freed and Landis, p. 92.

46. Sánchez and Calm, pp. 25, 27; Taufic, p. 70. Radio Agricultura broadcast a second flash at about 7:25 A.M. reporting the presence of carabinero troops outside the Moneda.

47. Varas and Vergara, p. 78. See also Sigmund, p. 229 and Dinges and Landau, p. 60.

48. Taufic, p. 91.

49. Sigmund, p. 186.

50. Sánchez and Calm, pp. 25, 29.

51. Ibid., p. 27.

52. Ibid., p. 25; Varas, p. 10.

53. Dinges and Landau, p. 64.

54. *FBIS*, Buenos Aires, 1302 GMT 11 Sept. 1973; Buenos Aires ANSA, 1354 GMT 11 Sept. 1973; Chavkin, p. 41; Freed and Landis, p. 21; Sánchez and Calm, p. 27; Taufic, pp. 67, 70; "La acción del ejército," p. 48; Fontaine and Zegers, p. 22; Chesnay, p. 68; Jorge Timossi, *Grandes alamedas: El combate del Presidente Allende* (Havana: Editorial de Ciencias Sociales, 1974), pp. 63, 73.

55. Taufic, p. 70; Freed and Landis, p. 21.

56. Dinges and Landau, p. 65; Freed and Landis, p. 21; Chesnay, p. 68.

57. Sigmund, p. 242; Taufic, p. 70; Chavkin, p. 19; Dinges and Landau, pp. 64–65; Freed and Landis, pp. 18–19, 21. Mrs. Allende describes the president calling the military "cowards and traitors," although she has Allende talking by phone with Pinochet. See Mrs. Allende's Mexico City interview of 19 September 1973, reported in the *New York Times*, 20 September 1973, p. 3. A Colombian journalist, Juan Gossaín, has essentially the same account. Gossaín, *Cromos* (Bogotá), vol. 141, 24 September 1973, p. 4.

58. Chavkin, p. 36; Sigmund, p. 243; *FBIS*, Havana PRELA, 1321 GMT 11 Sept. 1973; Madrid EFE, 1342 GMT 11 Sept. 1973; Chesnay, p. 56; Gossaín, pp. 2, 4. The quotation is a reconstruction of fragments taken from the sources. Timossi (pp. 73–74) quotes Joan Garcés as saying there was at least one and perhaps two additional broadcasts which may not have gotten on the air.

59. Sánchez and Calm, p. 27.

60. *FBIS*, 11 Sept. 1973, p. E12; White, p. 66.

61. Sánchez and Calm. p. 27. My family listened to the pro-UP stations, and my elder daughter kept a record of what they said.

62. Freed and Landis, p. 169.

63. White, p. 77.

64. Sánchez and Calm, p. 22; Taufic, p. 67; Freed and Landis, p. 20.

65. Chavkin, pp. 30, 33; Sánchez and Calm, p. 27; Varas, p. 10; Varas and Vergara, p. 34.

66. Sánchez and Calm, p. 27; Taufic, p. 95.

67. Dinges and Landau, p. 64.

68. Sánchez and Calm, p. 28; *Qué Pasa*, 8–14 September 1977, p. 15.

69. *FBIS*, Buenos Aires LATIN, 1315 GMT 11 Sept. 1973; Buenos Aires LATIN, 1445 GMT 11 Sept. 1973; *Qué Pasa*, 8–14 September 1977, p. 26; Freed and Landis, p. 221; Fontaine and Zegers, p. 23; Teresa Donoso Loero, ed., *Breve*

*historia de la Unidad Popular: Documento de "El Mercurio"* (Santiago: El Mercurio, 1974), pp. 416–17.

70. Dinges and Landau, p. 65; Sánchez and Calm, pp. 28–29.
71. Sánchez and Calm, p. 29.
72. Varas and Vergara, p. 41.
73. Chavkin, p. 41; Sánchez and Calm, p. 29.
74. Sánchez and Calm, p. 29.
75. Chavkin, p. 32.
76. Taufic, p. 59; Sánchez and Calm, pp. 25, 29.
77. Chesny, p. 56.
78. Luis Renato González Córdoba, as quoted in Laurence Birns, ed., *The End of Chilean Democracy* (New York: Seabury, 1974), p. 36. The González account contains numerous inaccuracies, but this particular statement appears credible. See also Taufic, p. 70.
79. Taufic, p. 70.
80. Sánchez and Calm, p. 32.
81. Chavkin, p. 36; *FBIS*, Santiago, Radio Cooperativa [Editorial Report], 1316 GMT 11 Sept. 1973.
82. *Qué Pasa*, 8–14 September 1977, p. 34; Taufic, p. 95.
83. Varas, p. 10; Varas and Vergara, p. 61; Taufic, p. 59.
84. Freed and Landis, p. 24; Varas and Vergara, p. 58; Taufic, p. 59.
85. Sánchez and Calm, p. 29; Varas and Vergara, p. 42; Taufic, p. 63; Fontaine and Zegers, p. 23.
86. Taufic, pp. 59, 67, and my daughter's records.
87. Varas and Vergara, p. 44. See also Taufic, p. 61.
88. For the Spanish version, see Taufic, pp. 268–69, and Florencia Varas and José Manuel Vergara, *Operación Chile* (Buenos Aires: Pomaire, 1974), pp. 75–77. For versions in English, see Varas and Vergara, *Coup!* pp. 51–53; Freed and Landis, pp. 98–99; Birns, pp. 30–32. Allende's appeal to the people not to "sacrifice" themselves appears to have been edited out of the text published by Birns, perhaps to avoid depicting the president as having had insufficient revolutionary fighting zeal.
89. Taufic, pp. 67, 71; Freed and Landis, pp. 26, 36. Dr. Bartulín appears to have been the source of the story that the president personally knocked out a tank with a bazooka. Actually, the doctor appears to have said only that he saw a bazooka protruding from the window of the president's private office and that a shot from that weapon hit a tank (Freed and Landis, p. 26). Most accounts have Allende firing his submachine gun, not a bazooka.
90. Varas and Vergara, *Coup!* pp. 42–43; Freed and Landis, p. 22; Sánchez and Calm, p. 29; *Qué Pasa*, 8–14 September 1977, p. 26; Taufic, pp. 70–71; Fontaine and Zegers, p. 23; "La acción del ejército," pp. 48–49. Chesnay, p. 56, places the time of Allende's interview with the aides as just before, rather than just after, his speech.
91. Freed and Landis, p. 23, quoting Dr. Bartulín.
92. Ibid., p. 79.
93. *FBIS*, Buenos Aires—Paris AFP, 1525 GMT 11 Sept. 1973; Freed and Landis, p. 23; Varas and Vergara, *Coup!* p. 56; Sánchez and Calm, p. 29; Taufic, pp. 59, 67, 71; interview with carabinero general Arturo Yovane, *Qué Pasa*, 8–14 September 1977, p. 34. A few leftist accounts assert that one or more of the carabineros actually tried to kill the president as they departed. They also

indicate that at least a few carabineros remained in the Moneda until about 11 a.m. See Timossi, pp. 84–88.

94. Freed and Landis, pp. 23–25. Rojas, p. 38, has another account of this assemblage. See also Taufic, pp. 68, 72, and Gossaín, p. 4.

95. Freed and Landis, p. 23; *Qué Pasa*, 8–14 September 1977, p. 15.

96. White, pp. 66–67.

97. Sánchez and Calm, p. 30; Taufic, p. 95; Varas and Vergara, *Coup!* p. 55; *Qué Pasa*, 8–14 September 1977, p. 27; Fontaine and Zegers, p. 23; Chesnay, p. 57.

98. *FBIS*, Bogotá Radio Santa Fé, 1445 GMT 11 Sept. 1973.

99. Robert J. Alexander, *The Tragedy of Chile* (Westport: Greenwood, 1978), appen. 2, pp. 453–54; Sigmund, p. 243; *FBIS*, Santiago, 1447 GMT 11 Sept. 1973 and Santiago, 1540 GMT 11 Sept. 1973; Thomas G. Sanders, "Military Government in Chile, Part I: The Coup," *Fieldstaff Reports*, vol. 22, no. 1, West Coast South America Series (Hanover, N.H.: American Universities Field Staff, 1975), p. 7; "La acción del ejército," pp. 31–37.

100. Sánchez and Calm, p. 30; Varas and Vergara, *Coup!* p. 63; Fontaine and Zegers, p. 23.

101. Sánchez and Calm, p. 30; Varas and Vergara, *Coup!* p. 62; *Qué Pasa*, 8–14 September 1977, p. 26; Taufic, pp. 59, 63; Gossaín, p. 4.

102. Freed and Landis, p. 98; *Qué Pasa*, 8–14 September 1977, p. 26; Chesnay, p. 56. Apparently Carvajal arranged a parallel carabinero pullback with Yovane.

103. Sánchez and Calm, pp. 32 and 36.

104. Ibid., p. 32; Taufic, p. 98. If pro-Junta accounts are to be believed, the carabinero station actually held out until it was relieved by police troops on the following morning. For other localities where resistance was said to have been offered, see Rojas, p. 216.

105. Taufic, pp. 95, 109–13.

106. Manuel Mejido, "Cowards Don't Head Revolutions—Allende's Final Words," *Chicago Tribune*, 20 September 1973 (interview with René Largo Farías), sec. 1, p. 7; Varas and Vergara, *Coup!* p. 60.

107. *New York Times*, 20 September 1973, p. 3; Sánchez and Calm, pp. 30–31; Taufic, pp. 59–60, 63–64; Chesnay, p. 57. The account in Taufic, pp. 63–64, claims that both La Payita and Marta González remained behind.

108. Freed and Landis, pp. 28–29. Isabel Allende suggested (Taufic, p. 68) that the military let the women pass, apprehending some men who were with them.

109. Taufic, p. 64; *New York Times*, 20 September 1973, p. 3.

110. Junta representatives have asserted in private that President Allende was under the influence of drugs (besides alcohol). I do not know if this was true.

111. Chesnay, pp. 56–57. Timossi, p. 111, puts the time of the opening of the carabineros' armory at after the bombing, or shortly after noon.

112. Sánchez and Calm, p. 31; Taufic, p. 73. The final autopsy said that the president's body showed a "90% level of alcohol toxicity," but Palacios allegedly said in an interview that the autopsy showed no alcohol in the blood. Rojas, pp. 28, 32; Taufic, p. 66. Palacios, talking with me on 5 July 1984, denied ever having said that the autopsy showed no alcohol. He said, in fact, that he

smelled alcohol in the Independence Salon, and he found a partly empty whiskey bottle there.

113. Sánchez and Calm, p. 30; *Qué Pasa,* 8–14 September 1977, p. 15; White, p. 66.

114. The army Noncommissioned Officers' School should not be confused with the carabineros' school, which reportedly was the scene of a loyalist rising.

115. Varas and Vergara, *Coup!* pp. 44, 50; Sánchez and Calm, p. 31; Taufic, p. 72; Fontaine and Zegers, p. 23.

116. Sánchez and Calm, pp. 31–32; Taufic, pp. 64, 72.

117. Sánchez and Calm, p. 32.

118. Ibid.; Taufic, pp. 60, 72–73; Fontaine and Zegers, pp. 23–24.

119. Freed and Landis, pp. 35, 92–93, 124; Varas, p. 10; Varas and Vergara, *Coup!* p. 67; Sánchez and Calm, pp. 32, 34; Taufic, p. 73.

120. Sánchez and Calm, p. 32; Freed and Landis, p. 35; Taufic, pp. 64, 73–74.

121. Varas and Vergara, *Coup!* p. 126; "La acción del ejército," pp. 41, 44.

122. Varas and Vergara, *Coup!* pp. 73, 81; Sánchez and Calm, p. 35; Freed and Landis, p. 36; Taufic, pp. 64, 74; Fontaine and Zegers, pp. 23–24. Some accounts, such as Rojas, p. 40, Chesnay, p. 58, and Taufic, p. 60, have the delegates going to the Ministry of Defense before the bombing, but it is unlikely. Fontaine and Zegers note that Flores called General Díaz and proposed the meeting before the bombing, but the delegates probably actually went after it.

123. Varas, p. 10; Sánchez and Calm, p. 32; Taufic, p. 66.

124. Sánchez and Calm, p. 32.

125. Varas and Vergara, *Coup!* p. 71; Sánchez and Calm, p. 33.

126. Varas and Vergara, *Coup!* pp. 71, 73; Sánchez and Calm, p. 32; Freed and Landis, pp. 122–23.

127. Quoted in Taufic, pp. 78–79.

128. Sánchez and Calm, p. 33.

129. Ibid. See also Freed and Landis, p. 36, and Taufic, p. 64.

130. Varas and Vergara, *Coup!* pp. 82–83. See also Gossaín, p. 9; and Chesnay, p. 58.

131. Gen. Ernesto Baeza Michaelsen stated publicly on 12 September that Allende offered to surrender unconditionally at 1:50 P.M. *FBIS,* Buenos Aires LATIN, 1708 GMT 12 Sept. 1973. Rojas, p. 35, quotes Baeza's announcement but has the time wrong. Baeza's statement also mentioned the "patrol" sent to the Moneda. See also *New York Times,* 13 September 1973, p. 18; *FBIS,* Buenos Aires LATIN, 1827 GMT 11 Sept. 1973; Varas and Vergara, *Coup!* pp. 82–83; Taufic, pp. 60, 68; Varas, p. 10; Sigmund, p. 5; Chesnay, p. 58; William Montalbano, "Allende Spent Final Hours Trying to Buy More Time," *Miami Herald,* 22 September 1973, p. 1 (from "sources close to the Allende family"). Rojas, p. 42, claims that Puccio was returning to the Moneda in the vehicle that had to turn back.

132. Sánchez and Calm, p. 33; Taufic, p. 60. Mrs. Allende confirmed, in an interview upon her arrival in Mexico on 16 September, that the surrender procession took place. She said the Junta gave Allende ten minutes to surrender. He then told his companions: "You others go on out; I will come right away. I will be the last." *New York Times,* 17 September 1973, p. 12. Colombian journalist Juan Gossaín (p. 9) quotes leftist sources describing how troops push-

ing through the Morandé door at 1:45 P.M. captured eight people and used a loudspeaker to demand that Allende surrender. Allende then ordered his companions to file down with their hands up, saying, "I shall come down last." Fontaine and Zegers (p. 24) report that the white flag fashioned from a doctor's coat was displayed and that the procession was emerging as Palacios approached the Morandé door. They also report the ten-minute ultimatum and Allende's assertion that he would come out last. For further discussion of the surrender procession and additional eyewitness reports that it took place, see chapter 11.

133. Varas and Vergara, *Coup!* pp. 84–89; Taufic, pp. 64–65. Soto's trip upstairs is also recounted in Freed and Landis, p. 37, and Fontaine and Zegers, p. 24. Fontaine says Allende passed on the message that he would be "last" to the military through Soto.

134. Sánchez and Calm, p. 33. See also *Qué Pasa*, 8–14 September 1977, p. 28; Sigmund, p. 246; Taufic, pp. 60–61.

135. Sigmund, p. 244. For varying accounts and speculation, see Varas and Vergara, *Coup!* pp. 117–18; Sigmund, p. 5; Rojas, p. 29.

136. Varas and Vergara, *Coup!* pp. 93–94. See also *Qué Pasa*, 8–14 September 1977, p. 28. Varas and Vergara, *Operación Chile*, have Palacios finding Allende "al centro del sillón rojo," so I have used a translation of that phrase in the quotation rather than the phrase in the English edition of the book, "in the red armchair." I have talked with General Palacios, and he confirms that it was a sofa, not an armchair.

137. Sánchez and Calm, p. 33; Alexander, p. 337; Donoso, p. 417; Taufic, pp. 61, 65, 69; Freed and Landis, p. 38.

138. *Qué Pasa*, 8–14 September 1977, p. 33; Taufic, p. 96.

139. Dinges and Landau, p. 65.

140. Sánchez and Calm, p. 34; Sigmund, p. 244.

141. Freed and Landis, pp. 170–71. A parallel account of the fighting at Sumar is given in Taufic, pp. 105–6.

142. Sánchez and Calm, pp. 34–35; Sigmund, p. 244.

143. Freed and Landis, pp. 170–72.

144. Alexander, p. 334; Sánchez and Calm, p. 32.

145. Alexander, p. 334. A listing of factories, office buildings, and other places where resistance was forcibly suppressed appears in Taufic, p. 97.

146. *Qué Pasa*, 8–14 September 1977, p. 31.

147. Sánchez and Calm, p. 36; Alexander, p. 331; Taufic, p. 108.

148. Sánchez and Calm, p. 34; Montalbano, p. 1.

149. Varas and Vergara, *Coup!* pp. 95–96.

150. Ibid., pp. 103, 105, 107, 110; Taufic, pp. 61, 69, 80; Rojas, p. 24; Sánchez and Calm, p. 34; Freed and Landis, p. 123; Sigmund, pp. 8, 244; Gossaín, p. 10.

151. Varas and Vergara, *Coup!* p. 111.

152. Taufic, p. 80; Gossaín, p. 10.

153. Varas and Vergara, *Coup!* p. 111.

154. *El Mercurio*, 19 September 1973, p. 19.

155. Sánchez and Calm, p. 36.

156. Ibid.

## Chapter 11. Assassination or Suicide?

1. Robinson Rojas Sandford, *The Murder of Allende* (New York: Harper & Row, 1976), pp. 25–37.
2. Rojas, pp. 1–2, 29.
3. See also the description of the surrender and procession in chapter 10, with endnotes.
4. Rojas, p. 29.
5. *El Mercurio*, 21 September 1973, p. 17. The *Foreign Broadcast Information Service* for 21 September 1973 and surrounding days carries nothing to confirm Rojas's account.
6. Pedro Pascual, "Chile de Allende y el golpe de estado," EFE, carried in *El Comercio* (Quito), 11, 12, 13, and 15 September 1983; Philippe Chesnay, "La verdad sobre la muerte de Salvador Allende," pt. 2, *Cosas* (Santiago), October 1983, p. 59. General Javier Palacios, whom I interviewed in New York on 5 July 1984, says that Guijón told him on the day of the coup that he had not seen Allende shoot himself, but had heard shots and went back. An additional curious element in Rojas's analysis is that he does not even mention the discrepancy. For his part, he criticizes Guijón's statement because he thinks it irrational for Guijón to have left the relative safety of the procession to fetch his gas mask and because Guijón removed his white coat (which the Rojas book, in a passage not quoted here, says he did). Rojas notes that the white medical coat indicated his noncombatant status and removing it would have jeopardized his life. In comment, one might observe that Guijón gave up his coat so it could be used as the surrender flag. *See also* Mary Zajer, "How Allende Died," *Cauce*, Santiago, 25 Sept. to 1 Oct., 1984, p. 11.
7. Florencia Varas and José Manuel Vergara, *Coup! Allende's Last Day* (New York: Stein & Day, 1975), p. 117. Others have heard this same story, including John Karkashian, a U.S. Foreign Service officer who headed a State Department working group on Chile in the 1973–1974 period. Karkashian to the author, letter dated 12 December 1983, quoted by permission.
8. Rojas, pp. 28, 33–34.
9. Paul E. Sigmund, *The Overthrow of Allende and the Politics of Chile, 1964–1976* (Pittsburgh: University of Pittsburgh Press, 1977), p. 246. Sigmund reports that Guijón told Briones about Allende's death on 11 September. In a newspaper interview in early November 1973 Briones says he learned of Allende's suicide at around 6 p.m. See Florencia Varas, "Last Feverish Hours of Allende Regime," *Times* (London), 6 November 1973, p. 10. This is probably earlier in the evening, however, than Briones and Guijón actually talked. More probably it was at about 11:30 P.M. or at about midnight. See Pasqual, pt. 4, 15 September.
10. Chesnay, p. 59.
11. Rojas, p. 27.
12. Ibid., pp. 32, 35–36.
13. Ibid., p. 29.
14. Manuel Mejido, "92 hs. de sitio a la embajada," *Excelsior* (Mexico City), 19 September 1973, p. 13.
15. Laurence Birns, ed., *The End of Chilean Democracy* (New York: Seabury, 1974), p. 40.
16. Mejido, p. 13.

17. Birns, pp. 35–41.

18. Camilo Taufic, *Chile en la hoguera* (Buenos Aires: Corregidor, 1974), p. 219.

19. Marta Sánchez and Lillian Calm, "El once, hora por hora," *Qué Pasa*, 10 September 1974, p. 34; Birns, pp. 38–39, 41; Taufic, p. 219. See also Sigmund, p. 246, for that scholar's conclusions.

20. Mejido, p. 13.

21. *El Mundo's* story is described in *Foreign Broadcast Information Service*, Daily Report, Latin America and Western Europe, Buenos Aires, LATIN, 2342 GMT, 12 Sept. 1973. As reported, a Peruvian ham radio operator was told of the Socialist party's charges by a Chilean colleague. The Peruvian passed the report on to Buenos Aires.

22. *New York Times*, 16 September 1973, p. 1.

23. Ibid., 17 September 1973, p. 12.

24. Ibid., 20 September 1973, p. 13.

25. Ibid., 13 September 1973, p. 18, carrying a 12 September Reuters dispatch.

26. Taufic, pp. 69, 75–76.

27. Ibid., p. 66. See also Jorge Timossi, *Grandes alamedas: El combate del Presidente Allende* (Havana: Editorial de Ciencias Sociales, 1974).

28. Judy White, *Chile's Days of Terror* (New York: Pathfinder, 1974), pp. 66–67.

29. A leftist would assert, of course, that the young Socialist's account omitted any reference to the surrender decision and procession because neither event took place. This position is difficult to sustain, however, as the evidence points strongly the other way.

30. Taufic, pp. 76–77.

31. Ibid., p. 69.

32. Gabriel García Márquez, "The Death of Salvador Allende," *Harper's*, March 1974, p. 53.

33. Ibid., p. 52.

34. In my interview with General Palacios in New York on 5 July 1984, he told me that he did not know any officer named Gallardo or Garrido and had never had an adjutant with any such name.

35. Arturo Fontaine Aldunate and Cristián Zegers Ariztía, *Cómo llegaron las fuerzas armadas a la acción del 11 de septiembre de 1973?* (Santiago: El Mercurio, 11 September 1974), p. 24; "La acción del ejército en la liberación de Chile," (Santiago: Historia inédita, circulated informally by senior Chilean Army officers, n.d.), p. 49.

36. Varas and Vergara, p. 85.

37. I am relying on my own recollection, the recollection of Chileans familiar with the pre-1973 presidential rooms in the Moneda Palace, and photographs of the old Red Room.

38. Rojas, pp. 1–3, 19–20.

39. The foreword of Rojas's original Spanish text is dated 20 June 1974, which was three months after García Márquez's article was published in *Harper's*. Robinson Rojas, *Estos mataron a Allende* (Barcelona: Martínez Roca, 1974), p. 10.

40. Rojas, *Murder*, pp. 18–37, 224–25.

41. Most witnesses described Allende as dressed in rust-colored, speckled

brown, or pepper-and-salt colored pants, while Rojas says the military removed Allende's "blue trousers and dressed his remains in dark gray ones." Donald Freed and Fred Simon Landis, *Death in Washington* (Westport: Hill, 1980) p. 23; Samuel Chavkin, *The Murder of Chile* (New York: Everest, 1982), p. 31; *Qué Pasa,* 8–14 September 1977, p. 28; Varas and Vergara, pp. 93–94; Rojas, *Murder,* pp. 19–20. The error may have been in part a translator's. The Spanish version of Rojas's text has the military removing his blue trousers and dressing him in "marengo" pants (Rojas, *Estos,* p. 35). "Marengo" is a textile-maker's term used in several languages and it means "speckled-brown" or "pepper-and-salt." Many people *think* it means "maroon" or "dark gray," however, and that is probably where the error arose. Nevertheless, this explanation does not account for the fact that hundreds of people saw or photographed Allende between early morning and 2 P.M. on 11 September and failed to describe him in "blue" trousers, as Rojas alleges, before the military changed his trousers to "marengo" ones. Juan Gossaín, in *Cromos* (Bogota), vol. 141, 24 September 1973, p. 4, like Rojas, describes Allende as wearing "dark blue" trousers during the Moneda battle.

42. Rojas, *Murder,* p. 2.

43. Ibid., pp. 45–46; *Que Pasa,* 10 September 1974, p. 22; Freed and Landis, p. 38; and *FBIS,* 9 October 1973, p. E-8.

44. Rojas, *Murder,* pp. 2–3, 18–19.

45. *Que Pasa,* 8–14 September 1977, pp. 25ff. The Carvajal-Pinochet conversation is given on p. 28.

46. The U.S. newspaperman in question has reviewed this text for accuracy but does not wish to be cited by name.

47. Rojas, *Murder,* pp. 18–19.

48. Guijón's explanation of *why* he moved the gun varies. At one point he was quoted as saying that he instinctively tried to take the dead president's pulse to see if there were signs of life, and moved the weapon in doing so. At another time he was quoted as saying that he pushed the gun away so soldiers coming upon him would not think he might use it against them. Varas and Vergara, pp. 117–18; Rojas, *Murder,* pp. 30–31; Sánchez and Calm, p. 33; Chesnay, p. 59.

49. Rojas, *Murder,* p. 26.

50. Ibid., pp. 26–27.

51. Ibid., p. 26.

52. I am indebted to Gary P. Paparo and Henry Siegel, former medical examiners of Westchester County, New York, for the comments in the text.

53. The Junta explained having suppressed publication of the photographs with a statement that the surviving members of the Allende family did not give permission for their release.

54. Rojas, *Murder,* p. 36.

55. *Qué Pasa,* 8–14 September 1977, p. 15.

56. Gossaín, pp. 8–9. See also Taufic, p. 84. "Estchborn" may be a misspelling of Eschborn, a town near the Taunus mountains west of Frankfurt a/M. (German postal zip 6236).

57. Gossaín, pp. 9–10.

58. See Rojas, *Estos,* p. 14, and *Murder,* p. 5.

59. *El Mercurio,* 21 September 1973, p. 17. The Junta representative was

Gen. Ernesto Baeza and the press conference in question was the same one the Rojas and El Mercurio quotations of Guijón's testimony are from.

60. See Rojas, Estos, pp. 36–37, and Murder, p. 21. See also Zajer, pp. 11–12.

61. Rojas, Murder, pp. 187–88.

62. Ibid., pp. 68–73.

63. Ibid., p. 73. See also pp. 74, 89, and 231–32, note 14.

64. Rojas, Estos, pp. 287ff. For Rojas's views on Allende and the UP, see chapter 4. Rojas expresses similar views in Murder, pp. 73ff., 89.

65. Taylor Branch and Eugene M. Propper, Labyrinth (New York: Viking, 1982), p. 65.

66. Similarities include the description of Pinochet's consultations with Baeza and Carvajal, the assault by the Infantry School Regiment supported by eight tanks, the infantry running up the stairs and coming on an armed civilian dressed in a turtleneck sweater, the string of wounds up the president's body, the confusion inside the Moneda, the sealed metal coffin flown to the coast for burial, and the army, navy, air force, and carabinero certification of death as a suicide. See the Branch and Propper account and Rojas, Murder, pp. 1, 4, 5, 19, 22, 23, 24, 25, and 39. A number of the circumstantial details are true, of course, and could have been learned from other sources besides Rojas, but the similarities are striking nonetheless.

67. Robert W. Scherrer (letter to the author dated 10 November 1983) tells me he furnished Taylor Branch with a copy of Rojas's book when Branch was writing the pages of Labyrinth discussed here, so there is no question that Branch had access to the Rojas account when he was writing his version.

68. Branch and Propper, pp. 64–65.

69. Rojas, Murder, pp. 21–22, 25, 37–38.

70. Ibid., pp. 34–35.

71. Ibid., p. 36.

72. Ibid., p. 35; FBIS, Buenos Aires LATIN 1708 GMT 12 Sept. 1973; El Mercurio, 13 September 1973; New York Times, 13 September 1973, pp. 1, 18. See also chapter 10.

73. Branch and Propper, pp. 336, 340.

74. El Mercurio, 21 September 1973, p. 17.

75. Branch and Propper, pp. 336–41, 448–49, 462–66.

76. Robert W. Scherrer to the author, letter dated 10 November 1983.

77. Rojas, Murder, p. 37. See also Sigmund, pp. 244, 246.

78. FBIS, Buenos Aires, ANSA, 0114 GMT 12 Sept. 1973, and 1624 GMT 12 Sept. 1973. Apparently the photographer was not allowed to take pictures.

79. Robert J. Alexander, The Tragedy of Chile (Westport: Greenwood, 1978), p. 337. The fireman told Alexander that he had seen Allende "with a gun under his chin," which could hardly have been an accurate description of the gun's location when the firemen were admitted.

80. Rojas, Murder, pp. 1–2.

81. See Varas and Vergara, p. 95.

82. Varas, p. 10.

83. Carlos Prats, Una vida por la legalidad (Mexico: Fondo de Cultura Económica, 1976), p. 105.

84. Taufic, p. 86.

85. Birns, p. 80.

86. Jonathan Kandell, "Chilean Officers Tell How They Began to Plan the Take-Over Last November," *New York Times*, 27 September 1973, p. 3.

87. *New York Times*, 16 September 1973, p. 1.

88. Paul Sigmund, interview, *Princeton Weekly Bulletin*, 13 February 1978, p. 4, and Sigmund, *The Overthrow of Allende*, pp. 246–47. See also Alexander, p. 338.

89. Qué Pasa, 8–14 September 1977, p. 29.

## Chapter 12. The Covert U.S. Role, 1971–1973

1. Flora Lewis, "Alas for Plausibility," *New York Times*, 8 April 1983, p. A31.

2. The chronological appendix to the staff report enumerates Forty Committee authorizations for the expenditure of covert funds, both in 1970–71 and subsequently. See U.S. Congress, Senate, *Covert Action in Chile, 1963–1973*, Staff Report of the Select Committee to Study Governmental Operations with Respect to Intelligence Activities (Washington, D.C., 1975), pp. 57–62. On p. 27 the staff report says that approximately $7 million was spent on covert action in Chile from 1970 to 1973, but that figure appears to include some moneys spent before and after Allende's period in office as well as some project funds that did not require Forty Committee approval.

3. U.S. Senate, *Covert Action in Chile*, p. 60.

4. Ibid., pp. 8, 60.

5. Ibid., p. 30.

6. Paul E. Sigmund, *The Overthrow of Allende and the Politics of Chile, 1964–1976* (Pittsburgh: University of Pittsburgh Press, 1977), p. 189.

7. U.S. Senate, *Covert Action in Chile*, p. 30. Small amounts of AID and other overt embassy funds were also used to commission economic research.

8. Ibid., p. 30.

9. Ibid., pp. 2, 28–39.

10. Ibid., pp. 30, 60.

11. Ibid., p. 31.

12. Ibid., p. 38.

13. Ibid., p. 28.

14. Ibid., p. 39.

15. Ibid., p. 38.

16. Ibid.

17. Laurence Stern, "CIA Role in Chile Revealed," *Washington Post*, 8 September 1974, p. A20. Stern was quoting Congressman Michael J. Harrington's account of CIA director William E. Colby's 22 April 1974 testimony before Congressman Lucien N. Nedzi's House Armed Services Subcommittee.

18. Seymour M. Hersh, "CIA Chief Tells House of $8 Million Campaign against Allende in '70–'73," *New York Times*, 8 September 1974, p. 26. Hersh identifies the Colby testimony from which his information came as a closed congressional hearing in October 1973. He may have been confusing Colby's testimony before the Latin American subcommittee of the House Foreign Affairs Committee in October 1973 with Colby's testimony to the Nedzi Subcommittee on 22 April 1974.

19. Time, 30 September 1974, p. 21; William E. Colby, *Honorable Men: My*

*Life in the CIA* (New York: Simon & Schuster, 1978), p. 304. Colby has told me categorically that "assistance to student and syndical groups" means students and unions affiliated with the Christian Democrats and with other parties of the center. Most of the assistance was to the Christian Democrats. The Church Committee's record of Forty Committee actions would support this interpretation, as aid to the truckers, for example, would have required Forty Committee authorization regardless of the conduit and country of transmission.

20. David A. Phillips, letter to the author, 25 February 1984.

21. U.S. Senate, *Covert Action in Chile*, p. 37. It may be recalled that Ambassador Korry had forbidden the station in 1970 to maintain contact with dissident officers. See chapter 1 and Thomas Powers, "Inside the Department of Dirty Tricks," *Atlantic*, August 1979, p. 50. Korry has subsequently indicated, however, that his instructions focused particularly on the period just before and after the 1970 elections.

My editor has expressed some surprise that ITT, Kennecott, and Anaconda have figured so little in this discussion. It should be remembered that Kennecott and Anaconda always did operate pretty much in the open. Besides, their representatives were gone from the scene. By 1972 ITT had been subjected to the Anderson revelations and the uproar in the U.S. Congress and was lying low. Of course, any of the three could have found ways to pour large amounts of money clandestinely to the opposition, the guilds, and the truckers, but I have not seen evidence that they did so. Besides, it is a truth—if one not always appreciated—that campaigns have their own dynamic and season. The subject of private covert financing from U.S. companies will be discussed a bit more later in this chapter.

22. For an earlier discussion of some of the issues raised in this section, see Nathaniel Davis, "US Covert Actions in Chile, 1971–1973," *Foreign Service Journal*, November and December 1978.

23. Sir Arthur Conan Doyle, "Silver Blaze," *The Complete Sherlock Holmes* (Garden City, N.Y.: Doubleday, 1930), pp. 347, 349. After drugging the stable boy on duty, the midnight visitor was leading the racehorse "Silver BLaze" out to lame it. If the dog had barked, it would have roused two other lads sleeping in the loft. It was silent because it was accustomed to the visitor.

24. David A. Phillips, *The Night Watch* (New York: Atheneum, 1977), pp. 252–53.

25. Hersh, pp. 1, 26; Stern, pp. A1, A20.

26. Colby, pp. 380–81. Phillips was standing at Colby's side during the conversation with Nedzi.

27. Hersh, p. 26.

28. Press Stenotypists' Association (Washington, D.C.), *Stenotype Transcript of Press Conference* (No. 2 of the president of the United States, 8 P.M., 16 September 1974, East Room), p. 6. See also *New York Times*, 17 September 1974, pp. 11, 22.

29. Richard R. Fagen of Stanford University subsequently quoted Kubisch as having said at this meeting that his hopes were that Unidad Popular would take Chile "into complete and total ruin" in the process, thereby proving that socialism does not work. Richard Fagen to Senator William Fulbright, letter of 8 October 1973, in Laurence Birns, ed., *The End of Chilean Democracy* (New York: Seabury, 1974), pp. 157, 175. Others at the meeting, including Kubisch himself and Henry A. Landsberger, president of the Latin American Studies

Association, recall that Kubisch did not express the sentiment Fagen described but emphasized that Chileans should be given the opportunity to determine their own destiny at the polls in 1976. Kubisch has provided me with a copy of Landsberger's letter to him of 8 November 1973, which makes Landsberger's position clear. For Kubisch's published testimony on this question, see U.S. Congress, House, Committee on Foreign Affairs, Inter-American Subcommittee, *United States and Chile during the Allende Years, 1970–1973*, Hearings, 20 September 1973 (Washington, D.C., 1975, GPO no. 39–180), pp. 97, 152.

30. William E. Colby, letter, dated 16 September 1974, to the editor, "Chile and the CIA," *New York Times*, 18 September 1974, p. 40.

31. Colby, *Honorable Men*, p. 382. See also Phillips, pp. 253–54. Former congressman Nedzi advises me that his long-held impression is that the word "destabilization" was coined by Harrington. Lucien N. Nedzi letter to the author, 26 October 1984.

32. Seymour M. Hersh, "Doubt on US Role in Chile Recalled," *New York Times*, 17 October 1974, p. 9.

33. Seymour M. Hersh, "CIA Said to Have Asked Funds for Chile Rightists in '73," *New York Times*, 21 October 1974, p. 2.

34. Daniel Schorr, *Clearing the Air* (Boston: Houghton Mifflin, 1977), pp. 132–33.

35. Daniel Schorr, letter to the author, 28 January 1978.

36. Seymour M. Hersh, "Washington Said to Have Authorized a 'Get Rougher' Policy in Chile in '71," *New York Times*, 24 September 1974, p. 2.

37. Edward M. Korry, "Statements and Discussion," U.S. Congress, Senate, Committee on Foreign Relations, *Nomination of Hon. Cyrus R. Vance to Be Secretary of State*, 11 January 1977, Hearing (Washington, D.C., 1977), p. 53.

38. Seymour M. Hersh, "CIA Is Linked to Strikers in Chile That Beset Allende," *New York Times*, 20 September 1974, p. 1.

39. U.S. Senate, *Covert Action in Chile*, p. 31.

40. Ibid., pp. 30–31.

41. U.S. Congress, Senate, Select Committee to Study Governmental Operations with Respect to Intelligence Activities (Senate Resolution 21), vol. 7: *Covert Action*, Hearings, 4 and 5 December 1975 (Washington, D.C., 1976), p. 22. See also U.S. Senate, *Covert Action in Chile*, p. 31.

42. Phillips, pp. 254–55; Cord Meyer, *Facing Reality* (New York: Harper & Row, 1980), p. 189; Colby, pp. 304ff. See also Phillips in the *New York Times*, 25 May 1975.

43. Hersh, "Doubt on US Role," p. 9.

44. *New York Times*, 22 October 1974, p. 39.

45. U.S. Senate, *Covert Action in Chile*, p. 31.

46. Robert J. Alexander, *The Tragedy of Chile* (Westport: Greenwood, 1978), p. 229.

47. Ray S. Cline, note to the author 23 October 1978.

48. I am told that the secretary briefly considered having William G. Hyland, chief of intelligence and research, initiate a top-secret recheck of the facts.

49. See for example, Penny Lernoux, *Cry of the People* (Garden City, N.J.: Doubleday, 1980), pp. 293–97; Mrs. Hortensia Bussi de Allende's speech of 5 April 1975 to the conference "The CIA and World Peace," Yale University, New Haven, Conn. Copies of Mrs. Allende's remarks were later disseminated.

50. U.S. Senate, *Covert Action in Chile*, p. 31.

51. Ibid., p. 30.

52. Ibid., p. 10.

53. Ibid., pp. 30–31.

54. Hersh, "CIA Chief Tells House," p. 26.

55. In a phone conversation on 31 August 1984 Jorden said he did not recall the conversation in question nor Kubisch having told him that he would be prepared to resign over the issue, but Jorden said his memory is not clear enough for him to dispute Kubish's recollection of what transpired.

56. Seymour M. Hersh, *The Price of Power: Kissinger in the Nixon White House* (New York: Summit, 1983), p. 295.

57. Ian Frykberg, "Aust. Spies Helped CIA Plan to Topple Allende," *Sydney Morning Herald*, 7 October 1974; *Sydney Morning Herald*, 8 October 1974 and 9 October 1974, pp. 1, 2; Paul Kelly, *The Unmaking of Gough* (Sydney: Angus & Robertson, 1976), p. 36.

58. Thomas Hauser, *The Execution of Charles Horman* (New York: Harcourt Brace Jovanovich, 1978), p. 247.

59. For accusations—and some refutations—that the CIA supported Tradition, Family, and Property, Richard Alexander Zanders (to upset the rythm of crops), Plan Delta (to contaminate water in Chilean irrigation ditches), Plan Centaur (to kill Castro in Chile), and efforts to persecute a UP-connected American in Switzerland named William P. Lynas, see the following references. So far as I know, there is no substance to any of these allegations. Lernoux, pp. 294–97; Phillips, pp. 240, 250; *Time*, 1 October 1973, p. 10; *New York Times*, 22 April 1976, p. 7; Thomas Powers, *The Man Who Kept the Secrets* (New York: Knopf, 1979), p. 13; Thomas Powers, "Inside the Department of Dirty Tricks," *Atlantic*, August 1979, pp. 33ff.; Warren Hinckle and William Turner, *The Fish Is Red* (New York: Harper & Row, 1981), pp. 293–94; "Unser Freund," *Der Spiegel*, 10 November 1975, pp. 132, 134.

60. Excerpts of Senator Frank Church's letter to Secretary of State Cyrus Vance were first published in Davis, p. 13, by permission of the late senator Church.

61. Marlise Simons, "The Brazilian Connection," *Washington Post*, 6 January 1974, p. B3.

62. Korry, pp. 56, 69–70. See also Edward M. Korry, "The Sell-Out of Chile and the American Taxpayer," *Penthouse*, March 1978, p. 116.

63. Edward M. Korry, "Confronting Our Past in Chile," *Los Angeles Times*, 8 March 1981, sec. 6, p. 5.

64. Tad Szulc, "The CIA and Chile," in Birns, p. 159. Seymour Hersh also reports that CIA director Colby, in congressional testimony, refused to rule out the possibility that Brazilian or other Latin American subsidiaries of U.S. corporations assisted anti-Allende demonstrators. See Hersh, "CIA Chief Tells House," p. 26. Colby has told me that the CIA did *not* use U.S. business subsidiaries as conduits for assistance to demonstrators or strikers.

65. Camilo Taufic, *Chile en la hoguera* (Buenos Aires: Corregidor, 1974), p. 215. Taufic notes that "Plan Z" (see chapter 14) was surprisingly similar to "Plan Cohen" in Brazil and "Plan Loto Rojo" in Bolivia (1971). See also Birns, p. 104; Raúl Ampuero, "The Military Counter-Revolution in Latin America," pp. 1–15, quoted in Lernoux, pp. 192–93 (Ampuero asserts that this collaboration was "particularly" evidenced after the coup).

66. *Qué Pasa*, 8–14 September 1977, p. 31.

67. Simons, p. B3.

68. Jonathan Kandell, "Foreign Companies Aided Anti-Allende Strikers, Chileans Say," New York Times, 16 October 1974, p. 8. It should be noted that the companies Kandell mentioned as donors denied that they had made contributions. Nevertheless, Kandell is a careful reporter.

69. Simons, p. B3; Robinson Rojas Sandford, The Murder of Allende (New York: Harper & Row, 1976), p. 125. See also Sigmund, p. 189. UP black market operations could have additionally contributed to fluctuations in the rate.

70. Washington Post, 9 September 1974.

71. Time, 30 September 1974, p. 21.

72. See Nathaniel Davis, "The Angola Decision of 1975: A Personal Memoire," Foreign Affairs, Autumn, 1978, pp. 109–24.

73. Daniel Drooz, "The CIA's Secret Iran Fund," Politics Today, March/April 1980, pp. 10–11.

74. Ray S. Cline, Secrets, Spies and Scholars (Washington, D.C.: Acropolis, 1976), p. 227.

75. U.S. Senate, Covert Action, Hearings, 4 and 5 December 1975, p. 27.

76. William V. Shannon, "The Politics of Death," New York Times, 3 August 1975, sec. 4, p. 15.

77. See Leslie H. Gelb, "U.S., Soviet, China Reported Aiding Portugal, Angola," New York Times, 25 September 1975, p. 1.

78. Editorial, Washington Post, reprinted in the International Herald Tribune, 13 January 1976, p. 6.

79. Time, 29 September 1975, p. 27.

80. Teresa Donoso Loero, ed., Breve historia de la Unidad Popular: Documento de "El Mercurio" (Santiago: El Mercurio, 1974).

81. Miami Herald, 26 October 1971; Henry H. Schulte, Jr., ed., Facts on File Yearbook, 1971 (New York: Facts on File, 1972), p. 857; Alexander, p. 241; Everett G. Martin, "Did the Chilean Press Need CIA Help?" Wall Street Journal, 8 September 1974; Thomas P. MacHale, El frente de la libertad de expresión, 1970–1972 (Santiago: Portada, 1972), pp. 55–56, 64–66.

82. Committee on Freedom of the Press, Report on Freedom of the Press in Chile, presented to the General Assembly, Inter-American Press Association (IAPA), Santiago meeting, 9–13 October 1972, documents presented at the meeting, pp. 3–4. See also MacHale, pp. 60–61.

83. Alexander, p. 240; MacHale, pp. 57–58.

84. IAPA report, pp. 3, 5; Alexander, p. 240; Colby, Honorable Men, p. 304.

85. Mark Falcoff, "Why Allende Fell," Commentary, July 1976, p. 43, note 16.

86. IAPA report, p. 3.

87. Sigmund, p. 142; Alexander, p. 239; MacHale, pp. 50, 110. Zig-Zag was affiliated with El Mercurio and the Edwards family's chain, and it could be argued that the Edwards's other interests should have bailed out Zig-Zag. El Mercurio itself was in financial trouble, however, and it was fairly clear that members of the Edwards family were not prepared to bankrupt themselves in an effort to save their Chilean publishing empire.

88. IAPA Report, p. 3.

89. Robert Moss, Chile's Marxist Experiment (Newton Abbot, England: David & Charles, 1973), p. 17.

90. MacHale, pp. 137–41. When MacHale wrote, three of the thirteen radio

stations had not been returned to their owners, apparently because the stations were in such financial straits that their owners were unwilling to press in the courts for their return. The Christian Democrats' Radio Balmaceda was harried off the air for a time. Schulte, p. 980.

91. In the end, the only program that remained open to opposition programing was a weekly congressional forum. MacHale, p. 20.

92. Martin, "Did the Chilean Press Need CIA Help?"; Donoso, p. 370.

93. It may be recalled that the Catholic University's unauthorized effort to extend its broadcasting to Concepción was countered by jamming, and Allende later vetoed a bill that would have officially authorized opposition TV broadcasting throughout the country. Alexander, p. 244.

94. Moss, p. 16; MacHale, pp. 27, 32.

95. *Economist*, 13 October 1973, p. 44.

96. See "Worldwide Bribe Disclosures Termed Only 'Tip of Iceberg,'" *International Herald Tribune*, 20 December 1976, p. 3.

97. See also Joseph Novitski, "CIA News Causes No Stir in Chile," *Washington Post*, 9 September 1974.

98. Sigmund, p. 263; Hermógenes Pérez de Arce, "Transnational Corporations Finance the UP," *Las Ultimas Noticias*, 11 June 1973, p. 5. *Qué Pasa* carried the same charges.

99. U.S. Senate, *Covert Action in Chile*, p. 20. See also Meyer, p. 177; Cline, p. 226.

100. Patrick J. Ryan, *1000 Bungled Days* (New York: American-Chilean Council, November 1976), p. 4.

101. Sigmund, pp. 103–4, 263–64.

102. Georgie Anne Geyer, "Helms and the Chile Question," *Washington Post*, 11 November 1977, p. A17.

103. U.S. Senate, *Covert Action*, Hearings, 4 and 5 December 1975, p. 21; see also p. 16, and U.S. Senate, *Covert Action in Chile*, p. 8. On p. 29 the Church Committee report takes a somewhat more jaundiced view.

104. See chapter 14.

105. Edward M. Korry, letter, published in U.S. Senate, *Covert Action*, Hearings, 4 and 5 December 1975, p. 117.

106. U.S. Senate, *Covert Action in Chile*, p. 10.

107. Thomas Powers, review of Cord Meyer's *Facing Reality*, New York *Times Book Review*, 26 October 1980, p. 34.

108. In 1976 I was trying to get Department of State clearance for "US Covert Actions in Chile, 1971–1973." Lawrence S. Eagleburger, acting for Secretary Kissinger, made me delete the following sentence: "Aside from the ethical question, there is a good deal of evidence accumulating to suggest that CIA money tends to corrupt and weaken our friends; and that in many situations it may, in the end, be no favor." I still feel that way.

109. Alexander, p. 230.

110. U.S. Senate, *Covert Action*, Hearings, 4 and 5 December 1975, p. 37.

### Chapter 13. U.S. Actions and the Coup

1. Press Stenotypists' Association (Washington, D.C.), *Stenotype Transcript of Press Conference* (No. 2 of the president of the United States, 8 P.M. 16 September 1974, East Room), p. 6.

2. U.S. Congress, Senate, *Covert Action in Chile, 1963–1973*, Staff Report of the Select Committee to Study Governmental Operations with Respect to Intelligence Activities (Washington, D.C., 1975), p. 2.

3. Ibid.

4. William E. Colby, *Honorable Men: My Life in the CIA* (New York: Simon & Schuster, 1978), p. 305.

5. U.S. Senate, *Covert Action in Chile*, pp. 6, 28.

6. Seymour M. Hersh, "CIA Chief Tells House of $8-Million Campaign against Allende in '70–'73," *New York Times*, 8 September 1974, p. 26.

7. Florencia Varas and José Manuel Vergara, *Coup! Allende's Last Day* (New York: Stein & Day, 1975), p. 121. See also *Foreign Broadcast Information Service*, Daily Report, Latin America and Western Europe, Paris AFP, 1823 GMT 21 Sept. 73.

8. C. L. Sulzberger, "The Unmaking of a President," *New York Times*, 30 November 1975, sec. 4, p. 13.

9. Colby, pp. 305 and 381.

10. *Newport Daily News*, 23 April 1981, p. 12.

11. David A. Phillips, letter to Hortensia Bussi de Allende, 10 May 1975, published in part by The *New York Times*, 22 May 1975, p. 37.

12. Phillips gave the date of the message to Washington reporters in a press conference on the day he retired, 10 May 1975.

13. David A. Phillips, *The Night Watch* (New York: Atheneum, 1977), pp. 238 and 274.

14. David A. Phillips, letter to the author, 25 February 1984.

15. Colby, p. 305.

16. Cord Meyer, *Facing Reality* (New York: Harper & Row, 1980), pp. 187–88.

17. Allegations of U.S. military involvement are discussed in several other places in chapter 12 and in this chapter, particularly Diane LaVoy's suspicions, the Arthur Creter case, and the allegations about Lt. Col. Patrick J. Ryan.

18. Editorial, "The CIA in Chile," *New York Times*, 7 December 1975, p. 14.

19. Giangiacomo Foa interview, published in *Excelsior* (Mexico City), 3 October 1973. See *FBIS*, Buenos Aires ANSA, 2313 GMT 3 October 1973, and Camilo Taufic, *Chile en la hoguera* (Buenos Aires: Corregidor, 1974), pp. 81–82. The same charge has been repeated by Mrs. Allende, who said that 150 North American "specialists in air acrobatics" arrived in Chile at the time of the coup. Hortensia Bussi de Allende, speech transcript, 5 April 1975, at the conference "The CIA and World Peace," held under the sponsorship of Promoting World Peace at Yale University, New Haven, Conn., pp. 42ff. Gabriel García Márquez asserted that the Moneda was bombed by U.S. flying-circus pilots in his "The Death of Salvador Allende," *Harper's*, March 1974, p. 53.

20. Laurence Birns, ed., *The End of Chilean Democracy* (New York: Seabury, 1974), p. 104.

21. Mrs. Allende, in her Yale speech, said U.S. Unitas warships were "standing by ready to help." See also Robinson Rojas Sandford, *The Murder of Allende* (New York: Harper & Row, 1976), pp. 187–88, and Thomas Hauser, *Missing* (New York: Avon, 1982), pp. 66–67, 76.

22. When I was teaching at the U.S. Naval War College I met one of the senior officers of the 1973 Unitas squadron, and he gave me the first-hand description that appears in the text. On 12 September State Department repre-

sentatives said the squadron left Ilo Bay (Peru) between 6 and 9 A.M., 11 September. *New York Times,* 13 September 1973, p. 18.

23. Hauser, p. 229, and Gary MacEoin, *No Peaceful Way* (New York: Sheed & Ward, 1974), p. 170.

24. Godfrey Hodgson and William Shawcross, "Destabilization," *Times* (London), 27 October 1974, p. 16.

25. Patrick J. Ryan, *1000 Bungled Days* (New York: American-Chilean Council, November 1976), p. 10.

26. Thomas Hauser, *The Execution of Charles Horman: An American Sacrifice* (New York: Harcourt Brace Jovanovich, 1978), pp. 65–66, 236. This is the hardback predecessor to *Missing,* with identical page numbering and central body of text.

27. *Joyce Horman et al. v. Henry A. Kissinger et al.,* CA 77-1748 (DDC), Exhibit A to Defendants' Response to Plaintiffs' Motion to Dismiss without Prejudice, 11 March 1977, p. 2; Terry Simon, "An American Girl in Chile's Revolution," *Senior Scholastic,* 6 December 1973, p. 14; and *Statement of Terry Simon,* notarized by Nancy Grossman, Queens County, N.Y., 11 April 1974.

28. The U.S. Military Group's telegram 211231Z of 21 August 1973, released to all parties, describes Arthur P. Creter's assignments.

29. Admin COMUSNAVSO/COMFIFTEEN FORT AMADOR CZ's telegram 212021Z of 21 November 1973. Fort Amador, Canal Zone, cable released to all parties.

30. *Joyce Horman et al.,* p. 2.

31. Mrs. Allende's Yale speech; Taufic, pp. 81–83; and MacEoin, p. 169.

32. Mrs. Allende's Yale speech.

33. The original source for these accounts and those cited in note 19 appears to have been the Argentinian magazine *Panorama.*

34. Max V. Krebs, letter to the author, 13 October 1982.

35. Henry Kissinger, *Years of Upheaval* (Boston: Little, Brown, 1982), pp. 404 and 1244.

36. Ibid., pp. 403–4.

37. The dinner was on 6 October 1971, and the press carried photographs of Kissinger and me talking with Almeyda and Letelier.

38. Bernard Gwertzman, "Kissinger Seeking Advice of Envoys," *New York Times,* August 1973, pp. 1 and 6.

39. Wireless file transcript, State Dept. Briefing (Hare), 6 September 1973, ARF-38, 350, 9/6/73/JN 306 P.M..

40. Dinges and Landau report my phone conversation with Letelier, no doubt having learned of it from talking with Isabel Letelier. They have the details and the dates slightly wrong, saying for example that I telephoned Letelier on 7 September while in actuality I left Santiago in the evening of the sixth. John Dinges and Saul Landau, *Assassination on Embassy Row* (New York: Pantheon, 1980), p. 58.

41. Kissinger, p. 404.

42. Ibid., pp. 1244–45.

43. Ibid., p. 1244.

44. Rojas, p. 253. See also Dinges and Landau, p. 58.

45. Kissinger, p. 404.

46. *Miami Herald,* 6 October 1973.

47. For example, see Birns, p. 150.

48. Tad Szulc, "The CIA and Chile," in Birns, p. 157.

49. Phillips, p. 246.

50. U.S. Senate, *Covert Action in Chile*, p. 39.

51. *New York Times*, 13 September 1973, p. 18. The same article said that there had been earlier warnings, which Kubisch was reluctant to credit, but they "reached a peak" on Sunday.

52. James Nelson Goodsell, "Latin America Points Finger at US," *Christian Science Monitor*, 17 September 1973.

53. David J. Morris, letter to the editor, *Washington Post*, 26 September 1973. *La Opinión* of Buenos Aires stated on 13 September that the U.S. government knew "two days in advance" (Taufic, p. 42).

54. Phillips, p. 246.

55. Bernard Gwertzman, "US Expected Chile Coup But Decided Not to Act," *New York Times*, 14 September 1973, p. 1.

56. Ibid.

57. *Miami Herald*, 6 October 1973.

58. A number of authors have quoted purported National Intelligence estimates (NIEs) written over a period of years to show that the estimates took a more benign and optimistic view of the Allende government's prospects than U.S. policy makers articulated. There is some truth to this assertion. I believe the NIE writers were occasionally overoptimistic in their assessments. See, for example, Freed and Landis, pp. 68–69. Of course, one can also explain the differences with devil theories.

59. Letter from David A. Phillips of 31 July 1984.

60. Marlise Simons, "The Brazil Connection," *Washington Post*, 6 January 1974, p. B3.

61. David Binder, "Chile's Junta Says It Kept US in Dark," *New York Times*, 15 September 1973, p. 11. The reason one can guess that the "cabinet-level official" was probably Ambassador Scali was because he was named in other contemporaneous news stories as the source of information about the coup and the U.S. posture.

62. Ibid.

63. Gwertzman, p. 1. *Exelsior* (Mexico City) also raised the question in the days after the coup whether the U.S. government should have warned Allende of the plot to overthrow him. That newspaper's conclusion was that the United States assumed a "grave responsibility in failing to do so." See Taufic, pp. 43–44.

64. Goodsell, "Latin America."

65. Phillips, p. 248.

66. A *New York Times* article of 13 September 1973, p. 18, intimates that this is what happened.

67. Phillips, p. 248.

## Chapter 14. Military Government

1. Marta Sánchez and Lillian Calm, "El once, hora por hora," *Qué Pasa*, 10 September 1974, p. 35; and *Foreign Broadcast Information Service*, Daily Report, Latin America and Western Europe, Chile Armed Forces and Carabineros Network, 1200 GMT 29 Sept. 1973 and Madrid EFE, 1936 GMT 4 Oct. 1973.

2. Alejandro Witker V., *El compañero Tohá* (Mexico City: Casa de Chile en México, 1977), pp. 31, 37–40; Camilo Taufic, *Chile en la hoguera* (Buenos Aires: Corregidor, 1974), p. 219; Donald Freed and Fred Simon Landis, *Death in Washington* (Westport: Hill, 1980), p. 107.

3. *FBIS*, Madrid EFE, 0324 GMT 21 Sept. 1973, and 2340 GMT 22 Sept. 1973; Madrid EFE, 1927 GMT 7 Oct. 1973.

4. Paul E. Sigmund, *The Overthrow of Allende and the Politics of Chile, 1964–1976* (Pittsburgh: University of Pittsburgh Press, 1977), p. 253; Laurence Birns, ed., *The End of Chilean Democracy* (New York: Seabury, 1974), pp. 67, 204–5; *Time*, 1 October 1973; Taufic, p. 8; "The Costs of Peace Run High," *New York Times*, 14 October 1973, sec. 4, p. 4.

5. Lewis H. Diuguid, "Chile Death Toll Said 750," *Washington Post*, 3 October 1973, p. A12; Birns, pp. 165, 199, 203, 216.

6. This phenomenon is as old as civilization. For example, see Thucydides, *History of the Peloponnesian War*, trans. Rex Warner, rev. ed. (Baltimore: Penguin, 1972), pp. 242–45.

7. Sigmund, p. 215.

8. *Economist*, 13 October 1973, p. 43.

9. Birns, p. 23.

10. Sánchez and Calm, p. 21; *Economist*, 13 October 1973, p. 44; Sigmund, p. 257; Taufic, p. 208. The second and third stories are also recounted in a letter from my wife to her mother dated 2 October 1973, in which she reports that death lists, on which my name appeared, were also said to have been part of the plans.

11. Sigmund, p. 257; Freed and Landis, p. 107. The number Freed and Landis give is "six hundred families."

12. Secretaría de Gobierno, *Libro blanco del cambio de gobierno en Chile, 11 sep. 1973* (Santiago: Empresa Editora Nacional Gabriela Mistral, n.d.) pp. 53–65.

13. See *Economist*, 13 October 1973, p. 44; Sigmund, p. 257.

14. Communist party of Chile, "To the People of Chile," in Birns, p. 98.

15. *Ercilla*, 13–19 March 1974, p. 16.

16. Benjamín Cate and Rudolph Rauch of *Time*, 29 October 1973, as reported in *Ercilla*, 7–13 November 1973, p. 14.

17. *Economist*, 13 October 1973, p. 44; Florencia Varas and José Manuel Vergara, *Coup! Allende's Last Day* (New York: Stein & Day, 1975), p. 123; Taufic, pp. 209–10.

18. Marlise Simons, "The Brazil Connection," *Washington Post*, 6 January 1974, p. B3. Freed and Landis, pp. 151 and 206, allege variously that Robert Moss, a militantly anticommunist British journalist, and David A. Phillips, chief of the Western Hemisphere Division of the CIA, were directly involved in the concoction of the document. The involvement of the latter, at least, is unlikely, as Phillips—so far as I know—did not come to Chile in the time between the coup and the document's publication. He and the CIA's station chief in Santiago have told me that CIA officers had no part in the drafting, although the Church Committee report says that "two CIA collaborators"— presumably Chileans—did assist in its preparation. U.S. Congress, Senate, *Covert Action in Chile, 1963–1973*, Staff Report of the Select Committee to Study Governmental Operations with Respect to Intelligence Activities (Washington, D.C., 1975), p. 40.

19. I was told that General Torres de la Cruz flew some of his troops north to Puerto Montt to join these reserve forces. Not needed, they apparently were sent back south.

20. Carlos Prats, *Una vida por la legalidad* (México: Fondo de Cultura Económica, 1976), pp. 91, 105.

21. *New York Times*, 16 September 1973, p. 3, and 1 October 1974, p. 14 (for Prats's death on 30 September 1974); Taylor Branch and Eugene M. Propper, *Labyrinth* (New York: Viking, 1982), pp. 66ff.

22. Jonathan Kandell, "Chile's Military Chiefs Abolish Nation's Largest Labor Group," *New York Times*, 26 September 1973, p. 10.

23. Robert J. Alexander, *The Tragedy of Chile* (Westport: Greenwood, 1978), p. 363.

24. Prats, p. 93.

25. Alexander, p. 342; Hortensia Bussi de Allende, speech transcript, 5 April 1975, at the conference "The CIA and World Peace," held under the sponsorship of Promoting World Peace at Yale University, New Haven, Conn., p. 46.

26. *New York Times*, 5 October 1973, p. 7.

27. The Reuter's dispatch is quoted by James N. Goodsell, "Latin America Points Finger at US," *Christian Science Monitor*, 17 September 1973.

28. My wife's mother saved her letters and returned them to Elizabeth some years later.

29. For example, see Thomas Hauser, *The Execution of Charles Horman; An American Sacrifice* (New York: Harcourt Brace Jovanovich, 1978), p. 120.

30. Carl T. Rowan, "Dumb Diplomatic Mess," *Washington Star-News*, 15 March 1975.

31. Transcript of State Dept. Briefing (King), 2 October 1973, ARF-22, 360; "US Envoy Expresses Concern to Chile Junta," *Washington Post*, 3 October 1973; Editorial, "Human Rights in Chile," *Washington Post*, 5 October 1973; Editorial, " Chile's Junta Is Raising Doubts," *Miami Herald*, 11 October 1973.

32. "Chile Defiant on Policy," *New York Daily News*, 4 October 1973.

33. *New York Times*, 24 September 1973, p. 4.

34. See chapter 13.

35. According to Hauser, "the trio walked to the bus station nearest their home. Joyce's transport came first, and she disappeared on board. . . ." According to Joyce Horman's formal legal complaint in 1977, "Charles Horman accompanied Terry Simon to town while Joyce Horman went with L, a friend of theirs, to do shopping and check on the safety of their other friends." It is not clear why Hauser represented Joyce Horman as having been alone, or why the complaint concealed the identity of "L." Hauser, p. 92. *Joyce Horman et al.* v. *Henry A. Kissinger et al.* CA 77-1748 (DDC), Summons in a Civil Action, 6 October 1977, p. 11.

36. Marvine Howe, "Chile's Military Holding 30 Allende Aides on Isle," *New York Times*, 23 September 1973, p. 3. See also Marvine Howe, "2 Americans Slain in Chile: The Unanswered Questions," *New York Times*, 19 November 1973, p. 20.

37. Terry Simon, "An American Girl in Chile's Revolution," *Senior Scholastic*, 6 December 1973, p. 16. What the article actually says is: "Charles Horman was taken from his home by Chilean soldiers about an hour after we parted. When Joyce got home, she found the house had been vandalized and

looted. The next day, neighbors told her Charlie was taken away by soldiers in a truck. . . ."

38. Hauser, p. 115.

39. Simon, p. 16.

40. Hauser, pp. 116–17.

41. Ibid., pp. 117–18, 130.

42. Chilean Foreign Ministry note of 13 December 1973, made available to all parties.

43. Chilean government statement of 18 October 1973, made available to all parties.

44. Joyce Horman et al., Motion to Dismiss without Prejudice, 10 December 1980, Memorandum of Frederick Smith, Jr., p. 4; Judd L. Kessler's memorandum of 19 July 1976, made available to all parties. See also Hauser, pp. 215–19.

45. Hauser, p. 169; *New York Times*, 19 November 1973, p. 21; Joyce Hormans's letter to Senator J. William Fulbright of 7 November 1973, *Congressional Record*, House (the letter was put into the record in the House), 14 November 1973, pp. 10039–40.

46. Frederick Smith, Jr., memo., pp. 3–4, and numerous U.S. Embassy Santiago telegrams, made available to all parties; Hauser, p. 203.

47. Hauser, pp. 103, 222–25, 228; Frederick Smith, Jr., memo., pp. 6–15; Joyce Horman et al., Plaintiffs' Exhibits, 94–97, pp. 19–20.

48. Joyce Horman et al., Plaintiffs' Exhibits, 94–97, p. 32.

49. Marvine Howe, "Lawmaker Visiting Chile Links US Economic Policies to Coup," *New York Times*, 28 October 1973, p. 11.

50. Pluto, "Chao, Mister Davis," *Las Ultimas Noticias*, 22 October 1973, p. 5.

51. The substance of what I said is recounted in this chapter. In addition, a number of the economic issues discussed in chapters 1, 3, 4, and 5 were touched on in my 9 November 1973 testimony, particularly copper nationalization, Chile's foreign debt, and Chile's credit situation.

52. Laurence Birns, "How to Lie in Washington and Get away with It," *New York Review of Books*, 17 July 1975, and Laurence Birns, letter to the author, 2 December 1975.

53. Popper's demarche was to Gonzalo Prieto, the Chilean minister of justice, on 14 March 1974.

54. Ernest W. Lefever and Roy Godson, *The CIA and the American Ethic* (Washington, D.C.: Ethics and Public Policy Center, Georgetown University, 1979), p. 103.

55. The text of the OAU ministerial council resolution was telegraphed to me.

56. See Rowland Evans and Robert Novak, " 'Ethnic' Foreign Policy," *Washington Post*, 7 April 1978, Op-Ed page.

57. So far as I know, all information passed or discussed was subsequently published by the Church Committee.

58. See Nathaniel Davis, "The Angola Decision of 1975: A Personal Memoir," *Foreign Affairs*, Autumn 1978, pp. 109–24.

59. Kissinger later publicly reiterated this statement.

60. My family and I flew to Bern on 1 January 1976.

61. Alexander, p. 361.

62. USIS Press Release, U.S. Mission, Geneva, "The Second Ford-Carter Television Debate," 6 October 1976, p. 5.

63. Brady Tyson drafted a telegram on 8 March 1977, containing the "text, reconstructed from extensive notes," of his comments. The quotations are taken from that text, as an informational copy of it was sent to me in Bern.

64. *International Herald Tribune*, 10 March 1977, p. 1.

65. Joseph L. Nogee and Robert Donaldson, *Soviet Foreign Policy since World War II* (Elmsford, N.Y.: Pergamon, 1981), p. 178, and Leon Gouré and Morris Rothenberg, *Soviet Penetration of Latin America* (Miami, Fla.: Center for Advanced International Studies, University of Miami, 1975), p. 109.

66. B. N. Ponomarev, "V. I. Lenin and the International Communist Movement," *Kommunist*, no. 2, January 1974, p. 17; Ponomarev, "The World Situation and the Revolutionary Process," *World Marxist Review*, June 1974, p. 11.

67. M. F. Kudachkin, "The Experience of the Struggle of the Communist Party of Chile for Unity among Leftist Forces and for Revolutionary Transformation," *Voprosy Istorii, KPSS*, no. 5, May 1974, p. 57.

68. Christopher S. Wren, "Moscow's Foreign Policy Fortunes," *International Herald Tribune*, 10 September 1976.

69. Flora Lewis, "Kremlin's European Policy," *New York Times*, 22 April 1980, p. A14.

70. Volodia Teitelboim, "Reflections on the 1,000 Days of Popular Unity Rule," *World Marxist Review*, January 1977, pp. 53, 60; Orlando Millas, "Stages of the Struggle," *World Marxist Review*, February 1977, p. 60; Rodrigo Rojas, "Psychological Warfare: A Political Weapon of Imperialism," *World Marxist Review*, March 1977, p. 48.

71. Corvalán followed up along the same lines in a February 1981 address to the 26th Soviet Party Congress in Moscow, and Teitelboim announced in Mexico City in March 1981 that the Manuel Rodríguez Patriotic Command was successfully carrying out acts of sabotage in Chile. Norma R. Harms, "Chile's Communist Party Opts for Revolution with Moscow's Blessing," Bureau of Intelligence and Research, U.S. Department of State, 1981 (Unclassified).

## Chapter 15. Reflections

1. Edward M. Korry, "Statement and Discussion," U.S. Congress, Senate, Committee on Foreign Relations, *Nomination of Hon. Cyrus R. Vance to Be Secretary of State*, 11 January 1977, Hearing (Washington, D.C., 1977), pp. 72, 76, 63–64.

2. Ibid., pp. 58, 61–62, 79. (According to Korry, the staffer who offered him a deal was Jerome Levinson of Senator Frank Church's multinationals subcommittee.)

3. David Pryce-Jones's political review of Jean-François Revel's "Censorship, New Style," *New York Times Magazine*, 11 December 1977, p. 116.

4. Philip W. Bonsal, *Cuba, Castro, and the United States* (Pittsburgh: University of Pittsburgh Press, 1971), p. 145.

5. Ibid., pp. 153–56.

6. Walter Lippmann, as quoted by Anthony Lewis, "Who Lost China?" *New York Times*, 15 May 1983, sec. 4, p. E21.

7. See Bonsal, p. 64.

8. Paul M. Sweezy and Harry Magdoff, *Revolution and Counter-revolution in Chile* (New York: Monthly Review, 1974), pp. 79–93.

9. The letter, which Cuban representatives have acknowledged is genuine, is reproduced in Castro's handwriting in Secretaría de Gobierno, *Libro blanco del cambio de gobierno en Chile, 11 sep. 1973* (Santiago: Empresa Editora Nacional Gabriela Mistral, n.d.), pp. 101–2.

10. See in chapter 10 the section entitled "Nine to Ten A.M.: Allende's Last Appeal."

# Index

# DATE DUE

| AP 25 '04 | | | |
|---|---|---|---|
| | | | |
| | | | |
| | | | |
| | | | |
| | | | |
| | | | |
| | | | |
| | | | |
| | | | |
| | | | |
| | | | |
| | | | |
| | | | |
| | | | |